The Hardest Battle

The Canadian Corps and the Arras 1918 Campaign

William F. Stewart

Helion & Company

To my wife who among her many virtues has been a constant support and wise counsellor.

Helion & Company Limited
Unit 8 Amherst Business Centre
Budbrooke Road
Warwick
CV34 5WE
England
Tel. 01926 499 619
Email: info@helion.co.uk
Website: www.helion.co.uk
Twitter: @helionbooks
Visit our blog at blog.helion.co.uk

Published by Helion & Company 2023
Designed and typeset by Mary Woolley (www.battlefield-design.co.uk)
Cover designed by Paul Hewitt, Battlefield Design (www.battlefield-design.co.uk)

ISBN 978-1-915113-66-5

British Library Cataloguing-in-Publication Data.
A catalogue record for this book is available from the British Library.

Contents

List of Photographs		viii
List of Maps		xi
List of Tables		xiii
Preface and Acknowledgements		xiv
Nomenclature		xv
List of Abbreviations		xvi
Foreword		xix
Introduction		xxi
	Key Questions	xxiii
	Sources	xxiv
	Structure	xxvii
Section One: Context		29
1	'It had life': The Canadian Corps' Commanders, Formations, and Arms	30
	Command Structure	30
	Divisions and Organisation	35
	Canadian Divisional Organisation	45
	Canadian Advantages	54
2	Ground, Foe, and Method: Where, Whom, and How the Canadian Corps Fought	60
	'Nothing but ruins': Arras 1918 Battlefield	60
	German Organisation and Leaders	68
	'*Alte Hasen*' and '*Korsettenstangen*' – Defences, Tactics, and Morale	71
	Canadian Doctrine	79
	Face of Battle	80
	Arras 1917	83
3	'Shake us out of the habits acquired by years in the trenches': Preparing the Corps For the Hundred Days	86
	German Spring Offensives	86
	Canadian Corps: January-May 1918	90
	Operation Delta	92

Open Warfare Training 95
Arras 1918's Precursor: Operation 'Thistle' 98
Amiens: Tanks, Surprise and Victory 100
Widening the Offensive 105

Section Two: To the Fresnes-Rouvroy Line 111

4 'To surprise the Enemy': Canadian Corps Operations Planning, 22-25 August 112
Canadian Corps Moves North 112
Planning Arras 1918 115
Haig Shifts the Spearhead 121
Corps' Plan 126
Divisional Plans 131
Highlanders! The 51st (Highland) Division 134
German Actions 135

5 'If Germany cannot hold us here': Canadian Corps Operations, 26 August 140
Right Flank: XVII Corps 140
2nd Division: Morning 142
2nd Division: Afternoon-Evening 145
3rd Division: Morning 150
7th Brigade 154
51st (Highland) Division 162
Results and Analysis 163

6 'Pressed with the greatest vigour': Failure Before the F-R Line, 27 August 167
Strategic Situation 167
Tempo 169
Germans 174
Corps Preparations 174
Flanking Forces 175
2nd Division 175
5th Brigade 178
4th Brigade 185
3rd Division 188
Highlanders 192
Results and Analysis 193

7 'A great importance was attached to its capture': Operations to Break the F-R Line, 28 August 196
Strategic Situation 196
Planning 198
Germans 203
XVII Corps 204
2nd Division Suffers 204

5th Brigade: Costly Failure 206
4th Brigade: More Failure 209
26th Reserve Division Account 212
3rd Division: Triumph 212
9th Brigade 214
7th Brigade 216
8th Brigade 218
Highlanders 221
Results and Analysis 221

Section Three: To the Drocourt-Quéant Line 225

8 'Totally overrun, overcome, and taken prisoner:' Approaching the D-Q Line, 29-30 August 226
Strategic Situation 226
German Situation 228
1st Division 230
4th British Division 233
Brutinel's Brigade 234
Relief: XXII Corps Takes Over the Northern Sector 237
Highlanders 238
Results 239
30 August: Task 2 Progress 239
Strategic Situation 241
German Situation 241
1st Brigade Planning 244
1st Brigade Strikes 246
German Counterblow 249
4th British Division: Task 3 Almost Completed 253
Results and Analysis 256

9 'Disorganised and thoroughly cowed': Gaining the Jump-Off Line, 31 August and 1 September 258
Preparing 258
Strategic Situation 261
Germans 261
1st Division: 'OCEAN WORK and Vicinity' Fall 263
4th British Division 265
4th Canadian Division Arrives 266
Results 269
Battle for the Jump-off Line: 1 September 269
Strategic Situation 271
Germans 271
1st Division: Gaining the Jump-Off Line 273
4th Canadian Division 279

4th British Division 283
Results and Analysis 284

Section Four: Breaking the D-Q Line 286

10 'Break the hinge': Planning the D-Q Line Attack 287
Conceptual Challenge 288
German Situation 292
Decisions 294
Planning Process 295
Corps' Plans 299
XVII Corps' Plan 301
1st Canadian Division's Plan 302
Canadian Independent Force's Plans 303
4th Canadian Division's Plan 304
4th British Division's Plans 307
Analysis 308

11 „Herr Leutnant, der Tommy ist hier": 1st Division and CIF, 2 September 311
Flanking Forces 311
3rd Brigade 313
German Southern Sector 319
2nd Brigade 320
1st Brigade 325
Air Operations 326
Canadian Independent Force 327
Analysis 332

12 'The most severe machine gun opposition': 4th Canadian and 4th British Divisions, 2 September 1918 336
12th Canadian Brigade 336
10th Canadian Brigade 341
11th Canadian Brigade 345
Unsupportive Support Weapons 351
4th British Division 353
Germans North of the Arras-Cambrai Road 354
Results and Analysis 356

13 'Impresses importance of pushing on': The Offensive Stalls, 3-5 September 360
Planning 360
4th Canadian Division 362
Dellmensingen's Decision 364
Strategic and Flanking Forces Situation 3-5 September 365
1st Division 365
4th Canadian Division 369

4th British Division 370
Offensive Sputters Out: 4-5 September 371

Section Five: Analysis 373

14 Analysis 374
Amiens-Arras 1918 Comparison 374
Outcomes 376
Casualties 382
Commander Assessment 386

Conclusion: 'The Hardest Battle' 392
Core Threads – Facilitators 393
Core Themes – Hindrances 398
Why the Greater Success of Arras 1918 versus Arras 1917? 404
Matériel, Manpower, Morale or Method 407
Did it Matter? 416

Appendices 418

I Historiographical Debate 419
II Comparison German and Canadian Divisions 421
III Formations, Units, Commanders, and Staff 423
IV Detailed Canadian Corps Orders of Battle, 26 August 1918 448
V Detailed Canadian Corps Orders of Battle, 2 September 1918 452
VI Canadian Independent Force Order of Battle, 2 September 1918 456

Bibliography 458
Index 475

List of Photographs

Lieutenant General Sir Arthur Currie and Field Marshal Sir Douglas Haig 31
General Sir Henry Horne 33
Marshal Ferdinand Foch 34
Major General Sir Archibald Cameron Macdonell 36
Major General Sir Henry Burstall and Haig 39
Major General Louis Lipsett 40
Major General Sir David Watson 43
Lewis Gun 47
Vickers Heavy Machine Gun 48
Major General E W B Morrison 51
6-inch Howitzer 52
18-Pounder Gun 54
CW Wireless Transmitter 56
River Scarpe 61
Cojeul River 63
Ruins of Wancourt 65
Tramways 67
Field Marshal Paul von Hindenburg 68
General der Infanterie Otto von Below 69
General der Artillerie Konrad Krafft von Dellmensingen 70
General Erich Ludendorff 87
Canadian Battalion on the March 96
General Sir Julian Byng 106
Lieutenant General Sir Charles Fergusson 108
Brigadier General A H Bell 118
Lieutenant Colonel A Ross 120
Arras-Cambrai Road 124
Sterilising Water 130
Brigadier General D C Draper 133
Panorama of Chérisy and Vicinity 146
View from Monchy-le-Preux 146
Lieutenant C Rutherford VC 152
Brigadier Generals 'Daddy' Dyer and W Griesbach 155
Lieutenant Colonel C Stewart 157

Brigadier General H A Panet 177
Brigadier General T L Tremblay 178
Lieutenant Colonel W H Clarke-Kennedy 180
Lieutenant Colonel A E G McKenzie 181
Lieutenant Colonel A Dubuc 183
Vis-en-Artois Ruins 185
Brigadier General D Ormond 188
Boiry-Notre-Dame Ruins 189
Major Georges Vanier 209
Brigadier General Rennie 210
Major R S Smythe 216
Generalmajor v Kemnitz 218
Infantry Advance Near Remy 219
Brigadier General Raymond Brutinel 235
Major A E Humphrey 236
Brigadier General H C Thacker 245
Lieutenant Colonel L McLaughlin 247
Generalleutenant Freiherr v Fritsch 255
Gridlock 259
Brigadier Generals Tuxford and Loomis 263
Brigadier General J H MacBrien 267
Lieutenant Colonel Dick Worrall 276
Brigadier General Ross Hayter 281
Barbed Wire of the D-Q Line 289
Dropped Bridge Across the Canal du Nord 290
Mark V Tank in Action in September 291
Generalmajor Paul Tiede 292
Bridge Building 296
Brigadier General A G L McNaughton 300
Brigadier General Victor Odlum 306
Lieutenant Colonel Cy Peck VC 314
Lance Corporal WH Metcalf VC 315
Sergeant W L Rayfield VC 321
10th Battalion Senior Leadership 323
Sergeant Arthur Knight, VC 325
Cost of Airpower 327
Lieutenant Colonel W K Walker 329
Canadian Independent Force 331
The Infamous Dury Windmill 338
Private Claude Nunney VC 340
Major 'Jock' Rankin 343
Lieutenant Colonel C Harbottle 347
Captain Bellenden Hutchenson VC 349
Private J F Young VC 350
Major Tido Brederlow PLM 356

Lieutenant Colonel R Davies 363
Tanks at Amiens 375
Tank Destroyed 379
Prisoners of War 381
Wounded 383
Currie and His Division Commanders 388
German Gun 396
Signallers 401
Minenwerfer 403
Arras 1917 406
Captured Machine Guns 409
Shell Dump 412
Dead Gunner 414

List of Maps

In Text

Map 1. Arras 1918 Terrain - The western sector of the battlefield. 62
Map 2. Arras 1918 Terrain - The eastern sector of the battlefield. 64
Map 3. German Defensive Positions August 1918 72
Map 4. Arras April-May 1917 82
Map 5. German *Michael* and *Mars* Offensives, March 1918 88
Map 6. Strategic Situation: Amiens, 8 August 102
Map 7. Strategic Situation: 9-20 August 104
Map 8. Strategic Situation: 21 August 107
Map 9. Operation Thistle 109
Map 10. *OHL* Situation Map: 25 August 114
Map 11. Strategic Situation: 22-25 August 116
Map 12. 6th Brigade and Neuville-Vitasse: 23-25 August 119
Map 13. The Most Important Operational Assignment of the Canadian Corps 122
Map 14. Canadian Corps Barrage Map: 23 August 127
Map 15. German Defensive Arrangements: 26 August 136
Map 16. Strategic Situation: 26 August 141
Map 17. Strategic Situation: 27 August 168
Map 18. Aggressive Operation Plan: 27 August 171
Map 19. Germans: August 27 173
Map 20. Strategic Situation: 28 August 197
Map 21. Another Aggressive Plan: 28 August 199
Map 22. German Situation: 28 August 202
Map 23. Strategic Situation: 29 August 227
Map 24. German Situation: 29 August 229
Map 25. 1st Division and XVII Corps: 29 August 232
Map 26. Strategic Situation: 30 August 240
Map 27. German Situation: 30 August 242
Map 28. Strategic Situation: 31 August 260
Map 29. German Situation: 31 August 262
Map 30. Strategic Situation: 1 September 270
Map 31. German Situation: 1 September 272

Map 32. German Situation: 2 September 293
Map 33. Flanking Forces: 2nd September 312
Map 34. The Offensive Peters Out: 3-5 September 366
Map 35. Canal du Nord Reached: 3 September 368

In Colour Map Booklet

Map C1. Opening Day Plan: 26 August 1918 V
Map C2. 2nd Division Success VI
Map C3. 3rd Division Takes Monchy-le-Preux: Morning VII
Map C4. 7th Brigade Frustrates *35th ID* Counterattack: Afternoon VIII
Map C5. 51st (Highland) Division Captures Mt Pleasant IX
Map C6. 2nd Division Mixed Success: 27 August X
Map C7. 3rd Division Makes Only Limited Gains: 27 August XI
Map C8. 51st (Highland) Division Stopped Before Greenland Hill: 27 August XII
Map C9. 2nd Division Repelled: 28 August XIII
Map C10. 3rd Division Breaks the F-R Line: 28 August XVI
Map C11. 4th British Division and Brutinel's Brigade: 29 August XV
Map C12. Highlanders: 29 August XVI
Map C13. 1st Brigade Attacks: 30 August XVII
Map C14. 1st Brigade: German Counterattack XVIII
Map C15. 4th British Division: 30 August XIX
Map C16. 1st Division and Flanking Forces: 31 August XX
Map C17. 4th British Division Takes St Servins Farm: 31 August XXI
Map C18. 1st Division and Flanking Forces: 1 September Morning XXII
Map C19. 1st Division and Flanking Forces: 1 September Afternoon XXIII
Map C20. 4th British Division Operations: 1 September XXIV
Map C21. Canadian Corps' Plan for 2 September XXV
Map C22. The 1st Division Responds: 2 September XXVI
Map C23. The CIF Flounders: 2 September XXVII
Map C24. The D-Q Line Broken: 2 September XXVIII
Map C25. The 4th Canadian and British Divisions Struggle: 2 September XXIX

List of Tables

3.1 Passchendaele-Hundred Days Comparison 93
5.1 Estimated Casualties For 26 August 1918 164
6.1 Estimated Casualties For 27 August 1918 194
7.1 Estimated Casualties For 28 August 1918 222
8.1 Estimated Casualties For 29 August 1918 239
8.2 Estimated Casualties For 30 August 1918 256
9.1 Estimated Casualties For 31 August 1918 269
9.2 Estimated Casualties For 1 September 1918 284
12.1 Estimated Casualties 2 September 1918 357
14.1 Amiens 1918 and Arras 1918 Comparison 376
14.2 Success Comparison Arras 1918 and Somme 1916 377
14.3 Support Weapons' Outcomes for Canadian Battalion Attacks 378
14.4 Tank Commitment and Loss Rate, Arras 1918 379
14.5 Average Casualties per Canadian Battalion Attack Outcome 380
14.6 German Divisions Defeated 380
14.7 Prisoners Captured 2 August-15 September 1918 382
14.8 Casualty Comparisons 383
14.9 Ratios of Canadian Wounded to Dead 384
14.10 Arras 1918 and Somme 1916 Loss Comparison per Battalion Attack 384
14.11 Average All Ranks Loss per Battalion by Canadian Division 385
14.12 Canadian Fatalities by Arm 1916 and 1918 386
C.1 Effect of Barrages on Outcomes All Attacks 394
C.2 Force Density Arras 1917 and 1918 and Amiens 399
C.3 Metres per Piece 30 August 1918 400
C.4 Arras 1917 and 1918 Comparison 405
C.5 Artillery Comparison Arras 1917, Passchendaele 1917, Arras 1918 408
C.6 Machine Gun Comparison 410
C.7 Aircraft Numbers 412

Preface and Acknowledgements

This volume is a logical progression from my first two Canadian Corps' books that explored its operations to the end of 1916. After the Somme's mud, blood, and multiple failures mixed with a few successes, I wanted to explore a period characterised by many more victories than stumbles. The campaigns in 1917 are well understood with two scholarly accounts on Vimy and Hill 70 and a popular one of the Canadian participation at Passchendaele.[1] The opening battle of the Hundred Days campaign has multiple treatments, but the battle that Currie believed a greater victory than Amiens––Arras 1918––has not received a comprehensive analysis. For the reasons elucidated in the Introduction, I believe this a critical battle to examine in-depth as it highlighted the immense changes to the way the Canadian Corps operated in 1918. As a further incentive, I obtained German documentation to add a more rounded view to the battle.

A book of this nature results from many scholars' generous assistance, but I am responsible for the errors and omissions. Leading the way was Tim Cook who provided incisive suggestions and continual encouragement for the project. Trevor Harvey and Patrick Dennis read the manuscript and delivered perceptive comments and recommendations that improved the argument and style. Robert Linnell of Nightfighter Productions provided a treasure trove of German documents from the archives in Stuttgart and Munich, and I want to acknowledge his generosity in sharing these invaluable files. Jan Vancoillie provided scans of a regimental history of the *4th Ersatz Division* that gave a missing perspective on its operations.

1 Geoffrey Hayes et al., *Vimy Ridge: A Canadian Reassessment* (Waterloo, Ont.: Wilfrid Laurier University Press, 2007); Serge Marc Durflinger, Douglas E. Delaney, and Nikolas Gardner, *Capturing Hill 70: Canada's Forgotten Battle of the First World War* (Vancouver: UBC Press, 2016); Daniel G. Dancocks, *Legacy of Valour: The Canadians at Passchendaele* (Edmonton: Hurtig, 1986).

Nomenclature

This study capitalises Corps in the Canadian Corps when used alone to denote a specific reference to the Canadian Corps. British infantry battalion designations can be daunting. To declutter the text, they are described by their full number and name in their first reference with subsequent ones in a shortened format. Thus, the 1/7th Argyll and Sutherland Highlanders are their full title on the first use but will be the 7th ASH from then on. National designations are used only where British and Canadian units or formations carry similar numerical designations. For instance, both the 4th Canadian and British Divisions served in the battle. Companies are denoted in the form A/49th or 1/2nd Machine Gun Battalion depending on the battalion practice for company designations. Italics are used to mark German formations so *4th Ersatz Division* and *II/361st Infantry Regiment*. Armies are spelled out, corps and battalions are listed as Roman numerals, and divisions, brigades, regiments and batteries or companies are given as Arabic numerals. Ranks are given as for the period under study. In accordance with usual customs, battle descriptions will move from right to left or in this case from the south to the north. They will usually follow the pattern of being grouped by division, then brigade and battalion before moving to the next formation. Times are given as a twelve-hour clock, as the Corps did not shift to the twenty-four hour system until October 1918. All times are on GMT with the German times shifted an hour to account for their being an hour ahead. The sometimes idiosyncratic spelling by Canadian officers in switching between British and Canadian versions is retained in quotations.

'Hundred Days' is used to describe the Allied march to victory in 1918 even as it overlooks the crucial role of the French counteroffensive on the Marne starting 18 July. The book's use is applicable as Canada's Hundred Days—John Livesay in his book on the Canadian operations first used the term in 1919.[1] The Canadians served at the front from the start of the Amiens offensive to the Armistice, a total of 96 days, so rounding up we get the Hundred Days. Secondly, the term is now so strongly entrenched in most readers' minds that trying to use another phrase would be counterproductive as any other term does not have its resonance.

1 John Frederick Bligh Livesay, *Canada's Hundred Days: With the Canadian Corps from Amiens to Mons, Aug. 8-Nov. 11, 1918* (Toronto: Thomas Allen, 1919); A.A. Montgomery, *The Story of the Fourth Army in the Battle of the Hundred Days, August 8th to November 11th, 1918* (London: Hodder & Stoughton, 1920).

List of Abbreviations

Text Abbreviations

AFA	Army Field Artillery
AR	All Ranks
ASH	Argyll and Sutherland Highlanders
BEF	British Expeditionary Force
BGGS	Brigadier General, General Staff
C-in-C	Commander-in-Chief
CAMC	Canadian Army Medical Corps
CBSO	Counter-Battery Staff Officer
CCCB	Canadian Corps Cyclist Battalion
CCHA	Canadian Corps Heavy Artillery
CDA	Canadian Division Artillery
CEF	Canadian Expeditionary Force
CFA	Canadian Field Artillery
CIF	Canadian Independent Force
CLH	Canadian Light Horse
CMGO	Corps Machine Gun Officer
CMMG	Canadian Motor Machine Gun
CMR	Canadian Mounted Rifles
CO	Commanding Officer
CRA	Commander, Royal Artillery
CW	Continuous Wave
CWNS	Canadian War Narrative Section
D-Q	Drocourt-Quéant Line
DA	Division Artillery
DSO	Distinguished Service Order
Dukes	Duke of Wellington's (West Riding) Regiment
EzD	*Ersatz Division*
F-R	Fresnes-Rouvroy Line
FA	Field Artillery
FAR	*Field Artillery Regiment*
FtABn	*Foot Artillery Battalion*

FtAR	*Foot Artillery Regiment*
FüR	*Füsilier Regiment*
GH	Gordon Highlanders
GHQ	General Headquarters
GOC	General Officer Commanding
GOCRA	General Officer Commanding, Royal Artillery
GRD	*Guards Reserve Division*
GrR	*Grenadier Regiment*
GRR	*Guards Reserve Regiment*
GS	General Service
GSO	General Staff Officer
HA	Heavy Artillery
HE	High Explosive
how.	howitzer
HWL	*Hauptwiderstandlinie - Main line of resistance*
ID	*Infantry Division*
IR	*Infantry Regiment*
KLR	King's (Liverpool) Regiment
KORL	Kings Own Royal Lancaster Regiment
LNL	Loyal North Lancaster Regiment
MC	Military Cross
MEBU	Mannschafts-Eisenbeton-Unterstände (Reinforced Concrete Shelters)
MGGS	Major General, General Staff
MT	Mechanical Transport
NCO	Non-Commissioned Officer
NWMP	North West Mounted Police
OHL	*Oberste Heeresleitung*
Pdr.	Pounder (weight of shell fired)
PF	Permanent Force
PPCLI	Princess Patricia's Canadian Light Infantry
R Warks	Royal Warwickshire Regiment
RAF	Royal Air Force
RB	Rifle Brigade
RCR	Royal Canadian Regiment
RD	*Reserve Division*
RFA	Royal Field Artillery
RFAR	*Reserve Field Artillery Regiment*
RIR	*Reserve Infantry Regiment*
RMC	Royal Military College
RMF	Royal Munster Fusiliers
RSM	Regimental Sergeant-Major
SD	*Schützen Division* (Dismounted Cavalry)
SLI	Somerset Light Infantry
SOC	Senior Officers Course, Aldershot
VC	Victoria Cross

Footnote Citation Abbreviations

AAQMG	Assistant Adjutant and Quartermaster-General
BWRA	Black Watch Regiment Archive, Montreal
CWGC	Commonwealth War Graves Commission
CWM	Canadian War Museum
GS	General Staff
LAC	Library and Archives Canada
loc	Location in an electronic book
McGill	McGill University Archives, Montreal
NLS	National Library of Scotland (UK)
OO	Operation Order
TNA	The National Archives (UK)
WD	War Diary

Foreword

The towering Canadian national memorial at Vimy Ridge stands as a silent sentry to the country's service and loss during the Great War. After nearly fifteen years of work, architect Walter Allward saw his memorial unveiled by King Edward VIII on 26 July 1936. The twin pylons that reached to the sky, the names of 11,285 Canadians with no known graves in France, and Canada Bereft, the central grieving mother, who, head bowed, stares down mournfully at the empty sarcophagus to represent Canada's over 66,000 wartime dead, come together in a powerful and evocative site of sorrow and pride. This memorial has stood for generations of visitors, and, when twinned with the successful battle from 9 to 12 April 1917, where all four Canadian divisions attacked together for the only time in the war, has created a national martial symbol for Canada.

While historians continue to investigate the Vimy legend, untangling the symbol from the battle and the memorial, historians of operations, tactics, and warfighting have observed that the long shadow of Vimy has obscured many other Canadian battles. The Hundred Days campaign, from 8 August to 11 November, a series of battles at Amiens, Arras, Cambrai, Valenciennes, and Mons, has been more rigorously examined in the 21st century and elevated from obscurity. In this first book ever written on the crucial 1918 Battle of Arras, Dr Bill Stewart, one of Canada's premier historians of Canadian Corps, offers new insight into the importance of the battle for the Allied war effort. Stewart has delved deep into British and Canadian archives to understand how the battle was planned, how it was fought, and how to situate it within the final victories that ended the war on the Western Front.

The Canadian Corps was a great fighting machine. It was also an organisation that learned in the cauldron of battle on the Western Front. Experienced staff officers, most of them British professional soldiers, helped to transform the Canadians into an effective fighting formation. Canadian militia officers, citizen soldiers, and some prewar professionals also rose through the ranks, learning their craft, melding infantry and artillery tactics, and mastering the importance of sound planning. Behind the lines, training was conducted steadily, while the essential work of support and logistical units allowed for increasingly complex operations. The bloody battles on the Somme through the Fall and early winter of 1916 revealed this evolution of combat power, with success and failure, and always new reforms instigated in the aftermath of that costly campaign.

The Canadian Corps, four divisions strong, was hurled against the seemingly impregnable Vimy Ridge in April 1917. The Canadians clawed their way up the fortified slopes, but a pre-battle evolution in warfighting tactics through large-scale raids, the training of infantry and artillery to fight with a creeping barrage, the introduction of scientific gunnery, the more effective arming of the infantry with light machine guns and trusting junior officers with more control over their platoons, all contributed to the celebrated victory. Hard-fought battles continued at Hill 70 in August and at Passchendaele at the end of the year, both under command of Canadian-born Corps commander Sir Arthur Currie.

General Currie was a fine battlefield commander, willing to postpone operations until plans and units were ready, and always demanding artillery support. But perhaps his greatest skill was his willingness to continuously learn from battle. He demanded that units engage in the process of learning from victory and defeat, and these and other lessons were brought together to update training in the summer of 1918 after the Corps was pulled from the line. The static war was changing, and the Canadians engaged in combined-arms, open warfare manoeuvres, which would inform the fighting by the Canadians, Australians, and other formations at Amiens on 8 August 1918. Whilst Amiens was a shocking victory, the stalemate was not broken. The battles of the final three months of the war were not defined by open warfare, but a hybrid model of set-piece battles, open advances, and then slow, grinding attritional combat.

The Canadian victories at Amiens have been studied in much detail, but what is less clear is how the Canadians evolved and transformed, the importance of weighing structural advantages of the Canadian Corps, or good officers, or the effectiveness of enemy formations. In this study of the Battle of Arras, with the heaviest fighting from 26 August to 2 September 1918, Stewart answers these questions, pulling the answers from the primary documents, including German ones, that were created by the fighting officers as they struggled to make sense of the chaos. These memoranda, orders, and doctrinal discussions are combined with after-action reports, casualty lists, and maps. Together, along with the eyewitness accounts of officers and the rank and file, they reveal the successes of the Canadians at Arras, as they strode forward, bitterly fighting a stubborn and effective enemy. As in almost all battles, and especially at Arras, the Germans were dug-in on ground of their choosing, having spent years fortifying it with trench systems, concrete machine gun positions, barbed wire, and situated artillery fire plans. Somehow the Canadians found ways to claw their way forward, alternating between set-piece battles, and more fluid, follow-on engagements of attack and counterattack. Stewart explores the entrails of the fighting, presenting new ways to understand the factors that contributed to the Canadians' effectiveness, not the least being the eye-watering bravery of a diminishing number of soldiers at the sharp end who were called upon to deliver victory in brutal conditions.

Tim Cook, CM, FRSC, Ph.D.

Introduction

I know no finer example of what can be done by courageous and determined men than this attack.

Major General Louis Lipsett, 30 August 1918[1]

At 3:30 p.m. on 24 August 1918, the Commander-in-Chief (C-in-C) of the British Expeditionary Force Field Marshal Sir Douglas Haig arrived at the Canadian Corps' headquarters west of Arras. He was there to dramatically recast its mission and give the Corps its most significant operational assignment of the war. More pivotal than Vimy, Passchendaele, or Amiens, its task was to smash through a 15-kilometre zone of five fortified positions including the formidable Drocourt-Quéant Line (D-Q Line). It would then storm across the Canal du Nord and seize the Bourlon Wood hill overlooking the vital communications hub of Cambrai. This would require a 27-kilometre advance. It would rupture the German defences on the Western Front as the Canadian Corps shattered its lynchpin. The commander of the Canadian Corps, Lieutenant General Sir Arthur Currie, considered the Corps' actions in the campaign as 'the hardest battle in its history.'[2] In his diary, he wrote he thought it a greater victory than Amiens.[3]

The German High Command, well aware of the sector's vital importance, defended it with all they had. The German formations that fought there deemed it momentous. Multiple elite divisional histories regarded it as one of the high points of their service in the First World War.[4] Three German commanders received the *Pour le Mérite*, the highest German military order, for their performance at Arras 1918.[5] German regimental histories would refer to the fighting as the 'hardest' and 'most glorious' of the war, and another noted the 'extraordinary achievements of the regiment.'[6]

1 Library and Archives, Canada (LAC): RG9 III-D-3 v4855: 3rd Division GS War Diary, 3rd Division Report on Operations from Aug. 26th to Aug. 28th, 1918.
2 A.E. Kemp, *Report of the Ministry, Overseas Military Forces of Canada, 1918* (London: Printed by authority of the Ministry, Overseas Military Forces of Canada, 1919), p.144.
3 LAC: MG30 E100 v43: Currie Fonds, Currie Diary, 3 September 1918.
4 Paul Tiede, *Die 1.Garde-Reserve-Division im Weltkriege 1914-1919* (Berlin: M. Galle, 1922), p.20; Generalmajor R Stühmke, *Die 26. (Württembergische) Reserve-Division im Weltkrieg 1914-1918* (Stuttgart: Bergers Literaisches Büro und Verlagsanstalt, 1935), II, p.71.
5 Generalleutenant Freiherr Albert von Fritsch, *26th Reserve Division*, Major Tido Brederlow, *1st Garde-Reserve-Regiment*, and Hauptmann Karl Seidel, *2nd Garde-Reserve-Regiment*.
6 Ernst Zillmer, Lothar Gitterman, Martin Grunau, *Das Feldartillerie-Regiment Nr. 71 Groß-Komtur im Weltkriege* (Zeulenroda: Sporn Verlag, 1936), p.305; Tido von Brederlow, *Geschichte Des 1st Garde-Reserve-Regiments* (Berlin: Gerhard Stalling, 1926), p.317.

As Corporal Albert West of the 43rd Battalion wrote in his diary on passing through the German defences after being relieved, 'If Germany cannot hold us here she cannot hold us at all.'[7] It represented the German's best opportunity to stop the Canadians during the Hundred Days. Unlike Amiens, the enemy expected an attack, defended a deep and heavily fortified zone, had ample reserves, and was fighting over terrain scarred by years of intense combat. Depleted in numbers, tired, and with lowered morale, German infantry – *Landsers* – still fought staunchly when they had the advantage. Their machine gunners continued to battle with skill and died hard. Hostile artillery was not the formidable force of 1916 and 1917, but it was difficult to fully suppress. It remained a factor despite the best Canadian efforts. Unlike Amiens, the famous tank battle, the Corps did not benefit from surprise, masses of tanks, or an elite corps on its flank. Instead, it experienced hard, brutal combat at an unrelenting pace. What is more, the battle opened with only two of the Corps' four divisions. At no point did Currie have all four Canadian divisions available to attack.

The book chronicles and analyses the nine-day campaign running from 26 August to 3 September 1918. The account extends the coverage to 5 September when it was clear the offensive was over. According to the postwar British Battles Nomenclature Committee, the campaign comprised the Battles of the Scarpe 26-30 August and of Drocourt-Quéant 2-3 September as part of the overall Second Battle of Arras. This naming, however, overlooks previous battles for Arras in 1914 and 1915 by the French. To simplify the naming, the campaign around Arras in 1917 is called Arras 1917 and this campaign is Arras 1918.

Historians typically subsume the battle into the larger account of the Hundred Days and give it a cursory treatment. Amiens, understandably given its importance, is the subject of multiple works.[8] Most books on the Canadian Corps cover Arras 1918 as a chapter or two in a history of the Hundred Days.[9] The Canadian Official History devoted the same number of pages to the Battle of Hill 70 in 1917 as to Arras 1918.[10] This despite Hill 70 being a relatively minor operation involving three divisions while Arras 1918 was far more important and employed the entire Corps. This history, unlike its coverage of earlier battles, made significant errors discussed in Appendix I Historiographical Debates.

Arras 1918 was not an unbroken record of success. It was a mix of large-scale operations, limited attacks, cleverly conducted engagements, bungled battles, and smashing successes. The Canadians could not treat the German defenders lightly. If the Corps did not employ the proper

7 LAC: MG30 E32 v1: A.C. West Fonds, A.C. West Personal Diary, 29 August 1918.

8 Charles Messenger, *The Day We Won the War: Turning Point at Amiens, 8 August 1918* (London: Weidenfeld & Nicolson, 2008); Alistair McCluskey and Peter Dennis, *Amiens 1918: The Black Day of the German Army* (Oxford: Osprey, 2008); Gregory Blaxland, Amiens: 1918 (London: W.H. Allen, 1981); N. M. Christie, *The Canadians at Amiens, August 8th to 16th, 1918: A Social History and Battlefield Tour* (Ottawa: CEF Books, 1999); A. Kearsey, *The Battle of Amiens, 1918, and Operations 8th August-3rd September, 1918:* Naval and Military Press, 2009); James L. McWilliams and R. J. Steel, *Amiens: Dawn of Victory* (Toronto: Dundurn Press, 2001).

9 Tim Cook, *Shock Troops: Canadians Fighting the Great War, 1917-1918* (Toronto: Viking Canada, 2008); Shane B. Schreiber, *Shock Army of the British Empire: The Canadian Corps in the Last 100 Days of the Great War* (Westport, Conn.: Praeger, 1997); Patrick M. Dennis, *Reluctant Warriors: Canadian Conscripts and the Great War* (Vancouver: UBC Press, 2017).

10 G.W.L. Nicholson, *Canadian Expeditionary Force, 1914-1919* (Ottawa: R. Duhamel, Queen's Printer, 1964), pp.284-297, 427-440.

attack methods, a stinging defeat could ensue. Currie was under pressure from Haig to pull off a massive victory with equally massive operational consequences. As a result, he took risks. This risk taking resulted in costly setbacks and brilliant successes. Ultimately, the Corps reached the canal despite facing serious obstacles.

Key Questions

The key question this work attempts to answer is why the Canadian Corps was more successful than were the British in their Arras 1917 offensive over the same ground. With fewer troops, less artillery and tanks, against a similar concentration of German forces, albeit weaker in numbers and in morale but stronger in machine guns, the Corps made greater gains at a lower cost. This flows into the larger question of why the Allies achieved significantly better results in the Hundred Days campaign than in the battles of 1916 and 1917. Historians have advanced four major reasons of manpower, matériel, morale, and method. Manpower refers to significant German manpower shortages during the Hundred Days. In this view, the Germans were so short of men that they could not stop an Allied attack. Matériel referred to the Allies' advantages in guns, munitions, tanks, aircraft, logistics, and all the material aspects required for combat. This was the prime factor that the Germans blamed for their defeat, especially tanks, as they were a *deus ex machina* that overwhelmed them. German regimental histories often referred to masses of machines at Arras 1918 when there were none present.[11] Morale ascribes the success to the collapse of the enemy's infantry's morale, so the Germans fought poorly and surrendered willingly. Method speaks to the Allies being better able to marshal their matériel advantages and to employ tactics that defeated the German defensive arrangements. While no reputable historian would suggest a mono-causal reason for the Germans' defeat, they attribute a greater responsibility to one or more of these factors. In focusing on a single campaign where the enemy had significant advantages, this volume provides the context to draw a limited conclusion on the preeminent factors for the victory.

Twelve threads that facilitated or hindered Canadian operations weave through the text and are vital to the analysis. These factors tend to wash out in accounts where Arras 1918 is part of a larger narrative. Facilitating the Canadian victory were the use of smoke, the importance of the field artillery barrage for success, and improved infantry tactics through better training. German errors and the declining effectiveness of their counterattacks also aided the Canadians. Foundational to the Corps' performance were important organisational and structural advantages that it enjoyed over its British counterparts. On the negative side were issues with traffic congestion, communications, insufficient forces for the task, British and Canadian command errors, challenges in integrating support weapons in offensive operations, and cooperation between formations. Sitting on both sides was a significantly higher operational tempo in the campaign over those in 1916 and 1917.

A key element of this work is setting the Canadian Corps within the context of the larger British Expeditionary Force (BEF) and the framework of Allied operations. The Canadian

11 For example, see Ernst Zillmer Lothar Gitterman, Martin Grunau, *Das Feldartillerie-Regiment Nr. 71 Groß-Komtur im Weltkriege* (Zeulenroda: Sporn Verlag, 1936), p.305; Stühmke, *26th Reserve Division* II, p.63; Fritz Pafferath, *Die Geschichte Des 6. Rheinischen Infanterie-Regiments Nr. 68 im Weltkriege 1914-1918* (Berlin: Druck und Verlag Franz Weber, 1930), p.692.

Corps was not a force apart, but a fully integrated component of the BEF. Its weapons, tactics, uniforms, nomenclature, rations, munitions, and administrative, disciplinary, and financial practices were those of the British Army. The only visible difference between a Canadian and a British soldier was the badge on their collar. Moreover, the General Headquarters of the BEF (GHQ) had to approve every organisational difference between the Corps and British formations, and these were in the form of a variation on a theme. Therefore, this work will examine the orders from GHQ to the First Army and the First Army's instructions and directions to Currie at the Corps. In addition, it will consider the role and actions of the neighbouring Third Army's formations and units, as they played a critical part. It is time to move beyond a narrow national focus on the Canadian Corps to recognise it was not operating independently but was an integral part of the BEF.

This is pre-eminently a history of the operations of the Canadian Corps at Arras 1918. All formations of the Corps, including the British ones, are part of the narrative, as they played critical roles in the campaign. One-third of the Corps' assault divisions were British, as were half of the field and almost all the heavy artillery. All the tank and heavy armoured car units, and half of the cavalry were British. Despite the large numbers of Canadians in the squadrons, the Royal Air Force (RAF) was a British organisation. The Canadian Corps could not have attacked successfully without its British component, including the added artillery, logistics, and transportation units. They were essential to the Corps' operations, so their story is told as well.

Sources

This volume's bedrock is the war diaries, maps, battle narratives, operational orders, training memoranda, and other content produced during and shortly after the campaign. The author consulted all the relevant documents for both combat and support arms from the battalion to GHQ. Supplementing this research were the administrative records of the Canadian Expeditionary Force (CEF) in France and in the United Kingdom, the personal papers of soldiers, commanders, and politicians, and transcripts of interviews for the CBC's 1963 radio series *In Flanders Fields*. Files related to prewar and wartime service of all the Canadian officers and men mentioned in the text proved to be a useful source as a basis of understanding their careers before this battle.[12] The author has also examined all the latest scholarship from Canada, United Kingdom, New Zealand, and Australia on the campaign.

In order to understand how and why the battle unfolded as it did, it was necessary to review the full gamut of the complex amalgam of interrelated systems. Thus, the book analyses not just the combat arms but logistics, training, doctrine, tactics, communications, intelligence, personnel policies, staff procedures, command, equipment, and organisation. These all had important impacts on how the Corps conducted operations and how the Germans defended. The author reviewed the war diary of every unit of the Canadian Corps. Even obscure elements, such as the 82nd Canadian Ordnance Workshop (Light), provided insights.

12 The attestation papers and service files are in the RG150 Acc1992–93/166 series at Library and Archives, Canada in Ottawa. prewar service records are based on the Department of Militia and Defence, *The Quarterly Militia List of the Dominion of Canada (Corrected to June 30, 1914)* (Ottawa: Department of Militia and Defence, 1914). In order to save space, all references to service records are from these sources, unless separately footnoted.

The major information sources for the book were the war diaries and after-action reports that almost every unit produced. Typically, the authors were the adjutant or his assistant at the battalion level and a junior staff officer in higher formations. While narrating the events and providing lessons learned, they also attempt to burnish the reputation of the unit and its commander. Based on information from survivors, these reports tried to pull a signal out of the noise. They had the burden of having to satisfy the conceits of the unit commander and their superiors. Thus, beyond the inaccuracy of relying on eyewitnesses under the stress of battle, an avoidance of uncomfortable facts shaped the accounts. If the report writer could not ignore these, they would provide an excuse to exculpate the unit. Therefore, the historian has to reconcile what the surviving evidence makes unreconcilable. This disinclination extended after the war, as Lieutenant Colonel W. Bovey explained regarding an article he wrote on Currie. He stated, '...some things had to be left out, since the National Defence Quarterly is an official organ, and many truths had to be put in a more or less veiled way because of feelings still existing.'[13]

In other cases, what commanders projected publicly differed dramatically from the internal reality. Brigadier General Raymond Brutinel in his report on the operations of the Canadian Independent Force for 2 September, for example, claimed they did splendidly. Yet, in a blistering letter to one of the force commanders, he chastised the unit's performance and doubted they even attempted to advance. Again, the historian has to assess what was likely to have occurred.

There is also the extent to which a unit or formation had a complete war diary. In the 4th Brigade, two sister battalions kept very different diaries, with the 18th comprising 112 pages in August 1918 versus the 314 pages of the 19th Battalion. Both battalions had similar combat experiences at Arras 1918. With units, such as the 22nd Battalion, that suffered heavy casualties, especially to officers and senior NCOs, it was difficult to produce any detailed account.

The author double checked all locations and distances mentioned in war diaries and reports as they sometimes were wrong or exaggerated. Given the hurried creation of these materials and disjointed sources of information, errors crept in. The historian cannot simply take statements in the narratives and war diaries at face value but must evaluate their accuracy and probability. Given the confusion, chaos, and stress of battle, it is not surprising that memory can play false. Basil Wedd, a Corps' staff officer writing just after the war, captured this best with 'Just about all these chaps are really sure of is that they were miles ahead of the units on either flank and they were being fired on from the rear!'[14] Despite these caveats, these are the best sources, because they have the advantage of immediacy, when memories were freshest and the need for accurate reports to relay to superiors were paramount. The Canadian Corps produced voluminous documentation that enables cross-checking of claims and assertions.

Another important information source was regimental histories, but historians must treat them with circumspection. They focus on their unit. Thus, their authors rarely portray the larger context in which they operated. Moreover, they tend to be reticent about uncomfortable topics. Seldom will a regimental history admit the unit was the first to break, was the last to penetrate the enemy line, or did not advance the furthest. They also have merits.[15] Those written between

13 Directorate of History and Heritage (DHH): 2001/10, VI F:82: Duguid Fonds, Bovey to Macdonell, 24 September 1926.

14 LAC: RG9 III-D-2 v4802, 138: CWNS Wedd to Duguid, [November] 1920.

15 For more on their merits, see Tim Cook, '"Literary Memorials": The Great War Regimental Histories, 1919-1939', *Journal of the Canadian Historical Association/Revue de la Société historique du Canada* 13,

the wars had access to large numbers of veterans who could provide insights seldom found in the official documents. Further, the audience, usually these veterans, would not tolerate an account straying too far from the facts. Therefore, there was a governor on the degree to which the history was fanciful.

A special category of information was the documents and analysis generated by the Canadian War Narrative Section (CWNS) in the immediate postwar period. Currie wanted to ensure that the story of the Canadian Corps and his role was appropriately told. To achieve this objective, he established the CWNS.[16] He placed Raymond Brutinel, the commander of the Canadian machine gun arm, in charge and assigned a group of staff officers to gather the information and write the account. Their working files and correspondence were invaluable, but the resulting product, however, had problems. Appendix I Historiographical Debate covers these.

The book also presents the German perspective where available. Most important of these being regimental and divisional histories, the German official history, archival documents from the Stuttgart and Munich archives, and parts of the diary of the German corps commander. The author reviewed regimental histories for half of the infantry and artillery regiments of the divisions fighting the Canadian Corps. Those units not covered either never had a history or were unavailable in Canada in any form. At least one infantry regimental history was reviewed per division, except for the *20th Infantry Division* (*ID*). The artillery regimental history for this formation was consulted. These sources give insights into the other side of the hill but have the same caveats of Canadian regimental histories and the coverage is, unfortunately, incomplete. Only rarely was there any attempt to distinguish between Tommies and Canadians—almost all references are to English troops. Further, while Canadian histories focus on the battalion, the German ones are exclusively on regiments of three battalions. Many of these regiments fought long, hard battles in every year of the war, so Arras 1918 was a minor part of their story. Often these accounts conflict with Canadian ones on timing, forces, and outcomes. German histories are replete with attacks by masses of tanks, where there were none, phantom assaults, and inevitably the Canadians suffer staggering losses when the actual casualties were light. Unless robust counter evidence exists, the German descriptions of their own forces, deployments, and intentions will supersede Canadian intelligence reports. Where there are differences in timing and outcomes, the author has selected the most probable solution.

The battlefield terrain was a crucial resource. While aspects of it have changed in the succeeding hundred years, the key heights, rivers, and other physical features have not. Walking the battlefield and seeing the relationship between the land features helps to explain the battle's orders and decisions. It is only on the battlefield that all the information elements come together. Even the finest-grain map does not show subtle folds in the ground that hid troops or blocked lines of sight.

The author created a detailed database that recorded each battalion-level attack. This database comprised over 40 factors including frontages, depth of advance, strengths, losses, time of day, barrage, and tank support. This database was then used to analyse operations and help arrive at conclusions on the critical factors for success and failure. Further, records of the Commonwealth

no. 1 (2002), p.184.

16 Tim Cook, *Clio's Warriors: Canadian Historians and the Writing of the World Wars* (Vancouver: UBC Press, 2006), p.29.

War Graves Commission (CWGC) were downloaded for all fatalities suffered by the Corps' units, both British and Canadian, and used to investigate casualty patterns in the Corps.

The author used contemporary maps at a 1/20,000 scale to create the maps in the book. They show all the critical terrain and defensive features and use British names for trenches and defensive positions. All trench names, locations, and features mentioned in the text are on the maps, except where they interfere with the clarity of presentation. Readers may notice that some German trenches have barbed wire belts on the east side. These were originally British trenches captured in March 1918, and the Germans had not moved them. The reversed colour scheme for defences may puzzle some readers in comparison with those used prior to June 1918. The maps reflect the practice during the Hundred Days. At an Inter-Allied conference held in Paris in June 1918, the attendees agreed to standardise on the Lambert projection system for all maps with a common symbology starting in November 1918. The colours used by the British to denote friendly and hostile positions were to switch immediately to correspond with the French and Belgian scheme. These were blue for the enemy and red for friendly forces.[17]

The result is the most detailed and complete research on this campaign to date. The sources, including the terrain, maps, Canadian, British, and German archival research, and extensive secondary works, provide the basis of the research and analysis.

Structure

The battle breaks down into three logical phases. The first was the period of 26 to 28 August, where the 2nd and 3rd Divisions supported by the 51st (Highland) made major strides. After three days of bloody fighting and mixed success, the 1st Canadian and 4th British Divisions, and later the 4th Canadian Division, relieved them. The 51st transferred to another corps. These divisions ground their way forward to reach jump-off lines for an attack on the D-Q Line. This ran from 29 August to 1 September. The final phase was the assault on the D-Q Line by these three divisions on 2 September and the battle's aftermath to 5 September. The book's organisation consists of 14 chapters grouped into a section of scene setting, three sections covering the major phases of the battle and a final analysis section. Providing context for the campaign, the initial section brings events up to the end of the Battle of Amiens and describes the Corps and its opponent. Planning and operations of the Corps from 22 to 28 August is the subject of the second section. Section three deals with the actions of the Corps in reaching the jump-off positions for the attack on the D-Q Line running from 29 August to 1 September. The fourth section covers the planning and execution of the D-Q Line attack on 2 September and the follow-on operations to 5 September. The last section includes the analysis of the battle and conclusion.

Arras 1918 was the most important operational assignment of the Canadian Corps in the First World War. As Currie discussed in his interim report, the breaking of the D-Q Line meant '…the retreat of the enemy became more accelerated, and our attacks met everywhere with less and less organised and determined resistance. The moral effect of the most bitter and relentless fighting which led to the capture of Cambrai was tremendous. The Germans had at

17 LAC: RG9 III-C-3 v4106, 21/3: GHQ Ic/11860/29, 24 June 1918.

last learned and understood that they were beaten.'[18] Its study will highlight both the nature of the Corps' achievements and its flaws. It will also provide a lens to examine why the Corps was so much more successful than the British had been in 1917 on the same ground. This then gives the necessary context to provide an answer to the larger question of men, matériel, morale, or method as the prime reason for the German defeat and Allied victory.

18 Kemp, *Report of the Ministry*, p.143.

Section One

Context

1

'It had life'
The Canadian Corps' Commanders, Formations, and Arms

I suppose you have read all about what took place on the 2nd … it was certainly the hardest scrap I've ever been through.

Lieutenant Clarence Gass, 85th Battalion, 9 September 1918[1]

On a showery and overcast night at 3:00 a.m. on 26 August 1918, 632 artillery pieces of the Canadian Corps opened the Arras 1918 battle with a deafening roar.[2] Lasting for nine days of almost continuous action, the Corps ground through 15 kilometres of some of the strongest defences on the Western Front and comprehensively destroyed nine German divisions and defeated another two. The force that accomplished this was by 1918 unique in the BEF in three respects. Its reputation as elite storm-troops put it into the first rank along with the other dominion formations and select British ones. It had an organisational structure that, although built on the British model, had important differences that provided critical advantages. Finally, it possessed a degree of semi-independence not afforded other dominion formations. This chapter examines the organisation of the Corps, its commanders down to the brigade level, its key weapons systems, and its advantages.

Command Structure

The Canadian Corps commanded the four Canadian divisions plus the 51st (Highland) for the first half of the battle and the 4th British for the second half. It also controlled additional British machine gun, artillery, cavalry, tank, and supply units. The Corps' commander was the Canadian Lieutenant General Sir Arthur William Currie (43). A successful Militia artillery officer but less so as a real-estate broker, he capably led the 2nd Brigade and 1st Division. His

1 'Gass, Clarence Reginald Letter: 1918 September 9th' <http://www.canadianletters.ca/content/document-3142?position=29&list=HmFlanQ-eZfN91UMM7eNscggOzGQwPovdkOhB0MLVUc> (12 April 2018).

2 LAC: RG9 III-D-2 v4800, 126: Artillery Statistics by Date.

Lieutenant General Sir Arthur Currie on the left was well suited to his role as the GOC Canadian Corps even though he made mistakes during the battle. Field Marshal Douglas Haig on the right had improved as an operational commander, but he still had critical blind-spots. (Canada. Dept. of National Defence/Library and Archives Canada/PA-002497)

obvious competence, the demands for a Canadian commander, and Haig's confidence in him resulted in his promotion to command the Corps on 9 June 1917. He would lead it to great victories in 1917 and 1918 and establish the Corps as one of the premier formations on the Western Front. Currie was a capable combat commander, a keen disciplinarian, and a gifted trainer, with a firm understanding of the tactical imperatives of fighting on the Western Front. He was well suited to his role as General Officer Commanding (GOC), Canadian Corps.[3]

Shy and somewhat awkward outside small groups or his inner circle and with a cold and aloof demeanour, he did not connect with the rank and file.[4] Currie lacked the man-management skills needed to earn the trust and affection of his soldiers.[5] His portly appearance also hampered him. 'He did not appear to me as a soldier, big, fat, and flabby - his belt away up his stomach,' wrote

3 Tim Cook, *The Madman and the Butcher* (Toronto: Allen Lane, 2010), pp.289–91. See also Chapter 7, William F. Stewart, *The Embattled General: Sir Richard Turner and the First World War* (Montreal & Kingston: McGill-Queen's University Press, 2015).

4 A.M.J. Hyatt, *General Sir Arthur Currie: A Military Biography* (Toronto: University of Toronto Press, 1987), p.97; Cook, *The Madman and the Butcher*, pp.240–241, 267–269.

5 Cook, *The Madman and the Butcher*, p.240.

Deward Barnes, a soldier in the 19th Battalion.[6] Currie was, however, respected by his staff, senior commanders and, most importantly, by Haig. Despite these limitations, he would be one of the finest corps commanders on the Western Front and arguably the best field commander Canada has produced. Beneath his bulk was an incisive mind – careful, deliberate, and, while perhaps not particularly imaginative, decisive. His considerable strengths aligned well with the circumstances of the Western Front. Currie believed in thorough pre-battle preparation and ample firepower to reduce losses. During Arras, however, he sometimes lost sight of these precepts. One of his principal merits was his great willingness to learn, listen to his experienced staff, and master his trade.[7] He devoured every GHQ treatise on tactics he could get his hands on – marking up many of them.[8] Currie's forte was the set-piece engagement. The increased tempo of open warfare meant more and more responsibility devolved to the divisional level. At times, the necessary control to ensure the divisions fought a coordinated battle was missing. He was no saint, had his favourites, mistrusted those outside his inner circle, and occasionally made mistakes. But he rarely made them twice.

Brigadier General Norman 'Ox' Webber (37), a Royal Engineer and Camberley-trained staff officer, was Currie's chief of staff or Brigadier General, General Staff (BGGS). He had capably served as the General Staff Officer (GSO) 1 of the 2nd Division from May 1916. He did so well that he succeeded Brigadier General Percy Radcliffe in April 1918, when Radcliffe became the Director of Military Operations at the War Office.[9] Webber worked well with Currie. There were, however, issues with focus during Arras 1918 that suggested the Corps had difficulties in conducting ongoing operations while planning a major offensive.

The Corps served in General Sir Henry Horne's (57) First Army, which reported to the BEF's GHQ. He was an artillery officer and the only BEF army commander who had not attended staff college.[10] The Canadians served in Horne's army from October 1916 to the war's end, except for the Passchendaele and Amiens campaigns. Horne was not a charismatic leader but had a 'consultative command style' that allowed his corps commanders leeway to run their battles.[11] He was quiet, reserved, and avoided publicity.[12] Generally, his working relationship with the prickly Currie was satisfactory. But Currie's 'swollen head' must have grated, as did the Canadian's propensity to go around him to appeal successfully to Haig.[13]

6 Bruce Cane, *It Made You Think of Home: The Haunting Journal of Deward Barnes, Canadian Expeditionary Force: 1916-1919* (Toronto: The Dundurn Group, 2004), pp.215-216.
7 McGill: MG4027 Acc.No391 Ref 1-2, 7j: Urquhart Fonds, Burstall Comments.
8 McGill: MG4027 C1, 13: Urquhart Fonds, General Webber Comments, 1934.
9 LAC: RG9 III-D-1 v4734, 144/10: Biography, Norman William Webber.
10 Simon Robbins, *British Generalship on the Western Front 1914-18: Defeat into Victory* (London: Frank Cass, 2005), p.28.
11 G. D. Sheffield, *Command and Morale: The British Army on the Western Front 1914-1918* (Barnsley: Praetorian Press, 2014), e-Book, loc.254.
12 Simon Robbins, ed., *The First World War Letters of General Lord Horne* (London: History Press for the Army Records Society, 2009), pp.13-16.
13 National Library of Scotland (NLS): Haig's Autograph Great War Diary, Part 1 No. 96: Haig Papers, Haig Diary, 18 April 1918.

General Sir Henry Horne, GOC First Army, on the right, was not a charismatic leader but had a 'consultative command style' that allowed his corps commanders leeway to run their battles. Currie is in the centre and on the left is King George V. (Canada. Dept. of National Defence/ Library and Archives Canada/PA-001502)

Historians often portray Horne as leaving the Canadians to run their battles.[14] There was some validity to this, but he provided the 'operational framework within which Currie and his Corps functioned.'[15] He left the details to the Corps, but he was not a passive participant. Almost every day, he met with Currie to review and approve future operations. Horne, also, visited division commanders regularly.[16] Crucially, he tried with intermittent success to coordinate actions with the Third Army. Additionally, he released and channelled reinforcements to Currie.[17] He also interceded on Currie's behalf regarding Haig's insistence in using the Cavalry Corps and persuaded Haig to back off.[18] Finally, the First Army's deception efforts north of the Scarpe caused the Germans to deploy valuable reserves in the wrong location. Horne's chief staff officer or Major General, General Staff (MGGS) was Major General Hastings Anderson (54), a

14 Cook, *Shock Troops*, p.458; J. P. Harris and Niall Barr, *Amiens to the Armistice: The BEF in the Hundred Days' Campaign, 8 August–11, November 1918* (London ; Washington: Brassey's, 1998), p.153.
15 Robbins, *British Generalship*, p.287.
16 The National Archives (TNA): WO 95-178-2: First Army GS War Diary, 31 August 1918.
17 For instance, Currie asked for the 1st British Division be made available east of Arras for the attack on the D-Q Line. Horne considered and agreed later. TNA: WO 95-178-2: First Army GS War Diary, Notes of Conference at Canadian Corps Headquarter, 30 August 1918.
18 TNA: First Army GS WD 178-3, Notes of Conference at Canadian Corps Headquarter, 28 August 1918.

trained staff officer unlike Horne.[19] Once Anderson had proven himself, Horne left him to deal with the staff work.[20]

Commanding the BEF was Field Marshal Sir Douglas Haig (57), who was the foremost British officer of the age. Trim and tall, with a soldiery deportment, he was a cavalry commander who had studied and thought deeply about war.[21] He was a better manager than a combat commander, perceptive but not original, dour but optimistic, and articulate on paper but far less so in person. Haig was not an inspiring leader in the traditional sense, but he was an effective executive.[22] He excelled in dealing with the day-to-day issues of managing a massive force on an ally's territory, and he had grown as an operational general. His staff were much stronger than the sycophants who surrounded him during 1916 and 1917.[23] He now listened to his army commanders because of his increased confidence in their ability. Finally, he had learned not to continue hammering away on the same sector as on the Somme, Arras 1917, and

Foch had a more acute strategic vision than did his German counterpart and successfully cajoled his strong-willed national commanders to execute that vision. (Underwood & Underwood, 1919 <https://www.wdl.org/en/item/19318/.)

19 Don Farr, *The Silent General: Horne of the First Army, A Biography of Haig's Trusted Great War Comrade-in-Arms* (Solihull: Helion, 2007), p.150; Robbins, *British Generalship,* p.144.
20 Robbins, *British Generalship*, pp.152-154.
21 Gary Sheffield, *The Chief: Douglas Haig and the British Army* (Aurum Press, 2011), e-Book, loc.3084.
22 For an in-depth but at times unconvincing examination of Haig as a manager, see Anthony John Vines, 'The Heroic Manager: An Assessment of Sir Douglas Haig's Role as a Military Manager on the Western Front' (PhD, King's College London, 2015).
23 Harris and Barr, *Amiens to Armistice,* p.31; Daniel Todman, 'The Grand Lamasery Revisited,' in Gary Sheffield and Daniel Todman, (ed.), *Command and Control on the Western Front: The British Army's Experience, 1914-1918* (Staplehurst: Spellmount, 2004), p.60.

Passchendaele. With a better logistical infrastructure and more matériel, Haig could shift his spearpoint without an excessive delay.

As an operational commander, he still had critical blind-spots. His excessive optimism and missing *coup d'oeil* meant he repeatedly misread the German situation and made his plans based on this misinterpretation. Haig was correct that the Germans were on their last legs and that the Allies could defeat them in 1918. He, however, translated this into assigning unrealistic goals to the Canadian Corps. He was a reverse mirror of the de facto German commander, General Erich Ludendorff, in that he had a strong sense of the correct operational objectives but a poor appreciation of how to reach them. The German knew how to break a line but not what to do with it.

The German success during their spring offensives finally compelled the Allies to agree to a Supreme Commander for the Western Front – Marshal Ferdinand Foch (67). Only a Frenchman could hold this role, as the French had the largest Allied army on the Western Front and the combatants fought on their territory. Foch was the only Frenchman the British would take orders from – hence his selection. He received his full title on 14 April, usually translated as Commander-in-Chief of Allied Armies. He did not have an enviable position as he 'was called on to herd his cat-like generals with their enormous egos.'[24] The national commanders' ability to appeal to their governments if they strongly disagreed with Foch constrained his control. Thus, he had to negotiate with and cajole his senior officers to get his way. They, however, could not ignore him or his directives. To do so, they would have to plead with their unsympathetic political masters. His appointment had an unexpected benefit for Haig in providing a cover, so he could command without having to go back to the politicians before each major operation.[25] Foch had a more acute strategic vision than Ludendorff and maintained a disciplined focus on what was critical for victory. Unlike Ludendorff, the allure of a temporary advantage did not distract him, but he remained committed to attacking the Germans at their key operational vulnerabilities. He delivered a unified view of the Western Front and played an important role in stopping the enemy from splitting up the coalition when the Germans attack the British.[26] After the costly German offensives of 1918, the aggressive Foch was quick to sense the change in tide and strike at the enemy while they were vulnerable. He masterfully managed his national commanders to deliver a series of staggering blows that defeated the Germans in 1918.

Divisions and Organisation

The 1st Division arrived in England in October 1914. It trained in appalling conditions on Salisbury Plain until crossing to the continent in February 1915. Its initial engagement was in the horrific gas warfare during the Second Battle of Ypres, where it suffered over 6,000

24 Cook, *Shock Troops*, p.402.

25 David R. Woodward, *Lloyd George and the Generals* (Newark, London: University of Delaware Press; Associated University Presses, 1983), p.326; Elizabeth Greenhalgh, *Victory through Coalition: Britain and France During the First World War* (Cambridge: Cambridge University Press, 2005), p.246.

26 Elizabeth Greenhalgh, 'General Ferdinand Foch and United Allied Command in 1918', *Journal of Military History* 79, no. 4 (2015), pp.1000-1002; Elizabeth Greenhalgh, *Foch in Command: The Forging of a First World War General* (Cambridge: Cambridge University Press, 2013), pp.305-316; Nick Lloyd, *Hundred Days: The Campaign That Ended World War I* (New York: Basic Books, 2014), p.20; Woodward, *Lloyd George and the Generals*, p.289.

Major General Sir Archibald Cameron Macdonell, GOC 1st Division, was unlike most of the grey and uncharismatic senior Canadian officers, and he placed his stamp on every formation he commanded. (Canada. Dept. of National Defence/Library and Archives Canada/ PA-006208)

casualties in battling against harrowing odds. It retook Mt Sorrel in June 1916 in an early portend of the Canadian way of fighting in 1917. Its initial engagement on the Somme in September 1916 highlighted its veteran status. It performed brilliantly in 1917 and at Amiens. After four years of hard fighting, each of its battalions had a strong identity and leadership at all levels.

The division's commander was Major General Sir Archibald Cameron Macdonell (54). According to his biographer, he was 'perhaps one of the most eccentric, indomitable, and beloved officers.'[27] A graduate of the Royal Military College (RMC) Kingston, 'Batty Mac' had long service in the North West Mounted Police (NWMP), fought in the Second Anglo-Boer War, and served in the Permanent Force – Canada's small regular army. He commanded a cavalry regiment and the 7th Brigade before replacing Currie as commander of the 1st Division in June 1917. A martinet at times, he was also loyal to his subordinates. He was unlike most of the grey and uncharismatic senior Canadian officers, and he placed his stamp on every formation he led.[28] Macdonell fostered an intense identification with the 1st Division. He referred constantly to the 'old Red Patch' from the red distinguishing cloth badge signifying the 1st Division worn on every soldiers' upper sleeve. He led an experienced formation with a strong leadership cadre further

27 Ian M. McCulloch, 'Batty Mac - Portrait of a Brigade Commander of the Great War, 1915-1917', *Canadian Military History* 7, no. 4 (1998), p.11.

28 McCulloch, 'Batty Mac', pp.11-23; LAC: MG30 E20 v1: A.C. Macdonell Fonds, Macdonell Biography, 140-155.

honed by open warfare training. His was a hard-hitting, tenacious, and resilient formation – arguably the best in the Corps. His command approach was to leave much to his brigade commanders. Where he shone was in developing the division, its *esprit de corps*, leadership, and training. The senior staff officer, the GSO 1, was the Canadian John 'Rowly' Parsons who according to Macdonell had a 'fine analytical mind.'[29]

Macdonell's brigade commanders were an experienced group with long service and success. Leading the 1st Brigade was the brilliant Brigadier General William Antrobus 'Billy' Griesbach (40). He was strict, brusque, and shrewd. From one of the first families of Alberta, he was a lawyer, the former mayor of Edmonton, ambitious, and a strong Conservative.[30] He raised and led the 49th Battalion with great success. He was savvy in ways both political and military, which probably accounts for him being 'respected rather than loved.'[31] His performance was such that he took over the 1st Brigade in February 1917. Macdonell called him 'the quickest officer that I have ever had anything to do with to grasp the tactical advantages or disadvantages of a given situation'.[32] He epitomised a particular strength of the Canadian Corps in analysing every action and taking lessons to bring to the next battle.[33] His 'Book of Wisdom' included a set of prescient observations of operations at Amiens on how to break a mesh of enemy machine gun posts.[34]

The GOC 2nd Brigade was Brigadier General Frederick Loomis (42) who ran the second largest contract construction company in Canada, based in Montreal.[35] An intensely ambitious officer, he took permanent brigade command in July 1916.[36] A strength of his was his open mind and willingness to improve. He had a trying, temperamental character, and there were complaints that he bullied his staff.[37] Loomis was a strict taskmaster, mercurial, and detailed oriented, but also well aware of the consequences of decisions on his men.[38] Like Currie, he believed in rigorous training and preparation. He would create a 'confident, cohesive, aggressive

29 Kenneth Radley, 'First Canadian Division, C.E.F., 1914-1918: Ducimus (We Lead)' (PhD, Carleton University, 2000), p.375.
30 His father was an ex-British military officer who was the first to join the NWMP in 1873, the forerunner of today's Royal Canadian Mounted Police, and he rose to a senior position in the Mounted Police.
31 Patrick Brennan, 'From Amateur to Professional: The Experience of Brigadier General William Antrobus Griesbach,' in Briton C. Busch, (ed.), *Canada and the Great War: Western Front Association Papers* (Montreal & Kingston: McGill-Queen's University Press, 2003), p.82.
32 Max Foran, 'W.A. "Billy" Griesbach and World War One', *Alberta History* 32, no. 3 (1984), p.4.
33 Patrick Brennan, 'Byng's and Currie's Commanders: A Still Untold Story of the Canadian Corps', *Canadian Military History* 11, no. 2 (2002), p.9.
34 LAC: MG30 E15 v3: Griesbach Fonds, Book of Wisdom, August 1918; Brennan, 'Amateur to Professional': pp.84-87.
35 LAC: RG9 III-A-1 v169, 6-L-3: Loomis Correspondence File, Carson to Alderson, 14 November 1915.
36 See for instance, LAC: Loomis Correspondence File, Loomis to Carson, 20 June 1915; LAC: Loomis Correspondence File, Loomis to Carson, 8 December 1915.
37 See Loomis's correspondence file for the veiled references of personality fit between Alderson, Carson, and Loomis. LAC: RG9 III-A-1 v169, 6-L-3: Loomis Correspondence File; Trevor Gordon Harvey, "An Army of Brigadiers' British Brigade Commanders at the Battle of Arras 1917' (PhD, University of Birmingham, 2016), p.121.
38 David R. O'Keefe, '"A Brutal, Soul Destroying Business:" Brigadier-General F.O.W. Loomis and the Question of 'Impersonal Generalship',' in Andrew B. Godefroy, (ed.), *Great War Commands: Historical*

and above all, successful 2nd Brigade.'[39] Currie thought him 'one of the most brilliant Canadian soldiers' in 1919.[40] But at Arras 1918, he would not shine as will be discussed.

The uncompromising George Tuxford commanded the 3rd Brigade. Born in Wales, the tall 48-year-old Tuxford emigrated to Moose Jaw, Saskatchewan in 1895 to take up ranching. With long service in the prewar Militia and command of the 5th Battalion, he took over the 3rd Brigade in March 1916. By 1918, he was an experienced commander. A no-nonsense officer who at times clashed with his subordinates and other officers in the division, he had a tendency to steal credit for other's successes.[41] He was aggressive, and on 2 September he was so far forward that he was out of touch with the division, his subordinates, and flanking forces.[42] Nevertheless, he was an effective leader.[43]

The 2nd Division started forming after the British acceptance of an offer of a second contingent on 31 October 1914.[44] The division's first major engagement was a failure at the Battle of St Eloi Craters running from 4 to 21 April 1916.[45] At the Somme, it performed superbly at Courcelette on 15 September 1916, winning the signal Canadian victory in the campaign. It fought well at Vimy, Hill 70, Passchendaele, and Amiens.

Its GOC was Major General Sir Henry Burstall (48). He was one of the most professionally qualified officers in the Canadian Corps having graduated from RMC and the Camberley staff college. He led the 1st Division's guns at the Second Battle of Ypres and at Festubert and later the Corps' artillery. The British commanders of the Corps thought highly of him and recommended him for a divisional command. He took over the 2nd Division on 15 December 1916 and remained in charge until demobilisation. While David Campbell in his PhD thesis on the division rated Burstall highly, Arras 1918 was not his best example of generalship.[46] He was an experienced officer having led it for over a year and a half. His division, however, would not get the extended training in open warfare afforded the other divisions. It was a sluggish formation, unable to maintain the tempo demanded by the Corps. There was nothing wrong with the battalion-level training, but the issues manifested themselves at the brigade and divisional level. He, also, appeared to be far too sanguine about his division's chances given the information available to him. The GSO 1 of the 2nd Division was Lieutenant Colonel William Bertram. He joined the 8th Battalion in 1914 and held a variety of staff and instructor positions

Perspectives on Canadian Army Leadership 1914-1918 (Kingston: Canadian Defence Academy Press, 2010), p.89.

39 Harvey, 'An Army of Brigadiers' p.121.

40 Canadian War Museum (CWM): 19801226-280/58A 1 61.3: Currie Fonds, Currie to Mewburn, 1 January 1919.

41 For an example of his critical nature, see W. W. Murray, *The History of the 2nd Canadian Battalion (East. Ontario Regiment), Canadian Expeditionary Force, in the Great War, 1914-1919* (Ottawa: Published for the Historical Committee, 2nd Canadian Battalion, C.E.F., 1947), p.95; Schreiber, *Shock Army*, p.105.

42 LAC: RG24 v1824, GAQ 5-45: Matthews Report, 2 September 1918.

43 Andrew B. Godefroy, 'Portrait of a Battalion Commander: Lieutenant-Colonel George Stuart Tuxford at the Second Battle of Ypres, April 1915', *Canadian Military Journal,* no. Summer (2004), p.56.

44 A. Fortescue Duguid, *The Canadian Forces in the Great War 1914-1919* (Ottawa: Minister of National Defence, 1938), 1, p.404.

45 For a detailed examination of St Eloi, see Stewart, *Embattled General,* pp.82-104.

46 See for instance, David Charles Gregory Campbell, 'The Divisional Experience in the C.E.F.: A Social and Operational History of the 2nd Canadian Division, 1915-1918' (PhD, University of Calgary, 2003), pp.557-559.

Major General Sir Henry Burstall, standing next to Haig in 1919, was the commander of the 2nd Division at Arras 1918. This battle highlighted his division's lack of open warfare training and his inadequacies with the faster tempo of the Hundred Days. (Canada. Dept. of National Defence/Library and Archives Canada/PA-002498)

until his promotion to GSO 1 in June 1918. Somewhat surprisingly, he did not appear to have had any formal staff training before or during the war. He was, thus, both quite young with relatively little experience and training for his important position.[47] Burstall wrote he 'could not overestimate the services' of Bertram.[48]

Burstall's brigade commanders had a mix of experience ranging from the longest-serving to one of the newest commanders in the Corps. Brigadier General Robert Rennie (56) was the solid and effective commander of the 4th Brigade for most of the war. The president of his family's eponymous seed company based in Toronto he had a prestigious command in the

47 Paul Martin Harris, 'The Men Who Planned the War: A Study of the Staff of the British Army on the Western Front 1914-1918' (PhD, King's College London, 2013), p.217.

48 LAC: RG9 III-D-2 v4795: 2nd Canadian Division: Narrative of Operations from March 13th to Nov. 11th, 1918, 71.

Militia in 1914. His leadership during Second Ypres in command of the 3rd Battalion resulted in his appointment to lead the 4th Brigade in November 1915. Thus, by the Hundred Days, he had almost three years' experience in command.[49]

Brigadier General Thomas-Louis Tremblay had only recently received the command of the 5th Brigade. A shell on 9 August at Amiens had decapitated the brigade leadership, and Tremblay took over.[50] He was an RMC graduate and had commanded the 22nd Battalion since January 1916. A highly regarded battalion commanding officer (CO), he was due for a promotion. He was also a rarity as a senior francophone officer in an anglophone army, one of a handful of RMC graduates leading infantry units, a Roman Catholic in a predominately Protestant service, and a young brigade commander at 32.[51] Although esteemed by his superiors,

British Regular Army officer Major General Louis Lipsett led the 3rd Division since 1916. His plans were the most innovative of the divisional commanders at Arras, and his division fought at a high level. (Canada. Dept. of National Defence/ Library and Archives Canada/PA-007442)

49 LAC: RG9 III-D-1 v4734, 144/10: Biography, Robert Rennie; 'Robert Rennie' <http://qormuseum.org/soldiers-of-the-queens-own/soldier-bios-q-r-s-t-u/soldiers-bios-r/rennie-robert/> (26 February 2013); 'The Clear Grit' <https://matthewkbarrett.com/2014/12/15/the-clear-grit/> (5 August 2019).

50 LAC: RG9 III-D-3 v4886: 5th Brigade War Diary, 9 August 1918.

51 Maxime Dagenais, 'Une Permission!...C'est Bon Pour Une Recrue, Discipline and Illegal Absences in the 22nd (French-Canadian) Battalion 1915-1919' (Masters, University of Ottawa, 2006), p.22;

respected by his officers, and adored by his men, Tremblay would have a rocky start to his command at Arras 1918.[52]

The commander of the 6th Brigade was Brigadier General Arthur Bell (43) who was a professional soldier. Bell raised and commanded the 31st Battalion with distinction until his promotion to command the 6th Brigade in April 1918. His performance at Arras 1918 showed him to be a solid and capable leader who could develop and execute a daring plan.[53]

The 3rd Division formed in France in December 1916 from battalions already stationed there and in England. Its first battle at Mt Sorrel in June 1916 was not a success similar to the initial engagements of the 1st and 2nd Divisions. The 3rd Division performed well in its first engagement in the Somme Campaign in September 1916 and in its battles at Vimy, Passchendaele, and Amiens. The British regular army officer Major General Louis James Lipsett (44) led the division. Lipsett was a trained staff officer, had extensive active service, and experience in staff positions. He commanded the 8th Battalion with great distinction and was 'a man long remembered with affection' by it.[54] He then led the 2nd Brigade and took over the 3rd Division in June 1916. Lipsett was an outstanding leader and an effective divisional commander, but there were issues. He was hard on his subordinates. Brigadier General James Elmsley, then GOC 8th Brigade, told Currie that all the brigade commanders and the GSO 1 were on the verge of quitting in 1918.[55] On the other hand, Lieutenant Charles Savage of the 5th Canadian Mounted Rifles (CMR) wrote: 'I never knew of any other officer of high rank who was more universally liked and respected.'[56] He brought a firm professionalism and competence to the 3rd Division.[57] His plans were the most innovative of the divisional commanders at Arras, and his division fought at a high level. His GSO 1 was the British officer, Lieutenant Colonel Christian Hore-Ruthven (38). An experienced staff officer with long service with the Canadians, he acted in a variety of staff roles before transferring to the GSO 1 position in the 3rd Division in August 1917.

Lipsett had two relatively new brigade commanders and one with over a year's experience. The senior commander was Brigadier General Hugh Marshall 'Daddy' Dyer (57) of the 7th Brigade. Born in Ireland and moved to Manitoba in 1881, Dyer served in the Militia. He took over the brigade, replacing Macdonell as part of the stream of promotions resulting from Currie moving up to command the Corps in June 1917. Despite his age, Dyer held up under the strain and performed solidly. Not a brilliant leader, he was a steady pair of hands. Major G

Raphaël Dallaire Ferland, 'Patriotism and Allegiances of the 22nd (French Canadian) Battalion, 1914-1918', *Canadian Military Journal* 13, no. 1 (2012), p.57.

52 Joseph Chaballe, 'Courcelette, the Glorious Battle Fought by the 22nd French-Canadian Battalion', *La Canadienne,* no. October & November, p.15c. LAC: RG9 III-B-1 v869, A-18-3: Staff Officers.

53 Marjorie Norris, ed., *Medicine and Duty: The World War I Memoir of Captain Harold W. McGill, Medical Officer, 31st Battalion, C.E.F.* (Calgary: University of Calgary Press, 2007), p.27; 'The Professional' <https://matthewkbarrett.com/2014/09/15/the-professional/> (4 August 2019).

54 Bruce Tascona, *Little Black Devils: A History of the Royal Winnipeg Rifles* (Winnipeg: Published by Frye Pub. for Royal Winnipeg Rifles, 1983), p.67.

55 Quoted in Brennan, 'Byng's and Currie's Commanders', p.16.

56 'Savage, Charles Henry Memoir: 1936' The Canadian Letters and Images Project <http://www.canadianletters.ca/content/document-8359> (24 September 2017).

57 LAC: RG24 v1815, GAQ 4-40: Record of Service of Louis Lipsett ; Robbins, *British Generalship,* p.453; 'Louis James Lipsett' < http://www.biographi.ca/en/bio/lipsett_louis_james_14E.html> (7 July 2016).

C D Kirkpatrick in the brigade claimed he 'knew his business as a commander.'[58] He remained in charge until September 1918, when the pressures of long service necessitated his transfer to England.[59]

Brigadier General Dennis Colburn Draper (43) commanded the 8th Brigade, but only took it over in June 1918. Draper was a farmer from the Eastern Townships of Quebec and also served in the Militia. His plan for the opening stages of the campaign was clever and resulted in overrunning of the German forward positions at a low cost.[60]

Brigadier General Daniel 'Dangerous Dan' Ormond (33) led the 9th Brigade. A prominent lawyer in Portage-la-Prairie Manitoba, he joined the 10th Battalion at the war's start. Wounded at Second Ypres, he served in and commanded the 10th Battalion. He led it with distinction until promoted to lead the 9th Brigade on 21 July 1918. An ambitious officer eager for promotion, 10th Battalion's regimental historian described Ormond, 'as the most dominant personality in the unit's history.'[61] He was a hard man. In the words of one of his soldiers, Private F C Bagshaw, Ormond 'had no tolerance or sympathy for anybody who isn't hard as far as war is concerned.'[62] A battle-tested battalion commander, Arras would be Ormond's second engagement as a brigade GOC.

The British accepted the offer of a fourth division in February 1916.[63] It formed and trained in England over the spring and summer of 1916 and crossed the channel in August. For reasons of further training, it initially served in Flanders when the Canadian Corps moved south to the Somme. Unlike the first three divisions, its first battle was a success and its record on the Somme was generally good. It had a rough experience prior to and at Vimy, where it took two days to capture its objectives. The division ran into more issues at Hill 70 with a series of ill-advised subsidiary attacks after the main assault. It did well at Passchendaele, however.

Its commander throughout the war was Major General Sir David Watson (47) whose appointment owed much to political influence and ties to the ruling Conservative Party.[64] A Militia officer commanding the 12th Regiment in Québec City in 1914, he was the wealthy

58 Quoted in Ian M. McCulloch, 'The "Fighting Seventh": The Evolution and Devolution of Tactical Command and Control in a Canadian Infantry Brigade of the Great War' (MA, Royal Military College of Canada, 1997), p.166.

59 Harvey, 'An Army of Brigadiers' p.75; 'Memorable Manitobans - Hugh Marshall Dyer' <http://www.mhs.mb.ca/docs/people/dyer_hm.shtml> (7 March 2016); LAC: RG9 III-C-3 v4051, 18/8: Hugh Marshall Dyer; William F. Stewart, ''Byng Boys': A Profile of Senior Commanders of Canadian Combat Units on the Somme 1916', *War in History* 23, no. 1 (2016), p.59; Ian M. McCulloch, 'Crisis in Leadership: The Seventh Brigade and the Nivelles "Mutiny", 1918', *The Army Doctrine and Training Bulletin* 3, no. 2 (2000), pp.223-225.

60 'Red Baiter' <http://matthewkbarrett.com/2015/10/07/the-red-baiter/> (4 December 2015); LAC: RG9 III-D-3 v4949: 5th CMR War Diary, September 1916.

61 He persuaded the important Conservative politician Arthur Meighen to write the political head of the Canadian administration in England to complain about his lack of promotion. RG9 III-A-1 v316, 10-O-58: Meighen to Kemp, 23 January 1918 ; Daniel G Dancocks, *Gallant Canadians: The Story of the Tenth Canadian Infantry Battalion, 1914-1919* (Calgary: Calgary Highlanders Regimental Funds Foundation, 1990), pp.90, 163.

62 LAC: RG41 v5, 3/3: F.C. Bagshaw Interview.

63 LAC: RG24 v1812, GAQ 4-3: Colonial Secretary to Governor General, 31 January 1916; LAC: RG24 v1812, GAQ 4-3: Cubitt to MacDougall, 121/Overseas/1604, 11 February 1916.

64 William F. Stewart, *The Canadians on the Somme, 1916: Canada's Neglected Campaign* (Solihull, West Midlands, England: Helion, 2017), pp.225-227.

Major General Sir David Watson, GOC 4th Division, whose appointment owed much to political influence, was not at the forefront of Canadian divisional commanders but he had grown in confidence and experience by 1918. (Canada. Dept. of National Defence/Library and Archives Canada/PA-002115)

managing director of the Conservative party aligned *Québec City Chronicle*.[65] He successfully commanded the 2nd Battalion and later the 5th Brigade from August 1915, but with less distinction. Often photographed with his hat at a rakish angle, this tall and athletic officer was a consummate political general with a mixed command history. He was 'wildly ambitious' and, while outwardly confident, he was insecure.[66] Even Patrick Brennan, in his generally positive chapter, indicated Watson's command would 'forever be associated with some of the most costly setbacks suffered by the Canadian Corps.'[67] While certainly not at the forefront of Canadian divisional commanders, he had grown in confidence and experience by Arras 1918.

Watson's GSO 1 was Lieutenant Colonel Édouard Panet (37), a Canadian gunner in the Permanent Force (PF), who was a graduate of the Camberley staff college. He was from a notable military family with his brother serving as the Commander, Royal Artillery (CRA) of the 2nd Division. According to Patrick Brennan, he was 'a very able staff officer.'[68] Panet had served with the division from its inception initially as the senior administrative officer, so

65 'Dictionary of Canadian Biography Online - Sir David Watson' <http://www.biographi.ca/009004-119.01-e.php?id_nbr=8411> (19 March 2013).

66 Cook, *The Madman and the Butcher*, p.124; Patrick Brennan, 'Major-General David Watson: A Critical Appraisal of Canadian Generalship in the Great War,' in Andrew B. Godefroy, (ed.), *Great War Commands: Historical Perspectives on Canadian Army Leadership 1914-1918* (Kingston: Canadian Defence Academy Press, 2010), p.122.

67 Brennan, 'Major-General David Watson': p.111.

68 Brennan, 'Major-General David Watson': p.135.

understood it well. Watson valued him in his confidential report as 'An excellent Staff Officer… Is painstaking, tactful, and efficient.'[69]

Watson's brigade commanders were all experienced and, judging from Arras 1918, an independent lot. Commanding the 10th Brigade was Brigadier General 'Ross' Hayter (41). He was an imperial officer who graduated from Camberley and was serving in Canada at the start of the war. Although born in India, he grew up in Canada and was an RMC graduate but transferred to the British army. Hayter served as a staff officer in the Corps and was the GSO 1 for the 1st Division. Learning that he was to receive a British brigade, Currie appointed him to command the 10th Brigade on 4 December 1917. He showed 'quick appreciation and sound judgement' and was 'extremely valuable' to the Corps.[70]

Brigadier General Victor Odlum (38) commanded the 11th Brigade. Prewar, he was a wealthy insurance broker and journalist from an influential family and a major in Vancouver's 11th Regiment. Odlum commanded the 7th Battalion with distinction until his appointment as GOC 11th Brigade on 6 July 1916.[71] An aggressive and energetic officer with determined views on how to fight battles, he was possibly too loyal to subordinates who had outlasted their usefulness.[72] Interestingly, when Odlum went on leave in June 1918, Watson sent Panet to command the brigade instead of the senior battalion commander. This suggests a lack of trust in the brigade's battalion COs.[73] Odlum was close to Currie from his period under his command. Currie would solicit advice from him on whether he should accept the offer to command the Canadians in England in November 1916. Watson's opinion of him was that he was 'Determined, very gallant, and with plenty of experience. Genl. Odlum is a splendid Brigade commander.'[74]

The commander of the 12th Brigade was Brigadier General James Howden MacBrien. A rising star in the PF, MacBrien (40) was a staff college trained officer. In 1914, he was serving at the War Office after graduating from Camberley staff college as part of a program of staff officer exchanges. He served in various administrative staff functions in the Corps until his selection to command the 12th Brigade on 13 September 1916. Watson regarded him as 'A gallant, determined, experienced Commander. Genl MacBrien is experienced in both the tactical and administrative side of war. He is tactful and efficient.'[75]

69 LAC: RG9 III-B-1 v2300, R-1-30 v1: GOC 4th Division Confidential Reports on Senior Officers, 1919.

70 Kenneth Radley, *We Lead, Others Follow: First Canadian Division 1914-1918* (St. Catharines, Ont.: Vanwell Pub., 2006), p.237; Brennan, 'Major-General David Watson': p.127; LAC: RG24 v1873: Ross Hayter; Robbins, *British Generalship*, p.431; Geoffrey Jackson, 'The British Empire on the Western Front: A Transnational Study of the 62nd West Riding Division and the Canadian 4th Division' (PhD, University of Calgary, 2013), pp.324-325.

71 LAC: RG9 III-A-1 v196, 6-O-12: Odlum Correspondence File.

72 E. L. M. Burns, *General Mud: Memoirs of Two World Wars* (Toronto: Clarke, Irwin, 1970), p.15.

73 LAC: MG30 E69: Watson Fonds, David Watson Diary, 18 June 1918.

74 LAC: 4th Div Confidential Reports.

75 LAC: 4th Div Confidential Reports.

Canadian Divisional Organisation

Canadian divisions were outsized formations in comparison with German ones. For both complete divisional establishments, see Appendix II. In comparison with the paper strength of a German division, a Canadian one had 1.8 times the infantry and artillery personnel, over 3.5 times the engineers/pioneers, and 2.3 times the support manpower like transportation, signals, supply, and medical.[76] In the field, German divisions were far weaker with the trench strength of companies as low as 50 men with only the rare unit with 120.[77] Their battalions averaged 635 men in August.[78] Owing to manpower and matériel shortages, the Germans had invested in supplying large numbers of their light machine guns to their *Landsers* (infantry) with 36 per battalion. Ludendorff emphasised: 'The light machine gun is the infantry weapon and that the company of infantry has become, so to speak, a company of light machine guns.'[79] The German High Command *Oberste Heeresleitung* (*OHL*) also supplied large quantities of trench mortars of multiple types to their troops – twelve times more on a per battalion basis. Not only did they have more, they used them to a greater extent, and they could do direct fire. Owing to issues with mobility and ammunition supply, only rarely did Canadian mortars contribute in open warfare conditions. The German regimental histories commonly referred to the use of *Minenwerfers* (trench mortars) in their accounts, unlike Canadian ones.[80]

In both cases, their respective high commands would reinforce formations with additional artillery, engineering, labour, signals, and transport resources, depending on the mission and expectations of enemy actions. Canadian divisions were far larger, sturdier, and capable of taking and inflicting greater damage than even a full-strength German division, and there were none of those available. This does not consider the Canadian training advantage nor their morale superiority. Another advantage was a disastrous shortage of animals handicapped German formations' mobility.[81]

The Canadian Corps was fully integrated into the BEF's command, discipline, and administrative structure. The British regimental system and ethos were the basis of the Corps' units, with battalions, such as the 48th and 72nd Battalions, copying their British counterparts.[82] Even when Canadians differed in their establishments – the approved quantities of personnel and equipment – GHQ had to approve it. The most significant variation from a soldier's

76 LAC: RG9 III-D-2 v4791: CWNS Intelligence Canadian Corps Battle Fronts Period Aug. 8th to Nov. 11th 1918.

77 Some examples, the *61st IR/35th ID* had an estimated company strength of 50 to 60 men on 28 September, the *I/360th IR/4th Ersatz Division* had 60 men on 2 September, but the *1st Guard Reserve Division* had 120-125 men. CWM: 19801226-274-58A 1 60.3: Currie Fonds, First Army Intelligence Summary - No. 1322, 28 August 1918; LAC: RG9 III-C-3 v4230, 22/3: 4th Division Intelligence Report in Connection with Operations, 10 September 1918.

78 Jonathan Boff, *Winning and Losing on the Western Front: The British Third Army and the Defeat of Germany in 1918* (Cambridge: Cambridge University Press, 2012), p.41.

79 A.E.F. Historical Sub-section General Staff, *Survey of German Tactics 1918* (Verdun Press, 1918), Kindle, loc.410.

80 Some examples: Dr. Otto Vogt and Karl Vogt, *3. Niederschlesisches Infanterie-Regiment Nr. 50 1914–1920* (Berlin: Bernard & Graefe, 1931), p.235; Pafferath, *Geschichte I.R. 68*, p.680; Alfred Vischer, *Das Württ. Infanterie-Regiment Nr. 180 im Weltkrieg 1914 - 1918* (Stuttgart: Belser, 1921), p.139.

81 D. Stevenson, *With Our Backs to the Wall: Victory and Defeat in 1918* (London: Allen Lane, 2012), p.224.

82 McCulloch, '"Fighting Seventh"' p.15.

perspective was that Canadian troops received four times the pay of their British counterparts. At the start of the war, Canada had only 12 staff college trained officers and so had to rely on British-supplied staff. By 1918, wartime trained Canadian staff officers had replaced many of the British officers. The senior staff officers at the Corps were British as were two of the four senior staff officers in the divisions. They were excellent as indicated by three future heads of the army – Dill, Ironside, and Alanbrooke – served in the Canadian Corps.[83]

The Corps was a complex amalgam of combat, support, and logistical elements, but the infantry was its foundation.[84] It was they who faced most of the enemy's fury and had to take and hold their positions. Foot soldiers suffered 87.6 percent of the fatalities at Arras 1918, down from 93 percent on the Somme in 1916.[85] The other elements supported the foot soldiers and supplemented their firepower. The basic infantry unit was the platoon with two Lewis Gun sections and two rifle sections comprising riflemen, grenadiers, rifle grenadiers, and scouts. A section was to include at least one leader, typically a Non-Commissioned Officer (NCO), and four to seven men.[86] The platoon was a mini-army capable of gaining firepower superiority from the two Lewis Gun sections, and indirect fire from rifle grenades so the rifle sections could use fire and movement to close with the enemy. GHQ doubled the number of Lewis Guns per platoon in the spring of 1918. With declining numbers of replacements, it was necessary to substitute firepower for manpower.

Four platoons formed a company, and four companies constituted a battalion. The battalion was the infantryman's world. It provided for his needs, trained him, and directed him. This was the highest echelon at which the commanding officer could directly place his imprimatur. Nominally, they had a strength of 1,066 all ranks with an additional 100 men for Canadian battalions as supernumeraries – these were personnel over the normal unit establishment. Battalions seldom reached that total. Canadian companies typically had a trench strength of 150-160 men with some as low as 124.[87] Trench or fighting strength was the term used for how many troops were in the firing line.

The higher levels of command comprised the brigade and division. Four battalions and a trench mortar battery with eight Stokes trench mortars made up a brigade. A brigadier general – a GOC – led it. The division, commanded by a major general, consisted of three infantry brigades and a full array of support elements. These included two field artillery brigades, an engineer brigade of three battalions, a divisional machine gun battalion with 96 Vickers heavy machine guns, a divisional signal company, three field ambulances providing medical care and evacuation, and supply units. Additional field artillery brigades and often one or two heavy artillery brigades supplemented the divisional artillery.

83 William F. Stewart, 'Attack Doctrine in the Canadian Corps, 1916-1918' (Masters, University of New Brunswick, 1982), pp.255–6. For more on British staff officers, see Douglas E. Delaney, 'Mentoring the Canadian Corps: Imperial Officers and the Canadian Expeditionary Force, 1914-1918', *Journal of Military History* 77, no. 3 (2013).

84 Kemp, *Report of the Ministry*, p.221; DHH: 990.013: Comments CEF, McNaughton, 9.

85 Stewart, *Neglected Campaign*, p.300.

86 LAC: RG24 v22009: SS 143 Training and Employment of Platoons, 1918, February 1918, p.8.

87 See for instance, LAC: RG9 III-D-3 v4909: 12th Brigade War Diary, 85th Battalion Report Scarpe Operation 30th Aug.-3rd Sept. 1918; LAC: 12th Brigade War Diary, 38th Battalion Report on Scarpe Operations 30th Aug-3rd Sep, 9 September 1918.

Two British divisions (51st and 4th) would serve directly under the Corps in offensive operations, with others on its flanks. By this stage, British divisions were considerably weaker in manpower and engineers than the lavish Canadian ones. GHQ reduced British infantry divisions to three battalions per brigade in the period prior to the March offensive because of manpower shortages. The British Official History was blunt: 'In many divisions the infantry formations adopted had the object of keeping control in the hand of the few efficient officers rather than tactical considerations.'[88] Infantry had to rely on the far more effective artillery to clear the way to advance. The average strength of a British division serving with the Canadian Corps was 14,011 men while the Canadian average was 21,485.[89] Thus, Canadian divisions were roughly half again as strong numerically as their British counterparts. The result was British units in heavy fighting melted away more quickly than Canadian ones. They simply were less durable. Despite all these limitations, the divisions serving with the Canadians fought well.

The key weapon in the platoon's arsenal was the Lewis Gun. 'We may attribute our successes to it and to the men who handle it' was Brigadier General W. Griesbach's assessment.[90] Relatively mobile at 13 kilograms, with fair accuracy, and a high rate of fire of 550 rounds per minute, it was a potent weapon. Its operators could keep up with the advancing infantry and fired it from the hip. German accounts speak of Lewis gunners leading a platoon emerging from smoke and fog firing from the hip and suppressing the defenders.

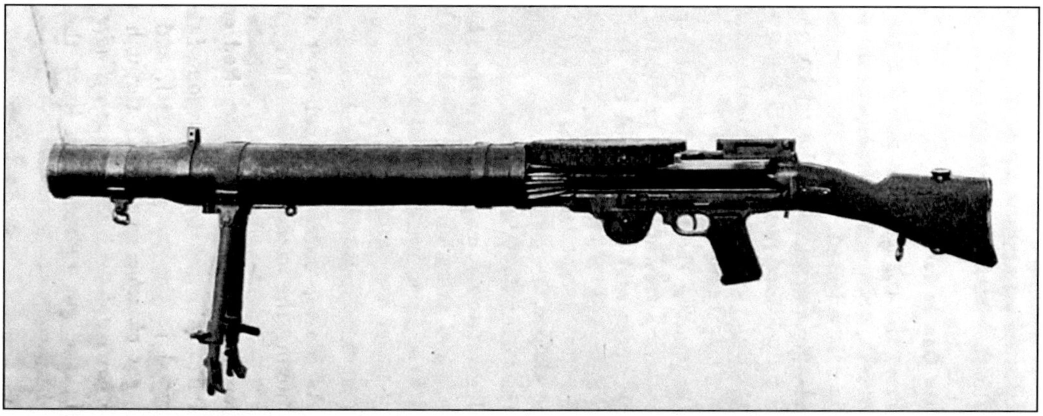

The key platoon weapon was the 13 kilogram Lewis Gun light machine gun. Brigadier General Griesbach, GOC 1st Brigade, attributed the Corps' success to it and the men that handled it. (An Instructor, The Complete Lewis Gunner, (Aldershot: Gale & Polden, 1918), 7.)

88 J.E. Edmonds, *Military Operations: France and Belgium, 1918* (London: Macmillan and Co., Limited, 1947), 4, p.183.
89 LAC: RG9 III-B-1 v1006, R-37-3 v1: Rations Issued at Refilling Points, 25 August and 1 September 1918.
90 LAC: MG30 E15 v3: Griesbach Fonds, 1st Brigade Lessons from Recent Fighting 1st Brigade, 24 August 1918.

In close support of the infantry were the trench mortars and the heavy machine guns. Trench mortars, organised in brigade trench mortar companies, deployed in the forward zone, and so were not dependent on the always vulnerable signals as was the artillery. The weapon was the 3-inch Stokes mortar, with the personnel drawn from the brigade's infantry battalions. Although it was roughly one-sixth the weight of its German counterpart and fired a round with more explosive filling than an 18-pounder shell, battalions seldom used it.[91] Poor crews hampered them, as battalions often sent their least effective soldiers to the batteries.[92] The biggest issue was that the small crews could not move the mortar and ammunition to keep up with the infantry. There was no ammunition column such as supplied the artillery, so the mortar crews handled their own supply. Multiple after-action reports called for a solution to the problem of transporting these powerful but under-used weapons.[93]

The Vickers heavy machine guns were organised into a divisional machine gun battalion with 96 guns. The Vickers heavy machine gun could sustain a high rate of fire but limitations

The Vickers heavy machine gun could sustain a high rate of fire but limitations in organisation, mobility, and communication meant their employment lagged the Germans in offensive actions. (Canada. Dept. of National Defence/Library and Archives Canada/PA-001017)

91 A.D. Harvey, 'Trench Mortars in the First World War', *The RUSI Journal* 174, no. 4, p.87.

92 LAC: RG24 v1862, 101: Trench Mortars; LAC: RG9 III-B-1 v972, O-1-83: Trench Mortar; Kemp, *Report of the Ministry*, p.238.

93 See for instance, LAC: RG9 III-D-3 v4873: 2nd Brigade War Diary, 2nd Brigade Narrative of Operations East of Arras August 25 to September 3, 1918; LAC: MG30 E300 v23: Odlum Fonds,

in organisation, mobility, and communication meant their employment lagged the Germans in offensive actions. A Canadian battalion was larger than the British 64 gun unit to account for the greater strength of a Canadian division. The Vickers fired both directly and indirectly and could sustain a high rate of accurate fire.[94] An effective weapon, it was heavy but far less mobile than the Lewis Gun. Machine gun officers such as the Corps' Machine Gun Officer, Brigadier General Raymond Brutinel, had successfully fought for greater independence of the machine gun service. By 1918, the authorities regarded it as 'a distinctive Arm with tactics of its own' [Underline in original].[95] The infantry resented this, because they could not control this potent source of firepower.[96] More significantly, the machine guns could not keep up with the infantry in an advance and so were of limited value in offensive operations.[97] Relying on the already overburdened infantry communications network, where their signals were a low priority, also hampered them.[98]

Brigadier General Raymond Brutinel (46) was a unique figure in the Canadian Corps. He was a French national living in Canada, with no connection to the Canadian Militia, having only served as a conscript in the French Army, and apparently with no formal experience with machine guns. He in effect acted as the Corps machine gun officer well before his formal appointment in October 1916. His policy of indirect fire was controversial then and now, but it became a standard element of all Canadian operations.[99] He was a strong advocate for the machine gun arm and had the ear of successive Corps' commanders including Currie.

An important support for the infantry were tanks, but they were not available in the numbers used at Amiens – the largest number fielded during Arras 1918 was 57 on 2 September. When used properly, they were devastating, and they demoralised German infantry. The dominant tank used at Arras was the Mark V, a 29 tonne, 8-metre long behemoth armed with either two 6-pounder guns or four Hotchkiss light machine guns. This new heavy tank had a longer range than the previous models and, in the right circumstances, could move somewhat faster than the infantry.[100] With an improved transmission and steering mechanism, it was far more nimble than previous versions.[101] It was still a trial to its crew as: 'The combination of heat, carbon

11th Brigade Lessons G.733, 1 September 1918 ; LAC: RG9 III-D-3 v4894: 7th Brigade War Diary, Summary of Lessons and Experiences Gained from Recent Operations, Undated [August 1918].

94 C.S. Grafton, *The Canadian "Emma Gees": A History of the Canadian Machine Gun Corps* (London, ON: Canadian Machine Gun Corps Association, 1938), pp.32, 60; LAC: RG9 III-C-3 v3937, 34/2: GHQ O.B./181, 16 July 1916.

95 LAC: RG9 III-C-1 v3832, 16/9: First Army Policy Regarding Employment of Machine Guns, 10 May 1918.

96 See for instance, LAC: RG9 III-D-3 v4900: 9th Brigade War Diary, 9th Brigade, Narrative of Operations from 25th to 30th August 1918, 15 September 1918; LAC: RG9 III-C-3 v4016, 31/5: 1st Brigade Report on Operations for the Period August 28th to September 4th, 1918, 6 September 1918.

97 See for instance, LAC: RG9 III-C-3 v4137, 2/16: 6th Brigade G.3/206, 31 October 1918; LAC: 12th Brigade War Diary, 12th Brigade Report Llandovery Castle Operation, 8-14 August 1918.

98 LAC: RG9 III-C-4 v4352, 6/15: Signals Discussion, 1 Bn CMGC, V.G. 15-43, 15 September; LAC: RG9 III-C-4 v4321, 15/1: Canadian Corps MG-G.22/582, 29 October 1918.

99 Yves Tremblay, 'Brutinel: A Unique Kind of Leadership,' in Bernd Horne and Stephen Harris, (ed.), *Warrior Chiefs* (Toronto: Dundurn Press, 2001).

100 LAC: RG24 v22020: SS 204 Infantry and Tank Cooperation and Training, March 1918, Introduction.

101 Christopher Byrnley Hammond, 'The Theory and Practice of Tank Cooperation with Other Arms on the Western Front in the First World War' (PhD, University of Birmingham, 2005), p.281.

monoxide and petrol fumes had an extremely debilitating effect on crews in action, and it could take several days before they were fit enough to resume.'[102] In addition, their slow speed meant little sleep for up to 36 hours for the crews in assembling, fighting, and rallying.[103] They were still a weapon of the set-piece attack, as they took time to get into position and even more to recover from operations.[104] Based on the costly experience of Amiens, the tanks were to trail the infantry by 100 to 200 metres and only move to the front when called to deal with machine gun posts.[105] At Amiens, the tankers found leading the advance without ample smoke and a barrage was suicidal. This new tactical approach was to shield the tanks with infantry and only commit them when absolutely necessary. While this reduced tank losses, it also meant the infantry would suffer losses as they first encountered the enemy's positions. This was a trade-off the BEF had to make if it were to maintain a viable tank force.

The key determinant of success was artillery support. As the German pre-and postwar expert on tactics, William Balck, stated 'as a matter of experience the infantry only gets as far as its artillery fire reaches.'[106] This was true for the Canadians at Arras. For all the improvements in tactics, organisation, and infantry fire power, the gunners were still vitally essential to overcome the machine gun defence-in-depth. Dick Worrall, the canny ex-ranker commander of the 14th Battalion, understood the secret to beating the Germans: 'Given a barrage and infantry close on its heels, it was the easiest thing in the world to absolutely overrun him.'[107]

Two significant changes make a sharp divide between artillery practices in 1917 and 1918 – predicted fire and smoke. Predicted fire enabled accurate shelling of distant targets without having to spot the fall of the shot and adjusting. Dependent on accurate maps and complex calculations, predicted fire enabled surprise bombardments and barrages. It was no longer necessary to go through the long-process of registering guns to ensure accuracy, which tipped off the enemy. It restored tactical and operational surprise. While the Canadians used smoke at Passchendaele, they employed it only for signalling locations or in the protective barrage once the advance had ceased.[108] During Arras 1918, the Canadians liberally fired it, except for the 2nd Division to its detriment. German post-battle accounts stressed the dislocating experience of fighting in smoke and fog and how it neutralised the defensive scheme and undermined morale. German commanders deployed defensive posts in-depth to provide mutual support and a deep mesh of machine guns. Smoke masked and broke down the mesh, allowing Canadian infantry to isolate and annihilate these posts.

102 Roger Blaber, 'Tanks in the 'Hundred Days' 1918 - A Diminishing Resource', *British Journal for Military History* 2, no. 1 (2015), p.113.
103 Shelford Bidwell and Dominick Graham, *Fire-Power: British Army Weapons and Theories of War, 1904-1945* (London: Allen and Unwin, 1982), p.138.
104 Hammond, 'Tank Cooperation' p.328.
105 LAC: RG9 III-C-4 v4357, 13/4: Preliminary Report on Lessons Learned During the Recent Operation, 18 August 1918.
106 W. Balck, *Development of Tactics--World War* (Fort Leavenworth, Kansas,: General Service Schools Press, 1922), p.251.
107 LAC: RG9 III-D-3 v4923: 14th Battalion War Diary, Report on Operation of September 1st, 6 September 1918.
108 LAC: RG9 III-D-3 v4957: War Diary, GOCRA Canadian Corps, October 1917 Appendix H Frontages of Barrage; LAC: GOCRA War Diary, Artillery Order No.95, 28 October 1917; LAC: GOCRA War Diary, Artillery Order, No.101, 4 November 1917; LAC: GOCRA War Diary, Artillery Order, No.92, 23 October 1917.

The artillery fired four basic shell types: shrapnel, high explosive (HE), smoke, and gas. Only 18-pounder and 60-pounder guns fired shrapnel, which consisted of small lead bullets contained in the shell. It relied on a time fuse to ensure the shrapnel burst over the target. All artillery pieces fired HE that comprised a shell containing an explosive mixture that detonated on contact or after a brief delay. The explosion would shatter the shell casing and scatter fragments. Gas shells comprised multiple types of poison gas filling and heavy artillery primarily fired them for counter-battery purposes. Field artillery, 18-pounders and 4.5-inch howitzers, fired a smoke shell consisting of a fuze and a white phosphorus filling that created thick white clouds.

The Corps' senior artillery commander, the General Officer Commanding, Royal Artillery (GOCRA), was Major General E W B Morrison (51), known as 'Dinky' for his short stature. A fascinating character combining a zest for journalism and combat, Morrison was the editor-in-chief for the *Ottawa Citizen*. He successively commanded the 1st Canadian Field Artillery Brigade (CFA), the 1st Canadian Divisional Artillery (CDA), and 2nd CDA. He moved up to lead the Corps' artillery in December 1916. His ferocious motto was 'Kill Boche.' While not brilliant or a scientific gunner, Morrison recognised and leveraged more talented subordinates

Major General E W B Morrison, commander of the Corps' artillery, while not a brilliant or a scientific gunner recognised and leveraged more talented subordinates to create a potent killing machine. (Canada. Dept. of National Defence/Library and Archives Canada/PA-007744)

to create a potent machine to kill the Boche.[109] Certainly, Canadian artillery was more effective under his command than under his predecessor, Henry Burstall.[110]

During Arras 1918, the Corps commanded 9 to 11 heavy artillery (HA) brigades. Unlike the field artillery (FA) brigades, they did not follow a standard pattern but comprised three to five batteries with one to six pieces depending on the calibre. During Arras 1918, the brigades assigned increased, but the number of pieces available declined. The decrease was due to their reduced availability and that the less mobile weapons remained in place as the front moved. On 26 August, the availability was 89 percent, while on 2 September it dropped to 79 percent – primarily from wear and breakdowns.[111] Typically, half of the HA brigades went to the divisions and the other half to counter-battery missions. These latter were the heavier and longer-range batteries. Those assigned to divisions were the more mobile 6-inch howitzer and 60-pounder brigades. The 6-inch howitzers accounted for 41 percent of the weight of shells fired in the

The 6-inch howitzer was the mainstay of the heavy artillery and was responsible for 41 percent of the rounds fired by weight by the Canadian Corps during the battle. (Canada. Dept. of National Defence/ Library and Archives Canada/PA-00313)

109 Campbell, 'The Divisional Experience' p.59; 'MGen Sir EWB Morrison KCMG, CB, DSO' <http://www.rcamuseum.com/English/Great%20Gunners/morrison.htm> (26 April 2013); 'Morrison, Sir Edward Whipple Bancroft' <http://www.biographi.ca/009004-119.01-e.php?BioId=41976> (26 April 2013); Cook, *Shock Troops,* p.34; Delaney, 'Mentoring the Canadian Corps', pp.931-932.

110 Stewart, *Neglected Campaign,* pp.283-285.

111 LAC: Artillery Statistics by Date.

Arras campaign, with the 18-pounders amounting to 22 percent.[112] The British Brigadier General R H Massie commanded the Canadian Corps Heavy Artillery (CCHA). Canadian histories portray him as a cypher giving considerable leeway to his Counter-Battery Staff Officer (CBSO) – the Canadian Lieutenant Colonel A G L McNaughton (31). Massie's temperament and illness contributed to this view.[113] McNaughton's role was to neutralise German artillery by collecting information on hostile battery locations, advising the GOCRA on the amount and dispositions of artillery to deal with enemy guns, issuing the detailed orders to accomplish this, and coordinating distant harassing fire.[114] An innovative, scientifically oriented, and assertive officer, McNaughton honed the Canadian counter-battery capabilities to a fine edge. By Arras 1918, Allied counter-battery efforts had forced the Germans to pull their batteries back or face destruction. The result was German guns played less of a role than in earlier battles.

The field artillery serving in a CDA comprised two FA brigades. Each brigade included three batteries of six 18-pounder guns and one battery of six 4.5-inch howitzers. A CRA directed the divisional artillery and the units attached to it. Typically, the GOCRA reinforced the CDA with up to six to seven additional FA brigades. These would be a combination of independent Army FA brigades (AFA) and brigades from unengaged divisions. Usually, there were too many units assigned to the division for the CRA to control directly, so instead he would group two to four brigades under a group commander.

Canadian Advantages

There were eight crucial differences between the Canadian Corps and equivalent British formations. First and critically, the semi-permanent nature of the Corps meant Canadian divisions served almost exclusively with it. If a division moved to another corps, they recognised it was only a temporary step. As a result, the Corps could develop shared knowledge, institutions, customs, and policies consistent across it. Commanders and staff were familiar with each other and knew each's strengths and weaknesses. The Corps' structure allowed a much higher degree of standardisation in tactics and doctrine. British divisions had no permanent assignment but moved at the whims of GHQ, and it repeatedly rotated elite units. For instance, when the 51st (Highland) Division joined the Canadians it was serving in its tenth different corps since arriving in France with fifty changes of corps.[115] As 'Ox' Webber, the Corps' BGGS and a British regular, later recalled the Corps had 'a life; there was a family feeling present,' while British corps were machines without one.[116]

112 LAC: MG30 E81 v4, Ammunition: Morrison Fonds, Statement of Ammunition and Guns Used from 7th August to 2nd October, 1918 Inclusive.

113 Paul Dickson, 'Leadership and Innovation: Andrew McNaughton and the Counter-Battery Staff Office,' in Andrew B. Godefroy, (ed.), *Great War Commands: Historical Perspectives on Canadian Army Leadership 1914-1918* (Kingston: Canadian Defence Academy Press, 2010), p.156; Schreiber, *Shock Army*, p.23.

114 LAC: RG9 III-C-1 v3903, 19/7: Organization and Procedure of Counter Battery Officer Canadian Corps Artillery, 28 January 1919.

115 TNA: WO 95-21-4: GHQ General Staff War Diary, Number of Times Division has Been in Different Corps in Order of Merit, 23 August 1918.

116 McGill: General Webber Comments, 1934.

The primary field artillery piece was the 18-pounder gun. The photo shows the measurement of a gun's muzzle velocity as one of the factors used to calculate predicted fire. (Canada. Dept. of National Defence/Library and Archives Canada/PA-008285)

Second, the Canadians had not undergone the organisational destabilisation of shifting from four battalions to three in each brigade. As a result, the Corps kept the fundamental tactical approaches they had used throughout the war, unlike British divisions that had to significantly revise theirs.

Third, the Corps often had more of everything – more radios, more guns, more trucks, more survey personnel, and more typewriters. They also had two tramways companies, discussed later, unlike British corps. A Second Army summary of the D-Q operation claimed the Corps received 80 percent of the new wireless equipment – likely because the Canadians had the best-trained operators and used the sets more extensively than other formations.[117]

117 LAC: RG9 III-C-1 v3911, 39/8: Second Army Note on First Army Fighting, 13 September 1918; LAC: RG9 III-D-2 v4805, 162: CWNS Canadian Signal Service with the Canadian Corps in the Field.

The Corps had two extra Mechanical Transport (MT) companies with over 100 lorries more than a British corps.[118] GHQ and armies, however, would assign additional MT companies to a corps when necessary. This meant that a British corps might have an equivalent number of vehicles depending on circumstances. The extra companies were still an advantage, as both the staff and MT companies well understood each other. This was an understanding unlikely to develop with units on short assignments. Further, the Corps staff could always count on them. British corps were at the mercy of their superior's determination of how much MT they required, so they could be reassigned at any time. Finally, the personnel in the Canadian MT companies were 'A' category men. These were troops capable of serving in the front lines compared with 'B' category in British MT units.[119] As a result, the Canadian MT Companies' personnel had greater stamina and so could operate around the clock. British units did not have the endurance to withstand these strains.[120]

The Corps had three additional permanent FA brigades. Like MT companies, FA brigades normally reinforced British corps. The exact number depended on the corps' mission, so the Canadians would not necessarily have more pieces. Like the MT, however, these three extra brigades were an advantage in that the GOCRA could count on them always being available. Further, their long service with the Corps meant a common understanding which was difficult for reinforcement FA brigades. This was particularly important as the communications and staff systems with the artillery were barely adequate for the assigned formations. During an attack, a division's artillery might have to manage seven or eight FA brigades – the equivalent of four times their normal strength with no extra resources.

One weapon the Corps did not have more of were machine guns on a per capita basis, although they did on an absolute one. Often Canadian Corps historians claim it had a significantly higher ratio of machine guns than a British division.[121] They tout this as showing how far ahead the Canadians were in recognising the necessity of increasing unit firepower.[122] Including the Corps' two motor machine gun brigades, the actual ratio was only slightly higher in the Canadian Corps. Based on 1,000-man battalions, the Canadian ratio was 21.9 men per gun versus the 23.2 men per gun in a British division – lower is better in this situation. In most cases, however, British divisions were under-strength with an average battalion comprising 750 men, so the British ratio was 17.4 men per gun.[123]

118 LAC: RG9 III-D-2 v4809, 7: CWNS Introduction to the Canadian Corps.

119 Michael Patrick Ryan, 'Supplying the Material Battle: Combined Logistics in the Canadian Corps, 1915-1918' (Masters, Carleton University, 2005), p.113.

120 McGill: MG4027 C1, 12: Urquhart Fonds, McAlpine to Urquhart, 12 November 1934.

121 Schreiber, *Shock Army,* p.20; J. L. Granatstein, *The Greatest Victory: Canada's One Hundred Days, 1918* (Oxford: Oxford University Press, 2014), p.7.

122 This misunderstanding likely stems from assuming the British retained the old establishment of one Lewis Gun per platoon and not factoring the reduction in the number of battalions in a British division.

123 This comparison is based on the standard establishment of 36 Lewis Guns per battalion in both the CEF and BEF. British machine gun battalions had 64 guns and Canadian ones 96. In addition, the Corps had two dedicated MMG brigades of 40 guns each. Non-infantry machine gun holdings are excluded.

Another sign of the Corps' lavish nature was typewriter availability. Today they are regarded as antiquated, but in 1918 they were a 'potent symbol of modernity and high technology.'[124] They were costly and so difficult to obtain.[125] The prevalence of them at a headquarters indicated the relative influence of the organisation. All Canadian infantry divisions', brigades', and 79 percent of battalions' war diaries for August 1918 used typewriters. For Western Front British units, 71 percent of infantry divisions and 47 percent of infantry brigades had their diaries typed.[126] This means a higher percentage of Canadian battalions had sufficient typewriters to use on a war diary than did British divisions.

The Canadian Corps had a unique 177-man Corps Survey Section that fulfilled three functions.[127] These were locating hostile batteries through flash spotting and sound ranging, gathering intelligence from observation of German rear areas, and precisely positioning friendly artillery in a process called resecting.[128] The section grew out of McNaughton's frustration with the army level field survey battalions at Passchendaele.[129] 'The Canadian Corps Survey Section…was organised with the intention of combining something of the accuracy of the Army Field Survey Battalion Observation Groups during trench warfare with the mobility required for moving battle conditions.'[130] In addition, the former Corps Topographic section that created maps and resecting battery positions had insufficient personnel. The new organisation addressed all these issues.[131]

At Arras, the section staffed three observation posts across the Corps' front at high points combining flash spotting, observation, and intelligence gathering. These posts used the latest technology Continuous Wave (CW) wireless sets. The broad availability of these sets within the Canadian Corps was invaluable as wire communications would not survive that far forward.[132] Each post had flash spotters, trained observers, and German speaking NCOs to debrief prisoners.[133] They deployed close to the front and kept up with the advance. In addition, scouts roamed forward searching for information and liaising with battalions. Finally, there were documentation collection posts that gathered captured German papers and forwarded the most valuable to Corps' headquarters by despatch rider. The result was an information gathering

124 Paddy Griffith, *Battle Tactics of the Western Front: The British Army's Art of Attack, 1916-18* (New Haven: Yale University Press, 1994), p.180.
125 LAC: RG9 III-B-1 v2892, O-153-3 v4: OMC Submissions, 6 August 1918; Brian N. Hall, 'The British Expeditionary Force and Communications on the Western Front, 1914-1918' (PhD, University of Salford, 2009), pp.94, 350.
126 This was based on a review of British war diaries on the Ancestry.com website of 48 of 48 British infantry divisions serving on the Western Front in August 1918 and 142 of 144 infantry brigades. One Canadian infantry battalion (116th) was not included in the Canadian figures.
127 British corps did have a survey section, but they had fewer personnel and did not have the sound ranging capabilities. The artillery had to rely on the army level survey battalions for resecting positions. LAC: RG24 v22003: Canadian Corps Survey Section War Establishment, May 1918.
128 Kemp, *Report of the Ministry*, p.273.
129 Dan Jenkins, 'Winning Trench Warfare: Battlefield Intelligence in the Canadian Corps, 1914-1919' (PhD, Carleton University, 1999), p.350.
130 LAC: Organisation CBSO 1919.
131 LAC: RG9 III-D-3 v5006: Canadian Corps Survey Section War Diary, 1-15 May 1918.
132 W Arthur Steele, 'Wireless Telegraphy in the Canadian Corps in France Part II Open Warfare', *Canadian Defence Quarterly* VIII, no. 3 (1931), p.394.
133 LAC: RG9 III-B-1 v2236, O-3-9 v3: Canadian Corps I.G.287, 24 August 1918.

The latest in signal's technology was a Continuous Wave Mark III* Transmitter. The Second Army claimed the Canadian Corps received 80% of the new wireless equipment. (The Wireless War on Land,' Marconi Heritage Group <http://marconiheritage.org/ww1-land.html> (7 August 2020).)

system that rapidly provided the artillery and Corps' general staff with data. This was a major leap in accelerating the flow of news back to the senior commanders and staff. It provided the Corps as one historian has noted, with 'its own ground-level "telescope" to the forward lines.'[134] The survey section claimed it provided over 70 percent of the information received by the Corps on 8 August.[135] Morrison took pride in keeping Currie informed of the situation at the front, with Currie often visiting the survey headquarters to get the latest news.[136]

Fourth, Currie had GHQ's approval to increase the quality and quantity of the Corps' infantry, logistics, engineering, machine gun, and artillery organisations. The British, with their straitened personnel reserves, could not implement these. These changes provided greater flexibility, effectiveness, and robustness. With the signal's organisation, GHQ refused permission for an increase, but Currie did it unofficially, anyway. The Corps' transfer of 1,000 personnel from its replacement pool to the signal service met these manpower needs.[137] He expanded the engineers in each division to brigade strength comprising three battalions. This reduced the strain on the infantry by freeing them from providing labour. Instead of having to rely on indifferent infantry work parties, the engineers supplied both the supervision and manpower resulting in the work getting done more efficiently and effectively. It also freed the infantry to rest and train. Currie viewed the increase in engineers so vital that he preferred 'to

134 Jenkins, 'Winning Trench Warfare' p.353.
135 LAC: Survey Section WD, 8 August 1918.
136 McGill: MG4027 C1, 13: Urquhart Fonds, Colonel Crear [Crerar] Comments, 1934.
137 LAC: CWNS Canadian Signal Service.

do without infantry than to go without Engineers.'[138] He added a third machine gun company of 32 guns to each divisional machine gun battalion. Historians have rightly praised Currie for his principled stance for pushing for the reorganisation instead of adopting a British proposal to expand the Canadian Corps.[139]

Fifth, the Canadian divisions had not suffered the extraordinary number of casualties and shattering defeats suffered by the British divisions in the German spring offensives. The 51st (Highland) Division was on his third 1918 rebuild when it joined the Canadian Corps. In contrast, the Canadians had suffered minimal casualties since Passchendaele. This resulted in for more experienced leadership at all levels. For instance, most platoon leaders in the 16th Battalion had served with the unit since January 1918. This gave them eight months of experience plus an extended period of open warfare training to learn their craft.[140]

Sixth, three of the four Canadian divisions had the inestimable advantage of having two months of open warfare training – an advantage not afforded British formations. The 51st (Highland) Division after suffering heavy casualties during the Marne offensive only conducted basic musketry instruction for its new replacements in August.[141] Contrast this with the Canadian's opportunity to conduct battalion and brigade-level open warfare exercises discussed in Chapter 3.

Seventh, despite the divisiveness and disruption caused in Canada, conscription provided sufficient reserves to keep the infantry up to strength.[142] The Amiens campaign resulted in many battalions losing 100 to 250 men, but most were close to their original strength by Arras. In some cases, such as the 2nd CMR, they emerged with more after Amiens than before owing to vagaries of manpower supply.[143] Moreover, the Canadians had the luxury of transferring men unfit for the front or overage out of the unit and having them replaced.[144]

Finally, the Canadian reputation plus Currie's obvious competence allowed the Corps far greater leeway than Haig afforded British formations.[145] For instance, Currie could postpone the initial attack by one day to allow more time for preparation, which Haig would likely not grant a less storied formation. This was especially surprising given Haig's anxiety regarding the Germans slipping away and that the Canadian attack was the BEF's spearhead. Haig well knew that Currie could call in the politicians if he did not get his way on an important matter. Further, the Canadian victories in 1917 were a powerful card for Currie. Currie also had a good relationship with the First Army commander, Horne.

138 LAC: RG9 III-B-1 v970, O-27-3: Currie to OMFC, 27 February 1918; H.F.H. Hertzberg, 'The Re-Organization of the Engineering Troops of a Canadian Division - Great War 1914-1918', *Canadian Defence Quarterly* 1, no. 4 (1923), p.39.

139 For more on the proposal, see Stewart, *Embattled General*, pp.220-222.

140 H. M. Urquhart, *The History of the 16th Battalion (the Canadian Scottish)* (Toronto: MacMillan, 1932), p.240.

141 F.W. Bewsher, *The History of the 51st (Highland) Division 1914-1918* (Edinburgh: William Blackwood and Sons, 1921), p.340; TNA: WO 95-2847-1/4: 51st (Highland) Division GS War Diary, July 1918.

142 For more on the larger role conscripts played in the Hundred Days, see Dennis, Reluctant Warriors.

143 G. Chalmers Johnston, *The 2nd Canadian Mounted Rifles (British Columbia Horse) in France and Flanders* (Vernon, B.C.: Vernon News Printing & Publishing Co., 1931), pp.68-69.

144 For instance, see LAC: RG9 III-D-3 v4911: Royal Canadian Regiment War Diary, 13 July 1918; LAC: RG9 III-D-3 v5001: 11th Battalion Canadian Engineers' War Diary, 6 June 1918; LAC: RG9 III-D-3 v5000: 10th Battalion Canadian Engineers' War Diary, June 1918.

145 McGill: General Webber Comments, 1934.

By the start of 1918, the Canadian Corps was the equal of the best forces on the Western Front. The Germans recognised this with the four Canadian divisions regarded as first-rate attack divisions – they rated only 7 out of 48 British formations this highly.[146] The German *121st Reserve Infantry Regiment* (*RIR*) marked the Canadian presence on the Arras front with 'The English had thrown fresh troops into battle, including their best Canadian attack divisions.'[147] It had a sterling and unbroken record of success in 1917, a strong and experienced leadership cadre, ample manpower reserves provided by conscription, an efficient learning orientation, and confidence in its superiority over the enemy. But, what of that enemy and the ground they had to fight over? That is the next chapter's topic.

146 'German Rating of BEF Divisions' <http://1914-1918.invisionzone.com/forums/index.php?/topic/34342-british-v-dominion/&page=2#comment-277580/jack> (9 February 2017).

147 Hauptstaatsarchiv Stuttgart: M109 Bü49 2009: Das III/R. 121 Auf Der Viser Höhe Vom 28-30.8.1918.

2

Ground, Foe, and Method
Where, Whom, and How the Canadian Corps Fought

It has often become the habit to cast the eyes towards the rear at even the smallest breakthrough, and under the pretence of 'flexible defence' retreat to positions in the rear.

Commander *Sixth Armee*, 12 September 1918[1]

The fundamental factors of ground, foe, and method powerfully shape land battles. Terrain affects observation, movement, and combat. The foe's forces, morale, defences, doctrine, and commanders play an instrumental role in the campaign's outcome. How one's own forces counter the enemy with their own approaches establishes the battle dynamic. It is, therefore, imperative to grasp how these foundational aspects influenced the campaign. This chapter examines the critical terrain on which the Canadian Corps conducted Arras 1918 and how it affected operations. It analyses the hostile forces, their defences, and how they fought. It also examines how the Canadian and British forces approached combat. The chapter briefly describes the Arras 1917 campaign to highlight how campaigning had changed since then.

'Nothing but ruins': Arras 1918 Battlefield

The Corps' front extended on both banks of the Scarpe. The northern section ran from 1,200 metres north of Gavrelle southwards to Fampoux on the Scarpe. South of the river, the line ran from Feuchy to the outskirts of Neuville-Vitasse. The 51st (Highland) Division defended the sector north of the Scarpe with the 3rd and 2nd Divisions on the southern front. The boundary between the First and Third Army shifted early in the offensive to the south-east to accommodate developments further south with the Fourth Army.[2] This greatly extended the Corps' front-line and had important effects. As the battle progressed, the Corps' advanced to the south-east centred on the Arras-Cambrai road.

The main campaign area was on the Canadian divisions' front, bounded in the north by the Scarpe, Trinquis Brook, and the Sensée Canal. The Scarpe was roughly 45 metres wide

1 Hauptstaatsarchiv Stuttgart: M93 Bü42: A.O.K.6 1a No 4448 Secret of 9.9.18.
2 Edmonds, *Military Operations, 1918* 4, p.299.

Tommies crossing the Scarpe in 1917. At 45 metres wide and with Germans damming it, there was no realistic possibility of a German counterattack from across it. ('Tommies Crossing the Scarpe,' National Library of Scotland <https://www.flickr.com/photos/nlscotland/4687950609/> (9 August 2020).)

and 2 metres deep, so it presented a significant obstacle. Private Glenn Irian thought it must have been a very beautiful stream before the war.[3] It had a series of locks to control levels and allow navigation. The Germans had dammed the river and it flooded its valley. With only a handful of crossing points through the marshes, there was no realistic possibility of a German counterattack from this direction. The height of Greenland Hill and its spurs north of the Scarpe, however, enabled German observation over sections of the vital supply line of the Arras-Cambrai road. Thus, long-range machine gun and, more dangerously, artillery fire would assail the Corps' left flank as it advanced south-east. To the south, the army boundary ran 4,000 metres south and parallel to the Arras-Cambrai road.

North of the river, the 80 metre Greenland Hill dominated the nearby terrain including the ground north of the Monchy-le-Preux ridge. Where the railway, with its high embankment at 21 metres, crossed the Scarpe, the river bent sharply to the south-east and created a complex

3 Glenn Irian, *In the Trenches, 1914-1918* (Kenora: Artbookbindery, 2008), p.257.

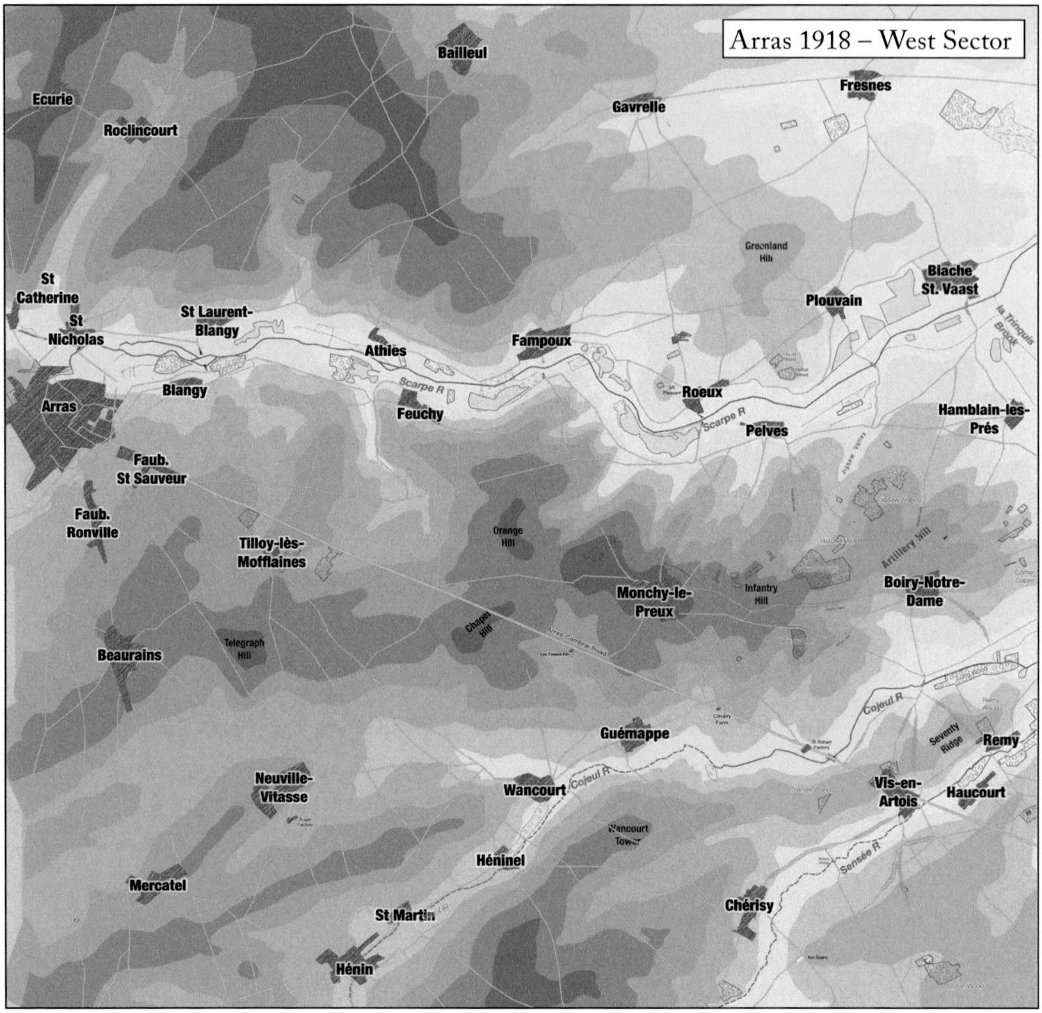

Map 1. The western sector of the battlefield. Note the dominating points of Greenland Hill, Monchy-le-Preux, Orange Hill, and Chapel Hill, and the numerous villages that were all potential strongpoints for the German defence. The villages east of Arras were all in ruins. (Author's Map)

Cojeul River in 2018. More of a stream than a river, both its and the Sensée's valleys were an obstacle to horse drawn and mechanical transportation. (Author's image)

salient pointed south-west.[4] There were a series of small woods and hills and the village of Roeux that overlooked the Canadian sector. The most important of these vantage points were Mt Pleasant, Hausa Wood, and Delbar Wood. Protected on the south and west by marshes and lakes, and the high railway embankment on the north, this sector was awkward to capture.

South of the Scarpe the terrain consisted of a series of ridges that compartmentalised the battle space. The result was that adjacent areas might not be observable from another. There were a series of ridges running roughly north-east obliquely across the Corps' advance. Each ridge complex was lower than the previous as the Corps advanced south-east. The first and largest ridge ran to the east with the steep, high point of Monchy-le-Preux with views extending from the Scarpe to the Cojeul River in the south. It contained Telegraph, Orange, and Chapel Hills, all were over 100 metres high, with Monchy-le-Preux at a steep 105 metres.[5] Orange and

4 TNA: WO 95-2868-1: 6/Gordon Highlanders War Diary, 19 August 1918.
5 LAC: RG9 III-D-3 v4855: 3rd Division GS War Diary, 3rd Division Report on Operations from Aug. 26th to Aug. 28th, 1918.

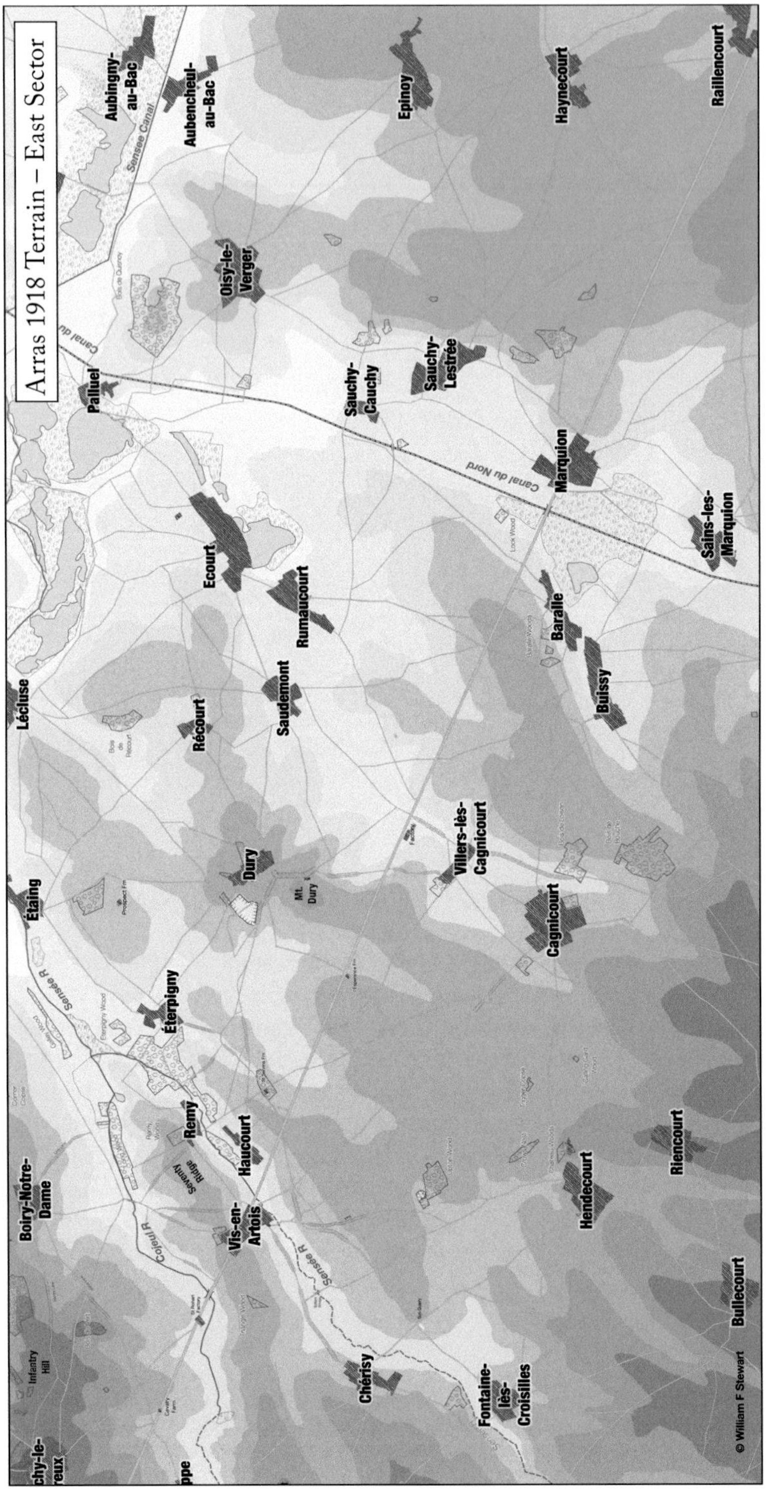

Map 2. The eastern sector of the battlefield. Note when moving east how each ridge is lower than the previous one. (Author's Map)

The ruins of Wancourt in 1919. Most of the villages in the battle area were blasted into a similar state of wreckage. (Canada. Dept. of National Defence/Library and Archives Canada/PA-004410)

Chapel Hills were like outworks protecting the major hill with a wide glacis giving great sight lines for machine gunners. To the north were a series of re-entrants that provided cover to the attacker from that direction.[6]

Two river valleys – the Cojeul and Sensée – divided these ridges until the streams joined in the northern part of the sector. These were more like a brook that a single stride could cross. These valleys created long slopes exposed to nearby heights, with deep ditches and tall rank grass at the bottom.[7] The streams were shallow but presented a major obstacle to horse-drawn transport, and this limited them to using bridges. These rivers were mostly dry in the summer until they

6 Ralph Wilfred Hodder-Williams, *Princess Patricia's Canadian Light Infantry* (Toronto: Hodder and Stoughton, 1923), 2, p.325.

7 D. J. Goodspeed, *Battle Royal: A History of the Royal Regiment of Canada, 1862-1979* (Toronto: Royal Regiment of Canada Association, 1979), p.246.

reached the Arras-Cambrai road where springs created marshy, wet bottom lands.[8] Their being dry was a disadvantage as it restricted where the troops and animals could obtain water.[9] Closer to the Scarpe, there were large swamps that created significant movement obstacles.

On the western outskirts of the combat zone lay the ancient city of Arras. Surrounded by ridges, this was the most important French city held by the British during the war.[10] The Canadian reporter John Livesay did not find it attractive, claiming: 'No stretch of imagination can render Arras beautiful.'[11] The fighting in 1917 and 1918 had flattened the villages in the battle zone, and those that were not yet soon would be. As the 2nd Engineer Battalion war diary phrased it, 'All villages including the famous MONCHY LE PREUX nothing but ruins.'[12]

The key transportation route was the Arras-Cambrai road running almost on a straight line from Arras to Cambrai on an old Roman road. It was vital as it was the primary all-weather highway in the operational area. East of Arras, the roads were in terrible shape from the heavy fighting. With the dense defences, horse transport, unlike at Amiens, had to keep to these battered routes. The rain affected the roads and tracks, and the First Army had to warn about loads damaging them.[13] A constant complaint in diaries, both personal and official, was the chaotic congestion of which more will be discussed.

Two Canadian tramways companies of 383 men each were a secret weapon crucial to maintaining the Corps' combat tempo. The compounding effect of insufficient road space, too much traffic, and poor control, discipline, and enforcement choked the transportation system. The Corps would have struggled without the tramway/light rail system that moved up to 1,800 tonnes of supplies a day.[14] It relieved pressure on the roads and allowed vital materials to reach the front regularly. The Canadian tramways organisation comprised No. 1 Company for construction and No. 2 for operations.[15] The construction company remained at Amiens, which handicapped the service.[16] In the BEF, GHQ controlled the tramways organisation, so having dedicated companies was a major advantage for the Corps. They would be responsive to the Corps' needs.[17] The Canadians were exempt from GHQ's limits on total maintained track mileage because of the British shortage of skilled personnel.[18] The transport authorities during the Hundred Days banned extending light rail to focus on standard gauge lines which had much higher capacity. This system, however, poorly served the sector south of the Scarpe. A First Army map of railway expansion on 28 August shows no intention of extending the line into the Canadian sector.[19] So, with the Corps having the resources to build and maintain the

8 LAC: RG24 v22007: Notes on the Valleys of the Scarpe and Sensee, March 1917.; LAC: RG9 III-C-3 v4052, 22/6: 4th Brigade BM 267, 29 August 1918.
9 LAC: Notes on Valleys, 28 August 1918.
10 Jonathan Nicholls, *Cheerful Sacrifice: The Battle of Arras 1917* (Barnsley, South Yorkshire: Pen & Sword, 2008), e-Book, loc.422.
11 Livesay, *Canada's Hundred Days*, p.120.
12 LAC: RG9 III-D-3 v4994: 2nd Battalion CE War Diary, 29 August 1918.
13 LAC: RG9 III-C-1 v3855, 75/2: First Army G148, 28 August 1918.
14 Kemp, *Report of the Ministry*, p.148.
15 LAC: RG24 v22003: Tramways Companies War Establishment, No. 1911, Part XVI.
16 LAC: RG9 III-D-3 v5006: No.1 and No.2 Tramways War Diaries, August 1918.
17 TNA: WO 95-39-3: GHQ QMG War Diary, 17 July 1918.
18 TNA: GHQ QMG War Diary, 9 July 1918.
19 TNA: WO 158-191: Map Accompanying First Army GS 1367/1, 28 August 1918.

The Canadian Corps' secret weapon were tramways. The Canadians had permission to extend their system, and it was the difference in enabling the Corps to maintain its high operational tempo. It could move 1,800 tonnes of supplies per day to the front without using the overloaded roads. (Canada. Dept. of National Defence/Library and Archives Canada/PA-003721)

lines, they again received an exemption.[20] Further, the Canadian service was far more efficient. It carried almost twice the tonnage per mile as the British service, and its personnel were four times more productive.[21]

The light rail system was especially useful in delivering ammunition to the front and for evacuating wounded. The 1st CDA reported that traffic congestion was a serious issue in supplying the guns until the engineers extended it. Tramways delivered just under half of the rounds dumped at the battery positions for the 2 September attack.[22] The Canadian Army

20 A. M. Henniker, *Transportation on the Western Front 1914-1918* (London: HMSO, 1937), p.453; WJK Davies, *Light Railways of the First World War: A History of Tactical Rail Communications on the British Fronts, 1914-18:* Newton Abbot (Devon): David & Charles, 1967), pp.98-99.

21 Davies, *Light Railways*, pp.56-57.

22 LAC: RG9 III-D-3 v4959: 1st Division Artillery War Diary, 1st Division Artillery Report on Operations 28 August to 4th September, 1918.

Medical Corps (CAMC) extensively used them on 2 September to evacuate the wounded. Heavy German shelling prevented use of many loading points and roads used by horse-drawn ambulances. This avoided the build-up of cases as at Amiens.[23] According to the official medical history of the CAMC, it saved the situation.[24] That the Corps assigned two to four engineer battalions to push the lines forward on each day indicates the tramway's importance.[25]

German Organisation and Leaders

The German forces facing the Canadians consisted of a revolving cast of divisions serving in the *II Bavarian Korps* under the Bavarian *General der Artillerie* Konrad Krafft von Dellmensingen. It reported to the Prussian *General der Infantrie* Otto v Below's *Seventeenth Armee*, which *Army Group Rupprecht* commanded by Field Marshal Crown Prince Rupprecht of Bavaria controlled. All were trained, experienced, and competent commanders with considerable success before

Head of the *OHL*, *Field Marshal* Paul v Hindenburg on the left with his chief of staff, *General* Erich Ludendorff. Ludendorff drove the day-to-day decision-making, while Hindenburg provided the gravitas and political cover. <http://loc.gov/pictures/resource/ggbain.20468/> (Accessed 26 August 2020))

23 LAC: RG9 III-D-3 v5025: Assistant Directory of Medical Services, 1st Division War Diary, 2 September 1918.
24 Arthur Evans Snell, *The C.A.M.C. With the Canadian Corps During the Last Hundred Days of the Great War* (Ottawa: Canadian Army Medical Corps, 1924), pp.128-130.
25 LAC: RG9 III-C-5 v4226, 3/12: CE Canadian Corps, Engineers Instructions No. 1, 28 August 1918.

March 1918. The German supreme high command was the *OHL* headed by Field Marshal Paul von Hindenburg with General Erich Ludendorff as his chief of staff.[26] Ludendorff drove the day-to-day decision-making, while Hindenburg provided the gravitas and political cover.

The Allied success at Amiens had caused a near-breakdown in Ludendorff's morale and mental balance. By Arras, he had recovered but was still subject to wild mood swings. These reflected the tension between his professional competence and recognition of situation's severity with his desire for reality to be otherwise.[27] *OHL* had exhausted the army and its spirit in its spring offensives, and with the arrival of Americans it was evident that Germany faced defeat. There were no tactical expedients that could overcome the Allied advantages. Ludendorff responded by meddling at low levels, sapping the initiative of his subordinates and forcing them into decisions with which they fundamentally disagreed.[28] He called v Kuhl, Rupprecht's chief of staff, four to five times a day.[29] Another unpleasant aspect of his personality was his tendency to search for scapegoats for defeats. The clear-eyed realist of 1916 had ossified into an inflexible martinet focused on tactical solutions to operational and strategic problems. Kuhl complained: 'What he said about his intentions was not at all clear, he gave no end-objectives or clear missions for the armies, just lots of tactical odds and ends.'[30]

General der Infanterie Otto von Below was the commander of the *Seventeenth Armee.* He was a successful offensive commander on multiple fronts but was less so at Arras 1918. His métier appeared to be offensive operations. <https://www.loc.gov/pictures/item/99403476/> (Accessed 26 August 2020))

26 Hermann Cron, *Imperial German Army 1914-18: Organisation, Structure, Orders-of-Battle* (Solihull, UK: Helion and Company, 1937), p.17.
27 Robert B. Asprey, *The German High Command at War: Hindenburg and Ludendorff Conduct World War I* (New York: W. Morrow, 1991), p.459.
28 Jonathan Boff, *Haig's Enemy: Crown Prince Rupprecht and Germany's War on the Western Front* (Oxford: Oxford University Press, 2018), e-Book, loc.408.
29 Boff, *Haig's Enemy*, loc.446.
30 Quoted in Boff, *Haig's Enemy*, loc.388.

The tall, angular Crown Prince Rupprecht (49) was the heir to the Bavarian throne and a professional soldier. During the Hundred Days, Rupprecht was detached and did not play a large role. He was on leave during Arras 1918.[31] Rupprecht was strongly supported by his chief of staff, *Generalleutnant* Herman von Kuhl.

Widely acclaimed as one of Germany's most accomplished generals, the army commander, v Below won victories on the Eastern, Italian, and Salonica fronts as an army commander. His victory with Krafft von Dellmensingen as his chief of staff at Caporetto, inevitably meant these two would move west to take part in Ludendorff's spring offensive. His operations in the offensive were disappointing, and his star was no longer in the ascendant. He misread the situation after the first day of the Third Army operation in August 1918 and launched costly counterattacks that exhausted his reserves.[32] Below's *métier* appeared to be offensive operations. Ludendorff pushed to replace him during Arras 1918 owing to the Canadian success.[33]

In charge of the *II Bavarian Korps*, v Dellmensingen was a key figure in the Royal Bavarian Army and a rising star. At the war's start, he was the chief of staff of Bavarian Crown Prince Rupprecht's *Sixth Armee*, where the 'two forged and maintained a close bond from the start.'[34] In the spring of 1915, *OHL* transferred Dellmensingen to command the *Alpenkorps*, an elite division-sized formation of mountain troops that performed superbly. He then moved to a staff role, including helping plan the highly successful Caporetto offensive that almost knocked Italy out of the war. He remained the chief of staff of the renamed *Seventeenth Armee* when it moved to the Western Front. Ludendorff blamed Dellmensingen for the

General der Artillerie Konrad Krafft v Dellmensingen commanded the *II Bavarian Korps* and the main opponent of the Canadian Corps. While a dynamic and capable officer, his insistence on fighting for the forward zone exhausted his formations for little benefit. (Viser, Jonathan. Konrad Krafft Von Dellmensingen.' http://prussianmachine.com/aka/krafft.htm (26 March 2020))

31 Boff, *Haig's Enemy*, loc.408.
32 Edmonds, *Military Operations, 1918* 4, pp.204-205.
33 Bundesarchive, Freiburg: RH 61/970: Herman Von Kuhl Kriegserinnerungen, 28 August 1918; 'Otto Von Below' <http://prussianmachine.com/aok/below_o.htm> (26 March 2017); Michael B. Barrett, ed., *Below, Otto Von (1857-1944)*, vol. 1, The Encyclopedia of World War I (Santa Barbara, CA: ABC-CLIO, 2005), p.198.
34 Boff, *Haig's Enemy*, loc.69.

army's poor performance in the March offensive.[35] On 19 April, Ludendorff transferred him to take over the *II Bavarian Korps* after the incumbent had disappointed in the Lys Offensive and who the Kaiser wanted removed.[36] The corps shifted to the Arras front in August 1918.

Dellmensingen would remain in command of the corps until almost the end of the war. He was clearly a dynamic and capable commander and staff officer. There were limits, however, to what even an elite commander could accomplish given the situation. From his diary, it was apparent that he frequently disagreed with his superior on the allocation of forces. Perhaps it was the close familiarity of serving as von Below's chief of staff that contributed to these tensions.[37] His insistence on fighting to restore the German outpost zone after every Canadian advance exhausted his formations for minimal benefit. While he had vastly more prewar training, Currie could match his battle experience in the Great War.[38] Also, at 56 he was 10 years older than Currie.

'*Alte Hasen*' and '*Korsettenstangen*' – Defences, Tactics, and Morale

The German defences comprised 15 kilometres of successive fortified zones. Fighting in the spring of 1917 and March 1918 had left prodigious devastation, defences, and the detritus of combat. The troops fought over 'all the debris of many overlapping battlefields,' as described by the 52nd (Lowland) Division's history.[39] As a result of the seesaw fights that swept up to and back from Arras, the defences were unusually deep and strong. Both sides created multiple fortified zones, each with many lines. In some cases, the Germans captured British trenches and did not move the wire, but these obstacles still presented a difficult obstacle. Adding to the challenge were numerous sunken roads and tracks between the fortified zones that the Germans would rapidly turn into improvised fortifications.

Five main fortified zones or positions made up the defensive system, each composed of multiple fire and communication trenches with dugouts and protected by belts of barbed wire. The engineers typically sited most of these defences on the reverse slope of a rise, making them more difficult to hit with artillery. The *II Bavarian Korps* held the Feuchy-Wancourt Line – a prominent objective for the offensive in 1917 – as their forward zone or *Vorfeld*. Running 1,000 to 2,000 metres further east, just short of Monchy-le-Preux, was the line lost by the British on 28 March 1918 German attack. It was also the *Hauptwiderstandlinie I* (*HWL*) or main line of resistance for the Germans. Another several thousand metres further east were the British and German lines before the 1918 German spring offensive. Both sides had lavished months of work to improve them. The next line, the Fresnes-Rouvroy (F-R) Line, was 2,000 metres further east and consisted of a strong set of defences south of the Cojeul River and more rudimentary ones north of it. Running south-east from Vis-en-Artois was the very strong switch named after the

35 David T. Zabecki, 'Operational Art and the German 1918 Offensives' (PhD, Cranfield University, 2004), p.259.
36 'Otto Von Stettin' <http://prussianmachine.com/akb/stetten.htm> (27 May 2018); Boff, *Haig's Enemy*, loc.390.
37 See for instance, Bundesarchiv, Freiburg: RH 61/918: Konrad Kraftt von Dellmensingen, Feldzug 1918: Entwürfe, Berichte, Betrachtungen Und Vormerkungen, 21, 28-30 August 1918.
38 'Otto Von Below'; Barrett, *Below, Otto Von (1857-1944)* p.198.
39 RR Thompson, *The Fifty-Second (Lowland) Division 1914-1918* (Glasgow: Maclehose, Jackson & Co. , 1923), p.521.

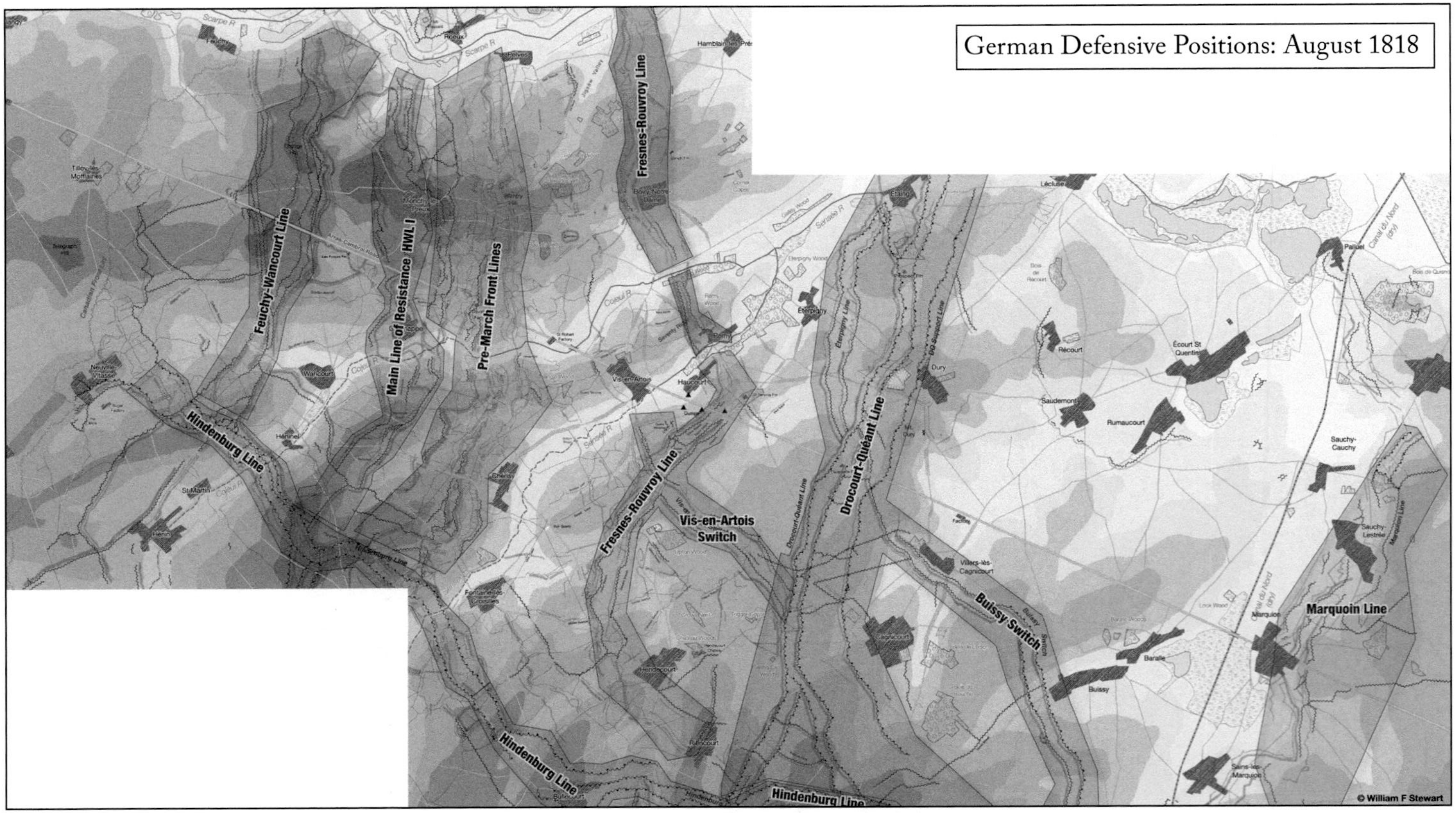

Map 3. The Canadian Corps had to breach five German defensive positions or lines to reach the Canal du Nord. Note the depth of the D-Q Line. Each position consisted of multiple trenches and thick barbed wire obstacles. Some, such as the D-Q Line featured concrete dugouts impervious to all but the heaviest shells. (Author's Map)

village that joined the D-Q Line. Finally, 1,500 to 3,000 metres behind the F-R Line was the D-Q Line and Buissy Switch. The D-Q Line generally ran north to south across the Canadians' attack front until it met the Hindenburg Line south of Riencourt. The Buissy Switch ran from the D-Q Line near the Arras-Cambrai road to the south-east. Barbed wire on the Switch was not as thick as on the D-Q Line, but it was well maintained.[40] These were the final organised defences before the obstacle of the Canal du Nord. Partially flooded, this canal sector limited crossing to existing bridges at small towns. Therefore, the Corps had to capture them before the Germans destroyed them.

The British and Canadian disquiet over the D-Q Line's strength overstated the reality. Often referred to as part of the Hindenburg Line, it was a separate switch. The Germans constructed it in the spring of 1917 on the same principles as the Hindenburg Line.[41] It was incomplete, as some sections had only holes for concrete emplacements. What was complete were wide belts of barbed wire entanglements, often set at angles like an 18th-century fortress to funnel attackers into kill zones. The engineers built them low to ensure they did not deflect traversing machine gun fire. There were up to three belts of wire each 10 to 30 metres deep made up of hardened steel difficult to cut by hand. Every 100 metres were steel reinforced concrete shelters called MEBUs (Mannschafts-Eisenbeton-Unterstände – reinforced concrete shelters for troops) or more colloquially pillboxes.[42] Designed to protect the occupants from bombardment, they were impervious to anything lighter than an 8-inch howitzer shell. While they had embrasures, the infantry were to fight not in but around them. There were up to five distinct trench lines. They were generally in pairs, with the first on the forward slope. The second was on the reverse 200 to 300 metres away, out of the enemy's view. German analysis found that long fields of fire were less important than avoiding observation.[43] Based on a captured example of the Hindenburg Line at Héinel in 1917, there were fears that tunnels linked these lines.[44]

By 1918 the Allied matériel and manpower advantages were so powerful that no forward defences could withstand the Allied gunners' pummelling. To counter this edge, the Germans adopted a flexible, defence-in-depth doctrine comprising three distinct defended zones. These were outpost or *Vorfeld*, battle, and artillery protection. The *II Bavarian Korps* laid out its defensive arrangements in accordance with *OHL* directives.[45] First introduced over the winter of 1916/17, *OHL* made constant adjustments to deal with the Allies' countermoves. The *Vorfeld* had a depth varying from a minimum of two to three kilometres but could extend to five.[46] During Arras 1918, the *II Bavarian Korps* endeavoured after every Canadian advance to recapture or recreate a new *Vorfeld*. Only a minimal garrison sufficient to repel probing attacks manned this zone. Its purpose was to absorb the blow of a major offensive and force the enemy to expend considerable effort in its capture. *OHL* instructions enjoined officers to escape the effect of a

40 Kim Beattie, *48th Highlanders of Canada, 1891-1928* (Canada: The Highlanders, 1932), p.362.
41 Patrick R. Osborn and Marc Romanych, *The Hindenburg Line* (Bloomsbury Publishing Plc, 2016), e-Book, loc.34.
42 Osborn and Romanych, *The Hindenburg Line*, loc.104.
43 Osborn and Romanych, *The Hindenburg Line*, loc.62.
44 LAC: RG9 III-C-1 v3959, 14/10: Hindenburg Line Notes from Chief Engineer, January 1918.
45 Boff, Winning and Losing, p.170.
46 Timothy T Lupfer, *The Dynamics of Doctrine: The Changes in German Tactical Doctrine During the First World War* (Fort Leavenworth, Kan.: Combat Studies Institute, U.S. Army Command and General Staff College, 1981), 4, p.13.

heavy bombardment by shifting forces forward or latterly, but never rearward.[47] The garrisons were to resist as long as possible, but sector commanders would order them back in the face of an all-out attack. These were sacrificial troops.

Next was a battle zone that was likewise deep and protected by a Main Line of Resistance or *HWL*. This was where the defenders would fight the main battle. Troops were to resist to the end to prevent any further penetration. The artillery protection zone covered the guns that provided the powerful defensive support needed by the infantry if they were to defeat the attackers. A further *HWL*, and usually referred to as *HWL II*, defended it. The principle was that the defence was not static but aggressively focused on disrupting the attacker. It would then snap back when the defenders had worn down and disorganised the assault troops. Key to the defensive scheme were divisions in this zone specially prepared to launch strong coordinated counterattacks. These *Eingreifdivisions* (intervention divisions) deployed in this zone out of the range of most Allied artillery fire.

Line-holding divisions typically employed all three regiments in line. This made it easier to add reserves instead of having to deal with inserting a regimental headquarters. Each regiment assigned one battalion to the *Vorfeld*, another to the *HWL I*, and the third in the rear to rest and train. In reaction to the increasing Allied firepower and capability, only portions of a battalion held the *Vorfeld*. The *214th ID* deployment on 26 August shows this development. Each regiment, with 12 infantry companies, committed two to the outpost zone, six to the battle zone, and four more in reserve in the artillery protection zone. Ideally, backstopping each line formation was an intervention division poised to drive back the attackers. During Arras 1918, the *II Bavarian Korps* seldom had the luxury of a full-strength intervention division behind each front-line formation.

The battle was not for specific ground but to inflict injury on the enemy. Ludendorff wrote that the growing power of the Allied attacks meant, 'we shall have to make up our minds to a greater extent than in the past to abandon outpost lines and forward systems in good time in such circumstances, and to give up the idea of retaking them [underline in original].'[48] This was an extraordinary admission of the decreasing effectiveness of the German infantry. Ludendorff stressed two other points. First, commanders had to exert maximum effort to combat the notion that fixed defences were of little value. Second, the army needed to pay utmost attention to resisting the new capabilities of Allied tanks. The defenders were to employ the entire gamut of countermeasures from gun fire, trench mortars, armour piercing bullets, to bundles of grenades for close-in fighting.

The German defensive doctrine relied on the artillery to inflict losses, machine gun posts echeloned in-depth to bring long-range cross fire from multiple directions on the advancing attackers, and well-supported counterattacks to strike over-extended Allied assault formations.[49] Flanking fire was essential owing to its disproportionate morale and casualty effects. Without smoke, the Canadian platoons had to deal with multiple machine gun posts firing from ranges

47 Historical Sub-section General Staff, *Survey of Tactics*, loc.682-689.
48 CWM: 19801226-274-58A 1 60.3: Currie Fonds, Experience of the Recent Fighting, Translation, 22 July 1918.
49 TNA: WO 94-2889-1/4: 52nd Division General Staff War Diary, News Sheet, 29 August 1918.

as much as 2,000 to 2,500 metres.[50] The Canadian infantry weapons had neither the reach nor firepower to suppress enemy nests more than about 250 metres out.

Eingreifdivisions remained out of the range of most Allied artillery but close enough to deliver a counterattack when the advance had slowed. These fresh troops would strike the powerful blows needed to restore the defensive system. In this scenario, the attackers were like a person running into the ocean. At first the going is easy, but it becomes increasingly difficult to make progress. The incoming waves initially are of no consequence, but as the runner gets deeper, the waves become more of a challenge until the person passes the point of equilibrium. Then, the next wave sweeps them back onto the beach.

German defensive artillery tactics were to support the outpost line with observed barrage fire. If attacked at night, in fog, or in smoke light signals would trigger pre-plotted annihilating fire on the enemy front-line and assembly areas. Company commanders and above alone were authorised to call for barrage fire and only after the annihilating fire program finished. Controlled, measured, and limited to the attack front, the artillery response conserved ammunition. Overall, this was a policy of poverty, where artillery pieces and munitions were at a premium, and where *OHL* prohibited speculative expenditure of shells.[51] To combat the scourge of Allied counter-battery fire, batteries established multiple dummy positions. They also left one gun behind in a known location while the remainder moved to a prepared site and remained silent.[52] Batteries would regularly change their location to confuse the enemy.[53]

The Germans also increasingly relied on gas shells to interdict communications instead of explosive rounds.[54] In some cases, they had no choice owing to ammunition shortages.[55] Often they targeted valleys and other depressions as the gas would linger there longer and these were choke points. For instance, the Sensée valley near Vis-en-Artois was the target of heavy gas shelling on the afternoon of 27 August that resulted in a minimum of 44 casualties.[56] Particularly devastating was the use of mustard gas that persisted longer than other forms and, while few died, it knocked out many.[57] Gas would not stop the Canadians, but it was another form of hate to wear down the attackers.

Jonathan Boff in his book on the Third Army claims the Germans weakened their artillery by stationing too many guns as anti-tank pieces.[58] This did not apply on the Canadian front. The Corps captured a relatively small number of guns that did not represent a significant portion of the sector's artillery park. For instance, the regimental history of the *221st RIR* of the *48th*

50 See for instance, LAC: RG9 III-D-3 v4227: 12th Brigade War Diary, 12th Brigade Report Llandovery Castle Operation, 8-14 August 1918.
51 LAC: RG24 v22011: German Artillery Tactics (Translation of Captured Order), 17 July 1918.
52 LAC: RG9 III-D-1 v4722, Summaries of Intelligence: GHQ Survey of Information, 20 August 1918.
53 CWM: 19801226-275/58A 1 60.4: Currie Fonds, General Staff Report for Period 6 A.M. 30 August to 6 A.M. 6th Sept.
54 LAC: RG24 v1826, GAQ 5-75: The Breaking of the Quéant-Drocourt Line by the Canadian Corps, First Army, 123.
55 For instance, see Karl Guth Otto Mathies, Urn Bunnemann, *Geschichte Des 3. Oberelsässisch. Feldartillerie-Regiments Nr. 80* (Berlin: Druck und Verlag von Gerhard Stalling, 1928), p.229.
56 LAC: RG9 III-C-1 v3978, 11/9: 2nd Division Report on Gas Shell Bombardments for Week Ending Saturday August 31 1918.
57 'Yellow Cross: The Advent of Mustard Gas In 1917' <https://simonjoneshistorian.com/2014/02/04/yellow-cross-the-advent-of-mustard-gas-in-1917/> (22 June 2017).
58 Boff, *Winning and Losing*, pp.176-177.

Reserve Division (*RD*) reported receiving two field guns to serve as anti-tank pieces to combat Allied tanks.[59] These weapons inflicted losses, knocked out many tanks, and slowed down the Canadian advance by firing over open sights. The difference was they were always eventually overrun with the crews killed or captured. If deployed in the rear, counter-battery fire would silence or knock out guns, but at least some crew would escape. German artillery over most of the period did not have the impact it did in 1916/1917. This was because the High Command deployed them out of range of many of the Canadian counter-battery pieces and munitions shortages. While this resulted in fewer guns lost to counter-battery efforts or outright capture, it also meant the forces in the outpost line received significantly less support. It was not the stationing of anti-tank guns that crippled the artillery threat, but the German withdrawal of pieces out of harm's way.

Tankschrecken – tank terror – dragged down German morale.[60] It had an outsized effect on the defender's psyche, far beyond their actual impact at Arras. The petrifying image of hundreds of virtually unstoppable leviathans spitting death emerging out of the smoke like some primeval horror was a constant fear. German reports reiterate masses of tanks accompanied Canadian attacks even when they were not present or only in small numbers. The average *Landser* did not know this, so the prospect of facing such terrors undermined morale. German countermeasures were effective in limiting the impact of tanks, but the Allied successes of 18 July and 8 August, featuring mass tank attacks, had already damaged morale.

By August 1918, German morale was suffering after the brief rise with the expectations and initial successes of the spring offensives.[61] The immense casualties of almost a million men, the offensives' ultimate failure, and the obvious increasing numbers of American troops depressed morale. Battle losses had hollowed out the German army. Exacerbating the situation was the influenza outbreak that incapacitated even more men – up to a million were on the sick list by mid-July.[62] The devastating successes of the French counteroffensive on the Marne on 18 July and the Allies at Amiens on 8 August further deflated morale.[63] There could be no question the Allies were now a potent threat. The average soldier was unlikely to know the details, but the impressions of defeat were widespread.

The fighters' spirit was depressed, but their willingness to fight on was contingent. Local factors like their last battle experience, exhaustion level, and circumstances would raise or lower morale.[64] Thus, while most Germans did not retire or surrender at the first sign of a Canadian, they did not fight with the same resolve as before. If cut-off or outflanked, they were far more likely to fall back or surrender than earlier. The decline in the numbers of *Landsers* willing to

59 Dr. Otto Hirschel, *Standhaft Und Treu! Geschichte Des Reserve-Infanterie-Regiments 221* (Berlin: Verlag Gehard Stalling, 1925), p.263.

60 Joseph Steuer, *Das 1. Unter-Elsassische Infanterie-Regiment Nr. 132 im Weltkriege* (Berlin: Tradition Wilhelm Kolk, 1931), p.399.

61 Jonathan Boff, 'The Morale Maze: The German Army in Late 1918', *The Journal of Strategic Studies* 37, no. 6-7 (2014), p.863.

62 Dennis E. Showalter, *Instrument of War: The German Army 1914-18* (Osprey Publishing, 2016), e-Book, loc.460.

63 Alexander Watson, *Enduring the Great War: Combat, Morale and Collapse in the German and British Armies, 1914-1918* (Cambridge: Cambridge University Press, 2008), p.197.

64 Carl von Clausewitz, Michael Howard, and Peter Paret, *On War* (Princeton, N.J.: Princeton University Press, 1976), p.189.

fight it out to the end contributed to the success of infiltration tactics. *OHL* recognised this and exhorted after Amiens: 'The principle that a Unit, even when enveloped, should hold in position if necessary all day to the last round and last man in the absence of orders to the contrary, has been forgotten.'[65]

One striking aspect of the Canadian battle accounts was the language used to describe German resistance was not markedly different from that used on the Somme 1916. Canadian accounts in 1916 and 1918 reported the German infantry would surrender readily once they lost the advantage, but that the machine gun crews would fight on. If bypassed, the German infantry would surrender in droves. As Alexander Watson phrased it, the average soldier was not fleeing from the front but finding ways to surrender.[66] The backbone of the German front defences were machine gunners and elite units like the Guards or Württemberg regiments, with the average quality of German infantry having declined. Dennis Showalter captures this: 'Battalions and companies depended increasingly and disproportionally on the remaining *alte Hasen* and the *Korsettenstangen*, the 'old hares' and the 'corset stays'—the machine gunners in particular.'[67] These old hares and corset stays could still fight hard, though. The regimental history of the 14th Battalion commented: 'The men who fought on this section of the front smiled grimly at the reports of lowered German morale.'[68]

Canadian reports support Alexander Watson's argument that Germans hid in their deep dugouts to surrender later. There were multiple comments of how bypassed pockets surrendered readily or hid in their dugouts until it was safe to submit.[69] The regimental history of the *68th Infantry Regiment* (*IR*) of the *16th ID* captures this experience describing a mixed group of survivors almost cut-off on 1 September. Two days of constant bombardment, fighting, and without food pounded them into apathy. Resigned to capture, most would hide out in their dugouts to await the Canadians' arrival. Only three would try to evade the enemy.[70] Previously, depending on their quality, they would fight on and aggressively launch immediate counterattacks. This made bypassing German units dangerous to the flanks. Now, they were more passive and would surrender when pressed. This meant Canadian infantry, as taught in their open warfare training, could strike out for distant objectives and ignore their flanks. When present, smoke aided these tactics by preventing aimed long-range machine gun fire, so flanks were less of a worry. In 1916, flanks were a constant worry and resulted in lost opportunities.[71]

By the end of 1917, the Germans had no suitable answer for a properly prepared and supported assault. Holding the outpost zone lightly meant its loss to nightly attacks, while doing so in strength resulted in heavy losses in an all-out offensive.[72] The Germans faced a terrible conundrum of trying to address strategic and operational problems with tactical palliatives.

65 Boff, *Winning and Losing*, p.168.
66 Watson, *Enduring the Great War*, pp.210-211.
67 Showalter, *Instrument of War*, loc.475.
68 R. C. Fetherstonhaugh, *The Royal Montreal Regiment: 14th Battalion, C.E.F. 1914-1925* (Montreal: The Gazette Printing Co. Limited, 1927), p.231.
69 See for instance, LAC: RG9 III-D-3 v4934: 26th Battalion War Diary, C Company Report, [31 August 1918].
70 Pafferath, *Geschichte I.R. 68*, p.725.
71 Stewart, *Neglected Campaign*, p.286.
72 Historical Sub-section General Staff, *Survey of Tactics*, loc.111-123.

Munitions shortages, manpower deficiencies, and slumping morale undermined their doctrine.[73] While the army replaced losses in artillery pieces there were severe shortfalls in ammunition. The *Second Armee* on the Amiens front fired 50,000 rounds a day while just the Canadian Corps averaged 95,000 shells a day.[74] Prisoner interrogations revealed complaints about serious German shortages during the battle.[75] Immediately after Arras 1918, the *Seventeenth Armee* warned its corps that ammunition for 100mm guns and 105mm howitzers would not keep up with expenditures due to raw material shortages. The troops were not to be told.[76]

The enormous losses suffered during the spring offensives and the influenza outbreak had left German divisions severely under-manned. Ludendorff's determination to hold as much ground as possible meant the Germans had few reserves available. By July, the German line was 120 kilometres longer than in March, with divisions defending large sectors, often with exiguous defences.[77] As a result, the German reliance on counterattack formations meant there were fewer troops available to deliver these hammer blows. Further, each division was weaker, so they had less effect. The infantry's morale, except for elite formations, had slumped. This resulted in more passive defensive forces, which surrendered more readily, and counterattacks delivered with less drive. Only the sullen desperation of the *alte Hasen* and the *Korsettenstangen*, machine gunners, and the artillery remained.

This tactical system was complex. It required a fine touch or, as in German, *Fingerspitzengefühl* and reliable, instant communications to know when to stand, when to fall back, and when to counterattack. The leaders with this fingertip instinct were now rare. They never had, nor would have, reliable instant communications. German post-battle reports concluded the subtleties of aggressively defending the different zones were beyond the weakened infantry and the decline in junior leadership. The commander of the *Sixth Armee* claimed 'It has often become the habit to cast the eyes towards the rear at even the smallest breakthrough, and under the pretence of 'flexible defence' retreat to positions in the rear.'[78] The defensive doctrine was too arcane and complex for the junior leaders to implement effectively. Moreover, it was in constant flux, with myriad instructions cascading down from *OHL*.[79] These changes undermined the troops' confidence and lowered their commitment to resist to the end.[80] It also gave troops an out to keep retreating in the guise of a flexible defence. A *12th ID* post-battle report highlighted that, as the army back peddled, the junior leadership and troops no longer believed a serious

73 Matthias Strohn, 'German Tactical Doctrine and the Defensive Battle on the Western Front,' in Matthias Strohn, (ed.), *World War I Companion* (Oxford: Osprey Publishing, 2013), p.118.

74 Boff, *Winning and Losing*, p.76; LAC: RG9 III-D-3 v4821: Canadian Corps AAQMG War Diary, September, Appendix D.

75 CWM: 19801226-274-58A 1 60.3: Currie Fonds, First Army Intelligence Summary - No. 1325, 31 August 1918.

76 Bundesarchiv, Freiburg: PH 8I/53: AOK 17 Radio Message to XVIII AK, 5 September 1918.

77 Watson, *Enduring the Great War*, p.187.

78 Hauptstaatsarchiv Stuttgart: A.O.K.6 1a No 4448.

79 *OHL* issued 11 different instructions for revisions to the defensive doctrine between July and September. Boff, *Haig's Enemy*, loc.412.

80 See for instance, Alfred Stenger, *Geschichte Des Kgl. Preuß. Trierschen Feldartillerie-Regiments Nr. 44, 1899-1919* (Freiburg: Poppen & Ortmann, 1934), pp.381-382.

resistance was possible. Retreat became the rule. When told to hold a line unconditionally, they no longer believed in the order or their ability to execute it.[81]

The steady rain of Allied blows forced German commanders to commit their divisions piecemeal, which reduced their effectiveness and added to their command burden. For instance, five other units separated two regiments of the *2nd Guard's Reserve Division* in the D-Q Line on 29 August.[82] Divisions scattered across the front could not deliver a coordinated and powerful counterblow or fight effectively.

The bitter response from Major Heinrigs, commander of the *68th IR*, to the demand for an investigation into its performance summarises all these issues. He highlighted that the High Command looked only at manpower numbers and not their training or integration into the unit. Troops did not know how to use or value their weapons. Junior leaders received promotions for valour but could not lead. There was an absence of mutual trust because of the lack of training. Finally, the continual insertion of new divisions destroyed cohesion.[83]

The situation on the opening day of Arras on 26 August 1918 illustrates these dire circumstances. The German artillery deployed far in the rear, so only the longest-range pieces covered the outpost zone. Subsequently, the *II Bavarian Korps* post-battle analysis indicated this was a mistake. It left the outpost zone unsupported, and it reduced their ability to defend.[84] Only one reserve division reached the battlefield in time to deliver a four-battalion counterattack on the 3rd Division's front. The counterattack was crushed before it could reach Canadian lines. On the 2nd Division's front, the intervention division had only one effective regiment. One regiment served to the south, and the other was out of the line owing to low strength.[85]

Fundamentally, the underlying premise of the superiority of the German army no longer was true, as the Allies had a matériel and tactical supremacy. Allied improvements in offensive doctrine and destructive capacity overwhelmed the German system of defensive tactics, fortifications, and firepower. The scheme of elastic defence-in-depth relied on the men to hold. As German *The Principles Of Command In Position Warfare* put it 'stout hearted men with iron nerves form the real backbone of defence.'[86] These were becoming increasingly rare.

Canadian Doctrine

The Canadian tactical doctrine and assault formations were based on British models. Reserves trailed by at least 500 to 1,000 metres to avoid getting caught in the battle. Typically, Canadian barrages made 100 metre jumps at 3 to 4 minutes per lift to pace the advance.[87] The Canadian doctrine was a phase line approach of distinct objectives and pre-planned barrages. While orders called for long advances, there was little expectation of an uninterrupted offensive. Conversely German attacks were non-stop and relentless, with divisions replaced only after days of combat.

81 Bundesarchiv, Freiburg: PH 8I/33-7: 12th ID Gefechtsbericht Für Dem 1 Und 2 September 1918.
82 Adolf Kümmel, *Res.Inf.Regt. Nr. 91 im Weltkriege 1914–1918* (Berlin: Verlag Gehard Stalling, 1926), p.422.
83 Pafferath, *Geschichte I.R. 68*, p.744.
84 Boff, *Winning and Losing*, p.177.
85 Stühmke, *26th Reserve Division* II, p.60.
86 Quoted in Lupfer, *Dynamics of Doctrine* 4, p.15.
87 Historical Sub-section General Staff, *Survey of Tactics*, loc.289.

Canadian offensives were spasmodic pulses, usually in the morning supported by artillery to crack the German positions. The *II Bavarian Korps* regarded this policy of phases with pauses as proving 'extremely handy for our defence and made it easier to organise our formations and set up the artillery defence.'[88] The doctrine was to defeat the expected strong counterattacks. An all-out attack without pauses created the risk that a counterattack would catch the troops off-balance and drive them back. Phase lines ensured the gunners could fire beyond that point without fear of fratricide.

Battalions typically attacked on a two-company front with either a company in support and one in reserve or two in support. The difference between the two was the support company commander could commit his troops without permission, while the battalion commander had explicitly to release a reserve company. Units would assault with three companies in line when they were short of men or had an extended front to cover. The GHQ tactical platoon manual called for each platoon to operate on a front of 100 metres with a battalion attacking a sector 200 to 600 metres wide.[89] At Arras 1918, actions by units of the Canadian Corps ranged on fronts of 200 to 2,000 metres, with an average of 815 metres.[90] This greatly exceeded the recommended limit, given these attacks typically faced significant fortifications. This was a function of the Corps' excessive frontage, which will be a recurring theme. The average depth of a battalion's advance was 3,200 metres, which was four times the depth at Passchendaele.

Unlike the Corps' 1916/1917 offensives, multi-day bombardments did not inevitably precede the attacks at Arras 1918. Instead, the offensive opened with no preliminary bombardment and without registering the guns. On subsequent days, the heavy artillery would bombard enemy positions for short periods before an attack. Only prior to the D-Q Line assault was a prolonged period of wire-cutting necessary. In most attacks, a rolling or lifting barrage led the infantry advance with the infantry trailing the barrage by 100 metres to minimise the effects of shorts. This safety margin was 200 metres for 4.5-inch howitzers and 600 for the heavy artillery.

Face of Battle

This book's focus is on the decisions and decision-making at the higher levels of command. Sight must not, however, be lost that each choice meant placing the humble private, bombardier, sapper, and others in harm's way. What then was the experience of combat or the face of battle?[91] After Amiens, the value of the new tactics was evident, and the battle's success confirmed the Canadian conceit that they were the better soldier. They did not regard German infantry highly, other than some elite units. Enemy machine gunners, however, were of a different calibre. Canadians greatly respected and feared them for their skill and determination. They would often fight to the death, so it was not uncommon to see dead gunners draped over their still steaming guns.

Often the approach march was a nightmare of fatigue, danger, and frustration in the dark, as the troops lugged over 30 kilograms of gear. Caught in the congestion on the roads, units

88 Quoted in Boff, *Winning and Losing*, p.226.
89 LAC: SS 143 Platoon, p.24.
90 Based on average of 83 contested battalion attacks conducted by the Canadian Corps during Arras 1918.
91 John Keegan, *The Face of Battle* (London: J. Cape, 1976).

averaged only a kilometre an hour. They frequently had to cross a river valley which the Germans flooded with persistent mustard gas. Men would have to put on their gas masks, which made the effort of marching more exhausting. German shelling of the road forced detours around still burning and exploding trucks and smashed horse teams with animals kicking in their final, frantic death throes. Open warfare involved long advances that tested the conditioning and endurance of the troops unlike before.

At Zero, the barrage opened with a mighty crack. Shells screamed overhead to crash into hostile lines a hundred metres in front of the waiting men. On the hand-motion of the platoon commander, they set out at a standard pace. The battlefield was a screeching cacophony of explosions, making it hard to hear orders. It was, however, apparently empty. The enemy were visible only by the flash of their firing. Troops only had the briefest glimpses of others in the dust and smoke. What was observable was the destruction wreaked by shellfire, smashed trenches, broken bodies of men and horses, and, most distressingly, those savagely wounded but not yet dead. Led by their scouts, the platoon's sections would advance in irregular columns or worms in a diamond formation.[92] Called an artillery formation, it minimised casualties when moving under enemy shelling. Enemy machine gunners would open up at all ranges but often, at about 400 metres distance, the assault troops would hear the dreaded mechanical chuck-a-chuck sound of a machine gun firing. The platoon's sections would extend into line and find cover. Its commander, based on the scout's reports or his own reconnaissance, would issue his orders. The two Lewis Gun sections would deliver covering fire while the rifle sections would spread out and advance in alternating rushes searching for dead ground. It was important for them to close the range. The troops advanced at double time, and the length of each rush diminished the closer to the post they got. The average dash was three to five seconds long and would cover 20 to 30 metres. Each rifle section would rise on command, sprint to the next cover, and pitch down. This was hot and physically taxing work. It took a fine touch to minimise the risk of enemy firing while accomplishing the military goal. Short bounds meant less immediate exposure, but it took longer to reach assault range, increasing the risk of an unlucky shot. The rushes had to be continuous but irregular to prevent the enemy predicting the next move. When the range was within 150 to 200 metres, the rifle grenadiers would fire explosive or smoke grenades to suppress the enemy. They might also have to fire on a flanking post to prevent it interfering. This cycle of heart pounding alternating rushes with fire constantly playing on the German post continued until the attackers were within bombing range of 30 metres. The bombers would then toss their grenades, and when these exploded, the section would rush the post with their bayonets flashing. Sometimes the defenders would shout *Kamerad!* and throw up their hands. If they delayed their surrender too long, however, they would pay the ultimate price for their defiance. Canadians were not magnanimous to defenders who fought on and inflicted casualties. This was just one of the hundreds of struggles to take out German machine gun posts.[93]

92 LAC: RG9 III-C-3 v4058: Diamond Formation, 1st Division G.7-113, 10 June 1918.
93 LAC: SS 143 Platoon, 22-24; LAC: RG9 III-C-3 v4069, 12/3: The Normal Formation of a Platoon and a Platoon in Attack, 7th Battalion, June 1918.

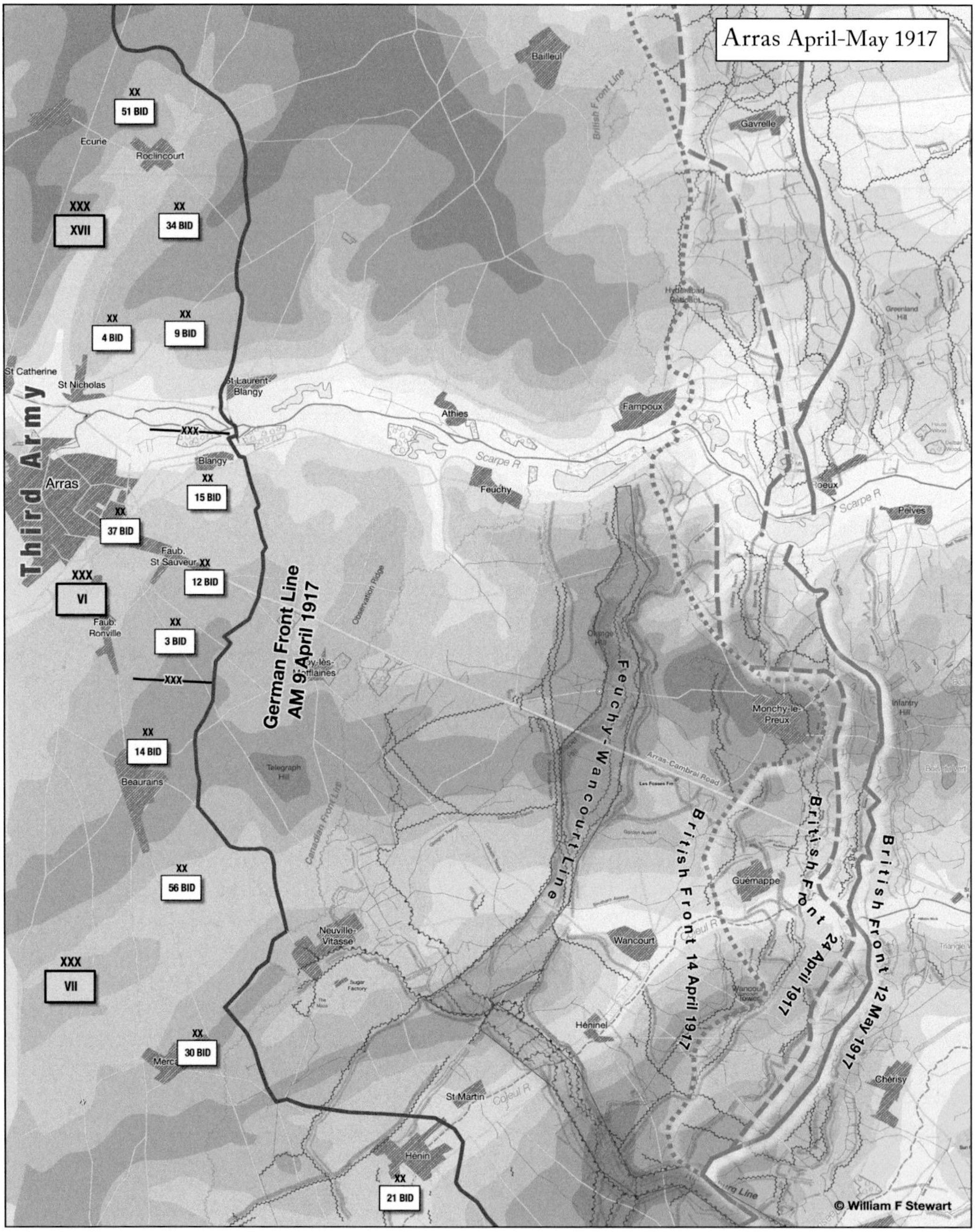

Map 4. Progress of the Battle of First Arras from 9 April to 12 May 1917. The zone south of the Scarpe River to Neuville-Vitasse was the 1918 Canadian Corps' attack front. (Author's Map)

Arras 1917

At Arras 1918, the Canadian Corps sector was the scene of intense fighting in April and May 1917 by General Sir Edmund Allenby's Third Army. The campaign of the 'Battles of Arras 1917' or Arras 1917 included three Battles of the Scarpe and two subsidiary operations on the north bank of the river. These coincided with the Canadian Corps' attack sector in August 1918. This section will focus on the engagements that corresponded to the Canadian Corps' 1918 combat zone.

As part of the Allies' 1917 offensive, the Arras operation's goal was to draw off German reserves prior to the primary attack by the French. The Third Army, with support of the First Army, was to break the enemy position north and south of the Scarpe. It would push to Cambrai and outflank the Hindenburg Line – a scheme Haig would return to in August 1918.[94] The Third Army would attack with 10 divisions on a 16-kilometre front with two more in reserve, along with the Cavalry Corps in GHQ reserve. Called by those who endured the campaign the 'most savage infantry battle of the war,' the Arras offensive lasted 39 days.[95] Poor staff and command decisions and increasingly slapdash and hurried preparations squandered a brilliant initial success. The result was diminishing returns and a lengthening casualty list. As Gary Sheffield wrote, the BEF at Arras 1917 was 'an army that had learned how to conduct successful set-piece operations, but lacked the skills to fight a mobile, or even semi-mobile, battle.'[96] British senior commanders tried to replicate the first day's success with a machine that could not respond to their tempo demands.

In the opening day of the First Battle of the Scarpe, the British won their greatest success in the war up to that point. This was due to a combination of improved infantry tactics, better preparation, and an intense bombardment and barrage, along with German deployment errors. The Third Army advanced three to five kilometres and captured key ground, including Neuville-Vitasse and most of Orange Hill – two prominent objectives in August 1918. It took part of the Feuchy-Wancourt Line in the north and reached it on most of its attack front.[97] The following days were less successful as weaker attacking forces with less artillery support, logistics issues, and increasing German reserves ensured the British made only small gains. Despite these issues, the 37th Division took Monchy-le-Preux which was more a testament to the increased infantry effectiveness than to the senior commanders' leadership.[98] Flanking attacks on the Hindenburg Line to the south forced the Germans to abandon Héninel and Wancourt and cross back over the muddy Cojeul River.

The final phase of the First Battle of the Scarpe on 14 April featured one of the periodic disasters that afflicted the Royal Newfoundland Regiment in the First World War. As part of the British 88th Brigade in the famous 29th Division, it and the 1/Essex struck east of Monchy-le-Preux in a poorly arranged and conceived operation. The two battalions attacked on a narrow

94 Nicholls, *Cheerful Sacrifice,* loc.551.
95 Nicholls, *Cheerful Sacrifice*, loc.195.
96 Sheffield, *Command and Morale,* loc.284.
97 Cyril Bentham Falls, *Military Operations: France and Belgium, 1917* (London: Macmillan, 1940), 1, pp.240-241.
98 Jim Smithson, *A Taste of Success: The First Battle of the Scarpe 9-14 April 1917: The Opening Phase of the Battle of Arras, 9-14 April 1917* (Solihull, West Midlands, England: Helion & Company, 2017), p.233.

front aimed at capturing Infantry Hill along the spur projecting east from Monchy-le-Preux. Under a thin barrage, they advanced 1,500 metres into a confined salient without adequate flank protection. The *3rd Bavarian Division* fell back before them. The Bavarians gathered reserves, prepared their artillery, and launched a devastating counterattack two hours after the initial assault. Supported by a strong barrage that severed communications, the Germans slashed the two battalions' flanks and engulfed them. The counterattack destroyed both units, with the Newfoundlanders losing 460 men and the Essex 661 all ranks or two-thirds of the battalion's total strength.[99] These units were the victims of the Germans' new elastic defence tactics and dreadful British staff work.[100]

The offensive now had to pause. Wet weather and depth of the advance meant the Third Army needed to restore its line of communications. Haig felt compelled to continue the slaughter because of his commitments to the French C-in-C. The British renewed the offensive on 23 April after delays due to weather and the need for more wire-cutting. The objectives were modest in comparison with the previous battles. They were to include Infantry Hill, Roeux, Chérisy, Bois du Sart, Pelves, and Greenland Hill – all would feature in the 1918 operation. In the centre, the army made a short advance of up 2,000 metres and took Guémappe in a fierce battle.[101] North of the Scarpe, the attackers gained ground up to the western slopes of Greenland Hill. But, they made little headway at Roeux and the Chemical Works. The 51st (Highland) Division briefly held the latter, but a German counterattack drove them back, a common occurrence in the campaign.[102] It would fight in this sector again in August 1918.

With the French offensive breaking down, Haig believed it was necessary to maintain pressure on the Germans to assist the French. The objective was now to obtain better defensible ground before stopping the offensive.[103] He ordered the Third Army to make another effort to break the defences before Boiry-Notre-Dame and advance as far as the D-Q Line.[104] The offensive involved from south to north the Fifth, Third, and First Armies.[105] Allenby wanted to capture Fontaine, Chérisy, Bois du Sart, St Rohart Factory, Pelves, and Plouvain Station – objectives again in August 1918. South of the Scarpe, the attack was generally a failure, with small German counterattacks able to drive back the assault troops.[106] At Chérisy, three German platoons evicted the attackers.[107] The attacks failed owing to the confusion of darkness, power of the re-invigorated enemy artillery, and weakened infantry. North of the Scarpe, the 4th and 9th (Scottish) Divisions again tried to capture the Roeux and the Chemical Works but poor timing thwarted the attempt.

99 Anthony McAllister, *The Greatest Gallantry: The Story of the Newfoundland Regiment at Monchy Le Preux* (St. John's, Nfld.: DRC Pub., 2011), pp.21-49, 130; Colin Fox, *Monchy Le Preux - Arras (Battleground Europe)* (Barnsley: Pen & Sword, 2000), pp.110-129, 138-139; Nicholls, *Cheerful Sacrifice,* loc.3720-3721.
100 Smithson, *Taste of Success*, p.242.
101 Nicholls, *Cheerful Sacrifice*, loc.3569.
102 Andrew Rawson, *The Arras Campaign* (Barnsley: Pen and Sword Military, 2017), p.166; Nicholls, *Cheerful Sacrifice,* loc.3947.
103 Falls, *BOH 1917* 1, p.427.
104 Rawson, *Arras Campaign*, pp.188-189.
105 Rawson, *Arras Campaign*, p.189; Nicholls, *Cheerful Sacrifice*, loc.3721.
106 Rawson, *Arras Campaign*, pp.198-201; Nicholls, *Cheerful Sacrifice*, loc.3721.
107 David Bilton, *Germans at Arras (Images of War)* (Barnsley: Pen & Sword, 2009), e-Book, loc.1381.

This was the last major effort to renew the offensive as Haig had shifted his attention to the north to begin his long desired Flanders operation. At the end of the battle, the British line ran 800 to 850 metres east of Monchy-le-Preux. The 4th British and 51st (Highland) Divisions, which would serve in the Canadian Corps at Arras 1918, suffered 6,304 and 6,477 casualties in the campaign.[108]

The Canadian Corps faced a formidable challenge at Arras 1918. Their foe was weaker in morale and numbers than in 1917. But experienced and skilled commanders led them, they defended powerful fortifications, and they were equipped with vast numbers of machine guns that partially offset their decreased ranks. German morale was situational where they would surrender 'in shoals' if they had to fight at a disadvantage.[109] While other units faced fierce, unyielding resistance. Canadian reports like this from the 3rd Battalion, 'The enemy fought hard throughout the operation and their morale appeared to be good' attested to this.[110] The difference in the German morale was the degree to which the Corps would force them to battle handicapped. Thus, the critical issue was could the Corps effectively employ the new open warfare doctrine that put the defenders at a disadvantage? How the Corps learned to wield the new open warfare doctrine and the reasons for the impaired German numbers and morale are the heart of the next chapter.

108 Nicholls, *Cheerful Sacrifice*, loc.4285.
109 LAC: RG9 III-D-3 v4878: 3rd Brigade War Diary, 16th Battalion, Narrative of Second Battle of ARRAS, 2 September 1918.
110 LAC: RG9 III-D-3 v4915: 3rd Battalion War Diary, 3rd Battalion Report 30 August 1918.

3

'Shake us out of the habits acquired by years in the trenches' Preparing the Corps For the Hundred Days

---

The Drocourt-Quéant operations and fighting for the jump-off line were all carried out in a much shorter time than would have been considered necessary for preparation for a trench raid the preceding winter.

Major General A C Macdonell[1]

This chapter focuses on the events and circumstances of 1918 that shaped both the Canadian Corps and its situation on the eve of Arras 1918, other than the already discussed structural changes. In the first half of the year, the Germans launched a series of smashing offensives that drove back the Allies and wreaked grave damage on the Allied armies. They also inflicted even more grievous injury on their own forces. While the Germans did not directly attack the Corps, the need to take over more ground meant at one point it covered a fifth of the British front. When Haig tried to break up the Corps to bolster his sagging lines, Currie protested to GHQ and the Canadian government. The latter intervened, and the British government forced the C-in-C to reunite it. This and other circumstances impaired the Canadians' and Currie's standing with Haig. The period also encompassed an indispensable two months of open warfare training. This instruction transformed its tactical approach from the deliberately paced offensives of 1917 to rapid-tempo open warfare. The chapter will also discuss the Battle of Amiens starting 8 August 1918, which tested and proved the efficacy of these new tactics.

German Spring Offensives

The German high command decided with the closing down of the Russian Front at the end of 1917 to shift divisions to the west. The intent was to launch a war-winning offensive before the Americans arrived in such numbers that victory was impossible. It believed the British were more vulnerable to an all-out attack and so targeted them. The Germans had a higher opinion of

1 A.C. Macdonell, 'The Old Red Patch at the Breaking of the Drocourt-Queant Line, the Crossing of the Canal Du Nord and the Advance on Cambrai, 30 Aug.--2nd Oct. 1918', *Canadian Defence Quarterly* IV, no. 4 (1927), p.391.

General Erich Ludendorff at the *OHL*. The clear-eyed realist of 1916 had ossified into an inflexible martinet focused on tactical solutions to operational and strategic problems. (Bundesarchiv_Bild_183-1992-0707-500,_Erich_Ludendorff.jpg)

the French Army's ability to handle the challenges of open warfare. Ludendorff focused on the immediate tactical requirements for a breakout instead of the strategic objectives and logistics for the operation, so selected a weakly defended sector of the Third and Fifth Armies south of Arras. The primary goal of the offensive was the will and cohesion of the British Army.[2] To ready the army for the offensive, the Germans conducted open warfare training for approximately a quarter of the divisions on the Western Front before the March operation. Much of this instruction was like what the Canadians would do later in May and June.[3]

OHL secretly concentrated three armies (*Seventeenth*, *Second*, and *Eighteenth*), 74 divisions, 6,600 guns, 3,500 mortars, and millions of shells on the assault front for operation *Michael.* For the Verdun offensive in 1916, *OHL* concentrated 1,204 pieces and 202 trench mortars and for the opening day at Passchendaele on 31 July 1917, GHQ deployed 2,266 pieces.[4] Eschewing a long bombardment, the attack opened on 21 March and was stunning. 'Well, we expected it [the

2 The best account of these offensives is David T. Zabecki, *The German 1918 Offensives: A Case Study in the Operational Level of War* (London: Routledge, 2006).

3 Historical Sub-section General Staff, *Survey of Tactics,* loc.184-187.

4 Alexander Watson, *Ring of Steel: Germany and Austria-Hungary at War, 1914-1918* (London: Allen Lane, 2014), p.294; Cyril Bentham Falls, *Military Operations: France and Belgium, 1917* (Nashville: Battery Press, 1948; repr., 1991), II, p.41.

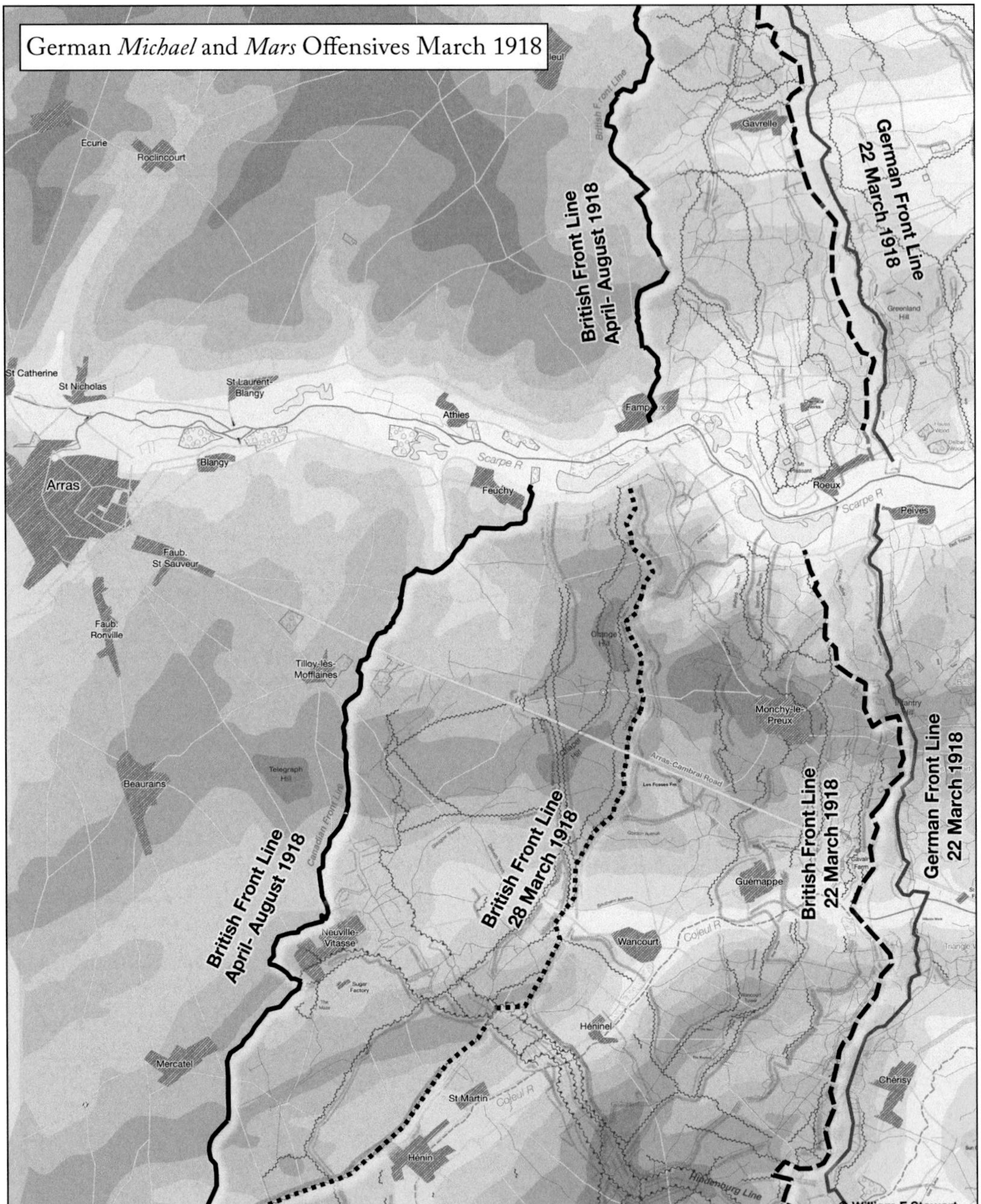

Map 5. Starting, intermediary, and final positions following the German Michael and Mars offensives in March 1918. Note how far the line was driven back south of the Scarpe River. (Author's Map)

German offensive] but were shocked at the advances made. They were so spectacular to anything that we had experienced before that we just couldn't understand it,' was how Canadian Brigadier General Alex Ross later described its impact.[5] The Germans made great gains, but they were strategically sterile, leaving the Germans defending a large salient. Belatedly, *OHL* recognised the central importance of Amiens as a logistics hub. By that point the opportunity to capture it had passed as French and British reserves stopped the offensive. Ludendorff ended the operation on 5 April. All three participants, British, French, and Germans suffered enormous losses with Allied casualties of 255,000 versus 239,000 German.[6] Catastrophically for the Germans, many of their losses were in their elite assault divisions, blunting the edge for future attacks.

On the Arras front, there was no significant change until the opening of the March 1918 offensive. The German success forced the XVII Corps, defending Arras, to fall back 3,500 metres to reduce the front held. This meant abandoning the high ground of Monchy-le-Preux, something the troops found 'particularly distasteful.'[7] This shortened the line and forced the Germans to change the preparations for their planned offensive on Arras, but also meant less developed defences.[8] The *Seventeenth Armee* launched another major attack on 28 March at Arras codenamed *Mars*. Launched on both sides of the Scarpe, Ludendorff intended this offensive to break the connection between the northern and southern British armies and to capture Arras. At 3:00 a.m., a tremendous bombardment opened, but it was a shadow of the 21 March program owing to munition shortages and lack of preparation time.[9] The attackers faced more defensible terrain, better defences, and a more intelligent force deployment than on 21 March.[10] The Germans made only limited gains while suffering crushing losses. South of the Scarpe, they drove back the Third Army line 5,000 to 6,000 metres and recaptured key positions taken in the 1917 Arras offensive. They now held the high points of Orange Hill, and Monchy-le-Preux, and their outposts were within six kilometres of Arras. North of the Scarpe, the German attack gained only 2,000 metres and the forward defensive zone. Ludendorff called the offensive off after just one day.[11] The *26th Reserve Division* (*RD*), which the Canadians would meet later, suffered heavy casualties in this abortive assault.[12] The result was the Germans had gained a wider glacis before the D-Q Line, and a risk that another German push could imperil Arras and key lines of communications. Haig was sensitive to this threat, and he repeatedly referenced intelligence reports on German preparations on the front and massing of reserves.[13]

5 LAC: RG41 v21: B.G. Ross, CBC Interview, Tape 3 p.13.
6 Zabecki, 'German 1918 Offensives' p.239.
7 J.E. Edmonds, *Military Operations: France and Belgium, 1918* (London: Macmillan and Co., Limited, 1935), 1, pp.41-42, 323.
8 Edmonds, *Military Operations, 1918* 1, pp.319-323; TNA: CAB 45-186: H Karslake to Edmonds, 23 February 1928.
9 Jackson Hughes, 'The Monstrous Anger of the Guns: The Development of British Artillery Tactics 1914 - 1918' (PhD, University of Adelaide, 1992), p.274.
10 Boff, *Haig's Enemy*, loc.360.
11 J.E. Edmonds, *Military Operations: France and Belgium, 1918* (London: Macmillan and Co., Limited, 1937), 2, pp.42-72; Zabecki, *German Offensives*, p.266; Martin Kitchen, *The German Offensives of 1918* (Charleston, SC: Tempus, 2001), p. 91; Bilton, *Germans at Arras (Images of War)*, loc.1613.
12 General Staff Intelligence Section, *Two Hundred and Fifty-One Divisions of the German Army Which Participated in the War (1914-1918)*: Government Publishing Office, 1920), pp.356-357.
13 NLS: Haig's Autograph Great War Diary, Part 1 No. 96: Haig Papers, Haig Diary, 10 March, 22 April, 7 May, 22-23 June 1918.

The shocking success of the German offensives had the merit of concentrating Allied minds to accept what was previously unacceptable – a unified command on the Western Front. On 26 March, the Allies selected General Ferdinand Foch to coordinate the national army commanders.[14]

The Germans would launch a further four offensives starting from 9 April to 15 July, with the first on the British Lys sector and the last three against the French Army. All but the last resulted in large gains in ground and heavy Allied casualties. The initial promise of these attacks lured Ludendorff in over-committing to and prolonging these actions. The Germans now held a series of extended salients difficult to supply and defend. Although lower than Allied losses, German ones were also heavy and were concentrated in their best units. They could not afford these casualties, nor the resulting hit to morale. The final offensive on 15 July was the least successful, as the French skilfully parried the blow. The defensive success resulted in Pétain, the French C-in-C, launching a counteroffensive on 18 July. This strike, supported by masses of tanks, was a total surprise and hit the vulnerable northern flank of the salient. It was the turning point of the 1918 campaign, as the initiative now passed to the Allies. The Germans barely prevented a collapse in the salient as they rapidly retired to avoid encirclement. They lost almost all their recent gains there.[15]

Canadian Corps: January-May 1918

The Corps spent the months after Passchendaele energetically focused on improving the Vimy sector defences. Building on the principles of defence-in-depth, it completed 400 kilometres of trenches, 480 kilometres of barbed wire obstacles, and 200 tunnelled machine gun emplacements.[16] In the German spring offensives, the line guarded by the Canadian Corps remained inviolate, so Currie's demands for effort paid off. The Canadian Cavalry Brigade and the 1st Canadian Motor Machine Gun (CMMG) Brigade were, however, heavily engaged and performed admirably there. GHQ stretched the Corps perilously thin by having it relieve British divisions on both its flanks. It also transferred the 2nd Division to serve in the neighbouring VI Corps. On 26 March, GHQ put the Corps in reserve with none of its divisions.[17] Currie protested, and GHQ relented to be discussed later. By 12/13 April, three divisions under the Corps' command defended a 29-kilometre front with the 2nd Division, in the VI Corps, defending another 6 kilometres. As a result, the Corps alone defended one-fifth of the British front as one of 18 corps in the BEF.[18] It was a highly stressful period on Currie and the troops as they anticipated a German attack on their stretched defences.[19]

Currie's relationship with Haig soured in the spring. He had already tested it in protesting the Corps' assignment to the Passchendaele campaign. Haig took the unusual step of meeting Currie to convince him of its necessity – an action that no British corps commander could typically expect.[20] Currie reacted strongly to the 26 March decision to transfer out all the

14 Foch received his Marshal's baton on 6 August 1918.
15 Zabecki, 'German 1918 Offensives' pp.461-483; Stevenson, *Backs to the Wall,* pp.113-118.
16 Kemp, *Report of the Ministry,* p.107.
17 NLS: Haig Diary, 26 March 1918.
18 Cook, *The Madman and the Butcher,* p.239.
19 Daniel G. Dancocks, *Sir Arthur Currie: A Biography* (Toronto: Methuen, 1985), p.137.
20 Cook, *The Madman and the Butcher,* p.206; Sheffield, *The Chief,* loc. 5502.

Canadian divisions. He 'made strong representations to First Army' and urged GHQ to reunite the Corps.[21] Currie, no political naïf, also copied the head of the Overseas Military Forces of Canada, Sir Edward Kemp to bring pressure. Kemp did so using diplomatic but unmistakable language that the Canadian government wanted the Corps reunited.[22] The British Secretary for War, Lord Derby, wired Haig to do so. Political interference was anathema to Haig, so this action increased his discontent with the Canadians.[23] Despite both Currie's and Kemp's statements that they did not presume to interfere in Haig's direction of the campaign, but they did so in requesting the Corps' reunification. Haig was under tremendous pressure from the Germans, so forced to keep the Canadian divisions together restricted his command flexibility.[24] Ironically like Currie, Haig baulked at calls from Foch to send divisions to serve under the French.[25] Haig was bitter about this constraint on his command. He later reminded Currie that the BEF fought off the German attacks unaided by the Canadians.[26] After the meeting on 18 April, Haig complained that Currie suffered 'from a swollen head Horne thinks!' and 'As a result Canadians are together holding a wide front near Arras but have not yet been in battle!'[27]

Adding to the fissure, Currie was vocal in disparaging British fighting prowess and this led to Horne's comment about Currie's swollen head.[28] The Canadian prime minister, Robert Borden, visiting England directed Currie to give him the 'unvarnished truth' on the situation at the front on 12 June.[29] He assured Currie that he would protect him against any repercussions.[30] Currie did not hold back. Borden then gave an impassioned speech at the Imperial War Cabinet meeting the next day based on this information. He also took Currie to speak with Lloyd George – the British prime minister – the next day. Lloyd George and his cabinet received the news positively as it aligned and reinforced their negative view of Haig and his generals. Likely Haig heard of Currie's denigration of his army, which would add to his irritation. Currie, however, was untouchable because of the Canadian Corps' victories in 1917, Borden's support, and the importance of the Canadian contribution to the war effort. Haig welcomed the combat prowess of the Dominion's troops, but not always their unique nature that differed from British ones. The subsequent victory at Amiens and the Canadian role in that great success helped to mend the fences. Nevertheless, the relevance of this contention was that it contributed to Currie's reaction to Haig's pressure for action during the battle. He was arguably more likely to agree to Haig's demands than he might have normally been, as Haig was unhappy with his actions during the spring.

21 Kemp, *Report of the Ministry*, p.112; Nicholson, *CEF*, pp.380-381; Cook, *The Madman and the Butcher*, p.238.
22 Desmond Morton, *A Peculiar Kind of Politics* (Toronto: University of Toronto Press, 1982), p.163.
23 Sheffield, *The Chief*, loc.1495.
24 John Bourne Gary Sheffield, ed., *Douglas Haig: War Diaries and Letters, 1914-1918* (London: Weidenfeld & Nicolson, 2005), p.389; Sheffield, *The Chief*, loc.6117-6211.
25 Greenhalgh, *Foch in Command*, pp.361-362; Sheffield, *The Chief*, loc.6386.
26 NLS: Haig Diary, 7 August 1918.
27 NLS: Haig Diary, 18 April 1918.
28 LAC: Currie Diary, 11 April 1918.
29 Robert Laird Borden and Henry Borden, *Robert Laird Borden: His Memoirs* (Toronto,: The Macmillan Company of Canada, Limited, 1938), p.813; Robert Laird Borden, *Letters to Limbo* (Toronto: University of Toronto Press, 1971), p.61.
30 Borden, *Letters to Limbo*, p.61.

Operation Delta

At the start of May, most of the Canadian Corps moved into reserve and began a critical two-month period of intense training for open warfare. Only the 2nd Division remained in line in this period and did not get the full benefit of practice in the new tactics. Preparing for Operation 'Delta' guided early training. This was a proposed attack by the First Army to drive back the Germans on its northern sector following the German Lys offensive.[31] The key component for this attack was the secret insertion of the Canadian Corps into the front. The plan went through multiple iterations from the end of April to June, and all had similar characteristics to the later Amiens attack.[32] Delta was, however, not executed due to Haig's uncertainty about German intentions and his resulting reluctance to commit the Canadians.

The importance of this open warfare training lay in its role in helping the Corps' commanders, staff, and troops transition from the careful step-by-step deliberate pace of the 1917 attacks to the more torrid tempo of 1918. Therefore, it is important to understand where they started. Meticulous preparation, days of bombardment and rehearsals, gathering detailed information on enemy positions, developing absolute firepower supremacy, and a measured pace characterised Passchendaele, along with the ubiquitous mud and terrible terrain conditions.[33] It featured short advances, narrow frontages, and dense artillery support and assault formations. Table 3.1 illustrates these crucial differences. The speed of preparations at Passchendaele was partly the result of the abysmal state of the line of communications, weather, and terrain conditions.

In the Hundred Days, frontages were two to three times wider than in 1917 and the advances 10 times deeper. While the field artillery density was half, smoke was part of most barrages instead of a merely ancillary munition, there was often no preliminary bombardment, and the artillery used predictive fire rather than registration.[34] The Corps took elaborate measures to ensure secrecy, something that was not possible in Flanders. Units entered the line only hours before an attack instead of days.[35] There was no opportunity for exhaustive intelligence collection or rehearsals. The operational tempo was blistering. The barrage lifts advanced at twice the rate as before. Rather than a four-day gap between attacks, or seven if there was a divisional relief, the Corps launched assaults on successive days. At Arras, the Corps launched division-scale operations within six and a half hours. Finally, at Amiens the Canadian Corps employed four battalions of tanks amounting to 162 fighting vehicles versus none at Passchendaele.[36] The contrast between the 1917 and 1918 engagements was dramatic.

31 For a detailed study of the impact on Operation Delta on the Canadian Corps, see William F. Stewart, '"The Most Vivifying Influence:" Operation Delta in Preparing the Canadian Corps for the Hundred Days', *Canadian Military History* 27, no. 2 (2018).

32 See for instance, LAC: RG9 III-C-1 v3854, 72/4: Canadian Corps G.979/2521, 29 May 1918.

33 Ian Malcolm Brown, 'Lieutenant-General Sir Arthur Currie and the Canadian Corps 1917-1918: The Evolution of a Style of Command and Attack' (Masters, University of Calgary, 1991), pp.41-42.

34 LAC: GOCRA War Diary, October 1917 Appendix H Frontages of Barrage; LAC: GOCRA War Diary, Artillery Order No.95, 28 October 1917; LAC: GOCRA War Diary, Artillery Order, No.101, 4 November 1917; LAC: GOCRA War Diary, Artillery Order, No.92, 23 October 1917.

35 LAC: RG9 III-C-1 v3859, 85/8: Canadian Corps G.724/27-3, 20 November 1917.

36 Nicholson, *CEF*, pp.396-397.

Table 3.1 Passchendaele-Hundred Days Comparison

	Passchendaele	Hundred Days Amiens/Arras 1918
Space		
Frontages	1,200-1,400 metres/division	1,200-1,400 m/brigade
Depth of advance	600-1,000 m/day	13,000 m/day (8 August) – 6,000 m/day (26 August)
Ground	Bottomless mud	Dry and fast
Defences	Prepared	Minimal at Amiens but deep and sophisticated at Arras 1918
Time		
Barrage lifts	8 min/100 m	3-4 min/100 m
Cycle time between attacks	4 to 7 days	Hours
Time to relieve division	7 days	1 day
Time in line prior to attack	Two days	Hours
Resources		
Smoke	Peripheral	Key
Artillery accuracy	Registration	Prediction
Field artillery barrage density	9 to 10 m/gun although more likely 12 to 13 m/gun*	Average of 25 m/gun
Counter-battery	Full panoply of techniques	Hastily arranged but effective
Preliminary bombardment	Prolonged	None except for wire-cutting for attack on Drocourt-Quéant line
Rehearsals	Extensive	None
Tanks	None	Yes
Engineering work parties	Infantry	Engineers
Surprise	Not attempted	Key element
Intelligence	Detailed	Adequate

* Many guns were not operational, hence the lower density.

There was a profound tactical and operational shift in the 10 months between Passchendaele and Amiens in the Canadian Corps. The soldier and section training did not alter dramatically as weapons' use was the same regardless of the tactics. The major changes were at the higher levels of command from battalion and above. Seven key doctrinal influences shaped this remarkable turnaround. Common across the BEF, including the Corps, was the British success at Cambrai, GHQ's new offensive doctrine codified in documents such as *SS 204* and *SS 135*, the shock of the success of the German offensives, the Hamel assault on 4 July, and the distribution of translated German orders as *Notes on Recent Fighting*.[37] The Corps analysed especially closely the translated German orders. According to Currie's 1919 Interim Report, they 'to a large extent, inspired our training.[38] For instance, he underlined text and made marginalia in his version of *Notes on Recent Fighting No. 14*.[39] Currie ordered his generals to review that document and have battalion commanders run schemes based on its principles.[40] The Canadian Corps also issued its own guidance for training divisions in open warfare such as G.135/14-3 on 30 April.[41] Again, the Interim Report referred to the Corps 'laying down a definitive Corps tactical doctrine.'[42] The commander of the 1st Division recorded spending 1 May reviewing this order.[43] The final influence was the open warfare training and the exercises for Delta.

According to Macdonell, the effects of trench warfare hung around officers' necks 'like a millstone' of whom few had prewar training relevant to open warfare.[44] The Corps had to instruct all ranks and arms to execute the new tactics, including ones never practised before like house-to-house fighting.[45] This training 'called for an exceptional degree of daring and resource in the infantry.'[46] The artillery had to instil the techniques of predicted fire, requiring precision and calculation of multiple factors far beyond what the field artillery attempted before. They also had to restore its mobility. Engineers had to rapidly repair and extend the lines of communications to keep up with the advance. Finally, they all had to execute the new doctrine at a tempo much higher than before. Rather than days to prepare for an attack, every echelon had hours. As Macdonell wrote, 'The Drocourt-Quéant operations and fighting for the jump-off line were all carried out in a much shorter time than would have been considered necessary for preparation

37 These were *SS 204 Infantry and Tank Co-operation and Training 1918* and *SS 135 The Training and Employment of Divisions 1918*. For the shock of the German offensive see LAC: RG9 III-C-1 v3854, 72/2: Notes on Conference of Corps Commanders Held by GOC First Army, 3 June 1918; Christopher Pugsley, 'Haig and the Implementation of Tactical Doctrine on the Western Front', *Sandhurst Occasional Papers* (2011), p.42; LAC: RG24 v22018: Notes Compiled by G.S. Fourth Army on the Operations by the Australian Corps against Hamel, Bois De Hamel, and Bois De Vaire, on 4th of July, 1918. See also Hammond, 'Tank Cooperation' pp.278-287.

38 Kemp, *Report of the Ministry*, p.123; Macdonell, 'Old Red Patch 1', p.388.

39 CWM: 19801226-273/58A 1 60.2: Currie Fonds, Notes on Recent Fighting No. 14 German Methods of Overcoming Machine Gun Defences.

40 LAC: RG9 III-C-3 v4187, 2/3: Currie to Lipsett, 23 June 1918; LAC: MG30 E100 v37, 167: Currie Fonds, 1st Division G.7-135, 24 June 1917.

41 LAC: RG9 III-C-3 v4201, 13/4: Canadian Corps G.135/14-3, 30 April 1918.

42 Kemp, *Report of the Ministry*, p.124.

43 LAC: MG30 E20 v1: A.C. Macdonell Fonds, A.C. Macdonell Diary, 1 May 1918.

44 Macdonell, 'Old Red Patch 1', p.389.

45 LAC: RG9 III-D-3 v4947: 2nd CMR War Diary, 8 May, 25 May and Appendix 2 1918.

46 Urquhart, *16th Battalion*, pp.262-263.

for a trench raid the preceding winter.'[47] The accelerated pace meant more responsibility pushed down to the lower echelons. This made greater demands on them and required a higher standard of training and experience than before.[48]

The 2nd Division did not have this opportunity for extended instruction – it had only two weeks of training out of the line in July.[49] It spent May and June still at the front in the VI Corps. David Campbell asserts that the division still conducted much training while it was in the line and that its aggressive raid policy ensured it was ready.[50] It was not, however, able to run battalion and brigade manoeuvres like the other three divisions.[51] It also did not get the same chance to physically harden its troops, as evidenced by complaints of too many men falling out during route marches.[52] Further, it ran its raids only after extensive planning and rehearsals, which did not prepare it for the faster tempo of the Hundred Days. This manifested itself in a slower response time to operations where its follow-on attacks on 27 and 28 August lagged the 3rd Division's by hours.[53]

Open Warfare Training

The 1st, 3rd, and 4th Divisions left the line starting on the 3 May 1918 and moved into the First Army's rear areas. They spent the rest of May, June, and part of July in training – a period unique in the Corps' history. Initially, they were to train for Delta, and then GHQ retained them in reserve in case of another strong German attack. At its core, the open warfare training involved explaining the new doctrine to all ranks and then practising it in schemes at the platoon and then up to the division level. Initially, units practised it slowly, so the troops understood it, and then later at battle speed.[54] The instructional focus was on infiltration tactics, penetrating machine gun defences by fire and movement, use of ground, support of nearby platoons, cooperation with tanks, forward artillery, and light and medium trench mortars, and exploiting smoke.[55] Most schemes included combinations of all these weapon systems and often aircraft to practice combined arms.[56]

47 Macdonell, 'Old Red Patch 1', p.391.
48 LAC: RG9 III-D-3 v4836: 1st Divison GS War Diary, Lessons Learned from Recent Fighting, ? September 1918.
49 LAC: RG9 III-D-3 v4846: 2nd Division GS War Diary, July 1918.
50 Campbell, 'The Divisional Experience' pp.404-405, 408-410.
51 For instance, the 5th Brigade was only able to conduct platoon and company level training while the 2nd Division was in the line. LAC: 5th Brigade W.D., May and June 1918.
52 LAC: RG9 III-C-3 v4186, 25/1: 6th Brigade G.5/833, 16 July 1918 and 27th Battalion A.1738, 17 July 1918.
53 Edmonds, *Military Operations, 1918* 4, p.327; LAC: 2nd Division Narrative, 8-9.
54 See for instance, LAC: RG9 III-D-3 v4942: 54th Battalion War Diary, 21 May 1918.
55 LAC: RG9 III-D-3 v4817: Canadian Corps GS War Diary, Canadian Corps Exercise No. 4, 29 June 1918.
56 For instance, LAC: 2nd Brigade War Diary, 23 May 1918.

A Canadian battalion on the march passes the Canadian prime minister, Sir Robert Borden, and Currie. Currie emphasised the importance of hard route marches to harden the troops for open warfare. (Canada. Dept. of National Defence/Library and Archives Canada/PA-002746)

At first, the training was intense, but later in May units switched to devoting the afternoons to sports to keep the men engaged, develop unit cohesion, and physical fitness.[57] Currie emphasised challenging long route marches to prepare them for extended advances.[58] The 102nd Battalion history declared: 'In short, nothing was neglected which might serve to harden the troops and fit them for long marching under the severest conditions.'[59] The effect was to make the troops well prepared for the demands of battle. 'I'd give anything if you can only have a look at this battalion as it is at present. I've never seen it in such fine shape physically before. The men are all as hard as nails,' boasted Major Ian Sinclair of the 13th Battalion in June 1918.[60]

57 For example, JBB [John Beswick Bailey], *Cinquante-Quatre; Being a Short History of the 54th Canadian Infantry Battalion* 1919), p.22; LAC: 3rd Brigade WD, May 1918; Edgar Stanford Russenholt, *Six Thousand Canadian Men: Being the History of the 44th Battalion Canadian Infantry 1914–1919* (Winnipeg: De Montfort Press, 1932), p.150.

58 LAC: Canadian Corps G.135/14-3, 30 April 1918.

59 L. McLeod Gould, *From B.C. To Baisieux: Being the Narrative History of the 102nd Canadian Infantry Battalion* (Victoria, B.C.: T.R. Cusack, 1919), p.89.

60 LAC: MG30 E153 v1: Sinclair Fonds, Sinclair to Dad, 22 June 1918.

It was not just the infantry that trained intensely, but all the arms to ensure they could deal with open warfare. The artillery and signals were part of the schemes as well as training on their own.[61] The instruction was as hard and demanding as that of the infantry.[62] It had the advantage, however, of a major break from holding the line and spending time in surroundings not savaged by war. 'Practicing going into action with speed and advancing and keeping communications up with visual signalling was all a pleasant change from the recent dug-out life,' was how the history of the 66th Battery described it.[63] The engineers were in the process of a major reorganisation into three battalions per division, which consumed much of their time.[64] But they did some open warfare training.[65]

One of the great advantages of the Canadian Corps was the ability to develop and instil a common doctrine. In the British army this was far more difficult with divisions transferred repeatedly between corps.[66] The CEF followed the British precept of command authority, where a unit's commander was ultimately responsible for training and the conduct of operations. Thus, it was not a hard and fast set of rules, but rather a starting point for a theme with many variations. The Corps had the means to inculcate a common doctrine in all ranks. Senior officers like Currie, staff, and the division commanders attended exercises to root out outmoded approaches.[67] Another mechanism of fostering a consistent approach was through platoon competitions that set an open warfare problem where senior officers could highlight and communicate both errors and successes to a larger audience.[68] First run at the battalion level, the competitions ran up to the division. Finally, Currie closely inspected troops and questioned subalterns about infantry regulations.[69] This was an impetus for field-grade officers to ensure their subordinates were up to speed or risk a sharp check from him. Thus, the Corps did not just handout doctrinal statements to the subordinate formations but took an active role in inculcating, monitoring, and enforcing them.

Operation Delta and its training provided a template to guide the doctrine and preparation of training exercises. Repeated references to Delta in the documents prove it was the basis of multiple tactical schemes.[70] It was also a reason why the Corps could conduct the Amiens operation with little preparation. The Corps had in effect been already rehearsing the attack

61 See for instance, LAC: 1st CDA W.D., 1 Division Artillery, G.2-2640, 3 May 1918; LAC: RG9 III-C-3 v4192, 15/4: 3rd Division G.89, 12 June 1918.
62 LAC: MG30 E345: Selwyn Wilson Fonds, The Diary of the 13th Battery, Canadian Field Artillery 1914-1919, 21 May 1918.
63 Anon., *The Story of the Sixty-Sixth C.F.A.* (Edinburgh: Turnbull & Spears, 1919), p.67.
64 See for instance, LAC: RG9 III-D-3 v4989: GOC Royal Engineers War Diary, May, June 1918.
65 LAC: RG9 III-D-3 v4989: 2nd Brigade Canadian Engineers War Diary, July 1918.
66 Boff, *Winning and Losing*, pp.61-62, 135.
67 LAC: 2nd Brigade War Diary, 15 May 1918; LAC: 2nd Brigade War Diary, 2nd Brigade OO No. 23, 13 May 1918; LAC: Currie to Lipsett, 23 June 1918; LAC: 3rd Division WD, 20, 27 May 1918; LAC: 12th Brigade War Diary, 21 May1918.
68 LAC: RG9 III-C-3 v4213, 6/6: 10th Canadian Infantry Battalion Platoon Competition Results, 23 May 1918; LAC: RG9 III-D-3 v4903: 10th Brigade War Diary, G-84-1, 21 May 1918; LAC: 3rd Brigade WD, 13 June 1918; LAC: 2nd Brigade War Diary, 5 June 1918.
69 The detailed instructions for Currie's formal inspection indicate how exacting he was, see LAC: RG9 III-C-3 v4025, 7/3: 1st Division G.369-11, 9 May 1918.
70 LAC: 2nd CMR W.D., 8 May, 25 May 1918, and Appendix 2; LAC: 2nd Brigade War Diary, 7-8 May 1918.

with the schemes and instruction shaped by the Delta plan. It provided the opportunity to crystallise the multiple doctrinal sources available in May into concrete policies that the Corps practised. The training for Delta and in the following months allowed all the formation levels and arms to rehearse the new doctrine, refine it, comprehend it, and gain confidence.

Formations, units, and commanders recognised the importance of the prolonged training period. There were multiple references in post-action reports of the value of the extended instruction in open warfare training. For instance, the 9th Brigade in its post-Arras report stated: 'Initiative and resolution as taught in practice in the Bomy Area were the great factors in success.'[71]

Lance Corporal Ken Foster (2nd Battalion), an old soldier who endured this prolonged training experience, should have the final word on the open warfare training's value. He remarked that by the middle of July 1918:

> We were pretty well fed up with attacking haystacks and windmills. It all seemed so un-necessary to us who had been through the same thing too often. On the contrary, it came in very useful when a little later on we came in contact with conditions such as we had been rehearsing, even to the extent of wheatfields, windmills and haystacks.[72]

Arras 1918's Precursor: Operation 'Thistle'

Haig was determined to regain the key ground south of the Scarpe lost in the March 1918 offensive and to reduce the threat to Arras. Initially, he conceived it as a limited attack by the First Army north and south of the Scarpe to give the Arras and Vimy defences more depth. He pushed this scheme from April to mid-August, but his army commanders kept raising objections. They believed the operation needed to extend further south into the Third Army's sector to capture the ridge north of Héninel.[73] Otherwise, the southern flank of the advance would be dangerously exposed. The problem was the ridge was an integral part of the Hindenburg Line defences and would require a major offensive to seize. In one of the later versions of the plan, the XVII Corps gave it a code name 'Operation Thistle,' and it is by this term it will be referred to.

The first iteration of what became Thistle was a Horne proposal in early April. He wanted the XVII Corps, now in the First Army, south of the Scarpe and the 1st Canadian Division north of it in early April to add depth to the Arras defences. They would advance to the limit of the artillery barrage of 2,000 to 3,000 metres and the high ground around Neuville-Vitasse, Telegraph Hill, and Orange Hill.[74] He needed the help of the Third Army to guard his flank with the vital Hénin Hill position overlooking the First Army's right flank. Before he could get the Third Army to agree the Germans struck his army on 9 April and the offensive was stillborn.

71 LAC: 9th Brigade War Diary, Narrative of Operations from 25th to 30th August 1918, 15 September 1918.

72 Foster joined the 2nd Battalion in July 1916. 'Foster, Kenneth Walter Memoir' The Canadian Letters and Images Project, <http://www.canadianletters.ca/content/document-4021> (18 April 2017).

73 Planning documents tended to refer to Hénin and Héninel and Hill and Ridge interchangeably. There were in fact two ridges one on each bank of the Cojeul River and it is not clear which, or both were discussed. For the sake of consistency, the term Hénin Hill will be used and refers to both locations.

74 TNA: WO 95-176-1 First Army GS War Diary, 6 April 1918.

GHQ held operations near Arras in abeyance until June. During this period, Haig remained anxious about another German offensive there. To forestall a potential blow, Haig directed Horne on 23 June to study attacking Orange Hill with, possibly, the Canadian Corps.[75] At this point, the Corps was in the GHQ reserve behind the First Army.[76] Instead of attacking, the Canadians took over the XVII front, including the sector south of the Scarpe on 15 July. That day, the Germans launched their final offensive against the French in the Champagne region. The least successful of these attacks, it still was of grave concern to Haig. He met with Horne and Byng the next day to instruct them to adopt an aggressive posture, to inflict losses, tie down enemy reserves, and gather intelligence. He also raised the notion of the attack on Orange Hill for the third time. Both protested it would be costly to launch and hold if the Third Army did not capture Hénin Hill as well. Haig ordered Horne to have the Canadian Corps work up a scheme and advance their line with step-by-step minor operations.[77] Horne translated this into a directive that the army needed 'an active offensive defensive attitude.'[78] In response, Currie ran a headquarters exercise on 22 July with his senior staff and divisional commanders to develop the plan.[79] This was the conference Currie used to surreptitiously prepare his divisional commanders for Amiens, although they did not yet know the secret.[80]

Currie then submitted a proposal the next day called Operation 'D.E.'. The attack would push the line north of the Scarpe and retake the old British battle zone that included Neuville-Vitasse, Chapel Hill, and Orange Hill. Three Canadian divisions would attack south of the Scarpe and one to the north if the neighbouring corps would temporarily take over its left brigade front. The plan depended on shock and tanks. Unlike at Amiens, the Canadians on this front would not be a surprise. Currie counted on efforts to hide the massing of artillery and the lack of a preliminary bombardment to stun the Germans. To overcome the resistance, Currie wanted a brigade of tanks with 108 machines – on 26 August only 13 tanks provided support. Currie also identified the issue of the right flank and suggested the Third Army's flanking corps take part.[81]

What is of interest in this plan was that many key elements of what the 26 August attack would be were already present. Currie referred to its value in preparing for the later operation.[82] It demonstrated the increasing attention on surprise, confidence in the artillery's power to suppress the enemy defences without a long bombardment, and in the infantry's ability to fight their way forward. Its dependence on tanks to do the wire breaking also presaged Amiens. There was a focus on secrecy, but not to the extent at Amiens. While the execution details showed more sophistication than the attacks in 1917, the limits of the field artillery range still restricted the advance's depth. The absolute limit of the barrage was 3,000 metres if the commanders accepted the risk of installing silent batteries within 1,000 metres of the front. Silent batteries moved forward at night, camouflaged, and did not register. They would not open fire until Zero

75 NLS: Haig Diary, 23 June 1918.
76 The 2nd Division was still in the line at this point.
77 NLS: Haig Diary, 16 July 1918.
78 LAC: RG9 III-C-1 v3854, 72/12: First Army GS 1313, 16 July 1918; TNA: WO 95-177-4: First Army GS War Diary, 16 July 1916.
79 Dancocks, *Sir Arthur Currie,* p.150.
80 CWM: D 547 C2 M38: "Flanders Fields" Transcribed Tapes by General A.G.L. McNaughton, p.135.
81 LAC: RG9 III-C-1 v3854, 72/12: Canadian Corps, G.648/25-22-1, 23 July 1918.
82 Kemp, *Report of the Ministry,* p.144.

Hour. In this plan, Currie was still envisioning the limited objective attacks of 1917 instead of the deeper operations conducted during the Hundred Days. This was also before the shattering defeats inflicted on the Germans at Amiens, so Currie did not want to take risks.

Horne tentatively approved the plan to take Orange Hill, but he could not set a date for the attack, yet.[83] The Corps was to make arrangements, but the Canadians' move south to Amiens suspended these.[84] In the interim, the XVII Corps replaced the Canadians on 30 July.[85]

Amiens: Tanks, Surprise and Victory

Amiens was the first battle of Canada's Hundred Days, but the second in a series of offensives that culminated in the Armistice. Marshal Foch masterminded these attacks. His framework for these offensives was his *battaille général* – to attack at vital points across the Western Front in successive blows and not just in one area. Two principles guided the campaign's conduct. First, the focus was not geographic locations but the destruction of the German army. Second, they would feature shallow advances on an ever-widening front to avoid the mistakes of previous campaigns. When one attack had drawn in nearby German reserves, the Allies would shift laterally to an adjacent sector. The series of consecutive cracks would exhaust the German reserves and army. In previous campaigns, the offensives continued driving into a salient where the equilibrium between the attacker and defender shifted to the defender's favour. *OHL* knew where the next blow would land and could manage their reserves accordingly. In Foch's scheme, the advantage would always lie with the Allies. Further, the follow-on battles would strike zones at least partially denuded of reserves sucked into the previous battle. The first day of Arras 1918 was an example of this scenario where the *II Bavarian Korps* had to strip a regiment from an *Eingreifdivision* to cover the front attacked by the Third Army the previous day.[86]

The genesis of the Amiens battle was Haig's order to General Sir Henry Rawlinson, GOC Fourth Army, on 17 May to investigate an attack on the Amiens front.[87] This was a particularly sensitive sector as critical rail lines for maintaining the BEF ran through the city. Three days later, Foch issued Directive 3 which included a proposal for an offensive to free up the Paris-Amiens rail line. The continued German offensives meant the Allies were in no position to launch an attack. In the interim, the Fourth Army continued exploring opportunities to exploit German weakness on the Amiens' front. On 4 July, the Australian Corps launched a strikingly successful but restricted-objective operation at Hamel near Amiens that featured many key aspects of the Amiens offensive. It was a surprise assault with no preliminary bombardment or registration, 60 tanks, and the heavy artillery concentrated on counter-battery missions.[88] The battle proved the efficacy of the new tactics and the weak state of the German defenders in the Amiens' sector.

83 LAC: Canadian Corps, G.648/25-22-1, 23 July 1918.
84 For instance, a 12th Brigade conference discussed the upcoming offensive. LAC: 12th Brigade War Diary, 26 July 1918.
85 TNA: WO 95-936-5: XVII Corps General Staff War Diary, 30 July 1918.
86 Boff, *Winning and Losing*, pp.23-24; Peter Simkins, *From the Somme to Victory: The British Army's Experience on the Western Front 1916-1918* (Barnsley: Pen & Sword, 2014), e-Book, loc.389.
87 NLS: Haig Diary, 17 May 1918.
88 LAC: Notes Compiled by the Fourth Army.

Immediately after this great success, Haig had Rawlinson continue to work on developing a major operation.[89] The planning crystallised when Foch met with Haig, Pétain, and Pershing the C-in-C of the American army. After the success of the 18 July counterattack on the Marne, Foch believed the tide had turned, and it was time to go over to the offensive.[90] He persuaded them to agree to a series of offensives, with the first at Amiens.[91] A key feature would be the secret transfer of the Canadian Corps from the Arras sector to Amiens. The Corps was the strongest formation in the BEF at this point. If the Germans detected its presence, it would be a sure sign of a major offensive. The Corps would only enter the line shortly before Zero Hour to prevent its discovery. Despite the concentration of masses of tanks, trucks, men, animals, guns, and munitions, the Germans did not detect the oncoming avalanche.

German defences were rudimentary and comprised little more than a *Vorfeld*. The defenders were strangely apathetic to improving them further. There was little expectation of an attack, so they took few precautions.[92] The Canadian sector of the offensive was 8,500 metres, and it received the mission of advancing south-east to capture the 1916 era British Outer Amiens Defence Line over 12 kilometres away.[93] Each of the three initial assault formations had an attached tank battalion with 42 tanks, and the reserve 4th Division had a 36-tank battalion. Thus, the Corps had 162 tanks. Supporting the attack was a powerful artillery park of 17 FA and 9 HA brigades with four long-range batteries – 646 pieces in total.[94] The barrage density worked out to a weak 28 metres per 18-pounder gun, but in line with the feeble defences and massive tank support.

Attacking out of the fog on 8 August, the operation was a complete surprise. The combination of shock, smothering counter-battery fire, huge concentrations of tanks, innovative tactics, and mediocre defences resulted in overrunning the German front-line divisions. The Corps advanced almost 13,000 metres and gained all its goals except on the right flank. While there were casualties, the battalions escaped the eviscerating numbers suffered in attacks in 1916 and 1917. Losses on the first day were 3,868 with 10 of the Corps' 12 brigades committed.[95]

Poor army command decisions, a resulting series of disjointed attacks, and a surprising success marked the second day. The result was a series of brigade-level assaults as late as 2:00 p.m. Intermittent artillery and tank support and exposed flanks affected these muddled attacks. The great gains of the previous day meant resupply was difficult. Despite all these liabilities, the infantry fought its way forward using its own firepower and tactical acumen, and they still gained over six kilometres of the aggressive 15-kilometre goal. While short of the day's objective, it was still an advance greater for the Corps than any previous day other than 8 August. The lesson was that even with a delayed start and a disjointed series of

89 NLS: Haig Diary, 5 and 16 July 1918.
90 Greenhalgh, *Foch in Command*, pp.407-408.
91 Stevenson, *Backs to the Wall*, p.117.
92 Edmonds, *Military Operations, 1918* 4, p.12.
93 Edmonds, *Military Operations, 1918* 4, pp.23, 134.
94 G.W.L. Nicholson, *The Gunners of Canada: The History of the Royal Regiment of Canadian Artillery* (Toronto: McClelland and Stewart, 1967), p.337; Nicholson, *CEF*, p.396.
95 Nicholson, *CEF*, pp.407, 414.

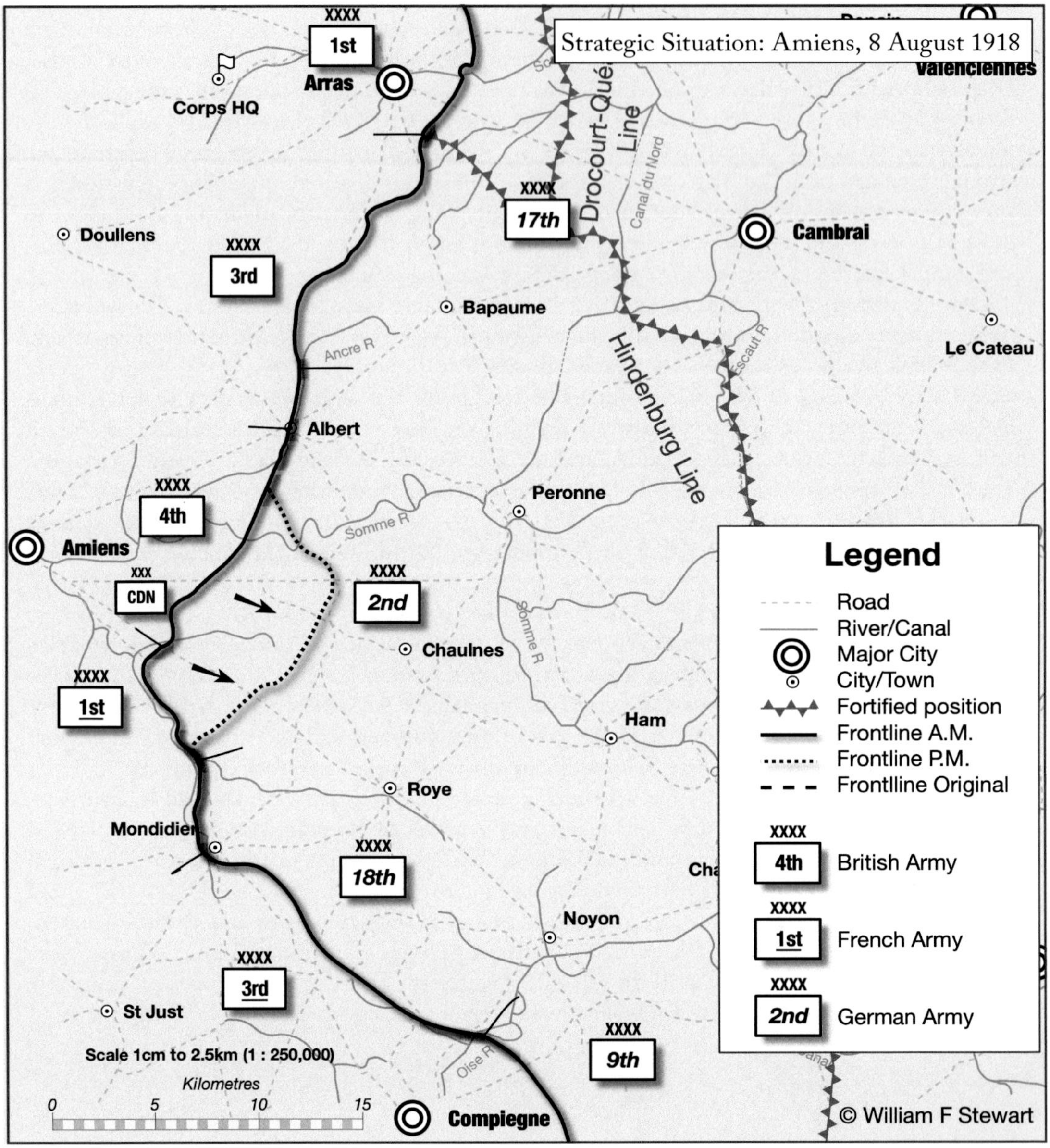

Map 6. Called by Ludendorff the 'Black Day of the German Army', the opening day of Amiens brought unprecedented gains in ground, prisoners, and matériel for the Allies. (Author's Map)

attacks, the Corps made considerable ground, inflicted heavy losses on the enemy, and suffered comparatively few of their own at 2,574.[96]

Canadian units in the latter part of the first and throughout the second day encountered German units in meeting engagements where the Canadians with their training and firepower had the advantage. Enemy reinforcements rushed to the front, often without their artillery and were split up to fill gaps.[97] As a result, the defences were less coherent and effective than usual. This second day, and opportunities squandered by the slow start, powerfully influenced how the Corps and its commanders viewed Arras 1918. Using their experience from Amiens, they reacted as if the Germans were in a similar state at Arras. Thus, it was more important to strike while the iron was hot rather than take the time to prepare a better attack.

The third day, resistance increased considerably as even more reserves arrived.[98] Although the Corps made some gains on 10 August, they were considerably less than the previous days. The offensive had clearly run its course and a halt was necessary. Rawlinson recognising this reality stopped it on 11 August, although formations could make local attacks to improve their situation.[99] The Fourth Army along with the Canadian Corps had scored a singular victory that resulted in great gains in ground, matériel, and captives. The Corps directly engaged 10 enemy divisions, parts of 5 more, and took 9,131 prisoners, 190 guns, and over a 1,000 machine guns.[100] It advanced 14 kilometres at a cost of 11,822 casualties for the period from 8 to 20 August.[101] The greatest effect of the battle was on Ludendorff's psyche. The defeat shook his confidence in his army. Calling 8 August the 'Black Day' of the German army, Ludendorff believed the defeats resulted from poor subordinate command decisions instead of endemic problems.[102]

Currie recommended that there be a pause to prepare a proper set-piece attack. He also suggested the Corps move to the Third Army front to strike toward Bapaume.[103] Instead, the Fourth Army was to renew the offensive on 15 August. The Corps conducted brigade-scale operations and probed the defences, while preparing for the set-piece. The prospect of another frontal attack alarmed Currie because of the scale of German reinforcements combined with the fortifications facing the Corps. Using air photos of uncut wire, he wrote a strong letter to Rawlinson arguing for the attack's postponement. With Monash, the commander of the Australian Corps, agreeing with Currie, the Fourth Army GOC persuaded Haig to postpone the attack on 14 August.[104]

The next day, Haig clashed with Foch over the continuation of the Amiens offensive, with Foch wanting the attack renewed. According to Haig, he had to put his foot down to get Foch to

96 Nicholson, *CEF*, pp.410-414; McWilliams and Steel, *Amiens: Dawn of Victory*, pp. 188-209; Cook, *Shock Troops*, pp.439-446.
97 *Der Weltkrieg 1914 Bis 1918* (Berlin: Ernst Siegfried Mittler and Sohn, 1944), 14.1, p.558.
98 Kemp, *Report of the Ministry*, pp.138-140.
99 TNA: WO 95-1053-1: Canadian Corps General Staff War Diary, 11 August 1918; Nicholson, *CEF*, p.418.
100 Kemp, *Report of the Ministry*, p.141.
101 Nicholson, *CEF*, p.419. The OMFC report gives a lower total of 11,362 which likely represents a shorter reporting period than the official history. Kemp, *Report of the Ministry*, p.140.
102 Erich von Ludendorff, *Ludendorff's Own Story, August 1914 - November 1918* (New York: Harper and Brothers Publishers, 1919), e-Book, loc.4194; Boff, *Haig's Enemy*, loc.235.
103 Kemp, *Report of the Ministry*, p.140.
104 Nicholson, *CEF*, pp.422-423; Lloyd, *Hundred Days*, p.61.

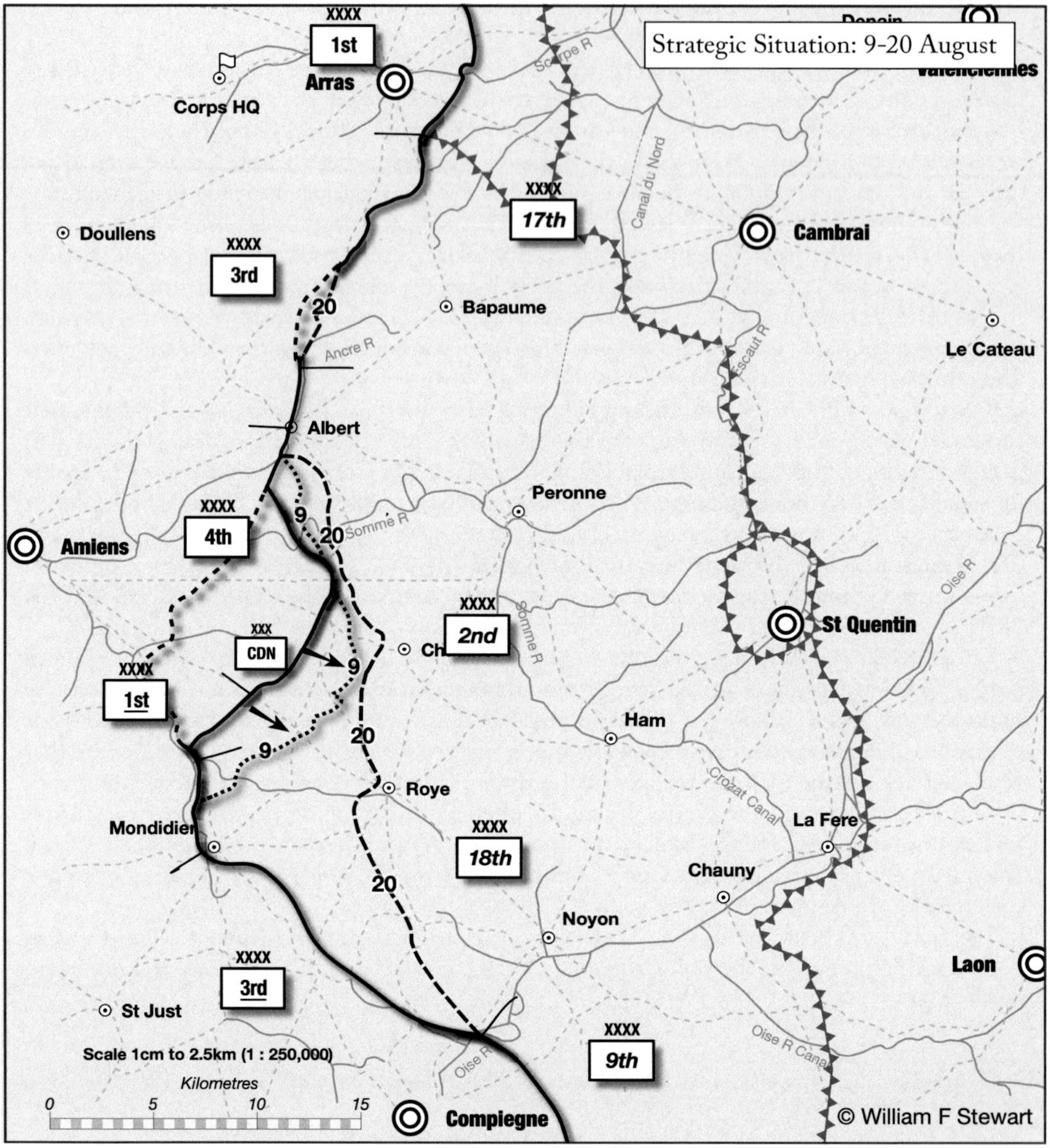

Map 7. The Amiens offensive runs out of steam, and Rawlinson persuades Haig to call off a further attack. (Author's Map)

back down.[105] The most recent English biographer of Foch convincingly suggests he just wanted Haig to attack somewhere and not wait to shift his forces north to Flanders.[106] Information that the 1st French Army's commander also had grave reservations about the attack as he had insufficient gun ammunition persuaded Foch to cancel the operation.[107]

In the aftermath of the disasters of 18 July and 8 August, German soldiers and *OHL* recognised they were in a perilous position. The heavy fighting and losses resulted in a warning from *OHL* on 18 August that the former policy of resting formations was no longer possible. According to German calculations on the vital 200-kilometre central sector, they faced seven enemy armies massing 86 infantry and 3 cavalry divisions supported by 700 tanks with ample guns, munitions, and aircraft. Further, Ludendorff and Rupprecht thought a British attack in Flanders on Mount Kemmel was likely. Thus, *OHL* had to allocate reserves for another potential attack vector, stretching them further.[108]

Widening the Offensive

Two days into the Amiens operation, Foch pressured Haig to widen the offensive to the neighbouring Third Army rather than Flanders.[109] Foch's plan had two advantages. First, it was much faster to transfer forces to the Third Army than to Flanders, which would take at least three weeks. Second, the Amiens disaster sucked German reserves from neighbouring armies, leaving them stripped of ready reinforcements. On 13 August, Haig issued the order to the Third Army to attack east toward Bapaume on 20 August.[110] Included in this order were the instructions to the First Army to plan a support attack – Thistle. Delays in transferring forces meant Byng did not attack until 21 August. It was a limited operation with four divisions, but they captured the German's outpost zone and 2,700 prisoners.[111] Before the attack, the limited scope of Byng's plan dissatisfied Haig, and his disquiet increased when Byng halted further operations on 22 August to bring up the guns.[112] Byng was cautious given the weak and under-trained state of his infantry but was too cautious for the C-in-C. Haig directed Byng to attack 'with the utmost vigour at the earliest possible moment.'[113] The Third Army had to scramble to launch operations on 23 August. The result was a ragged series of attacks. Nevertheless, they gained considerable ground and took 5,000 prisoners.[114] As part of this broader scope, the next day the VI Corps on the Canadians' right flank was to advance on Vis-en-Artois, with the Canadians to conform.[115] This will be important in the lead up to the Canadian attack and will be discussed in the next chapter. In summary, Haig had extended the breadth of the Amiens

105 NLS: Haig Diary, 15 August 1918.
106 Greenhalgh, *Foch in Command*, p.426.
107 Edmonds, *Military Operations, 1918* 4, pp.167-170.
108 *Der Weltkrieg* 14.1, pp.572, 578.
109 Greenhalgh, *Victory through Coalition*, p.250; Greenhalgh, 'United Allied Command', p.1008; Edmonds, *Military Operations, 1918* 4, pp.133-134.
110 Edmonds, *Military Operations, 1918* 4, p.584.
111 Edmonds, *Military Operations, 1918* 4, pp.183-194.
112 NLS: Haig Diary, 19, 21 August 1918.
113 TNA: WO 158-227: OAD 907/10, GHQ to Byng, 22 August 1918.
114 Edmonds, *Military Operations, 1918* 4, p.233.
115 Edmonds, *Military Operations, 1918* 4, p.242.

General Sir Julian Byng, GOC Third Army, was the revered former commander of the Canadian Corps. Despite this connection, the coordination between his formations and the Canadian Corps was lacking. (Canada. Dept. of National Defence/Library and Archives Canada/PA-001284)

offensive by directing the Third Army to attack towards Bapaume and later to drive north-east to Vis-en-Artois. He had high hopes for the Third Army operations, but Byng's advance was too measured and careful.

Horne handed the assignment to support the Third Army to Lieutenant General Sir Charles Fergusson, the GOC of the XVII Corps. He was decidedly unenthusiastic about it. In the notes for his outline plan, he claimed it was 'not tactically sound' and not worth the cost in launching it.[116] It was only viable if the Third Army attacked as well to take the high ground on the Hénin and Wancourt Ridges – the same objections Horne and Byng raised earlier. Further, 'We are at the present very much in the dark as regards the enemy dispositions, and his machine gun nests, and the latter cannot therefore be dealt with effectively by artillery.' His comment on being in the dark was puzzling. His corps had been on this exact sector for months, with only a two-week

116 TNA: WO 95-178-1: First Army General Staff War Diary, XVII Corps G.X.1, 16 August 1918.

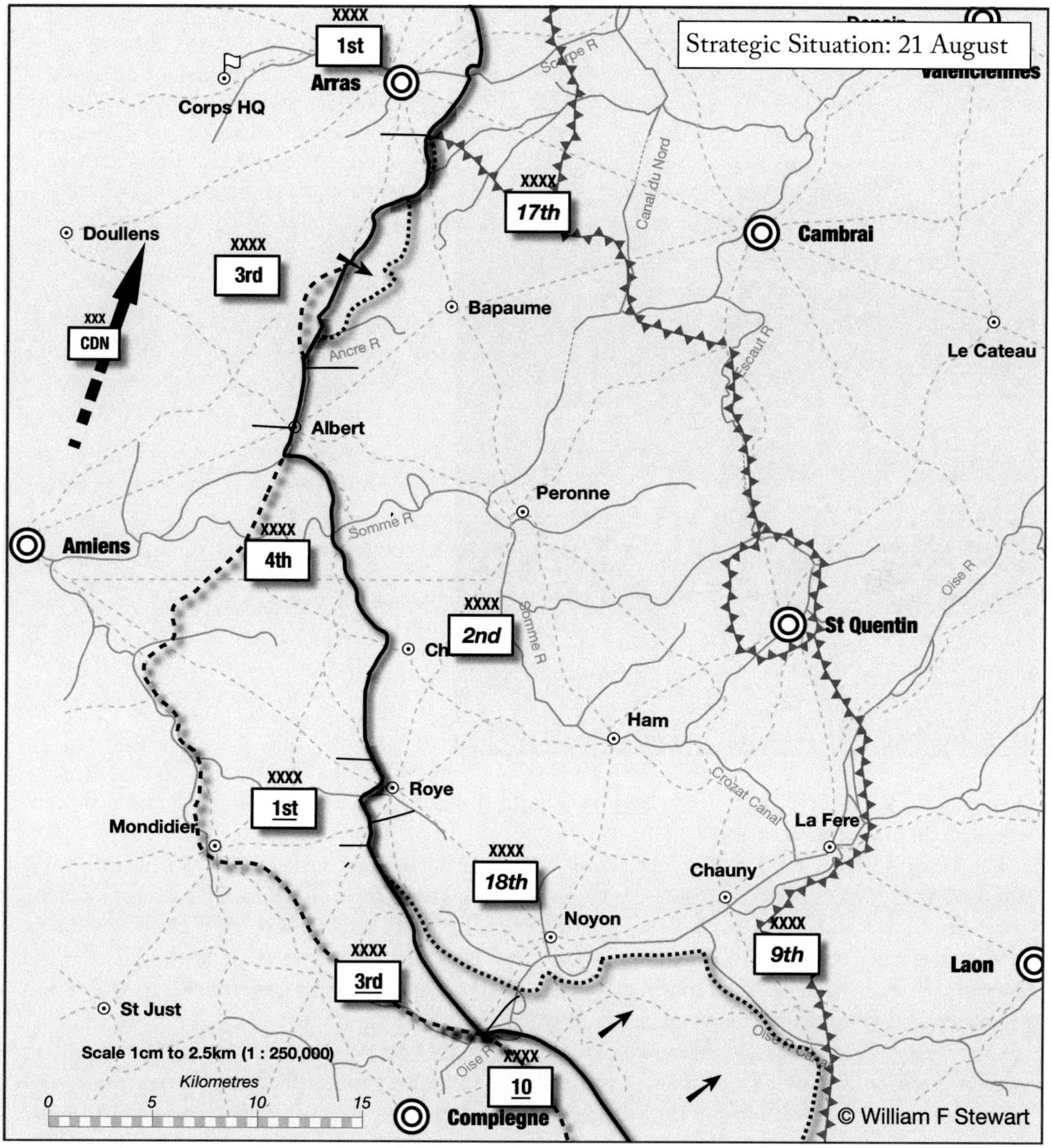

Map 8. To the south of Noyon, the French make great gains. Byng's Third Army has success in its attack towards Bapaume. (Author's Map)

Lieutenant General Sir Charles Fergusson, GOC XVII Corps, pictured in 1926 as the Governor-General of New Zealand. He and Currie did not work well together. (Herman John Schmidt <http://find.natlib.govt.nz/primo_library/libweb/action/display.do?ct=display&doc=nlnz_tapuhi1236927/> Lieutenant General Sir Charles Fergusson

period in GHQ reserve from 15 to 30 July. That it did not know its front suggests a significant intelligence failure on its part.

Fergusson's plan called for an attack by three territorial divisions (52nd, 56th, and 57th) supported by tanks to cut the wire as there would be no preliminary bombardment. Horne chose not to pass on all Fergusson's reservations to GHQ. He did stress there was no possibility of surprise other than its timing, that support by the Third Army was essential, and that the 'enemy artillery is strong.'[117] In the interim, the XVII Corps worked on establishing dumps and preparing the ground for the attack without warning the enemy.

One key difference stands out when comparing the planned attack with the Canadian operation on 26 August. In concept, both relied on an unregistered barrage, on surprise, and tank support. But in ambition, the Canadian operation was strikingly different. With fewer troops and tanks, the Canadians conducted an offensive that penetrated twice as far as the 'Thistle' plan called for on its first day.[118] This suggests either Fergusson overestimated the extent of the German resistance or the Canadian Corps was significantly better than the XVII Corps believed its forces were. The artillery plans were similar and with no dramatic differences other than the depth of the advance. The core concepts were similar, which suggests the Canadian

117 TNA: First Army GS WD, First Army, GS 1376/8, 17 August 1918.

118 Canadian divisions were larger, but the XVII Corps committed more divisions and brigades than the Canadian plan.

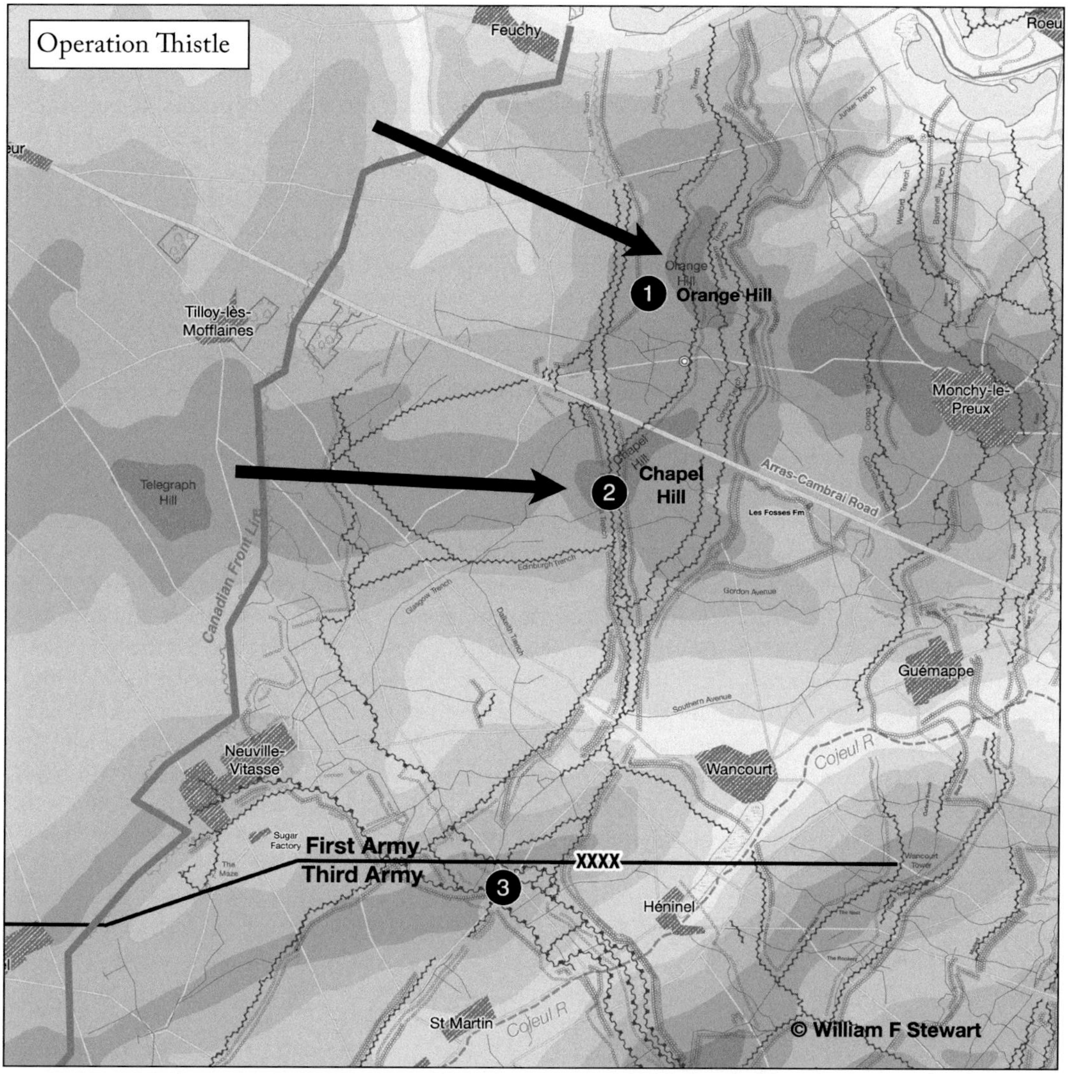

Map 9. Operation Thistle objectives and challenges:

1. Orange Hill overlooks sectors on both banks of the Scarpe and into Arras
2. Chapel Hill provides observation into Arras
3. Hénin Hill in the Third Army sector provides observation of any advance on Chapel Hill (Author's Map

Corps developed the plan, passed it to the XVII Corps, and who then handed it back. While the First Army did not execute Thistle, it was the basis of the Canadian attack on 26 August. Even the code name used by Lipsett for the 3rd Division's instructions was Operation 'T' and likely based on Thistle. As Currie's Interim Report stated, 'In addition to a detailed knowledge of the ground, which we had held before, we were particularly benefited by all the reconnaissances and plans made for the capture of Orange Hill during the period of simulated activity at the end of July.'[119]

Meanwhile, on 19 August, with the situation rapidly changing across the front, Haig ordered the First Army to move the XVII Corps' three territorial divisions out of the line into GHQ reserve.[120] They moved to the Third Army and participated in its renewed offensive on 23 August in the VI Corps. This decision had the effect of suspending Thistle until the Canadian Corps was in position on 23 August. In the interim, the XVII Corps commanding the 2nd and 3rd Canadian Divisions would continue to prepare ammunition dumps and improving roads.[121] Once the Canadians had relieved the XVII Corps, it moved to the Third Army and took over the three Territorial divisions in the afternoon of 24 August.[122]

The Corps had prepared, was tested, and had passed at Amiens. It had the inestimable advantage of a prolonged training period to hone its methods, and these had proven their effectiveness at Amiens. The Corps emerged with even greater confidence in itself, its doctrine, and in its capabilities. The gain in ground and captures of masses of Germans and matériel proved the merit of the new approaches. Amiens was, however, not the model for future attacks but an outlier. In this battle, the Allies struck a uniquely vulnerable German salient, with total surprise, and supported by hundreds of tanks. Subsequent attacks would not have the benefit of shock, the absence of defences, and the numbers of tanks to smash the defenders. Still, the Germans were vulnerable, but the Allies had to maintain the pressure. Thus, unlike previous campaigns in 1917 where long periods of rest separated offensive operations, the Corps would plunge straight into another gruelling battle.

119 Kemp, *Report of the Ministry*, p.144.

120 TNA: First Army GS WD, GHQ OAD 907/6, 19 August 1918.

121 LAC: RG9 III-C-1 v3912, 40/5: XVII Corps No.G.22, 22 August 1918; LAC: RG9 III-C-1 v3912, 40/5: RA XVII Corps No RA X/8, 23 August 1918.

122 TNA: 51st Div. GS WD, 23 August 1918.

Section Two

To the Fresnes-Rouvroy Line

4

'To surprise the Enemy' Canadian Corps Operations Planning 22-25 August

The object of this attack will be to pierce the Drocourt-Queant line

GHQ OAD 907/13, 24 August 1918[1]

With the Amiens offensive on hiatus, the Canadian Corps transferred back to the Arras sector. Its mission was the oft-discussed attack on Orange Hill with a possible extension to Monchy-le-Preux. It would have three days to prepare a set-piece operation much different from Amiens. Surprise was not possible. The Germans had strong fortifications in-depth, and there were few tanks available. Two factors made the operation feasible on short notice; an existing plan with preparations under way and a fully developed infrastructure. Then, the afternoon before the action, Haig dropped a bombshell. He tasked the Canadian Corps with the far more ambitious objective of crossing the distant Canal Du Nord. This entailed a rapid recasting of the plan with far more aggressive goals. This chapter discusses the events that led to the Corps' move back to Arras and the circumstances that explain the different directives it received. It will also examine the Corps' actions prior to 26 August, its planning, and its dysfunctional interactions with the Third Army on its right flank.

Canadian Corps Moves North

The Canadian Corps' transfer north was ironically the result of General 'Blackjack' Pershing's demands. On 16 August, he requested the return of three of the five US divisions training with the BEF. He required them to carry out a Foch directive. This put a serious crimp into Haig's calculations. While these formations were green, they were twice the size of a British division and were fresh.[2] Haig used this demand as a bargaining chip to reduce the BEF's line. He told

1 TNA: First Army GS WD, GHQ OAD 907/13, 24 August 1918.
2 An American infantry division consisted of just under 28,000 men versus a British division of about 14,000 men. 'Basic Fighting Unit of the AEF the Square Division' <http://www.worldwar1.com/dbc/squarediv.htm> (10 February 2018).

Foch that to continue the offensive, he needed to reduce his front by 18,000 metres, or the equivalent of three good divisions. The next day Foch agreed and ordered Marshal Pétain to take over that frontage. This was the location of the Canadian Corps on the BEF's right flank. Foch stipulated that all the non-divisional artillery was to remain in place, which trapped two of the three Canadian HA brigades on the Amiens front until after Arras.[3] Somewhat surprisingly, the Corps' non-divisional field artillery (5th CDA, 8th CFA) accompanied the Corps north.

Currie had recommended the Corps fight in Byng's army. Instead, he received 'intimations' on 19 August that the Corps was returning to Arras to serve under Horne again.[4] Simultaneously, GHQ shifted three territorial divisions from the First Army to the Third Army. Likely the reason for this formation swapping was that without the Canadians the First Army lacked sufficient combat power to strike a strong blow. Horne's army in comparison with the Third and Fourth Armies had a significantly smaller artillery park. On 21 August, its concentration of field and heavy artillery was 54 and 116 metres per piece. Only the Fifth Army in a purely defensive posture had a lower concentration of heavy artillery. The average density across the rest of the BEF was 35 and 100 metres per piece – a lower number was better.[5] With the British infantry's dependence on overwhelming artillery support, Horne had no choice but to rely on the Canadians.

The Canadian Corps handed over its front at Amiens to the Australian Corps at noon on 22 August and transferred north to the First Army. There was a complex reshuffling of fronts as the French and Australians took over the Canadian sector. The CCHA headquarters did not move until 25 August, and this affected battle planning.[6] After an intermediary stop, the Corps headquarters moved to Noyelle Vion about 20 kilometres from Arras on 23 August where it would remain.[7] It relieved the XVII Corps at noon on 23 August and took over the famous 51st (Highland) Division.[8]

The 2nd and 3rd Divisions left the front-line first at Amiens and started moving into reserve on the night of 16/17 August. Burstall's division spent the next three days resting, which would have recharged the troops. GHQ's authorisation for the 2nd Division's move to the First Army came on 19 August.[9] It started its move on 20 August under instructions that 'the strictest secrecy would be observed as to the movements of the Canadian Corps.'[10] All the moves by train, bus, and road were at night. There were multiple delays and confusion in loading and moving because of the masses of transport on the roads. This would be a continuing issue throughout the Arras 1918 campaign.[11] The 3rd Division experienced a similar set of travails in entraining and moving north starting on 20 August after four days in reserve. GHQ's transportation system of

3 Edmonds, *Military Operations, 1918* 4, p.171.
4 LAC: MG30 E100 v1: Currie Fonds, Currie to Borden, 26 November 1918; LAC: Currie Diary, 19 August 1918.
5 Edmonds, *Military Operations, 1918* 4, p.180.
6 TNA: WO 95-1053-2: Canadian Corps General Staff War Diary, Canadian Corps OO 227, 21 August 1918.
7 LAC: Canadian Corps AAQMG WD, 22-23 August 1918.
8 TNA: 51st Div. GS WD, 23 August 1918.
9 WO 95/39-9 QMG WD 18-21 August 1918.
10 LAC: RG9 III-D-3 v4847: 2nd Division General Staff War Diary, 19 August 1918.
11 LAC: RG9 III-D-2 v4794, 54: 2nd Division Report Battle of Arras.

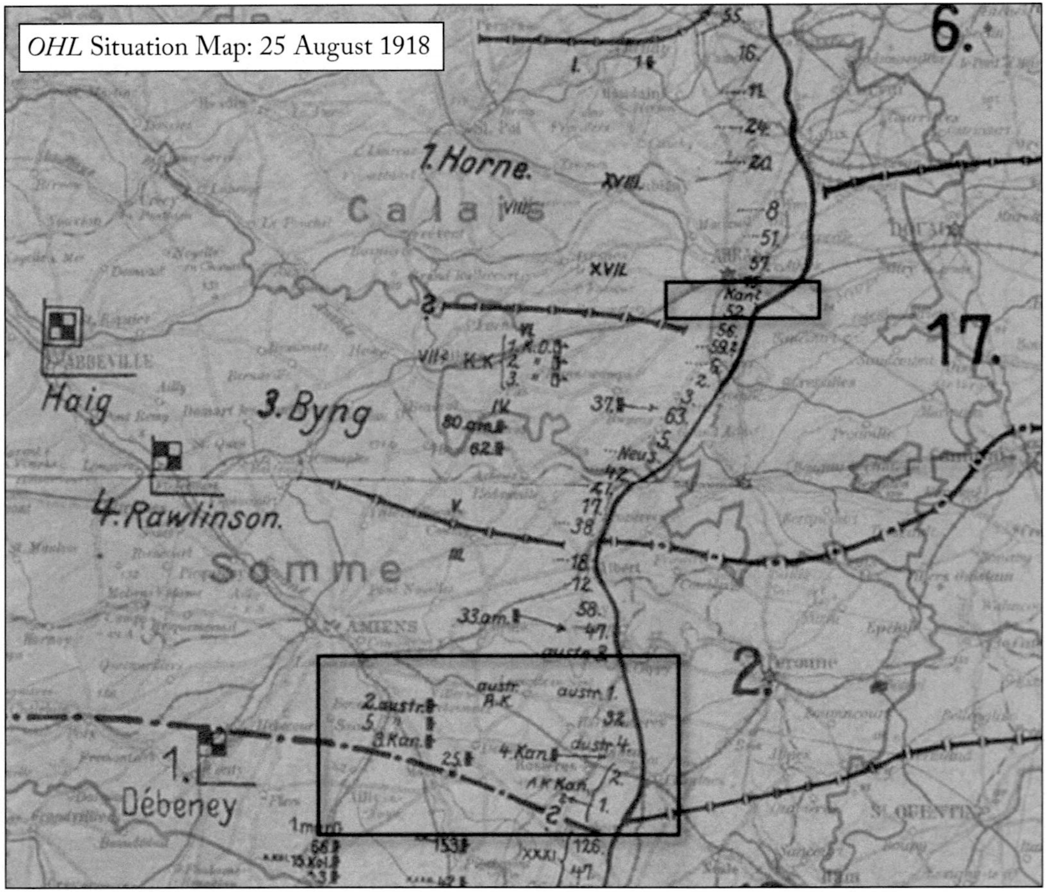

Map 10. Excerpt of the *OHL* situation map on 25 August 1918 showing how badly German intelligence had misplaced the locations of the Canadian Corps, its divisions, and the XVII Corps. The two boxes highlight where *OHL* believed the Canadian were. ('Akte Nr. 256. Übersichtskarte Des Chefs Des Generalstabes Des Feldheeres – Abteilung Fremde Heere Zur Verteilung Der Französischen, Englischen Und Belgischen Streitkräfte an Der Westfront Vom 25.08.1918.' <http://tsamo.germandocsinrussia.org/de/pages/39222/map> (6 March 2018).)

trains and buses had difficulty in accommodating the larger Canadian brigades with their four battalions.

The Corps endeavoured to thwart the standard German intelligence gathering methods of wireless interception and air observation to hide the move. Unless in trains, units moved at night to foil aerial observation. Artillery batteries moved into silent positions and did not register or fire before Zero Hour. Wireless stations remained offline until the attack. Traffic analysis of wireless messages, even enciphered ones, was a powerful means of discerning enemy shifts.[12] The XVII Corps did not have CW sets while the Canadians did. Therefore, they remained shut down until the attack, as their presence would signal a change.[13]

Canadian secrecy paid off. The 2nd Division entered the line on the night of 22/23 August with the 6th Brigade. Lipsett's division followed the next night with its 8th Brigade on the left of the 2nd Division.[14] The *OHL* situation map for end of day 25 August 1918 showed the Germans had not discerned the transfer.[15] This demonstrated the degree to which the German high command was operating blindly. They had not identified that the 2nd Division had departed the line nor its entry in a new sector over eight days. Given the stormtrooper reputation of the Canadians, especially after Amiens, this was a serious oversight. They also had not noticed the XVII Corps with its three divisions had left the line.

Planning Arras 1918

Now, Haig and Horne needed to decide what to do with this powerful formation. On 21 August, the C-in-C envisioned the Third Army attacking the D-Q Line while the First Army took Monchy-le-Preux and advanced as far as Vis-en-Artois.[16] This indicated that despite extending the scope of the First Army operation, it was still not the primary thrust. Evidence of its limited nature was it would have the support of a composite tank company for a one-day operation.[17] Horne understood his role was subsidiary when he instructed Currie on 22 August to prepare to attack Orange Hill in three days similar to the Thistle operation.[18] The long-standing objections regarding the need to capture the Hénin Hill were moot as this was one of the Third Army's objectives in their offensive.

While Canadians were working on their scheme, the Third Army resumed its offensive. This had ramifications for the Corps' planning. On 23 August, the VI Corps' left division, the 52nd (Lowland), was to cover the main thrust of the 56th Division aimed at Vis-en-Artois on the

12 John Ferris, 'The British Army and Signals Intelligence in the Field During the First World War', *Intelligence and National Security* 3, no. 4 (1988), p.21.
13 W Arthur Steele, 'Wireless Telegraphy in the Canadian Corps in France Part II Open Warfare', *Canadian Defence Quarterly* VII, no. 4 (1930), p.387.
14 LAC: 3rd Division WD, 20-24 August 1918.
15 'Akte Nr. 256. Übersichtskarte Des Chefs Des Generalstabes Des Feldheeres – Abteilung Fremde Heere Zur Verteilung Der Französischen, Englischen Und Belgischen Streitkräfte an Der Westfront Vom 25.08.1918' <http://tsamo.germandocsinrussia.org/de/pages/39222/map> (6 March 2018).
16 NLS: Haig Diary, 21 August 1918.
17 TNA: WO 95-103-4: 14th Tank Battalion, N.780, 16 September 1918.
18 NLS: Haig Diary, 19, 21, 24-25 August 1918; TNA: First Army GS WD, First Army GS 1378/20, 22 August 1918; TNA: First Army GS WD, Canadian Corps G.512/2525-4, 25 August 1918; TNA: First Army GS WD, GHQ OAD 907/13, 24 August 1918.

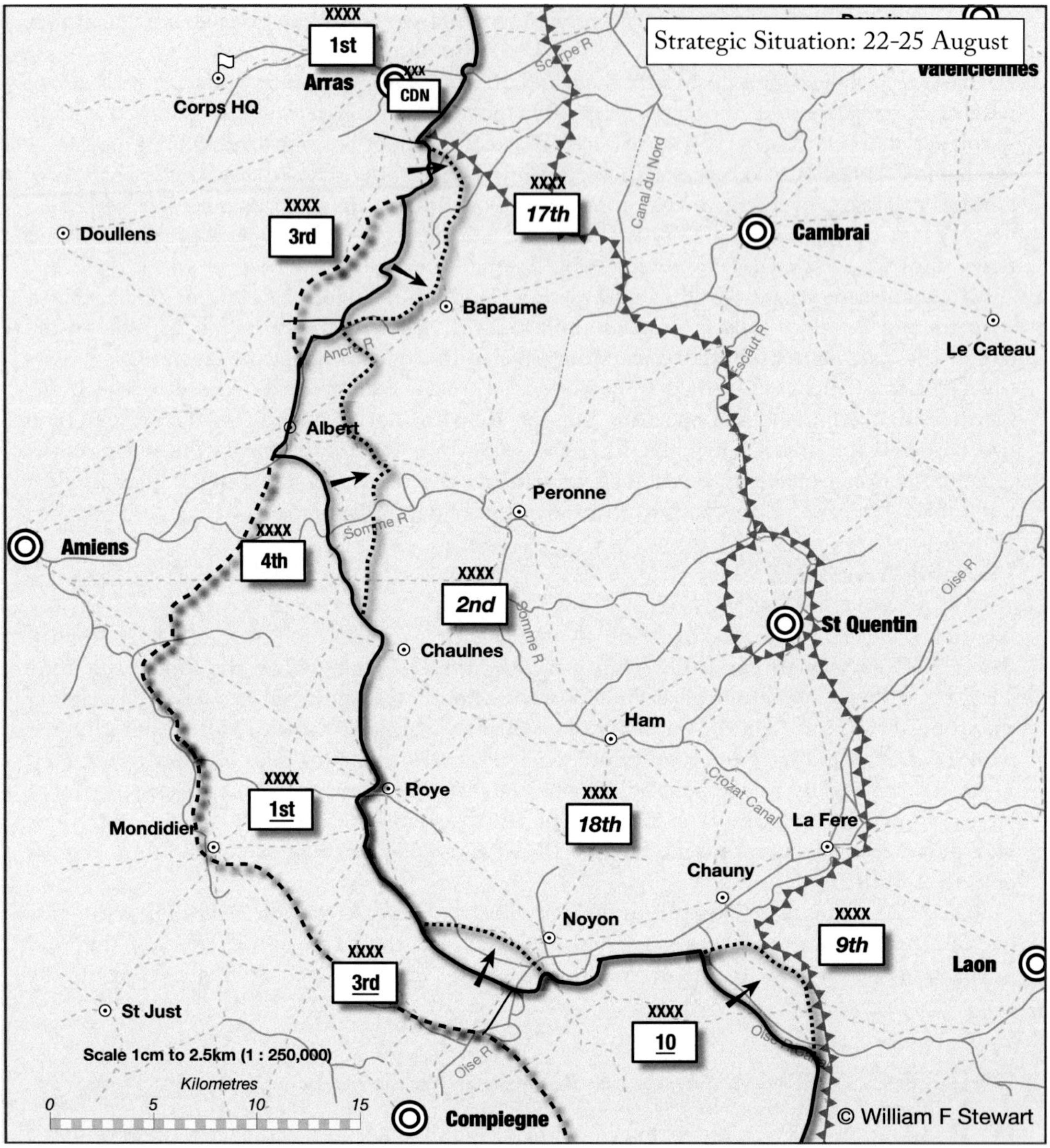

Map 11. Strategic situation from 22 to 25 August with advances by the British Third and Fourth Armies and the Third and Tenth French Armies. Despite the great gains, the Germans still hold much of the ground gained in the spring offensives. (Author's map)

Arras-Cambrai road.[19] Both divisions would have to pierce the Hindenburg Line. These were two of the three divisions Haig had ordered Horne to transfer to the Third Army. The German hold of Neuville-Vitasse in the 2nd Division's sector close to the boundary with the Third Army threatened the 52nd's advance. This small agricultural village sat on a spur and dominated the nearby terrain. The First Army ordered the Canadians to conform to the 52nd's advance and place pressure on the Germans.[20] At this point, Burstall's division had just entered the line. Lieutenant General A Haldane's VI Corps made progress on 23 August but was still far from having broken the Hindenburg Line. The 52nd Division complained that the Canadians did not push forward as promised and that the Germans held positions the Canadians claimed they possessed.[21] Despite the Germans lightly holding the Hindenburg Line, a standing British heavy artillery barrage thwarted an attempt by the 52nd to bounce it.[22] The VI Corps ordered the division to continue its attack the next day.

The 52nd Division's attack would affect the 31st Battalion. It moved into the line around Neuville-Vitasse on the night of 22/23 August. In response to the 6th Brigade's orders, it aggressively pushed out patrols to gauge the enemy's posture and found them 'holding in fairly heavy strength with instructions to hold the line at all costs.'[23] That night 23/24 August it sent out patrols that enveloped a complex of trenches to the south of Neuville-Vitasse called the Maze that was a long-standing point of contention.[24] The patrols then jumped it before the Germans could react, capturing it along with one officer and 23 other ranks.[25]

The First Army had renewed the directive to the Corps to conform to the Third Army advance late on 23 August.[26] What followed was a concerted effort by every level of the Canadian chain of command to avoid carrying it out. This was a case of 'Consent and Evade' where subordinates accept an order but delay and dodge its execution until its cancellation. The reason for the Corps' reluctance was its major attack scheduled for the next day. Typically on a per-unit basis, these small-scale attacks were more costly and resource-intensive than an all-out battle. The foot dragging would have implications for its own operations.

'Ox' Webber, following the First Army order, called on the 2nd Division to make up as much ground as possible. Burstall pushed back, but the BGGS was unwavering that the division capture Neuville-Vitasse. Brigadier General Bell, GOC 6th Brigade, warned his battalion commanders they might have to attack.[27] Based on an erroneous 24 August VI Corps' report that the Germans were falling back, the Corps ordered the 2nd Division to capture Neuville-Vitasse.[28] Burstall protested that he would have to take parts of the nearby Hindenburg Line

19 TNA: WO 95-774-3: VI Corps General Staff War Diary, VI Corps OO N. 367, 22 August 1918; TNA: VI Corps GS WD, VI Corps GS 73/71, 22 August 1918; Thompson, *Fifty-Second*, pp.521-522; TNA: First Army GS WD, First Army G973, 23 August 1918.
20 TNA: First Army GS WD, First Army G449, 23 August 1918.
21 TNA: 52nd Division GS WD, 23 August 1918.
22 Thompson, *Fifty-Second*, pp.522-524.
23 LAC: RG9 III-D-3 v4937: 31st Battalion War Diary, 23 August 1918.
24 For instance, the 20th Battalion raided it in June. LAC: RG9 III-D-3 v4833: 4th Brigade War Diary, 3rd June 1918.
25 LAC: 31st Battalion War Diary, 23-26 August 1918.
26 TNA: First Army GS WD, First Army G973, 23 August 1918.
27 LAC: RG9 III-C-3 v4139, 7/13: 6th Brigade G. 3/985, 23 August 1918.
28 LAC: RG9 III-C-1 v3855, 75/3: Canadian Corps G.453, 24 August 1918.

Brigadier General A H Bell, GOC 6th Brigade, was a solid and capable leader who could develop and execute a daring plan. (Canada. Dept. of National Defence/Library and Archives Canada/PA-006940)

and that would be costly.[29] Nevertheless, he passed the instruction to Bell, who questioned the order's basis, as his troops had not seen a German retreat.[30] What is more, Bell would require three battalions to execute the order. Probably shocked that Bell would need almost his entire brigade, Burstall told him to hold off while he discussed it with Webber and Currie.[31]

On 24 August, the 31st Battalion continued to push into Neuville-Vitasse, but the Germans held on. The battalion reported patrols penetrated as far as Hénin Trench well within the Third Army's sector, as per the 6th Brigade's orders.[32] By the end of the 24 August, they had a good portion of the village, but the Germans were obstinately holding the remainder. Given the imminence of the set-piece attack and the stiffening German resistance, Bell ordered the battalion to stand down.

Meantime, Anderson, the First Army MGGS, contacted the Corps early on 24 August and directed it to take Neuville-Vitasse so as not to delay the Third Army. Clearly, Byng was

29 LAC: 2nd Division Arras Report.
30 LAC: 2nd Division GS WD, 10:40 a.m. 24 August 1918.
31 LAC: 2nd Division Arras Report.
32 LAC: RG9 III-D-3 v4891: 6th Brigade War Diary, 6th Brigade G.3/987, 23 August 1918.

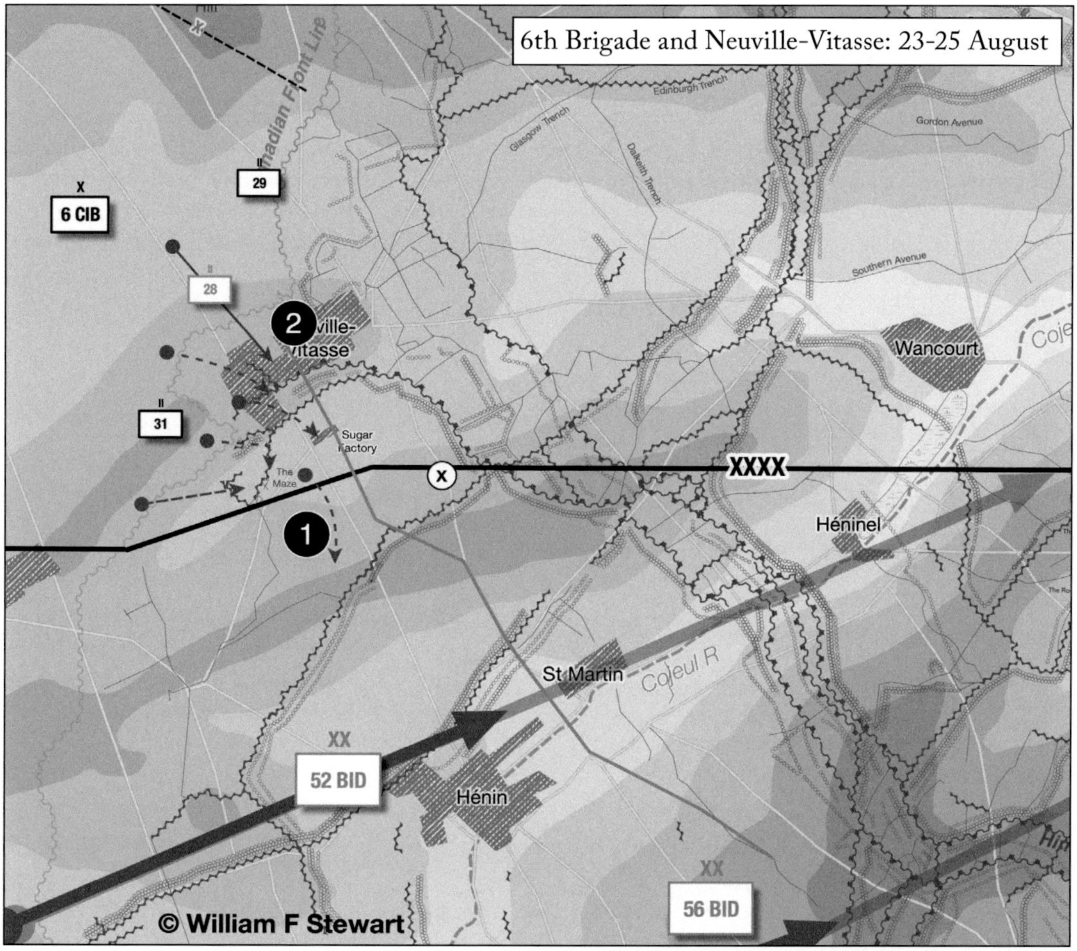

Map 12. The actions of the 6th Brigade prior to the 26 August attack.

X. The location the 52nd Division claimed it reached on 23 August.

1. The active patrols and probes of the 31st Battalion including the capture of the Maze
2. The proposed attack by the 28th Battalion. Note how exposed its assembly area is to German observation from Neuville-Vitasse (Author's map)

pressuring Horne to get the Canadians going. The 52nd Division had to refuse its flank because the Canadians had not taken the village. Anderson reiterated the order to take it, despite the need for a full-scale attack.[33] The 2nd Division was to do so soon as possible and not wait for the set-piece attack. The Corps had no choice but to pass on the directive.[34] Currie, suspicious of the VI Corps' claims based on the information from the 6th Brigade, sent Webber to the British corps to get the real story. Meanwhile, he told Burstall that the 6th Brigade could use up to two battalions for the attack.[35] Each level in the chain of command objected to the order as there was insufficient preparation time and the troops would have to assemble in daylight under observation from the village.[36] The objections were overruled, but the operation was whittled down to a single battalion – the 28th. Its commander, Lieutenant Colonel Alex Ross, was adamant that a daylight attack would fail, and especially one made with so little preparation time.[37] All these protests and delays finally paid off as Webber called the 2nd Division just

Lieutenant Colonel A Ross, CO 28th Battalion, was adamant that a daylight attack on Neuville-Vitasse would fail, and especially one made with so little preparation time. (Canada. Dept. of National Defence/Library and Archives Canada/PA-004144)

33 LAC: 2nd Division GS WD, 8:50 a.m. 24 August 1918.
34 LAC: 2nd Division GS WD, 11:05 a.m. 24 August 1918.
35 LAC: 2nd Division GS WD, 11:25 a.m. 24 August 1918.
36 LAC: 2nd Division GS WD, 24 August 1918; LAC: 2nd Division Arras Report.
37 Donald George Scott Calder, *The History of the 28th (Northwest) Battalion, C. E. F. (October 1914-June 1919) from the Memoirs of Brigadier General Alexander Ross* (Regina, Sask.: Regina Rifle Regiment,

before 4:00 p.m. from the VI Corps' headquarters to postpone the operation by 24 hours. He found the 52nd Division was not as far forward as claimed.[38]

Horne and Haig met with Currie at the Corps headquarters that day at 3:30 p.m. and Haig revealed a far more ambitious scheme – to be discussed below. Likely, it was at this meeting that Currie persuaded the two that given the scale of the new assignment it was essential to stop the Neuville-Vitasse attack.[39] The Corps cancelled the action that night.[40] The Saskatchewan regiment's history pulled no punches in stating with the cancellation: 'The 28th Battalion was saved from heavy, useless casualties.'[41]

Haig Shifts the Spearhead

Between 22 and 24 August, Haig decided to shift the primary thrust of the BEF's offensive to the Canadian's sector. While he provided no rationale for this change, there was considerable circumstantial evidence pointing to frustration with Byng's unhurried progress. Haig was operating under an apprehension that the Germans might fall back to the Hindenburg Line, and he wanted his army commanders to be aggressive.[42] It was not accidental that GHQ issued OAD 911 on 22 August calling for his commanders to take greater risks.[43] He demanded, 'Risks which a month ago would have been criminal to incur, ought to be incurred as a duty.' Even before the attack, Haig had concerns with the limited scope of Byng's offensive. Adding to Haig's anxiety, the defenders stymied the VI Corps' efforts to break through the Hindenburg Line on 23 and 24 August. The VI Corps lacked the tanks, massive artillery support, and prolonged preparation needed for the action. Haig wanted a more rapid tempo. If Byng could not provide, then possibly Horne and the powerful Canadian Corps would. As a result, the Canadian attack's scope changed from a subsidiary action to be the spearhead. It was not clear from either Haig's diary or the orders issued, if he expected the Corps to crack the D-Q Line in one day or if it would take multiple days. An advance only slightly longer than that achieved on the first day of Amiens would mean the capture of the objective. Certainly Currie did not expect an advance of this scale, based on the Corps' orders – the 1st Division issued orders on 26 August for an expected attack on the D-Q Line on 28 August.[44] A close reading of the plans for the 2nd and 3rd Divisions suggests that the instructions related to pursuit to the D-Q Line were perfunctory. They were not to the level of detail usually associated with Canadian orders, indicating little expectation of their being executed. It made sense to set longer-range goals in the event of a German collapse, especially after the second day experience at Amiens. Judging from the comments of Burstall to Haig prior to the offensive discussed below, the commander of the 2nd Division did not understand the improbable nature of the order for the furthest objective.

1961), p.209.
38 LAC: 2nd Division GS WD, 3:55 p.m. 24 August 1918.
39 NLS: Haig Diary, 24 August 1918; LAC: Currie Diary, 24 August 1918.
40 TNA: First Army GS WD, First Army G991, 24 August 1918.
41 Calder, *28th (Northwest) Battalion*, p.209.
42 Boff, *Winning and Losing*, p.27.
43 TNA: WO 95-575-1: Cavalry Corps General Staff War Diary, GHQ OAD 911, 22 August 1918.
44 LAC: 1st Division W.D., 1 Canadian Division G.3-93/3, 26 August 1918.

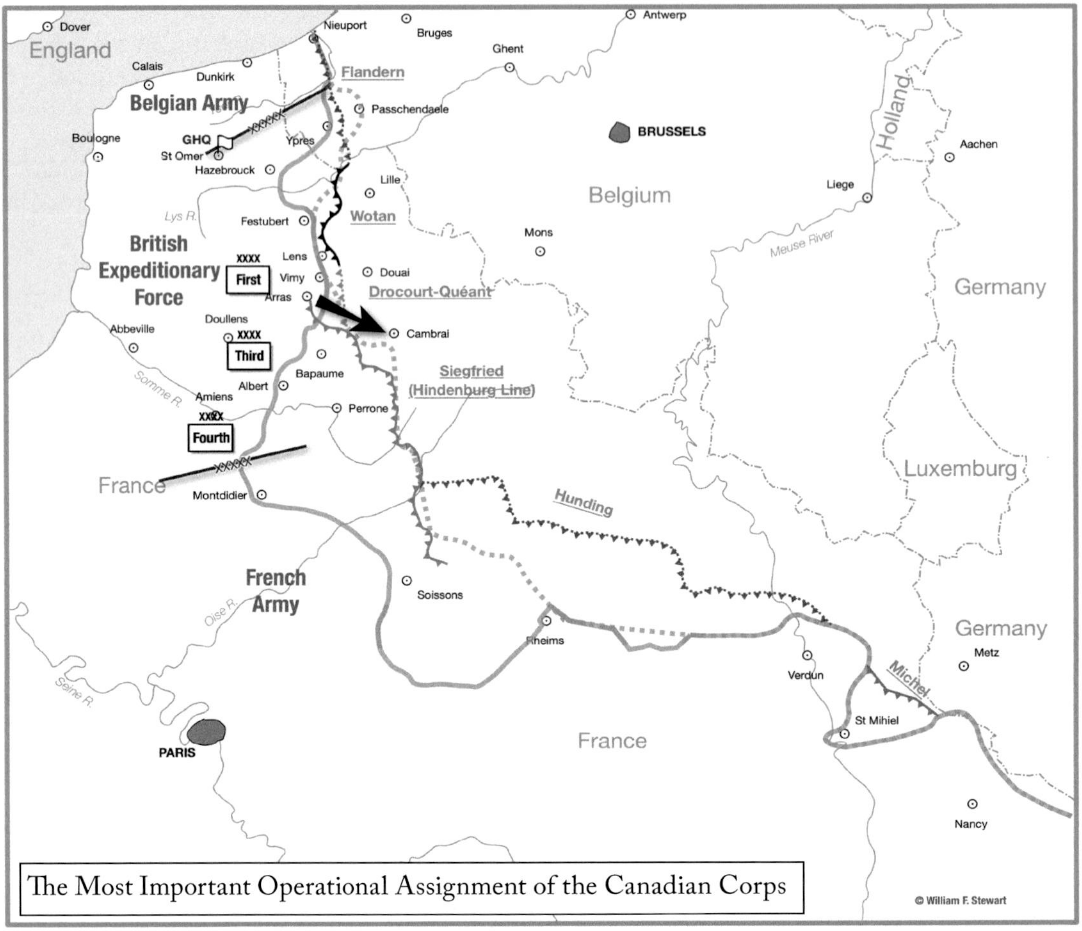

Map 13. Breaking the D-Q Line and capturing Cambrai would unhinge the German defences on the Western Front. The Canadian capture would force the Germans to fall back on an extended front or risk being encircled. It was the most important operational assignment the Canadians received in the First World War. (Author's map)

Haig met with Currie and Horne on 24 August and expanded the Canadian attack's ambitions.[45] This was the Corps' most important operational assignment in the war – certainly Currie believed it to be so.[46] It was to drive south-east from the outskirts of Arras and cross the Canal Du Nord centred on the Arras-Cambrai road. It had to punch through five defensive zones comprising 15 kilometres of defences and then cross the canal to capture the *Seventeenth Armee*'s supply depots around Cambrai. This action would unhinge the German defences in the centre of the Western Front. Instead of the Canadians supporting the flank of the Third Army as it battered through the Hindenburg Line, the Corps would lever open the door for Byng. In line with previous policy, Haig stipulated the Corps was not to attack until the Third Army captured Hénin Hill.

Haig's transfer of the Cavalry Corps to Horne from Byng's army indicated how important he regarded this operation. More evidence was Haig's refusal to reinforce the Fourth Army, as he stated the BEF's spearhead was along the Arras-Cambrai road.[47] The C-in-C wanted the Corps to attack on 25 August, but Currie argued for a one-day postponement. The Corps needed another day to bring up the needed artillery, and Currie was reluctant to attack on the Sabbath.[48]

What was striking was Haig's acceptance of a one-day delay when he was so anxious that the Germans were going to get away. The Canadians enjoyed three critical advantages that ensured Haig would grant the delay – a similar British formation would not normally receive this much consideration. First, being a Dominion formation meant Haig had to treat it somewhat differently. He was aware of the ramifications of a set-to with the Canadian government if he overruled Currie. Second, Haig had confidence in Currie. While he did not look like the prototypical British general preferred by Haig with his pear shape and jowls, he behaved like one.[49] He won victories, instilled discipline, and was punctilious about his troops' appearance – all attributes Haig demanded. Finally, the Corps had a brilliant record of success, so it received more leeway.

Currie briefed his commanders following the meeting with Haig. The Corps issued its operation order on 24 August, laying out a somewhat more aggressive plan. It was a tame set of orders as it stipulated two objectives – the old Feuchy-Wancourt line from 1917 and the German main line of resistance short of Monchy-le-Preux. The first was the Green Line and the second the Red Dotted Line – after their colours on the map. Both divisions were to exploit any weaknesses beyond the second objective. The order did not mention breaking through the D-Q Line or of employing tanks.

The First Army's orders, concise at 56 words including stops, arrived after the Corps had issued its instructions and was similar in scope.[50] Owing to its limited resources, Horne's army had to rely on the Canadian Corps. Haig was explicit that artillery and divisional reinforcements

45 NLS: Haig Diary, 24 August 1918; LAC: Currie Diary, 24 August 1918; TNA: First Army GS WD, GHQ OAD 907/13, 24 August 1918. The Official History misdates this. For more, see Appendix I Historiographical Debate. Nicholson, *CEF*, p.426; Kemp, *Report of the Ministry,* p.14.
46 LAC: Currie Diary, 3 September 1918.
47 NLS: Haig Diary, 25 August 1918.
48 The Canadian Corps had not made any major attacks on a Sunday up to that point. Kemp, *Report of the Ministry,* p.143.
49 Hyatt, *General Sir Arthur Currie,* pp.22-23.
50 TNA: First Army GS WD, First Army G.991, 24 August 1918.

The Arras-Cambrai road at Haucourt. Note the shattered trees lining the road, the traffic, and the German signs from their occupation. The road was the main supply route of the Corps and was vital to keeping the offensive advancing. (Canada. Dept. of National Defence/Library and Archives Canada/ PA-003185)

were limited.[51] This in turn meant that Horne ceded detailed planning for the operation to the Corps. The First Army provided only the broad outline of the task, with Canadian planners having to fill in the details. As there was already the Thistle plan, there was little reason to interfere.

On 25 August, Haig, after meeting with Horne, gathered Currie was 'a little sticky.' He told Horne that he had met with Burstall who understood what he wanted and would do what was right 'whatever Currie might feel!'[52] He did not explain the reason for the 'sticky' comment. There were four possible alternatives: the offensive's start date, the Canadian's reluctance to support the Third Army, that the Hénin Hill was still in German hands, or Currie's operational plan was insufficiently aggressive. In his *Shock Troops*, Tim Cook argued Haig's objection was to

51 LAC: Breaking the Quéant-Drocourt Line, p.121; Bernd Horne, ed., *Fortune Favours the Brave: Tales of Courage and Tenacity in Canadian Military History* (Toronto: Dundurn Press, 2009), p.10.
52 NLS: Haig Diary, 25 August 1918.

the one-day postponement.[53] This was unlikely the cause, as Haig did not complain in his diary about the delay the previous day.[54] Another possibility was the Canadian's failure to support the Third Army.[55] It was plausible but does not explain the reference to Burstall ignoring Currie's views as he was equally reluctant to storm the village.

The third alternative was the long-standing objection to attacking with Hénin Hill held by the enemy.[56] The Third Army did not have the hill nor was it planning to take it on 26 August.[57] In his instructions to Currie, Haig had directed the Corps was not to attack until this hill fell but later directed the attack to proceed regardless of the hill situation.[58] This circumstantial evidence suggests Currie raised objections about the Hénin Hill situation. It does not, however, explain Burstall's promise to Haig.

The fourth possibility was Currie was not aggressive enough. The Corps' operation order No. 228 issued on 24 August was less aggressive than Haig intended. GHQ's order directed the Corps 'to pierce the DROCOURT - QUEANT line' and operate against the enemy holding up the Third Army.[59] Instead of an aim of breaking the D-Q Line, the Corps just instructed that once they took the second objective: 'Divisions will exploit as far East as possible.'[60] This was far less ambitious than Haig demanded. Following the afternoon meeting with Haig on 25 August, the Corps issued a further document on the policy for future operations. It was bolder. It explicitly stated the offensive's aim was to drive south to break the D-Q Line and reach the Canal Du Nord. Further, it exhorted 'utmost vigour' and 'as much ground as possible must be gained.'[61] Likely, the Corps issued it in reaction to Haig's dissatisfaction with the Canadians' modest plan. This aligns with Burstall's statement to Haig about ignoring Currie's views and following the Field Marshal's wishes to push hard. It was this order where Currie laid out his plan that each division was to attack on the front of one brigade and the Corps would pause before each major defensive zone to bring up the heavy artillery. In summary, Haig's view of Currie's stickiness was probably a combination of Currie's reluctance to attack with the Germans holding Hénin Hill and the Corps' cautious plan.

Complicating operations over the next three days was a GHQ change in the boundary between the First and Third Army to take effect on 25 August.[62] The border shifted from running due east to running south-east, with the effect of greatly widening the Canadian front as it advanced. This was a critical decision as it meant stretching the Corps' forces and not allowing a concentration of troops on a narrower front. Most of the Corps' units did not pick up this boundary change until well into the next day – the 2nd Division reported the shift at 10:15 a.m. on 26 August.[63] A former staff officer suggested that the staff so hurriedly assembled the

53 Cook, *Shock Troops*, p.458.
54 NLS: Haig Diary, 24 August 1918.
55 Robbins, *The First World War Letters of General Lord Horne*, pp.30-31.
56 Farr, *The Silent General*, p.200.
57 TNA: First Army GS WD, MGGS First Army Telephone Conversation, 25 August 1918.
58 LAC: Currie Diary, 24 August 1918.
59 TNA: First Army GS WD, GHQ OAD 907/13, 24 August 1918.
60 TNA: Cdn. Corps GS WD, Canadian Corps OO No. 228, 24 August 1918.
61 LAC: RG9 III-C-1 v3964, 28/7: Canadian Corps G.512/2525-4, 25 August 1918.
62 TNA: First Army GS WD, First Army S.S.1376/24, 25 August 1918.
63 LAC: 2nd Division Arras Report.

plans for 26 August that they muddled the boundaries.[64] Even the Canadian Official History's colour battle map did not recognise the change. The poor communication of this change would lead to some later acrimonious exchanges between the 5th Brigade and elements of the 52nd Division. Apparently, the British division or at least its subordinate units were unaware of the change as late as 28 August. GHQ had instructed formations not to adhere to boundaries rigidly, as a 'certain amount of play is necessary for manoeuvre.'[65] This injunction was applicable when all formations understood the correct boundaries. When they did not grasp these bounds, this flexibility created confusion and rancour.

Corps' Plan

The Corps' plan was essentially the same as the earlier 'Thistle' iterations, but with more aggressive follow-on attacks. It was not an involved order as it comprised just nine items contained on two pages.[66] There were two set, named phase lines – Green and Red Dotted – with the 2nd and 3rd Divisions exploiting as far east as possible. For more, see Map 4.5 Opening Day Plan: 26 August in the colour map booklet. The plan tasked the 51st Division commander to leverage any Canadian success by trying to gain Mt Pleasant. Corresponding to the Feuchy-Wancourt Line, the Green Line represented a 2,000 to 3,000 metre advance. The planners expected the attackers to reach it at 0+131 minutes. After a pause of 14 minutes, the advance would continue for a further 1,000 to 2,000 metres to the Red Dotted Line by 0+184 minutes. The artillery would then fire a protective barrage 300 metres in front until 0+208 minutes. This represented the limit of the artillery support. The remaining actions depended on the battle's course, and the divisions would set the pace and commitment of forces. One of the major divergences from 1916/17 planning was passing decision-making responsibility down to the division commanders. Previously, orders were more prescriptive and laid out the whole course of the operation.

Webber, based on an earlier Third Army success, suggested to Currie attacking in moonlight to shield the advancing infantry from long-range machine gun fire. Currie discussed it with his senior commanders and altered the attack's Zero Hour from 4:50 a.m. to 3:00 a.m. This change did not reach the 8th Brigade until 8:00 p.m. on 25 August.[67] His rationale for the last-minute adjustment was he was 'hoping in this way to surprise the enemy,' and that the darkness would mask Canadian infiltration of the forward enemy machine gun positions.[68] He was counting on clear skies and bright moonlight to make the attack possible – the skies would be clouded over with showers. This late change 'created a dangerous situation' for the 8th Brigade as there was little time to warn the attack battalions of the alteration or for the troops to get sufficient rest.[69]

The time change also triggered a further unusual intervention. On learning of the alteration, according to Webber, GHQ sent a former Corps' staff officer, Brigadier General John Dill, to get the Corps to revert to the original time to coordinate with the Third Army's operation.

64 LAC: RG9 III-D-2 v4800, 121: Wedd to Duguid, [January-February 1919].
65 TNA: First Army GS WD, First Army, GS 1376/24, 25 August 1918.
66 TNA: Cdn. Corps GS WD, Canadian Corps OO No. 228, 24 August 1918.
67 LAC: RG9 III-D-3 v4897: 8th Brigade War Diary, 25 August 1918.
68 LAC: Currie Diary, 25 August 1918; Kemp, *Report of the Ministry*, pp.147-148.
69 LAC: RG9 III-C-3 v4163, 12/1: 8th Brigade G.80/9, 25 August 1918.

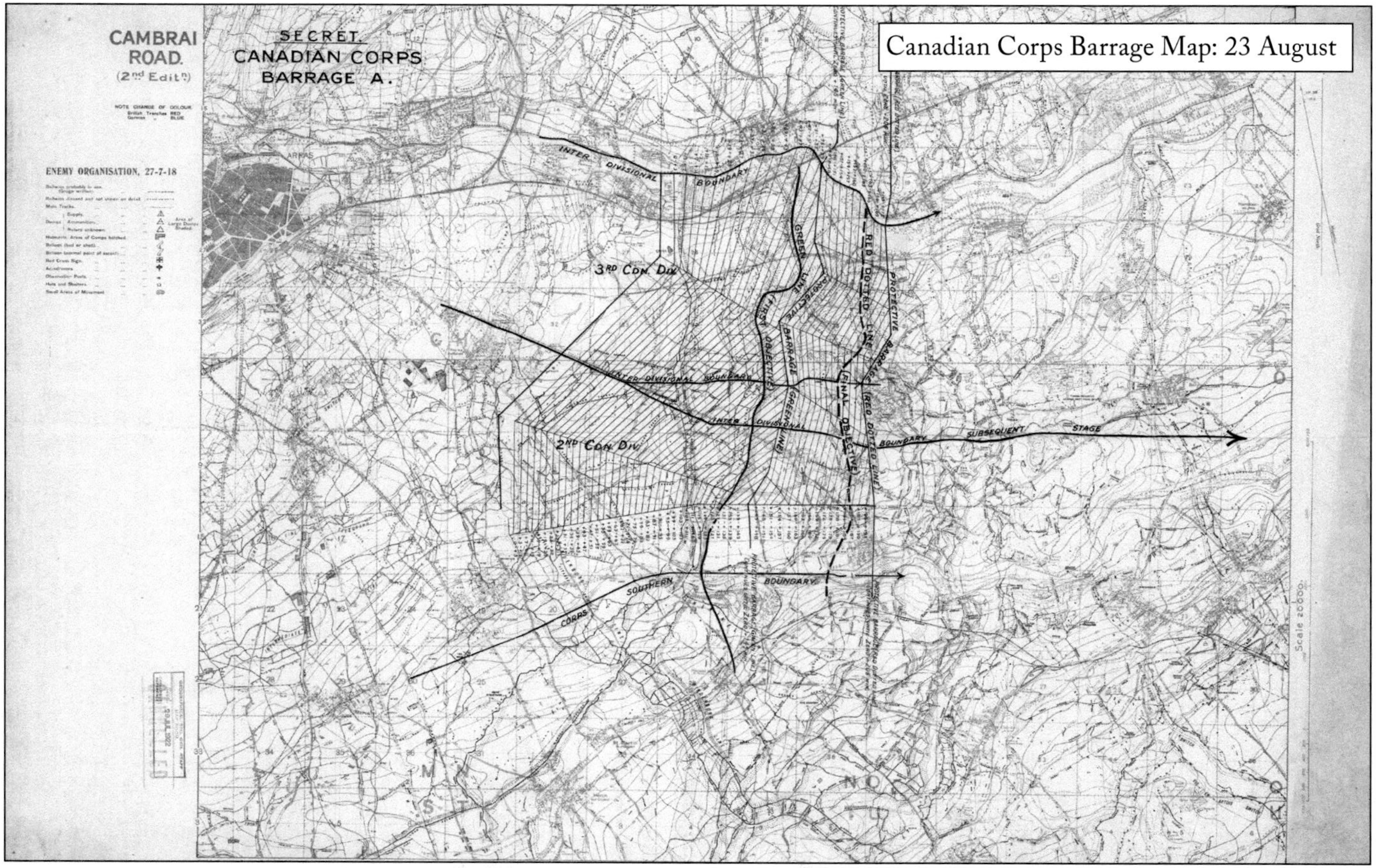

Map 14. The Canadian Corps barrage map for the attack on 26 August. Three things are of interest. First note how the barrage does not cover the entirety of the 2nd Division's sector. Second, the later change in the boundary between the First and Third Army did not appear on this map. It would run parallel to the Arras-Cambrai road. Finally, the barrage only reaches the second objective and does not cover Monchy-le-Preux or further east. ('Canadian Corps Barrage A, 23 August 1918,' McMaster University, <http://digitalarchive.mcmaster.ca/islandora/object/macrepo%3A71695> (27 May 2018))

Currie refused, and the early start remained.[70] The story is curious as there was almost no time for GHQ to receive the message, to task Dill, and for him to travel to the Corps' headquarters to meet Currie. Dill did not mention this intervention in his correspondence regarding the Canadians.[71]

The key element of the Corps plan was the artillery instructions issued by the GOCRA.[72] They set the basic parameters of the attack, including boundaries, objectives, and timing. The artillery support for the attack consisted of 14 FA brigades with 2 more as close support artillery and 9 HA brigades. This amounted to 384 field artillery and 270 heavy artillery pieces, although only 241 were operational.[73] See Appendix IV 26 August Order-of-Battle for more. The plan was a hybrid mix of centralised control for the 18-pounder creeping barrage and counter-battery efforts with the remaining pieces assigned to the divisions. The GOCRA controlled only the field artillery for the barrage, while McNaughton, the CBSO, directed five heavy artillery brigades for counter-battery missions. Four 4.5-inch howitzer batteries were to fire smoke to screen the Corps' south flank and on Mt Pleasant and Monchy-le-Preux. The gunners fired no preliminary bombardment or registration. To ensure accuracy, the Corps Survey Section resected each battery position. The orders specified batteries were to sort all ammunition into similar lots. Also, 'Section commanders will check constantly the laying of the guns with field clinometer and inspection of switch angles.'[74] To minimise ground destruction, the creeping barrage used shrapnel mixed with 10 percent smoke unless crossing defences where it fired HE shells with the No. 106 fuze.

Two aspects of the plan are of interest. First, there were insufficient 18-pounders to cover the entire Corps front in sufficient density. Therefore, Morrison limited the barrage to the fronts of the 3rd Division, the 4th Brigade, and a small portion of the 6th. Even with this reduced breadth, the barrage density was just under 24 metres per gun – roughly half of Passchendaele's concentration. This would have critical implications for the 2nd Division's planning. Second, although the plan went through four iterations, the basic outline remained unchanged, because of the restricted range of the field guns. The 18-pounders maximum barrage range was normally 2,500-3,000 metres, which was the first objective. By installing batteries close to the front-line and using the longer-range 18-pounders with air recuperators, the artillery could stretch the barrage to reach just short of Monchy-le-Preux – the Red Dotted Line.[75] The new air-recuperator guns extended their range from 6,200 to 9,500 metres over models equipped with springs.[76] Both served in the Corps. Thus, whether the advance was 5,000 or 10,000 metres, the barrage remained unchanged. The major alteration was the release of most of

70 Daniel G. Dancocks, *Spearhead to Victory: Canada and the Great War* (Edmonton: Hurtig, 1987), p.94; Hugh MacIntyre Urquhart, *Arthur Currie, the Biography of a Great Canadian* (Toronto: J.M. Dent & Sons (Canada), 1950), p.245; McGill: General Webber Comments, 1934.
71 McGill: MG4027 C1, 13: Urquhart Fonds, General Dill Comments, 1934.
72 LAC: RG9 III-C-1 v3943, 55/3: GOCRA Artillery Instructions 132 No. 1-4, 23-5 August 1918.
73 LAC: Artillery Statistics by Date.
74 LAC: RG9 III-C-1 v3943, 55/3: GOCRA Artillery Instructions 132 No. 4, 25 August 1918.
75 LAC: RG9 III-D-3 v4960: 2nd CRA War Diary, 2nd CDA Arty, Instr. No.2, 25 August 1918.
76 The equivalent to the 18-pounder in the German service was the 77mm gun which had a range of 9,952 metres when firing HE and 11,702 if shrapnel. LAC: RG9 III-D-2 v4810: CWNS Comparison of German and Canadian Artillery.

the FA brigades to divisional control when the barrage ended. Before only two brigades would advance.

The counter-battery office had a far more challenging assignment than at Amiens. There, the German guns deployed to be within range of their outpost zone, and the Allies had located the majority of them. As a result, the counter-battery results were superb. At Arras, the German high command moved most field artillery pieces back, so were harder to locate and hit. This meant, however, hostile artillery fire would not be a factor until the Canadians approached the second objective.

Brutinel planned a strong machine gun barrage extending as far as the first objective. The indirect barrage consisted of 22 batteries with 176 guns, with six of these batteries advancing into enemy territory following the infantry to extend the barrage. It moved at a rate of 100 metres every four minutes with a density of 35-47.5 metres per gun. A striking aspect of the barrage was the degree to which batteries on the northern portion had to fire at eccentric angles. This indicates Brutinel's confidence in the technical proficiency of his crews, but he miscalculated with the 51st Machine Gun Battalion as will be seen.[77] It is questionable how effective was the barrage, given the Germans were holding the *Vorfeld* with so few troops. The 2nd Machine Gun Battalion argued that if the enemy main line of resistance was over 1,000 metres from the front, it was better to fire on known targets than fire an indirect barrage.[78]

The administrative situation was far better than at Amiens as the Corps had the dual benefit of attacking from a fully developed infrastructure with preparations for 'Thistle' under way. In addition, the railheads were closer so there were not the long hauls necessary as at Amiens.[79] With a complete light rail system, an extensive network of water supply sources, and roads in far better shape than in April 1917, the Corps had a strong base. Much of the required ammunition was already at the battery positions or in dumps.[80]

The Chief Engineer forecast the battle would be more difficult for the engineers than at Amiens. There, the terrain was relatively unmarked by war, so horse transport could move off-road.[81] At Arras, the ground was so torn up and crossed by barbed wire and trenches that horse transport could only travel on roads and tracks. Thus, two of the three priorities for the engineers related to improving the transportation infrastructure. First, he wanted sufficient manpower concentrated at road chokepoints to ensure rapid repair. Second, the engineers were to aggressively push the tramways with one track per divisional front. Finally, the speed of the advance would likely outpace the ability to bring piped water to the troops. Hence, it was essential to develop a local supply by bringing in pumps and sterilising lorries. The force allocation reflected these priorities with 60 percent of the field companies working on roads, 18 percent on tramways and 7 percent on the water supply. The remaining companies worked

77 LAC: RG9 III-D-3 v4981: CMGO War Diary, Canadian Corps G.483.2525-4, 24 August 1918; LAC: CMGO WD, Canadian Corps MG-G.21-4/670-673, 24 August 1918; 'M.G. Barrage Map No. 25, 24 August 1918' McMaster University <http://digitalarchive.mcmaster.ca/islandora/object/macrepo%3A71696> (27 May 2018).

78 LAC: RG9 III-C-4 v4359, 18/11: 2nd Machine Gun Battalion Lessons Learned, August 1918.

79 LAC: RG9 III-D-2 v4810, A&Q Arras: 3rd Division AAQMG Report on Move to Arras Area and Operation from 16th to 29th August 1918.

80 LAC: GOCRA AO 132.

81 LAC: RG9 III-D-3 v4989: GOCRE War Diary, Canadian Corps CE 408-21-1, 25 August 1918.

Engineers sterilising water pumped from a dirty stream. Clean and abundant water was essential to maintain the offensive. (Canada. Dept. of National Defence/Library and Archives Canada/PA-003111)

on inspecting dugouts, reconnaissance, and assisting field artillery to advance.[82] Crucially but unstated, the order did not require any work parties from the infantry. Currie's decision to form the engineering brigades paid off handsomely here.

Divisional Plans

Divisional plans evolved as the GOCs worked in collaboration with their brigade commanders to hammer out the details. The increase in the attack's ambition forced a major transformation, with the two divisions solving it differently. Burstall had three connected complications for his two assault brigades – 6th on the right and 4th on the left. Only about 1,000 metres of the 6th Brigade's had a barrage, leaving 1,800 metres unsupported. The second was the contentious

82 LAC: RG9 III-D-3 v4991: 2nd Brigade CE War Diary, 25 August 1918; LAC: RG9 III-D-3 v4991: 3rd Brigade CE War Diary, 3rd Brigade CE T. Instructions No.3, 25 August 1918.

village of Neuville-Vitasse sat in this unshelled zone. The issue for the planners was how to deal with this sector and the village. Burstall, Bell, and their planners would not arrive at a final decision until late on 25 August. Finally, there was uncertainty about whether the 52nd Division and XVII Corps on the right flank would advance.

Initially, the XVII Corps would not attack, in part because the Canadian Corps could not provide tanks to it to assault the Hindenburg Line.[83] The British corps wanted the full panoply of support weapons, especially tanks to make the assault. There was to be a running issue of poor cooperation between the Canadians and the XVII Corps. There was a definite subtext that Currie and Fergusson did not get along.[84] Simon Robbins in his landmark study of senior British leadership gave Fergusson as an example of a corps commander kept only because there were no better alternatives.[85]

After dragging their feet to help the Third Army earlier, the Corps now wanted their assistance. Horne sped off to Byng's headquarters to persuade him to cooperate.[86] Judging from the results, the outcome was unsatisfactory, and he relayed his concern to Haig. The C-in-C responded by stressing to Byng it was in his interest to help the Canadians.[87] What resulted were instructions to XVII Corps to roll up the Hindenburg Line.[88] Instead of attacking it directly, the 52nd Division was to pivot on St Martin-sud-Cojeul and strike south-east along it and to meet the Canadians near Wancourt.[89] The XVII garbled these instructions as Wancourt was in the Canadian sector.

Staff and commanders of the 6th Brigade had a particularly strenuous day on 25 August with plans undergoing constant revision. The initial scheme was for a broad attack with two battalions to advance east to the Corsica-Minorca trench system and to capture Neuville-Vitasse and Wancourt.[90] It was a direct assault with only weak artillery support and no tanks. Burstall visited Bell at 7:00 p.m. on 25 August, and the scheme was 'revolutionised.'[91] Instead, the brigade would now bypass the defenders and then sweep down from the north and pocket the lot. The 27th Battalion would advance with two companies on the narrow barrage sector until it reached the Red Dotted Line or second objective. The other two companies and 28th Battalion were to follow behind. At the Red Dotted Line, the 27th and 28th battalions would wheel right and strike south, taking Wancourt and outflanking the defences.[92] Neuville-Vitasse would fall as a matter of course without a direct assault. It was a daring plan that required considerable skill to execute and relied on the Germans holding the outpost line lightly. In effect, the brigade was advancing on the front of two companies to a depth of 4,500 metres in the dark, while leaving

83 LAC: RG9 III-C-1 v3855, 75/3: Canadian Corps G.527, 25 August 1918.
84 Dancocks, *Spearhead to Victory*, p.108; Cook, *The Madman and the Butcher*, pp.236-237.
85 Simon Robbins, 'British Generalship on the Western Front, 1914-1918' (PhD, King's College London, 2001), pp.29, 65.
86 TNA: First Army GS WD, MGGS First Army Telephone Conversation, 25 August 1918.
87 NLS: Haig Diary, 25 August 1918.
88 TNA: WO 95-178-4: First Army GS War Diary, Third Army GS 73/73, 25 August 1918.
89 TNA: First Army GS WD 178, XVII Corps Order No. 152, 25 August 1918.
90 LAC: 6th Brigade WD, 6th Brigade Instructions No.1, 25 August 1918; LAC: RG9 III-D-3 v4936: 29th Battalion War Diary, A Narrative of the Operations Undertaken by the 28th Canadian Infantry Battalion August 27/27th, 1918.
91 LAC: 6th Brigade WD, 25 August 1918.
92 LAC: 6th Brigade WD, 6th Brigade Instructions No.2, 25 August 1918.

remaining the 1,800 metres of the brigade front unengaged. The 29th and 31st Battalions would pull back from their forward positions to avoid the counter-barrage. The battalions had less than seven hours to prepare and move up. It was a testament to the Canadians' excellence that the brigade could pull off such a complex program with so little preparation time.

For the 4th Brigade, the major terrain consideration was Chapel Hill astride the Arras-Cambrai road. The brigade would attack in an east-south-east direction, with its first objective 3,500 metres away on an almost 2,000 metre front. It would first have to capture the old Feuchy-Wancourt system, called the Nova Scotia trench, and then descend to the old British front-line system during the *Mars* offensive. This was the Green Line. The brigade would then advance, with the looming mass of the Monchy-le-Preux hill on its left flank. Its second objective, the Red Dotted Line, was a further 1,700 metres away and was the German's main line of resistance. Each of the leading battalions would encounter one to one and half companies defending the outpost zone and a support battalion along the Green Line from the *363rd IR* and *50th IR*. The boundary between the 2nd and 3rd Division's was eccentric. It swung north around Chapel Hill and followed a series of trenches roughly 300 metres parallel north of the Arras-Cambrai road. Likely the planners drew this complex boundary to ensure Chapel Hill was the exclusive responsibility of the 2nd Division.

The brigade would attack on a two-battalion front with the 21st Battalion on the right and the 20th on the left. The 18th Battalion conditionally was to take Guémappe in the Cojeul River valley, but not until it saw the 3rd Division advancing on Monchy-le-Preux. It would be exceedingly rash for a single battalion to assault, if the 3rd Division had not neutralised the observational advantage of Monchy-le-Preux.[93] Three tanks of the 9th Tank Battalion and two Stokes mortars would assist each unit, with two tanks supporting the 18th Battalion. In reserve was the 19th Battalion.[94] The brigade hastily assembled this plan, so it made no mention of tanks. The battalion orders reflected this scramble, with the 20th's not revised and the 21st's amended in handwriting.[95]

Lipsett's division's challenge was it had to not only take the Green and Red Dotted Lines but also Monchy-le-Preux, Boiry-Notre-Dame, and Dury – an advance of 13 kilometres. He divided the operation into two major stages. The first conducted by the 8th Brigade would advance the line to past Monchy-le-Preux. Then, the 7th Brigade would pass through and seize the distant objectives of breaking the F-R and D-Q Lines. The expectation must have been that the Germans held these positions lightly.

During planning, Lipsett and Draper, GOC 8th Brigade, viewed Orange Hill and Monchy-le-Preux from the north bank of the Scarpe.[96] The British held the north bank east to the first objective. They examined the attack front from an angle rarely afforded to planners. What they saw was forbidding. 'Honeycombed with a powerful trench system,' the long western slope of Orange Hill would bring masses of machine guns to bear from multiple posts. It was apparent

93 LAC: 4th Brigade War Diary, 4th Brigade OO No. 254, 25 August 1918.
94 LAC: 4th Brigade War Diary, 4th BRIGADE Narrative of Operations South of Scarpe, 26, 27, and 28 August, 1918.
95 LAC: RG9 III-C-3 v4109, 30/3: 20th Battalion OO No.197, 25 August 1918; LAC: RG9 III-C-3 v4109, 30/4: 21st Battalion OO No.209, 25 August 1918.
96 Johnston, *The 2nd CMR*, p.68.

then that a frontal assault on the Orange Hill ridge would be 'hazardous.'[97] Instead, they would make the main thrust along the south bank of the Scarpe and outflank these positions from the north. The terrain near the river was more broken and provided more cover. Moreover, the defences were not as developed. Only when the division advanced beyond the Green Line would it have to refuse its left flank to avoid enfilade fire from the high ground across the Scarpe. The 'T' Instruction called for a rolling barrage with a slower rate of advance on the norther sector to accommodate the tougher terrain.[98]

GOC 8th Brigade, Brigadier General D C Draper's plan for the opening stages of the campaign was clever and resulted in overrunning the German forward positions at a low-cost. (Canada. Dept. of National Defence/Library and Archives Canada/PA-007253)

This plan and its bold objective setting reflected the experience of Amiens. There, the German defences there were front-loaded and once cracked the Canadians made a deep advance. At Arras, the main line of resistance was along the Red Dotted Line. The expectation was probably that once taken, the Germans would have few forces left, and the assault troops would meet disorganised and fragmented defenders. Arras, however, was different. First, the Germans had pulled most defenders back from the outpost zone, so the barrage would catch few of them. Second, the enemy artillery deployed further to the rear than at Amiens and was out of the infantry's reach. The success at the earlier battle was partly due to the capture of much of the enemy's field artillery. Finally, unlike on 8 August, the German defences were far more formidable and deeper, so that even small parties of defenders had secure positions to fight from.

It was late in the planning cycle that the Corps assigned tanks to the operation.[99] The 3rd Division received a composite tank company

97 LAC: 3rd Division WD, 3rd Division Report on Operations from Aug. 26th to Aug. 28th, 1918.
98 LAC: 3rd Division WD, T. Instructions No. 1, 23 August 1918.
99 LAC: RG9 III-C-3 v4154, 6/8: 7th Brigade Report on Operations East of Arras, August 26th, 27th and 28th, 13 September 1918.

with only five tanks of the 11th Tank Battalion which it allocated to the 7th Brigade. The change in the start time for the attack meant they could not move in time to support the 8th Brigade.[100]

Highlanders! The 51st (Highland) Division

The famous 51st (Highland) Division, regarded by the enemy and itself as a crack division, was a shadow of its former self. It had already fought three desperate battles in 1918 that each required its rebuilding. Its nine battalions comprised only about 1,500 men after the March offensive.[101] The division's war diary described the lamentable condition of the infantry as 'lacking in training in the elementary duties of an infantry soldier and were unable to apply the lessons learnt.'[102] As David French described the division was 'almost obliterated' in the March offensive and what continued was 'bludgeoned to extinction the following month at the battle of the Lys'[103] It suffered 3,863 casualties in the Champagne offensive in July 1918 but received only 993 replacements that month.[104] The 1/6th Black Watch on reaching Arras had a ration strength of 13 officers and 359 other ranks – indicating the parlous state of the infantry.[105] It was brought up close to strength later. The division had only a short period of 10 days to reform, refit, and retrain after it reached the Arras sector. Not surprisingly, it wished it had more time to rest and ready the troops for the next onslaught.[106]

The Highlanders entered the line on 14 August holding a 3,500-metre sector north of the Scarpe. The forward positions of the division were about 2,000 metres further east of the line south of the Scarpe. This resulted from the German attack on 28 March making less progress on the north side of the Scarpe than the south. With the high ground of Orange Hill and Monchy-le-Preux looming over their sector, the Highlanders could not advance until the Canadians controlled these heights. The 51st had no great numerical or material advantage over its opponent, the *48th RD*. During the Arras operation, four field artillery brigades, one heavy artillery brigade, its own machine gun battalion, and one or two additional machine gun companies supported it. It had no tanks. The limited gunnery support meant it could only assault on at most a 1,500-metre front. What it could do though was concentrate its forces on a portion of the sector, confident that it was unlikely the Germans would strike back.

On entering the line and after some minor actions, it appeared the sector would remain quiet. On the understanding that the 51st would not take part in an attack, the division GOC, Major General G T C Carter-Campbell went on leave. In his place, the CRA, Brigadier General L. Oldfield, took over and would lead it during the Arras operation.[107]

100 LAC: RG9 III-D-2 v4798, 103: 3rd Tank Brigade Report on Operations of 26th August 1918, ? September 1918.
101 Bewsher, *History of 51st (Highland)*, p.292; TNA: WO 95-2849-1/4: 51st Division AAQMG War Diary, March 1918.
102 TNA: 51st Div. GS WD, Lessons Learned, April 1918.
103 Craig French, 'The 51st (Highland) Division During the First World War' (PhD, University of Glasgow, 2006), pp.288-289.
104 TNA: 51st Div. GS WD, Casualty Summary July 1918.; TNA: 51st Div AAQMG WD, July 1918.
105 TNA: WO 95-2876-1/4: 1/6th Black Watch War Diary, Appendix 'C' Ration Strength 2 and 17 August 1918.
106 Bewsher, *History of 51st (Highland)*, p.357.
107 Bewsher, *History of 51st (Highland)*, p.360.

The division continued to launch small-scale, successful attacks leading up to 26 August that chipped away at the German outpost zone, advancing 500 to 700 metres.[108] These actions, the artillery preparation, and the presence of an elite division would have contributed to misleading the Germans where the next attack would land. The *48th RD* held the zone with just enough force to prevent a successful probe so that a formal attack was necessary to advance.[109] While the fighting was fierce at times, there were only small-scale counterattacks to retake the lost ground.

The 51st's role was to protect the flank of the Canadian advance with the prime objective of taking the three high points of Mt Pleasant, Greenland Hill, and its spur running south where Hausa and Delbar Woods sat. A high embankment of the Arras-Douai railway bisected the attack front. The division history characterised this as 'a commanding place admirably suited for purposes of defence, which lent itself perfectly to the German genius for improvising strong points of resistance.'[110] The division, however, could not advance until the Canadians took the key position of Monchy-le-Preux. As a result, their planning had to consider multiple contingencies. It would take the form of three advances of 500 to 800 metres each. The final jump would take the trench system on the reverse slope of Greenland Hill and the spur with the two woods. As their attack would follow the Canadian one, there was no opportunity for surprise.

German Actions

OHL was clearly cognisant of trouble brewing on the *Seventeenth Armee*'s front, so it heavily reinforced the sector.[111] During the 10-day period from 11 to 20 August, the army gained thirteen divisions and lost one. In the last eleven days of August, it received another seven and lost three.[112] Prisoner interrogations showed the Germans expected an attack on the Scarpe front as early as mid-July, given the presence of the Canadian Corps.[113] The *39th ID* facing the 2nd Division expected an attack from 19 August. In response, the division command ordered the *II/132nd IR* to pull out of Neuville-Vitasse. When the Canadians did not follow up, a small detachment reoccupied the village on 25 August.[114]

Prisoners captured on 26 August revealed that the Germans expected an attack for some time, but the location and timing were a surprise.[115] The commander of the *II Bavarian Korps*, von Dellmensingen, briefed Hindenburg on 21 August that he expected an attack north of the Scarpe and south of the Arras-Cambrai road.[116] The location of reserves predominantly on the wrong side of the river, and the transfer of one *Eingreifdivision* to a neighbouring corps just

108 *Canada in the Great World War: An Authentic Account of the Military History of Canada from the Earliest Days to the Close of the War of the Nations* (Toronto: United Publishers of Canada, Limited), pp.153 Infantry Brigade Narrative of Operations from 18th to 28th August, 1918.
109 Hirschel, *Geschichte RIR 221*, p.261.
110 Bewsher, *History of 51st (Highland),* p.364.
111 Ludendorff, *Ludendorff's Own Story*, loc.4280.
112 *Der Weltkrieg 1914 Bis 1918, Beilagen* (Berlin: Ernst Siegfried Mittler and Sohn, 1944), 14.2, pp.12-16.
113 TNA: WO 95-1052-7: Canadian Corps General Staff War Diary, Daily Summary of Intelligence, No. 4, 27 July 1918.
114 Steuer, *I.R. Nr. 132 History,* pp.393-394.
115 TNA: Cdn. Corps GS WD, Daily Summary of Intelligence, 27 August 1918.
116 Bundesarchiv, Freiburg: Feldzug 1918, 21 August 1918.

Map 15. German defensive arrangements for 26 August, based on Canadian intelligence. Each unlabelled blob represents a company. (Author's map)

before the attack, supports this.[117] Given the position of the Canadian Corps to outflank the Hindenburg Line, it is even more surprising that the Germans did not anticipate Haig's plan. A glance at the map should have demonstrated its vulnerability to an outflanking manoeuvre. The combination of misplacing the Corps, the Third Army's attack, and the actions north of the Scarpe confused the Germans, and they misaligned their reserves.

The German tactical arrangements in the face of the imminent offensive were two-fold. First, they dramatically thinned out their forward defences. On 18 August, the 57th Division reported a German deserter claiming just two companies defended a regimental front – the normal allotment was four.[118] The German command moved most of this sector's artillery back to Sailly, nine kilometres from the front. This was in keeping with the *Seventeenth Armee*'s actions during the opening stages of the Third Army offensive.[119] North of the Scarpe, the *48th RD* reorganised its defences into greater depth.[120] The defensive scheme was to hold the pre-March front as the main line of resistance, with the western zone lightly held. This was a reaction to the Allied successes in their offensives in capturing German artillery and the increasing success of Allied counter-battery efforts. The Germans reported the loss of 13 percent of their artillery park to Allied counter-battery fire in July – an unsustainable loss rate.[121]

Second, as early as July, intelligence reports indicated the troops in the *Vorfeld* were to fall back in a major offensive. They would thin out the zone during the day when British attacks tended to occur and reinforce it at night to contest any probing attacks.[122] This approach would minimise losses in a full-scale onslaught while forcing the attackers to commit significant resources to take the outpost zone. It would challenge the Australian tactic of peaceful penetration at night, where they whittled away at a lightly held outpost zone.

The 2nd Division faced the *132nd IR* of the *39th ID* reinforced with machine gun marksmen detachment with 36 machine guns and in the afternoon elements of the *176th IR*.[123] A prewar active division, it had spent all its time on the Western Front. It lost heavily in the March offensive against the Third Army and less so during the Lys operation. Entering the line on the night of 2/3 August, it needed relief by the time of the Canadian attack, but there were no reserves available.[124] The American's rated it as a solid second-class division out of five rating levels, but the British thought it poor. Based on prisoner interrogations, 'In no case was 'morale' good.' Like all such reports, this has to be viewed sceptically given it did not fold up facing attacks from multiple directions on 26 August.[125]

Facing most of the 2nd and all the 3rd Division, the *214th ID* had been in the line since 19 May. Its commander had requested its relief, but the high command refused. With the paucity

117 LAC: RG9 III-C-1 v3859, 85/8: First Army Lessons Learned GS 1331/1, 31 August 1918; Stühmke, *26th Reserve Division* II, p.59.
118 TNA: WO 95-2967-1: 57th Division General Staff War Diary, 18 August 1918.
119 LAC: RG9 III-C-1 v3859, 85/8: Notes from the Battle 21/23 August, [?] August 1918.
120 Hirschel, *Geschichte RIR 221*, pp.258-260.
121 Edmonds, *Military Operations, 1918* 4, p.8.
122 TNA: WO 95-178-3: First Army GS War Diary, XVII Corps Weekly Operations Report, 23 August 1918.
123 Steuer, *I.R. Nr. 132 History*, p.394.
124 TNA: 52nd Division GS WD, News Sheet, 29 August 1918.
125 General Staff Intelligence Section, *251 Divisions,* pp.43643-4348; '39. Infanterie-Division 1914-1918' <http://www.militaerpass.net/39id.htm> (12 December 2017).

of reserves, they did not want to burn up these holding the front. It defended the sector south from the Scarpe to the boundary with the *39th ID* at the Cojeul River. It deployed with all three regiments in line with one battalion forward, another on the *HWL* west of Monchy-le-Preux, and the third in reserve. The Corps engaged all nine battalions during the day. The division formed in September 1916 from Prussian regiments of three other formations. It fought in the Lys offensive in 1918 and moved into the Monchy-le-Preux sector in May. Allied intelligence rated it as a solid line-holding division, with the *50th IR* regarded somewhat lower because of the prevalence of Poles in its ranks. Based on prisoner interrogations in July, the Poles in *I/50th IR* were 'very bitter against Germans.'[126]

The division made special efforts to prepare anti-tank measures, but order and counter-order wore out the troops. Some measures were unfamiliar, which increased their uncertainty. As the Bible quotation states, 'For if the trumpet gives an uncertain sound, who shall prepare himself to the battle?'[127] The result was the troops lacked the usual confidence in the defensive arrangements. Compounding the issue was the three-month period in line left the division stale and tired.[128]

The *II Bavarian Korps* had two *Eingreifdivisions* – *35th ID* and *26th RD*. South of the Scarpe, the battle-hardened *26th RD* guarded the F-R Line, while the *35th ID* was south-west of Douai. Originally, the *II Bavarian Korps* had three such formations, but the success of the Third Army's offensive forced the *Seventeenth Armee* to transfer one to a neighbouring corps. This meant on 26 August Dellmensingen lacked the resources to launch a strong counterattack. A Württemberg division and regarded as an equal to an active division, the *26th RD* had defended the Thiepval height at the Somme for almost three months in 1916. This epic performance cost it over 10,000 men. In 1918, it fought during the Mars offensive where suffered 60 percent casualties, but it did not participate in another attack after. Its *119th RIR* fought at Amiens with its battalions reduced to a trench strength of 120 men each. In the evening of 26 August, the *II Bavarian Korps* transferred the *180th RIR* and a field artillery battery to serve with the *39th ID* south of the Canadian sector. The battered *119th* moved into the F-R Line to replace the *180th*.[129]

The *35th ID* was north of the Scarpe holding the D-Q Line near Vitry, six kilometres north-east of Jigsaw Wood. It had reached there from the Flanders front on 23 August. It was mis-positioned to intervene promptly. A Prussian prewar active division, its performance at Arras 1918 demonstrated a hard-fighting formation. It defended in most of the Allied offensives in 1917 and participated in the Lys offensive in April 1918. It remained on that front until moved to Lille where it rested for almost a week.[130]

126 LAC: CWNS Intelligence Canadian Corps Battle Fronts Period Aug. 8th to Nov. 11th 1918; CWM: 19801226-274-58A 1 60.3: Currie Fonds, Summary of Information Gained During to-Day's Operations, 26 August 1918; General Staff Intelligence Section, *251 Divisions*, pp.679-81; LAC: 1st Divison W.D., Information Concerning the 50 IR 214th Divn., 30 July 1918.

127 *King James Bible,* 1 Corinthians 14:8.

128 Stenger, *Geschichte F.A.R. Nr. 44*, pp.381-382.

129 General Staff Intelligence Section, *251 Divisions,* pp.365-367; Stühmke, *26th Reserve Division* II, pp.58-60.

130 Edmund Schulemann, *Das Kulmer Infanterie-Regiment Nr. 141 im Weltkriege* (Berlin: Gerhard Stalling, 1926), p.190; Wilhelm Preusser, *Das 9. Westpreussische Infanterie-Regiment Nr. 176 im Weltkrieg* (Berlin: Tradition Wilhelm Kolk, 1931), p.273.

Deployed behind the *26th RD* in the D-Q Line, the gravely weakened *2 Guards Reserve Division* (*GRD*) acted as a backstop. Contrary to what its name might indicate, it was an inferior formation.[131] It suffered heavily in attacks by the Third Army to the point that its *91st RIR* comprised two half 'position' battalions with only 100 and 125 men. The regiment had even lost its commander.[132]

North of the Scarpe, the *48th RD* held the line with all three regiments. Formed at the start of the war from primarily Hessian units, it held the line in the Lys offensive but was preparing for another attack when it transferred to holding positions north of the Scarpe late in July.[133] Allied intelligence rated as a second-class formation, but it performed creditably. A captured document showed the trench strength of the *2nd Company I/222nd IR* was a mere 3 officers, twelve NCOs, and 26 OR with one medical orderly and 3 stretcher-bearers. This was likely a particularly feeble company, but it was evidence of the weakness of German units.[134]

Field Marshal Haig had set the Canadian Corps a formidable task and with minimal time. While the Canadians had the advantage of an existing plan, and ongoing preparations, they had to accelerate the normal battle procedures. Unlike at Amiens, they would have to contend with an alert enemy, entrenched in a deep, defensive zone, and fighting over ground torn and shattered by war. Moreover, only half of the Corps was available, and the weather worse than at Amiens. The resulting plans were innovative and daring and would place severe demands on the officers and men, many of whom were new to their units. Would the Corps' open warfare training prior to the Hundred Days and its experience at Amiens enable it to overcome these obstacles? As Private Donald Reid wrote his father: 'It's great fun to see the German run but not so much fun before we get them going.'[135] Would the Canadians get to see the Germans run?

131 General Staff Intelligence Section, *251 Divisions*, p.55; LAC: MG30 E40 v1: Erlebach Fonds, SS 644b Classification and Engagement of Enemy Divisions in the Western Theatre, 21 March - 12 October 1918.

132 Kümmel, *Res.Inf.Regt. Nr. 91*, pp.406-418, 421.

133 Hirschel, *Geschichte RIR 221*, p.257.

134 '48. Reserve-Division 1914–1918' <http://www.militaerpass.net/48rd.htm >(12 December 2017); General Staff Intelligence Section, *251 Divisions*, pp.479-481; CWM: 19801226-274-58A 1 60.3: Currie Fonds, First Army Intelligence Summary – No. 1319, 25 August 1918.

135 'Reid, Donald Calderwood Letter: 1918 August 24th' The Canadian Letters and Images Project <http://www.canadianletters.ca/content/document-6437?position=92&list=of77sNO263Y0LsfRfsi9NzXeugSiZuhy7PN7ewfmIVs> (12 April 2018).

5

'If Germany cannot hold us here' Canadian Corps Operations 26 August

If Germany cannot hold us here, she cannot hold us at all.

Private A C West, 43rd Battalion[1]

Assaulting in the pitch black of a rainy and cloudy early morning, the Canadian Corps decisively outflanked the Hindenburg Line, advanced 6,500 metres, and took over 1,000 prisoners. In the process, they captured a lightly held outpost zone, broke the German's main line of resistance, and gained significant territory. As Private Reid wished, they saw the Germans run. Using daring tactics, only a handful of tanks, but with powerful artillery support, the Canadians smashed the *214th ID* and seriously damaged the *35th* and *39th IDs*. Haig crowed, 'We have given the Germans a severe blow.'[2]

Right Flank: XVII Corps

On the Canadian's right flank, the 52nd Division was to cooperate with them and strike the Hindenburg Line from the north.[3] A key factor was the change in the boundary between the Third and First Armies. It created confusion as XVII Corps' units encroached into the Canadian sector. The British corps did not recognise the shift, and it set objectives on the Corps' side of the boundary. For instance, both of the 52nd Division's objectives were in the 2nd Division's sector. This would create more disarray in an already chaotic battlespace with the possibility of misplaced barrages hitting friendly troops or leaving open flanks.

The 52nd Division, attacking at 3:00 a.m. with the Canadians, penetrated the Hindenburg Line north of St Martin against minimal resistance. Its barrage at 10 metres per gun was more than twice the concentration of the Canadian one.[4] The war diary reported the Germans 'cleared

1 LAC: West Diary, 29 August 1918.
2 NLS: Haig's Autograph Great War Diary, Part 150-157: Haig Papers, Haig Letters to Wife, 27 August 1918.
3 TNA: First Army GS WD 178, XVII Corps Order 152, 25 August 1918.
4 Edmonds, *Military Operations, 1918* 4, p.304.

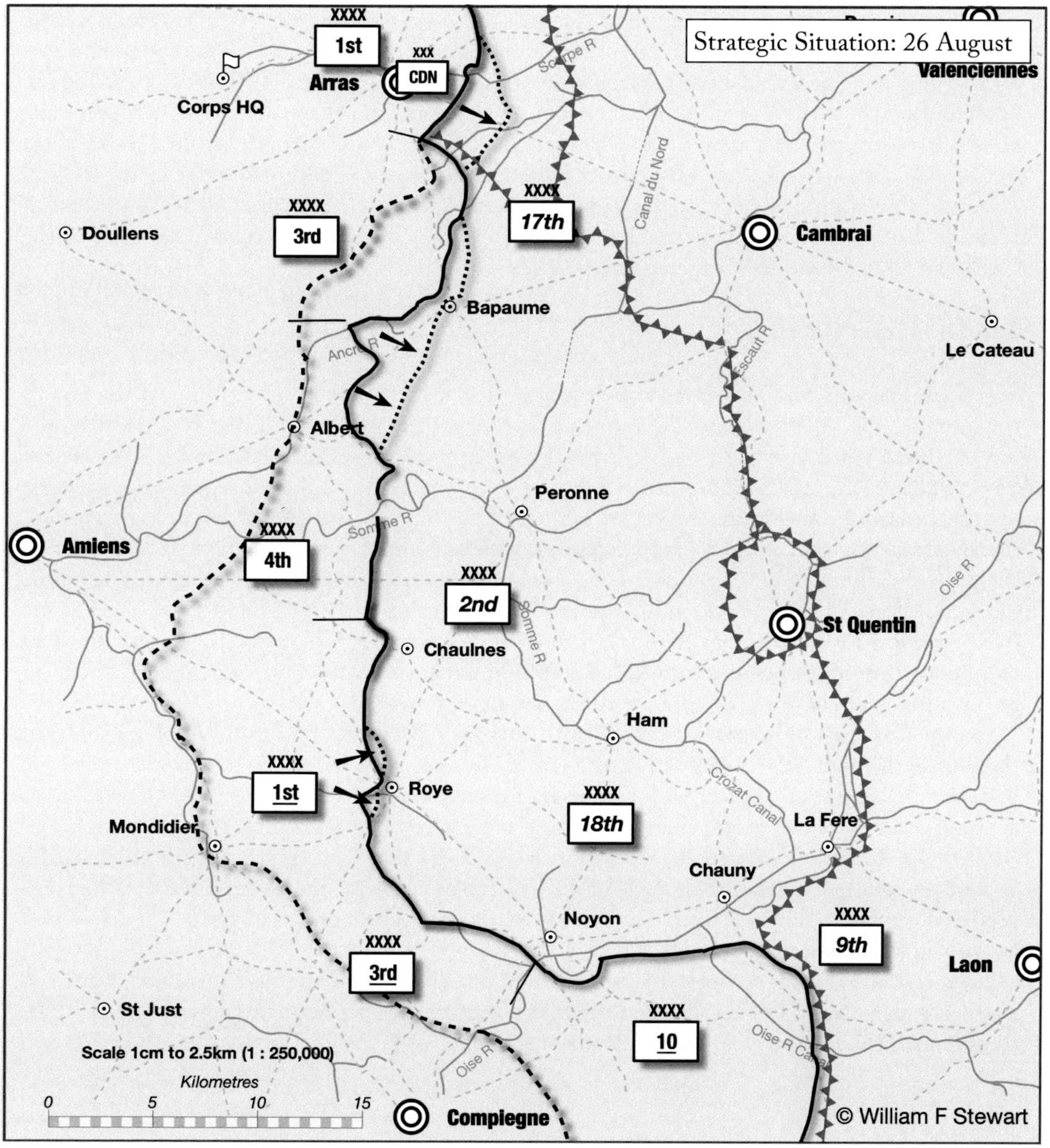

Map 16. Strategic situation 26 August with significant advances by the Canadian Corps and the British Third and Fourth Armies. (Author's map)

off in front of our advance.'[5] Given the success of the 2nd Division, there was no reason for the Germans to stand and fight. Thus, the British outflanked the defences that had stymied them for two days at a fraction of a frontal attack's cost. In mid-morning, the XVII Corps ordered the 52nd to conform to the Canadian advance south-east to take the Wancourt Tower Ridge – most of which was in the Canadian Corps' sector. The division could advance but had a challenge in clearing out part of Hénin Hill.[6] Its reported position at the end of the day again showed evidence of confusion. Its line supposedly extended to west of Wancourt and fell just short of Héninel. Both were well within the 2nd Division's sector. Nevertheless, it had kept up with the Canadian advance and had inflicted sharp losses on the *39th ID*.

2nd Division: Morning

Seven FA brigades and two HA brigades supported the 2nd Division's attack. At the end of the barrage, one FA brigade would move up to support the 4th Brigade and two the 6th. The field artillery density was 20 metres per 18-pounder, which was less than the 13 metres at Passchendaele. The division used smoke in the initial barrage, unlike subsequent ones.[7] There was an extensive indirect machine gun barrage with 96 guns firing.[8] With the high ground, there were multiple locations to fire on enemy positions without the advancing infantry masking them. The darkness and smoke from the barrage, however, limited how much the machine guns could accomplish. The conundrum was in poor visibility the guns had to be close to the front – within 100 to 200 metres – to be effective, but it made the crews easy targets. In these conditions bringing up the gun and ammunition exhausted the crew and exposed them 'to heavy losses without doing a proportionate amount of good.'[9]

On the division's right attack front, the 6th Brigade's 27th Battalion from Winnipeg entered the line on the night 22/23 August. Lieutenant Colonel Harold Riley (31) now commanded the battalion. Riley was a barrister with no prewar military experience who rose from lieutenant to command the battalion in less than three years and already had a Distinguished Service Order (DSO). The battalion entered the operation in excellent shape, having lost only 71 casualties at Amiens and had a trench strength of 637 all ranks.[10] It was, therefore, a well-trained and prepared formation for the extreme test it was to undergo. For more, see Map 5.2 2nd Division Success in the colour map booklet.

Its operation plan was complex and not resolved until late on 25 August.[11] It would advance on a two-company front. Once it reached the first objective, two trailing companies were to wheel south and push down to clear out the Wancourt pocket with the 28th Battalion. The other two

5 TNA: 52nd Division GS WD, 26 August 1918.
6 Thompson, *Fifty-Second*, pp.525-527; TNA: XVII Corps GS WD, 26 August 1918.
7 LAC: RG9 III-C-1 v3911, 39/3: Chronological Table of Artillery Distribution, August 26th to Sept. 8th, 1918; LAC: RG9 III-C-3 v4020, 44/1: 2 CDA Arty, Instr. No.1, 25 August 1918; LAC: RG9 III-C-1 v3923, 11/2: Narrative of Operations of the 2nd Canadian Divisional Artillery from Arras in the General Direction of Cambrai, Aug. 26th. To Sept. 3rd. 1918.
8 LAC: RG9 III-D-3 v4985: 2nd MG Battalion War Diary, 2nd Battalion CMMC, OO No.116, 25 August 1918.
9 LAC: 2nd MG Bn WD, Report on Operation From August 26-29th.
10 LAC: RG9 III-D-3 v4935: War Diary, 27th Battalion, 25 August 1918.
11 LAC: WD 27th Bn, 27th Battalion Instructions for the Offensive No.2, 25 August 1918.

companies were to defend the east face of the front. The plan indicated strong confidence in the infantry's ability to carry out complicated manoeuvres in the face of the enemy.

At Zero Hour, the defender's barbed wire was intact, but the officers and NCOs found gaps that allowed the troops to keep up with the barrage. They met little resistance in the dark and wet conditions, with the enemy having 'little stomach to fight.'[12] Stokes mortars demonstrating their potential knocked out two machine guns posts with just eight and two rounds. Usually, the overloaded trench mortar crews fell behind in an attack. The battalion swept up large numbers of prisoners with one company taking 130 alone from the *132nd IR*. At 6:00 a.m., the two trailing companies faced south and advanced on a 1,000 metre front and cleared out the Wancourt pocket with their left on the Cojeul River. The Germans were too occupied fleeing to resist.[13] By 9:00 a.m., the battalion had captured all its objectives.

Following the 27th was Saskatchewan's 28th Battalion. Commanded by Lieutenant Colonel Alexander Ross (38), it did well at Amiens and escaped the fighting with minimal losses of 130 all ranks. By 1918, Ross was an experienced and capable commander, having led the unit with success since 1916. The last-minute changes to the 6th Brigade plan meant Ross had to hurriedly outline the scheme to the company commanders that night without a written order.[14] Assembly and the advance were difficult in the dark, rain, and churned up, slippery soil. The darkness did, however, mask their advance, so they encountered no flanking fire. Once it reached the Green Line about 6:00 a.m., the battalion changed facing south. It then advanced on a two thousand metre front clearing an area of two square kilometres by 9:00 a.m. Signaller Claude Craig wrote of advancing 4,000 metres in the morning with the enemy 'running before us.'[15] They killed 70 Germans and captured 150 Germans, including a staff officer.

The 6th Brigade destroyed the *II/132nd IR*. Ordered to remain in line to help hold Hénin Hill, the 6th Brigade's breakthrough to the north deeply compromised the Germans' position. The battalion commander finally convinced the regiment to allow it to retreat, but the reprieve came too late. His troops had to scramble back through the closing trap, and the Canadians shot or captured most. It lost three-quarters of its strength.[16]

On the 4th Brigade's front, the 21st Battalion was on the right. It had suffered few casualties at Amiens, other than the critical loss of a beloved CO.[17] The new commander was Lieutenant Colonel H E Pense (29), whose initials led battalion wags to call him 'High Explosive'. This would be his first major engagement as a CO. The battalion entered the line in the Telegraph Hill sector on the night of 24/25 August, with a trench strength of 23 officers and 593 men. Given the unit's frontage, Pense committed three companies to lead the attack. The three tanks in support did not catch up to the battalion during the battle. Navigating primarily by compass in the dark and light rain, the assault troops met few Germans and limited resistance in the abandoned outpost zone. At Nova Scotia Trench, the battalion's Lewis Guns and rifle grenades

12 LAC: RG9 III-C-3 v4128: 6th Brigade, Narrative of Operations in Front of Arras from August 23rd to 28th 1918, 9 September 1918.
13 LAC: RG9 III-C-3 v4132, 12/14: 27th Battalion Narrative of Attack South East of Arras 25-28th Aug. 1918; LAC: 6th Brigade Narrative.
14 LAC: RG9 III-D-3 v4936: 28th Battalion War Diary, Warning Order, 24 August 1918; LAC: 28th Battalion War Diary, 28th Battalion Instructions for the Offensive, 25 August 1918.
15 LAC: MG30 E351: Craig Fonds, Craig Diary, 26 August 1918.
16 Steuer, *I.R. Nr. 132 History*, pp.393-396.
17 LAC: RG9 III-D-3 v4931: 21st Battalion War Diary, 8 August 1918.

overcame the machine gun posts. The next enemy stand was at the final objective at Southern Avenue. There, the 21st overran an anti-tank battery capturing three guns and 20 gunners. The forward German guns claimed to have inflicted heavy losses, but they were all overrun, with their crews either fleeing, taken prisoner, or killed. They were, however, effective in knocking out tanks.[18] The 21st reached the outskirts of Guémappe by 7:30 a.m. and consolidated the position under heavy shelling.[19] It captured two German positions and penetrated five kilometres at a cost of 9 officers and 135 other ranks.

The 20th Battalion, from Toronto, on the brigade's left, had experienced considerable command turbulence before the Hundred Days. It had undergone three changes from June 1918, with Lieutenant Colonel B Hooper (39) of the 19th Battalion taking over on 22 July.[20] Parachuting in an outsider indicated senior commander dissatisfaction with the 20th's leadership. The battalion suffered few losses at Amiens, and as the regimental history claimed: 'Everyone was becoming so confident of success that no thought of failure existed.'[21]

It moved into the line on the night of 24/25 in the Tilloy sector – the same sector it held prior to Amiens. Given the 1,100 metre width of its sector, Hooper employed three companies and three tanks. It met little resistance in the dark, and it was not until the first objective that it faced a fight. The Torontonians overwhelmed the machine gun posts along Minorca and Corsica Trenches in a shower of rifle grenades and fire from Lewis Guns. They captured a battery with three guns and 30 gunners near Columbus Trench. As they approached this final objective in daylight, the defenders directed considerable long-range machine gun and sniper fire from both sides of the highway. As per standard doctrine, the tanks followed the infantry and when called up, one swiftly crushed those south of the road, but a German gun knocked it out as it crossed over to the north side. Despite this setback and heavy fire from Guémappe, the battalion reached its final goal by 7:30 a.m.

The division assigned its eight tanks to the 4th Brigade. They started behind the infantry and did not catch up to them until they were attacking the first objective. The delay was not critical, as the Germans were not strongly defending the outpost zone. The tanks' effect was minimal as attested by the absence of comment in infantry reports, other than from the 20th Battalion. German after-action reports and regimental histories stressed the critical importance of tanks to their defeat even when there were few, if any, present. Essentially, every battle was a repeat of Amiens with its hundreds of tanks.[22] Of the eight machines committed, two reached the Red

18 Stenger, *Geschichte F.A.R. Nr. 44*, p.384.

19 Stephen J. Nichol, *Ordinary Heroes: Eastern Ontario's 21st Battalion C.E.F. In the Great War* (Almonte, ON: Stephen J. Nichol, 2008), pp.189-191.; LAC: 21st Bn. WD, Report on 21st Canadian Battalion Operations of August 26-27-28.; LAC: 21st Bn. WD, 21st Canadian Battalion OO No. 209, 25 August 1918.

20 David James Corrigall, *The History of the Twentieth Canadian Battalion (Central Ontario Regiment) Canadian Expeditionary Force: In the Great War, 1914-1918* (Toronto: Stone & Cox Limited, 1935), pp.205, 210-212.

21 Corrigall, *Twentieth Canadian Battalion*, p.236.

22 Some examples of these spurious claims are Lothar Gitterman, *F.A.R. Nr. 71*, p.305; Otto Mathies, *Geschichte Des 3. Oberelsässisch. Feldartillerie-Regiments Nr. 80*, p.228; Stenger, *Geschichte F.A.R. Nr. 44*, p.383.

Dotted line, two turned back early, one broke down, and the Germans knocked out three.[23] The tanks undoubtedly were of value in isolated cases. They did not have the effect as at Amiens, in part because of the darkness and few numbers.

Initial reports to the 2nd Division were of rapid progress against minimal resistance. At 8:15 a.m., Webber reported the capture of Monchy-le-Preux by the 3rd Division and suggested that Burstall employ the 5th Brigade to capture the Wancourt Tower Ridge. Burstall wanted to keep it for the D-Q Line, so he tasked the 6th Brigade with taking the ridge.[24] Rennie announced a few minutes later it appeared his formation had taken all its objectives. As a result, he ordered the 18th to seize Guémappe and the 19th to advance to the pre-March British line on the north side of the Arras-Cambrai road.

All seemed to be progressing well. Then, the division finally either learned of or recognised the shift of the Corps boundary to south-east. This significantly widened the 2nd Division's sector by almost 2,000 metres, and this grew as it pressed on. To deal with the wider front, the 2nd Division wanted the 3rd Division to shift the shared boundary to the Arras-Cambrai road. Webber agreed as soon as the situation allowed, but this was unacceptable to Burstall. He called the 3rd Division at 11:30 a.m. to peremptorily demand, 'We want the boundary adjusted at once.' The 3rd Division was experiencing its own issues and could not respond quickly. Burstall would not accept excuses. He thundered that he 'would order our troops to withdraw and 3rd Division must conform.'[25] He got the Corps to make an immediate change, and this meant Lipsett's division had to scramble to replace the shifting 2nd Division units.

To help fill the resulting gap, the Corps sent forward two batteries of the 1st CMMG Brigade, supported by two cyclist platoons, until the 3rd Division could respond. These gunners and cyclists were part of the Canadian Independent Force (CIF). The force was also to probe down the Arras-Cambrai road. Officer and motorcycle patrols found the road impassable and the resistance too great. Another attempt in the early afternoon had the same result.[26]

2nd Division: Afternoon-Evening

The division was aggressive and kept pressuring for more ground. At noon, Burstall ordered the 4th and 6th Brigades to advance to the south-east. The dividing line between the brigades was the light rail line running south of the Cojeul River. The 6th Brigade did not pick up on the boundary change as there was later contention. Burstall was also having to deal with an embarrassment, as the division had inaccurately informed the Corps of Guémappe's seizure. This was over seven hours premature. The 4th Brigade was having to organise artillery and machine gun support for another attack, which took time. No further advances were possible until the division removed this obstacle.

23 TNA: WO 95-107-4: 9th Tank Battalion War Diary, 23-26 August 1918; TNA: 9th Tank WD, Report on Operations 'B' Company, 26/8/18; TNA: WO 95-107-5: 9th Tank Battalion War Diary, History of the 9th Tank Battalion From November 1916 to December 1918; LAC: RG9 III-D-2 v4802, 128: 20th Battalion Report on Operations of 26/27/28 August, 1918, 31 August 1918.

24 LAC: 2nd Division GS WD, 26 August 1918; LAC: 2nd Division Narrative.

25 LAC: 2nd Division GS WD, 26 August 1918.

26 LAC: MG30 E537 v1: Sansom Fonds, Narrative Covering Operations of the 1st Canadian Machine Gun Brigade, the Canadian Independent Force, the Composite Brigade, and Brutinel's Force, 1926.

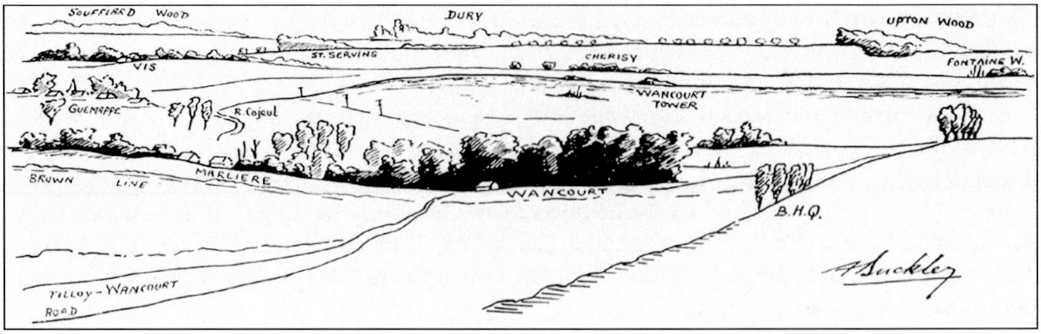

This panorama captures the series of ridges and valleys that the Corps had to capture on its way to the Canal du Nord. Drawn before Arras 1917, this woods and villages shown in the sketch were flattened by Arras 1918. (Francis Buckley, *Q.6.A and Other Places: Recollections of 1916, 1917 and 1918*, (London: Spottiswoode, 1920), p.128.)

The observation advantage from Monchy-le-Preux. Observers on the hill could call down artillery fire in all directions deep into the Canadian lines. It had to be captured. (Canada. Dept. of National Defence/Library and Archives Canada/PA-00443)

On the right, the 6th Brigade was to capture Wancourt Tower Ridge that afternoon and then push on as far as Chérisy 3,500 metres away. The operation required reorganising the assault battalions and assembling along the Cojeul River under the observation of the ridge.[27] The brigade would then have to cross two ridges defended by four zones of trenches, so it was a formidable objective. But, without Wancourt Tower, it would be difficult to advance along the Arras-Cambrai road given its surveillance capabilities. The Corps stressed it was 'Vitally important' to capture the ridge as soon as possible.[28] This was asking a lot of the 28th on the right and the 27th on the left who had fought since the early morning. Zero hour was 4:30 p.m., as it took time to arrange the artillery barrage and resupply. Knowing the ridge was the German main line of resistance, the brigade arranged for a barrage using the 5th and 6th CFA brigades assigned to it. The two needed to get into position and to avoid the heavy counter-battery fire resulting from observers on Monchy-le-Preux.

Observers on the hill could call down artillery fire in all directions deep into the Canadian lines. It had to be captured. Time was so tight that the 2nd CDA did not produce a barrage map. The resulting barrage was a mere 97 metres per gun – less than one-third the concentration of the morning one.[29] At Bell's request, it was twice as fast as the usual rate.[30]

With the 6th Brigade fighting for the Wancourt Tower Ridge, Burstall received reports from the 52nd Division that it had reached the Sensée River and captured Chérisy as the Germans were falling back. Note, the village was well within 2nd Division's boundaries. Despite his doubts about the report's reliability, Burstall ordered the 6th Brigade to push on to the next river valley – the Sensée – and join up with the 52nd Division. His scepticism was justified as the report was false.[31]

The two battalions attacked on a 2,500 metre front under a barrage that 'was scattered and weak.'[32] Six companies of the already battered *132nd IR* opposed them.[33] The 27th and 28th crossed the Cojeul River's dry bed and climbed the slope up to Wancourt Tower Ridge. They faced minimal resistance until they crested it. Sheets of machine gun and artillery fire then met them from the front and flank. They fought forward as far as Crow Trench but arriving Germans reserves drove out the small lodgements made in the next trench – Egret. Attesting to the poor staff work of the 52nd Division, two companies of the 1/7th Cameronians from the 52nd Division had ended up in the Canadian sector not knowing about the boundary change. In the later afternoon, a combination of artillery, Lewis Gun, and rifle fire stopped a prospective German counterattack before it could get going. The *132nd IR* history claimed the counterattack sealed off the gap in the defences.[34] In this campaign, the Germans usually launched their counterattacks too late or with insufficient strength and preparation to have an

27 LAC: 6th Brigade Narrative.
28 The instruction arrived after the brigade had already captured the ridge. LAC: RG9 III-C-1 v3855, 75/3: Canadian Corps G.552, 26 August 1918.
29 LAC: 2nd CDA Narrative.
30 LAC: RG9 III-D-3 v4968: 5th Brigade CFA War Diary, 26 August 1918; LAC: RG9 III-D-3 v4968: 6th Brigade CFA War Diary, Close Support of Infantry Commencing 26 August, ? September 1918.
31 LAC: 2nd Division Arras Report.
32 Bruce Tascona, *From the Forks to Flanders Field: The Story of the 27th City of Winnipeg Battalion, 1914-1918:* Bruce Tascona, 1995), p.55.
33 Steuer, *I.R. Nr. 132 History*, pp.397-398.
34 Steuer, *I.R. Nr. 132 History*, p.398.

impact. Their capacity for ripostes was fading as the morale, numbers, and capability of their infantry declined.

Burstall needed the second set of trenches for jump-off positions for the next day's operation. It was essential that the 6th Brigade attack again. Rather than organising another barrage, the two battalions assaulted in the early morning hours with no artillery support to catch the Germans off-guard. It worked, and Egret and the Rookery set of trenches fell.[35] This last operation added a further 1,500 metres to the distance the brigade had advanced. An exhausted Signaller Craig wrote in his diary after taking the ridge, 'We had lost a lot of men and were very tired.'[36] The strain on the signallers in these operations was severe. They not only had to carry heavy reels of wire, they had to maintain the connections throughout the night. This tempo left troops bone-weary and operating in conditions of constant fatigue.

The performance of the two battalions was impressive. They had fought for 27 hours straight, performed two 90° face changes, and advanced 3,500 metres. Given the depth of the advance, the 28th Battalion's 105 casualties and the 27th's 115 all ranks were an astonishingly low total for a First World War battle. The 27th captured 264 prisoners in its three assaults along with 20 machine guns.[37]

In the morning, Rennie issued new orders to the 18th and 19th Battalions, after taking the final objective and with the capture of Monchy-le-Preux. The 18th was to take Guémappe, and the 19th was to advance to the pre-March British line north of the Arras-Cambrai road, well within the 3rd Division's sector.[38]

The 18th Battalion, originally in support, had emerged from Amiens with relatively light casualties so was in good shape. Its commander was Lieutenant Colonel Louis Jones (41), a civil engineer and prewar Militia officer. Judging from his awards, by Arras he was an experienced and effective leader.[39] When Monchy-le-Preux fell, the 4th Brigade ordered the 18th to take Guémappe. Expecting little resistance, two companies advanced around noon, but lacking artillery support, the attack failed.[40] It would need more support. The 19th's advance had to wait to Guémappe fell.

The reserve battalion – 19th – had confidence in its leaders based on their performance according to the regimental history.[41] Its long-term commander Lieutenant Colonel Lionel Millen (42) embodied the expected values of service to the troops, loyalty to the regiment, and pride in his battalion. He already had a DSO by Arras and would gain another in the Hundred

35 LAC: 28th Battalion War Diary, A Narrative of the Operations Undertaken by the 28th Canadian Infantry Battalion August 27/27th, 1918; LAC: 28th Battalion War Diary, 12, 28 August 1918; Calder, *28th (Northwest) Battalion*, p.210.

36 LAC: MG30 E341 v: Craig Fonds, Claude Craig Diary, 26 August 1918.

37 Tascona, *Forks to Flanders*, pp.55-57; LAC: 27th Battalion Narrative of Attack South East of Arras 25-28th Aug. 1918; LAC: 6th Brigade Narrative.

38 LAC: RG9 III-D-3 v4927: 19th Battalion War Diary, Operations of the 19th Canadian Battalion August 25th-29th 1918.

39 He had a D.S.O. with a Bar and CMG. The CMG was the Companion of the Order of St Michael and St George that was typically given to brigade commanders and above.

40 LAC: 4th Brigade War Diary, 4th Brigade Narrative of Operations South of Scarpe, 26, 27, and 28 August, 1918; LAC: RG9 III-D-3 v4926: 18th Battalion War Diary, 26 August 1918; LAC: 2nd Division GS WD, 26 August 1918.

41 David Campbell, *It Can't Last Forever: The 19th Battalion and the Canadian Corps in the First World War* (Waterloo, ON: WLU Press, 2017), p.380.

Days.[42] The battalion made two attacks at Amiens and suffered 230 casualties all ranks – the most in the brigade. It went into battle with a trench strength of 20 officers and 584 other ranks with replacements filling the gaps from the Amiens attack.[43] These consisted of two types – conscripts and returned wounded. The return of wounded veterans mitigated to a degree the dilution of experience caused by heavy casualties.

In the afternoon, Rennie ordered it to slide to the right of the brigade front and attack with the 6th Brigade. The problem was that the objective line for the attack extended 1,000 metres into the 6th Brigade's sector. There were serious problems in the 2nd Division's staff work in determining what were the proper boundaries. Before the action, Corporal Deward Barnes and his comrades received their pre-attack rum, dispensed by Sergeant Newell who clearly got into the supply himself. Barnes observed, Newell 'was feeling good.' This would later have fatal consequences.[44] The battalion advanced at 4:45 p.m., well after the 6th Brigade jumped off. A/19th ended up in Curlew Trench in the 6th Brigade sector across the Cojeul under heavy fire along with the 27th Battalion. On finding the 27th had the same mission as it, the battalion ordered it back across the river. Exhausted from a full day of marching and fighting, and with little chance for rest, the battalion would have to fight on.[45]

This was the second time the 4th Brigade had issued orders for units to advance into other brigade's and division's sectors. This was another example of how the tempo of operations had strained the divisional and brigade staff. They did not have the same opportunity for open warfare training as did the other divisions.

To take Guémappe, the 4th Brigade arranged for a barrage, and the 18th overran the battered ruins in just 17 minutes.[46] Rennie had not finished yet, and the 18th advanced in the evening, taking Stag and Rake trenches. Given its multiple commitments, the battalion suffered surprisingly few casualties – 10 killed and 15 wounded.[47] The Germans in his sector were few and not combative, leading to the low loss total.

To cover the 3rd Division's flank, Rennie ordered Hooper's 20th Battalion to advance on Rake Trench almost 1,500 metres ahead.[48] It attacked against limited resistance and captured Rake Trench along with two 150mm howitzers. By now, the Canadians had battered the sector's defenders.[49] The result was feeble resistance. The 20th suffered an estimated loss of 5 officers and 140 men that day. They lost only one man in taking Rake Trench as the German

42 'Lt-Col Lionel Herbert Millen, DSO (1876–1956)' <https://www.argylls.ca/history/millen.html> (29 July 2018).
43 LAC: 19th Battalion War Diary, Strength of Bn by Platoons. 24 August 1918.
44 Cane, *It Made You Think of Home,* p.242.
45 LAC: 19th Battalion War Diary, Operations of the 19th Canadian Battalion August 25th-29th 1918; LAC: RG9 III-D-2 v4802, 138: CWNS Millen to Rennie, 1 December 1920; Campbell, *It Can't Last Forever,* pp.422-427; LAC: 4th Brigade War Diary, 4th Brigade Narrative of Operations South of Scarpe, 26, 27, and 28 August, 1918.
46 LAC: 4th Brigade War Diary, 4th Brigade Narrative of Operations South of Scarpe, 26, 27, and 28 August, 1918; LAC: 18th Battalion War Diary, 26 August 1918; LAC: 2nd Division GS WD, 26 August 1918.
47 Patrick Dennis, 'A Canadian Conscript Goes to War—August 1918: Old Myths Re-Examined', *Canadian Military History* 18, no. 1 (2009), p.30.
48 LAC: RG9 III-D-3 v4930: 20th Battalion War Diary, 26 August 1918.
49 LAC: 4th Brigade War Diary, 4th Brigade Narrative of Operations South of Scarpe, 26, 27, and 28 August, 1918.

machine gunners aimed too high. The prisoner total was about 150 with a large haul of matériel, including 10 artillery pieces.[50]

3rd Division: Morning

North of the Arras-Cambrai road, the 3rd Division had the support of seven FA brigades (126x18-pounder guns and 42x4.5-inch howitzers) and two HA brigades (48 pieces). Two FA brigades of the 5th CDA acted as mobile guns attached to the assault formations.[51] The field artillery support density was 24 metres per 18-pounder. The barrage unusually moved at a different rate, with the northern sector slightly faster.[52] There were likely two reasons for this. First, the defences to the south were better developed so the advance would be slower. Second, the quicker northern pace allowed the troops to outflank the defenders distracted by dealing with the southern force.

The main means of communications of the 3rd Division was by wire, but its signal company using every measure available to keep the system going. This included recovering the buried network used before the March offensive. The signal company discovered that poled lines were easier to maintain than those laid on the ground, even with the greater effort needed to set them up.[53] With the improved communications, the forward units could keep their superiors and artillery relatively well informed. As a result, the commanders and the artillery could intervene more effectively in the battle than in 1916/17. On the German side, Canadian shelling and smoke disrupted German wire and light signals. This forced the Germans to depend on unreliable wireless connections.[54]

The 8th Brigade attacked with three battalions stretching from the Arras-Cambrai road north to the Scarpe on a front of 2,400 metres. On the right, the 5th CMR would advance south-east along the divisional boundary to maintain ties with the 2nd Division and seize the col between Orange and Chapel Hills. The 2nd CMR in the centre would punch through the German outpost line. It would then swing south to take Orange Hill from the north in a series of turning movements. On the left, the 4th CMR swept along the south bank of the river to protect the brigade's flank. On reaching the Green Line, the 1st CMR would pass through the 2nd and 4th CMR at Zero +145. It and the 5th CMR would secure the second objective and Monchy-le-Preux. The 1st CMR would repeat the outflanking and capture the village from the north while the 5th CMR attacked its face and from the south.[55] For more, see Map 5.3 3rd Division Takes Monchy-le-Preux: Morning in the colour map booklet.

Three aspects of this plan are of particular interest. First, the daring use of a turning manoeuvre to outflank the defenders signified the planners' confidence in the troops. It demonstrated that, while the Corps had not escaped Amiens unscathed, enough of the troops and leaders trained in

50 LAC: 20th Battalion Report; Corrigall, *Twentieth Canadian Battalion*, pp.235-237; LAC: RG9 III-D-2 v4802, 138: CWNS Hooper to Rennie, 22 November 1920 ; LAC: RG9 III-D-2 v4802, 138: CWNS Wedd to Rennie, 19 November 1920.
51 LAC: Chronological Table.
52 LAC: 3rd Division WD, T. Instruction No. 1, 23 August 1918; LAC: RG9 III-D-3 v4962: 3rd Canadian Divisional Artillery War Diary, 3rd CDA Operation Order No.198, 24 August 1918.
53 LAC: RG9 III-D-3 v5005: 3rd Division Signal Company War Diary, 26 August 1918.
54 Stenger, *Geschichte F.A.R. Nr. 44*, p.383.
55 LAC: 8th Brigade WD, 8th Brigade, OO No. 11, 25 August 1918.

open-warfare remained to execute this potentially hazardous action. The second point was the lack of time for preparation and rehearsals. This reinforces the importance of the open warfare training. Finally, the willingness of commanders to commit all four battalions of a brigade to an operation shows the conviction that the Germans were not a significant threat. This was a major departure from the policy on the Somme where formations kept substantial reserves in hand.[56]

The 5th CMR's Amiens losses were only 2 officers and 63 men and these were replaced.[57] Arras was just the second battle for its new commander, Lieutenant Colonel William Rhoades (44), who was an experienced prewar ranker. He was a rarity in the command ranks of the Canadian Corps as a commissioned ranker in charge of a battalion.[58] The battalion attacked on a two-company front, starting from an abandoned light rail deep in No Man's Land. It had an aggressive series of objectives of the Green, Red Dotted Lines, and half of Monchy-le-Preux.[59] This required a 4,500 metre advance, the capture of eight trench lines, and a fortified village. Reflecting this, the brigade heavily reinforced the battalion with artillery, machine guns, and medium mortars.

The dark night with the rain meant it was not possible to see over 10 to 15 metres ahead. While this made movement and control difficult, it also rendered much of the German use of overlapping machine gun fire impossible. Resistance flared as they approached the first trench. Infiltration tactics relying on Lewis Guns and rifle grenades overcame these defenders. Here, the battalion took 60 prisoners, 8 machine guns, and 2 light trench mortars – likely the survivors of the two German companies defending this sector. The account of the *50th IR* mirrors the Canadian description of visibility of only a few metres, isolated German posts overwhelmed from the flanks, and the annihilation of the *Vorfeld* defenders.[60]

The battalion then encountered a particularly troublesome strongpoint guarding the third set of trenches. Again, the infiltration tactics of smoke grenades to blind the defenders, with Lewis Gun delivering covering fire, enabled the attackers to work their way within assault distance. They rushed it, and the defenders died or surrendered. As dawn approached at 5:30 a.m., the first objective and fifth defensive line fell. Again, resistance increased as they reached the second objective – Congo Trench. By 6:20 a.m., the battalion had taken it along with one hundred prisoners, two 105mm howitzers, and five machine guns. This was the main line of resistance, hence the larger haul of prisoners and matériel.

Next was Monchy-le-Preux, with one party attacking from the west, and the other from the south. It was here that Lieutenant Charles Rutherford, scouting ahead alone, convinced 80 Germans to surrender through a 'masterly bluff.' He first encountered a group of 40 Germans milling around a strongpoint and not in the trenches. Believing any hesitancy was fatal, he boldly advanced and ordered them to surrender. An English-speaking German officer disputed who was who's captive, but Rutherford's audacious assertion that they were surrounded persuaded them to drop their weapons. With his brave front, Rutherford captured 2 officers,

56 Stewart, *Neglected Campaign*, pp.219-220.
57 LAC: 5th CMR War Diary, 10-11 August 1918.
58 'Wiliam Rhoades Fonds' <https://memoryns.ca/william-rhoades-fonds> (31 July 2018); Department of Militia and Defence, *Quarterly Militia List*, pp.33, 93, 418.
59 LAC: 5th CMR War Diary, 25 August 1918; LAC: 5th CMR War Diary, 5th CMR, Summary of Operations, 3 September 1918.
60 Vogt, *I.R. Nr. 50*, p.234.

Lieutenant Charles Rutherford received the VC for his 'masterly bluff' in capturing eighty Germans. (Canada. Dept. of National Defence/ Library and Archives Canada/PA-006703)

43 other ranks, and 3 machine guns. Not yet finished, he sent most of his men on to attack Monchy-le-Preux. Seeing another pillbox holding up the right-hand platoon, he took a Lewis Gun section, attacked it, and secured another 35 prisoners and 4 machine guns. He received the Victoria Cross for these intrepid actions. What this episode demonstrates was both Rutherford's sangfroid and the depressed, dreadful morale of these defenders.[61]

Meanwhile, the rest of the 5th CMR swept through its portion of Monchy-le-Preux capturing more prisoners and two machine guns. The battalion reached its final objective of East Trench on the eastern outskirts of the village by 8:00 a.m. A German artillery observer at Monchy reported the village's fall as of 8:15 a.m.[62] The German *50th IR* described the defences beyond Monchy-le-Preux as reduced to fragments.[63] The enemy spent the rest of the day and the next relentlessly shelling the already ruined village in revenge.[64]

Illustrating the major change in command evident during the Hundred Days, the battalion headquarters pushed forward three times. It kept in touch with the brigade via visual signalling, while retaining contact with the advancing troops. On the Somme, the high command tied battalion commanders to their immobile headquarters stationed well back from the front-line. They had little or no opportunity to direct operations during an attack.[65] The battalion had performed superbly in capturing all its objectives, while claiming 300 prisoners, 15 machine guns, 2 field howitzers, and 4 trench mortars. Its losses of 6 officers and 176 other ranks were surprisingly

61 Rutherford was the last Great War VC winner to die in 1989 at age 97. LAC: RG9 III-D-2 v4811: Victoria Cross Winners; 'Charles Smith Rutherford' Directorate of History and Heritage <http://www.cmp-cpm.forces.gc.ca/dhh-dhp/gal/vcg-gcv/bio/rutherford-cs-eng.asp> (4 June 2018).
62 Stenger, *Geschichte F.A.R. Nr. 44*, p.385.
63 Vogt, *I.R. Nr. 50*, p.235.
64 LAC: 8th Brigade WD, 26 August 1918.
65 Stewart, *Neglected Campaign*, p.294.

low considering the defences it had to overcome. This was a well-trained and effective unit with strong aggressive leadership, as evident by Lieutenant Rutherford's performance.

In the centre, the 2nd CMR emerged from Amiens stronger than it entered, despite suffering 242 casualties. The battalion commander, Lieutenant Colonel G C 'Whizbang' Johnston (44), had led it through all the battles in 1917 and was a capable veteran and esteemed by his men. The 2nd CMR attacked on a two-company front, each on a one platoon front. This meant a compact but dense formation that was easier to control. No Man's Land was 1,600 metres deep here, so the battalion formed up far into the zone. At each trench system encountered, one company wheeled right and pushed down the trench to the 5th CMR. A small party faced left and advanced north along the trench to meet the 4th CMR. In the darkness and rain, the Germans did not see the advance and were surprised. In flashes from the barrage, assault troops saw the enemy machine guns firing straight into the distance at phantoms. The 2nd also captured a field gun serving as an anti-tank piece. They turned it around and banged away at its former owners until out of ammunition. By 5:10 a.m., the battalion signalled its success from Orange Hill in taking the Green Line.[66] Given that it was assaulting a key defensive position, its losses of 143 all ranks were low.[67] The battalion claimed only 83 prisoners along with 1 field gun, 8 machine guns during its three-day commitment.[68] Its advance was an impressive performance of field craft and tactical cunning.

On the left, the 4th CMR had done well at Amiens and suffered fewer than 100 casualties. The regimental history recorded it had 'never left a battlefield in such splendid trim.'[69] Its commander was Lieutenant Colonel William Patterson (34) who had received the DSO for service on the Somme in 1916. Having led the unit from May 1917, he was an experienced leader by Arras.[70]

A German gas attack rocked it before the battle. The Germans discovered the battalion's entry into the line on 23 August and heavily shelled D/4th CMR overnight with mustard gas and HE. Despite an intense and prolonged bombardment, the unit only lost 10 men. In the morning, the sunlight vaporised the condensed gas, and 5 officers and 106 other ranks had to be evacuated. A further 50 men had to replace their clothing. This knocked it out of action for the foreseeable future.[71]

The battalion attacked on a two-company front, supported by an excellent barrage that 'gave heart to the men as they went over the top.'[72] Wire, darkness, and detritus slowed the attack, but there was little opposition except from a misplaced barrage from the 51st Machine Gun Battalion across the Scarpe. At Indian Trench, they met heavy German machine gun fire from across the Scarpe. Despite this, the battalion captured the Green Line 5:30 a.m. At 7:17 a.m., Draper ordered it to protect the 1st CMR's flank by taking Welford and Bayonet Trenches

66 LAC: 2nd CMR W.D., August 1918; LAC: RG9 III-C-3 v4163, 12/1: 2nd CMR Report on Operations, 26-29th August 1918; Johnston, *The 2nd CMR*; LAC: 2nd CMR Report, 26 August 1918.

67 It was primarily engaged in the first day, so most losses were incurred then, as was the capture of prisoners.

68 LAC: 2nd CMR Report.

69 S. G. Bennett, *The 4th Canadian Mounted Rifles, 1914–1919* (Toronto: Murray Printing, 1926), p.125.

70 'William Reginald Patterson DSO' <http://www.doingourbit.ca/profile/william-patterson-dso> (30 July 2018).

71 LAC: 8th Brigade WD, 23 August 1918; LAC: 8th Brigade WD, 126.

72 Bennett, *4th CMR*, p.127.

running south from the river. By noon, the advance was complete. Resistance overall was weak, and losses were minimal at 85 all ranks. In advancing three kilometres, its casualties were fewer than in the gas attack.[73]

The 1st CMR, tasked with taking Monchy-le-Preux from the north, had suffered relatively few casualties at Amiens, and they were replaced. It had performed well there, including the complex capture of Hangard Wood in the early morning fog of 8 August. Its commander was the recently appointed Lieutenant Colonel Burnett Laws (41) who had service in the NWMP and in the Boer War. He joined the 1st CMR at its formation, and he took it over in June 1918.[74]

The battalion attacked with two companies advancing in artillery formation. It crossed the Green Line at 0+145 minutes under a 'dandy barrage.'[75] It pushed on rapidly, inflicted many casualties, but made no claims of captures. The battalion reached the second objective by 7:00 a.m. and pushed on to take the northern portion of Monchy-le-Preux an hour later. It then advanced to hold a line of trenches 200 metres east of the village. Like the 5th CMR, the Germans heavily shelled it. Its losses for the full three days were 10 officers and 140 men. Given that it advanced 2,500 metres, secured the German main line of resistance on this front, and seized part of the fortified village on a high hill, its losses were relatively light.[76]

7th Brigade

Visual signalling from the battalion headquarters kept Draper, the 8th Brigade's commander, abreast of the situation. He informed Lipsett of the battle's progress, so Lipsett could determine when to insert the 7th Brigade. Another information source was Captain E L M 'Tommy' Burns.[77] Acting as a reconnaissance officer for the 3rd Division staff, he rode forward to find Monchy-le-Preux captured. He reported this to the division and urged the brigade's prompt commitment.[78] The challenge was timing. Too early and the 7th Brigade could get sucked into the 8th's battle and could not carry out its mission. Too late and the Germans would recover. The lag of up to two hours in both getting information and disseminating orders complicated the decision. There were two ways to shortcut this. Senior officers could grant latitude to the forward reserve commanders to decide when to advance. As will be seen later in the campaign, this could lead to a premature commitment. The other alternative was to adopt the German method of not stopping at phase lines and to continue to push on. This was a sharp departure from British practices, and the Corps had not trained using it. Thus, it was not a workable option.

73 Note if the 8th Brigade created a battle narrative, it has not survived. It did not produce a narrative for Amiens or Canal du Nord. Bennett, *4th CMR*, pp.128-130; LAC: 8th Brigade WD, 26 August 1918.

74 'Tribute To: Colonel Burnett Laws' <http://www.rcmpveteransvancouver.com/tribute-to-colonel-burnett-laws/> (31 July 2018); *The Quarterly Army List for the Quarter Ending 31 March 1914* (London: HMSO, 1914), pp.142, 409.

75 'Maharg, Ivan Clark Diary: 1918 August' <http://www.canadianletters.ca/content/document-9511> (18 April 2017).

76 LAC: RG9 III-D-3 v4946: War Diary, 1st CMR, 1st CMR OO 134, 25th August 1918; LAC: WD, 1st CMR, 26 August 1918; LAC: 8th Brigade WD, 26 August 1918; LAC: RG9 III-D-2 v4802, 138: CWNS Burnett Laws to Duguid, 9 February 1921; 'Maharg Diary' 26 August 1918.

77 Burns was a corps commander in the Second World War.

78 Burns, *General Mud*, p.77.

At 8:10 a.m., Lipsett ordered the 7th Brigade to pass through the 8th.[79] Burns would later claim Dyer and his brigade-major were out of touch, so Dyer issued the order late losing an opportunity.[80] Dyer had to use the 8th Brigade's signal lines, but shelling had severed the lines. It was not until 9:25 a.m. that the signallers could send the message.[81] Lieutenant Ivan Maharg, 1st CMR, also thought Lipsett missed an opportunity, so the 'Hun has a chance to regain

On the left, Brigadier General H M 'Daddy' Dyer, GOC 7th Brigade, despite his age held up under the stream and was a steady pair of hands. On the right, Brigadier General W 'Billy' Griesbach, GOC 1st Brigade, was strict, brusque and shrewd. His division commander thought him the quickest officer to understand the tactical situation. (Canada. Dept. of National Defence/Library and Archives Canada/ PA-007103)

79 LAC: RG9 III-C-1 v3855, 75/9: 3rd Division G.24, 26 August 1918.
80 Burns, *General Mud,* p.78.
81 LAC: 8th Brigade WD, 26 August 1918.

himself.'[82] These criticisms have merit. For more, see Map 5.4 7th Brigade Frustrates *35th ID* Counterattack: Afternoon in the colour map booklet.

The 7th Brigade's mission was to break the pre-March German front-line and seize the ridge spur running east from Monchy-le-Preux. This entailed three key objectives: Jigsaw Wood, Bois du Sart, and the village of Boiry-Notre-Dame.[83] All three were on high ground and would entail advancing four kilometres and breaking the F-R Line. Both of the brigade's flanks were open, with the right particularly dependent on the 2nd Division keeping pace. The brigade would employ the Royal Canadian Regiment (RCR) on the right, Princess Patricia's Canadian Light Infantry (PPCLI) on the left and 49th Battalion guarding the long-left flank. In reserve initially was the 42nd Battalion. The divisional boundary shifting to the Arras-Cambrai road compromised the plan. This change extended the 7th Brigade's front by over two kilometres, so Dyer had to commit the 42nd Battalion on his right to cover his flank.

The brigade had only limited firepower support with two CFA brigades (48 pieces), one machine gun company, and five tanks. While the guns were useful in firing on point targets, they could not replicate the advantages of a barrage. Here again the experience at Amiens, where follow-on forces made large gains with minimal artillery support, was misleading.

The composite tank company with five tanks of the 11th Tank Battalion had to cover eight kilometres to reach the front.[84] Following doctrine, the tanks trailed the infantry to avoid the increasingly effective German anti-tank measures. When needed, the tank liaison officer would bring them forward. Here, as soon as they crossed the front-line, the RCR called up two, which the Germans promptly destroyed.

The RCR on the right had a formidable task. It was to take the mass of entrenchments that comprised the old German front-line, most of Bois du Sart, and Boiry-Notre-Dame. This required a 4,000 metre advance across strong defences, down into a valley, and then back up to the village. The RCR had a relatively new CO in Lieutenant Colonel C R E Willets (38). He was a professional soldier not given to many words and who maintained his predecessor's focus on maintaining PF norms.[85] He had attended the Aldershot Senior Officers Course (SOC) and so was an experienced and well-trained battalion commander.[86] The battalion had returned to Arras having suffered minimal losses at Amiens and those all replaced. It had enough time that the 'Shino Boys' – named for their spit and polish – underwent saluting and smartening up drill.[87]

At Orange Hill, a brigade staff captain gave the orders to advance at 9:35 a.m. and, after a 10-minute conference, it attacked on a three-company front.[88] Crossing the start line, they faced heavy machine gun and artillery fire. As they pushed forward, a German attack from Arrow Copse surprised and briefly slowed them down.[89] This was an example of the aggressive posture

82 LAC: CWNS Millen to Rennie.
83 LAC: 7th Brigade Report.
84 LAC: 3rd Tank Brigade Report.
85 McCulloch, 'Crisis in Leadership', p.39.
86 Department of Militia and Defence, *Quarterly Militia List,* pp.85, 114, 115, 364, 426; 'Lt.-Col. Charles Richard Edward Willets, D.S.O.' <http://regimentalrogue.com/rcr_great_war_officers/rcr_offr_willets_cre.html> (1 August 2018).
87 LAC: RCR WD, 21 August 1918.
88 LAC: RG9 III-D-2 v4802, 138: CWNS Captain Fenton to Duguid, ?[1920].
89 LAC: CWNS Fenton to Duguid.

Lieutenant Colonel Charlie Stewart, CO PPCLI, was a magnificent battlefield leader but a weak administrator and trainer away from combat. (Canada. Dept. of National Defence/Library and Archives Canada/PA-007031)

of the newly arrived *35th ID*. Resistance from Bois du Sart was particularly strong, and the battalion could only make slow progress. The right company had to form a flank guard as the unit advanced. By the afternoon, the left and centre companies were beyond Long Trench. To slow them down, the Germans threw everything they had at them, including a strafing attack by 15 German fighters. Disorganisation and casualties wore away at the forward companies, and Willets had to send his only reserve to bolster them. By early afternoon, the Germans had stopped the RCR.

The PPCLI in the centre had lost 144 all ranks at Amiens, with replacements received for most.[90] The battalion commander, Lieutenant Colonel Charlie Stewart (44), was a magnificent battlefield leader but a weak administrator and trainer away from combat. Described as an 'army in himself' he had a colourful and somewhat disreputable past and was popular with the troops and officers, but not Currie.[91] Currie thought him 'Falstaffian.'[92]

The battalion was to advance on a 1,000 metre front on the brigade's left to take the north portion of Bois du Sart and Jigsaw Wood. The Germans usually made good use of woods to mass for counterattacks. Bois du Sart was particularly important as it covered the final portion of the ridge running from Monchy-le-Preux.[93] The PPCLI advanced with little opposition in heavy rain until it reached Faction Trench, the pre-March 1918 German front-line. There, machine guns positioned along the ridge line, in nearby trenches, and from Pelves to the north assailed it. To defeat the stubborn resistance, the 'Pats' cleared the trench in hand to hand fighting. Its left flank was exposed, and it suffered heavily from there. Two of its three tanks

90 LAC: 7th Brigade W.D., Amiens Casualties, August 1918.

91 James S. Kempling, 'Birth of a Regiment: Princess Patricia's Canadian Light Infantry 1914-1919' (MA, University of Victoria, 2011), p.45; 'Stewart, Charles James Townshend' <http://www.biographi.ca/en/bio/stewart_charles_james_townshend_14E.html> (1 August 2018).

92 Jeffery Williams, *First in the Field: Gault of the Patricias* (St. Catharines, Ont.: Vanwell Publishing, 1995), pp.134-135.

93 LAC: 7th Brigade W.D., 7th Brigade OO No.167, 25 August 1918.

were almost immediately knocked out, and the third ditched. Their crews later reported that the Germans were on the run as long as the tanks were functioning but once stopped the enemy recovered their courage.[94] By noon, the battalion could no longer make any headway. The resulting battle was like a typical trench battle.[95] The *141st IR* of the *35th ID* reinforced the remnants of the *214th ID* defending this sector. Shelling and machine gun and sniper fire took a steady toll of the forward companies, so Stewart had to feed in reserves to bolster them. Even with these reinforcements, companies comprised 25 to 35 rifles with a platoon sergeant in command. Officer losses were particularly heavy.[96] The situation was dire as the 7th Brigade had only two companies in reserve. A strong German counterattack was a real threat.

In support on the left, the 49th Battalion, from Edmonton, returned to the Arras front relatively unscarred by the Amiens offensive.[97] Its commander was Major C Y Weaver (34), while its regular leader, Lieutenant Colonel Palmer, was attending the Aldershot SOC. Dyer and the senior commanders had sufficient confidence to leave him in charge of the battalion while Palmer was on his course.[98] The 49th's initial role was to protect the brigade's left. Two companies would screen the village of Pelves and Jigsaw Valley, while the other two remained under Dyer's control.[99] The 'Eddys' trailed the PPCLI by 800 to 1,000 metres. This was close enough to rapidly respond to orders or enemy actions without getting caught up in the leading battalion's battle. By noon, it was clear that the PPCLI was unlikely to gain more ground. To shield the flank and counter the German fire from the village, Dyer ordered the two reserve companies to refuse the flank on the left of the 'Pats' and cover it to the Scarpe. The Germans in Pelves and on Mt Pleasant responded by shifting their fire to the 49th. An artillery bombardment on the village somewhat diminished this fire. The 49th's role was necessary, but not one that would gain it much acclaim.[100] As long as the 51st (Highland) was still lagging the now advanced Canadian positions; the elongating left flank was subject to German artillery and machine gun fire from across the Scarpe.

By late afternoon, the 7th Brigade situation was a perfect illustration of both the German defensive doctrine in action and why it failed. The lightly manned outpost line would act like a shock absorber and soak up the enemy artillery fire and attacking forces, causing casualties and disorganisation while minimising German losses. The follow-on assault forces with only limited artillery and tank support would pour out their strength in fighting increasingly strong defences. At that point, counterattacks would strike the attackers at their weakest and drive them back.

94 LAC: 3rd Tank Brigade Report.
95 McCulloch, '"Fighting Seventh"' p.219.
96 LAC: RG9 III-D-3 v4912: Princess Patricia's Canadian Light Infantry War Diary, PPCLI Narrative of Operations August 5th/29th August 1918; Hodder-Williams, *PPCLI 2*, pp.327-339; Aaron Taylor Miedema, 'Bayonets and Blobsticks: The Canadian Experience of Close Combat 1915-1918' (Masters, Royal Military College of Canada, 2010), pp.150-151.
97 LAC: RG9 III-D-3 v4940: 49th Battalion War Diary, 17 August 1918.
98 'Major C. Y. Weaver, D.S.O. 49th (Edmonton Regiment) Battalion' <https://matthewkbarrett.com/2018/05/03/lt-col-weaver/> (1 August 2018); Department of Militia and Defence, *Quarterly Militia List,* p.139.
99 LAC: 49th Battalion WD, 49th Battalion OO 182, 25 August 1918.
100 G. R. Stevens, *A City Goes to War; [History of the Loyal Edmonton Regiment (3 PPCLI)* (Brampton: Charters Publishing Co., 1964), pp.126-127; LAC: 49th Battalion WD, Report of Operations Conducted by 49th Canadian Battalion - Edmonton Regiment, east of Arras on the 26th, 27th, 28th August 1918; LAC: 49th Battalion WD, 26 August 1918; LAC: 7th Brigade Report.

The German doctrine called for flexibility that accepted the short-term loss of positions with the promise that fresh reserves would regain them. This was exactly the 7th Brigade's situation except it did not work.

The deep, lightly manned outpost line absorbed the Canadian artillery barrage and the resources of a full infantry brigade. Admittedly, the 8th Brigade had taken the main line of resistance, but it was in no shape to push on. The 7th Brigade got sucked into a vicious static battle without the necessary gunnery support. The result was that the PPCLI and RCR were over-extended with both flanks open, disorganised from the loss of men and leadership, exhausted, and low on ammunition. With only two companies in reserve, the brigade was vulnerable. On 14 April 1917, on the same ground, the Germans destroyed two battalions, including the Royal Newfoundland Regiment, with such a counterattack. In August 1918, there was a very different result.

The *35th ID* would launch the counterattack. It moved to the 3rd Division's front shortly after the fall of Monchy-le-Preux.[101] Reinforcing the shattered *214th ID*, it was the reason the 7th Brigade had so much difficulty in advancing. At 3:00 p.m., the *II Bavarian Korps* ordered it to drive back the Canadians and possibly retake Monchy-le-Preux. It massed two battalions each of the *141st IR* and *61st IR* in Jigsaw Wood and Bois du Sart.[102] By this point, only the 214th ID's *III/44th Field Artillery Regiment* (*FAR*) and a foot artillery battery were still combat effective. The other two battalions had withdrawn.[103]

Sniper patrols of the PPCLI, having worked their way forward unnoticed, observed the Germans assembling.[104] They passed this information back, and Canadian field and heavy artillery and the RAF pounded the woods. The Germans made up to five separate attempts to advance from 6:35 p.m. to 7:30 p.m. The *141st IR* did not receive the order to attack until 4:30 p.m., and it took ninety minutes to get ready. By that point, the artillery was running out of ammunition, so it delivered little gunnery support. The *71st FAR* of the *35th ID*, owing to the hurried move to the front and scattered commands, did not get the order for the attack preparation until too late. It was further hampered by a shortage of ammunition.[105] The combination of hurricane artillery fire and massed Lewis Guns prevented any Germans from reaching the Canadian lines.[106] Rather than rolling back the Canadians, the Germans had wrecked four vital battalions for no gain.

The counterattack should have been successful. Canadian defenders were exhausted and greatly reduced in effectiveness. The four attack battalions reached the assembly areas within striking distance without interference. German artillery was in position and was already firing on the Canadians – albeit short of munitions.[107] Why then was this attack a failure when those

101 Schulemann, *I.R. Nr. 141*, p.190.
102 General Staff Intelligence Section, *251 Divisions*, pp.413-415; '35. Infanterie-Division 1914-1918' <http://www.militaerpass.net/35id.htm> (12 December 2017); TNA: Cdn. Corps GS WD, Daily Summary of Intelligence, 27 August 1918; LAC: RG9 III-D-2 v4791, 23: CWNS Intelligence Report.
103 Stenger, *Geschichte F.A.R. Nr. 44*, pp.385-388.
104 Leslie P. Mepham, 'Making Their Mark: Canadian Snipers and the Great War. 1914-1918' (Masters, University of Windsor, 1997), p.110.
105 Lothar Gitterman, *F.A.R. Nr. 71*, pp.305-306.
106 Schulemann, *I.R. Nr. 141*, p.191.
107 The Germans attacking from Jigsaw Wood could use Jigsaw Valley to get within assault distance of the Canadian line without being observed.

in 1917 were so fruitful? Four factors were crucial: timing, differences in infantry strength, signals, and artillery. The attack would likely have been more successful if the order to carry it out came earlier.[108] The 7th Brigade was most vulnerable in the period after noon when the advance stopped, and its units were off-balance. Six additional hours enabled them to recover their equilibrium and to consolidate.

Unlike British infantry in the later stages of Arras 1917, the Canadians in 1918 were better trained, better led, and had more firepower. Most of the 7th Brigade's officers and men had the advantage of two months of open warfare training. This contributed to units continuing to fight even when battle had culled the leadership. They entered the battle far fresher than the British units and were almost at full strength. Finally, the addition of a second Lewis Gun per platoon meant even severely weakened units could generate the firepower needed to stop an attack. While the Canadian infantry had improved, the Germans had declined. Their heavy losses had hollowed out German formations, leaving them short of men committed to fight. Nevertheless, the 35th ID pressed its attacks despite the Canadian firepower.

Canadian front-line units could communicate with the rear to a greater extent than in 1917. While still slow and subject to interruption, signals had improved to the point where commanders and the artillery could intervene. Both could react promptly to looming counterattacks, and the guns could crush them before they could do any damage. It was now possible even to bring the RAF into battle.[109] Finally, the artillery was far more mobile and able to respond than in 1917. Again, the open warfare training meant the field artillery could follow an advance as deep as on 26 August and fire accurately during the battle.[110] Even the more mobile heavy artillery batteries – 6-inch howitzers and 60-pounders – advanced to west of Orange Hill by the afternoon.[111] Also, the logistic support could keep the guns supplied.[112] The additional firepower of several brigades of field artillery was devastating.

On the brigade's right flank, Dyer committed the 42nd Battalion. It had an easy time initially at Amiens but had a fierce fight at Parvillers on 12 August. It emerged, however, in strong shape with a relatively low total of 148 casualties, and its morale was never higher.[113] A shell killed its beloved battalion commander on 3 August, and Major Royal Ewing (39) replaced him.[114] A prewar real-estate agent, Ewing was known for his 'initiative and absolute disregard for personal danger.'[115] He later clashed with Dyer's replacement as brigade commander, suggesting an officer with strong opinions and self-confidence.[116]

108 The author of the history was the regiment's commander in the battle. Preusser, *Nr. 176 Im Weltkrieg*, p.282.
109 LAC: RG9 III-C-1 v3912, 41/15: RA Canadian Corps Messages, 26 August 1918.
110 LAC: RG9 III-D-3 v4963: GOCRA War Diary, Report of the Action of Close Support Brigades of 5th Canadian Divisional Artillery During Operations Commencing Aug. 26 1918.
111 LAC: RG9 III-D-3 v4974: Canadian Corps Heavy Artillery War Diary, 26 August 1918.
112 For more on the mobile warfare side for artillery, see Anon., *Sixty-Sixth C.F.A.*, pp.89-90.
113 C. Beresford Topp, *The 42nd Battalion, C. E. F., Royal Highlanders of Canada, in the Great War* (Montreal: Gazette Printing Co., Limited, 1931), pp.234-237.
114 Paul P. Hutchison, *Canada's Black Watch: The First Hundred Years, 1862-1962* (Bloomfield, Ont.: Museum Restoration Service, 1987), p.121.
115 'Lieutenant Colonel Royal Ewing, D.S.O., M.C.' <https://matthewkbarrett.com/2017/11/06/lt-col-ewing/> (1 August 2018).
116 McCulloch, 'Crisis in Leadership', p.30.

The battalion's initial role was as a reserve for the brigade, and it followed the RCR. The brigade ordered the battalion to take over the extension of the front at 2:30 p.m. and to attack. It would have to grind through a complex maze of trenches consisting of 10 separate lines to reach its final objective of Factory Trench. The 2nd CMR would support it to provide a defensive flank as the 2nd Division was not advancing. This was an exceedingly aggressive objective requiring the Black Watch to advance 2,800 metres on a front of 2,000 metres. The planners' expectation must have been that the Canadians had comprehensively defeated the Germans. As at Amiens, with the defensive crust broken, the advance would be a pursuit.

The battalion's approach, however, was more prudent with the cut-up the terrain and defences. Instead of a frontal attack, the decision was to follow the precedent of Parvillers at Amiens, and bomb down the front defences to the Arras-Cambrai road using two companies.[117] Once they took the first set of trenches including Shovel, Sod and Spade, they would push on to take the complex warren of defences to Saddle Trench. The reserve companies would then leapfrog, and capture Factory Trench another 1,500 metres distant.

While machine gun and sniper fire were fierce from the start of the attack at 4:30 p.m., the battalion easily overcame the resistance. Distant defenders would fire on the Canadians but were not willing to engage at close range. Any advance along a trench was a slow process, and it took the two companies until 8:30 p.m. to reach Saddle Trench. It was a protracted fight, with few losses. But, it was too late in the day to exploit any further. There were two wrinkles to the action. In the battalion centre and on its left, German strongpoints held out. Efforts to evict them were unsuccessful, so the 42nd had to extend its flank almost 700 metres back to East Trench to meet with the RCR. That night the Germans pulled out recognising the futility of retaining this section.

The 42nd Battalion captured 6 artillery pieces, a light trench mortar, and 18 machine guns. Its losses were surprisingly light at 3 officers and 42 other ranks, and they counted at least 20 prisoners. It was evident from the casualty totals that the defenders were unwilling to confront them at close range. The relatively few captives and casualties indicated a German force that was fighting a delaying action. At Arras, the extensive defences enabled small parties of Germans to slow down the advance to a crawl.[118]

Despite their counterattack's failure, but the Germans kept coming. They even tried camouflaging their helmets with leaves to sneak through the thick grass. They were unsuccessful.[119] Nevertheless, the relentless pressure and the risk of exposed flanks resulted in the two forward RCR companies falling back to Long Trench. The regimental history refers to a 'seething front,' which captures the confused and contested situation.[120] Despite the desperate conditions, the battalion suffered the loss of only 9 officers and 187 other ranks over the course

117 Topp, *42nd Battalion*, p.242.

118 LAC: 7th Brigade Report; Topp, *42nd Battalion*, pp.242-246; LAC: RG9 III-D-3 v4938: 42nd Battalion War Diary, Narrative of Operations Carried Out By the 42nd Canadian Battalion, RHC on August 26th 1918.

119 Bernd Horn, *Establishing a Legacy: The History of the Royal Canadian Regiment, 1881-1953* (Toronto: Dundurn Press, 2008), pp.101-102.

120 R.C. Fetherstonhaugh, Stevens, G.R.B., *The Royal Canadian Regiment* (London, Ont.: London Print. & Lithographing Co., 1936), p.344.

of the three days, with most on 26 August.[121] It is telling of the vicious, chaotic fighting that the battalion reported no captures of enemies or matériel, but it lost five men as prisoners.[122]

After the defeat of the German counterattack, the *141st IR* tried a different scheme against the PPCLI. Using the trench system and one of the disabled tanks as covered approaches, they tried five bombing attacks, but the 'Pats' repulsed them all.[123] The bruising fight had exhausted the battalion and reduced it to 300 men in the line. The battalion's losses for three days of intense fighting were lower than expected at 15 officers and 182 other ranks.

51st (Highland) Division

On learning that the Canadians held Monchy, the 51st Division ordered the 152nd (1/6th Gordon Highlanders) on the right and 153rd (1/6th and 1/7th Black Watch) Brigades on the left to attack at 10:30 a.m. This was the first of the three stages planned by the division that would capture the vital Greenland Hill position. On the 153rd Brigade's front, the advance was only 500 to 700 metres and was in line with the division's capabilities. The 152nd's 6th Gordons had a far more challenging assignment in matching the 153rd. It had to cross the railway embankment to the south and seize the Mt Pleasant height. Based on spurious reports that the Germans had pulled back, the Gordon's had no gunnery support.[124] Only three FA brigades assisted the 153rd as the other one assigned to the division was still supporting the Canadian attack. In addition, 24 machine guns added their firepower.[125] For more, see Map 5.5 51st (Highland) Division Captures Mt Pleasant in the colour map booklet.

The operation went in on schedule and met limited resistance, with all the objectives captured within an hour. With reports of a German withdrawal from the next set of defences, the division ordered the 153rd Brigade to complete the last two phases that night. The success of the Canadians south of the Scarpe forced the *48th RD* to abandon the outpost zone at 1:30 p.m.[126] At 7:00 p.m., this time under a strong barrage, the two forward battalions plus a company of the 1/7th Gordon Highlanders reached the second objective at the foot of Greenland Hill. Casualties were light, but confusion in the darkness was significant. The attackers believed they had captured Greenland Hill and reported its seizure. This caused an acrimonious exchange between the 6th Gordons and its brigade over why it had not advanced farther to match the 153rd Brigade.[127] It was not until a staff officer toured the sector in the early morning that he

121 LAC: RCR WD, RCR Narrative of Operations, 25/28 August 1918; Fetherstonhaugh, *The Royal Canadian Regiment*, pp.342-344.

122 One man died the next day in German captivity. Edward H. Wigney, *Guests of the Kaiser: Prisoners of War of the Canadian Expeditionary Force 1915-1918* (Ottawa: CEF Books, 2008).

123 Hodder-Williams, *PPCLI* 2, p.338.

124 TNA: WO 95-2864-1/4: 152nd Brigade War Diary, 152nd Infantry Brigade Account of Operations from 20th to 30th August 1918, 11 September 1918; TNA: WO 95-2868-1/4: 1/6th Gordon Highlanders War Diary, 6th Gordon Account of Operations from August 20th to August 28th 1918, 15 September 1918; TNA: 51st Div. GS WD, Report on the Operations North of the Scarpe by the 51st (Highland) Division August 18th - 30th 1918, 9 September 1918.

125 TNA: WO 95-2854-4: 256th Field Artillery Brigade War Diary, 26 August 1918; TNA: WO 95-2857-2: 51st MG Battalion War Diary, 26 August 1918.

126 Hirschel, *Geschichte RIR 221*, p.261.

127 TNA: 6th Gordon WD, 26 August 1918.

determined the 153rd was short of the hill. The 6th Gordons got as far as taking Roeux and the Chemical Works, which were major battle zones the brigade captured in 1917 but could not link up with the 153rd Brigade.[128] The fighting on this front lasted until early the next morning.[129] Given its constrained resources and the limitations of its troops' training, the 51st had done well. Nevertheless, two out of the three high points critical to the Canadian advance remained in the enemy's hands.

Results and Analysis

Reflecting the confusion of battle, the Corps overestimated that it took 2,000 prisoners on 26 August.[130] The actual total was still a respectable 1,129 made of 37 officers and 1,092 other ranks.[131] The attentive reader would have noticed that the captive claims by the battalions far exceeded this total. Units could be extremely liberal in their interpretation of numbers captured. In most cases, it was the friction of war and the focus of officers on fighting the battle rather than precise prisoner counts.

The Corps suffered an estimated 1,827 casualties on 26 August. The 3rd Division had almost double the deaths as did the 2nd Division. This reflects the desperate fighting of the 7th Brigade in taking on a fresh German division. The limited nature of the 51st (Highland)'s engagement resulted in its low casualty figures. During the day, the Corps used 13 Canadian battalions in attacks. Sometimes, as with the 28th and 29th Battalions, they conducted multiple operations. Thus, the casualty totals average just under 100 men per battalion attack which was a considerable drop from those in 1916 and 1917. On the Somme in 1916, battalions lost half of their troops in an attack with an average loss of 295 men.[132]

128 Bewsher, *History of 51st (Highland)*, p.364.
129 TNA: 152nd Brigade WD, 26 August 1918; TNA: WO 95-2875-1/4: 153rd Brigade War Diary, 153 Infantry Brigade Narrative of Operations from 18th to 28th August, 1918; TNA: 51st Div. GS WD, Report on the Operations North of the Scarpe.
130 TNA: Cdn. Corps GS WD, 26 August 1918.
131 LAC: RG9 III-C-1 v3950, 80/3: Prisoners of War, Battle of Arras.
132 Stewart, *Neglected Campaign*, pp.297-298.

Table 5.1 Estimated Casualties For 26 August 1918

	Killed*	Wounded†	POW‡	Total
1st CID				
2nd CID	104	616		720
3rd CID	193	683	7	883
4th CID				
51st HD‖	15	98		113
4th BID‖				
Tank Corps¶	8			8
Other	10	93		103
Estimated Total	**330**	**1,490**	**7**	**1,827**

Sources:
* Battle of Arras Main Dressing Station Report to 6 A.M. September 8th, MG30 E5 v2, Bovey Fonds; LAC.
† 'Find War Dead' <http://www.cwgc.org/find-war-dead.aspx?cpage=1> (4 March 2018).
‡ Edward H. Wigney, *Guests of the Kaiser: Prisoners of War of the Canadian Expeditionary Force 1915–1918* (Ottawa: CEF Books, 2008).

‖ 51st (Highland) and 4th British Division totals do not include prisoners lost
¶ Tank Corps wounded are included in the other category
BID=British Infantry Division
CID=Canadian Infantry Division
HD=Highland Division

The first day of the offensive was a significant success, albeit not to the extent demanded by the high command. The two Canadian divisions smashed one German division and elements of two more, advanced 5,500 to 6,500 metres, and captured 1,129 prisoners as well as significant quantities of matériel. They also killed and wounded substantial numbers of Germans. There was a high probability that the Germans suffered heavier casualties than did the Canadians. Battles where the defenders' losses exceeded the attackers' were a rarity in the First World War. This was especially the case when occupying strong defences.

Why was the Corps so successful? It was a combination of effective combined arms with well-trained, well-led, and spirited infantry, Canadian minor tactics, timing, morale differences, and German command mistakes. The Canadian use of combined arms was the key factor. The artillery was powerful, especially when firing barrages with smoke. Barrages delivered three critical advantages. It kept those being shelled in their trench or dugout and not firing on the attackers. Second, it provided a morale boost to the Canadians and decreased German morale. Finally, it shielded the attackers from observed long-range machine gun, sniper, and artillery fire. The combination of explosions, dust, and smoke concealed the attackers' advance. This enabled the minor tactics of isolating and annihilating enemy machine gun strongpoints. A platoon having to manoeuvre in the face of more than a handful of machine gun posts was a recipe for disaster. Individual batteries or even guns could destroy, devastate, and demolish point targets, but they could not neutralise a zone as a barrage could.

Tanks were useful when they were available. There were, however, so few that contrary to German claims their effect was minimal. They knocked out some strong points and encouraged the infantry and depressed German morale, but they lacked the numbers to have a significant impact. Out of the 13 tanks allocated, only 4 were functional at the end of the day. This was a 70 percent loss rate, although many of these were mechanical breakdowns. No force, no matter how committed, could remain effective at this loss rate.

The training in open warfare paid off in major dividends as units executed daring schemes with a fraction of the time usually devoted to major operations. Canadian tactics of attacking from the flanks worked well. These approaches consistently surprised the defenders, who could not put up a sustained resistance before being overwhelmed. These flanking attacks also resulted in relatively low losses. Currie's insistence on physical training was crucial.

The decision to advance the start time on Webber's suggestion was correct, despite the strife it caused. The efficacy of Canadian training overcame the dark, sloppy, and rainy conditions. Darkness neutralised the German tactic of long-range fire. As a result, the outflanking tactics worked well. Whether they would have been as successful in broad daylight is debatable.

In what will be a consistent theme throughout the campaign, the German *Landsers* fought when they believed they had the advantage. When that no longer applied, they would flee or surrender. The best example of this was Rutherford's capture of so many Germans. If the attackers faltered, however, it would embolden the defenders to continue to fight. The machine gunners were made of sterner stuff and battled on regardless of the situation in most cases. Contributing to the weakness in German morale was the method of dispersing troops in small units in-depth. This made it extremely difficult for leaders to lead. This was a repeated complaint by German commanders that small detachments 'left on their own fall easily into panic.'[133] Critical to success, therefore, was the combination of infiltration tactics, Canadian infantry endurance, a strong artillery barrage, and occasional tank support that would compel the Germans to retreat or surrender.

German command mistakes aided the attack. The withdrawal of artillery to the rear prior to the battle meant it had only a nuisance effect in the morning. As the Canadians advanced, the volume and effectiveness of the gun fire increased. Essentially, the high command took their own artillery out of the battle for half of the day. This was a victory for Canadian counter-battery efforts. This was a critical factor to the commander of the *132nd IR* in its inability to stop the attack.[134] Another error was the misplacement of the intervention divisions. The *26th RD* was reduced to effectively a single regiment to cover the Canadian divisions' attack front, and this was far too weak to influence the battle. On the wrong side of the Scarpe, the *35th ID* could not reach the front in time to make a timely counterattack.

The attack was a success but not on the scale of Amiens. What was different? The Corps was attacking with just two Canadian divisions with no substantial reserves. Unlike Amiens, the attack did not have the advantage of a surprise attack against unprepared divisions at the end of an uncertain supply line. While the German command poorly positioned their reserves,

133 For instance, see Steuer, *I.R. Nr. 132 History*, pp.400-401; Hauptstaatsarchiv Stuttgart: Battle Report on the Enemy Attack on the I and III Batt. R/121st in the Hochwaldstellung on 30.8.1918.

134 Steuer, *I.R. Nr. 132 History*, pp.400-401.

they intervened much sooner than at Amiens. Enemy artillery survived substantially intact and affected the battle later in the day while the Canadian artillery was still moving up. The defences were far more developed and in-depth. Even weak German units could retard an advance when fighting from a prepared position. The Canadians did not have the advantage of an elite corps of Australians on their flank. Finally, the amount of tank support was significantly less. Instead of a full-strength tank battalion supporting each division, each got a reduced composite company.

The Corps had another triumph and had made substantial progress towards the objective of the D-Q Line. Another similar advance as 26 August would bring the Corps up to their goal. The issue facing Currie and his commanders was whether the conditions were like Amiens' day two. There, the Germans were off-balance and without sufficient reserves to seal the breach. Could the Canadians take advantage of the semi-open warfare and launch a coordinated assault early in the morning to exploit the apparent German disorganisation and disorder? Or was this a different battle with different conditions that required a different approach?

6

'Pressed with the greatest vigour' Failure Before the F-R Line, 27 August

Colonel Dubeque [Dubuc] had been wounded in the temple and he was in awful bad shape, terrible bad shape.

George Level, CBC Interview[1]

The second day of the offensive saw a hardening of the defences as the Corps made disjointed and uncoordinated attacks. It gained ground, but nowhere as deep as required and at a high cost. 27 August would turn out much differently than the second day at Amiens, as the Germans had fresh reserves embedded in strong defences. Complicating matters, GHQ's earlier shift of the army boundary exerted a malign effect on the Corps' operations. With a line widened by 40 percent on 27 August and by 85 percent the next day, the Corps had too much front to overwhelm the defenders.[2] This greatly enlarged line did not bring with it any reinforcements. The reduced force density combined with disorganisation from a day of hard fighting meant the relative ratio of combat power was shifting to the German's favour, factoring in the fortification's impact.

Strategic Situation

Strategically, the Germans were withdrawing on a 50-kilometre front on the Third and Fourth Armies, while pivoting on the D-Q Line. They were doing so more rapidly on the southern and central portions to escape a possible encirclement. This was Haig's great fear realised. While the Germans were losing matériel and prisoners, the British could not get to grips with them. The two British armies made progress, but not as much as the Canadian Corps in its attacks on 26 August. A further stress on Haig was Foch and his desire that the BEF do more than push the enemy back. As described by the British Official History, Foch sent Haig a letter 'couched in friendly terms yet containing some advice with a little dash of criticism about the steady advance

1 LAC: RG41 v1: Interview with George Level, p.7.
2 The front south of the Scarpe on 26 August was 6,500 metres, 9,100 on 27 August, and 11,500 on 28 August.

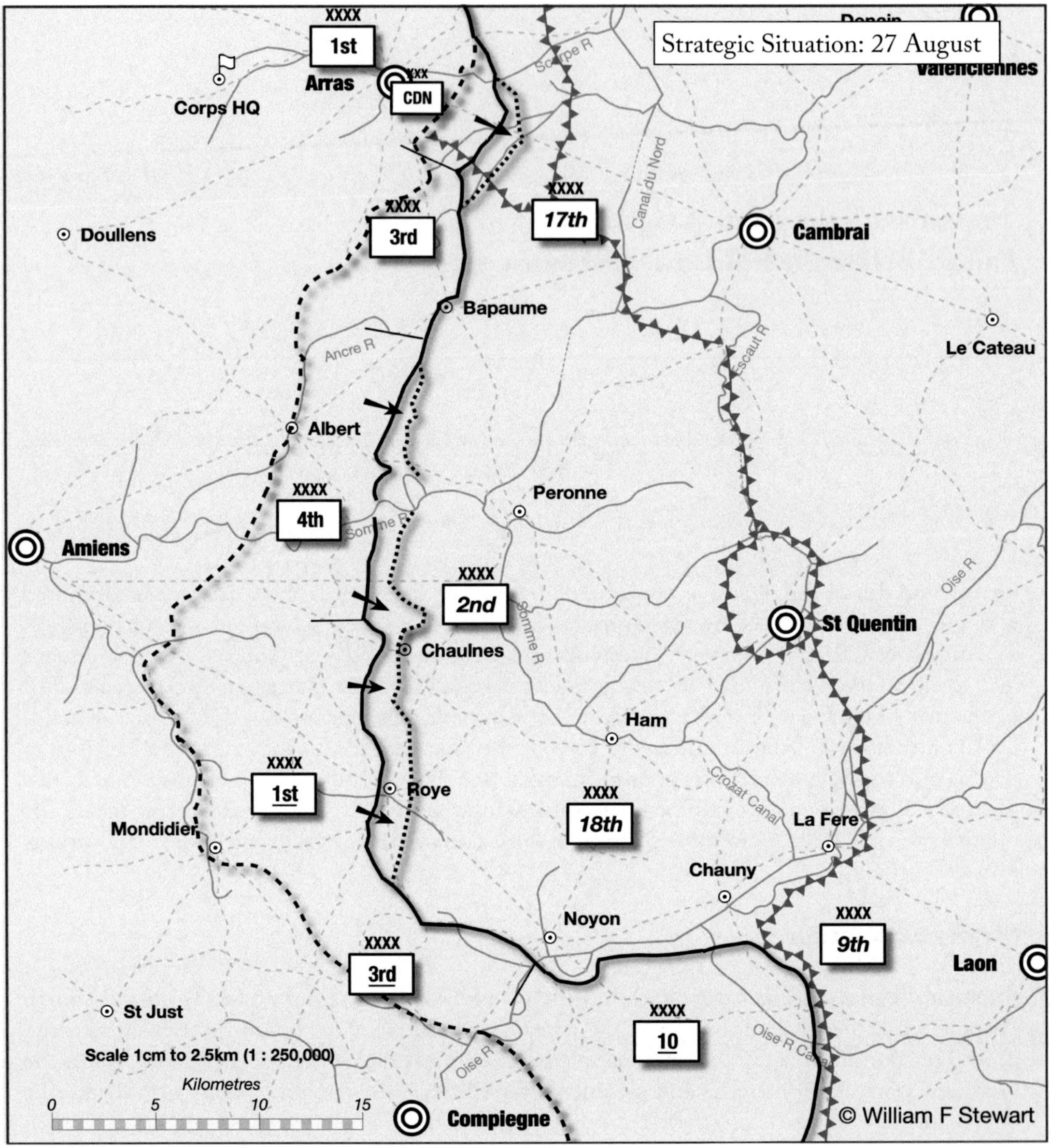

Map 17. Strategic situation 27 August with a general advance across the front. The reason for Foch's concern that the offensive was pushing the Germans back and not destroying them is evident from the map. (Author's map)

in line.'[3] Haig's response to Foch testified to his confidence in the Canadian attack, and his serious underestimation of the resources needed. He declared, 'I am especially strong S. of the Scarpe in order to pierce the DROCOURT-QUEANT line and reach MARQUION.'[4] While some legerdemain might be expected when dealing with his French superior, the C-in-C was exaggerating. The Canadian Corps was not 'especially strong' given its frontage and the defences it faced. It was further evidence of Haig's poor grasp of time, force, and space factors. Foch's pressure made Haig anxious that the Canadians complete their mission quickly. He visited the Canadian Corps and held a conference on 24, 26, and 27 August with senior commanders and staff. He also called on Burstall on 25 August. It was his common practice to make multiple calls on a corps in a critical sector.[5] It meant Currie was under considerable pressure to deliver results.

Tempo

One striking characteristic of Canadian operations during Arras 1918 was its tempo. Instead of days of preparation, the Corps launched daily, hastily arranged attacks. Higher commands could only issue concise written orders covering the essential details, while lower levels often had time for only verbal instructions. The best example of this was the sequence of decisions, orders, and actions leading to the 27 August attack.

A major challenge for commanders at Arras was they had to make many decisions based on incomplete information. The limited time to assimilate, discuss, decide, document, and disseminate orders at each level had three critical implications. First, decisions, especially at the higher levels, were of necessity based on early results and impressions of progress. These were often misleading and contributed to poor decision-making. Assuming a dawn attack, the First Army had to issue its plans in the previous early evening to ensure the battalion and battery levels got instructions in time. If there were extensive troop movements then even more time was necessary. Reserve units replacing a forward unit had to move in a congested, cut-up, and contested battle space at night over unknown ground. They also had to prepare for the assault. Finally, the tight timeframes meant there was not enough time for detailed orders. They had to be succinct and cover only the essential aspects. The Corps left important matters like timing to the divisions. It also placed much greater responsibility on more junior officers.[6] The result was an abbreviated battle procedure and truncated orders. For instance, the Canadian Corps Operation Order G.475 for operations on 27 August comprised a mere 18 lines of typed text that easily fitted on a standard message form.[7] Contrast this with the 20 to 30 page orders in 1917. The Corps so hurriedly composed the plan that the version in the Canadian Corps' War Diary refers mistakenly to the 31st instead of the 51st Division.[8] Also, it did not state a start time or the coordination between the divisions.

3 Edmonds, *Military Operations, 1918* 4, p.315.
4 TNA: WO 158-29: Haig to Foch, 27 August 1918.
5 See for instance, Innes-Robbins, 'Henry Horne as Corps Commander on the Somme': p.262-263.
6 LAC: 1st Divison W.D., Arras Operations Night 28/29 August to Night 4/5 September 1918.
7 LAC: RG9 III-B-1 v968, O-19-3 v1: Canadian Corps G.475, 26 August 1918.
8 TNA: WO 95-1053-2: Canadian Corps G.475, 26 August 1918.

The sequence of decision-making and plans started with Currie visiting the divisional headquarters during the afternoon of 26 August.[9] He briefed each commander of their likely missions to give them a head start on preparations.[10] While Currie was away from the headquarters, Haig and Horne met with Webber at the Corps headquarters to discuss future policy. Haig expected the Canadian attack to break through that day, as demonstrated by the pressure he placed on Horne to ensure the Cavalry Corps exploited it. Horne raised concerns about the lagging action of the XVII Corps. Haig called on Fergusson to tell him that 'the door into the Hindenburg Line' was open, and he should roll up the line.[11]

At the conference, Horne instructed Webber to continue the operation the next morning. The First Army order G.36 issued at 7:10 p.m. formalised this in a single page instruction.[12] This order directed that should the Germans strongly hold the D-Q Line, the Corps would attack it on 28 August. It suggested the First Army expected the Canadians would at least reach the jump-off line to attack it. This was unlikely. While undoubtedly preliminary planning was already underway, these were the formal instructions that set the parameters for the operation. This left just under 10 hours between issuing the order and the attack for three separate command levels to make their preparations. Sometimes, lower echelons raised objections that required revisions. They might also have coordinate timing with another formation. Doing this through the Corps would take too long, so it had to be decentralised.

It took the Corps an hour to issue its G.475 tasking the two divisions to break the D-Q Line.[13] The plan left timing to the divisions. Even with wire signals, it took time to receive orders. It was much longer if the headquarters used despatch riders to send them to forward positions like battalions and batteries. Owing to German wire interception, the high command prohibited passing critical information over wires within 3.2 kilometres of the front-line.[14]

Lipsett and Burstall jointly decided on a 4:55 a.m. start time.[15] That was the beginning of morning twilight.[16] The divisions took an hour to prepare their plans. The 2nd Division's GSO 1, Lieutenant Colonel W. Bertram, called the brigades to warn them of the timing and their mission. Tremblay, GOC 5th Brigade, then in reserve, challenged the timing. He argued his brigade could not reach the start line until 6:00 a.m. at the earliest, the supporting tanks would be even later, and his officers and men had not viewed the ground. Tremblay suggested a 10:00 a.m. attack time to surprise the Germans, allow for reconnaissance, and enable the tanks to assist. Burstall agreed to the change. Thus, creating a five-hour gap between attacks, leaving the 3rd Division's flank open. In effect, the Corps' operation broke down into individual divisional attacks.

9 In his diary, Currie did not list what time he visited, but likely he would wait to the afternoon when more information was available. LAC: Currie Diary, 26 August 1918.
10 Based on a reference in the 9th Brigade War Diary that Lipsett told the brigade at 5:30 p.m. of what was expected of it the next day. LAC: 9th Brigade War Diary, 26 August 1918.
11 NLS: Haig Diary, 26 August 1918.
12 TNA: First Army GS WD, First Army G.36, 26 August 1918.
13 LAC: 2nd Division GS WD, 26 August 1918.
14 LAC: RG9 III-C-1 v3951, 83/1: First Army Instructions Regard Communications in the Danger Zone, 1918.
15 LAC: 2nd Division Narrative.
16 LAC: RG9 III-C-3 v4061, 6/4: Daylight and Light Conditions July, August, September 1918.

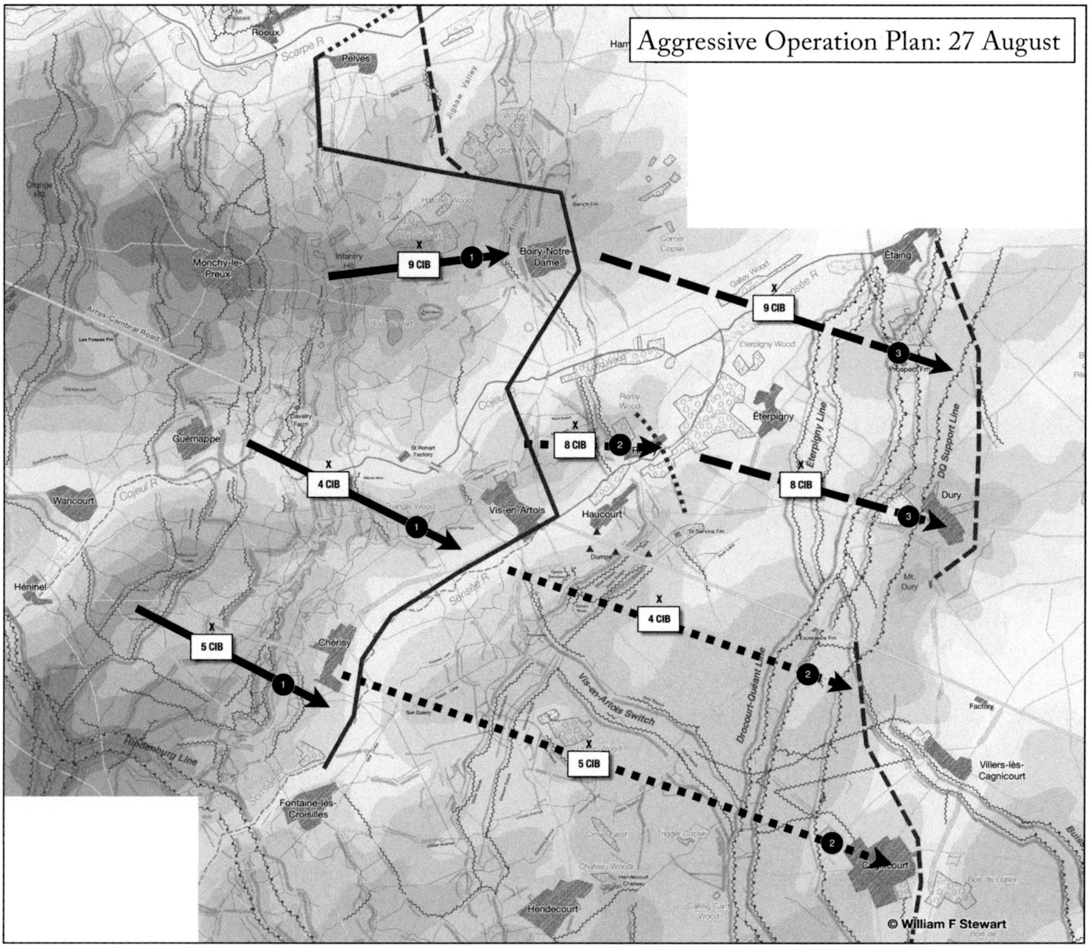

Map 18. The Canadian Corps' aggressive plan for the second day of the offensive called for the capture of the Fresnes-Rouvroy and Drocourt-Quéant Lines in one day:

1. The 2nd Division was to reach the Sensée River and the 3rd takes Boiry-Notre Dame
2. Next, Burstall's division would break both the F-R and D-Q Lines, while the 8th Brigade completed the capture of the remaining portion of the F-R Line north of the Arras-Cambrai road.
3. The 3rd Division would break through the D-Q Line north of the Arras-Cambrai road.

(Author's map)

The 2nd Division issued its OO #248 at midnight. Burstall expected 'every effort to be made for troops to advance as far as possible.'[17] Also, they could expect relief in the evening. The 5th Brigade received this order three hours later at 3:10 a.m., which left Tremblay with only enough time to issue verbal orders. The 4th Brigade issued a brief handwritten order at 5:40 a.m. that only covered the briefest of details.[18] This gave the attacking battalions a little over four hours to plan, move, resupply, and brief their troops.

The 3rd Division issued its G.49 at 10:30 p.m. detailing the attack, but it took almost three hours (1:15 am) to reach the 9th Brigade. This gave it just over three-and-half hours to prepare. However, the brigade was getting its battalions ready long before this. It warned its battalions the previous afternoon of the area where it would attack.[19] Later that afternoon, it directed them to advance to Orange Hill to prepare for the next day.[20] Unlike the 2nd Division, this was an instance where the division gave its brigades advance notice of their probable mission that allowed them to accelerate preparations.

Both divisions had similar amounts of preparation time, but the 3rd attacked at dawn. The reason for the 2nd Division's delay was to allow more time for the 5th Brigade to get into position. This indicates either Burstall underestimated or Tremblay overestimated the time needed. Unlike the 3rd Division, which ordered its reserve brigade to move forward in the late afternoon, the 2nd Division left its reserve brigade west of Chapel Hill. This was about four kilometres away as the crow flies, so it could not get to the jump-off line for 4:55 a.m. As Currie visited both divisions' headquarters in the afternoon and likely told both that the attack would continue the next day. Burstall mistakenly did not move up his reserves as did Lipsett, so misplaced them.

Another issue was the Corps' plan for the two divisions was reckless. If both reached their objectives, they would have dangerously exposed flanks. On the left, the flank would run from Pelves to Boiry-Notre-Dame. This was seven kilometres – a divisional front. The only reserves were the depleted 7th Brigade – one battalion served with the 9th Brigade – the CIF with 80 machine guns, and the Canadian Corps Cyclist Battalion. Lipsett committed the 8th and 9th Brigades to the attack that day. The nearest other reserve was the 1st Division deployed south of Arras. It would take hours to reach that sector. The same issue existed on the right as the XVII Corps was unlikely to keep up fighting through the Hindenburg Line. The result was another potential open flank of seven kilometres. Here, the 6th Brigade was at hand, and the leading elements of the 1st Division were close by. The Corps was vulnerable to devastating counterattacks, from the north, centred on Boiry-Notre-Dame and from the south aligned on Hendecourt. Currie and Webber were too experienced to be unaware of the risk and its potentially devastating consequences. Why then did they keep pushing the two divisions given these circumstances? Likely, if the Canadians reached the distant objectives, the Germans could not take advantage of the open flank. They would be too busy trying to salvage something from the disaster. This was taking Haig's instructions to accept risks to the maximum extent.

17 LAC: 2nd Division GS WD, 2nd Division OO 248, 26 August 1918.
18 LAC: RG9 III-C-3 v4108, 28/2: 4th Brigade OO No.5, 27 August 1918.
19 LAC: RG9 III-C-3 v4199, 6/1: 9th Brigade G.11, 26 August 1918.
20 LAC: RG9 III-C-3 v4199, 6/1: 9th Brigade G.12, 26 August 1918.

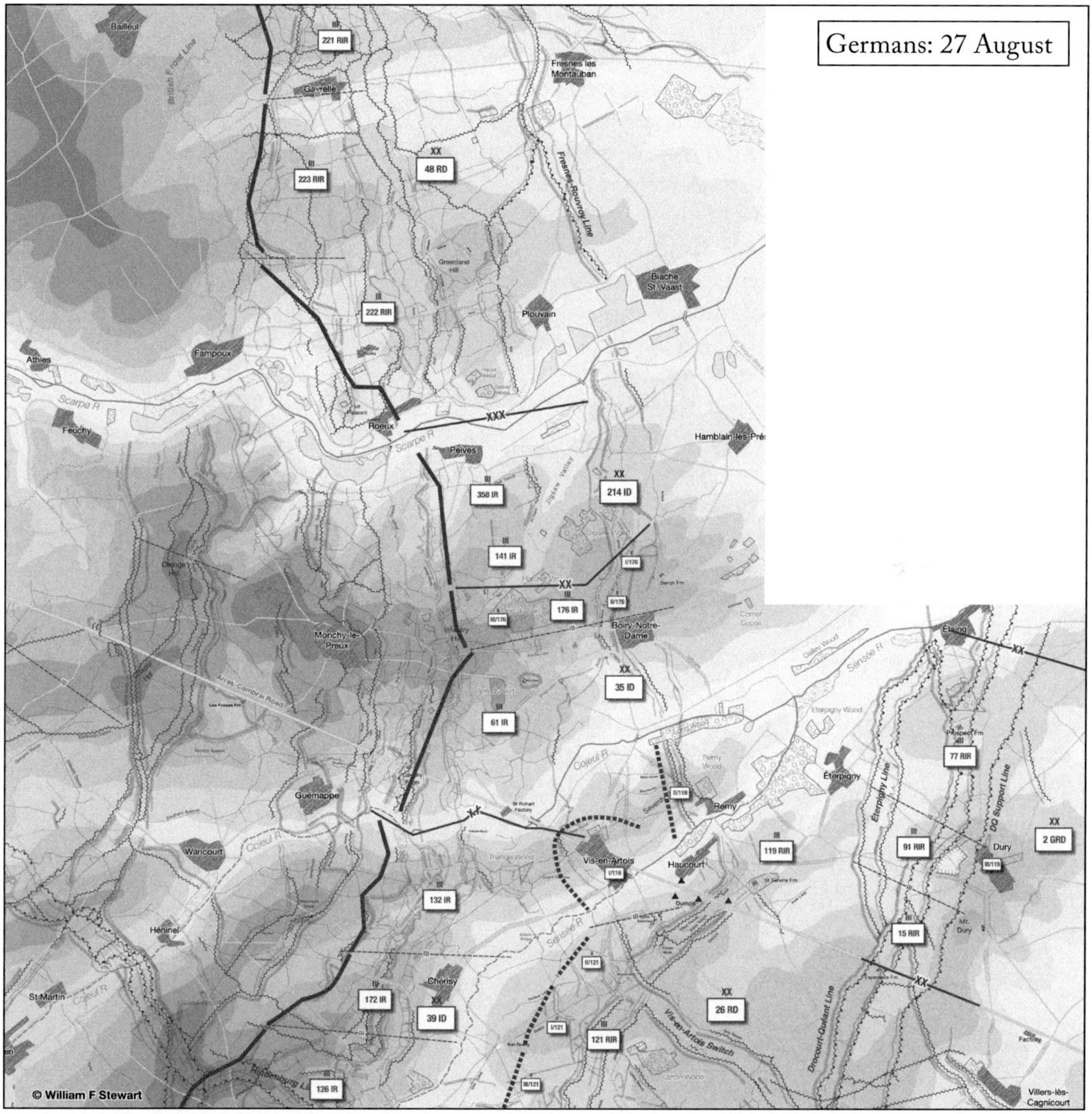

Map 19. The *II Bavarian Korps* had a serious issue with the loss of its *Vorfeld* and main line of resistance the previous day. The presence of two fresh divisions in a strong defensive line, with the *35th ID* and the *26th RD, saved it*. (Author's map)

Germans

The *II Bavarian Korps* had a serious issue. The *Vorfeld* and the *HWL*'s loss meant it needed to rebuild its defensive system. Fortunately, it had two relatively fresh divisions in strong positions. South of the Cojeul River, the remnants of the *132nd IR* and *172nd IR* defended the front.[21] Behind it, the *121st RIR* and *119th RIR* of the crack *26th RD* manned the F-R Line. North of it, the *35th ID* held the line with elements of the shattered *214th ID*. For instance, the *II/50th IR* of the *214th ID* consolidated its four companies into two.[22] The *35th ID*, with its *61st IR* and the *III/176th IR*, defended from the Cojeul to Infantry Hill. The rest of the *176th IR* were in reserve holding the F-R Line.[23] After the failure of the counterattack on 26 August, the artillery of the *35th ID* moved back to ease ammunition supply and escape the relentless Canadian counter-battery efforts.[24] The *214th ID* defended the sector from Infantry Hill to the Scarpe with the *141st IR* of the *35th ID* and its *358th IR*.[25] The *II Bavarian Korps* would pull out the exhausted *214th ID* that day. North of the Scarpe, the *48th RD* still faced the Highlanders.

Behind these formations, five other divisions – *16th ID, 1st GRD, 2nd GRD, 111th ID, and 4th Ersatz Division* (*EzD*) – lurked holding the D-Q Line or were close enough to intervene.[26] Even if the Corps broke through the F-R Line, there was still a formidable mass of enemies ready to contest any further advance. Canadian intelligence identified three divisions in reserve on the Corps' front on 26 August, but Currie ignored or overlooked this in his plan.[27] Thus, the Corps' objective of breaking the D-Q Line was illusory on 27 August.

Corps Preparations

On the first day, the 6-inch howitzer and 60-pounder batteries of the heavy artillery trundled forward to positions west of Orange Hill and Neuville-Vitasse to support the next attacks.[28] The heavier pieces remained in position as they took too long to move and tied-up the roads.[29] Expecting open warfare conditions on 27 August, the GOCRA passed artillery control to the divisions.[30] Likewise, there were no operations instructions issued by the commander of the heavy artillery or the Corps Machine Gun Officer (CMGO). In open warfare, the Corps could only set the boundaries and objectives while the divisions handled all the other details. Thus, the faster tempo of open warfare negated much of the Corps' ability to coordinate and direct the battle. The engineers continued to be to rehabilitate the road system, extend the tramways, and

21 Steuer, *I.R. Nr. 132 History*, p.400.
22 Vogt, *I.R. Nr. 50*, p.235.
23 Preusser, *Nr. 176 Im Weltkrieg*, p.274.
24 Lothar Gitterman, *F.A.R. Nr. 71*, pp.305-306.
25 Schulemann, *I.R. Nr. 141,* p.191.
26 Kümmel, *Res.Inf.Regt. Nr. 91*, p.420.
27 CWM: Summary of Information Gained During to-Day's Operations, 26 August 1918.
28 LAC: CCHA WD, 26-27 August 1918.
29 9.2-inch howitzers took 18 hours to breakdown for movement and another 18 to prepare to fire. LAC: RG9 III-C-1 v3911, 39/7: Artillery Notes on Operations - August 26th to Sept. 4th 1918.
30 LAC: Artillery Notes on Operations - August 26th to Sept. 4th 1918.

supply water.[31] By the end of the day, the Arras-Cambrai road was open to two-way lorry traffic to Tilloy and was in fair condition for two-way traffic south of Monchy-le-Preux.[32]

Flanking Forces

The Third Army's instructions to the XVII Corps were to continue to advance down the Hindenburg Line in concert with the Canadians. Fergusson's divisions, facing strong defences, were tired and would have no tanks. As the British Official History observed: 'Without tanks tired infantry could not be expected to accomplish anything decisive.'[33] The 52nd (Lowland) Division was to capture Fontaine-lès-Croisilles and ideally Hendecourt a further 3,000 metres away and Riencourt 1,250 metres beyond there.[34] Should the Canadians take the F-R Line and threaten the D-Q Line, it was essential that the 52nd seize these two villages to protect the Canadian flank. It attacked at the same time as the 2nd Division.[35]

The Lowlanders captured the contentious Hénin Hill and pushed south-east along the Hindenburg Line. At noon, it reported the enemy were fleeing, and that it was approaching the Sensée. It claimed the capture of high ground across the Sensée, and that the 2nd Division had stopped just east of the river. Its 157th Brigade could not push much beyond Fontaine-lès-Croisilles, and it requested reinforcements. The 156th Brigade moved to the left to act as a link with the 2nd Division. According to the divisional history, this brigade took Chérisy and 500 prisoners. This was fanciful as the Canadians reported no British units in this sector. Further, the *176th IR* defending the sector was clear that its line collapsed owing to attacks from the north. Like the 2nd Division, the 52nd could not make any progress against the F-R Line.[36] Five days of constant fighting required its relief that night by the 57th Division. By the end of the battle, the 52nd had lost half of its infantry complement.[37]

2nd Division

The 2nd Division's attack front was 3,500 metres, with the first objective of the Sensée River requiring an advance of 2,500 to 3,500 metres. To get there, Burstall's division, with the 5th Brigade on the right and the 4th on the left, had to punch through the pre-March British and German front lines. The 5th had to reach the Sensée River and seize Chérisy – a scene of fierce fighting in 1917. The 4th Brigade had an even more challenging mission. It had to pierce the same set of enemy defences, but it had to cross the Cojeul River on part of its front. This section was wet from springs supplying a thin trickle of water. It would also have to capture the village of Vis-en-Artois on the west side of the Sensée.

31 LAC: GOCRE WD, Tramways Report, September 1918 ; LAC: RG9 III-C-5 v4387, 11/4: Narrative of Operations of the 3rd Brigade CE, 11 January 1919.
32 LAC: RG9 III-D3 v4992: 3rd Brigade CE War Diary, 27 August 1918.
33 Edmonds, *Military Operations, 1918* 4, p.323.
34 TNA: 52nd Division GS WD, 27 August 1918.
35 LAC: 2nd Division GS War Diary, 27 August 1918.
36 TNA: 52nd Division GS WD, 27 August 1918.
37 TNA: 57th Division GS WD, 28 August 1918; TNA: XVII Corps GS WD, 27 August 1918; LAC: RG9 III-D-2 v4799, 111: CWNS XVII Corps August Narrative; Thompson, *Fifty-Second,* pp.528-532.

After a 30-minute pause, the attack would resume without a barrage. The second objective was the F-R Line, 1,400 metres away on the 4th Brigade front and 2,000 metres on the 5th's. Three mobile FA brigades would engage point targets. The infantry having descended to the Sensée River valley had to climb a short bank and then advance across an exposed slope to reach the second goal. They would be subject to long-range fire from the moment they topped the ridge overlooking the Sensée on the west. It was an ideal killing zone, and the Germans had carefully positioned the line to exploit it. For more, see Map 6.4 2nd Division Mixed Success: 27 August in the colour map booklet.

The ultimate objective was Cagnicourt, which entailed advancing 10 kilometres and breaking the F-R and D-Q Lines. The 2nd Division was committing its only fresh reserve and would have to rely on the 4th Brigade for the second day. It was an unrealistic set of objectives. The division thought it feasible because of the Third Army's attack and Canadian success in seriously disorganising the enemy.[38] The challenges, however, were substantial. It attacked in the mid-morning, reducing the daylight available. It could only provide a weak barrage for the first third of the advance and none for the rest. There were only a handful of tanks available, and it faced three sets of defences with the Germans moving up reinforcements. One of its assault brigades was tired after a day of fighting, and its reserve was still recovering from a long tour. This would not turn out like Amiens' second day.

The 2nd Division's CRA, Brigadier General H A Panet, had only enough pieces to provide a barrage density of just 30 metres per gun. The artillery comprised seven FA brigades with 126x18-pounders and 42x4.5-inch howitzers.[39] Barrages placed a considerable burden on the horses and men bringing up the ammunition. This barrage required a minimum of 1,260 rounds per 18-pounder battery and there were 21 batteries.[40] That amounted to 12 General Service (GS) wagon loads per battery; hauled at night over slippery, shell-damaged roads while contending with other traffic and enemy bombing and shelling.[41] Three brigades of heavy artillery also supported the operation.

Panet decided that after 26 August to stop using smoke in the rolling barrage. He would still use it in the final protective fire and in smoke screens. The rationale was it was 'found to confuse infantry and tanks.'[42] The other divisions continued to use it in their barrages, and they did not complain. This was a consequence of not conducting extended open warfare training, and they had no experience with smoke barrages at Amiens.[43] Three field artillery brigades would support the attack on the second objective. Owing to the short pause on the first objective, there was insufficient time for another barrage. Instead, they would act as mobile field artillery to fire on individual targets. All reportedly did good work, but they could not stop the deadly fire from

38 LAC: RG9 III-D-1 v4794, 54: 2nd Canadian Division Narrative of Operations from March 13th to Nov. 11th 1918.

39 LAC: RG9 III-C-1 v3911, 39/8: Narrative of Operations of the 2nd Divisional Artillery, August 1918.

40 A barrage extending 3,000 metres moving at 100 metres every 3 minutes with a standard rate of fire of 2 rounds per minute would require 180 rounds per piece. Adding in a 30-minute protective barrage with a ROF of 1 round per minute adds another 30 rounds.

41 LAC: MG30 E81 v4, Ammunition: Morrison Fonds, Ammo Loads by Vehicle.

42 LAC: 2nd CDA Narrative.

43 Smoke was used to screen key observation points away from the infantry advance on 8 August in the 2nd Division but in no barrages at Amiens by the division. LAC: RG9 III-D-3 v4959: 2nd Canadian Division Artillery War Diary, 2nd CDA Artillery instruction No.4, 6 August 1918.

Brigadier General H A Panet was an RMC graduate from a notable French-Canadian military family. His decision, with Burstall's concurrence, to stop using smoke was an unfortunate consequence of the 2nd Division's lack of open warfare training. (Canada. Dept. of National Defence/ Library and Archives Canada/ PA-003918)

the F-R Line. Mobile artillery could suppress or destroy point targets but could not neutralise an area.[44]

The 14th Tank Battalion had to provide one company of eight tanks to each division. On 26 August, it had 10 fit tanks, along with six worn-out ones without guns from the driving school. It would receive eight tanks from another battalion at 6:00 p.m., giving it little time to get into position.[45] The composite company supporting the 5th Brigade comprised only six tanks, and their tracks were troublesome. The division and brigade staff ignored the company commander's attempts to get orders until divisional instructions arrived at 1:11 a.m. In moving to the Cojeul valley, tracks on two tanks broke. The four remaining tanks did not cross the start line until 30 minutes after Zero. They advanced trailing the infantry and attracted a great deal of artillery

44 LAC: GOCRA WD, Report of the Action of the Close Support Artillery Brigades Operating Under 2nd CDA in the Operations Commencing August. 26th, 1918 ; LAC: Artillery Notes on Operations - August 26th to Sept. 4th 1918.

45 TNA: WO 95-103-5: 14th Tank Battalion War Diary, History of the Fourteen Battalion, Tank Corps, 1919.

fire. Another vehicle's tracks broke, so only three fought, and the Germans knocked out two of them. So, for a five-hour delay, the brigade gained the use of only four tanks. These four, of which only three engaged the enemy, fought across a frontage of 3,000 metres meant they had only a limited, localised effect. The infantry accounts did not mention any assistance rendered by them.[46] As per orders, they only advanced to the Sensée.

5th Brigade

The 5th Brigade returned from Amiens having suffered a serious blow to its leadership. A shell on 9 August wounded the brigade commander and the intelligence staff captain and killed the brigade-major.[47] Lieutenant Colonel T L Tremblay (32) took control.[48] In addition, the 25th

Brigadier General T L Tremblay, GOC 5th Brigade, had just received the 5th Brigade. Although esteemed by his superiors, respected by his officers, and adored by his men, Tremblay would have a rocky start to his command at Arras 1918. (Canada. Dept. of National Defence/Library and Archives Canada/PA-002666)

46 TNA: 14th Tk. Bn. WD, History of the Fourteen Battalion, Tank Corps, 1919; LAC: 2nd Division Narrative.

47 LAC: 5th Brigade W.D., 9 August 1918.

48 LAC: Staff Officers.

Battalion's CO suffered a severe wound at Amiens. As a result, the brigade headquarters was going into battle with an untested leadership cadre. It would suffer even greater losses at Arras, where the three remaining battalion commanders died or suffered wounds.[49]

The brigade did not fight on 26 August. It moved up to the area west of Chapel Hill in the morning and remained there, suggesting Burstall planned to use it along the Arras-Cambrai road. Instead, he replaced the tired 6th Brigade with Tremblay's, but he had poorly positioned it for a quick relief. The forward battalions were 4,000 metres from the jump-off line, so the three forward battalions took over four hours to reach their assembly positions.[50] This was as an error by the 2nd Division in mis-positioning its only reserve so far from its likely battle sector.

The 5th attacked on a three battalion front with the 26th Battalion on the right, 24th in the centre, and 22nd on the left. One battery of the 1/2nd Machine Gun Battalion accompanied each unit. The 25th Battalion was in support, and the 6th Brigade's 29th Battalion was the reserve. This battalion was wearied after holding the line prior to 26 August and complained of the 'exhausted condition' of the men.[51] As a result, it was likely Tremblay was chary of using them. With time tight, Tremblay had to orally brief the battalion commanders.[52] At 4:00 a.m., the battalions started their move to the assembly areas.

The barrage opened well with a strong German reaction by their long-range artillery. Initially, the assault troops met little resistance with the *Vorfeld* held lightly by the battered *39th ID*. The morning reports were positive, with minimal opposition and many prisoners. After a thirty minute pause, the attacked continued by crossing the Sensée. This was the critical point, because if the 5th Brigade captured the F-R Line it would have a decisive effect. It would mean outflanking an 8,000 metre section of the Hindenburg Line, disrupting German defensive arrangements, and accelerating the attack on the D-Q Line. A failure here would delay the latter assault by days.

The good news changed when Clarke-Kennedy, CO 24th Battalion, arrived at the brigade headquarters to report the second phase of the attack had stalled 500 metres beyond the Sensée due to intense machine gun and artillery fire. The bad news did not stop there, as the 22nd's commander was wounded, and it and the 24th had many casualties. The attackers observed Germans rushing reinforcements to the sector, so the task was becoming even more difficult. Then, to add to the doleful situation, the 156th Brigade on the right flank indicated they were pulling back from Fontaine-lès-Croisilles because of a flanking formation failure. It did not do so and kept the village.[53] Even if erroneous, the report had to influence Tremblay. The village was on the east bank of the Sensée and dominated the valley. The 5th's brigade-major considered it was impossible to advance if the British did not hold it.[54]

Meanwhile, field artillery batteries were moving up and were available for fire missions. The 6th CFA opened up on enemy guns in Upton Wood and reinforcements moving on the Hendecourt-Dury road. Lieutenant Colonel C F Constantine CO of the 5th CFA arranged for

49 Lieutenant-Colonels Dubuc (22nd Battalion) and Clark-Kennedy (24th Battalion) suffered severe wounds and McKenzie (26th Battalion) died.
50 LAC: 5th Brigade W.D., Narrative of Operations, August 19 to 26, 3 September 1918.
51 LAC: 5th Brigade W.D., B.I. 32, 27 August 1918.
52 LAC: 5th Brigade W.D., OO No. 268, 26 August 1918 and OO No. 268/1, 27 August 1918.
53 Thompson, *Fifty-Second*, pp.528-529.
54 LAC: 5th Brigade W.D., B.M. 130, 28 August 1918.

Lieutenant Colonel W H Clarke-Kennedy, CO 24th Battalion, was an inspired leader and received a VC for his command during the battle. The after-effects of his serious wound still show in his face in this image. (Canada. Dept. of National Defence/Library and Archives Canada/ PA-003909)

the heavy artillery to pound these locations. Tremblay and his brigade-major, Major J C Kemp, scouted the front-line to determine if they could re-energise the attack.[55] Trembly tried to organise a barrage, but there was insufficient time before dusk to do so. He decided to try again the next morning with a proper barrage.[56] At nightfall, the front held was 400 to 950 metres east of the Sensée but still short of the F-R Line. On the left, the brigade lacked a strong connection with the 4th Brigade and the 22nd Battalion was weak.[57]

The 5th Brigade punched through the *39th ID*, and the German commanding officer had to report on its failure.[58] Once the brigade crossed the Sensée, it met the far more formidable *26th RD*. This division reported von Dellmensingen ordered them to take over the front as survivors of the *39th ID* poured through their positions. The Canadian and British attack destroyed the *39th ID*'s *172nd IR* and reduced its three battalions respectively to a 'handful of troops', 32, and 70 all ranks. Almost 80 percent of its losses were prisoners.[59]

55 R. C. Fetherstonhaugh, *The 24th Battalion, C.E.F., Victoria Rifles of Canada, 1914-1919* (Montreal: Gazette Print. Co., 1930), p.239.

56 LAC: 2nd Division Narrative; LAC: 5th Brigade W.D., Narrative of Operations, August 19th to 29th 1918, 3 September 1918.

57 LAC: 5th Brigade W.D., B.M. 130, 28 August 1918.

58 German divisions like Canadian and British ones drafted battle accounts as a matter of course. That the corps commander would explicitly mention it in his diary suggests a matter of some unusual importance. Bundesarchiv, Freiburg: Feldzug 1918, 30 August 1918.

59 Hans Wegener, *Die Geschicte Des 3. Ober-Elsässischen Infanterie-Regiments Nr, 172* (Zeulenroda: Bernard Sporn, 1934), pp.254-258.

Lieutenant Colonel A E G McKenzie, CO 26th Battalion, was an experienced commander with a strict attitude. He is sitting with three of this battalion officers. (Canada. Dept. of National Defence/Library and Archives Canada/PA-006801)

Despite suffering 227 casualties at Amiens, the 26th Battalion on the brigade's right returned to the Arras sector at almost the same strength as it had left with.[60] It was under the experienced command of Lieutenant Colonel A E G McKenzie (40) who had led it since May 1916. McKenzie was a veteran, brave, and capable officer with a strict attitude to service reflecting his Scots Presbyterian upbringing.[61] It attacked on a two-company front with an eccentric front expanding to 1,300 metres and shrinking to 900. The field artillery barrage was excellent, but the battalion complained that its machine gun battery never showed up.[62] There was a brief battle in the German front-line, but the troops killed or captured any defenders not fleeing. The

60 LAC: 26th Bn WD, 25 August 1918; S. Douglas MacGowan, Harry M. Heckbert and Byron E. O'Leary, *New Brunswick's Fighting 26th: A History of the 26th New Brunswick Battalion, C.E.F., 1914-1919* (Saint John, N.B.: Neptune Publishing Company, 1994), p.263.

61 'Dictionary of Canadian Biography Online - McKenzie, Archibald Ernest Graham' <http://www.biographi.ca/en/bio/mckenzie_archibald_ernest_graham_14E.html> (26 September 2018).

62 LAC: 5th Brigade W.D., 5th Brigade, W.14, 27 August 1918.

major resistance was from enemy artillery fire, but losses were minimal. Some Germans hid in dugouts as the leading waves passed over them and meekly surrendered and marched to the rear without defiance.[63]

After a brief pause, the battalion crossed the Sensée and reached the Fontaine-Haucourt road a couple hundred metres east of the river. There, it met much stiffer resistance. Heavy machine gun fire from the front and from the high ground in the British sector slowed them down and inflicted losses. German field guns fired over open sights from Upton Wood, and the battalion could not get beyond Una Lane, 350-400 metres beyond the Sensée.[64] The open right flank was a threat, and the combination of fire from the front and on the right kept it from advancing.[65] The battalion losses, however, were relatively light at 1 officer and 135 other ranks.[66]

In the brigade's centre, the 24th Battalion had suffered considerable casualties at Amiens – 242 all ranks.[67] Commanded by Lieutenant Colonel W H Clarke-Kennedy (38) a prewar company manager, it had spent 21 days in July in open warfare training and was one of the better-prepared battalions in the 2nd Division.[68] After holding staff positions, Clarke-Kennedy took over the 24th Battalion in December 1917 with only minimal command experience. Nevertheless, his seniors valued him as his DSO with bar and Victoria Cross (VC) earned at Arras would later attest.

With an initial front of over 800 metres, it was to take Chérisy. The barrage opened at 10:00 a.m. and was accurate. A veteran battalion with confidence in the gunners, its officers led their troops into No Man's Land before the artillery made their first lift. This was to get a jump on reaching the German defences. Despite this, it faced a tough battle in taking Mallard Trench – the front-line defence. The enemy machine gun broke up the battalion's formation but did not stop the attackers, though, and they took the trench, many prisoners, and machine guns. The regimental history declared the German machine gunners, 'fought bravely and well, in contrast to the German infantry, who at some other points, revealed evidence of approaching demoralisation.'[69] Until the Sensée, it was German artillery opposing the advance. The 24th crossed the almost dry river bed and waited for the final protective barrage to finish. This allowed the battalion to reorganise after a 2,700 metre advance.

The nature of the battle changed completely, however, as the Montrealers advanced up the slope towards the F-R Line. Machine gun and artillery fire from three sides flayed the battalion, and it struggled on to reach within 150 metres of the heavily-wired Ulster Trench. Clarke-Kennedy, recognising the impossibility of breaching the wire, ordered his men to drop back. This was especially necessary as the enemy rapidly reinforced the sector with more troops and guns. He went to the brigade headquarters to describe the dispiriting situation. Contrary to

63 LAC: 26th Bn WD, C Company Report [31 August 1918]; LAC: 26th Bn WD, 25 August 1918.
64 The regimental history generously claims its final position was 600 metres beyond the river. The actual measured distance was half of that.
65 LAC: 26th Bn WD, B Coy 31 August 1918.
66 LAC: 26th Bn WD, Operations east of Arras, August 26th -29th Inclusive ; MacGowan and O'Leary, *Fighting 26th*, pp.271-274.
67 LAC: RG9 III-D-3 v4932: 24th Battalion War Diary, Response to 5th Bde AQ_11/150, 18 August 1918.
68 LAC: 24th Battalion W.D., 1-10 July 1918.
69 Fetherstonhaugh, *24th Battalion*, p.237.

Lieutenant Colonel A Dubuc, CO 22nd Battalion, suffered a severe head wound in the battle. (Canada. Dept. of National Defence/Library and Archives Canada/PA-002819)

expectations, the Germans were not in disarray and had established a strong defence.[70] Without gunnery support, there was little chance for success. The battalion suffered in one day as many casualties – 242 – as it did during the entire Amiens operation. Losing 10 officers meant considerable shuffling of leaders overnight to ready it for the next day.[71]

It is difficult to tell the 22nd's story because so few of its leaders survived to describe what happened. With the promotion of its former commander Tremblay, Lieutenant Colonel A E Dubuc (38) took over. He had previously led the battalion but was in England in a training command when the authorities recalled him hurriedly to France. Covered by a 'strong and effective artillery barrage' on a 600 metre front, it advanced.[72] Owing to its low strength, it attacked with all its companies in line.[73] It reached the Sensée valley with little trouble, although it was suffering losses. Contrary to some accounts, it did not lose men fighting for Chérisy, as the

70 George vom Holtz, *Das Württembergische Reserve-Infanterie-Regiment Nr. 121 im Weltkrieg 1914-1918* (Stuttgart: Chr. Belsersche Verlagsbuchhandlung, 1922), p.75.
71 Fetherstonhaugh, *24th Battalion*, pp.236-239; LAC: 24th Battalion W.D., 26-27 August 1918.
72 LAC: RG9 III-D-3 v4931: 22nd Battalion War Diary, 27 August 1918.
73 LAC: RG9 III-D-2 v4802, 138: CWNS Vanier to Duguid, 9 March 1920.

village was in the 24th's sector.[74] After the 30-minute pause, it started up the slope towards the F-R Line, when the situation unravelled. It faced direct fire and from flanking positions south of Vis-en-Artois that the 4th Brigade had not yet reached. It took crippling losses, especially in officers. German fire knocked out 15 including Dubuc. He suffered a wound to the temple that most thought mortal – he would survive. According to one soldier, 'he was in awful bad shape, terrible bad shape.'[75] With the loss of so many officers, the attack broke up. Leadership was so thin that Clarke-Kennedy assumed effective control of the battalion until Major Georges Vanier could take over.[76] The first day of fighting badly battered the 22nd with a loss of 240 all ranks.[77] The death or wounding of 13 officers meant the battalion had to advance next day with minimal officer supervision. That it continued to attack in such negative circumstances was a testament to the courage and determination of its troops.

4th Brigade

Now on its second day of fighting, the 4th Brigade was tiring and had three challenges. It straddled the Cojeul with one battalion on each side. It had to advance 2,400 metres before both were on the same bank. While not much of an obstacle to infantry, it had flowing water and was more of a barrier than upstream.[78] The brigade had a long advance of 3,800 metres. It had to cross over a ridge separating the Cojeul and Sensée valleys with many trenches and wire obstacles to reach the Sensée and its first objective. The left battalion had to capture the village of Vis-en-Artois – partially in the 3rd Division's sector. It too needed to charge up a bare slope to reach the F-R Line's complex of defences. The German engineers positioned it to sweep the slope with machine gun fire, and the *119th IR* adeptly defended it.[79] Finally, the 3rd and 2nd Division's advance diverged with the 3rd going north-east and the 2nd south-east. This would expose the brigade's left flank.

The 19th Battalion would attack on the right and the 18th on the left, each with an 800 metre front. The 19th was initially in reserve on the first day of the offensive because it had led two attacks at Amiens. Millen, the battalion CO, only learned of the upcoming attack at 5:00 a.m. and its commitments on 26 August had scattered its companies. It would have to scramble to get ready. With the hurried preparations, Millen did not realise the barrage ended at the Sensée, and the war diary complained about the poor barrage beyond there.[80] It attacked on a two-company front, giving it a thin concentration of only 0.8 men per metre. This should

74 See for instance, Carl Pépin, 'The Need to Advance: The Battle of Chérisy and the Massacre of Québécois Troops (August 1918)', *Canadian Military Journal* 15, no. 3 (2006).
75 LAC: 22nd Bn. WD, 27 August 1918; LAC: Interview with George Level, 7.
76 Vanier would be the first French-Canadian Governor-General. Robert Speaight, *Vanier: Soldier, Diplomat and Governor General: A Biography* (London: Collins, 1970), p.77; Pépin, 'Need to Advance'.
77 LAC: 22nd Bn. WD, 27 August 1918; LAC: 5th Brigade W.D., 5th Brigade Narrative of Operations, August 19 to 29, 3 September 1918.
78 A series of springs fed the river from a marshy area. LAC: RG9 III-C-1 v3920, 2/19: Notes on the Area between the Scarpe, La Sensée Canal, Canal De l'Escaut and Cambrai-Bapaume Road, [1918].
79 Matthäus Gerster, *Das Württembergische Reserve-Infanterie-Regiment Nr. 119 im Weltkrieg 1914-1918* (Stuttgart: Chr. Belsersche Verlagsbuchhandlung, 1920), pp.118-119.
80 LAC: 19th Battalion War Diary, Operations of the 19th Canadian Battalion, August 25th-29th 1918.

The ruins of Vis-en-Artois shown in 1919. Only the shells of buildings remain standing. (Canada. Dept. of National Defence/Library and Archives Canada/PA-004436)

dispel the German claims of defeating masses of Canadian troops in the attack.[81] Despite the complex set of trenches and barbed wire obstacles, the battalion made excellent progress to its first objective at the Sensée. It inflicted heavy casualties while suffering few of their own, and it took 268 prisoners. The defenders were too weak to properly resist, and the thin barrage neutralised the already demoralised Germans. The *132nd IR* history blamed breakthroughs on each flank for its collapse. According to the *26th RD,* survivors flooded in a disorganised panic through their positions.[82] After this debacle, the *132nd IR*'s three battalions totalled 15 officers and 180 men. The situation, however, was so desperate that the regiment marshalled the remnants as a reserve until the morning. After the standard pause, the 19th crossed the Sensée, but thick willow breaks slowed its progress. Once out of the valley, telling machine gun fire from the heavily-wired Ocean Works, Opera, and Olive Trenches and from the flanks shredded

81 See for instance, Stühmke, *26th Reserve Division* II, p.61.
82 Steuer, *I.R. Nr. 132 History,* pp.400-402; Stühmke, *26th Reserve Division* II, p.62.

the battalion. It could not advance without artillery support, and its flank was open because of the 22nd's problems. Millen would assert that the 5th Brigade was never in contact during the attack.[83] By 3:00 p.m., the Germans had definitely stopped the assault, and the battalion fell back across the river. It had just five company officers still standing and had lost over 210 other ranks.[84]

On the left, the 18th Battalion went into battle with its second-in-command, Major J A McIntosh – a capable and experienced officer.[85] The 18th had lost only 25 all ranks in the capture of Guémappe the day before, so other than fatigue it was battle ready. It attacked on a two-company front with its first objective the Sensée and the little village of Vis-en-Artois. The battalion faced elements of the *176th IR* of the *35th ID* and the *I/119th RIR* of the *26th RD*. Like the 19th, the attack initially went well with the Germans surrendering in masses. Private Hilaire Dennis wrote of this stage that: 'We took a big bunch of prisoners one morning and I thought it was good for a little lot of Canadians to take so many great Big husky germans.'[86] The battalion took Vis-en-Artois by noon. Unfortunately, the 18th's records are scanty, so only the German side has any detail, and it was flawed. Two batteries of the *26th RFAR* deployed north of Vis-en-Artois reported that the defenders before them had vanished, but it wanted to remain defending the vital town. The *26th RD* agreed and moved up the *I/119th RIR* to Vis-en-Artois to protect them. The battalion could not hold the town against an attack from the south supported by 15 tanks, and it fell back across the Sensée.[87] Rennie's brigade had no tanks, so this was another example of the Germans seeing tanks everywhere. With the break at the village, the *26th RD* had to throw in its last remaining reserve to seal the gap. The Germans pulled out most of the guns before the Canadians overran them. The *I/119th RIR* paid a steep price, with the two companies defending Vis-en-Artois reduced to 40 men each.[88] Again, the battle changed when the 18th tried to cross the river. Fierce machine gun fire from the F-R Line hit them hard. The battalion could not advance and only held a small bridgehead on the Arras-Cambrai road across the Sensée. During the battle, Major McIntosh was wounded along with 160 others killed or wounded.[89]

With the forward battalions gone to ground and with no chance of a further advance, the brigade ordered the units to consolidate their positions. They would wait until the division would arrange another set-piece attack with a barrage and indirect machine gun fire.

Initial reports coming into the division, as often was the case, were optimistic with the two brigades making good progress. The preliminary statements indicated the operation was on schedule with few losses and many German prisoners. After 3:00 p.m., however, the tenor

83 LAC: CWNS Millen to Rennie.
84 Campbell, *It Can't Last Forever*, pp.430-432; LAC: 19th Battalion War Diary, Operations of the 19th Canadian Battalion August 25th-29th 1918; LAC: 4th Brigade War Diary, 4th Brigade Narrative of Operations South of Scarpe, 26, 27, and 28 August, 1918.
85 'Senior Officers' Course Confidential Report on Major J.A. McIntosh, 3 March 1918' <https://18thbattalioncef.wordpress.com/soldiers-listed-in-diary/mcintosh-john-alexander-major/> (27 September 2018).
86 Dennis, 'Canadian Conscript', p.30.
87 Stühmke, *26th Reserve Division* II, p.61. The regimental history of the *119th IR* only reported a number of burning tanks in the distance. Gerster, *RIR Nr. 119*, p.118.
88 Gerster, *RIR Nr. 119*, p.118.
89 LAC: 18th Battalion War Diary, 27 August.

of the accounts changed for the worse, with both brigades reporting difficulties and heavy casualties. Both blamed the other brigade for leaving a gap between them. It was apparent the attack was foundering. Currie called the division headquarters at 5:45 p.m. and spoke with Bertram to discuss the situation. The Corps commander disingenuously said there was no long advance intended for the day – he was already trying to shape the battle's narrative. This was certainly not the case, judging from the Corps' orders and Haig's intent. The Corps had copies of the divisional orders, and Currie did not raise any objections to the long advances. Bertram explained the division was held up in front of the F-R Line and suggested the troops make good the Sensée. Currie agreed and called off any further actions that day.[90]

3rd Division

The 3rd Division's task was formidable. It was to take three objectives, advance 8,000 metres, and break through the F-R and D-Q Lines. The 9th Brigade would capture the woods that had stopped the 7th Brigade the previous day – Bois du Sart and Bois du Vert – and seize Boiry-Notre-Dame and Artillery Hill north of the village. This was a 3,000 metre advance to break the F-R Line starting at 4:55 a.m. The 8th Brigade would then take Remy Wood south-east to the woods near St Servins Farm across the Sensée River. Once completed the 9th Brigade would break the D-Q Line and hold a line from Étaing south to Dury. Complicating matters, with the 2nd Division not attacking until 10:00 a.m., the 3rd Division's right flank would be exposed for five hours. For more, see Map 6.5 3rd Division Makes Only Limited Gains: 27 August in the colour map booklet.

The 9th Brigade's plan was careful to avoid taking on Jigsaw Wood to the north of Artillery Hill. A woodland of this size would require more forces than available. The barrage density was 26 metres per gun, but it would fire for only 48 minutes, giving it a depth of just 1,600 metres at the lift rate of 100 metres every 3 minutes. Thus, the barrage would cease beyond Bois du Sart.[91] There were three possible explanations for this short barrage. The division thought it only necessary to cover the first phase of the advance. There was a shortage of ammunition – the 3rd Division's CRA, Brigadier General J S Stewart, commented in his diary that 'The gunners and horses are getting tired.'[92] Finally, multiple barrages would constrain the following phases to a specific timeline when flexibility was needed. Likely all three were a factor in the decision.

The 9th Brigade remained in reserve on 26 August, and Lipsett issued verbal orders to it at 5:30 p.m. for an attack in the early morning. The 3rd Division's order G.49th confirmed it was to take the two woods, Boiry, and Artillery Hill. Owing to the wide 2,500 metre attack front, Lipsett reinforced the 9th with the 49th and 2nd CMR Battalions.[93] Ormond, GOC 9th Brigade, met with his battalion commanders at 7:30 p.m. to plan. Note the difference in the

90 LAC: 2nd Division GS WD, 27 August 1918.
91 LAC: 3rd CDA WD, OO 198-15, 26 August 1918.
92 John Smith Stewart, *Memoirs of a Soldier: Brigadier-General John Smith Stewart* (Lethbridge, AB: S.I., 1979?), 27 August 1918.
93 LAC: RG9 III-D-3 v4986: 3rd Machine Gun Battalion War Diary, 3rd MG Battalion Report on Operations August 26th to 29th 1918.

Brigadier General 'Dangerous Dan' Ormond, GOC 9th Brigade. He was a hard man and a battle-tested leader. (Canada. Dept. of National Defence/ Library and Archives Canada/ PA-003900)

tempo between the 2nd and 3rd Divisions. While the 5th Brigade's first notice was at 9:00 p.m., Ormond had already had a planning session 90 minutes earlier.[94]

The 9th Brigade's plan had to consider the 2nd Division's late start, so it instructed the 43rd Battalion to cover the exposed flank. On the right, the 52nd Battalion would take Bois du Vert and Vert Work beyond it – an advance of 1,300 metres. The 58th Battalion would capture Bois du Sart – a slightly longer distance of 1,500 metres. Both attacks were under the shelter of the artillery barrage. Once the brigade had these, the 116th would pass between them centred on the sunken Infantry Lane and take both Boiry-Notre-Dame and Artillery Hill. The ridge would shield it from fire from Jigsaw Wood. Given the lack of barrage support and the commitment of a single battalion, the plan must have assumed that there were few troops defending the F-R Line.[95] Also, the line north of the Arras-Cambrai road was weaker than the southern portion.

On the right, the 52nd, under the command of Lieutenant Colonel D M Sutherland (39), attacked on a three-company front. The battalion's main objective was Bois du Vert overlooking the nearby terrain. It was necessary to capture this before attempting Boiry-Notre-Dame. Two

94 LAC: 9th Brigade War Diary, Narrative of Operations from 25 to 30 August, 15 September 1918.
95 LAC: 9th Brigade War Diary, Narrative of Operations from 25 to 30 August, 15 September 1918.

The ruins of Boiry-Notre-Dame shown in 1919. The only standing structures were the school and church. (Canada. Dept. of National Defence/Library and Archives Canada/PA-004508)

companies would seize the woods with the third protecting the exposed flank. The battalion took the woods, but at 7:00 a.m., both companies reported the Germans counterattacking the battalion's right. With the 2nd Division not attacking, the unit had a long open flank. The *61st IR* of the *35th ID* hit the battalion's right and took prisoners. The battle reduced the right company to one officer and 35 other ranks. Sutherland shifted his support company and restored the situation. The 2nd Division's offensive at 10:00 a.m. finally neutralised the flank threat. When the 43rd attacked as described below, it freed the captives. They had the satisfaction of marching their former captors to the rear.[96]

96 George F. G. Stanley, *In the Face of Danger: The History of the Lake Superior Regiment* (Port Arthur, Ont.: Lake Superior Scottish Regiment, 1960), pp.33-34; LAC: RG9 III-D-3 v4941: 52nd Battalion War Diary, 27 August 1918; LAC: 9th Brigade War Diary, Narrative of Operations from 25 to 30 August, 15 September 1918.

This engagement presents an interesting case study where two assigned tanks arrived over an hour late. The barrage had finished, and the battalion was on its objective. German anti-tank guns promptly dispatched the two tanks without the protection of smoke or a barrage.

On the left, the 58th Battalion's commander was Temporary/Major Rolsa Smythe, who was acting for the wounded CO. Only 23, he joined the unit as a lieutenant at the end of November 1916. This was an extraordinarily rapid rise and indicates a competent officer. It is an example of how command selection had shifted to proven capability instead of age, political connections, social standing, and prewar experience.[97] He also exemplified Andrew Groves' term 'rat-catchers' who had risen to positions of command. These were aggressive, self-sure, and empirical officers who got the job done, but perhaps not with the graces of a regular officer.[98]

The battalion's objective was the high ground of Bois du Sart sitting on the spur projecting from Monchy-le-Preux. Using the new open warfare tactics, three companies carried out their missions and captured the wood by 6:50 a.m. Patrols then probed Hatchet Wood to the north-east. The onslaught destroyed the *III/141st IR*, and its survivors fell back to the F-R Line.[99] The *35th ID* could not passively accept the loss of this vital ground and launched a powerful counterattack with two reserve battalions of the *176th IR* at 7:00 a.m. supported by heavy machine gun fire from flanking positions. Overrunning the scouts in Hatchet Wood, one battalion drove in on the north-east corner of Bois du Sart. The other crashed into the south and south-east portions of the woods. The *176th IR* was trying to pocket the 58th Battalion. These counterblows pushed the two companies holding the woods to its centre. Smythe sent his reserve company along Infantry Lane to the edge of Bois du Sart. The two companies in the woods attacked in unison and pushed out the Germans, with the woods cleared by 7:30 a.m. The *176th IR* blamed tanks and the failure of flanking units for its withdrawal.[100] But there were no tanks involved.[101]

Next up was the 116th Battalion, which was to take Boiry-Notre-Dame. It was fully-manned with a trench strength of 27 officers and 885 other ranks. The second-in-command Major John Sutherland led the unit.[102] He was a 30-year-old law student who had attended the SOC in France in April, indicating he was being groomed for promotion. He was a brave and conscientious officer. Like the other battalions, it had a hard march in a light drizzle to reach the jump-off line with only 35 minutes to spare. Its history credited the open warfare training and night manoeuvres for reaching the line in time.[103]

97 For more on the earlier process of promotion to battalion commander, see Stewart, 'Byng Boys'.

98 Andrew Gordon, 'Ratcatchers and Regulators at the Battle of Jutland,' in G. Sheffield, (ed.), *The Challenges of High Command* (London: Palgrave Macmillan, 2003), p.26.

99 Vogt, *I.R. Nr. 50*, p.236; Preusser, *Nr. 176 Im Weltkrieg*, p.274.

100 Preusser, *Nr. 176 Im Weltkrieg*, pp.275-276.

101 LAC: 49th Battalion WD, Report of Operations Conducted by 49th Canadian Battalion - Edmonton Regiment, east of Arras on the 26th, 27th, 27th August 1918; LAC: 9th Brigade War Diary, 58th Battalion Narrative, 1 September 1918; LAC: RG9 III-D-3 v4942: 58th Battalion War Diary, 27 August 1918; Kevin R. Shackleton, *Second to None: The Fighting 58th Battalion of the Canadian Expeditionary Force* (Toronto: Dundurn Group, 2002), pp.255-256.

102 Reginald Herbert Roy, *For Most Conspicuous Bravery: A Biography of Major-General George R. Pearkes, V.C., through Two World Wars* (Vancouver: University of British Columbia Press, 1977), p.74.

103 The Adjutant, *The 116th Battalion in France* (Toronto: E.P.S. Allen, 1921), p.74.

It was to trail the two forward units by 15 minutes until they had taken the two woods. It would then advance on a 500 metre front on the axis of Infantry Lane running between the two. The plan fell apart almost immediately. One company got sucked into the Bois du Vert fight and was lost to the battalion. Along the lane, two centre companies crossed a ridge crest and 'were literally mowed down by intense machine gun fire from Artillery Hill and Boiry Village' and could make no progress.[104] With no artillery support and the defenders unshaken, the unit had no chance for success. Repeated attempts to advance brought only further casualties. In complete disregard for his safety, Major Sutherland tried to rally the battalion, but a German sniper killed him. At 10:30 a.m., two tanks tried to break the stalemate, but they were quickly destroyed. After a 50 minute bombardment of the village, it tried again at 1:00 p.m. The *176th IR* was in position and, with links to the artillery restored, the defences were too strong.[105] Only small isolated parties could push ahead. At no point, however, did the battalion get close to the wire protecting the village. To add further misery, Canadian artillery started pounding the troops, and they had to drop back 150 metres to escape it. Scattered in shell holes and affected by gas lingering in the long grass, the attack stalled. Over the course of two days fighting, it suffered 295 casualties – mostly on 27 August. This indicated the impossible situation the plan placed the battalion in, trying to take on fortifications with minimal support.[106]

The 43rd Battalion, in reserve initially, suffered heavily at Amiens with the loss of 357 men.[107] Its companies comprised just 80 men each. As it moved up, 316 replacements arrived but there was no time to integrate them, so they remained in the rear. Hence, Private A C West's comment that 'surely we thought this decimated unit can not be put "over again."'[108] Lieutenant Colonel W K Chandler (35), was the battalion's new commander, although he had led them at Passchendaele. He was a battalion original and the only officer to return with the battalion in 1919.[109] At 7:45 a.m., the brigade ordered it to attack with the 2nd Division. Reinforced by the 2nd CMR, it was to advance to the Cojeul with the 2nd Division. A feature of the sector was it was 'seamed with the Old British and German line trenches where the line had become stationary after the Battle of Arras in 1917.'[110] There was only time for a quick conference with the company commanders and the 2nd CMR before the attack. A characteristic of Arras 1918 was the reliance on face-to-face meetings for orders in lower-echelon units. The battalion used the same tactical approach as the 42nd the previous day in pushing east along a communications trench and then working down a trench to the Arras-Cambrai road. Each of the two forward companies had a company in support. The fighting was hard with many Germans killed, but the progress was steady. With no reserves left after the failed counterattack at Bois du Vert, the

104 Adjutant, *The 116th Battalion in France*, p.75.
105 Preusser, *Nr. 176 Im Weltkrieg*, pp.275-276.
106 Adjutant, *The 116th Battalion in France,* pp.74-77; LAC: 9th Brigade War Diary, Narrative of Operations from 25 to 30 August, 15 September 1918; LAC: 9th Brigade War Diary, 116th Battalion 26 to 29 August, 1 September 1918; LAC: RG9 III-D-3 v4945: 116th Battalion War Diary, 27 August 1918.
107 LAC: RG9 III-D-3 v4939: 43rd Battalion War Diary, 8-16 August 1918.
108 LAC: West Diary, 26 August 1918.
109 'Memorable Manitobans: William Kellman Chandler (?-1948)' www.mhs.mb.ca/docs/people/chandler_wk2.shtml, (26 July 2018).
110 LAC: 9th Brigade War Diary, 43rd Narrative of Operations, Augst 26th -29th, 1918.

61st IR had little remaining combat power.[111] This kind of fighting was slow but produced results with few casualties. It took five hours and twenty minutes to reach and cross the Cojeul – an advance of 2,400 metres. An attempt to bounce the F-R Line at Remy broke down due to the strength of the defence, officer casualties, and disorganisation after a long advance. The 43rd was well in advance of the rest of the brigade. With its lines stretched thin, it complained that the 2nd CMR had not followed up as ordered. Ormond hustled it up into position west of the Cojeul to act as a connection between the 43rd and 52nd Battalions. The 43rd reported that although at the outskirts of Vis-en-Artois it had no contact with the 2nd Division. Its losses reflected the relatively low cost of its tactics, losing 11 officers and 133 other ranks in the two days of fighting.[112]

Why did the 9th Brigade take only half of its objectives? It was a combination of a strong and aggressive German division holding strong defences against a weak attacker. The tank support for the brigade did not arrive on time and accomplished little before getting knocked out. German counterattacks hit the 52nd and 58th which keeping them off-balance and unable to assist the 116th, Thus, its attack was essentially unsupported and unlikely to succeed. The combative German actions did not permanently retake the lost ground, but it disrupted the attack. With two long unprotected flanks, the 9th advanced deeply into a salient that opened it to fire from three directions. The Germans were too strong, and the 9th Brigade could only advance as far as the barrage could take it. When the 2nd Division attacked, its barrage had the effect of assisting the 43rd in its push, so it could reach the Cojeul with relative ease. Thus, the barrage was essential to success, while tanks were a worthwhile adjunct if used properly and in mass. Neither of which applied here.

Highlanders

Given the ambitious plans of the Canadian Corps, it was essential for the 51st Division to capture the remaining high ground overlooking the Corps' rear. If not, the Germans would deliver observed fire into the Corps' rear areas. This would put a serious crimp in logistics and moving up the field artillery. As it was, the 3rd Division had to rely on pack animals forward of Monchy-le-Preux.[113] Given its limited artillery, the 51st had to stagger its attacks. Three FA brigades supported its morning attack and four in the afternoon. This despite the morning frontage was 2,000 metres and the afternoon 1,200 metres.[114] For more, see Map 6.6 51st (Highland) Division Stopped Before Greenland Hill: 27 August in the colour map booklet.

The centre brigade, the 153rd, attacked at 10:30 a.m. – well after the 3rd Division. Its objective was Greenland Hill. The 7th Gordons would capture the yellow line – its third goal from the previous day. Observers saw troops advancing up the hill and then rocket signals indicating 'Objective Gained.' These were, however, not British rockets but German ones calling for

111 Preusser, *Nr. 176 Im Weltkrieg,* p.277.

112 LAC: 9th Brigade War Diary, 43rd Narrative of Operations, August 26th-29th, 1918; LAC: 43rd Bn WD, 27 August 1918; LAC: West Diary, 26 August 1918; LAC: 9th Brigade War Diary, Narrative of Operations from 25 to 30 August, 15 September 1918.

113 LAC: 3rd Division AAQMG Report on Move to Arras Area and Operation from 16th to 29th August 1918.

114 TNA: 256th FA WD, 27 August 1918.

artillery fire. The signals were identical, and so the brigade reported Greenland had fallen. Likely, few troops penetrated beyond the first set of trenches. The Germans stubbornly held on to the defences at the foot of Greenland Hill. Later in the afternoon, they took advantage of the railway embankment to infiltrate and strike the 7th Gordons' right flank, and it had to fall back. This caused considerable bitterness in the brigade's account. The 6th Gordons of the 152nd Brigade had to pull back as well.[115]

Based on the erroneous report of Greenland Hill's capture, the 152nd Brigade ordered the 6th Seaforths to capture the spur running south from it. On it were the vital Hausa and Delbar Woods which overlooked the Canadian's left flank. Based on previous experience, the planners expected the enemy would hold this sector lightly. Up to this point, the *48th RD* defended its outpost zone with minimal forces and accepted any ground loss. On 27 August, the Highlanders were approaching terrain that the defenders had to retain. So, the division reinforced its forward defences and launched counterattacks. In the attack, one of Seaforth's two assault companies arrived late, so there was a staggered assault. This, plus too broad a front for one battalion and a strong defence, meant the battalion reached only halfway to the spur. A single weak British battalion even with the support of four FA brigades would not get far if the Germans resisted strongly.[116] The result was frustrating as the Highlanders did not take the needed high ground.

Results and Analysis

The offensive's second day featured hard fighting often at a Canadian disadvantage. Prisoners taken and casualty totals reflected the action's severity and decreased success. The Corps captured 23 officers and 758 other ranks.[117] Most of these were likely from the *39th ID* when the 2nd Division overran it. The Corps suffered an estimated 2,419 casualties on 27 August. The 2nd Division this time suffered more fatalities than did the 3rd. This reflects the desperate afternoon engagements. The battles south of the Scarpe were hard and unrelenting with casualties increasing by a third over the previous day for less ground gained. The 51st's casualty figures reflected the limited troop numbers committed.

115 TNA: 51st Div. GS WD, Report on the Operations North of the Scarpe by the 51st (Highland) Division August 18th - 30th 1918, 9 September 1918; TNA: 153rd Bde. WD, 6th Black Watch, Narrative of Operations for Period from 25th August, 1918 to 29th August, 1918; TNA: 153rd Bde. WD, 7 Gordon Highlanders, Narrative of Events during Operations North of the Scarpe from 26th to 28th August 1918; TNA: 153rd Bde. WD, 153 Infantry Brigade Narrative of Operations from 18th to 28th August, 1918.

116 TNA: 152nd Brigade WD, 152nd Infantry Brigade Account of Operations from 20th to 30th August 1918, 11 September 1918.

117 LAC: POW Arras.

Table 6.1 Estimated Casualties For 27 August 1918

	Killed	Wounded	POW	Total
1st CID	6	13		19
2nd CID	240	1031	2	1,273
3rd CID	141	633	3	777
4th CID	4			4
51st HD*	28	194		222
4th BID*				0
Tank Corps†	6			6
Other	5	113		118
Total	**430**	**1,984**	**5**	**2,419**

* 51st (Highland) Division and 4th British Division does not include prisoners lost
† Tank Corps wounded are included in the other category

In comparison to the opening day, the Corps gained less ground, captured fewer prisoners and matériel, and suffered more casualties. In addition, the two primary divisions they faced, while damaged, retained considerable combat power, unlike on 26 August. The Corps, however, had inflicted further damage on the opening day's two defending divisions forcing their relief. The *214th ID*'s *50th IR* was so battered that its *I* and *II/50th* had only the strength of a company.[118]

A key factor was the force ratio was not as favourable as on 26 August. A combination of fewer tanks and a weak to non-existent barrage meant less combat power. Both divisions overran the initial set of defences, but the Germans stopped them when the attackers passed beyond the barrage. On the 3rd Division's front, the 9th Brigade took on the *35th ID* and elements of the *214th ID*. While the four German regiments engaged were little more than battalion strength each, they stopped the Canadians. With a broader front on the second day and limited artillery support, Lipsett's division was too weak to punch through. Lipsett misread the situation and conducted operations as if it were more of a breakthrough rather than a break-in operation. On the 2nd Division's front, Burstall made three fundamental errors. First, he mis-positioned the 5th Brigade so that it could not attack on the agreed time. His agreement with Lipsett to attack at dawn reveals his misunderstanding of time and space. By delaying the start time, he left Lipsett's division with a wide-open flank for five hours. Finally, he misconceived the situation and conducted his attack as if the capture of the F-R Line were a simple matter. Intelligence had located the *26th RD*, so Burstall's blithe assumption that his men would take the F-R Line without a barrage was excessively optimistic.[119]

118 Vogt, *I.R. Nr. 50*, p.236.
119 CWM: Summary of Information Gained During to-Day's Operations, 26 August 1918.

The Corps' command control was lacking in allowing the 2nd Division to attack far after the 3rd. Unlike the previous day, there are no records of Currie visiting the divisions. The Corps played a hands-off role. Even Currie's comment to Bertram that the Corps had not intended a deep advance was at variance with its orders and intent. Currie and staff appear to have focused on the D-Q Line in the expectation that the capture of the F-R Line was a sure thing. Further, both commanders worked on the assumption their relief would be that night after they had committed all their brigades. Currie did not communicate to his commanders he was delaying their relief.

The defenders were better than on the previous day. The *35th ID* was a prewar active division and while not highly regarded, it fought far more effectively and aggressively than the *214th ID*. On the 2nd Division's front, the attackers easily brushed aside the feeble *39th ID*. When the 2nd Division met the superb *26th RD* positioned in strong defences the Württembergers cut them to pieces. There was no risk of the defenders cowering in their dugouts, especially without an artillery barrage.

Only in isolated situations were Canadian infantry able to advance through prepared German defences without the support of a creeping barrage. On both division's fronts, the infantry advanced only as far as the gunners could take them. The fundamental issue with the Arras sector was the depth of fortifications meant there were few places where defenders did not have their protection. Where they did not exist, there were sunken roads that made excellent extemporised defensive positions. Where the guns were effective, the German infantry would provide only perfunctory resistance, but in its absence, they would resist far more stoutly.

The Corps set a high tempo to take advantage of both the offensive's momentum and the supposed disruption of the German's defensive arrangements. A staggered set of attacks that reduced their effectiveness resulted. The fundamental issue was that despite the damage done to the enemy they still had two good divisions in strong positions. Dellmensingen had stitched together enough of a line with one fresh division and another relatively rested one to contest the advance. The firepower support for the attack was inadequate to overcome the defenders' advantages.

The Corps had made progress on the second day of the offensive but had not met its aggressive objectives. Its two primary attack divisions had committed all their brigades and failed to take the F-R Line. Currie now had a difficult decision. Should he pause to replace the assault divisions, relieve only the 2nd Division, or renew the offensive with the existing forces? All three alternatives had potentially negative consequences, so there was no obvious choice. Which he chose, and the outcome is next.

7

'A great importance was attached to its capture' Operations to Break the F-R Line, 28 August

It is impossible to overestimate the results achieved by the valour and leadership of this officer.

Victoria Cross Citation for Lieutenant Colonel W H Clarke-Kennedy[1]

A day of mixed success, 28 August featured planning and decisions that reflected poorly on almost every command level. Haig, Horne, Currie, Burstall, and Tremblay all blundered to different degrees resulting in a sharp repulse of the 2nd Division. This defeat disrupted the Corps' progress and delayed operations for days. The only senior officer to emerge with a burnished reputation was Lipsett, GOC 3rd Division. In a series of daring and clever manoeuvres, Lipsett's division performed superbly in smashing through its portion of the F-R Line, while the 2nd Division failed across its whole attack front crippling two brigades. Currie, Burstall, and Tremblay each had a key decision to make, and they chose badly.

Strategic Situation

With the Third Army confronting the Hindenburg Line on its left flank, Haig ordered it stood down. It was to wait until the Canadian and XVII Corps' turning movement weakened the Germans' grip.[2] Thus, it was imperative that the Canadians succeed. On the BEF's right wing, the Fourth Army continued to push back enemy rearguards. The Germans still held territory taken in the spring and were trading space for time. They were pivoting their line back on Quéant, the southern terminus of the D-Q Line. *OHL* was warning its armies it might be necessary to retire to the Hindenburg Line given the shortage of reserves.[3]

1 LAC: CWNS, VC Winners.
2 Edmonds, *Military Operations, 1918* 4, p.335.
3 *Der Weltkrieg* 14.1, p.581.

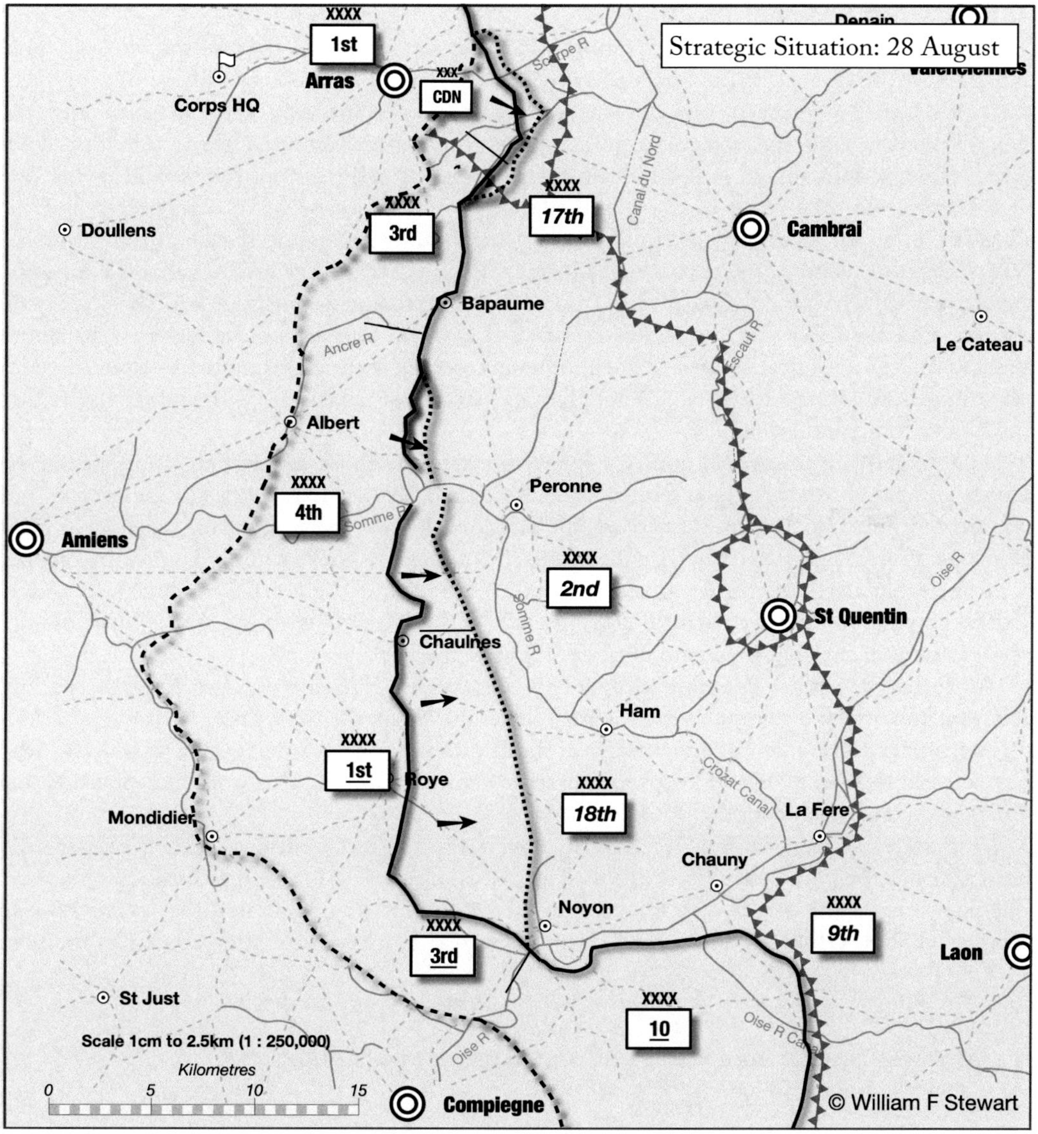

Map 20. Strategic situation 28 August depicts the French making large gains against a retreating enemy on the front of the French First and Third Armies. The British Fourth Army pushed back German rearguards as they fell back, while Haig had the British Third Army stand down to wait the success of the Canadians and its XVII Corps in clearing the Hindenburg Line. (Author's map)

Planning

There was an odd disjoint in the planning this day accompanied by multiple errors. Haig, Horne, and Currie met in the afternoon of 27 August and prepared the outline of a set-piece attack on the D-Q Line in one to two days' time.[4] Simultaneously, the Corps' ordered the two divisions to take that objective on 28 August. The British Official History called the First Army's instructions for 28 August 'curiously worded.'[5] It assigned objectives well to the rear of a set-piece to take place in two days. It was prudent to ready for contingencies, but the divisions' program, especially the 2nd's, were predicated on breaching the D-Q Line. Burstall was so eager to secure the line that he exhorted: 'The G.O.C. is very anxious that the Division capture the QUEANT-DROCOURT Line today.'[6] Contrast this with the 3rd Division's more realistic statement that the Corps wanted the F-R Line 'as a great importance was attached to its capture.'[7] As a result, the need to keep forces in reserve for the D-Q Line distorted Burstall's planning. Thus, there were three different battles planned on 28 August – the two divisions and the higher command levels.

Haig, in shifting the army boundary to the south-east without adding forces, dissipated the Corps' combat power across too wide a front. At almost 12 kilometres south of the Scarpe, this was far too much for two weakened assault divisions – these were defensive frontages.[8] Haig recognised somewhat belatedly that the Corps' front was too great. On 27 August, he ordered a corps headquarters to the Arras sector to take over part of the Corps' frontage.[9] The XXII Corps, however, did not arrive until 30 August.[10] With his army stretched then, Horne did not provide another division to Currie until the night of 29/30 August.[11]

Currie had a critical decision to make for 28 August. He could pause, replace the 2nd Division and attack, or employ the existing forces. He chose the last option. This was a serious misjudgement and condemned the troops of the 2nd Division to a hopeless task. Historians who have closely studied Arras 1918 agree.[12] Patrick Dennis claimed, 'this was the worst decision Currie would make during the 'Hundred Days'.'[13]

To understand the decision, we have to review the Corps' situation. First, the Corps did not carry out the planned relief of the 2nd and 3rd Divisions on the night of 27/28 August.[14] The plan was for the 4th British Division to relieve the 3rd Canadian and the 1st Division to replace the 2nd. GHQ, however, had mispositioned the British formation too far in the rear.

4 NLS: Haig Diary, 27 August 1918; LAC: Currie Diary, 27 August 1918.
5 Edmonds, *Military Operations, 1918* 4, p.337.
6 LAC: RG9 III-C-1 v3923, 11/2: Narrative of Operations of the 2nd Canadian Divisional Artillery Supporting the Attacks of by the 2nd and 1st Canadian Divisions in the Advance of the Canadian Corps from Arras in the General Direction of Cambrai, Aug. 26th. To Sept. 3rd. 1918, Inclusive.
7 LAC: 3rd Division WD, 3rd Division Report on Operations from Aug. 26th to Aug. 28th, 1918.
8 For instance, the defensive fronts of the 52nd and 57th British Divisions on 2 August were 6,400 and 6,600 metres. TNA: WO 153-458: First Army Deployment Map, 2 August 1918.
9 NLS: Haig Diary, 27 August 1918.
10 TNA: Cdn. Corps GS WD, OO No. 233, 29 August 1918 Canadian Corps.
11 TNA: First Army GS WD, First Army, G617, 29 August 1918.
12 Schreiber, *Shock Army*, p.76; Cook, *Shock Troops*, p.474; Dennis, *Reluctant Warriors*, p.98.
13 Dennis, 'Canadian Conscript', p.30.
14 LAC: 1st Divison W.D., 1st Division G.3-93/3, 26 August 1918.

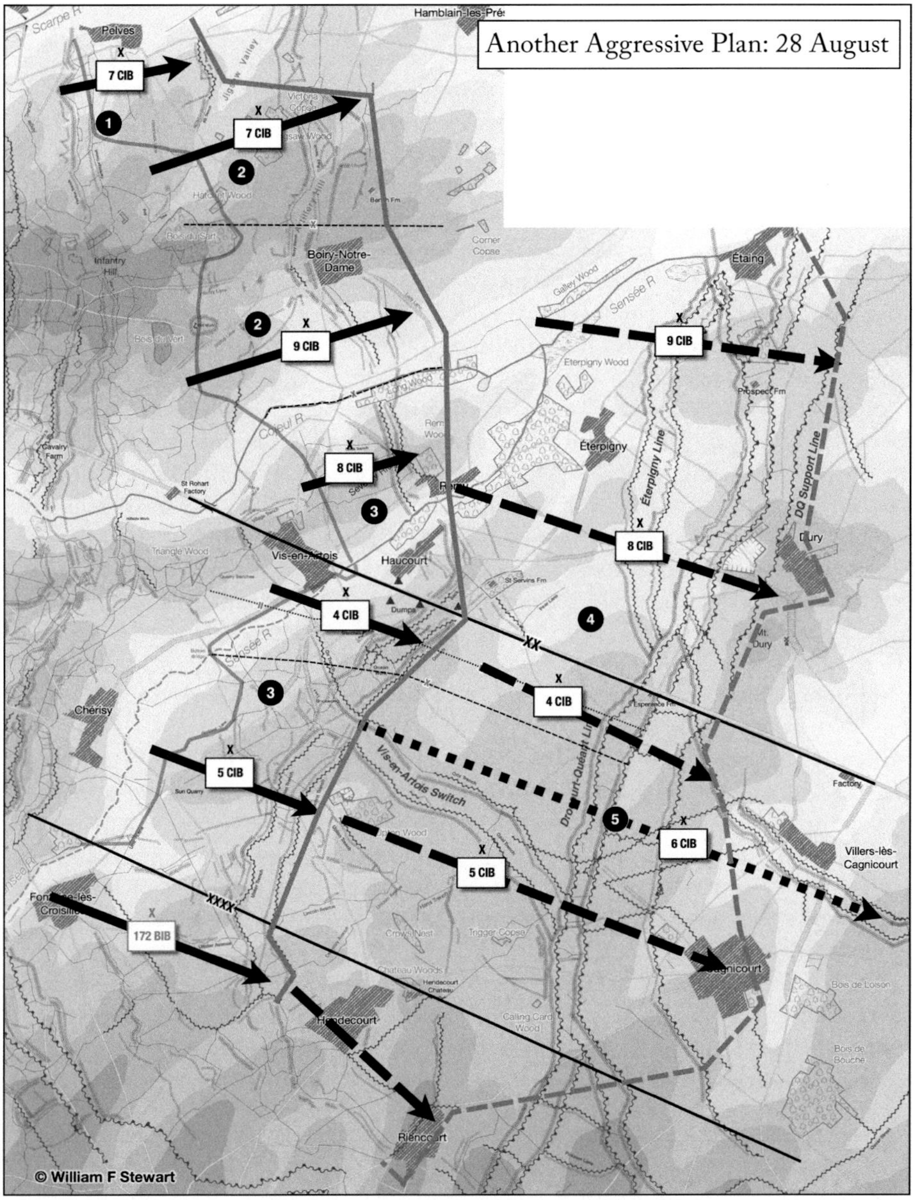

Map 21. The Canadian Corps again planned an aggressive set of objectives for the 2nd and 3rd Divisions:

1. The 49th Battalion would take Pelves and protect the 3rd Division’s flank in a dawn attack.
2. The 9th Brigade under the protection of all the division’s assigned artillery attacks with the 7th Brigade to break the F-R Line at 11:00 a.m.
3. At 12:30 p.m., the 8th, 4th, and 5th Brigades attack to capture the remaining portions of the F-R Line.
4. After a short pause, the 2nd and 3rd Divisions attack south-east to capture the D-Q Line with the 4th, 5th, 8th and 9th Brigades.
5. The 6th Brigade takes over the attack on the 2nd Division’s front. (Author’s map)

In GHQ reserve, it moved from Flanders to Villers au Bois about 15 kilometres north-west of Arras by noon 26 August.[15] Its infantry would have a 32-kilometre march to relieve the 3rd Division the next night. Given the congested roads and traffic control issues, this was too distant. The division's misplacement angered Haig, after he found out from its commander, Major General T G Matheson.[16] The First Army assigned it to the Corps at 7:30 p.m. on 26 August.[17] Shortly after this, Currie postponed the 3rd Division's relief by a day, based on a 4th British Division's warning order issued early next morning. The order stated that it would relieve the 3rd Division the night of 28/29 August – a 24-hour delay.[18] Matheson would have only sent it after discussions with the Corps. The 1st Division had arrived from Amiens and was in position to relieve the 2nd Division on the night of 27/28. Further, it was expecting to attack the D-Q Line on 28 August.[19]

The second consideration was what information Currie had on 27 August. Before going into another conference with Haig at 3:00 p.m., Currie knew the following. The initial reports were positive, but he likely knew the 3rd Division was encountering difficulties. With the lag in communications, it was unlikely he appreciated the problems the 2nd Division had beyond the Sensée. Further, the noon casualty estimate showed the 2nd Division in better condition than the 3rd. Thus, by the early afternoon, Currie and his staff had a sense of unit strengths. Currie saw the 3rd Division's infantry had suffered 1,425 losses with seven battalions losing over 150 men each.[20] The 2nd Division was apparently in much better shape with casualties of only 700 men. This report was misleading as most of the casualties sustained by the 2nd Division were in the afternoon. On the following day, the 2nd's casualty total had soared to 1,850 with eight battalions with at least 150 casualties.

The discussion at the conference focused on taking the D-Q Line. Haig's concern was not breaking the line, but its proper exploitation.[21] During the meeting there were conflicting reports flooding into the Corps that losses were heavy, but artillery statements had the 2nd Division taking the F-R Line and advancing beyond.[22] Currie got much of his near real-time information from the artillery channels, so he was likely still optimistic.[23] So, the negative reports did not affect the conference. This continued until he spoke with Bertram in the late afternoon and learned of the 2nd Division's failure.

Currie now had to decide what to do. He could follow his original plan codified in his policy for future operations. This entailed pausing before the major defensive systems, like the F-R Line, and preparing a set-piece attack with full artillery support.[24] He could relieve the 2nd Division with the 1st while keeping the 3rd in place. Both would attack on 28 August. Originally, the

15 TNA: GHQ GS WD, Major, GS to BGO, 8 August 1918; TNA: GHQ GS WD, LTC, GS to MGO, 23 August 1918; TNA: GHQ GS WD, 24 August 1918.
16 NLS: Haig Diary, 27 August 1918.
17 TNA: WO 95-1448-1/3: 4th British Division General Staff War Diary, 26 August 1918.
18 LAC: RG9 III-C-1 v3912, 40/1: 4th (British) Division Warning Order, 27 August 1918.
19 LAC: 1st Divison W.D., 1st Division G.3-93/3, 26 August 1918.
20 PPCLI, RCR, 4th CMR, 52nd, 58th, and 116th Battalions. LAC: MG30 E5 v2: Bovey Fonds, Estimated Casualties to Noon 26 August to 5 September 1918.
21 NLS: Haig Diary, 27 August 1918.
22 LAC: RA Canadian Corps Messages, 26 August 1918.
23 McGill: Colonel Crear [Crerar] Comments, 1934.
24 Dennis, *Reluctant Warriors*, pp.94-98.

1st expected to assault the D-Q Line that day, so it was possible for it to do so for the nearer F-R Line. Finally, he could continue the offensive with the existing forces. Each option had significant advantages and disadvantages. Pausing meant losing the offensive's momentum, risking Haig's ire at the slow progress, and allowing the Germans time to recover. Currie was under considerable pressure from Haig directly and through Horne to get to Cambrai rapidly. As discussed earlier, he was still dealing with the tensions from the spring and Haig's evident displeasure with the Canadians' attitude. There was likely a residual effect even after the success at Amiens. The C-in-C visited the Corps headquarters three times in four days to impress his will on Currie. Pausing was sure to upset him. The pause would lose the momentum the Corps had built up, but in reality, there was no momentum left. The Germans had stopped both divisions and decisively so before the F-R Line. With a lull, however, the Corps could arrange a fully coordinated set-piece attack with a proper barrage. There is little doubt that it would have succeeded.

A partial relief carried the risk that the 1st Division could not attack concurrently with Lipsett's, leaving it to face the full fury of the defences. Even if the 1st attacked, it would require a challenging relief of the 2nd Division and hasty preparations. Relieving a division meant shuffling up to 30,000 personnel and 9,000 horses from the two divisions. Replacement also risked these engagements wearing out the 1st Division prematurely. Currie wanted to preserve his best division for the D-Q Line. This approach had the advantage of adding impetus by changing a wrecked formation with a fresh division. He rejected this option as he thought it 'undesirable' to employ a fresh division alongside a tired one.[25] This was not a convincing argument.

Continuing the attack with the existing formations meant there was no disruption from a relief, answered Haig's pressure, and was the easiest option to implement. The 2nd Division was operating with critical handicaps, however, which should have been evident to Currie and Burstall. Its infantry was exhausted, bled out, and disorganised. With no tanks or effective artillery support, it was doubtful it could take on the strong F-R Line. It was clearly too weak to attack such a strong position without equally strong support.[26]

Currie decided to continue with the existing forces based on three considerations. First, he was under considerable pressure to advance. Currie and Haig operated under the flawed conceit that the situation was like Amiens with a broken enemy unable to respond to a high-tempo attack. Second, the Corps' focus appears to be on the looming attack on the D-Q Line. The Corps ceded battle control to the divisions with little oversight. Things were happening too fast for Currie and his staff to manage the process and prepare a major set-piece attack as well. Finally, Burstall's determination to keep attacking, please Haig, and his ebullient mood likely influenced the Corps commander. There was, however, significant evidence available to Currie that not all was well with the 2nd Division. Experience with the German ability to recover and the difficulty of breaking organised defences should have given Currie pause.

Another error was the two divisions were to advance in divergent directions, with the 3rd striking north-east while the 2nd pushed south-east. This created the situation where enfilade fire from Haucourt and St. Servins Farm would strike the open flank of the 4th Brigade. The

25 Kemp, *Report of the Ministry*, p.149.
26 Cook, *Shock Troops*, p.474.

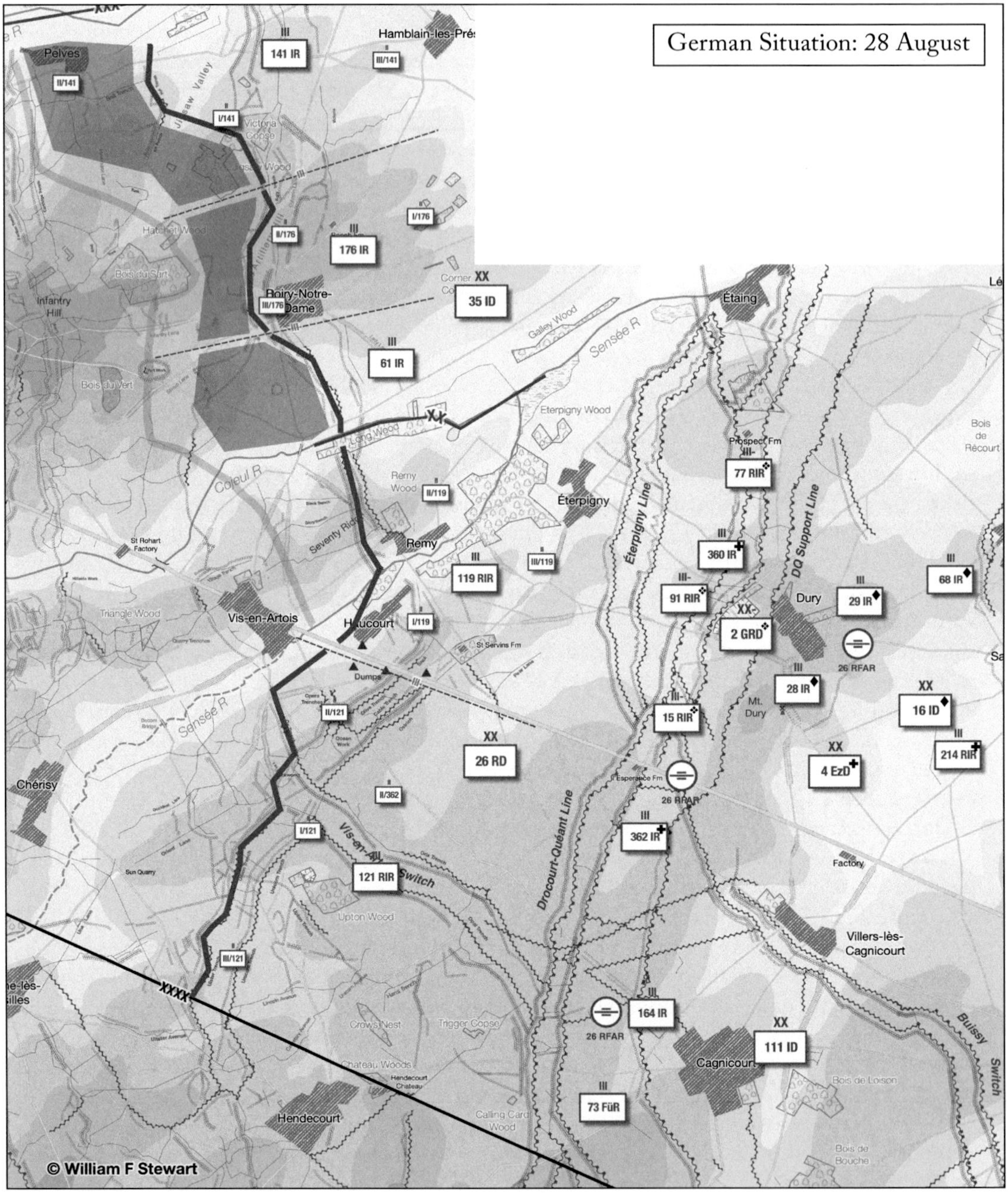

Map 22. The German situation with the tired *26th RD* and *35th ID* holding the line for another day but backstopped by significant reserves deployed in the D-Q Line. Any hope of a major breakout by the Canadian Corps was illusory. (Author's map)

26th RD took advantage of this to strike the open wing of the 4th Brigade during the battle. There was also a risk of a riposte by the reserves holding the D-Q Line. There were three divisions there – *4th EzD*, *2nd GRD*, and *16th ID*. This was a case where the Corps needed to coordinate the divisions' operations but did not.

Germans

The *II Bavarian Korps* could look at the situation with some satisfaction. While it had lost ground and suffered casualties the previous day, it had decisively repulsed the Canadian attack on the F-R Line. It had substantial reserves available, and the two forward divisions while tired had performed well. The *26th RD* still faced the 2nd Division. On its left, the *121st RIR* continued to defend with all three of its battalions in the line and on the right, the *119th RIR*. Dellmensingen reinforced it with two battalions of the *362nd IR* and the artillery of the *39th ID* and *2nd GRD*.[27]

The *35th ID* continued to battle the 3rd Division with all three of its regiments in line. The *61st IR* held the line from the Cojeul to south of Boiry-Notre-Dame, the *171st IR* held from the *61st* north to Hatchet Wood, with the *141st IR* responsible from Hatchet Wood to Pelves. Each regiment had one battalion in reserve, but there was no nearby *Eingreifdivision*. The *44th FAR* reinforced its artillery component.[28] Exhausted after two days of intense combat, the division was weak. The *176th IR* comprised only 27 officers and 711 other ranks or the equivalent of the trench strength of a battalion. Likely the *61st IR* was even in worse shape after getting mauled in its counterattack on 26 August and defeat on 27 August.[29]

Positioned in the D-Q Line, the *II Bavarian Korps* had four divisions backstopping the main front. The weakened *2nd GRD*, the strong *16th ID*, and the *4th EzD* defended the D-Q Line. Overnight, the *111th ID* had arrived with two regiments positioned near Cagnicourt. Its *76th IR* served against the Third Army south of the Corps' boundary.[30] The division had suffered heavily in fighting the Third Army near Bapaume, and its *73rd Füsilier Regiment* (*FüR*) consisted of two weak battalions.[31] Overall, the strength of German forces defending these positions made any Canadian success in taking it highly unlikely. During the evening of 27 August, the *II Bavarian Korps* ordered the *16th ID* to move from south of Douai to the D-Q Line. It was to act as an *Eingreifdivision* north of the Arras-Cambrai road, but was quite distant from the *35th ID*'s sector.[32] Units were piling up near the D-Q Line as von Dellmensingen broke up formation

27 Stühmke, *26th Reserve Division* II, pp.62-64.

28 Stenger, *Geschichte F.A.R. Nr. 44*, p.386; Schulemann, *I.R. Nr. 141*, p.392; Preusser, *Nr. 176 Im Weltkrieg*, p.277.

29 Unfortunately, the *61st IR* did not produce a regimental history.

30 Herbert v. Sydow, *Das Infanterie-Regiment Hamburg (2. Hanseatisches) Nr. 76 im Weltkriege 1914/1918* (Berlin: Gerhard Stalling, 1922), pp.194-198.

31 Ernst Jünger, famous for his book *Storm of Steel,* served in the regiment. Max v. Szczepanski, *Erinnerungsblätter Aus Der Geschichte Des Füsilier-Regiments Generalfeldmarschall Prinz Albrecht Von Preußen (Hann.) Nr. 73 Während Des Weltkrieges 1914-1918* (Berlin: Druck und Verlag von Gerhard Stalling, 1923), pp.150-151.

32 Paul Münstermann and Robert Begau, *Infanterie-Regiments Von Goeben (2. Rhein.) Nr. 28 im Weltkrieg 1914-1918* (Monchen Gladbach: Buch- und Kunstdruckerei Küppers and Knoben, 1932), p.234.

integrity to garrison the defences. The *91st RIR* complained there were five other regiments between it and the rest of the *2nd GRD*.[33]

XVII Corps

On the Corps' southern flank, there was a testy clash between the British and the Canadians regarding unit locations. On 27/28 August, the XVII Corps replaced the exhausted 52nd Division with the 57th. There were, however, British battalions deployed in the Canadian sector resulting from the boundary confusion. Eager for relief, the 52nd made a pointed query to the 2nd Division when Canadian troops would replace these units. There were a series of messages between the two divisions and the 5th Brigade, with the 5th Brigade adamant that the British did not know where their units were. The 5th's brigade-major on the strength of his tour of the front was obdurate that the 5th was in the correct position. He reported on the 7th Royal Scots headquarters that 'I am not impressed by their knowledge of the situation.'[34] Eventually, the 57th took over the front and relieved these wayward units.[35] Confusion and testiness were not uncommon across boundaries, but the extent of this ill-feeling was more than normal. This suggests the 52nd Division, despite its good work in pushing down the Hindenburg Line, had not completely adjusted to the challenge of Western Front fighting having arrived from Palestine.

The 57th Division had more success than the 2nd Division this day. The British territorials reached the outskirts of Hendecourt, and it used just two battalions of its 172nd Brigade on a 2,000 metre front. It had the advantage of six FA brigades with a density of 18.5 metres per 18-pounder for its barrage, almost twice the 2nd Division's concentration. The brigade attacked with the 2nd Division and reached the first objective west of Hendecourt. Small parties of its 2/4th South Lancashire Regiment even entered Hendecourt. In doing so they forced the *III/121st RIR* to throw back its right flank to Union Avenue.[36] This created a vulnerability that the attackers could exploit.[37]

2nd Division Suffers

Burstall also blundered with operations on 28 August. The 2nd Division's tasks were to advance 1,500 metres on a 3.7 kilometre front and take the heavily-wired F-R Line. Then after a 30-minute pause, it would push 4.5 kilometres to break the D-Q Line. Its resources were two exhausted, weakened brigades and a feeble artillery barrage for the first phase. The weather for the attack was dull with showers that restricted RAF operations.[38] Thus, it had a difficult mission, and Burstall had three choices. He could, as Patrick Dennis strongly argues,

33 Kümmel, *Res.Inf.Regt. Nr. 91*, p.422.
34 LAC: 5th Brigade W.D., 5 Brigade B.M. 130, 28 August 1918.
35 LAC: 2nd Division GS WD, 28 September 1918.
36 Hauptstaatsarchiv Stuttgart: Visher Höhe.
37 TNA: 57th Division GS WD, 57th Division Narrative of Operations August 20th to September 7th 1918; Edmonds, *Military Operations, 1918* 4, pp.335-336; Franz Theodor Poland, *Das Kgl. Sächs. Reserve-Infanterie-Regiment Nr. 103* (Dresden: Wilhelm und Bertha v. Baensch Stiftung, 1922), p.142.
38 LAC: 3rd Division WD, 28 August 1918.

demand Currie keep to his policy of pausing before attacking a major defensive position like the F-R Line.[39] Ample cause existed to request more time based on the division's circumstances. Alternately, Burstall could use the relatively fresh 6th Brigade or continue the engagement with the existing forces.

According to the commander of the 1st Division, Burstall on 28 August was in a 'jubilant mood' expecting great results.[40] That strongly indicates he overestimated his formation's capability and underestimated enemy resistance. He had earlier promised Haig that he would be aggressive 'regardless of what Currie might feel.'[41] Thus, he would not ask for a delay. Tim Cook suggested traffic congestion prevented replacing the 5th Brigade with the 6th in time.[42] If true, the division again poorly positioned its reserves. Two battalions of the 6th Brigade were only two kilometres behind the 5th Brigade, so the division had over 15 hours to replace the 5th Brigade in time for the attack. There was ample time.[43] Finally, he could use the forces already in line, and he chose that alternative. The reason Burstall gave was that he wanted to keep the 6th Brigade unengaged for breaking the D-Q Line.[44] With a misplaced confidence that the Germans were on the run and in the strength of his units, Burstall plunged ahead. All of which was an indictment of his judgement in open warfare conditions.

The field artillery supporting the attack comprised seven FA brigades for the 12:30 p.m. start time. They would fire a barrage with a concentration of just 30 metres per gun with four minutes per 100 metre lift and without smoke. This was a brisk pace indicating the division expected a rapid advance. Only air-recuperator guns could reach the distant second objective, so the artillery support would be even thinner there.[45] Two HA brigades would bombard the F-R Line from 9:00 a.m. and then join the barrage. They would lift with the field artillery, but with a 600 metre safety zone, they would only briefly fire on the F-R Line.[46] Overall, the artillery support was inadequate for the fortifications facing the 2nd Division. For more, see Map 7.4 2nd Division Repelled: 28 August in the colour map booklet.

Initial reports were of mixed success. Rennie believed the brigade was fighting for Olive Trench, while Tremblay reported his brigade was doing well. Based on this, the division reported that it was in the F-R Line in the centre and likely on the left. In response, Burstall directed the 6th to cross the Sensée to be ready for further advances. A few minutes later, the 57th Division stated it had its first objective halfway to the F-R Line. Thus, the 2nd Division's right flank was at least partially protected. Then, the front reports turned negative. The 4th Brigade got stuck in front of Olive Trench and was getting hit hard and needed a fresh battalion to restart the advance. On Tremblay's front, the 26th and 24th Battalions were fighting in or just before the F-R Line, but ominously, there was no report from the 22nd. Tremblay was arranging with the artillery to bring back the barrage – a sure sign of a faltering attack. Finally, Bell reported the Germans had blocked the offensive, and that he doubted his brigade could restore the situation.

39 Dennis, *Reluctant Warriors*, p.94.
40 Macdonell, 'Old Red Patch 1', p.391.
41 NLS: Haig Diary, 25 August.
42 Cook, *Shock Troops*, p.473; LAC: 2nd Division Narrative.
43 LAC: 2nd Division GS WD, 27 August 1918; LAC: 6th Brigade Narrative.
44 LAC: 2nd Division Narrative.
45 LAC: 6th Brigade WD, 6th Brigade M28/3, 28 August 1918.
46 LAC: 2nd CDA Narrative; LAC: 2nd CRA War Diary, OO No. 208 by C.R.A., 2nd Canadian Division, 27 August 1918.

By 4:35 p.m., Tremblay interpreted scattered reports to mean the brigade held Union and Ulster Trenches – the first of the F-R Line trenches and the second line – Unicorn. Bertram instructed him to consolidate the first trenches, and he would get another battalion to help take Unicorn. The 6th Brigade sent the 28th Battalion deployed west of Chérisy to restore momentum and the 31st Battalion to the 4th Brigade.[47] Shortly after, Rennie tried to break the deadlock in front of Olive Trench by requesting a new intense artillery barrage and later tanks from the division. The answer was no. Instead, based on Tremblay's supposed success, the division would arrange an attack from the south – the 5th Brigade's sector. Rennie tried a further attack at 6:00 p.m., along with artillery support. It failed. A plan to employ the 31st Battalion with a bombardment by 4.5-inch and 6-inch howitzers to take Olive Trench foundered when the brigade learned the enemy still held a vital flanking position – the Brickworks. The result was neither brigade used the 6th Brigade battalions – supposedly because of ammunition shortages.[48] More likely the reason was committing these units would only increase the casualty list to no benefit.

Shortly before 8:00 p.m., the Germans hit the exposed left flank of the 4th Brigade from Haucourt. They drove back the exhausted 18th and 20th Battalions. They could retain only a small bridgehead pivoting on the sunken road west of the Opera Trenches and then back to Bottom Bridge. Thus, the brigade had made only a minor gain at a bitterly high cost.[49] The division into the evening believed it held Union and Ulster Trenches with posts in Unicorn, but the situation was obscure late into the night.[50] In reality, the division's position was much worse than it imagined.

5th Brigade: Costly Failure

The 5th Brigade received its attack orders early in the morning. Essentially, the plan was unchanged with the same units, same boundaries, and same two objectives – the F-R and D-Q Lines. The only exception being the addition of the weak barrage. In another blunder, Tremblay left the same three battalions in place. There are four explanations for his choice to continue to use the cut-up 22nd Battalion. First, Tremblay as its long-standing commander thought it could handle the strain. Second, possibly he was unaware of its weakness given the heavy leadership losses. Third, he could only replace one battalion, so he may have feared the appearance of favouritism if he relieved it. Especially, as he was one of the few senior French-Canadian officers in the PF and the 22nd was the Corps' only francophone battalion. Finally, given the weak state of the 25th Battalion and that its colonel was untested and ill, he thought the 22nd was a better choice.[51] The 25th had a new CO, Lieutenant Colonel F P Day (37), who would only command it briefly before illness caused his evacuation to England. He did not appear to have any active service experience, so Tremblay was unlikely to rely on an inexperienced CO with health issues. Tremblay explained he wanted to keep the 25th fresh to support the attack and wanted to shield

47 LAC: 6th Brigade WD, 28 August 1918.
48 LAC: 6th Brigade WD, 28 August 1918; LAC: 6th Brigade Narrative.
49 LAC: 2nd Division GS WD, 28 August 1918.
50 Macdonell, 'Old Red Patch 1'.
51 LAC: RG9 III-D-3 v4933: 25th Battalion War Diary, 25 August 1918.

it from German artillery. Rather improbably, the brigade claimed the 22nd and 24th battalions were 'both anxious to continue the attack.'[52]

Initially, the reports were positive, with flares signalling success seen at 2:20 p.m.[53] By 4:00 p.m., it was clear the 24th was in trouble. A wounded NCO reported that the 24th Battalion was stopped and taking heavy losses. The CO was seriously wounded but was directing operations and encouraging his troops from a shell hole. No manner of innovative or brilliant tactics would solve the problem of uncut wire. The artillery preparation was insufficient and the barrage too weak to neutralise the defenders. Despite this discouraging news, Tremblay reported again that he had units in the front-line trenches and posts in the second. Bertram directed the brigade to secure that first line. Tremblay reacted by ordering the 25th forward to take Unicorn, but he split it across the brigade front, so it had no impact.[54] It was not until the late afternoon that Captain J F MacKay, a brigade staff officer, toured the front to determine the situation. His assessment was dire. He could find no information on the 22nd Battalion and reported 'They are in a very bad shape.'[55] Contrary the prevailing optimism, the brigade did not hold the front-line trenches and it needed 'heavy reinforcements.' All units were incapable of further efforts but claimed positions far beyond what they held. After a personal reconnaissance close to midnight, the interim commanders of the 24th and 25th Battalions found three belts of uncut wire and the Germans in strength and alert in Union and Ulster Trenches.[56] Leadership losses, scattered troops, and dominating enemy fire meant a confused situation. So confused that the 3rd Brigade sent to relieve the 5th decided it was easier to take over the line held by the 29th along the Sensée. It then pushed out patrols to find the locations of the forward units, which took most of the night.

The 26th Battalion on the right faced intense machine gun and rifle fire as they rushed 1,000 metres up the bare slopes to Ulster Trench. Their two companies had never seen such concentrated masses of machine guns. The *III/121st RIR*'s machine gunners and snipers took a heavy toll of the battalion's command cadre. It was the unit's worst day of the war, with 12 officers and 244 other ranks cut down. Leadership losses contributed to the brigade's misunderstanding of the situation on its right. Among those lost was the CO, Lieutenant Colonel McKenzie, killed instantly as he crossed the Chérisy-Hendecourt road. The right-hand company briefly seized a lodgement in Ulster Trench, but without support the Germans drove it out.[57]

In the brigade's centre, the previous day's fighting had badly shaken the 24th Battalion's leadership, forcing considerable reorganisation. Fortunately, its commanding officer had the dynamism, charisma, and skill to ready it for another day of fighting. He would earn the Empire's highest accolade for courage – the Victoria Cross – for his inspired leadership. He

52 LAC: 5th Brigade W.D., 5th Brigade Narrative of Operations, August 19th to 29th 1918, 3 September 1918.
53 LAC: 5th Brigade W.D., 5th Brigade Narrative of Operations, August 19th to 29th 1918, 3 September 1918.
54 LAC: 29th Battalion War Diary, 28 August 1918.
55 LAC: 5th Brigade W.D., 5th Brigade S.C. 42, 28 August 1918.
56 LAC: 5th Brigade W.D., 5th Brigade OO No. 269, 28 August 1918; LAC: 5th Brigade W.D., 5th Brigade D1, 28 August 1918.
57 R.W. Gould and S.K. Smith, *The Story of the Fighting 26th*: St. John News Co., 1918), pp.275-279; LAC: RG9 III-D-3 4933: War Diary, 26th Battalion, Operations east of Arras, August 26th -29th Inclusive [1918] and A, B, C and D Company Reports.

led his battalion forward on 28 August but received a crippling bullet wound that fractured his lower leg early in the battle. Despite his pain and immobility, he encouraged his men and directed the battle from a shell hole. Seeing the futility of further attempts to advance, he ordered his men to consolidate. He refused evacuation for five hours despite his loss of blood and pain. As the citation read: 'It is impossible to overestimate the results achieved by the valour and leadership of this officer.'[58] Opposition was more intense than the previous day. German wire and machine gun fire stymied every attempt to reach the trenches. Small groups infiltrated in, but the defenders soon drove them out.[59] By the late afternoon, it had only 3 officers and 150 men trying to attack on a 950 metre front. Its losses were 9 officers and 152 other ranks on 28 August. During the two days it was in the line, the battalion lost 5 officers and the Regimental Sergeant-Major (RSM) killed, and 17 more officers wounded.

The 24th leadership losses were devastating and unsustainable. Comparable losses on the Somme quickly rendered battalions ineffective.[60] The challenge was two-fold. First, while there were replacement officers available, they lacked experience and training. Second, battalions could not so easily replace senior NCO's. There were no large-scale external sources for these vital leaders. Units developed them internally from junior NCOs. With so many casualties, the only supply was the depleted ranks of the junior NCOs. Thus, less experienced juniors replaced senior casualties, further draining the pool of capable junior NCOs. Another drain on quality personnel was the requirement to send potential officers to England for training and commissioning. For instance, the 50th Battalion had to send 11 NCOs on 21 August.[61] The Corps risked undermining its ability to employ advanced tactics. The blade was getting dull from over-use.

On the brigade's left, Major Georges Vanier found the 22nd Battalion in poor shape and scattered in isolated shell holes. He and Clarke-Kennedy formed a joint battalion headquarters as both battalions were short of leaders. The battalion attacked under a weak artillery barrage that did nothing to suppress the concentrated machine gun fire. It made little headway before losses stopped the advance. Vanier suffered a grave wound and lost his leg.[62] Officer losses were so great that the battalion's medical officer, Dr Albéric Marin, tore off his medical badges and took charge of a group of men. Only the quartermaster and the doctor survived uninjured from the officer corps. The 22nd had ceased to exist except as small parties of stalwart fighters but with no higher-level leadership.[63] Shortly before midnight, the temporary commander of the combined 24th and 22nd Battalions claimed he could find only 40 other ranks of the 22nd. Casualties of 193 all ranks, after the previous day's losses, brought the battalion down to its knees. The CWGC reported the battalion lost 124 men killed – the most of any battalion in the campaign.

The 25th was in support for the attack again. Tremblay tried to re-energise the attack with it but sent one company to each of the assault battalions. This was a curious decision, reinforcing

58 LAC: CWNS, VC Winners.
59 LAC: 24th Battalion W.D., 28 August 1918; Fetherstonhaugh, *24th Battalion*, pp.240-244.
60 Stewart, *Neglected Campaign*, pp.297-298.
61 LAC: RG9 III-D-3 v4941: 50th Battalion War Diary, 21 August 1918.
62 LAC: 5th Brigade W.D., 5th Brigade D4, 28 August 1918; Speaight, *Vanier: Soldier, Diplomat and Governor General: A Biography*, pp.77-78; LAC: 22nd Bn. WD, 28 August 1918.
63 Fetherstonhaugh, *24th Battalion*, p.243.

Major Georges Vanier took over the 22nd Battalion and found in poor shape. He would later become the first French Canadian Governor General. (Canada. Dept. of National Defence/Library and Archives Canada/ PA-002777)

the notion that Tremblay had little confidence in the battalion commander. The best way to influence the battle was to commit fresh troops at a key point rather than reinforcing the failures.[64] They accomplished little.[65]

Tremblay's first command from the start of the battle had not gone well. He was not responsible for the optimistic planning on 27 August, but he was culpable in two respects for 28 August. There is no evidence he raised any objections to the second day's attack. Supported by only a weak artillery barrage, the battered brigade would have little chance of success. An experienced commander, like Tremblay, would have known this. Possibly given his recent promotion, he was unwilling to rock the boat. Secondly, his decision to rely on the broken 22nd Battalion was a mistake. Its failure left the flanks of both the 4th Brigade and 24th Battalions exposed to German fire. Tremblay should have realised the 22nd was at the end of its tether and needed replacement.

4th Brigade: More Failure

On the division's left, the 4th Brigade in its third day of fighting was to capture the F-R Line – 1,700 metres away. Then, it would storm the D-Q Line – a further 3,000 metres. Owing to

64 Robert N. Clements and B. D. Tennyson, *Merry Hell: The Story of the 25th Battalion (Nova Scotia Regiment), Canadian Expeditionary Force 1914-1919* (Toronto: University of Toronto Press, 2013), p.296.

65 LAC: 25th Bn. W.D., Company Narrative A, B, and C Companies 25th Battalion From Aug. 25th to Aug. 29th, 1918.

Brigadier General Robert Rennie was the original commander of the 4th Brigade so by Arras 1918 was an experienced leader. (Courtesy of John Stephens, Curator, The Queen's Own Rifles of Canada Regimental Museum)

the brigade's weak state, Burstall reduced its front at the F-R Line to only 700 metres. It would attack on a two-battalion front with the 21st on the right and 20th on the left. The 19th and 18th Battalions would follow in close support. With units badly debilitated, Rennie committed all his battalions and the batmen and cooks.[66] The condition of the formation plainly worried him as shortly after the advance began, he told the division he was 'very anxious' for a rapid relief.[67]

It faced a complex system of three heavily-wired trenches with the last two on a reverse slope. There were up to seven different barbed wire belts to penetrate. The 21st had an especially difficult task as it had to overrun two outerworks first and then Ocean Work, a strongly fortified set of trenches. To add to the difficulty, the divergent advance by the 3rd Division would expose the 4th Brigade's flank.

A torrent of machine gun and artillery fire slashed the troops as they crossed the Sensée. They quickly overran Ox Trench, but the two battalions could not breach the thick wire before the main trenches. Its troops faced the infantrymen's nightmare of an advance up a bare slope against an unsuppressed enemy protected by thick uncut wire. Although parties entered Opera and Ocean Work, they could not hold on when they ran out of hand grenades. The brigade had the barrage restarted several times, but it had no effect. Adding to the misery, the 22nd's

66 LAC: 4th Brigade War Diary, Narrative of Operations South of Scarpe, 26, 27, and 28 August, 1918.
67 LAC: 2nd Division GS WD, 28 August 1918.

challenges meant enfilade fire from Ox Trench in the 5th Brigade's sector assailed them as well. Casualties and disorganisation were severe, and there were no palliatives available. Rennie called for tanks, but none were available.

The 21st Battalion on the brigade's right was so weak it used three companies to attack a 350 metre front. It stalled in front of the thick wire although small parties entered Olive Trench. The unit report cited the fatigued condition and low strength of the companies as well as the poor artillery preparation for failure.[68] The battle hit the battalion's leadership hard with only three-company officers left standing. Over the three days of fighting it suffered 55 percent losses, including 16 officers and 331 other ranks.[69] The 19th Battalion in support got sucked into the engagement. Leadership casualties in officers and senior NCOs were so severe that Corporal Deward Barnes led two exhausted platoons. The battalion lost 13 officers and 272 other ranks in the battle.[70]

The 20th Battalion on the left had a 350 metre front and attacked with two companies. German artillery fire was so severe that the battalion lost 90 percent of its runners in trying to relay information across the Sensée. 'The enemy's barrage and Machine Gun fire was severe and intense at all times,' stated the battalion report.[71] To add to the misery, German ammunition dumps in the area kept exploding. This forced the troops to fall back. Attempts to use section rushes to advance resulted in high losses. Short of an effective barrage, there was little a battalion could do once it had lost its momentum and had scattered into shell holes.[72] The battalion's officer corps took a beating with 14 out of the 24 officers killed, wounded, or gassed. Estimated casualties for the campaign were 14 officers and 423 other ranks. The battalion comprised just 8 officers and 120 men and 4 serviceable Lewis Guns at the end – its establishment was 36. In effect, what was happening to German regiments was occurring to Canadian battalions with the difference the Canadians had sufficient replacements. Next day, the 20th was back to strength in Lewis Guns.[73] In support of the 20th Battalion, the 18th got involved in the battle and suffered surprisingly heavy losses of 6 officers and 80 men. The battalion referred succinctly to the problem as, 'machine gun nests and wire in the German line being equally heavy.'[74]

The eventual line held ran from Bottom Bridge on the brigade's right flank to a sunken road just short of the Opera Trenches and then refused back to Vis-en-Artois. Elements of the *121st RIR* and *119th RIR* hit the brigade's exposed flanks in the evening and cleared out the attackers from the area close to the F-R Line.[75] Overnight, the Germans took advantage of the fact the

68 LAC: 21st Bn. WD, Report on 21st Canadian Battalion Operations of August 26-27-28 [1918].
69 LAC: 21st Bn. WD, Report on 21st Canadian Battalion Operations of August 26-27-28 [1918] and 21st Canadian Battalion OO No. 211, 28 August 1918; Nichol, *Ordinary Heroes*, pp.192-194.
70 Cane, *It Made You Think of Home*, p.245; LAC: CWNS Millen to Rennie; LAC: 19th Battalion War Diary, Operations of the 19th Canadian Battalion August 25th-29th 1918; Campbell, *It Can't Last Forever*, pp.434-436.
71 LAC: 20th Battalion Report.
72 Corrigall, *Twentieth Canadian Battalion*, p.242.
73 LAC: 20th Battalion War Diary, 20th Battalion OO No. 199, 28 August 1918; LAC: 20th Battalion War Diary, 28 and 31 August 1918; LAC: 20th Battalion Report; Corrigall, *Twentieth Canadian Battalion*, pp.241-243.
74 Dennis, 'Canadian Conscript', p.31; LAC: 18th Battalion War Diary, OO 352, 28 August 1918 and 28 August 1918 Entry; LAC: RG9 III-D-2 v4802, 138: CWNS J.H. Bell to Duguid, 7 September 1919.
75 Holtz, *Reserve-Infanterie-Regiment Nr. 121*, p.75; Gerster, *RIR Nr. 119*, p.119.

brigade occupied a low-lying area and flooded it with gas. This forced the tired men to wear their gas masks and thus added to their afflictions.[76]

26th Reserve Division Account

According to the division's history written by its last commander, it was only now, after the capture of several Canadians and the recovery of bodies, that they recognised the Corps' presence.[77] Based on the diary of the corps commander and the division's history, German Intelligence poorly appreciated what the *II Bavarian Korps* faced. Dellmensingen on 30 August believed his corps was fighting six divisions in the Canadian Corps – the four Canadian and the 4th and 15th British Divisions.[78] Only the 4th British and 1st Canadian Divisions were in the line on that date, with the 4th Canadian moving up.

The *121st RIR* regarded its repulse of the 4th and 5th Brigades as a glorious day in the regiment's history. It reported that the Canadians only entered the *Vorfeld* in a couple of locations, and it drove them out. They correctly diagnosed that they had badly damaged the 2nd Division.[79] Contemporary reports of *II/121st RIR* credited their success to the prompt and effective fire of their light and heavy machine guns. At 8:30 p.m., the battalion commander reported the Canadian losses were 'enormous', while his battalion's were light. He was confident he could hold against any further attacks in his strong position. His only two complaints were the urgent need for machine gun ammunition and for the artillery to stop shooting short.[80] These reports highlight how the 2nd Division failed to create the conditions for a successful attack.

3rd Division: Triumph

Currie was insistent that the 3rd Division take the F-R Line.[81] The 3rd had the same liabilities as did the 2nd Division, but with a longer front of 7,800 metres. It too was exhausted, with many units disorganised and having suffered substantial casualties. Moreover, its battalions were scattered after the complex fighting. A broad front attack would likely fail as the gunnery support was too weak to neutralise the Germans. Instead, Lipsett decided to make two risky sequential narrow-front assaults, each supported by the divisional artillery. He contended the 'Germans did not seem sufficiently well organised to concentrate their Artillery against it effectively.'[82] If he were right, the division would strike under a dense barrage and punch its way through the defences. If wrong, the assault would fall apart under concentrated German machine gun and artillery fire. With the wide sector, Lipsett committed every battalion, leaving

76 LAC: 4th Brigade War Diary, Narrative of Operations South of Scarpe, 26, 27, and 28 August, 1918.
77 Stühmke, *26th Reserve Division* II, pp.62-64.; Gerster, *RIR Nr. 119*, p.120.
78 Bundesarchiv, Freiburg: Feldzug 1918, 30 August 1918.
79 Holtz, *Reserve-Infanterie-Regiment Nr. 121*, p.75.
80 Hauptstaatsarchiv Stuttgart: M109 Bü49 2009: II/121 RIR Bericht Über Die Gefechts Des Batls. Vom 27.-30.9.18.
81 LAC: 3rd Division WD, 3rd Division Report on Operations from Aug. 26th to Aug. 28th, 1918.
82 LAC: 3rd Division WD, 3rd Division Report on Operations from Aug. 26th to Aug. 28th, 1918.

no reserves. It would be an all-or-nothing action. For more, see Map 7.5 3rd Division Breaks the F-R Line: 28 August in the colour map booklet.

The division's mission was to take the F-R Line and then the D-Q Line from Étaing south to the Arras-Cambrai road. Its initial objective required a push of 1,200 to 2,000 metres and the second a further 4,000 to 4,500 metres and a realignment of its advance from north-east to east. Lipsett in the afternoon of 27 August assigned each brigade its own sector with the 8th on the right, the 9th in the centre, and the 7th on the left. As an early step in the planning, the commanders of the 8th and 9th Brigades and the GSO 1, Hore-Ruthven, elected to spare exhausted units a further march. Thus, the 43rd Battalion remained with the 8th Brigade and 4th CMR with the 9th.[83]

Lipsett's plan, issued at 3:00 a.m., specified three separate attacks.[84] The 7th Brigade's 49th Battalion would seal the division's left flank by capturing Pelves and trenches north of Jigsaw Woods at 5:00 a.m. Six hours later, the 9th Brigade would strike south of Boiry-Notre-Dame, then wheel and take the village from the south supported by a brief but concentrated barrage. Simultaneously, the 7th Brigade would attack north of Boiry and take Jigsaw Wood, but without gunnery support. At 12:30 p.m., the 8th Brigade supported by another short but intense barrage would capture the line between the Cojeul and Sensée Rivers, including Seventy Ridge, Remy, Remy Wood, and St. Servins Farm.

The division decentralised artillery support with the group commanders coordinating the two barrages with the brigade commanders.[85] The first would last for 30 minutes on a front of 1,000 metres with a density of under 10 metres per 18-pounder. This was three times more than the 2nd Division, and it used smoke. The second would fire for 26 minutes on a 1,200 metre front with a concentration of 22 metres per gun, again with smoke. Thus, owing to Lipsett's daring decision, the artillery support was markedly superior to that afforded Burstall's division. The barrage could not go deeper because of range limitations.[86] The 51st Division had not eliminated German observation from the north, so the FA brigades could not move beyond Monchy. As it was, the 10th CFA lost 20 men and 21 animals to German counter-battery fire from 26 to 31 August.[87] During the battle, the enemy artillery shelling was heavy but slackened soon because of ammunition shortages and counter-battery fire.[88] Lipsett was correct that the *35th ID* could not concentrate on the separate attacks. Only the batteries dedicated to a front-line regiment would support, because the signals were in poor shape and this made coordination impossible.[89]

To eliminate the flanking fire that bedevilled the PPCLI on 26 August, the 7th Brigade's 49th Battalion would capture Pelves starting at 5:00 a.m.[90] It had field artillery support for ninety minutes and the heavies would pound Pelves for 30 minutes from the 5:00 a.m. start time. The Germans were not holding the town in strength but as a forward zone, especially

83 LAC: RG9 III-D-3 v4894: War Diary, 8th Brigade, 27 August 1918.
84 LAC: RG9 III-C-1 v3855, 75/9: 3rd Division G.80/1, 28 August 1918.
85 LAC: 3rd CDA WD, OO 198-19, 28 August 1918.
86 LAC: 3rd CDA WD, 3rd CDA, G.-48, 28 August 1918; LAC: RG9 III-D-3 v4970: 9th CFA War Diary, 28 August 1918.
87 LAC: RG9 III-D-3 v4971: 10th CFA War Diary, 10th CFA Battle of Arras August 26th to September 1918.
88 LAC: GOCRA WD, 28 August 1918.
89 Lothar Gitterman, *F.A.R. Nr. 71*, pp.305-306.
90 LAC: RG9 III-C-3 v4155, 10/6: 7th Brigade OO No.168, 27 August 1918.

as the 51st's advance north of the river meant it was untenable. The 49th pushed north along Cartridge Trench to reach the village. By doing so its advance was slow, but it minimised casualties. It cleared the village after an hour and a half. Then, it advanced along Belt Trench in a classic trench warfare operation, with the C/49th leading the charge. The company gained 11 recommendations for awards for its performance. It had a fierce fight for the German main defensive line as it bombed (using grenades) – it no longer had any artillery support. This fight took another four hours but ensured the defenders could not interfere with the 11:00 a.m. assault. In response to the loss of the *HWL*, the *141st IR* launched a counterattack, but it failed. The relatively low number of prisoners suggests that the battalion pushed the Germans back more than overran them. The battalion estimated its losses at 5 officers and 60 other ranks. It had fought effectively, with its report stating: 'The morale and tone never better in the history of the Battalion.'[91]

9th Brigade

The 9th Brigade made the next attack at 11:00 a.m. It was to take Boiry-Notre-Dame and Artillery Hill as the first objective. Its second was to capture the D-Q Line as far as north as Étaing. The brigade chose a clever approach of outflanking Boiry-Notre-Dame instead of taking it head on. Possibly contact patrols identified the boundary between the *176th* and *61st IR*s, and the brigade used this to focus on the battered *61st*. The brigade would punch through the F-R Line south of Boiry and advance to Lady Lane. This entailed a 2,400 metre gain. After outflanking Boiry, the 58th would wheel north and strike the village's defenders in the flank. The barrage, while brief at 30 minutes, was far stronger than the previous day's barrages, and it played an important role in the overrunning of the German defences.[92]

The 4th CMR on the right would strike east and capture Lady Lane and hold a defensive flank until the attack by the 8th Brigade. It had a long approach march of six kilometres and shelling delayed the two assault companies. The support company commanders, showing great initiative, committed their units, instead. Despite being 800 metres from the start line, they caught up to the barrage, and avoided some of the strong initial German artillery counter-barrage. The support companies smashed the *61st IR* and consolidated a line along Lady Lane by late afternoon. It was so successful that the neighbouring German regiment complained of having to rally fleeing *61st* troops.[93] The advance stopped at Lady Lane as heavy machine gun and artillery fire made a further advance hazardous. The 52nd CFA effectively responded to calls for fire support. This was an instance when an assigned mobile battery worked well. The battalion claimed at least 60 prisoners, but its losses were heavy at 12 officers and 154 other ranks. The

91 LAC: 7th Brigade Report; LAC: 49th Battalion WD, 28 August 1918 and Report of Operations Conducted by 49th Canadian Battalion - Edmonton Regiment, east of Arras on the 26th, 27th, 27th August 1918; Stevens, *A City Goes to War*, pp.127-128.

92 LAC: 9th Brigade War Diary, 9th Brigade, Narrative of Operations from 25th to 30th August 1918, 15 September 1918.

93 Preusser, *Nr. 176 Im Weltkrieg*, pp.277-284.

ratio of wounded to dead was 10-1, which demonstrated the decreasing effectiveness of enemy shelling. Artillery fire usually resulted in a higher percentage of deaths than did bullets.[94]

The 116th Battalion supported the 4th CMR. It had multiple orders whipsaw it in the morning, so the battalion had to scramble to get into position. This meant no time for reconnaissance and little opportunity to brief the men already exhausted from the previous day. Nevertheless, the battalion advanced and ended up taking over the northern portion of Lady Lane. There were no claims, however, for prisoners or matériel captured suggesting it spent most of the battle in support. Losses in the battle were 10 officers and 285 men, with most suffered the previous day in the failed attack on Boiry-Notre-Dame.[95]

The 52nd Battalion on the left was down to just 220 bone-tired men. It was so weak that all four companies were in the line. The fighting and night marches resulted in men getting lost and separated from the battalion, hence its weakness. Despite this, it cut through the *61st IR* and forged on to Lady Lane. By the end of the day, it was down to 100 all ranks. Casualties for the whole tour were 11 officers and 266 other ranks, with most suffered the previous day. It made no prisoner claims, which signified how little resistance the *61st IR* put up.[96]

The 58th Battalion was to support the 52nd and then take Boiry-Notre-Dame and Artillery Hill. Its relief at Bois du Sart only finished at 5:00 a.m., which exhausted the men. In moving into position, one company ended up advancing with the 4th CMR.[97] The battalion now down to three companies followed the 58th and wheeled north. By noon, it had secured the village. The operation caught the *III/176th* in the flank and crushed it. In the fighting around Boiry-Notre-Dame and Artillery Hill, two snipers, Privates Anderson and Oliver, knocked out four German machine gun positions along with 20 Germans at ranges of 300 to 600 metres.[98]

The 58th then attacked Artillery Hill. The advance ground forward until the leading companies encountered two pillboxes near the road junction north of the village. They could not take or bypass them. At the 58th's request, the 42nd Battalion outflanked and captured the two. The advance resumed, with most of the hill cleared by 1:50 p.m. In response, the Germans attacked centred on Culverin Lane in the afternoon with the *I* and *II/176th IR*.[99] The counterattack dangerously pushed back the Canadians into the village. Smythe called up two reserve RCR companies at 2:45 p.m. to help bolster him.[100]

94 Gary Sheffield, *Forgotten Victory: The First World War: Myths and Realities* (London: Review, 2002), p.111; Bennett, *4th CMR*, pp.130-132; LAC: 9th Brigade War Diary, 9th Brigade, Narrative of Operations from 25th to 30th August 1918, 15 September 1918.

95 Adjutant, *The 116th Battalion in France*, pp.76-77; LAC: 9th Brigade War Diary, 116th Battalion Arras Narrative, 1 September 1918 and 9 Brigade, Narrative of Operations from 25th to 30th August 1918, 15 September 1918; LAC: 116 Bn WD, 28 August 1918.

96 Stanley, *In the Face of Danger*, p.34; LAC: 52nd Battalion War Diary, 28 August 1918; LAC: 9th Brigade War Diary, 52nd Battalion Narrative of Operations from 25th to 30th August 1918, 15 September 1918.

97 LAC: RG9 III-D-2 v4802, 138: CWNS Lamb to Duguid, 11 February 1921.

98 LAC: RG9 III-C-3 v4192, 15/3: 9th Brigade Response to Canadian Corps I.G.527, 5 January 1919.

99 The Canadian and German accounts generally harmonize on the course of the battle except for the usual exaggerations. They do not, however, match as to timing. Using the principle that preference is given to the accounts discussing their own actions, the German timing was more likely accurate. Preusser, *Nr. 176 Im Weltkrieg*, p.280.

100 LAC: RCR WD, RCR Narrative of Operations, 25/28 August 1918.

Major R S Smythe, the 23-year-old commander of the 58th Battalion, led his battalion with great skill on 28 August. (Canada. Dept. of National Defence/Library and Archives Canada/ PA-007377)

After a fierce 45 minute struggle, the Canadians repulsed the counterattack and eventually regained the ground in the evening. This was after the Germans had pulled back behind Trinquis Brook. The battalion claimed 300 prisoners, 50 machine guns, and an anti-tank gun. It suffered 102 casualties. The 58th performed superbly, and its commander, the 23-year-old Major Smythe, received a DSO for this achievement.[101]

7th Brigade

In concert with the 9th Brigade, the 'Pats' on the left and 42nd on the right struck east to seize Jigsaw Wood and the F-R Line north of Boiry-Notre-Dame. Lipsett counted on the thick woods shielding the attackers, so they had no artillery support. The 42nd had a four kilometre march in the pitch black through badly cut-up terrain and woods' close vegetation to relieve the 58th Battalion. Despite these handicaps, the 42nd was in position before first light. It attacked on a three-company front along the spur running from Infantry Hill. It was to conform to the actions of the 9th Brigade without waiting for instructions. This was another example of the decentralisation that open warfare demanded. Initial resistance was minimal, and by 1:40 p.m., the battalion had secured the ridge crest overlooking the F-R Line. C/42nd then leapfrogged and took Boiry Trench north of the town by 2:00 p.m. Its assistance to the 58th Battalion resulted in a German withdrawal because of encirclement fears. By 4:00 p.m., Boiry Trench to Jigsaw Wood was under the battalion's control. Artillery fire repulsed the final counterattack down Culverin Lane at 7:00 p.m., and the battle died down. The 42nd's losses were surprisingly low at just 109 all ranks with 280 prisoners claimed. Contrary to claims of a brave battle, many enemy surrendered without a fight, For instance, a signal detachment of three captured 60 Germans hiding in dugouts.[102]

101 Shackleton, *Second to None*, pp.260-261; LAC: 9th Brigade War Diary, 58th Battalion Narrative, 1 September 1918; LAC: 58th Battalion WD, 28 August 1918.

102 LAC: 7th Brigade Report; Topp, *42nd Battalion*, pp.247-251; LAC: 42nd Battalion War Diary, 28 August 1918 and 42nd Battalion Report on Operations 27th/28th August about JIGSAW WOOD, ARTILLERY HILL and BOIRY NOTRE DAME.

The PPCLI in the 7th Brigade's centre was to take Jigsaw Wood. If the 'Pats' failed, the Germans could use it as a covered assembly area for a counterattack. The *35th ID* had already done so in its 26 August counterattack. A scouting party pushed ahead and pre-empted a German counterattack on the 49th. Enemy counterattacks to re-establish the position resulted in a seesaw battle that they lost.[103] At 11:00 a.m., two companies advanced on Jigsaw Wood in section rushes in concert with the 42nd Battalion. German resistance broke under the heavy pressure and the 'Pats' cleared the woods with 175 prisoners taken. The fight was not a walk over as one company took over two hours to clear its sector. There was a gap on the left between the PPCLI and the 49th Battalion, and Charlie Stewart used a company of the RCR to plug it. Sixty hours of intense fighting exhausted the battalion, but it had carried out its mission. Losses this day were moderate with it losing 15 officers and 182 other ranks during its tour.[104]

The initial role of the RCR was in reserve, but that changed. With such a wide front, Lipsett had to use all his battalions in the days' operation. Normally, this would be a dangerous policy, but Lipsett was correct that the Germans could not disrupt his operations. The shortage of forces meant the RCR split into two with two companies to the PPCLI. At 9:00 a.m., the brigade assigned the two remaining companies to the 58th Battalion. The battalion overall suffered 196 casualties with most on 26 August.[105]

The three German regimental histories of the *35th ID* – *141st IR*, *176th IR*, and *71st FAR* – conflict with the Canadian records as to timing, forces, and results. For instance, they described repulsing a frontal assault with two tanks at 9:00 a.m. on Boiry-Notre-Dame. There was, however, no attack then, nor a direct assault on the town, and no tanks on 28 August. The accounts do confirm how the 9th Brigade overran the *61st IR*, then struck the *III/176th IR* in the flank, and inflicted heavy losses.[106] Recognising the threat presented by losing Boiry, the reserve *I/176th IR* counterattacked to reach the eastern outskirts. Reinforced by a pioneer company, the battalion contested the Canadian hold. The *II/176th IR* deployed north of Boiry had to refuse its flank as the 58th Battalion pushed out of the town. It drove the Canadians back into Boiry and restored a semblance of a line. With all its companies committed, the regiment continued to hold off the Canadians until 4:00 p.m. Repeated counterattacks failed because of the lack of artillery support due to ammunition shortages at the batteries. With the failure of the *141st IR* on the regiment's right, the *II/176th* was at risk of encirclement with the 7th Brigade threatening its right. At 4:45 p.m., the *II Battalion* fell back along the road to Hamblain. The Canadian attack reduced the regiment's battalions to about 100 men each. Under severe shelling, the regiment pulled back behind the Trinquis Brook in the late evening. It reported losses of 602 all ranks including 351 missing – an 80 percent loss rate.[107] Dellmensingen or von Below relieved the division commander von Kemnitz on 5 September possibly to placate

103 The *141st IR* account described multiple successful counterattacks driving back the attackers, which did not show up in Canadian reports. In the end, the Canadians advanced and the Germans retreated. Schulemann, *I.R. Nr. 141*, pp.192-194.

104 LAC: 7th Brigade Report; Hodder-Williams, *PPCLI* 2, pp.344-349; LAC: PPCLI WD, PPCLI Narrative of Operations August 5th/29th 1918.

105 Fetherstonhaugh, *The Royal Canadian Regiment*, pp.345-346; LAC: RCR WD, Narrative of Operations, 25/28 August 1918.

106 LAC: War Diary, 8th Brigade, 28 August 1918.

107 Preusser, *Nr. 176 Im Weltkrieg*, pp.277-284.

Generalmajor v Kemnitz commander of the *35th ID* in happier times at an inspection by the Kaiser in April 1918. He is to the left of the Kaiser. His relief was likely a way of placating the raging Ludendorff at failing to stop the Corps. (Wilhelm Preusser, *Das 9. Westpreussische Infanterie-Regiment Nr. 176 im Weltkrieg*, (Berlin: Tradition Wilhelm Kolk, 1931), p.273)

Ludendorff. Following the Canadian success, von Kuhl reported that Ludendorff 'raged the army [*Seventeenth*] was badly run.'[108]

On the German's right, the *141st IR* account mentions relentless counterattacks to drive back the Canadians, but heavy losses finally forced the regiment to retire. This history did not mention the loss of Jigsaw Wood but did claim to seal off the gap created by the 7th Brigade attack until the division ordered it back across the Trinquis Brook.[109] It emerged in better shape than the *176th IR* with a strength of 1,087 all ranks. The two regimental histories blame the other for failing to hold. Judging from the hard fighting the 9th Brigade faced in Boiry-Notre-Dame and the scores of prisoners taken in Jigsaw Wood, it is likely that the *176th IR* account was the more accurate.

8th Brigade

On the 3rd Division's right flank, the 8th Brigade attacked at 12:30 p.m. on a 1,200 metre front at the F-R Line. The 43rd Battalion was on the right and 5th CMR on the left, and three FA and two HA brigades supported the operation. Instead of the by now traditional creeping barrage, Draper arranged a standing bombardment on the forward defences for 30 minutes

108 Bundesarchive, Freiburg: Herman Von Kuhl Kriegserinnerungen, 28 August 1918.
109 Schulemann, *I.R. Nr. 141*, pp.192-194.

followed by another 3 minutes on the support line.[110] His reasoning was with the jump-off positions 1,000 metres from the objective and the wire needing cutting, it was better to focus on making breaches. He was confident his troops could deal with any Germans in No Man's Land, and that they could manoeuvre better without the barrage's constraints. He was correct. The Germans concentrated their defence along the F-R Line. Meeting the battered survivors of the *II/119th RIR*, the 8th Brigade rapidly overran the defenders. The only issue was on the right flank where the 43rd did not have contact with the 2nd Division.[111]

8th Brigade infantry advancing in section worms near Remy on 28 August. (Canada. Dept. of National Defence/Library and Archives Canada/PA-003140)

On the brigade's right, the 43rd's mission was to take Remy and Remy Wood 1,400 metres away. The 2nd CMR would support the battalion and cross the Sensée at Remy to exploit the success. The 43rd had already fought for 26 hours, endured heavy shelling overnight, and its companies comprised 40 to 50 men each. Moreover, it believed its relief was that night. Its initial front was 900 metres which shrank to 600 metres at the objective. With such a low combat strength, the battalion attacked on a three-company front, with one in reserve. The battalion surged forward and, despite enemy fire from ahead and the flank, the battalion took the two objectives. Private West recalled 'This was the only stirring and thrilling moment of my war experience.' He described in his diary a thin line of khaki moving with determination led by Lieutenant K D Miller who 'seemed to pay so little heed to the shooting.'[112] The 2nd CMR did not move in support, however. Diplomatically, the 43rd's report described they 'apparently misunderstood their orders, never coming up with the Battalion.'[113] The 43rd lost half its men and all but one officer per company, with D Company reduced to 13 men and 1

110 LAC: War Diary, 8th Brigade, 28 August 1918.
111 LAC: War Diary, 8th Brigade, 28 August 1918; LAC: 3rd Division WD, 3rd Division Report on Operations from Aug. 26th to Aug. 28th, 1918.
112 LAC: West Diary, 28 August 1918.
113 LAC: 9th Brigade War Diary, 43rd Narrative of Operations, August 26th -29th, 1918.

Lewis Gun. Despite the weak strength of the battalion, the brigade reported the 43rd's losses for the campaign as only 11 officers and 133 men.[114]

The 5th CMR attacked east on a two-company front with an 800 metre front. It was advance 850 metres to take the F-R Line north of Remy Woods. It would also have to contend with Long Wood in the Cojeul River valley. As it crossed the Cojeul River to get in position, heavy machine gun fire and shelling hit it. This included a dense gas bombardment in the valley forcing the men to mask up while marching. Assembly was 'under extremely difficult conditions and many casualties were sustained.'[115] The attackers did not cross the start line until zero plus 20 minutes to give the bombardment sufficient time to bite and cut lanes in the wire. The timing worked well as the leading edge of the battalion reached the Germans just as the barrage lifted. It found enough gaps in the wire to get at the Germans. Small parties spread out and moved north and south along the forward and support trenches to take out enemy positions from the flank. The battalion reported that their Lewis Guns provided 'splendid' cover for their rushes. It took only forty-five minutes to overwhelm the defenders. The battalion, however, suffered heavily. It had 10 officers and 129 other ranks killed or wounded with another four missing on 28 September. It claimed a modest 20 prisoners, 5 trench mortars, and 10 machine guns, although it asserted German dead filled the trenches.[116]

The 2nd CMR's role was to support the assault battalions, but the 43rd believed it had not carried out its mission. This was possibly the result of the hurried nature of the planning and constant shifting of orders. The brigade split the battalion's companies across its front in support or reserve. When B Company arrived at Remy to cross the Sensée, German machine gun fire from the south bank prevented a crossing. In the evening, the 43rd called up D/2nd CMR to establish a bridgehead across the river.[117] Captain R E Gunn commanding the company did not comply believing there were Canadian troops already across. Further, the battalion relief would happen soon. This oddly passive attitude was likely a consequence of exhaustion from three days of fighting and a refusal to throw lives away. There was little possibility of a single company crossing and holding a bridgehead at this point.[118] The battalion claimed 83 prisoners and suffered losses of 143 over the three days of combat.[119]

Draper properly read the situation, and the 8th Brigade conducted a textbook operation accompanied by overwhelming firepower. Sections manoeuvred around the scattered German artillery barrage and swept over the defences. The German account has the *II/119th IR* resisting stoutly but Canadians outflanking them by crossing the Cojeul from the north. No Canadian reports support this statement. More likely, the 5th CMR and 43rd used infiltration tactics to find gaps in the defences and attack the defenders' flanks. With the loss of the northern sections of the F-R Line, the few survivors of the *II Battalion* withdrew across the river valley.

114 LAC: 9th Brigade War Diary, 9 Brigade, Narrative of Operations from 25th to 30th August 1918, 15 September 1918.
115 LAC: 5th CMR War Diary, 5th CMR, Summary of Operations, 3 September 1918; LAC: War Diary, 8th Brigade, 28 August 1918.
116 LAC: 5th CMR War Diary, 5th CMR, Summary of Operations, 3 September 1918; LAC: War Diary, 8th Brigade, 28 August 1918.
117 LAC: 2nd CMR Report; Johnston, *The 2nd CMR*, p.69.
118 Gunn moved to the Corps school as an instructor in September.
119 LAC: 2nd CMR Report.

The *III/362nd IR* from the *4th EzD* bolstered the shattered line by defending the zone from Éterpigny to St Servins Farm.[120]

Highlanders

The 51st Division spent the day reorganising and repositioning for a new attack. Two days of fighting had worn out the 152nd and 153rd Brigades, while the 154th defend the division's northern sector. To solve this, Horne arranged for the 8th Division to take over the 154th Brigade's front on the night of 27/28 August. Oldfield, the temporary divisional commander, planned a neat manoeuvre to lever the Germans off of the heights they held, but this took time to arrange. Thus, the 51st would not attack until the next day.[121] The slow progress of the Highlanders was interfering with the Canadians' advance. Later that day, Horne and Currie visited Oldfield to impress upon him the necessity of taking these positions. This was after a conference at the Corps headquarters where Currie likely complained about the 51st's tardiness to Horne.[122]

Results and Analysis

The offensive's third day featured mixed success with the 3rd performing brilliantly and the 2nd rebuffed. Casualties and prisoners were similar to the second day – the Corps captured 791 Germans.[123] Most of the captives would have been from the mauled *35th ID*, as it was unlikely the 2nd Division took many prisoners. The Corps suffered an estimated 2,293 casualties. The 2nd Division lost substantially more including 60 percent more fatalities than did the 3rd Division. Its ratio of dead to wounded at 2.7 versus Lipsett's division ratio of 3.7 illustrated the costs of desperate and unsuccessful fighting. The ratio of dead to wounded dropped – lower is worse – when the attackers' failed and they did not control the battlefield. Thus, some of those died who in other circumstances would have survived – one of the many costs of failure. The 51st Division made no attacks and so suffered even fewer losses than the day before. In Currie's view, the Canadians were bleeding, while the 51st dawdled.

120 Gerster, *RIR Nr. 119*, pp.119-120.

121 Bewsher, *History of 51st (Highland)*, p.367; TNA: 51st Div. GS WD, 51st Division OO No. 303, 28 August 1918 and Report on the Operations North of the Scarpe by the 51st (Highland) Division August 18th - 30th 1918, 9 September 1918.

122 TNA: First Army GS WD, Notes of Conference at Canadian Corps Headquarter, 28 August 1918.

123 LAC: POW Arras.

Table 7.1 Estimated Casualties For 28 August 1918

	Killed	Wounded	POW	Total
1st CID	6	30		36
2nd CID	299	820	3	1,122
3rd CID	184	687		871
4th CID	3	4		7
51st HD*	34	56		90
4th BID*	7	8		15
Tank Corps†	1			1
Other	85	143		15
Total	**542**	**1,748**	**3**	**2,293**

* 51st (Highland) Division and 4th British Division does not include prisoners lost
† Tank Corps wounded are included in the other category

This was the last battle for both Canadian divisions at Arras 1918. Lipsett's division suffered 20 percent fewer casualties than did Burstall's. Some of this difference was due to the better defences and defenders facing the 2nd Division, but a large part was due to the 3rd's better leadership.

Haig, Horne, Currie, Burstall, and Tremblay erred in their key decisions for 28 August. Haig and Horne did so in not providing the resources needed for the mission assigned the Corps. Currie blundered in continuing the offensive with the weakened 2nd Division. The essential reason for the failure was his faulty appreciation of the strength of the 2nd Division versus the German defenders. The ready availability of replacements – the product of conscription – was a factor as Patrick Dennis argues in *Reluctant Warriors*, but it was not the primary reason for Currie's aggression.[124] Currie mistakenly thought the Germans were weaker and the 2nd Division stronger than it was. Further, the Corps did not manage the battle so, the two divisions' attacks continued on diverging angles. Burstall went astray in neither demanding a pause nor at least using the fresher 6th Brigade. Tremblay's mistakes were to not protest the use of his battered brigade, the reuse of the hollowed out 22nd Battalion and scattering the 25th Battalion across his front.

What if Currie had the 1st Division replace the 2nd? The 1st was in position and prepared to attack the D-Q Line on 28 August, so it was possible. Whilst the 1st was fresher, much stronger than Burstall's division and had the capable 57th Division on its flank, it would still encounter the same liabilities as did the 2nd. Breaking the line was contingent on first outflanking or breaching the barbed wire defences. On the Somme in 1916 not a single Canadian infantry

124 Dennis, *Reluctant Warriors*, p.98.

battalion attack succeeded when it faced uncut wire.[125] This calculus still applied in 1918. There was no opportunity to outflank, so artillery and tanks needed to break the wire, but the First Army ordered the Corps to conserve tanks for the D-Q operation.[126] The 1st Division would have the same artillery resources as the 2nd, so it also would have too few guns for its front. An approach like Lipsett's of a series of sequential narrow-front attacks was problematic. The *26th RD* was less damaged than the *35th ID*, and a continuous front made this type of operation risky. The 1st Division was unlikely to have succeeded. This would have imperilled its full participation in the D-Q Line operation. The best alternative for Currie was to pause, bombard the line, and attack the next day.

Why was the 3rd Division so much more successful than the 2nd? The 3rd took all its first objective and effectively destroyed the *35th ID*. Lipsett's formation had a front twice the width of the 2nd's and faced four regiments while the 2nd Division only one.[127] Burstall's division could not hold the small lodgements it made in the F-R Line. The Germans decisively repulsed it with heavy losses to the two assault brigades. There were five primary reasons for this difference. The F-R Line was not as strong north of the Sensée River as south. Lipsett's troops did not have to contend with as many trenches and wire belts as did the 2nd, and they were not as well maintained.[128] Second, by 28 August the *35th ID* had already lost substantial casualties and was exhausted. The *26th RD* was fresher and had not suffered greatly in the engagement the day before. Third, Allied intelligence rated the *26th RD* as a much superior division to the *35th ID* – although it performed well at Arras. Fourth, the 3rd's attack was better considered and executed than Burstall's. The concentration of attacks on narrow fronts supported by the divisional artillery was a masterstroke. Instead of a density of 30 metres per gun, the barrages were 10 to 20 metres, and all used smoke. The result was the 3rd's assault troops had little trouble overrunning the enemy's defences. Bypassing the main defensive position at Boiry and outflanking it meant avoiding a potentially difficult fight for the town. It meant Lipsett's division secured its first objective, despite the repeated counterattacks by the *35th ID*, without the heavy losses of Burstall's division. The 2nd Division's 5th CFA highlighted the issue with its devastating comment 'This attack plainly showed the inadvisability of attacking commanding ground strongly held by M.G.s in broad daylight without the protection of [sic] creeping barrage. The need of a heavy smoke screen to protect advancing infantry was apparent from the start.'[129]

Burstall's bull rush approach that failed the previous day was an indictment on his competence. Fundamentally, the only change was the addition of a thin artillery barrage. This to support a force numerically weaker, further disorganised, and more exhausted than on 27 August. It was not a plan that suggests Burstall had a firm understanding of the requirements for success. There can be no question about the courage and determination of the 2nd Division's officers and men, the defeat was not theirs but of their senior leadership. It is difficult to envision a scenario where any combination of juggling of forces would lead to victory. Only far more artillery and tanks

125 Stewart, *Neglected Campaign*, p.296.
126 TNA: First Army GS WD, Notes of Conference at Canadian Corps Headquarter, 28 August 1918.
127 The 3rd Division fought the three regiments of the *35th ID* and the *119th RIR* of the *26th RD* while the 2nd only faced the *121st RIR* of the *26th RD*.
128 LAC: Notes on the Area between the Scarpe, La Sensée Canal, Canal De l'Escaut and Cambrai-Bapaume Road, [1918].
129 LAC: 5th CFA WD, 28 August 1918.

or a fundamentally different approach would solve this challenge. Finally, the 2nd Division was weaker than the 3rd. It had suffered more losses and was using two exhausted and battered brigades. Although tired, the 3rd Division had more manageable losses. It had no battalions in as bad a shape as the 22nd. As the 2nd Division's historian David Campbell stated, 'It is difficult to see how events could have turned out much worse if more time had been taken to prepare follow-up attacks after 26 August.'[130]

There were consequences for the failure south of the Sensée. First, it meant delaying the D-Q Line attack, as the Corps had to first break the F-R Line and capture jump-off positions. This would take time and risked wrecking the 1st Division to accomplish this. It also gave space for the Germans to prepare their defences and move up reserves. Second, it meant the 2nd Division would need considerable time to recover and train its replacements. Third, it removed some of Currie's lustre after the successes of Amiens and the opening stages of Arras. Haig would crow with *schadenfreude* that the 57th Division reached Riencourt on 29 August a kilometre south of the Corps boundary and were 'right ahead of the Canadians! This will do the latter good.'[131]

Currie recognised the day was a mix of triumph and tragedy. He called the taking of Boiry-Notre-Dame 'a very important operation.' He also admitted the failure south of the Sensée, 'will seriously interfere with future events.'[132] It meant the 1st Division had to break that line before it could get into position for the more formidable D-Q Line. There was a substantial risk that Macdonell's division would burn-out like what happened to the 2nd. If this occurred, it would leave Currie with just the 4th British and the soon to arrive 4th Canadian Division to assault the D-Q Line. These would not be enough to do so. Thus, the key question was whether the 1st Division could take the F-R Line and advance to the jump-off positions while remaining combat effective. Given the skill and ferocity with which the Germans had defended on 27 and 28 August, it would require a remarkable performance by the 'old Red Patch.'

130 Campbell, *It Can't Last Forever*, p.438.
131 NLS: Haig Diary, 30 August 1918.
132 LAC: Currie Diary, 28 August 1918.

Section Three

To the Drocourt-Quéant Line

8

'Totally overrun, overcome, and taken prisoner' Approaching the D-Q Line, 29-30 August

The breaking of the F-R LINE. The way in which it was done was his own idea and was literally a Bde. [brigade] tactical masterpiece.

Macdonell Confidential Report on Brigadier General W. Griesbach, 1919[1]

Beginning on 29 August, the Canadian Corps had four interrelated tasks to complete before tackling its prime mission of breaking the D-Q Line. It had to finish them rapidly while limiting losses. Task 1 was the seizure of the high ground north of the Scarpe. Task 2 was the capture of the F-R Line south of the Sensée. The third task required advancing to within assault range of D-Q Line, and the final one was to breach the wire protecting the D-Q Line. To add to the challenge, the Corps could not tackle Tasks 3 and 4 until completing the first two. For Task 1, the 51st Division had to capture Greenland Hill and the Hausa and Delbar Woods to eliminate German observation across the Scarpe. Completing this would allow the field artillery to advance beyond Monchy-le-Preux to support Tasks 3 and 4. With Task 2, the 1st Division had to capture the F-R Line without breaking any battalions. This chapter focuses on the Corps' efforts to finish Tasks 1 and 2 and start on Task 3 over the two days of 29-30 August. It includes a brilliant operation on 30 August by the 1st Brigade that a well-timed German counterattack almost reversed.

Strategic Situation

Haig reiterated the existing orders for the First Army to attack the D-Q Line and exploit to Bourlon Wood across the canal. The Cavalry Corps would then swing behind the Hindenburg Line and 'operate against the lines of communications of the hostile troops opposing the Third and Fourth Armies.'[2] Those armies were to maintain their pressure to hold the enemy in place. The plan did not specify the main assault's date, but clearly time was of the essence given Haig's apprehensions of a German retreat.

1 LAC: MG30 E15 v1: Griesbach Fonds, Griesbach Confidential Report, 19 January 1919.
2 TNA: First Army GS WD, GHQ OAD 907/16, 29 August 1918.

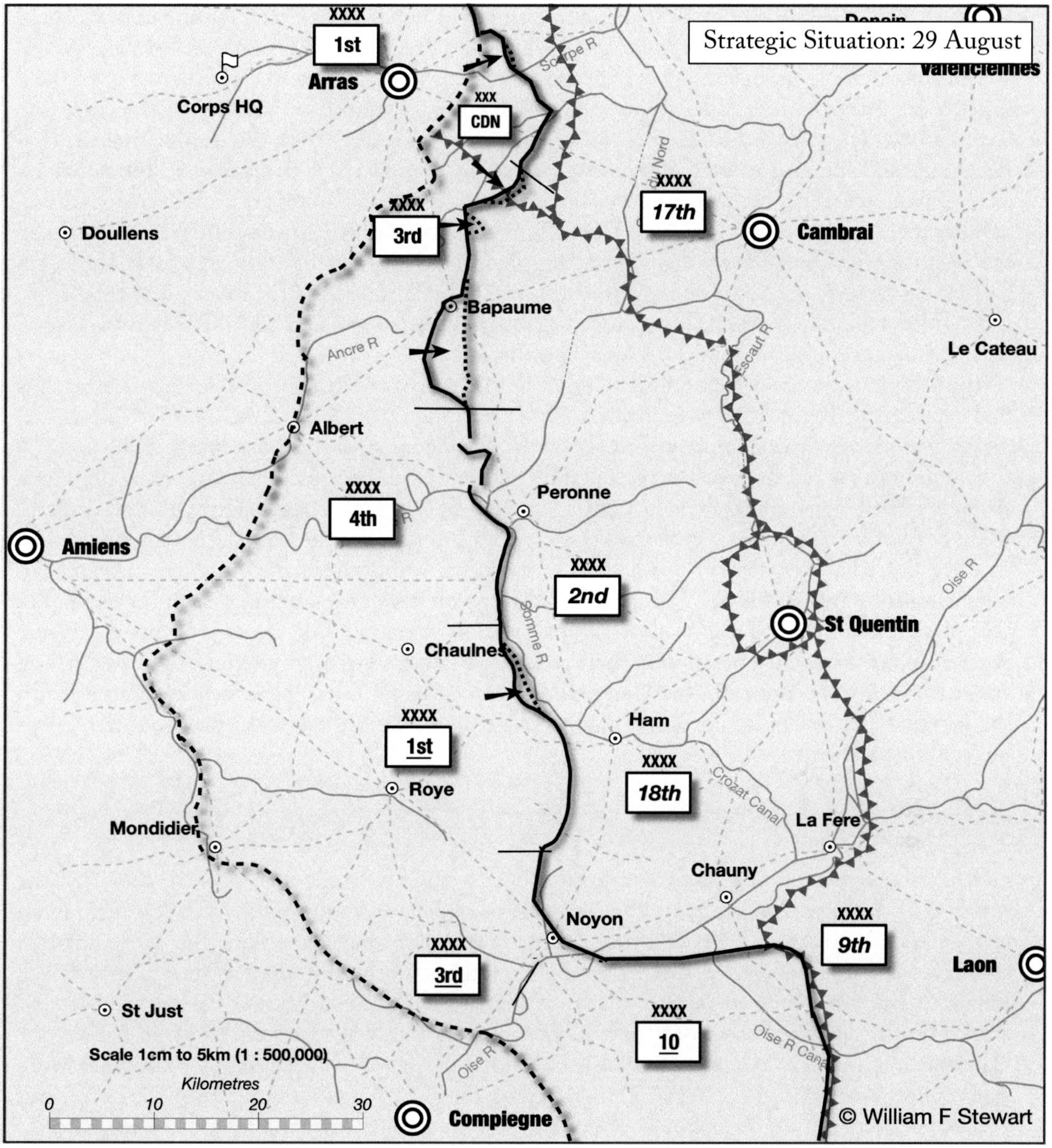

Map 23. To the south of the Canadian Corps, the British Fourth and Third Armies followed up the withdrawing Germans. On the Third Army's left flank, the VI and XVII Corps made some gains, including the capture of sections of the Hindenburg line. (Author's map)

South of the Somme forty kilometres from the Corps' location, the Germans retired six to six and a half kilometres. North to Bapaume they did not fall back to the same extent. These withdrawals allowed the Fourth and Third Armies to follow up with minimal fighting. North of Bapaume, the Germans still held the line in strength and contested the British advance.[3] On the left wing of the Third Army, the XVII Corps was well in advance of the forces on each flank which constrained its operations. Fergusson tasked the 57th Division with capturing Riencourt and the spur beyond. This meant an advance of its 170th Brigade of 1,700 metres on a two-kilometre front. Fergusson's corps hoped the 1st Division would attack, but the operation would proceed, regardless. The 2/4th Loyal North Lancashire Regiment (LNL) on the left and the 2/5th Kings Own (Royal Lancaster Regiment) (KORL) on the right attacked. The 2/5th KORL captured Riencourt. On the left, the German fire annihilated the first ranks of the 2/4th LNL. Nevertheless, the battalion pressed through Hendecourt and took Greyhound Trench with patrols reaching the spur north of Riencourt.

The Germans ascribed their failure to other British forces outflanking the defenders after they had captured Bullecourt. In the middle of the night, the *103rd RIR* of the *58th ID* committed its reserves along with a company of the *107th IR* and elements of the *7th Schützen Division* (*SD*) to a counterattack.[4] It was successful, and it drove the British back over 1,500 metres. The 170th Brigade's final gains ranged from just 200 to about 1,500 metres, but the 57th Division was still well ahead of its neighbours. It blamed the 1st Division for not attacking, although it was clear that the Canadians would not do so. This was another symptom of the difficulties inherent in operating on army boundaries. While the 57th Division did not retain its gains, its performance still pleased Haig, as it brought down the Canadians by a peg. He claimed in his diary that 'Canadians seem to have postponed their attack without giving 57th warning.'[5] He was wrong about the lack of notification, but Currie did critique the 1st Division for not keeping up with the British.[6] While he did not know about Haig's diary, Currie was sensitive about the Corps not pulling its weight.

German Situation

Dellmensingen was troubled on 29 August. While content with the success of the *26th RD*, the rest of the front was unsatisfactory. The *35th ID* was no longer combat effective, but the ground it now defended across the Trinquis Brook was unsuitable for offensive action. The sector north of the Arras-Cambrai road needed reinforcements. On his southern flank, pressure from the 57th Division had threatened to rupture his front there. Facing the Canadian Corps, the battered *26th RD* still defended the front from Hendecourt to the Sensée River. South of the Arras-Cambrai road, its *121st RIR* still stoutly defended its front. It received two battalions from different regiments from the *4th EzD* to help plug the gap on its southern flank. The pernicious practice of breaking up formations because of the desperate situation meant scattering three of the Ersatz division's battalions across the *26th RD*'s front. North of the Arras-Cambrai road, the *119th RIR* defended to the Sensée River. To its frustration, just as it had finished reshuffling,

3 Edmonds, *Military Operations, 1918* 4, pp.338, 343.
4 Poland, *RIR Nr. 103 History*, pp.142-143.
5 NLS: Haig Diary, 30 August 1918.
6 LAC: RG9 III-C-3 v4052, 31/5: 1st Division G.3-93, 29 August 1918.

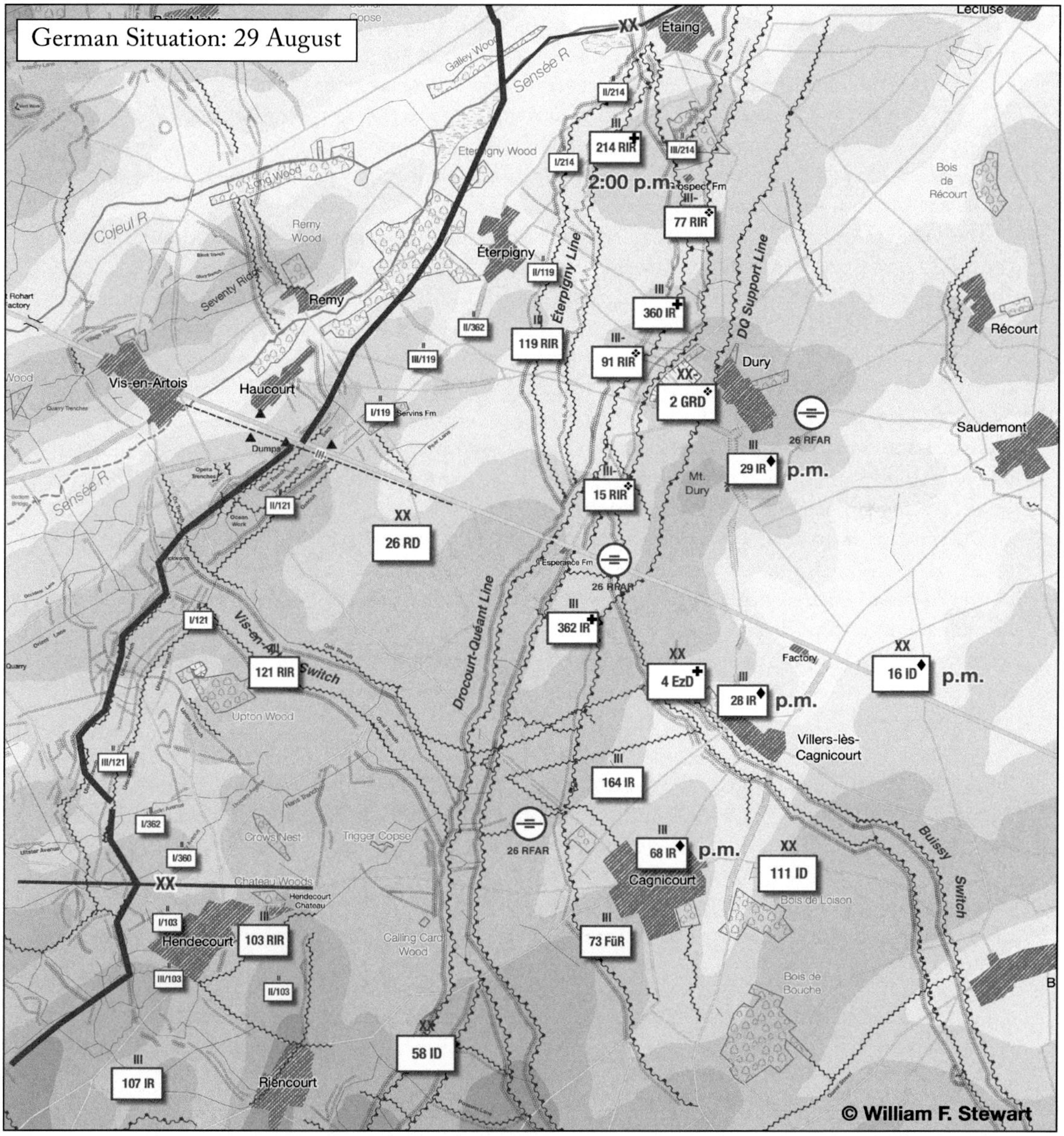

Map 24. The *26th RD* continued to staunchly defend its front, with the *2nd GRD* and the *111th ID* in reserve. Over the course of the day, the *4th EzD* and the *16th ID* arrived to reinforce the *II Bavarian Korps*. (Author's map)

as the regimental historian wryly phrased it, 'The Leader Far Behind the Front with the Blue Pencil' ordered the lines adjusted again. The historian complained these leaders had little idea of the hardships they inflicted on the troops by 'their light strokes' on a map.[7] The *III/362nd IR* of the *4th EzD* reinforced the *119th*.[8] In reserve were the remainder of the *4th EzD*, *2nd GRD*, *16th ID*, and *111th ID*. The *7th SD* was also moving up to backstop the *II Bavarian Korps*. It was a dismounted cavalry division with a strength of approximately a regiment. In the afternoon, the *II Bavarian Korps* subordinated the *214th RIR* of the *4th EzD* to the *26th RD*, and it deployed in the sector from Éterpigny north to Étaing.[9]

The *4th EzD* formed at the start of the war from men who had not received prewar military training.[10] It served two tours on the Somme where it faced the Canadians on 1 and 8 October 1916, and it performed credibly. The British battered it during Arras 1917 in defending Roeux in April 1917. In 1918, it attempted to capture Givenchy as part of the Lys offensive but suffered a significant defeat.[11] It was then heavily engaged in the Marne offensive and to bolster it, *OHL* in early August assigned the *214th RIR* from the disbanded *46th RD* to replace its broken up *361st IR*. The remaining members of the broken-up regiment ended up in the *360th IR*.[12] *OHL* was so short of replacements that it had to breakdown multiple battle-tested units to make one whole. Allied intelligence rated the *4th EzD* as a third-class division. By Arras 1918, it was weak, having suffered heavy losses in 1918.[13]

During the day, the *II Bavarian Korps* shifted the *16th ID* to around Villers-lès-Cagnicourt to act as an *Eingreifdivision* for the sector south of the Arras-Cambrai road.[14] The Canadians observed it and shelled it regularly as it moved south. It suffered few losses, but it took most of the day to get into position. The division's orders were to prepare to counterattack on the sector from the Arras-Cambrai road to Hendecourt – an operation needed the next day.[15]

1st Division

With the 2nd Division burned out, it was now the 1st's turn, but the situation was unclear and disordered. Thus, Macdonell's division would not attack. It first had to stabilise the front. An additional factor was a shortage of ammunition at the gun positions because of delivery difficulties. The traffic congestion in the rear was becoming out of hand with insufficient road space and poor traffic discipline. On 28 August, the 1st CDA reported no ammunition had arrived that day and there was no estimate when it would.[16] Further, the horse transport and

7 Gerster, *RIR Nr. 119*, p.120.
8 Stühmke, *26th Reserve Division* II, p.65.
9 Stühmke, *26th Reserve Division* II, p.65.
10 Unfortunately, only one regiment of the division produced a regimental history and it was not accessible in Canada.
11 LAC: RG9 III-C-3 v4076, 2/22: Notes on Recent Fighting—No. 7, 24 April 1918.
12 Hanns Bastanier, *Geschichte Des Großherzoglich Mecklenburgischen Reserve-Infanterie-Regiments Nr. 214* (Dessau: Selbstverlag, 1933), pp.409-411.
13 LAC: RG9 III-C-4 v4031, 3/3: 1st Division I.G.514, 2 September 1918; General Staff Intelligence Section, *251 Divisions*, pp.96-98.
14 Begau, *IR 28 in Weltkrieg*, p.234.
15 Pafferath, *Geschichte I.R. 68*, pp.690-691.
16 LAC: 1st CDA W.D., 28 August 1918.

MT had long hauls, with the Corps' supply head at Agnez-lès-Duisans – 10 kilometres on the far side of Arras.[17]

The French had relieved Macdonell's division over the nights of 19-21 August at Amiens. It slowly moved away from the fighting with ample time for the troops to rest. It moved by train and completed the transfer to the Arras sector on 27 August. Currie briefed Macdonell and his GSO 1 at the Corps Headquarters on 25 August. Based on the briefing, the division issued orders to relieve the 2nd Division on the night of 27/28 August and to attack the D-Q Line that day.[18] In light of the failure to take the F-R Line, Currie had to issue new orders that pushed the D-Q Line attack to 1 September. So, it would have three days (30 August to 1 September) to complete Tasks 2 and 3.[19] Macdonell envisioned this stage as three separate 1st Brigade actions: take the F-R Line; seize Ocean Work and advance a kilometre on the left; and capture the Crow's Nest on the right. This approach would keep the other two brigades fresh at the risk of wrecking the 1st Brigade.[20]

The division arrived at Arras essentially as strong as it left for Amiens. It had a ration strength of 21,294 men and 4,607 horses, with only 165 men and 419 horses fewer than on 3 August.[21] There are multiple references in this text to battalions returning from Amiens at full or almost full strength despite suffering hundreds of casualties. One of the Corps' advantages was a sufficiency of replacements owing to conscription. The system held up during Amiens, but strains appeared by the third day of Arras. Against the 6,209 men lost during the first three days of the offensive, there were only 41 officers and 801 replacements available. In the period 1-3 September according to Corps' records, another 100 officers and 3,812 men would arrive from England, but they would have 12 and not the normal 14 weeks of training. The following week, a further 2,500 would come, but with just 10 weeks of instruction. These would provide sufficient replacements but leave only 904 available for additional losses. The Corps was running short of men. Therefore on 31 August, it reduced the infantry battalion establishment by 100 men back to the standard 966 all ranks.[22]

Macdonell's division took over a front that was fluid. There was no clear idea of where the line lay, so the relief was a time-consuming affair. The 3rd Brigade on the right and the 2nd on the left deployed along the previous day's start line and then cautiously advanced. Scouts led the infiltration forward to find the scattered survivors of the day's battle. There was a strong risk they would miss the handful of troops there and blunder into the enemy. It took most of the night to find out where the line lay and replace the exhausted 2nd Division. The long relief meant the 2nd and 3rd Brigades adopted a defensive posture while the artillery cut gaps into the F-R Line's wire.

17 LAC: RG9 III-D-3 v4840: 1st Division AAQMG War Diary, 1st Canadian Division Report on Administrative Arrangements for Operations East of Arras, August 28 - September 4th, 1918.
18 LAC: 1st Divison W.D., 1st Canadian Division G.3-93/3, 26 August 1918.
19 LAC: 1st Divison W.D., Arras Operations Night 28/29 August to Night 4/5 September 1918.
20 Macdonell, 'Old Red Patch 1', pp.390-392.
21 LAC: 1st Division AAQMG War Diary, Ration Strength, August 1918.
22 LAC: MG30 E5 v5: Bovey Fonds, Reinforcements in Sight, 31 August 1918; LAC: MG30 E5 v5: Bovey Fonds, Canadian Corps A.105-150, 31 August 1918.

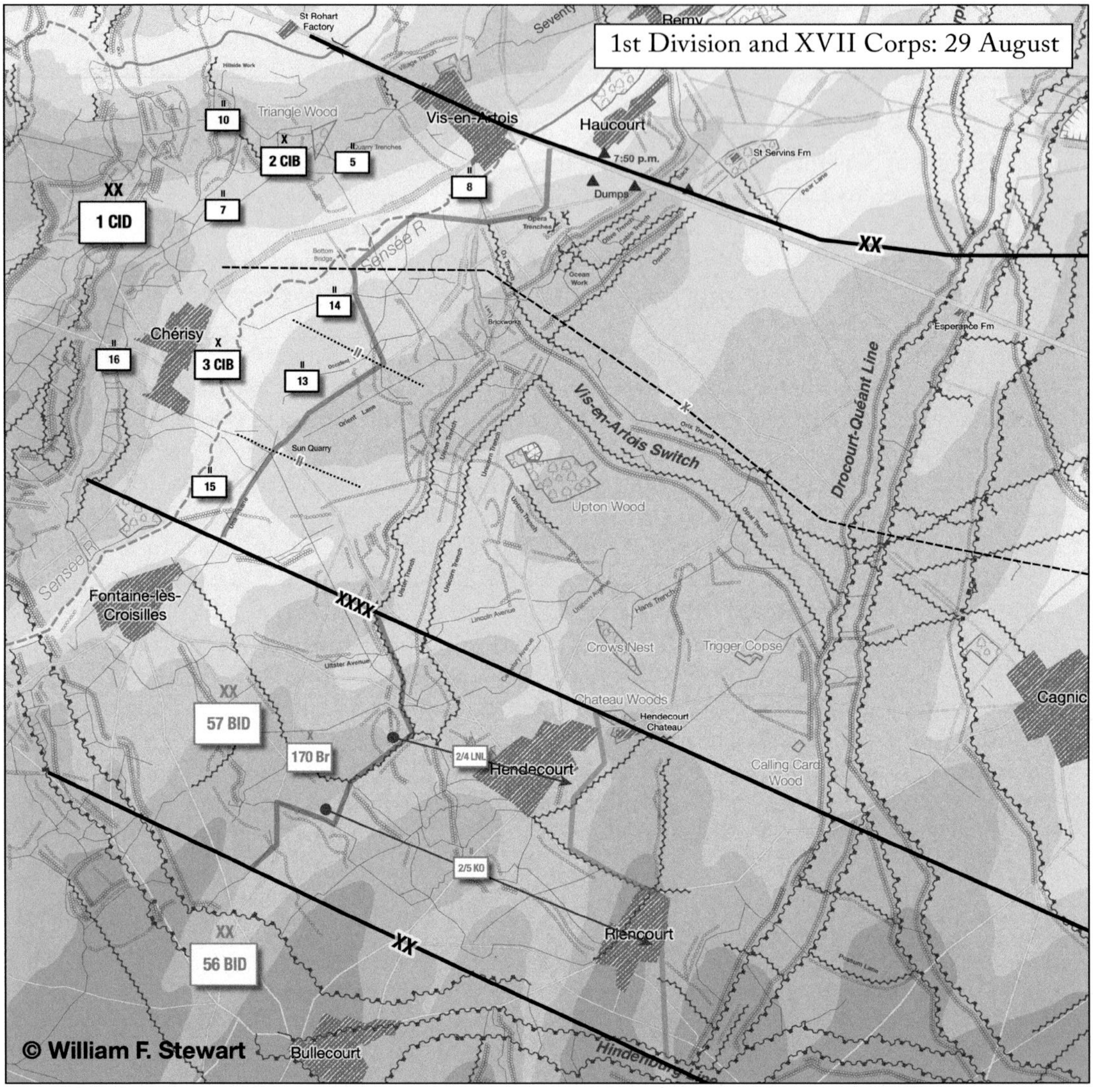

Map 25. The 1st Division relieved the 2nd Division but fell back to allow the artillery unfettered freedom to shell the F-R Line. On its right, the 57th Division took Hendecourt and Riencourt, thus outflanking the F-R Line. This pleased Haig as it brought the Canadians down a peg. (Author's map)

The division controlled nine FA brigades (216 pieces), which spent the day preparing gun positions and bringing up ammunition.[23] Its field artillery was out of range so could not cut the D-Q Line wire entanglements.[24] The heavy artillery was busy cutting wire in the F-R and D-Q Lines.

4th British Division

The 4th British Division's relieved Lipsett's formation on the night of 28/29 August. It was a regular army formation that had fought in most of the war's major battles through 1917. In 1918, it successfully defended the sector north of the Scarpe in the XVII Corps during *Mars*. There, it suffered 2,216 casualties from 21 March to 5 April – one of the lower totals for formations in the March offensive.[25] In the April offensive, it suffered another 2,568 casualties. While not light, the division did not endure the crushing losses that destroyed the leadership cadres of other divisions. Its commander was Major General Torquhil Matheson – a Guards officer – who Haig thought had 'made the 4th Division into one of the best in the army.'[26] Lipsett replaced Matheson after Arras 1918.[27] Ostensibly, this was to give Lipsett a career boost in commanding a British division. It was more likely that he and Currie had fallen out over Lipsett's supposed undermining of him post-Passchendaele.[28] Currie also complained in his diary about a petty incident after Amiens where Lipsett had infringed on his *amour propre*.[29] The British general in his final speech to his troops expressed his disappointment at being 'forced to leave the Third Canadian Division.'[30] This indicates that his transfer was not his choice. Lipsett moved to command the 4th British Division on 14 September while Matheson transferred to the Guards Division.[31] While a lateral move, his selection to command the Guards, the elite British division, signified Haig's esteem. Thus, the 4th British Division was one of the better BEF formations with a strong, capable commander.

On 28 August, the division moved by brigades by bus to Arras. The changing situation and orders meant its move was needlessly wearing. Due to order changes, the British 10th Brigade had a 16-kilometre march including passing through the congestion of the city to reach the 3rd Division's front.[32] The British division relieved the 3rd on the night of 28/29 August, with it officially taking over the line at 6:30 a.m. Like the 1st Division, the relief was difficult because of

23 LAC: 1st Divison W.D., Arras Operations Night 28/29 August to Night 4/5 September 1918; LAC: RG9 III-D-3 v4959: 1st Canadian Division Artillery War Diary, 1st CDA Report of Operations 28 August to 4th September 1918.
24 LAC: 1st CDA War Diary, 30 August 1918.
25 Edmonds, *Military Operations, 1918 v2* 2, pp.492, 591.
26 NLS: Haig Diary, 20 May 1918.
27 Jonathan Boff, 'British Third Army, the Application of Modern War, and the Defeat of the German Army, August-November 1918' (PhD, King's College London, 2010), p.259.
28 McGill: MG4027 C1, 2: Urquhart Fonds, Draft Currie Biography, 13; McGill: McAlpine to Urquhart, 12 November 1934.
29 LAC: Currie Diary, 17-18 August 1918.
30 'Savage, Charles Henry Memoir: 1936'.
31 Boff, 'British Third Army' p.261.
32 TNA: 4th British Div GS WD, 4th British Division, OO 153, 28 August 1918.

the darkness and the obstacles of trenches, shelled terrain, and barbed wire.[33] The 4th Division had at its disposal nine FA brigades (216 pieces). The CRA also had the 42nd and 50th HA brigades with six batteries of 6-inch howitzers and one of 8-inch howitzers.[34] For more, see Map 8.4 4th British Division and Brutinel's Brigade: 29 August in the colour map booklet.

From Currie, Matheson got his orders to seize jump-off positions to assault the D-Q Line – Task 3. The division deployed its 10th Brigade on the right to cover the front primarily from the Arras-Cambrai road along the Sensée valley. It positioned the 2nd Duke of Wellington's (West Riding Regiment), known as 2nd Dukes on the right and the 1st Royal Warwickshire (R Warks) on the left. The 11th Brigade took over the front from the Cojeul river to just north of Boiry-Notre-Dame with the 1st Somerset Light Infantry (SLI) on the right and the 1st Hampshire on the left.

Unlike the 1st Division, Matheson's formation made minor advances where the Germans had withdrawn. During the night of 29/30 August, the 2nd Dukes occupied the ruins of Haucourt without meeting much resistance. It suffered only 10 casualties in the operation.[35] The German defensive line sat on a spur that overlooked the village. Trying to defend at the river's edge while under observation from Seventy Ridge was not a mistake the Germans would make. In the afternoon, the 1st R Warks occupied the rest of Remy, as there was no opposition other than shelling.[36] On the division's left, the 11th Brigade also pushed into what was essentially No Man's Land but suffered losses due to shell fire.

Brutinel's Brigade

Currie had a problem with the flank south of the Scarpe – he lacked the infantry to cover it. The 4th British Division with nine battalions was replacing the 3rd Division with twelve. Without reinforcements, the British would not have the forces to conduct offensive actions. Therefore, he needed a force to protect a 3,200-metre front from the Scarpe down to Boiry-Notre-Dame. While the Germans were unlikely to attack, someone had to guard it. To do so, Currie deployed his abundant machine gun resources as an extemporised force with 100 machine guns commanded by Brigadier General Raymond Brutinel. Initially called the Canadian Composite Brigade, later Brutinel's Brigade, it comprised the 2nd CMMG Brigade, the Canadian Corps Cyclist Battalion (CCCB), two companies of the 101st Life Guards Machine Gun Battalion, and six trench mortars. Brutinel divided the force into three, each built around one of the major units.[37] This unit was a formidable defensive force, but it had limited tactical mobility. It was hard for the crews to move the bulky weapons, ammunition, and supplies. An infantry major attending the GHQ Machine Gun School reported back in the summer of 1918 that after

33 TNA: 4th British Div GS WD, Narrative of Operations of 4th Division from 26 August to 4th September 1918.
34 TNA: WO 95-1460-4/5: 4th British Divisional Artillery War Diary, 4th Divisional Artillery Order No. 126, 28 August 1918 and 28-9 August 1918; TNA: WO 95-1466-5: 29th Field Artillery Brigade War Diary, 29 August 1918 and Narrative of Operations of 4th Divisional Artillery From 26th August to 4th September, 1918.
35 TNA: WO 95-1482-3: 2nd Duke of Wellington's War Diary, 29 August 1918.
36 TNA: WO 95-1484-1/7: 1st Royal Warwickshire War Diary, 29 August 1918.
37 LAC: RG9 III-C-1 v3943, 55/3: Canadian Composite Brigade OO No. 1, 28 August 1918.

Brigadier General Raymond Brutinel (46) was a unique figure in the Canadian Corps. He was a strong advocate for the machine gun arm and had the ear of successive Corps' commanders including Currie. (Allen L Churchill, *The Story of the Great War Victory with the Allies*, vol. VIII (NY: PF Collier and Son, 1920), p.421.)

carrying a machine gun 1,000 metres, he realised they were not as mobile as he thought.[38] A constant refrain in infantry after-action reports were complaints about the machine gun arm, as they were 'fast becoming an Arm apart.'[39] The infantry's dissatisfaction with the direction of the machine gun arm had merit. Only the British Army would continue to treat heavy machine guns as separate into the Second World War. Every other army ensured they were an integral part of each infantry battalion.

The 2nd CMMG Brigade comprised five batteries of eight Vickers machine guns, each only formed 5 June with an attached MT company.[40] These lorries gave it tremendous mobility away from the front-line but were of scant value tactically. There was a great reluctance to risk the loss of these vehicles to enemy fire.[41] Lorries were so valuable and scarce that only a corps commander had the authority to write one off. Also, with narrow tires and weak transmissions, they were unsuited for cross-country travel. The brigade's commander was Lieutenant Colonel

38 LAC: RG9 III-C-3, 2/6: Major Meredith Notes on GHQ MG School, 18 July 1918.
39 For instance, see LAC: RG9 III-D-3 v4836: 1st Division GS War Diary, Lessons Learned from Recent Fighting, ? September 1918; LAC: 9th Brigade War Diary, Narrative of Operations from 25th to 30th August 1918, 15 September 1918; LAC: 12th Brigade War Diary, Report Llandovery Castle Operation, 8-14 August 1918.
40 LAC: RG9 III-D-3 v4987: 2nd Canadian Motorised Machine Gun Brigade War Diary, June, July 1918; University of British Columbia Archives: D547.M3 L63 1919a.: Harry T Logan Fonds, Machine Gun History, 126-127.
41 LAC: 2nd CMMG WD, Lessons Learned [Amiens] August 1918.

W J A Lalor (38), a prewar farmer who served primarily in the 1st Division as a machine gun officer.

The other major Canadian element was the reinforced company-sized Canadian Corps Cyclist Battalion. Comprising three companies of three platoons each, it had a strength of only 321 all ranks. It had not received additional Lewis Guns as did the infantry, so it had less firepower than a comparable infantry unit.[42] Compared to the lumbering machine gun crews, it had the merit of greater combat mobility, but it was reliant on passable roads to fulfil its mobility potential. Major A E Humphrey (38) commanded it and was a rare graduate of RMC in command of a unit in the Corps.

Major A E Humphrey commanded the Canadian Corps Cyclist Battalion. He was a rare RMC graduate in a command of a battalion. (Canada. Dept. of National Defence/Library and Archives Canada/ PA-007363)

Brutinel received orders in the afternoon on 28 August to form his unit and replace the 7th Brigade that night. The relief was time consuming, and it took over a line to the rear of the forward forces. With the 7th Brigade exhausted and in the process of occupying the front, the Canadians did not realise the *35th ID* had already slipped across the Trinquis. The result was when the brigade advanced first on the right and then the left it met only long-range fire. On the right, the brigade took Victoria Trench and Bench Farm to protect the 4th British Division's flank – a 500 metre advance. The push was in the open with little cover, so it was cautious and slow to avoid casualties. Only two machine guns moved at a time to ensure there was sufficient covering fire. The approach worked as the group suffered only 13 casualties.[43] They also captured 20 prisoners. In the later afternoon, the left group attacked to clear the trenches north of Victoria Trench to the Scarpe River. Two platoons of the CCCB did most of

42 LAC: RG9 III-B-1 v972, O-78-3: Cyclist Battalion War Establisment.

43 LAC: Narrative Covering Operations of the 1st Canadian Machine Gun Brigade, the Canadian Independent Force, the Composite Brigade, and Brutinel's Force, 1926; LAC: 2nd CMMG WD.

the fighting, as they complained the 101st MG Battalion made little effort to assist.[44] They suffered but nine casualties.[45] Ironically, the *48th RD* incorrectly interpreted the action as an attempt to cross the river and roll up their wing, which they gallantly repulsed.[46]

In the morning, Brutinel learned the incoming 11th British Division that night would take over the frontage from the Scarpe to just north of Boiry-Notre-Dame. The 101st MG Battalion would remain in place, with the 11th Division assuming its command. Brutinel's force would slide south and take over the 11th British Brigade's sector from the Hamblain road junction to where the Cojeul and Sensée Rivers joined. Both the CCCB and CMMG would go into reserve, and he would instead get the 39th Machine Gun Battalion to cover this approximately 1,500-metre front.[47] When it reached the 11th Brigade's sector on the night of 29/30 August, it found few to no troops there. Apparently, the British had cleared out without waiting for the machine gunners to the battalion's disdain.[48]

Overall, Brutinel's Brigade had provided yeoman service in filling a gap, while suffering less than 30 casualties. Without it, the 4th British Division would have had to cover that front. The brigade's actions highlighted the weaker state of British divisions. Whereas the 3rd Division attacked successfully on the full front, the 4th needed it reduced by 3,200 metres to undertake even limited operations. It required giving up another 1,500 metres before it could seriously challenge the German defences. With just nine battalions, British divisions did not have the offensive punch and resilience of the Canadian ones.

Relief: XXII Corps Takes Over the Northern Sector

Having registered the Canadian Corps had too much frontage for its forces, Haig arranged for the XXII Corps in First Army reserve to take over the northern sector.[49] A Canadian staff officer working on the CWNS project suggested Currie instigated the action, and given the entry in Haig's diary, it was likely at the meeting at the Corps headquarters on 27 August.[50] The XXII Corps would comprise the 51st (Highland) Division and the 11th British Division. It took over the 51st (Highland) Division at noon on 29 August, and with it the Corps handed over four FA and two HA brigades.[51] The 11th British Division defended the sector held by Brutinel's Brigade, which it assumed on 29/30 August.[52] It was a New Army formation that had first fought at Suvla Bay during the Gallipoli campaign. By Arras, it was a veteran of the Western Front. It only had two brigades, as Haig had transferred its 34th Brigade and some artillery to the Cavalry Corps and motorised them.[53] The transfer of front and forces did not

44 LAC: RG9 III-C-1 v3944, 56/4: Canadian Corps Cyclist Battalion Report on Operations from August 26th to September 4th, 1918.
45 LAC: CMGO WD, Summary of Operations. Canadian Independent Force 28-8-18 to 31-8-18.
46 Hirschel, *Geschichte RIR 221*, p.236.
47 LAC: CMGO WD, Brutinel's Brigade OO No.2, 29 August 1918.
48 TNA: WO 95-2577-4: 39th Machine Gun Battalion War Diary, 28-30 August 1918.
49 NLS: Haig Diary, 27 August 1918.
50 LAC: RG9 III-D-2 v4800, 121: [Basil Webb] Notes to Duguid, Undated [1919].
51 LAC: Chronological Table; TNA: Cdn. Corps GS WD, Canadian Corps OO No. 233, 29 August 1918.
52 TNA: First Army GS WD, First Army, G.88 28 August 1918.
53 LAC: RG9 III-C-1 v3912, 40/1: First Army GS 1376/25, 26 August 1918.

bother Currie. 'This shortened the line considerably and relieved me of the anxiety caused by the length and vulnerability of the northern flank,' according to his Interim Report.[54] The insertion of the XXII Corps greatly simplified his command and decreased the Corp's frontage to 8,350 metres south of the Scarpe.

Highlanders

Although the 51st would pass from the Corps' control during the day, it still had to complete Task 1 – the capture of Greenland Hill and its spur. The challenge was Oldfield had two objectives with the resources for one. The 154th Brigade were his only fresh troops. With one battalion in reserve, the 154th deployed the 1/7th Argyll & Sutherland Highlanders (ASH) and the 1/4th Gordon Highlanders (GH) on the right for an attack. With four FA brigades and one HA brigade, the assault frontage was 1,600 metres – a density of 22 metres per 18-pounder. Oldfield's solution was to exploit the marshes and bodies of water south of Plouvain that constricted the German lines of communication to the spur. If he could threaten the capture of Plouvain, the Germans holding the woods on the spur would retreat or risk capture. The plan was to advance on both sides of the railway embankment to stop the Germans using it as an infiltration route and capture Greenland Hill. It would thus outflank the Hausa and Delbar Wood positions.[55] For more, see Map 8.5 Highlanders: 29 August in the colour map booklet.

At 6:30 a.m., the two battalions attacked on each side of the railway. The success of the 3rd Division on 28 August had outflanked the *48th RD*'s defences from the south. As a result, the Germans held this zone lightly as a *Vorfeld*. South of the railway, the 4th GH took their objective along Clod Trench by 9:30 a.m., while the 7th ASH seized Greenland Hill by 8:00 a.m. The attackers captured just 2 officers and 109 other ranks, indicating how weakly the *48th RD* held these positions.[56] The two battalions suffered 124 casualties.[57] Recognising the futility of trying to hold on to the two woods, the Germans started pulling back early in the afternoon to the F-R Line north of the Scarpe.

Oldfield's scheme effectively dealt with the twin issues of the hill and its spur, while he had only a thin margin of superiority over the defenders. It had pushed the *48th RD* off the vital ground and had advanced over three kilometres, but it had not pushed hard. The division reported total losses of 827 all ranks for the period from 25 to 29 August. An observer could interpret this as an economical use of manpower or a symptom of an unwillingness to hazard casualties.[58] Its low level of training and lack of artillery resources restricted what it could do.

Currie acknowledged the success of the Highlanders, but he wanted them to have pushed further, faster. He complained in his diary that the lack of substantial progress north of the Scarpe impeded the Corps. He mused that taking the northern F-R Line with fresh forces

54 Note the timing of the handover given in the Interim report was incorrect. Kemp, *Report of the Ministry*, p.151.
55 TNA: 51st Div. GS WD, Report on the Operations North of the Sc; TNA: 51st Div. GS WD, 51st Division OO No. 303, 28 August 1918; Bewsher, *History of 51st (Highland)*, pp.367-369.
56 TNA: 51st Div. GS WD, 29 August 1918.
57 TNA: WO 95-2886-1: 1/7th Argyll & Sutherland Highlanders War Diary, 29 August 1918; TNA: WO 95-2886-2: 1/4th Gordon Highlanders War Diary, 29 August 1918.
58 TNA: 51st Div. GS WD, Casualties Sustained by Division during Operations 25th to 29th August, 1918.

would allow the heavy artillery to move to the Fampoux area. Many larger pieces remained far to the rear behind Vimy Ridge and this distance reduced the effectiveness of the counter-battery fire. Further, his main supply route, the Arras-Cambrai road, was 'practically under enemy field artillery fire.' This constrained the further advance of the Corps, so it was necessary to shift north.[59] This was not realistic. There were no fresh forces available, as Currie knew, and it would take too long to shift the Corps there.

Results

The casualties on 29 August reflected the reduced effort by the Corps. Only the 4th British Division conducted offensive operations south of the Scarpe, and these were primarily occupying undefended ground. Nevertheless, the First World War battlefield during active operations was hazardous, as the 1st Division's 123 casualties indicate. Overall, the Corps' losses dropped by a factor of four over the previous day with an estimated 557. The 51st Division's totals were not recorded as it passed to the XXII Corps. The Corps reported many captives with 5 officers and 575 other ranks.[60] This was anomalous. For a day of limited action, the total was high. This may be an artefact of the reporting period and included prisoners taken the previous day.

Table 8.1 Estimated Casualties For 29 August 1918

	Killed	Wounded	POW	Total
1st CID	47	75	1	123
2nd CID	36	64		100
3rd CID	47	42		89
4th CID	5	3		8
4th BID*	34	121		155
Tank Corps†				0
Other	7	75		82
Total	**176**	**380**	**1**	**557**

* 4th British Division totals do not include prisoners lost.
† Included in the Other category are Tank Corps wounded.

30 August: Task 2 Progress

With the insertion of the XXII Corps, Currie's command span and front shrunk. He and the Corps could now focus on preparing to assault the D-Q Line. First Army issued two orders to the Corps. It was to continue to reach the jump-off line and close up with the XVII Corps

59 LAC: Currie Diary, 29 August 1918.
60 LAC: POW Arras.

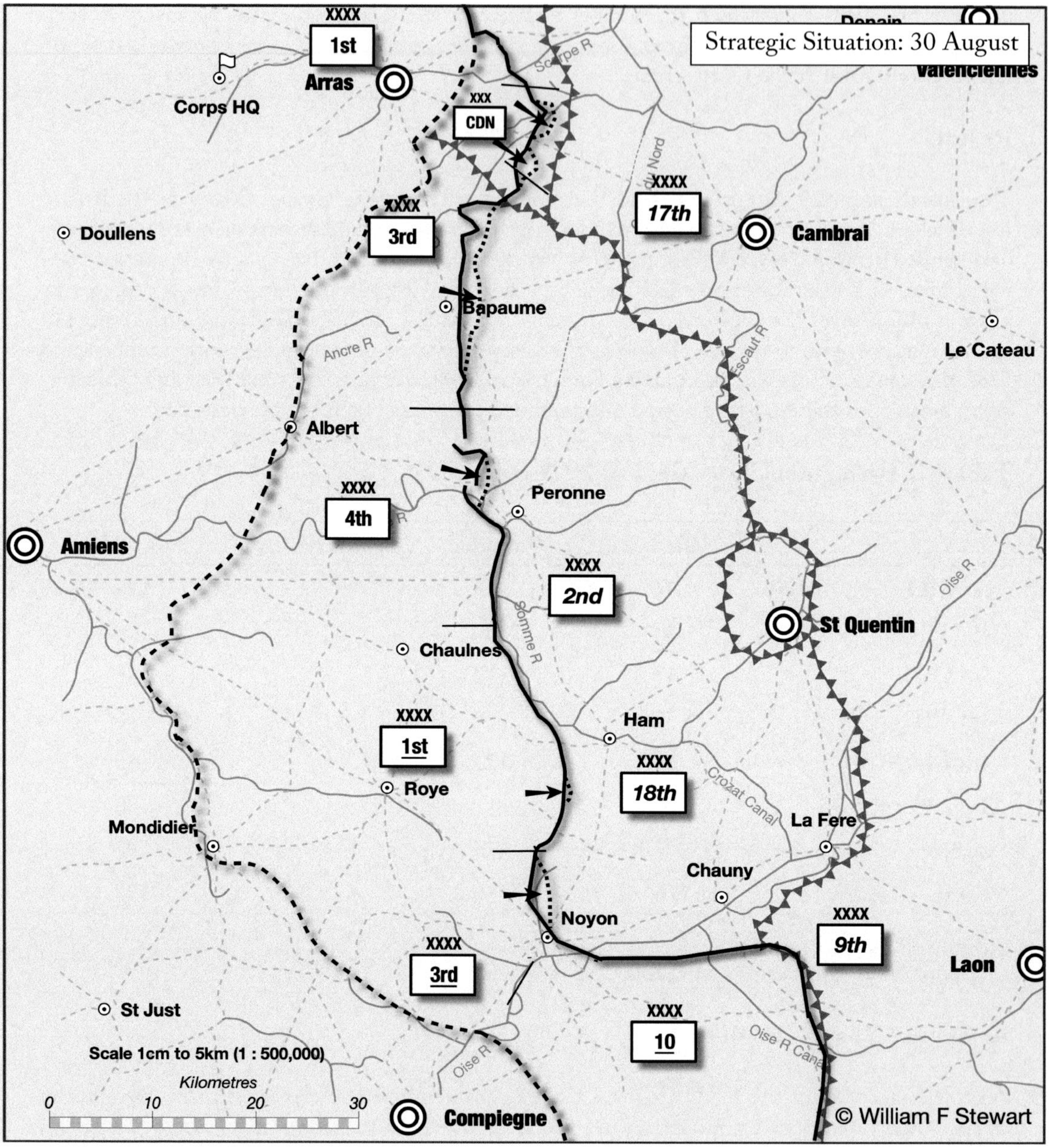

Map 26. North of the Somme, the Germans fell back to a strong ridge position they intended to hold for the winter. The British Fourth and French First and Third Armies made limited gains. (Author's map)

around Hendecourt.[61] The Corps' orders for the day reflected Horne's instructions with a concentration on pushing eastwards.[62] Note how these objectives were far less aggressive than those set for the 2nd and 3rd Divisions. It was imperative that 1st Division capture the F-R Line to complete Task 2 and make progress on Task 3, while linking up with the XVII Corps. Macdonell's division had to advance through the F-R Line 2,200 metres on the left to 3,500 metres on the right to reach its jump-off line. The division had also to contend with the Vis-en-Artois Switch and the fortified Crow's Nest. These defences lay on high ground dominating the nearby terrain and gave unobstructed fields of fire. Likewise, the 4th British Division had to gain jump-off positions that required a push of 800 metres on its left to 1,800 on the right. This advance had to climb several spurs and valleys from the main ridge. This gave opportunities for enfilade fire and to bring up counterattack forces shielded from observation. Much would depend on the extent to which von Dellmensingen would defend the forward zone.

Strategic Situation

With the Germans falling back across the Somme, the Fourth Army tried to seize crossings without success. North of there, the enemy retired to a line based on a strong ridge position they intended to keep. They wanted to hold this 50-kilometre line, extending north to the D-Q Line, for the winter. Ludendorff refused to retire farther because of the political and psychological consequences. If the Canadians could break the D-Q Line, it would unhinge this position and force another significant retreat or risk being pocketed. The Third Army encountered this new position and made progress in places, but it was uneven. German resistance was strong. On the army's left, the XVII Corps was to consolidate its gains given it was ahead of the corps on each side. In the French sector, only the centre of the 10th Army advanced towards Soissons while elsewhere gains were minimal.

On Byng's left, the 57th Division was hard pressed to hold the line near Hendecourt and could not attack. The Germans held the village with a mix of companies from the *103rd IR* and *26th Dragoon Regiment* of the *7th SD*. Who held Hendecourt was uncertain, as the fighting spluttered on. It meant that the 1st Brigade did not recognise the opportunity to outflank the F-R Line, as communications between the divisions were poor to almost non-existent.[63]

German Situation

For the Germans, the previous day was a welcome relief from the constant attacks. Dellmensingen recognising the exhausted state of the *26th RD* tried to hand over the sector north of the Arras-Cambrai road to the *4th EzD* on the night of 29/30 August. They could only do so on the northern portion.[64] As a result, the commander of the *26th RD* remained the sector commander for the entire front. The corps commander blamed inexperienced staff officers in the *4th EzD* for the delay. This was the mark of a less capable formation.

61 TNA: First Army GS WD, First Army, G110, 29 August 1918.
62 TNA: Cdn. Corps GS WD, Canadian Corps G.749, 29 August 1918.
63 TNA: 57th Division GS WD, Narrative of Operations August 20th to September 7th 1918; Poland, *RIR Nr. 103 History*, p.143; LAC: CWNS XVII Corps.
64 Bundesarchiv, Freiburg: Feldzug 1918, 30 August 1918.

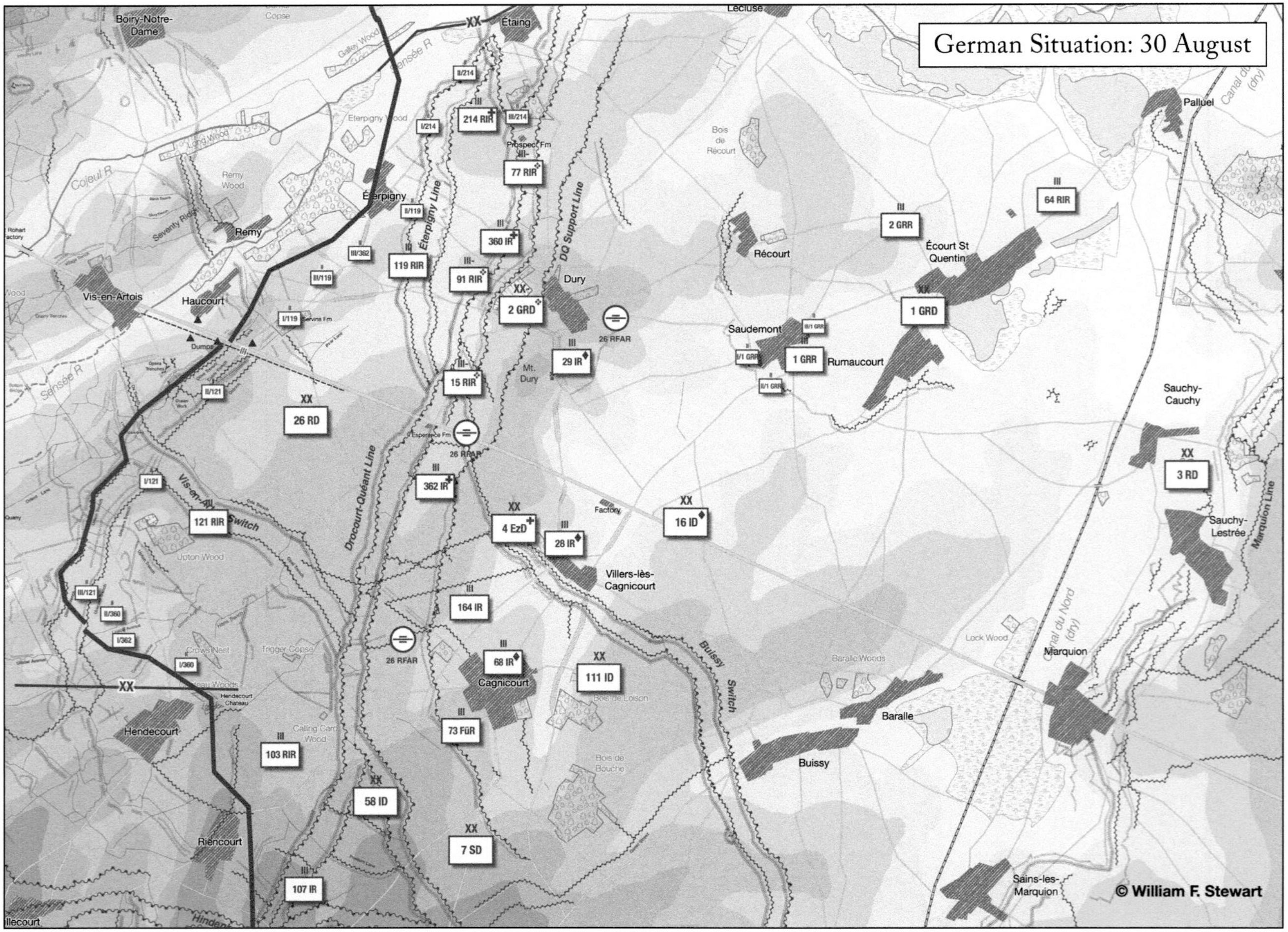

Map 27. The *II Bavarian Korps* had to leave the exhausted *26th RD* in the line, with the *4th EzD* taking over the northern sector and reinforcing the *26th RD* with four battalions. The *2nd GRD*, *111th ID*, *and 16th ID* held the D-Q Line. The *3rd RD* was in reserve across the Canal du Nord. (Author's map)

The German order-of-battle for the day ran from the south with *7th SD* and *58th ID* at Hendecourt after retaking the village. The *121st RIR* then held the sector from Hendecourt to the Arras-Cambrai road reinforced by three battalions from two regiments of the *4th EzD*. North of the Arras-Cambrai road, the *119th RIR* defended to Éterpigny reinforced by another battalion of the *4th EzD*. The *214th RIR* from the *4th EzD* held the zone from Éterpigny to Étaing.[65] The *35th ID* continued to control the Trinquis Brook. In addition, Canadian reports indicated the Germans were reinforcing their artillery park.[66]

The *2nd GRD*, *16th ID*, and *111th ID* remained in the D-Q Line. The key division on 30 August, the *16th ID*, was a prewar active formation from the Rhineland. It served on the Western Front throughout the war, and it was the division that overran two 51st Division brigade headquarters in April 1918. GHQ rated it as a 'Very Good' division and a view *OHL*'s agreed with as it reinforced it with one battalion per regiment from the disbanded *364th IR*. This action brought each battalion up to a strength of 700 men each, and fully equipped with machine guns (36), and trench mortars (12). They did not, however, have time to train together before their next battle. The *16th ID*'s regiments were among the strongest the Canadians would face.[67]

Dellmensingen was in a running conflict with the *Seventeenth Armee* over the provision of another *Eingreifdivision*.[68] The army would not supply one, and he stated the corps would not be responsible for its front in those circumstances. His concern relied on German intelligence's identification of a formidable mass of enemy formations of six divisions. Moreover, he grumbled about the quality and quantity of his reserves in the D-Q Line. He had grounds for anxiety. His chief of staff, *Oberst* von Seißer, made a convincing case to the army that it was possible that the attackers might penetrate the D-Q Line without better reserves.[69] In response, the *Seventeenth Armee* rushed the *1st GRD* to the area around Ecourt St Quentin and Saudemont. Originally meant for the sector north of the Scarpe, the *35th ID*'s defeat meant the *1st GRD*'s redirection south.[70] The army also moved up the *3rd RD* to east of the canal as army reserve.[71] Dellmensingen complained the division would take up to 12 hours to intervene on his front. He thought it a repeat of the 1917 mistaken positioning of reserves too far to the rear.

Rather than fighting the six divisions in the intelligence report, the *II Bavarian Korps* faced just the 4th British and 1st Canadian. While Canadian intelligence did not have a full picture of the enemy's forces, they were markedly better in their assessments than the Germans. His intelligence service poorly served von Dellmensingen. They missed the Canadians arriving on 23 August and, according to the *26th RD* history, did not identify their presence until the

65 Stühmke, *26th Reserve Division* II, p.65.
66 LAC: RG9 III-D-3 v4972: 13th CFA War Diary, 31 August 1918; LAC: RG9 III-D-3 v4669: 6th CFA War Diary, 29 August 1918.
67 Edmonds, *Military Operations, 1918 v2* 2, p.287; Pafferath, *Geschichte I.R. 68*, pp.679-681; '6. Rheinisches Infanterie-Regiment Nr. 68' <http://genwiki.genealogy.net/IR_68> (6 October 2018); LAC: SS 644b Classification; General Staff Intelligence Section, *251 Divisions*, pp.262-264.
68 Bundesarchiv, Freiburg: Feldzug 1918, 30 August 1918.
69 Bundesarchiv, Freiburg: Feldzug 1918, 30 August 1918.
70 Tido von Brederlow, *Geschichte Des 1st Garde-Reserve-Regiments* (Berlin: Gerhard Stalling, 1926), pp.313-314.
71 Döring v. Gottberg, *Das Grenadier-Regiment König Friedrich Wilhelm IV (1. Pommersches) Nr. 2 im Weltkrieg* (Berlin: Verlag Tradition Wilhelm Kolk, 1928), p.456.

third day of the offensive. Once identified, the intelligence service then wildly exaggerated the number of front line divisions in the Canadian Corps.[72]

1st Brigade Planning

It was time for the 1st Division to complete Task 2 and take the F-R Line. Macdonell informed Griesbach, GOC 1st Brigade, early on 29 August that his brigade would take the fortification from Ox Trench south to the division boundary the next day. Griesbach faced the same challenges as did the 2nd Division of capturing a strong defensive position without tanks and with limited artillery. He prepared three plans during the day, but he then learned later in the afternoon that the 57th Division had captured Hendecourt. The 1st Machine Gun Battalion claimed one of its officers scouting for guns positions discovered the situation.[73] It was telling of the poor liaison between corps that the 1st Brigade did not learn about this from the 57th Division. The result was a more daring version.[74] Instead of a frontal assault, Griesbach took advantage of the defenders' exposed side and would hit them from two directions. The 1st and 2nd Battalions would strike north from the vicinity of Hendecourt and roll up the German line. Simultaneously, the 3rd Battalion would punch through at the junction of the Vis-en-Artois Switch and the F-R Line to distract the Germans. The scheme entailed a long flank march by two battalions across a congested and unknown battlefield in the dark. While potentially risky, it would place the defenders at a fatal disadvantage. It would also lead to the capture of a good portion of the Vis-en-Artois Switch, which was not part of the 1st Division's directive but necessary.[75]

Griesbach quickly got Macdonell's approval for the plan, but it did not issue its final orders until 6:00 p.m. This left little time to get the units assembled for the 4:40 a.m. start time. It meant the troops would attack in pitch-black visibility with morning twilight not until 4:47 a.m.[76] The 2nd Battalion would complain it was too dark to see the ground, but it had the merit of shielding attackers from German fire from Hendecourt.[77]

Not only would the timing be tight for the infantry, Griesbach's plan meant a complex barrage. There was little time for Thacker, the CRA, to prepare it, disseminate the instructions, and supply the batteries. To prevent interception of orders, the division artillery sent the directive by despatch rider. The instructions arrived in some cases with only minutes to spare.[78] There was doubt to the end whether the eight batteries of 4.5-inch howitzers firing the vital smoke shells would get a sufficient supply. The 2nd CFA reported supply was the most difficult of the

72 Bundesarchiv, Freiburg: Feldzug 1918, 30 August 1918.
73 LAC: RG9 III-C-4 v4031, 3/3: 1st Bn CMGC, Report on Offensive Operations from August 28th to Sept 4th 1918.
74 Lieutenant Colonel McLaughlin 2nd Battalion was out scouting.
75 LAC: MG30 E15 v1: Griesbach Fonds, W.A. Griesbach Diary, 29 August 1918; Macdonell, 'Old Red Patch 1', p.392; LAC: RG9 III-C-3 v4040, 3/7: 1st CIB OO No.242, 29 August 1918; LAC: RG9 III-D-3 v4869: 1st Brigade War Diary, 1st Brigade G.469-8, 31 August 1918.
76 LAC: Daylight and Light Conditions July, August, September 1918.
77 LAC: RG9 III-C-3 v4016, 31/5: 2nd Battalion Report on Operations between 28 August and 1 September 1918, 9 September 1918.
78 LAC: 1st CDA War Diary, 1st Division Artillery Report on Operations, 28 August to 4th September 1918.

Brigadier General HC Thacker, CRA 1st Division, pictured here in 1926 as Chief of the Canadian General Staff. The division commander thought Thacker's barrage was ingenious. (Library and Archives Canada, Public Domain, <https://commons.wikimedia.org/w/index.php?curid=64583847>)

campaign as congestion, dead horses, and confusion blocked the roads in the dark night.[79] Not until 4:00 a.m. did the wagons arrive with the last of 400 rounds for each 18-pounder.

The barrage comprising two lines shaped like a L on its back closing in on itself with one line moving north and the other east. It featured elements of 9 FA brigades with 28x18-pounder batteries firing a 50 percent mix of shrapnel and HE, with 8x4.5-inch howitzer batteries firing smoke shells.[80] The barrage density was a crushing 16 metres and almost double of the 2nd Division's. Dellmensingen admitted in his diary that Canadian counter-battery efforts paralysed his artillery during the day.[81] It was a testament to Canadian gunners' capabilities that they could organise a barrage of this complexity so quickly. Unit reports were universal in their praise of its effectiveness. Griesbach later called it a 'masterpiece' and Macdonell 'ingenious.'[82]

In the rush to get the orders out, someone took a forbidden shortcut and telephoned them, and the Germans overheard it an hour before Zero.[83] There was insufficient time, however, to relay that information, so it had no effect on the battle. A tension always existed between maintaining signal security and ensuring subordinates received orders in time. An overheard

79 LAC: RG9 III-D-3 v4965: 2nd Brigade CFA War Diary, Report on Operations from August 27th to Sept. 6th, 1918.
80 LAC: 1st CDA War Diary, 1st Division OO No.87, 29 August 1918.
81 Bundesarchiv, Freiburg: Feldzug 1918, 30 August 1918.
82 LAC: MG30 E15 v5, 34 (b): Griesbach Fonds, Griesbach to Macdonell, 2 February 1927; Macdonell, 'Old Red Patch 1', p.392.
83 LAC: RG9 III-C-3 v4112, 40/1: 2nd Division GS 244, 2 September 1918.

order could have devastating consequences, but so would orders that arrived too late. In the communications environment of 1918, there were no good options.

1st Brigade Strikes

On the brigade's right, the 1st Battalion faced fewer defences and defenders but a larger area to cover than the other units. At Amiens, it did not suffer heavy losses and praised the open warfare training for its few casualties.[84] Its commander, Lieutenant Colonel A W Sparling (27), had a curious path to command. A farmer from Saskatchewan, Sparling joined in 1914, but did not reach the front until November 1916. Despite his youth and lack of command experience, he took over the 1st Battalion at Hill 70 in August 1917. He earned a DSO for his performance there and would gain two bars for his service during the Hundred Days. His rapid rise and multiple awards show a strong officer. For more, see Map 8.8 1st Brigade Attacks: 30 August in the colour map booklet.

The 1st Battalion led the march to the assembly positions north of Hendecourt. It and the 2nd Battalion had to navigate in the dark over unknown roads amid congestion and German shelling. This shelling resulted in A Company and the headquarters being cut-off and not arriving until Zero Hour. It found that the Germans had retaken Hendecourt and so adjusted its deployment.[85] It attacked on a two-company front striking to the north-east on a 750-metre front to a depth of 2,300 metres to capture the two trenches of the Vis-en-Artois Switch – Opal and Orix. Included was the dense forest on the high point of Upton Wood.

Behind an intense barrage, the troops advanced at 4:40 a.m. A heavy German protective barrage crashed down within five minutes and inflicted losses on the reserve company. The battalion punched through the *I/362nd IR* and took 40 prisoners, including a company commander. He claimed the battalion's companies had only 50 men each. The battalion reported taking all its objectives by 9:30 a.m. Machine gun and artillery fire from the high ground to the south-east presented the most effective resistance, causing numerous casualties. This was the challenge of long-range fire from unengaged sectors interfering with the attack. The battalion reorganised with two companies guarding the Vis-en-Artois Switch, one in reserve, and two platoons holding the long-exposed flank from the Switch to the division boundary.[86]

To the left of the 1st Battalion, the 2nd was responsible for taking the F-R Line. It did not have a hard struggle at Amiens, so it was in good shape. Its leader was the veteran but diminutive Lieutenant Colonel Lorne McLaughlin (39) with 15 months' command experience.[87] He took over the 2nd Battalion in May 1917 and would earn a DSO with two bars for his service. He was clearly well-regarded by the authorities and an inspiring leader. The 2nd Battalion followed the 1st to the assembly position and experienced the same heavy shelling. It only reached the assembly point minutes before Zero Hour. The battalion had a 400-metre front and would

84 LAC: RG9 III-D-3 v4913: 1st Battalion War Diary, 1st Battalion Report on Operations on 9 August 1918, 13 August 1918.

85 LAC: RG9 III-C-3 v4033, 4/1: 1st Battalion Report on Operations 30 and 31 August, 1918, 9 September 1918; LAC: 1st Battalion War Diary, 30 August 1918.

86 LAC: 1st Bn Report 30-31 August; LAC: 1st Battalion War Diary, 30 August 1918.

87 LAC: Griesbach Diary, 12 June 1918; 'The Iron Man' <https://matthewkbarrett.com/2015/11/14/the-ironman/> (6 February 2019).

Lieutenant Colonel L McLaughlin 'Little Mac', CO 2nd Battalion, restored order with his pistol and leadership when the Germans counterattacked. (Canada. Dept. of National Defence/Library and Archives Canada/ PA-007537)

advance 2,100 metres along Ulster and Union Trenches to meet the 3rd Battalion pushing south. It attacked with two companies, each on a front of just one platoon. On the left, the opposition was more intermittent as: 'The enemy, somewhat bewildered by the unusual direction of the attack, left his line in great numbers and retreated overland.'[88] The support company commander deployed a platoon to shoot the fleeing enemy and inflicted heavy losses. It took time for the Germans to recognise the threat, and resistance hardened only after about a kilometre's advance. The battalion reported: 'It is noted that in many instances German machine guns remained in action until the infantry had entirely surrounded them and killed their crews.'[89] It reached its objectives by 6:30 a.m., and redeployed in Unicorn Trench, with one company in Opal Trench. It took most of its estimated 200 prisoners in the morning as well as a three-piece battery of 105mm howitzers and 25 machine guns.[90]

In the morning, the *121st RIR* reported repulsing a frontal assault except for a small section where the 3rd Battalion struck. There was, however, only a frontal attack on the 3rd Battalion's sector. The *I/121st RIR* claimed to have erased the foothold but at the cost of its commander's death. The single-minded attention to the direct front was a characteristic of trench warfare.

88 LAC: 2nd Bn Report 28 August-1 September.
89 LAC: 2nd Bn Report 28 August-1 September.
90 LAC: 2nd Bn Report 28 August-1 September; Murray, *2nd Battalion History*, pp.277-285; LAC: RG9 III-D-3 v4985: 2nd Battalion War Diary, 30 August 1918; LAC: RG9 III-C-3 v4027, 13/7: 2nd Battalion Ref 7-46, 31 August 1918.

Then, according to German reports, the attackers rolled up the defenders unexpectedly from the south when the Canadians broke through another regiment. Fleeing troops racing north tried to warn of the oncoming onslaught, but the defenders did not believe them. The Canadians surprised and outflanked them. Small groups tried to infiltrate the Canadian cordon while the machine guns fought to the end to hold off the attackers. Essentially, the *III* and *I/121st RIR* ceased to exist with only about 50 men from the two battalions escaping the disaster.[91]

The battle report of the *I* and *III/121st RIR* provides insight into Canadian tactics and their devastating effectiveness. Fog and smoke used effectively by the Canadians was the greatest threat to the defence. A platoon would emerge from the mist led by two Lewis Gun teams firing from the hip to keep the defenders' heads down. These tactics were 'very effective both materially and on morale.' Troops bravely defending the front were 'totally overrun, overcome, and taken prisoner.' Further, flexible defence opened gaps in the lines that the attackers exploited to isolate and annihilate the defenders. Given the state of their morale, retreating broke up units and rendered them ineffective.[92]

To the north, the 3rd Battalion was to drive east to capture the junction of the Vis-en-Artois Switch and F-R Line. It did well at Amiens with 205 casualties.[93] It was a veteran unit with a strong record. A gauge of this status was a return from May 1918 showing 116 officers and men in the unit with two wounds – including its CO.[94] Its long-term commander was on leave, so Major Douglas Mason (35) was in charge for Arras 1918. While this was his first stint in command during a battle, he was an experienced and capable officer with a DSO already.[95]

The Toronto battalion had the difficult task of a frontal attack on the F-R Line with no flank support. It attacked on a two-company front along communications trenches leading to the line on a 700-metre sector. The unit met little resistance in the darkness until it approached Ox and Ulster Trenches. Strong forces emerged from their dugouts and opened fire when the barrage lifted. The result was a hard battle to take the objectives. Despite heavy fire from Ocean Work to the north, the Torontonians were consolidating their positions by 8:30 a.m. They cut-off several hundred Germans and some surrendered and some had to be killed. It reported the enemy fought with tenacity, and 'their morale appeared to be good.' This was not surprising given the elite nature of the Württembergers of the *121st RIR*. The battalion paid a steep price for its success with the loss of 13 officers and 225 men.[96]

After the morning's success, Macdonell instructed the 1st Brigade to take Ocean Work and Olive and Ostrich Trenches.[97] At 1:10 p.m., Griesbach ordered the 3rd Battalion to capture the position supported by artillery at 2:00 p.m. It is possible that he envisioned it as a probe

91 Hauptstaatsarchiv Stuttgart: Visher Höhe; Stühmke, *26th Reserve Division* II, p.95; Holtz, *Reserve-Infanterie-Regiment Nr. 121*, p.75.
92 Hauptstaatsarchiv Stuttgart: M109 Bü49 2009: Gefechtsbericht Uber Den Feindlichen Angriff Auf I. Und III. Batl. R./121 in Der Hochwaldstellung am 30.8.1918.
93 LAC: 3rd Battalion War Diary, 3rd Battalion Report, Amiens August 1918.
94 LAC: 3rd Battalion War Diary, 1 May 1918.
95 He was in temporary command of the battalion while Rogers was away on a month's leave in early 1918.
96 LAC: RG9 III-C-3 v4016, 31/5: 3rd Battalion Report on Operations between 28 August and 1 September 1918, 9 September 1918; Goodspeed, *Battle Royal*, pp.246-248; LAC: 3rd Battalion War Diary, 3rd Battalion Report 30 August 1918.
97 LAC: 1st Div GS WD, Appendix G August 1918.

to test if the Germans had abandoned the sector.[98] There was not enough time for the gunners to prepare, and the brigade delayed the operation an hour. Due to the constricted space, only four platoons from two companies conducted it. A deadly crossfire quickly stopped this hurried and ill-prepared assault with substantial losses. The 8th Battalion's assessment from its position facing the defences was the operation had little chance of success.[99]

Burstall's division twice failed to breach the F-R Line in a frontal assault. Why was the 3rd Battalion able to punch through the same defences with no flank support? The Germans were weaker after four days of defending the line, and the 3rd Battalion was fresher than the 5th Brigade. Crucially, the cover provided by a predawn attack allowed the attackers to reach the defences without interference. Finally, the barrage was far stronger, and smoke shielded the attackers by interfering with the effectiveness of long-range machine gun fire.

German Counterblow

Griesbach's final plan had a serious flaw that created conditions for what should have been a devastating counterattack. His mistake was to leave his 2,200 metres south-east flank weakly defended. He should have assigned a full battalion to it, instead of two platoons. This was an instance where the 'millstone' of trench tactics seriously affected operations.[100] Typically in trench to trench attacks, the line of communications ran along the axis of advance and with no exposed flanks. Given the boundary with the 57th Division ran south-east, the advance north-east left a long, unprotected flank that the Germans would exploit. For more, see Map 8.9 1st Brigade: German Counterattack in the colour map booklet.

Griesbach described 10 years later that the attack route taken by the 1st and 2nd Battalions had 'a curious psychological effect on all ranks.'[101] It affected him too. The two battalions oriented their defences primarily facing the direction of the advance. Thus, when the Germans struck from the south-west, it was potentially calamitous. Employing four battalions, they struck the 1st Battalion in the flank and rolled it up. Elements of the 1st and 2nd Battalions understandably broke, just like the *121st RIR* did in the morning. The German counterattack reached the southern boundary of Upton Wood along the Switch. It also pushed forces into the wood and got as far as a line running from the south-west along the Vis-en-Artois-Hendecourt Road.

To recover from the morning's disaster, the *16th ID*, the sector's *Eingreifdivision*, ordered a two-regiment counterattack. The *68th* and *28th IR* would advance centred on a line running from Villers-lès-Cagnicourt to Upton Wood. This was what the Canadian defensive arrangements were ready for. The *26th RD* and *4th EzD* were to participate but were too battered to do so. Just as the *68th IR* reported its readiness, new information from officer patrols and the *26th RD* forced a reconsideration. The Canadian breakthrough was not at the centre but on the left, so the counterattack shifted to strike from the south-west and hit the Canadians' vulnerable flank.

98 LAC: 1st Div GS WD, Appendix G August 1918.
99 LAC: 3rd Bn Report 28 August-1 September; Goodspeed, *Battle Royal*, pp.246-248; 'Mason, Douglas Herbert Campbell' <https://qormuseum.org/soldiers-of-the-queens-own/mason-d-h-c/> (7 February 2019); LAC: RG9 III-C-3 v4052, 22/6: 8th Bn to 2nd Bde, 30 August 1918.
100 Macdonell, 'Old Red Patch 1', p.389.
101 LAC: Griesbach to Macdonell.

Note the German's ability to identify the opportunity. The *68th IR* would strike to the north-west along the Vis-en-Artois Switch and take Upton Wood with two battalions. To its left, the *29th IR* would punch west with two battalions in a staggered configuration. Its left battalion would trail to protect the regiment's left flank because it was uncertain who held Hendecourt. This new scheme meant a major reshuffling of forces, as the *29th IR* moved up from reserve while the *68th IR* sidled south.[102]

At 11:00 a.m., the Canadians reported a fierce bombardment of their positions that interfered in getting up supplies. Concerned the opportunity was passing, the *68th IR* received orders to attack despite that neither the *29th IR* and nor the gunners were ready to fire a barrage. Nevertheless, the two battalions of the *68th IR* advanced and struck the vulnerable two front companies of the 1st Battalion in the flank. Griesbach sheepishly confessed 10 years later, that he neglected to inform Macdonell of the rout worried about a 'strafe from the old man.'[103] The brigade report claimed it restored the situation by 2:15 p.m. – at least eight hours early.[104] The *II/68th* described the Canadian infantry falling back 400 metres but the machine gunners remaining in action until the counterattack was within 60 to 80 metres when they tried to get away. Delays in the advance of the *29th IR* meant the *I/68th* filled the gap on the left, while the *I/29th IR* pushed to the outskirts of Hendecourt.[105] The attackers faced little resistance until they approached the Hendecourt-Dury road. From then on severe fire assailed them. For instance, the 2nd CFA expended all its dumped ammunition, and its battery wagons were busy through the afternoon keeping it firing SOS barrages.[106]

The situation was serious as this blow imperilled all the gains made by the 1st Brigade. This was where the commander of the 2nd Battalion, McLaughlin, decisively intervened to change the battle's course. As Griesbach wrote '"Little Mac" happened to be around at this moment, as good men have a habit of doing, and pistol in hand drove the bolters back in a counter attack which restored the line.' He led forward two and half companies of his unit plus other remnants that crashed into the advancing Germans and stopped them. He received a serious wound that immobilised him. Despite the blood loss and pain, he refused evacuation. He remained in a shell hole directing and encouraging his men until the situation had stabilised. 'Little Mac' earned a second bar to his DSO for his courage and leadership. By 2:45 p.m., there was a stalemate, with both sides pounding the other's infantry with shells and machine gun fire. With the Canadians having far more artillery and shells available, the Germans got worn down.

It took time for information to reach Griesbach so he could properly fashion a response.[107] After 1:00 p.m., on learning of the German success, he had the 3rd Brigade send up two battalions to garrison F-R Line trenches. In the afternoon, he had the 4th Battalion send two companies each to 1st and 2nd Battalions.[108] This was a curious decision as he knew an adjutant commanded the 2nd Battalion. This suggests a reluctance to thrust a new and untested

102 Pafferath, *Geschichte I.R. 68*, pp.692-693.
103 LAC: Griesbach to Macdonell.
104 LAC: 1st Brigade War Diary, Appendix G August 1918.
105 Pafferath, *Geschichte I.R. 68*, pp.693-696.
106 LAC: 2 CFA WD, Report on Operations from August 27th to Sept. 6th, 1918.
107 LAC: 1st Brigade Report 28 August-1 September.
108 LAC: 1st Brigade Report 28 August-1 September; LAC: RG9 III-C-3 v4016, 31/5: 4th Battalion Report on Operations for the Period August 28th to September 4th, 1918, 6 September 1918.

battalion commander into a confused situation. Major George Blackstock (35) took over at Amiens when the incumbent commander was wounded. He attended the SOC Aldershot during Passchendaele, so his service and training qualified him for command. The battalion suffered substantial losses at Amiens with 285 all ranks including the commander and 18 other officers, but it was the second strongest battalion in the brigade by Arras.[109]

With the situation stalemated and with the 4th Battalion's reinforcements, it was the Canadians' turn. There were three separate actions starting after 7:00 p.m. First, two companies of the 2nd Battalion under the new commander, Major R Vanderwater, pushed south-east along the Vis-en-Artois Switch clearing out the *III/68th IR*.[110] Sparling decided on two separate operations using the two 4th Battalion companies. B/4th attacked at 7:40 p.m. through Upton Wood. There was little resistance in the woods until they emerged into the open. While the attackers rooted out most Germans, there were still 30 lurking who did not surrender until 1 September. The company occupied a position 100 metres south of the wood. A wise precaution, as the Germans pounded Upton Woods with gas and shells over the next days.[111] D/4th cleared up the situation on the right flank along Cemetery and Unicorn Avenues and claimed the capture of 150 Germans. It stitched up the remaining hole in the line.[112] The three operations left the Canadians holding a front running along Cemetery Avenue to the Vis-en-Artois Switch.

From the German perspective, a Canadian standing barrage across the Hendecourt-Dury road made it difficult to resupply, move up reinforcements, and pass messages. Adding to the misery was a consistent pattern of short shooting by their own gunners. In a fluid situation, it was hard to separate friends from foes at a distance. Closer to the fighting, Canadian snipers and machine gunners identified the *III/68th*'s leadership group and cut them down, which contributed to its defeat. Few of its men escaped from Upton Wood after the 2nd Battalion counterattack. With the right breaking down, two companies from the *29th IR* reinforced the sagging line. Determined to retake the lost ground, the *16th ID* at 6:30 p.m., ordered a new counterattack with two and a half battalions. Three hours later, only two infantry and one machine gum companies from the *II/29th* were in position. One battalion was unavailable, and the other could not be found. The officer on the spot wisely refused to attack with such a feeble force.

In the evening, the *II Bavarian Korps* ordered the *16th ID* to take over from the battered *26th RD* overnight on the front south of the Arras-Cambrai road. The *28th IR* would defend the right sector and the *68th IR* the left. Dellmensingen issued explicit instructions that machine guns were to deploy in a checkerboard fashion in the sector west of the D-Q Line. The counterattack and the Canadian ripostes badly battered the *68th IR* with its *II* and *III Battalions* reduced to a strength of 120 personnel each.[113]

The 1st Battalion claimed 60 prisoners and 6 machine guns, and they lost 7 officers and 160 men including 4 prisoners. These totals were surprisingly low given a full day of fighting

109 LAC: RG9 III-D-3 v4916: 4th Battalion War Diary, 4th Battalion Report, 12 August 1918; LAC: RG9 III-C-3 v4027, 13/7: 1st Brigade Strength of Units, 27 August 1918.
110 LAC: 2nd Bn Report 28 August-1 September; Murray, *2nd Battalion History*, pp.277-285; LAC: 2nd Battalion WD, 30 August 1918; LAC: 2nd Battalion Ref 7-46, 31 August 1918.
111 LAC: 4th Bn. WD, Narrative B Coy Operations 30 August 1918, 5 September 1918.
112 LAC: 4th Bn. WD, D Coy Narrative of Operation from August 28th to September 4th 1918.
113 Pafferath, *Geschichte I.R. 68*, p.710.

including having their flank rolled up. The 2nd Battalion estimated its casualties at 12 officers and 200 other ranks. While, the 4th Battalion had few losses with just 1 officer and 13 men although it also lost 11 more to gas and had two men captured. Griesbach's report gave the total casualties for the operation as 22 officers and 620 other ranks with the capture of 10 officers and 351 other ranks.[114] The hard fighting and toll taken on the 1st Brigade meant Macdonell could not rely, as he planned, on the 1st Brigade to complete Task 3 reaching the jump-off line. He would have to employ his other two brigades.

The German counterattack even more so than that on 26 August was the epitome of a perfectly positioned and timed *Eingreifdivision* action. Striking the 1st Brigade's wide-open flank with four strong battalions from a crack division, the counterattack should have steamrolled the Canadians. It certainly drove them back, but it did not restore the original line. Why did it fail while the Canadian action was successful? The principal factors were operational circumstances, barrage, visibility, firepower, and reaction. Griesbach's brigade had the benefit of a coordinated and prepared formal operation. The German's hasty arrangements, revisions, and premature launch reduced its effectiveness. As a result, the attack lacked the full effect of a two-regiment action. Moreover, concerned with the possibility of another offensive in the afternoon, von Dellmensingen ordered the *16th ID* to commit no more battalions to the attack.[115] The Canadians engaged with the protection and firepower of a powerful artillery barrage while the Germans had only a bombardment of suspected Canadian positions. Darkness and smoke disrupted the defensive system, as acknowledged by the Germans. While, their counterattack was fully visible to Canadian artillery spotters to see the SOS calls and the attacking Germans. This enabled the full panoply of Canadian firepower to flay the advancing enemy. For instance, three machine gun batteries supporting the brigade fired 18,000 rounds, with most being fired during the German counterattack.[116] The increase to two Lewis Guns per platoon greatly added to each platoon's firepower. The British estimated a Vickers machine gun had the equivalent firepower of 40 riflemen.[117] With a lower rate of fire, less range and accuracy, the Lewis Gun was likely half as effective as the Vickers. This gave a 30-man platoon, the firepower effect of 66 rifleman.[118] Finally, McLaughlin's leadership stemmed the incipient rout and restored his troop's determination. His action stopped the German advance so additional reserves could arrive. Even in a mass war, individual actions could have outsized effects on the battle.

4th British Division: Task 3 Almost Completed

The 4th British Division's mission for 30 August was to reach its jump-off line. It had less ground to take than the 1st Division as it only had to advance 800 to 1,800 metres. The deepest section was on the right along the Arras-Cambrai road but required the 1st Division to keep

114 LAC: 1st Brigade War Diary, 1st Brigade G.469-8, 31 August 1918; LAC: 1st Battalion War Diary, 30 August 1918; LAC: 2nd Bn Report 28 August-1 September; LAC: 3rd Battalion War Diary, Report 30 August 1918.

115 Bundesarchiv, Freiburg: Feldzug 1918, 30 August 1918.

116 LAC: 1st Brigade War Diary, 1st Brigade G.469-8, 31 August 1918; LAC: 1st Bn CMGC Report.

117 Bidwell and Graham, *Fire-Power*, p.28.

118 This was based on two men per crew operating the Lewis Gun and the remaining 26 counting as riflemen.

pace. During the day, the division's 4.5-inch howitzers focused on wire-cutting, with each piece allocated 300 rounds for the task. The gunners had many complaints at this stage about road congestion and poor traffic control with vehicles banked four-deep in places. This bottleneck was choking off the supply of ammunition, and units received instructions to use their shells judiciously. There were ample rounds at the dumps, but it was difficult to move them forward.[119] Further, while the 51st Division had driven off the observers on Greenland Hill, there were long-range guns to the north that routinely shelled the Arras-Cambrai road.[120] A major task of the 4th British Division's engineers on 31 August was burying dead horses found along the road because of this fire.[121] What the 51st Division's success meant was that the field artillery started moving to positions south of Boiry-Notre-Dame without crushing observed counter-battery fire.[122] The Germans instead concentrated their guns on the division's infantry and inflicted considerable casualties and disorganisation.[123] For more, see Map 8.10 4th British Division: 30 August in the colour map booklet.

In the morning, the 10th and 11th Brigades sent out fighting patrols to gain ground. They made limited progress across the Sensée, as only a fully supported attack would dislodge the enemy. In response, the division ordered the two brigades to attack at 4:00 p.m. – each with two battalions. The attack had three objectives, with the last being the D-Q jump-off line. A 15-minute bombardment of Éterpigny would precede the advance and a slow-paced barrage moving at 50 metres every two minutes supported it.[124] The 10th Brigade attacked with the 2nd Dukes on the right and 1st R Warks on the left. This was on a front of 1,700 metres to a depth of 900. The 2nd Dukes advanced with two companies and reached St Servins Farm and the woods that surrounded it but got no further. Fire from the last sections of the F-R Line along the open right flank doomed any further advance. The Dukes would hold the farm until German pressure in the evening forced it back to Sack Trench. It took one officer and 42 other ranks prisoners but lost heavily for a limited operation with 7 officers and 205 men.[125]

On the left, the 1st R Warks had a rough time. The Germans spotted its assembly and pounded it to the point that two of its companies were down to 30 men each. Another company had to lead the assault, and it had to cross the Sensée and a marshy area. Slowed down by waist-high water, the attackers lost the all-important barrage. Casualties and the lost barrage meant the battalion took only portions of the second objective, leaving an open flank on the left. Reduced to 4 officers and 150 men, the battalion reorganised on a two-company basis. The Seaforths

119 LAC: 1st Division AAQMG War Diary, 30 August 1918.
120 TNA: 4th British Divisional Artillery War Diary, 30 August 1918 and Narrative of Operations of 4th Divisional Artillery From 26th August to 4th September, 1918.
121 TNA: WO 95-1464-1/4: 4th British Division CRE War Diary, 31 August 1918.
122 LAC: War Diary, 12 CFA, 30 August 1918; Anon., *Sixty-Sixth C.F.A.*, p.91; TNA: WO 95 95-167-4: 32nd Brigade RFA War Diary, 30 August 1918; LAC: RG9 III-D-3 v4964: 8th Brigade CFA War Diary, 30 August 1918; LAC: 3rd CDA WD, 3rd CDA, BM 27-1, 30 August 1918.
123 TNA: 4th British Div GS WD, 30 August 1918 and Narrative of Operations of 4th Division from 26 August to 4th September 1918.
124 TNA: WO 95-1494-1: 11th British Brigade War Diary, 30 August 1918 and OO 69, 30 August 1918.
125 TNA: 2nd Duke of Wellington's War Diary, 30 August 1918 and 2nd Duke of Wellington's Regiment Operation Order No. 109, 30 August 1918.

relieved it overnight. Surprisingly, the battalion reported losses of only 218 all ranks.[126] This should not have forced it to go to two companies, unless there were other factors. Men may have been separated or were ill. The 10th Brigade insisted its officers had to pay strict attention to the troops going sick before, during, and after an action.[127] The battalion's inability to keep pace meant both the Dukes and the 1st RB had to defend a longer front than normally and this contributed to the 2nd Dukes' retirement from St Servins. After the battle, the battalion commander, Lieutenant Colonel G B Marriott, transferred to command a Labour Group. This move suggests either he was not standing up to the strains or there was dissatisfaction with the battalion's performance.

The 11th Brigade was more successful and gained most of the ground to the jump-off line. On the right, the 1st RB was to take Éterpigny and its woods on a front of 750 metres to a depth of 900. The artillery adjusted the barrage at the last minute and caught elements of the unit causing casualties. It shook off this tragedy and poured into Éterpigny capturing it shortly after Zero. It captured 35 prisoners and 3 machine guns. The battalion did not list its losses except as 6 officers. Based on its casualties for its whole tour, its losses were about 136 other ranks for this action. It too had to endure prolonged shelling and lost many men through the day.[128] The defending *I/214th RIR* suffered heavy losses with its *3rd Company* effectively wiped out. Ordered to counterattack to retake Éterpigny, the *III/214th RIR* was preparing when the higher authorities cancelled it due to the uncertain situation.[129] This was a repeated theme where events overtook the Germans command's responses causing cancelled counterattacks or delays.

To the left, 1st SLI had a 750 metre front with an 800 metre advance. It reported the prospects for the attack 'were not bright' because of the men's exhaustion and loss of many NCOs. The Germans fell back when the battalion advanced, but it still took 30 prisoners. The enemy held this sector lightly as a *Vorfeld*. Given the lack of direct resistance, it suffered high losses of 5 officers and 190 men.[130]

The *119th RIR* believed the fighting patrols of the 10th Brigade were an all-out assault that they repulsed. What they could not stop was the persistent bombardment of the area around St Servins Farm by their own artillery. Flares and messages had no effect on the pounding, and the German commander ordered his troops to withdraw. The regiment stubbornly remained close to St Servins Farm as its loss would imperil the position south of the Arras-Cambrai road. It suffered heavy losses and only firm leadership kept troops in place under the force of the shelling. The divisional commander ordered an investigation into the short shooting. It found that a newly arrived division had misunderstood where the front-line was and had ignored ceasefire signals.[131]

126 The battalion did not produce a narrative for the battle. TNA: 1st Royal Warwickshire War Diary, 30 August 1918; TNA: WO 95-1483-1-7: 1st Seaforth Highlanders War Diary, 30 August 1918.
127 TNA: WO 95-1480-1/6: 10th British Brigade War Diary, Report on Operations Carried out by the 10th Infantry Brigade East of Monchy-les-Preux During August and September 1918.
128 TNA: 11th Br Bde WD, 1st Rifle Brigade Account of Operation at Arras August 28th - September 2nd 1918.
129 Bastanier, *Geschichte RIR 214*, p.414.
130 TNA: WO 95-1499-1/7: 1st Somerset Light Infantry War Diary, 30 August 1918.
131 Gerster, *RIR Nr. 119*, pp.120-122; Kümmel, *Res.Inf.Regt. Nr. 91*, p.423; Max Klaus, *Das Württembergische Reserve-Feldartillerie-Regiment Nr. 26 im Weltkrieg 1914-1918* (Stuttgart: Chr. Belse AG, 1929), p.107.

Generalleutenant Freiherr v Fritsch commander of the *26th RD*. His division performed so well in stopping the 2nd Division that he received the highest military award of merit in the Imperial army the *Pour le Mérite*. (Generalmajor R Stühmke, *Die 26. (Württembergische) Reserve-Division im Weltkrieg 1914-1918*, vol. II (Stuttgart: Bergers Literaisches Büro und Verlagsanstalt, 1935), p.67.)

Overnight, the *26th RD* handed over its line to the *4th EzD* and *16th ID* and it went into a well-deserved rest for a month. The division had done well, very well. So well, that the German authorities awarded its commander, *Generalleutenant* Freiherr v Fritsch, the *Pour le Mérite* or 'Blue Max' in acknowledgement of its accomplishments. The Blue Max was the highest military order of merit in the Imperial army.[132] The division's regimental histories referred to this period as the most glorious in its history. This was striking as this was the formation that held Thiepval for 10 weeks against everything the British could throw at it on the Somme in 1916.[133]

Results and Analysis

With renewed action, the Corps' casualty totals increased by almost threefold over the previous day. The Corps' losses were 1,488 all ranks with the 1st Division paying the highest price reflecting the 1st Brigade's hard fighting. The day's prisoner total was 9 officers and 147 men.[134]

132 Unlike the Victoria Cross, it was not awarded for gallantry but sustained excellence. About one-quarter of these during the war were to senior military officers. 687 were awarded in the war in a much larger army versus 628 Victoria Crosses.

133 Otto Mathies, *Geschichte Des 3. Oberelsässisch. Feldartillerie-Regiments Nr. 80*, pp.108-109; Holtz, *Reserve-Infanterie-Regiment Nr. 121*, p.75; Gerster, *RIR Nr. 119*, p.123; Stühmke, *26th Reserve Division* II, p.71.

134 LAC: POW Arras.

Again, this total was an anomaly as it seriously understated the number of prisoners. Even with discounting battalion reports, the figure was less than half of what it should have been. This probably again reflects an artefact of the reporting period.

Table 8.2 Estimated Casualties For 30 August 1918

	Killed	Wounded	POW	Total
1st CID	201	522	6	729
2nd CID	12	19		31
3rd CID	14	14		28
4th CID		8		8
4th BID*	161	417		578
Tank Corps				0
Other	6	108		114
Total	**394**	**1,088**	**6**	**1,488**

* 4th British Division totals do not include prisoners lost.
† Included in the Other category are Tank Corps wounded.

By the end of 30 August, the Canadian Corps had made good progress towards the D-Q Line. It had almost completed Task 2 – the capture of most of the F-R Line, repulsed a dangerous German counterattack that weakened the *16th ID*, the 4th British Division had seized half of its jump-off line for the major offensive, and the Corps frontage was substantially reduced. Additionally, von Dellmensingen had to withdraw the hollowed out *26th RD* and draw down his reserves by committing the *4th EzD* and *16th ID*. The negatives were both the 4th British and 1st Canadian Divisions had suffered substantial casualties on 30 August considering how few forces fought. In addition, the units participating were wearing down. This was the longest battle fought by the 2nd Battalion since Second Ypres in 1915. It was in action for 24 hours along with the rest of the 1st Brigade.[135]

The day's operations also highlighted an issue with the Corps' poor coordination between its divisions. The 3rd Battalion's attack at 3:00 p.m. was not synchronised with the 4th British Division's action an hour later. A combined attack would likely have been far more successful. The 3rd Battalion was repulsed, while an hour later the British took St Servins Farm. Defending south of the Arras-Cambrai road, the *II/121st RIR* retired to avoid encirclement leaving the remaining portion of the F-R Line undefended. The 3rd was unaware of this and took no advantage of it. The 2nd Dukes fell back to their start line, in part because of the threat of encirclement from south of the road. Had the two attacks been simultaneous, the Germans

135 Murray, *2nd Battalion History*, p.285.

would have pulled out from the salient, thus saving another attack. Each division ran its own operations with no coordination to the detriment of the cause.

The 1st Brigade's operation was both a brilliant tactical scheme and a defensive blunder that hard fighting salvaged. Griesbach's stroke caught the Germans in a vulnerable position that destroyed multiple battalions.[136] His mistake was not to reinforce his right wing properly. The counterattack was dangerous but achieved less than it should have. What it illustrated was the diminishing effectiveness of even a well-timed and placed counterattack from a strong formation.

The Corps pushed back the D-Q Line attack by two days. Thus, the forward divisions had more time to complete Task 3. The same strictures as before applied to gaining the necessary ground without exhausting their forces. David Watson's 4th Canadian Division was arriving, but Currie preferred it remain uncommitted in readiness for the main offensive. The next two days would see whether Currie could keep it fresh for the D-Q operation. Could the 4th British and Macdonell's 'Old Red Patch' pull it off or would von Dellmensingen's Germans keep the wolves at bay and away from the vital D-Q Line?

136 There are no available casualty figures for the *4th EzD* for this operation, but it is unlikely many survived from the three battalions overrun in the attack.

9

'Disorganised and thoroughly cowed' Gaining the Jump-Off Line, 31 August and 1 September

---

Given a barrage and infantry close on his heels, it was the easiest thing in the world to absolutely overrun him.

Lieutenant Colonel Dick Worrall, 8 September 1918[1]

On 31 August, the Canadian Corps was struggling to reach the jump-off line for the D-Q operation. It made progress the previous day, but there was still hard fighting ahead. By postponing the D-Q attack, it gained time to complete Tasks 3 and 4. This was an odd twilight period that featured heavy fighting and not inconsiderable losses on both sides but fell outside an officially named battle.[2] The Germans were well aware of the Canadian intention to attack the D-Q Line. They were striving to secure time to improve the defences, gather reserves, and most importantly wear out the attackers. According to German intelligence, the Corps had committed all the Canadian divisions. This meant that a wearing battle for the *Vorfeld* would erode the attackers' strength and weaken the assault on the D-Q Line. More significantly, it meant the Canadian field artillery could not fire a barrage to the fortification's full depth. The Corps fight to gain the jump-off line and the German defence of the *Vorfeld* characterised the next two days' actions. A critical issue was to what degree would Watson's division get entangled in this and sap its strength.

Preparing

Gridlock constrained operations. The combination of too much traffic, not enough road space, inadequate staff work, and insufficient control personnel, created it. Sustained fighting on every day but one exacerbated the issue. There was not enough of a break to recover. As a result, battalions moving up averaged only 20 to 30 percent of their normal march rate. Excessive

1 LAC: 14th Battalion War Diary, Report on Operation of September 1st, 6 September 1918.
2 The British Battles Nomenclature Committee determined the Battle of the Scarpe ran from 26-30 August and the Battle of Drocourt-Quéant 2-3 September. Strangely, they ignored the hard combats of 31 August and 1 September.

Gridlock on the Arras-Cambrai road as lorries, transport, and troops try to push through the traffic. This congestion was threatening to strangle the offensive. (Canada. Dept. of National Defence/Library and Archives Canada/PA-040207)

loads and traffic ground down captured roads, so the engineers spent much effort keeping them operational. Delivering the immense quantities of shells stressed the road system. For instance, the Canadians expended 11 trainloads of ammunition on 29 August amounting to over 3,600 tonnes and numbering about 150,000 shells. The Corps received more rounds than it could clear from the supply heads.[3] The wet weather also adversely affected the roads.[4]

A major factor was poor traffic control. Typically, each division received two Canadian Light Horse (CLH) troops of 26 men each, as despatch riders and for road duty.[5] Not surprisingly then, traffic control was not a Canadian strength. In contrast, the IX Corps at Messines in 1917 had 447 personnel committed to the task.[6] Currie, also, severely censured the second-in-command of the 1st Machine Gun Battalion for violating traffic regulations during Arras to stop this too common practice.[7]

To address the gridlock, the thousands of engineers in 12 battalions continued improving the existing road network, creating new tracks, and extending the light rail system. They were busy building bypasses around watering stations and ammunition dumps to reduce traffic congestion. The sappers' extension of light rail to Wancourt on 31 August was another major boon to the Corps' logistics.[8] This saved the MT companies the lengthy drive to the previous supply head west of Arras, and it reduced the bottlenecks at the dumps.[9]

Heavy guns and howitzers continued the dual tasks of cutting the dense barbed wire protecting the D-Q Line – Task 4—and beating down enemy guns. The counter-battery

3 TNA: WO 95-188-3: First Army AQ War Diary, August 1918 Summary.
4 LAC: First Army G148, 28 August 1918.
5 The CLH was the Corps' cavalry regiment.
6 Sheffield, *Command and Morale,* loc.425.
7 CWM: 19801226-284 58 A1, 61.7: Currie Fonds, Canadian Corps, A.101-M-105, 20 May 1919.
8 LAC: 1st Division AAQMG War Diary, 31 August 1918.
9 LAC: 1st Division AAQMG War Diary, Report on Administrative Arrangements for Operations East of Arras, August 28 - September 4th, 1918.

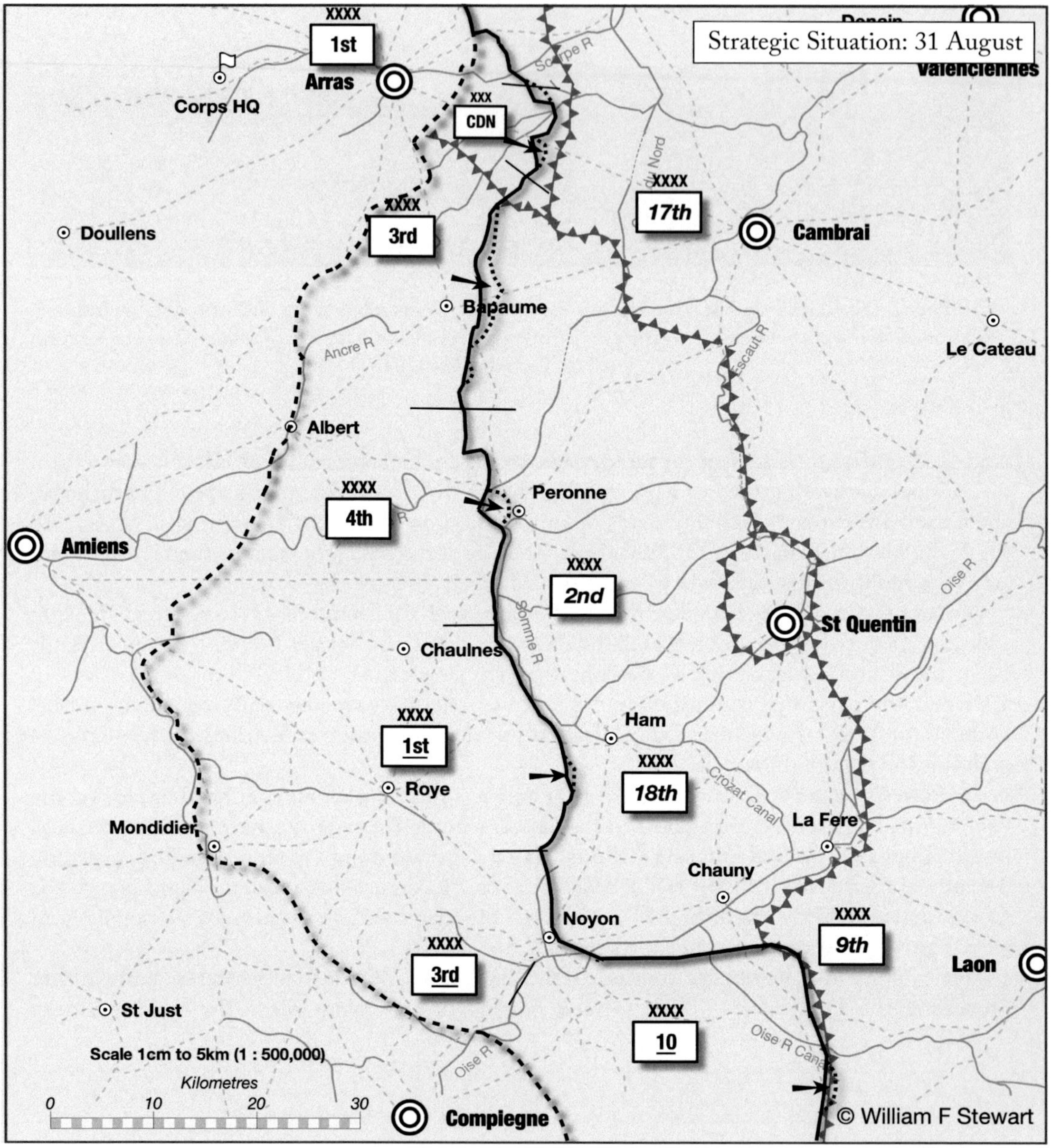

Map 28. Strategic situation 31 August with only minor gains made across the front with the Australian Corps establishing a bridgehead on the far bank of the Somme. (Author's map)

effort was challenging. The Germans kept dispersing and moving their batteries to disguise their locations, and the Canadian heavy artillery still sat well to the rear. Further, the enemy was reinforcing the front.[10] The result was the absolute artillery domination of the first day of Amiens was absent at Arras 1918.

Strategic Situation

On 31 August, the Australians in the Fourth Army had a signal success in establishing a bridgehead on the south bank of the Somme north of Peronne. The Third Army remained in place except for minor operations on its left flank.[11] On the XVII Corps' front, the 57th Division swapped the 171st Brigade for the 172nd overnight, which squabbled with Hendecourt's defenders.[12] Overall, while the British armies were still pushing, they were waiting for the Canadian capture of the D-Q Line to re-energise their offensives. Thus, Haig's urgency in getting the Canadians to attack the line.

Germans

Early in the morning, the *Seventeenth Armee* transferred most of the *3rd RD* to *II Bavarian Korps*' control. Dellmensingen ordered it to move south of the Arras-Cambrai road, less one regiment, to be the *Eingreifdivision* for the southern sector.[13] The *3rd RD* underwent a major overhaul just before the battle. In place of its disbanded *2nd RIR*, the full-strength *2nd Grenadier Regiment* (*GrR*) joined it on 20 August. It was one of the strongest regiments at Arras 1918, with a ration strength of 89 officers and 2,295 men and 306 horses.[14] It remained in army reserve in Sauchy-Cauchy on the far side of the canal. Each *3rd RD* regiment received the personnel from its dissolved *2nd RIR*.

Throughout 31 August, von Dellmensingen organised his forces into three zones, with two divisions guarding each zone north and south of the Arras-Cambrai road. In the first zone, the *16th ID* defended the *Vorfeld* on the left and the *4th EzD on* the right. The latter covered the Éterpigny Line and St Servins Farm. Defending the second zone – the D-Q Line – were the *111th ID* on the left and the *2nd GRD* on the right. Placed well back to avoid Canadian artillery, the third zone had the *3rd RD* with two regiments south of the road and the *1st GRD* north. He believed the sector north of the Arras-Cambrai road was a more difficult section to attack, so he weighted his forces on his left.[15] Two of the three divisions north of the road – *4th EzD* and *2nd GRD* – had neither quality nor quantity of personnel. The *1st GRD* was an excellent division, however. South of the road, all three divisions, although weakened, were all average to above-average formations.

10 CWM: GS Report 30 Aug-6 Sep 1918.
11 Edmonds, *Military Operations, 1918* 4, pp.356-364, 385.
12 TNA: 57th Division GS WD, 31 August 1918.
13 Generalleutnant a.D. Kraehe, *Das Füsilier-Regiment Königin Victoria Von Schweden (Pommersches) Nr. 34 im Weltkriege* (Stettin: Verlag von F. Heffenland, GmbH, 1931), pp.431-432.
14 Gottberg, *Grenadier-Regiment Nr. 2*, pp.453-455.
15 Bundesarchiv, Freiburg: Feldzug 1918, 30 August 1918.

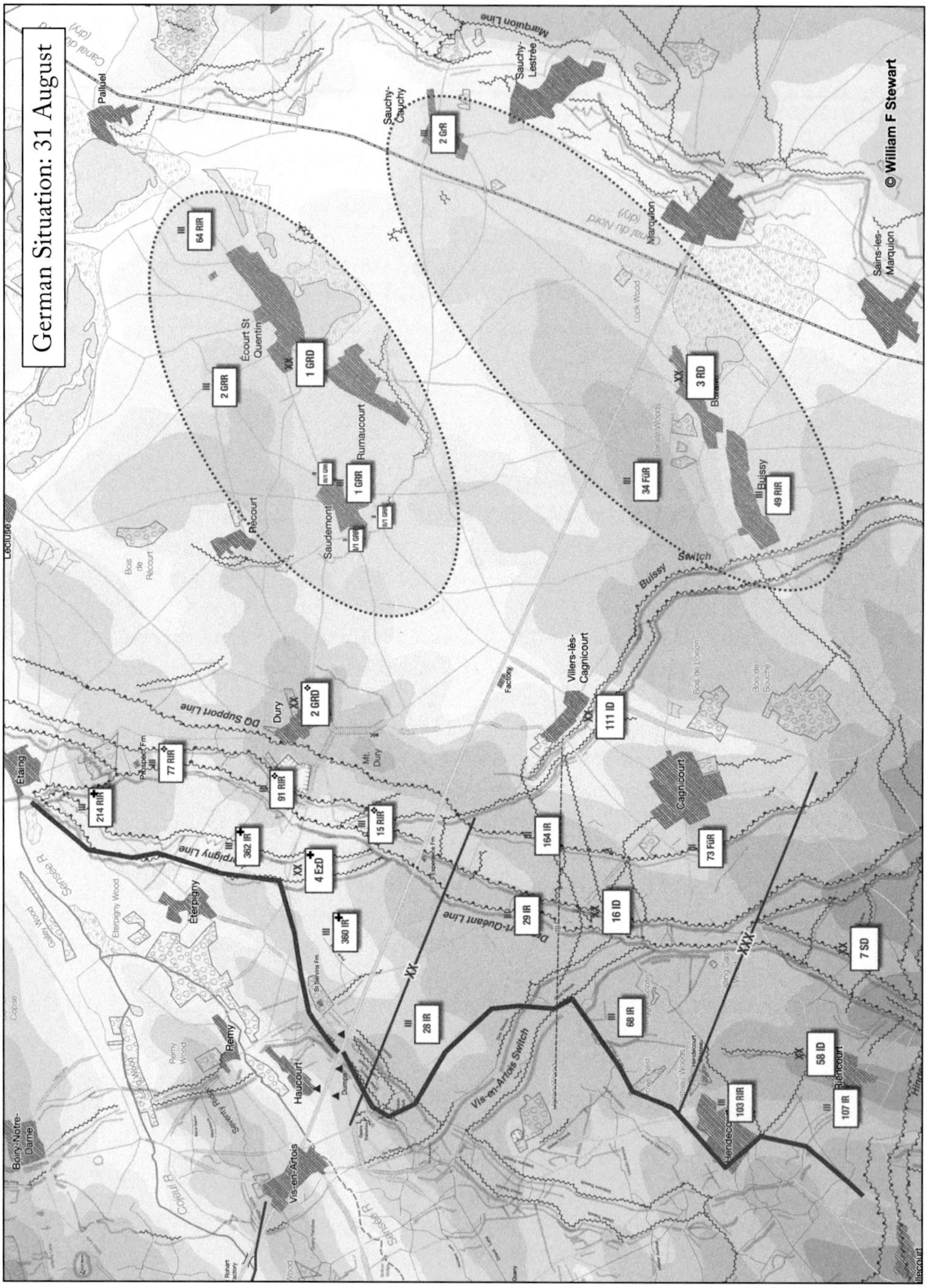

Map 29. The *II Bavarian Korps* created a three-deep division deployment north and south of the Arras-Cambrai road. One division each defended the *Vorfeld*, one the D-Q Line, and one acted as an *Eingreifdivision* positioned in depth behind the D-Q Line. (Author's map)

1st Division: 'OCEAN WORK and Vicinity' Fall

On the 1st Division's right, it was a day of heavy shelling by the Germans, as they prepared another counterattack. The *II Bavarian Korps* ordered the *16th ID* to recapture Upton Wood and sent a *29th IR* battalion and two companies to carry it out. The Canadians easily rebuffed two weak preliminary attacks. As a result, the *16th ID* did not launch the large-scale operation.[16] These actions were so small that the 1st Brigade did not note them in their reports. The 3rd Battalion tried to advance down the Vis-en-Artois Switch with the equivalent of a one-company attack, but the Germans defeated it too without comment.[17] For more, see Map 9.3 1st Division and Flanking Forces: 31 August 1918 in the colour map booklet.

On the division's left, the 2nd Brigade was to take the last vestiges of the F-R Line. After the repulse of the 3rd Battalion attempt, Macdonell instructed Loomis, GOC 2nd Brigade, to capture the position the next morning. The 8th Battalion received the assignment and would attack with two companies supported by four FA brigades, two HA brigades, and one machine

Brigadier Generals George Tuxford is on the left and Frederick Loomis on the right. Tuxford was a no-nonsense officer who at times clashed with his subordinates but was effective. Loomis was a strong leader on 30 August and 1 September but faltered badly in his planning for 2 September. (Canada. Dept. of National Defence/Library and Archives Canada/PA-007580)

16 Pafferath, *Geschichte I.R. 68*, pp.708-715.
17 LAC: 3rd Battalion War Diary, 3rd Battalion Report, 30 August 1918.

gun battery.[18] The density of the gunnery support was impressive with a concentration of 16 metres per gun and 44 heavy pieces totalling 140 barrels for a two-company operation. A key factor in the plan was the British still held St Servins Farm. There was no indication that the 4th British Division had informed Macdonell's division that it lost the Farm.[19]

The 8th Battalion suffered exceptionally heavy casualties at Amiens at two-thirds of its trench strength. Its casualties included its commander, 14 other officers, and its RSM.[20] The battalion was still under-strength with 28 officers and 901 other ranks present.[21] Major Alex Saunders replaced the former CO on 9 August. The hard nature of the war resulted in *novus homo* emerging who had non-traditional routes to command. 'Bug' Saunders (30) was one such example and was unique in two respects.[22] First, he was not an officer prior to the war, whereas on the Somme 1916, all but one of the Canadian battalion commanders were officers prior to the war.[23] Second, he had served in and commanded a trench mortar battery. These had the reputation as a dumping ground for battalions to discard unwanted personnel. He must have impressed in the role, as he later attended SOC Aldershot. He remained in command to the end of the war and received a DSO and Military Cross (MC) with bar. With a new commander and many new men, the battalion was likely expecting time to recover – it did not.

Originally scheduled for 2:00 a.m., the battalion learned of a three-hour postponement with minutes to spare. It barely had time to notify its companies. None of the brigade or division documents mentioned the postponement. There may have been issues with the artillery. One supporting FA brigade only got its orders at 2:00 a.m.[24] In the evening, Loomis noticed a perceptible slackening in the rate of fire on the position. He got Macdonell to increase the shell allocation to resume firing.[25]

At Zero Hour in intermittent rain and misty conditions, two companies attacked with one advancing north from Orix Trench and the other from the east. Both rapidly overran the defences with the battalion reporting slight opposition and the entire garrison wiped out. It expected to meet the British at the junction of Ostrich Trench and the Arras-Cambrai road. Instead, they encountered sheets of German machine gun fire. Its support company had to deploy along the road to cover the open flank, as the 2nd Dukes had lost St Servins Farm. The 8th would complain it was impossible to get a definitive answer of where the British lines were. The 2nd Dukes did not finally take St Servins Farm until the evening after another failed

18 15th DA (70th RFA, 71st RFA), 39th (174th RFA, 186th RFA), 48th HA, and 91st HA. LAC: 2nd Brigade War Diary, 2nd Bde OO No. 311, 30 August 1918.

19 LAC: 2nd Brigade War Diary, 30 August 1918 and 2nd Brigade Narrative of Operations East of Arras August 25 to September 3, 1918 and 2nd Brigade OO 175, 30 August 1918; Black Watch Regimental Archives (BWRA): Loomis Diary, 30 August 1918.

20 LAC: RG9 III-D-3 v4918: 8th Battalion War Diary, 8-9 August 1918 and Narrative of Events No. 2, 10 August 1918.

21 LAC: RG9 III-C-3 v4069, 11/11: 8th Battalion Strength Return Week Ending 30 August 1918.

22 'The Bug' <https://matthewkbarrett.com/2015/04/17/the-bug/#more-1480> (29 January 2019).

23 The one exception was Lieutenant Colonel PJ Daly of the 28th Battalion. Stewart, 'Byng Boys', p.64.

24 LAC: 2 CFA WD, 31 August 1918.

25 BWRA: Loomis Diary, 30 August 1918; LAC: 8th Bn WD, Narrative of Events Phase 1, [September 1918].

attempt. This was one more example of the lamentable ignorance of what was happening on the flanks.[26]

With the success of the attack, Loomis ordered the 8th to push out its outposts 1,400 metres to the D-Q jump-off line. In the mist, the scouts could not see and blundered into the German machine gun nests and suffered 50 percent casualties. Saunders wisely called off the advance. The scouts fell back to an outpost line 600 to 1,000 metres from the jump-off line. The battalion had finally captured the remaining elements of the F-R Line. It lost 5 officers and 93 men, with a claim of 21 prisoners and many more who the British snaffled.[27] Why was this attack so much more successful than the three preceding assaults? Because only the advance parties of a relieving battalion defended the sector. The previous day, the *II/121st RIR* withdrew to escape the risk of encirclement with the temporary fall of St Servins Farm. The *III/28th IR* was to reoccupy the sector overnight. It was unclear if the Canadians had occupied the line, so scouts had to patrol ahead. Further, Canadian artillery was pounding the area, so the advance was slow. The battalion was still moving into position when the 8th Battalion swamped it.[28] Its regimental history indicated only light forces were in place when the Canadians hit. The rapidity of the push and the low number of captives show there were few defenders in position. When the 8th tried to push out its patrols, they encountered the enemy's main body, who stopped the advance cold.

4th British Division

On the Corps' left flank, the 4th British Division still had to reach the jump-off line on its 10th British Brigade's front. The primary feature was St Servins Farm – a set of buildings surrounded by a copse situated just off the Arras-Cambrai road. Neither division could advance without significant risks if the enemy occupied it.[29] After the success of the 8th Battalion, there was no longer any excuse that an exposed flank prevented the Farm's seizure. But the 4th British Division was wearing down, with 540 casualties the previous day, along with another 138 evacuated ill.[30] In this casualty total were 59 officers giving a casualty ratio of 8.1 other ranks to officers – the Corps average over the battle was 20.9.[31] This suggests the division's officers had to exhibit conspicuous gallantry, exposing them to excessive casualties. It was entering its third day of fighting, and the 10th and 11th British Brigades were getting exhausted. For more, see Map 9.3 1st Division and Flanking Forces: 31 August in the colour map booklet.

The British attacked seven hours after the 8th Battalion assault. If synchronised with the Canadian operation, it would likely have been more successful than it was. It appeared that the 1st Canadian and 4th British Divisions were fighting their own war. This should have been the

26 Tascona, *Little Black Devils*, p.117; LAC: 8th Bn WD, Narrative of Events Phase 1, [September 1918]; LAC: RG9 III-C-3 v4052, 22/6: 2nd Brigade BM X1, 31 August 1918.
27 LAC: RG9 III-C-3 v4052, 22/6: 2nd Brigade BM X3, 31 August 1918; LAC: 8th Bn WD, Narrative of Events Phase 1, [September 1918].
28 Begau, *IR 28 in Weltkrieg*, p.235.
29 LAC: Breaking the Quéant-Drocourt Line, p.122.
30 TNA: WO 95-1452-3: 4th British Division AAQMG War Diary, 31 August 1918.
31 LAC: MG30 E5 v2: Bovey Fonds, Battle of Arras Main Dressing Staton Report to 6 A.M. September 8th.

responsibility of the Corps. With its focus on the upcoming D-Q action, it had abrogated its responsibilities for coordination.

On the right flank, the 10th British Brigade traded blows with the *4th EzD* as it tried to capture and hold St Servins Farm. The first strike was a small-scale attack at 2:30 p.m. by the 2nd Dukes with no artillery barrage. It reached the edge of the copse but no further. A German counterattack, at 6:30 p.m., drove them back to their start line. The division then ordered another attempt with artillery support. This final assault worked with the 2nd Dukes and the 2nd Seaforth Highlanders advancing at 8:45 p.m. with the protection of a barrage. The Dukes took and finally held the Farm. On the right, the Seaforths matched the advance except for a strongpoint in a sunken road. When the Canadians later overran the area, they found 100 dead Germans and 19 machine guns indicating the scale of resistance.[32]

The 11th British Brigade had to endure a long trying bombardment by shells and gas. On the 10th British Brigade front overnight, the 12th Canadian Brigade took over the southern portion of its sector. The 4th Canadian Division had now arrived. With two divisions and their brigades with the same designations, there was a great potential for confusion. To combat this, the Corps issued a directive that the correct nomenclature for formations and units was by number, nationality, and type, for example, the 10th British Brigade and 10th Canadian Brigade.[33] This policy will be employed as well.

In the afternoon, Brigadier General J Greene, GOC 10th British Brigade, reported his brigade was unfit to attack because of casualties and fatigue. In addition, the 11th British Brigade's 1st SLI was down to 300 officers and men.[34] Matheson had to inform Currie that his division was too weak to attack the D-Q Line on a two-brigade front. This put a major crimp in Currie's plans to be discussed in Chapter 10.[35]

4th Canadian Division Arrives

The 4th Division remained on the Amiens front until French formations relieved it over the nights of 23/24 to 24/25 August. It reached Arras late on 29 August, with an expectation of entering the line on a single brigade front once the F-R Line fell.[36] While the division was working its way north, its commander, David Watson, had time to visit Paris and attend the *Folies Bergère*.[37] The 12th Brigade received its orders to take over a 1,500-metre sector that straddled the Arras-Cambrai road on the night of 31 August/1 September. It would be a complicated operation as the 12th would replace elements of two brigades from two divisions in a heavily contested sector. The 10th British Brigade misunderstood how much of their front the Canadians were assuming and thought they would relieve all the 2nd Dukes.[38]

32 TNA: 1st Seaforth Highlanders War Diary, 31 August 1918; TNA: 2nd Duke of Wellington's War Diary, 31 August 1918; TNA: 10th Br Bde WD, 31 August 1918.
33 TNA: WO 95-1234-1/6: 1st British Division War Diary.
34 TNA: 1st Somerset Light Infantry War Diary, 1 September 1918.
35 TNA: First Army GS WD, BGGS, Canadian Corps, 31 August 1918; LAC: Currie Diary, 31 August 1918; TNA: 4th British Div GS WD, Narrative of Operations of 4th Division from 26 August to 4th September 1918.
36 LAC: RG9 III-D-3 v4861: 4th Canadian Division War Diary, 23-31 August 1918.
37 LAC: Watson Diary, 25-26 August 1918.
38 TNA: 10th Br Bde WD, 31 August 1918.

Brigadier General J H MacBrien, GOC 12th Brigade. A rising star in the PF, MacBrien was one of the few staff college trained officers in the Canadian military. (72nd Battalion, CEF. Twitter Post. 14 April 2017, 12:35 PM. <https://twitter.com/72ndbn/status/852968472841736192>)

MacBrien's 12th Brigade had relatively few casualties at Amiens with losses of 45 officers and 773 men. Its 78th Battalion, however, suffered over half of this total. When the brigade entrained for Arras, the 78th had a strength of 868 all ranks while the average of the other three was 1,006.[39] This explains why it was initially in reserve on 1 September. The 12th went into the line with three battalions (72nd right, 38th, and 85th left). This was the order in which they would attack on 2 September.

Its 72nd Battalion deployed on the brigade's right. Its CO was the veteran Lieutenant Colonel John Arthur Clark (32). A lawyer in Vancouver, he raised the 72nd and brought it out to France in August 1916. A leader with high ideals and demanding of his men, he was an effective commander who made his battalion a success. Its losses at Amiens were 172 all ranks.[40] It went into the line on the night of 31 August having to fight for its position, and the brigade ordered it to push out outposts. The result was the relief did not finish until almost dawn.[41]

39 LAC: RG9 III-C-3 v4233, 28/17: Entrainment Strength Reported 25 August 1918.

40 LAC: RG9 III-D-3 v4943: 72nd Battalion War Diary, 10 August 1918; Bernard McEvoy, *History of the 72nd Canadian Infantry Battalion, Seaforth Highlanders of Canada* (Vancouver: Cowan & Brookhouse, 1920), pp.118-119.

41 LAC: 12th Brigade War Diary, 72nd Battalion Scarpe Operation 29th Aug.-3rd Sept. 1918; McEvoy, *72nd Battalion History*, p.120.

The 38th deployed in the brigade's centre. Its commander was the wealthy lumberman from Ottawa, Lieutenant Colonel Cameron Edwards (37). Travelling in the highest Canadian social circles, Edwards formed and led the 38th Battalion with distinction. The 38th had manageable losses at Amiens, so it was close to a full complement with 35 officers and 978 men.[42] Ever-present problem of traffic congestion and issues with guides delayed the relief of the 2nd Brigade to 3:30 a.m.

The 85th Battalion suffered only 136 casualties at Amiens, but German fire devastated its command structure. In the course of 24 hours, it lost its CO, second-in-command, and the senior company commander. Commanding it at Arras 1918 was Major John Millar (35), a prewar civil engineer. He joined the 85th in December 1915 as a ranker and received his commission in February 1916, so his rise from a ranker to battalion commander was rapid. Like the other battalions in the brigade, its takeover of the front was difficult as there was no sign of the 2nd Dukes. Instead, they found the Germans in strength and so close that the artillery could not support them. They had a tiring battle with one particularly powerful strongpoint along the Arras-Cambrai road that they could not budge.[43]

In reserve was the 78th Battalion. Its commander was Lieutenant Colonel James Kirkcaldy (52). Born in Scotland and with service in the Black Watch, Kirkcaldy moved to Canada in 1891. After recovering from a severe chest wound at Second Ypres, he raised the 78th Battalion and arrived in France in command in August 1916. He was a rare example of a British ranker rising to lead a battalion. The 78th had a tough tour at Amiens, losing 15 officers and 325 men.[44] To add further injury, German night bombers struck it overnight on 24 August inflicting a demoralising 19 killed and 40 wounded.[45] The German air service repeatedly conducted night bombing missions during the Arras campaign. While the matériel and personnel effects were minuscule, the consequences on morale and energy were not. The regimental history of the 44th Battalion explicitly referred to its unnerving effects as night-time bombing nonplussed even veterans of repeated bombardments.[46] Watson referred to the night bombing and its effects in his private diary.[47] These missions were relatively recent, and the troops had not had time to adjust to this fresh horror. The drone of aircraft overhead at night prevented sleep. Further, there was little warning of falling bombs, so it was difficult to take protective action. Units in the rear were more likely to be bombed than those at the front; thus, reversing the usual risk. In May 1918, three night raids hit hospitals well to the rear inflicting 982 casualties including the deaths of six Canadian nurses.[48] Finally, these raids could inflict losses that devastated small units. For instance, H Battery of the 4th Machine Gun Battalion was effectively knocked out of the battle on the night of 1/2 September by three German bombs.[49]

42 LAC: RG9 III-D-3 v4938: 38th Battalion War Diary, 31 August 1918.
43 LAC: RG9 III-D-3 v4944: 85th Battalion War Diary, 8-10, 31 August 1918; Joseph Hayes, *The Eighty-Fifth in France and Flanders* (Halifax N.S.: Royal Print & Litho, 1920), pp.121-122.
44 LAC: 12th Brigade War Diary, 12th Brigade Report Llandovery Castle Operation, 8-14 August 1918.
45 LAC: Watson Diary, 24 August 1918.
46 Russenholt, *6000 Canadian Men*, p.173.
47 LAC: Watson Diary, 24 August, 1 September 1918.
48 T. Robert Fowler, 'The Canadian Nursing Service and the British War Office: The Debate over Awarding the Military Cross, 1918', *Canadian Military History* 14, no. 4 (2012), pp.32-36.
49 LAC: MG30 E537 v1: Sansom Fonds, 4th Machine Gun Battalion Narrative, 59-60.

Results

In comparison with the previous day, the Corps committed fewer troops and the casualty list reflected this. The losses dropped by 50 to 765 all ranks, with the 4th British Division suffering more than the 1st Canadian. Prisoner totals increased to 213 all ranks, but with only two officers captured.

Table 9.1 Estimated Casualties For 31 August 1918

	Killed	Wounded	POW	Total
1st CID	58	190		248
2nd CID	7	17		24
3rd CID	9	16		25
4th CID	3	10		13
4th BID*	84	231		315
Tank Corps				0
Other	7	133		140
Total	**168**	**597**	**0**	**765**

* 4th British Division totals do not include prisoners lost.
† Included in the Other category are Tank Corps wounded.

Battle for the Jump-off Line: 1 September

With one day left to the big push, only the left brigade of the 4th British Division was on its jump-off line. There was, therefore, urgency in reaching it, while the Germans would do all they could to prevent that. Having to clear out a deep *Vorfeld* zone before hitting the D-Q Line would consume troops and munitions needed for cracking the fortifications. It would also mean the field artillery might not fire its barrage through to the first objective. The day's stakes were high.

Strategic Situation

Overall, 1 September was a day of some gains but primarily one of marking time and preparing for another general offensive.[50] On the Third Army's left flank, the 57th British Division attacked with the 1st Division with the same objectives as on 29 August. There were the usual misunderstandings as the Canadians thought the British would not assist. The 171st Brigade attacked with a barrage on a two-battalion front – 1/8th King's (Liverpool) Regiment (KLR)

50 Edmonds, *Military Operations, 1918* 4, pp.371-381, 385.

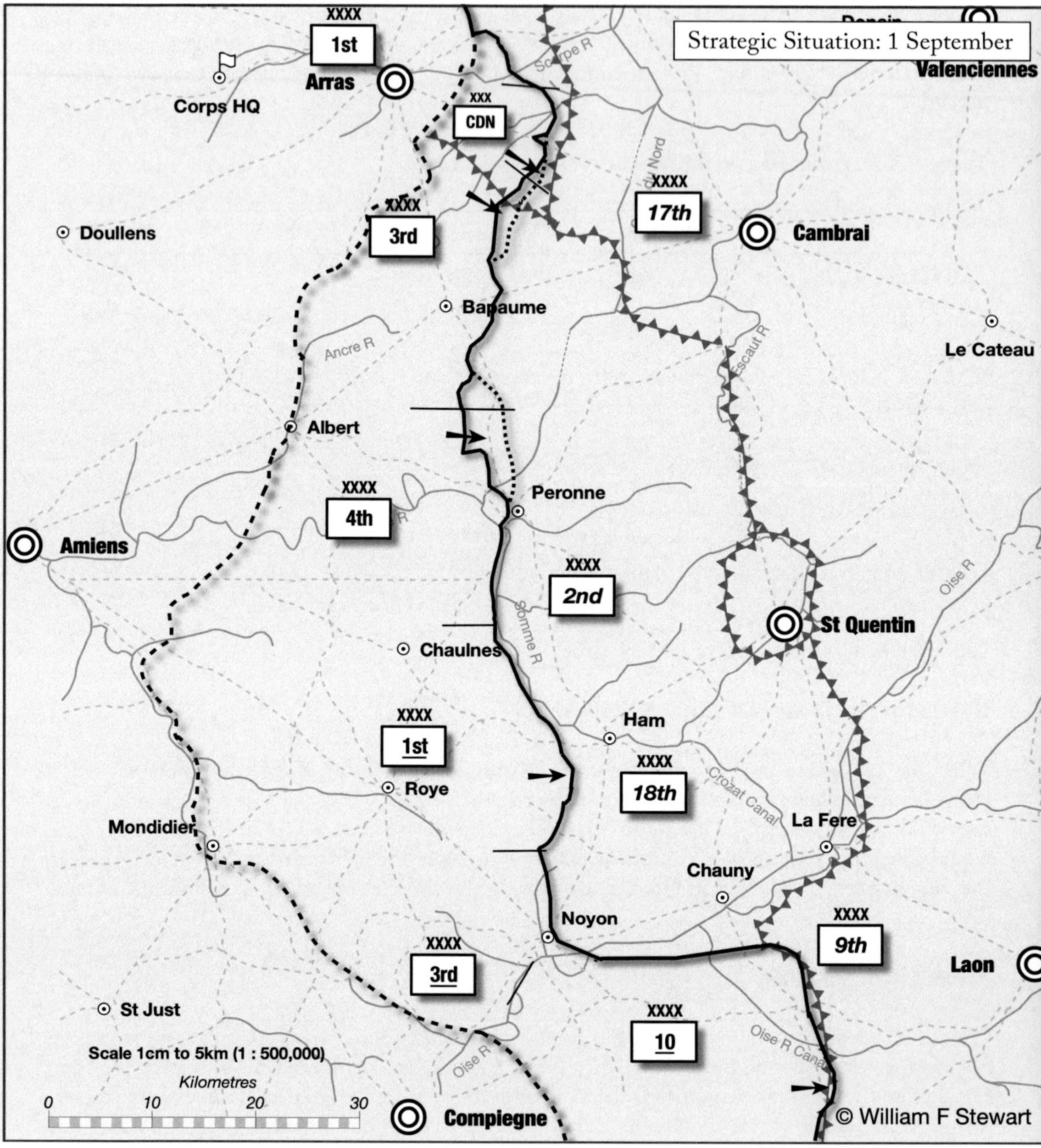

Map 30. Strategic situation 1 September with most of the British armies waiting for the Canadian attack to loosen the German hold on their forward positions across the front. (Author's map)

right and 2/7th KLR left. They took Hendecourt and advanced to Greyhound Trench by 9:00 a.m., sometime after the Canadian 3rd Brigade had seized its objectives. The brigade advanced again at 6:15 p.m. with two battalions taking Riencourt and the spur running north. This brought the British line up to the Canadian advance. This success removed the risk of a flanking counterattack. The Germans tried a local counterattack at 8:30 p.m. that the brigade drove off.[51]

Germans

The Canadian Corps' attacks on 31 August broke down von Dellmensingen's tidy defensive scheme. Adding to its disintegration, he committed substantial forces to retake Upton Woods and the F-R Line. In doing so, he dangerously drew down his reserves and burned out multiple regiments trying to restore the situation. *OHL* recognised the looming threat to the D-Q Line and were doing all they could to rush their last reserves to the *Seventeenth Armee*. Kuhl thought the situation was on a 'knife edge,' but there was no choice but to strip forces from the northern armies.[52] The circumstances were so grave that the *20th ID* spent only one day in line north of the *48th RD* before orders arrived to rush south to reinforce the *II Bavarian Korps*.[53] Withdrawing newly arrived forces from potentially active sectors indicated a desperate situation. On the southern wing, the *22nd ID* transferred north to the *XVIII Korps* as an *Eingreifdivision*, and it would get involved in the fighting on 2 September.[54]

Dellmensingen, anticipating further blows, shifted up elements of his *Eingreifdivision* centred near the Arras-Cambrai road. He rightly regarded it as the sector's centre of gravity. North of the road, the *1st Guards Reserve Regiment* (*GRR*) moved up to east of Mont Dury. South of the road, the *3rd RD*'s *34th FüR* and *49th RIR* deployed forward near Cagnicourt and Villers-lès-Cagnicourt.[55] This had the advantage of reducing the time to engage the enemy but risked being engaged prematurely and exposed them to shelling.

The German order-of-battle starting in the south included the *7th Schützen Division* and elements of the *68th IR* replacing the burned out *58th ID* defending Riencourt and Hendecourt. South of the Arras-Cambrai road, the *16th ID* defended the sector, with the *68th IR* and *28th IR* in line and the *29th IR* in reserve. The *111th ID* remained in position in the second line. The *Eingreifdivision*, the *3rd RD*, had two regiments, with the newly joined *2nd GrR* still across the Canal du Nord as an army reserve. It was a Pomeranian division badly mauled by the French during their July counteroffensive. Both GHQ and the Americans thought it an average division with a susceptibility to haemorrhage captives in action.[56]

North of the Arras-Cambrai road, the *4th EzD* continued to hold the line from 500 metres south of Haucourt to Étaing. Behind it, the *2nd GRD* sat with three attenuated regiments. This division had fought from the start of the war on the Western Front and faced the Canadians

51 LAC: RG9 III-D-3 v5072: XVII General Staff War Diary, 1 September 1918.
52 Bundesarchive, Freiburg: Herman Von Kuhl Kriegserinnerungen, 1 September 1918.
53 Oscar Winter Karl Dieterich, *Das Niedersächsische Feld-Artillerie-Regiment Nr. 46 im Krieg 1914-1918* (Braunschweig: George Westermann, 1934), pp.440-442.
54 Walter Seebohm, *Geschichte Des Oberelsässischen Infanterie-Regiments Nr. 167* (Jena: Walter Viedermann, 1932), p.140.
55 Brederlow, *1st Garde-Reserve-Regiments*, pp.313-314; Szczepanski, *Geschicte FüR No. 73*, p.154.
56 LAC: SS 644b Classification; General Staff Intelligence Section, *251 Divisions*, pp.600-603.

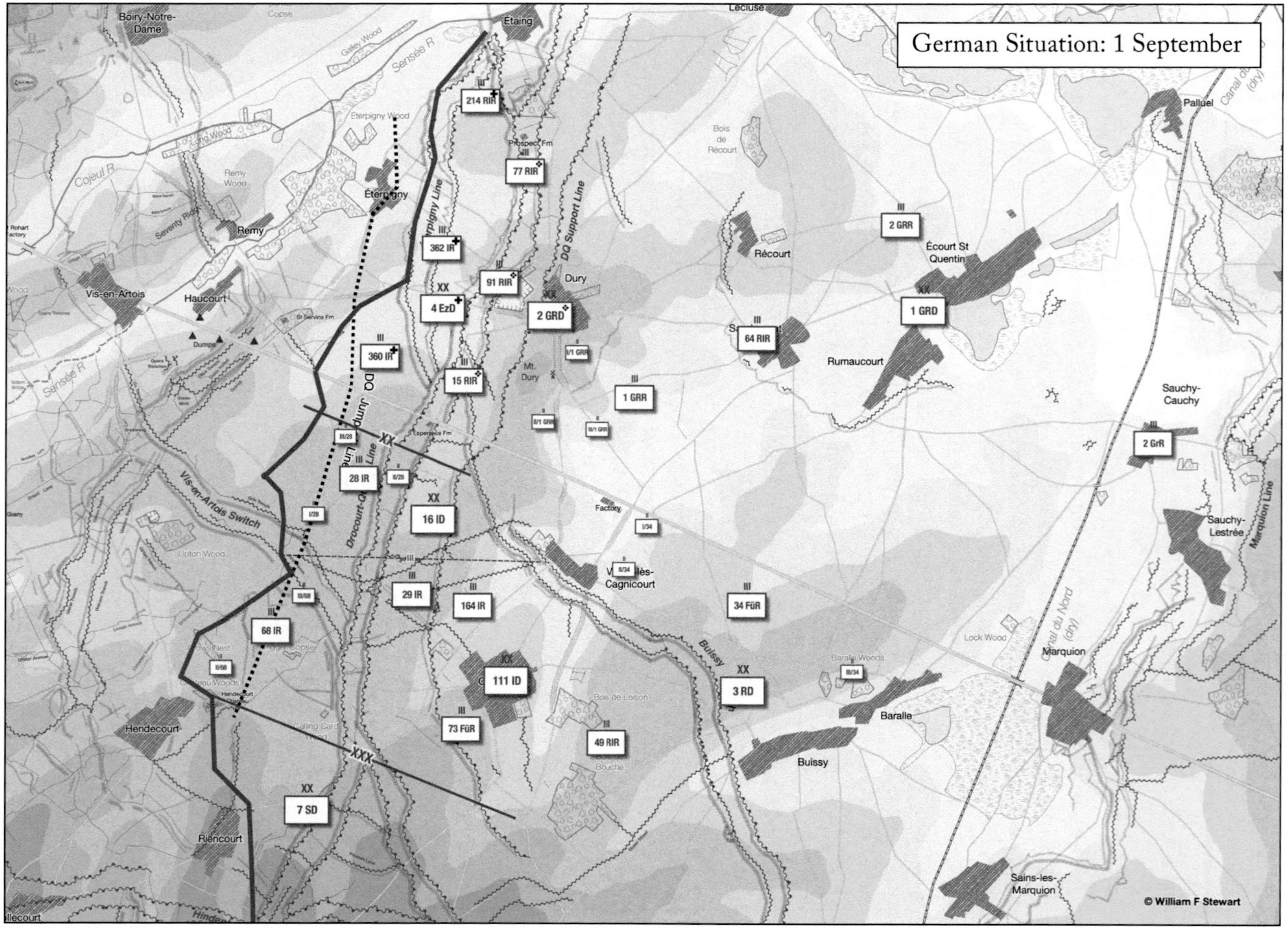

Map 31. The *II Bavarian Korps* defensive arrangements were under strain as the Canadian Corps pressed hard its forward forces. Dellmensingen pushed his *Eingreifdivisions* closer to the front to promptly intervene if the Canadians launched a major attack. (Author's map)

on the Somme. The Third Army mauled it in its August attacks, but *OHL* was so desperate for formations it committed it to defend the D-Q Line. Its *91st RIR* was in such terrible shape that it comprised just two half battalions with a total strength of 225. The regimental commander, *Oberstleutnant* v Keizer, pleaded for the regiment's relief given the troops' poor health, exhaustion, lack of trained machine gunners, and low strength in spirit and numbers. Moreover, their officers were too inexperienced to influence the troops. The division ignored Keizer's pleas.[57] This did not presage a determined struggle when attacked.

The sector's *Eingreifdivision* was the crack *1st GRD*. Formed at the war's start, and it fought in all the major battles including on the Somme around Mouquet Farm against the Canadians in 1916. It got the better of the 1st Division there.[58] The *1st GRD* was one of the specially trained assault divisions and attacked at the start of *Michael*. It later replaced the *4th EzD* at Givenchy in April, and the division's commander received a *Pour le Mérite* for its performance. GHQ regarded it as a 'Very Good' formation.[59]

Dellmensingen did not accept the loss of the Upton Wood or the F-R Line and ordered the *16th ID* to retake them. The *28th IR* received the assignment and was to attack with three battalions along with a company of pioneers at 5:33 a.m. with a barrage. Once the *28th* had taken the woods, the *68th IR* was to advance to the Hendecourt-Vis-en-Artois road. The Canadians pre-empted the operation with their own assault launched at 4:50 a.m. that threw the *16th ID* into a calamitous defensive struggle.[60]

1st Division: Gaining the Jump-Off Line

The 1st Division was still a distant 800 to 1,100 metres from the jump-off line. Macdonell had to conduct a complex operation with elements of three brigades (2nd, 3rd and 12th) from two divisions (1st and 4th) relieving a single brigade (1st) overnight. Then the two 1st Division brigades had to conduct an assault in the morning. This action required capable leadership and staff work. The Corps ordered the 1st Division to take Crow's Nest and Hendecourt Chateau woods on 1 September. The Crow's Nest was a wood dominating the valley to the west that could disrupt the D-Q operation. Judging from the fire received from this location, the enemy held it in strength. The Corps' order instructed the 1st Division to work out the details with the XVII Corps for a coordinated strike.[61] Likely, Macdonell, busy in the detailed planning for the D-Q operation, verbally passed the responsibility to Tuxford's 3rd Brigade – there were no 1st Division instructions. Tuxford tried to make arrangements with the British but failed.[62] Major J P Girvan, the 15th Battalion's CO, only found out that the 57th would not cooperate at the last minute.[63] Curiously, the British formation attacked as already described, so either there was

57 Kümmel, *Res.Inf.Regt. Nr. 91*, pp.425-427.
58 Stewart, *Neglected Campaign*, p.75.
59 LAC: SS 644b Classification; General Staff Intelligence Section, *251 Divisions*, pp.22-25.
60 Pafferath, *Geschichte I.R. 68*, p.719; LAC: RG9 III-C-3 v4152, 2/15: Translation of Divisional Order 16th Infantry Division, 31 August 1918; Begau, *IR 28 in Weltkrieg*, pp.236-238.
61 LAC: RG9 III-C-1 v3855, 75/3: Canadian Corps G.856, 31 August 1918.
62 LAC: 3rd Brigade WD, 31 August 1918.
63 Beattie, *48th Highlanders*, p.349.

a late change of heart or there was a significant misunderstanding. For more, see Map 9.7 1st Division and Flanking Forces: 1 September Morning in the colour map booklet.

Zero Hour was 4:50 a.m., and the time worked well. First, it masked the advance initially, as there was no smoke.[64] Likely, shortages of smoke shells meant reserving them for the main offensive.[65] Second, it pre-empted the planned *28th IR* counterattack scheduled for 5:33 a.m. On the division's right, the 3rd Brigade took over the southern part of the 1st Brigade's front. It would attack with two battalions to take the dominant positions of the Crow's Nest and Hendecourt Chateau and its woods. The 2nd Brigade would employ its 5th Battalion to seize a further 800 metres of the Vis-en-Artois Switch up to the jump-off line. Five FA brigades would fire in support of the 3rd Brigade and two the 2nd – giving a density of 23 metres and 25 metres per gun for the two attacks.[66]

On the 3rd Brigade's right, the Highlanders of Toronto's 15th Battalion had the tough assignment of taking on the Crow's Nest. It had suffered relatively few casualties (190 all ranks) at Amiens and was effectively back to full strength (31 officers and 993 other ranks).[67] It, however, experienced major command turbulence, as it was on its third CO from the start of Amiens.[68] The new CO, Major John P Girvan (31), was an example of a new generation of battalion commanders with no prewar military experience who rose through the ranks. He joined the unit in 1914 as a private and only received his commission in September 1915. Currie called him 'an exceptionally fine soldier, and I regarded him as one of the most outstanding officers in the Corps.'[69]

The 15th Battalion had an 800 metre front with an advance of 1,100 metres on its right by its two companies. Given the hasty arrangements and lack of information about the defences, Girvan decided to rush the primary objective. Using the standard tactics, scouts screened the advance and found enemy resistance points. Behind these skirmishers, the rest of the platoon followed in columns of sections in artillery formation. Firing HE, the enemy protective barrage came down promptly, but the section worms worked their way through it with minimal losses. The Highlanders were on the Germans before they could react. They captured twenty machine guns ready to fire but did not have time to open up.[70] The enemy's poor morale in this sector contributed to the rapid success, with the Canadians reaching their objectives within an hour. Assisting the operation were rapid communications via a lamp from a reporting centre south of the Crow's Nest back to the battalion headquarters and then to the brigade. This would be of great value during the battle. For instance, at 8:30 a.m. an artillery battery, responding to a request, silenced a German machine gun strongpoint in Trigger Copse just beyond the objective line. In earlier battles, this would have taken hours to arrange. The enemy tried two counterattacks, but SOS flares brought a prompt shelling that defeated them. The unit's losses were surprisingly low at 80 all ranks. It did not keep track of how many prisoners it took. The

64 LAC: RG9 III-C-3 v4077, 3/14: 15th Battalion Report on Attack of September 1 1918 on Crows Nest and Chateau Wood, 6 September 1918.
65 TNA: WO 95-2570-1/5: 39th Divisional Artillery War Diary, 1 September 1918.
66 TNA: 39th DA WD, 1 September 1918; LAC: 1st CDA W.D., 1 Division Artillery OO No. 89, 31 August 1918.
67 Beattie, *48th Highlanders*, p.338.
68 LAC: RG9 III-D-3 v4924: 15th Battalion War Diary, 8-23 August 1918.
69 LAC: RG9 III-A-1 v279, 10-G-269: Currie to Secretary, OMFC, 13 May 1920.
70 LAC: 1st Divison W.D., 1st CDA Report of Operations, 28 August to 4th September 1918.

3rd Brigade claimed 300 captives, including a battalion commander and staff. Girvan ascribed his battalion's success to the 'dash of the men and the good leadership of the junior Officers.'[71]

The Canadian accounts describe a far less magnificent stand than did the *68th IR*'s history. In its version, the Highlanders emerged from the fog under an 'insane' barrage. The defenders stopped repeated attacks until assault troops outflanked them. In an impossible situation, the defenders had to fight their way back but had to leave their wounded behind. The attack reduced one company to a sergeant, a corporal and seven men. The regiment had no choice but to retire to the D-Q Line. Given the 15th Battalion's few casualties, the rapid capture of the objectives, and the large haul of prisoners, the German account seems more aspirational than accurate.[72]

The 14th Battalion on the brigade's left suffered heavily at Amiens with the loss of 21 officers and 278 men.[73] It quickly recovered its strength in other ranks but losing so many officers, including two-company commanders, strained the battalion's leadership. Fortunately, it had a strong leader in Lieutenant Colonel Dick Worrall (28). It is hard to imagine a more unlikely commander than Worrall. He came from an English working-class background, had extensive tattoos on arms and a leg at a time when that was rare in command ranks, and he was a deserter from the US Army.[74] An example of the rat-catcher that rose from the ranks and succeeded in the rough and tumble of active duty, he took over the battalion in April 1918. His rise from humble beginnings, his winning of two DSOs and two MCs and the performance of the battalion at Arras 1918 attest to a skilled and courageous officer.[75] His reports on the battles show a keen insight and thoughtful perspective.

The 14th Battalion would attack on a single company front with a frontage of 650 metres and an advance of 900 regulated by the 15th Battalion's movements. It expected little resistance, and the Germans complied. The unit blew through a scattered set of shell-hole defences and the defenders 'surrendered eagerly.' In some cases, they even ran forward to surrender, but they were well equipped. In one 100 metre section of Hans Trench packed with defenders, the battalion captured 13 light machine guns. Worrall wrote that the lead company had many recent replacements who were keen, and they 'joyfully bayonetted' the enemy.[76] British and Canadian recruits received intensive training in bayonet fighting. Recruits spent 10 percent of their training time on bayonet fighting as a means of fostering an aggressive spirit.[77] Further battalions regularly practised it in the field.

71 LAC: 3rd Brigade WD, Narrative of Events - 26th August - 3rd September 1918 and 31 August-1 September 1918; Beattie, *48th Highlanders*, pp.346-355; LAC: 15th Bn Report, Crows Nest.

72 Pafferath, *Geschichte I.R. 68*, pp.719-731.

73 LAC: 14th Battalion War Diary, 8-9 August 1918.

74 He attested as Richard but declared in late 1918 his true name was Dick.

75 James Daly, *Portsmouth's World War One Heroes: Stories of the Fallen Men and Women* (Stroud, UK: The History Press, 2013), Chapter 4; '1915 Battlefield Commissions for Two Future RMR Co's' <http://www.royalmontrealregiment.com/1915-battlefield-commissions-for-two-future-rmr-cos/> (31 January 2019); Fetherstonhaugh, *14th Battalion, C.E.F.*, pp.201-202.

76 LAC: 14th Battalion War Diary, 1 September 1918 and OO No 242, 31 August 1918; LAC: 3rd Brigade WD, 14th Battalion Report on Operation of September 1st, 6 September 1918; Fetherstonhaugh, *14th Battalion, C.E.F.*, pp.234-236.

77 For opposing views on the utility of bayonet fighting, see Paul Dominick Hodges, "They Don't Like It up 'Em!': Bayonet Fetishization in the British Army During the First World War', *Journal of War and Culture Studies* 1, no. 2 (2008), p.83; Miedema, 'Bayonets and Blobsticks: The Canadian Experience of

An unlikely commander from humble origins, Lieutenant Colonel Dick Worrall, CO 14th Battalion had a keen insight and a thoughtful perspective. (Canada. Dept. of National Defence/Library and Archives Canada/ PA-003788.)

Thinking the Canadians were aiming to breach the D-Q Line, the *16th ID* ordered the *29th IR* to defend it.[78] When it was clear, the attack was going no further the division changed the regiment's mission. It was now to counterattack and retake at minimum, the ground lost in the morning. The *29th IR* plus surviving fragments of the *68th IR* attacked and reached Canadian lines about noon. On the 14th Battalion front, the attack centred on Hans Trench. The battalion reported repulsing three enemy counterattacks and using a captured supply of potato masher grenades to defeat a bombing attack. It defended a line of multiple shell holes, so movement was difficult in daylight. Worrall pointed out that three wounded officers remained at duty, and he claimed this inspired 40 other ranks to continue at their posts despite their wounds. After the failed attacks, the Germans shot gas shells all day, so the troops had to wear gas masks – a fatiguing experience. The battalion claimed 300 prisoners, 100 dead enemy, and 35 machine guns for a loss of 5 officers and about 100 men. Worrall reported: 'Never in my experience have I seen him so disorganised and thoroughly cowed.' This was more evidence that the *68th IR*'s account was fanciful.[79]

On the division's left flank, the 2nd Brigade deployed a single battalion, the 5th, to attack on a 650 metre front to a depth of 900 metres. Its mission was to push down the Vis-en-Artois Switch to the south-east along Orix and Opal Trenches to reach the jump-off

Close Combat 1915-1918'; LAC: RG9 III-B-1 v3111, T-25-36 v1: Training in Canadian Reserve Battalions, Revised Edition, 1 October 1917.

78 Pafferath, *Geschichte I.R. 68*, pp.727-728.

79 LAC: 14th Battalion War Diary, 1 September 1918 and OO No 242, 31 August 1918; LAC: 3rd Brigade WD, 14th Battalion Report on Operation of September 1st, 6 September 1918; Fetherstonhaugh, *14th Battalion, C.E.F.*, pp.234-236.

line.[80] It would attack with one platoon each on the outside of the two trenches and one through the zone between. Without guides, scouts, or a map, the battalion got into line with less than an hour to spare before the attack.

Despite losing 297 men at Amiens, it received so many replacements that it was over-strength and passed 80 to the 8th Battalion.[81] Its commander was Lieutenant Colonel Lorn Tudor (42), who joined the 5th as a lieutenant and took over the battalion in June 1917. By Arras, he was an experienced battalion commander already with a DSO and would win another for his conspicuous gallantry and ability to command on 1 September 1918.[82]

At Zero, it faced redoubts on each flank and trenches packed with defenders and machine guns. German fire whittled away the lead company, and a party of 100 Germans, seeing an open flank, took advantage and tried to envelop it. The support company intervened and captured or killed the lot. Tudor had to commit a third company to the battle as losses mounted. The last hurdle was a series of redoubts along the Hendecourt-Dury road that the battalion overran. By 5:45 a.m., the Western Cavalry had reached its objective, but the lead company was down to just 20 men. The 5th destroyed the *I/28th IR* and claimed 200 prisoners. With a long-left flank, however, the Germans used the road running north of the trench system to infiltrate through gaps to try to retake Orix Trench. The battalion had to commit most of its reserves to repel the attempt, thus stretching it thin. About 9:00 a.m., the Germans started bombarding the Canadian positions. This allowed them to position multiple machine guns to gain fire superiority in the area. The *29th IR*, assisted by *II/28th IR* and survivors of *I/28th IR*, counterattacked at 11:30 a.m. It hit the 5th hard and rolled it back up Orix. One of the major differences between the assault tactics of the Germans and Canadians was the use of machine guns in the offensive. The *28th IR*'s history highlights how the battalion's machine gun companies were an integral part of the attack instead of them lagging behind, as with the Canadian guns.[83] For more, see Map 9.8 1st Division and Flanking Forces: 1 September 1918 Afternoon in the colour map booklet.

At this point the flexibility and initiative of Canadian infantry asserted itself. The 5th Battalion, with the assistance of a platoon from the 72nd, launched a counterattack at 1:00 p.m. The officers on the spot extemporised it without reference to their superiors. Under a barrage of rifle grenades, the two forces advanced on each side of the trenches and drove the Germans back to the Hendecourt-Dury road. By attacking overland, only a few defenders in the trench could fire on the attackers, and so the assault troops outnumbered them locally. Using sectional rushes, the advance was slow and cautious but relentless. The battalion restored the line by 4:00 p.m. along with the capture of another 60 prisoners.[84]

80 'Wilson, Andrew Diary: 1918 September 1st' <http://www.canadianletters.ca/content/document-2201?position=312&list=epFid7A8SEhIegQkhQL_b_xvfyKN_K2Nr20IiYMYOOY> (12 April 2018).

81 LAC: RG9 III-D-3 v4916: War Diary, 5th Battalion, 8-20 August 1919.

82 'Flag Bearer' <https://matthewkbarrett.com/2015/07/01/the-flagbearer/> (30 January 2019).

83 Begau, *IR 28 in Weltkrieg*, pp.236-238.

84 LAC: RG9 III-C-3 v4052, 22/6: Narrative of Operations Carried out by the 5th Canadian Battalion ((Western Cavalry) September 1 and 2nd 1918, 9 September 1918; LAC: RG9 III-D-3 v4916: 5th Battalion War Diary, 1 September 1918; LAC: 2nd Brigade War Diary, 2nd Brigade Narrative of Operations East of Arras August 25 to September 3, 1918; BWRA: Loomis Diary, 1 September 1918; Begau, *IR 28 in Weltkrieg*, pp.236-238.

The German counterattack was initially successful as it hit an off-balance battalion. Lacking ammunition and with most of its reserves committed, the 5th recoiled from the initial blow, but like a spring it slammed back. Without a barrage, it broke the enemy who streamed through the D-Q Line, as German observers noted. The battalion's losses reflected the hard fight with a loss of 10 officers and 225 other ranks. They claimed 300 prisoners taken but lost 5 of their own. In the failure's aftermath, the *28th* and *29th IRs* took over defence of the D-Q Line. The *68th IR*'s few survivors moved back to Cagnicourt. While the *16th ID* had abandoned the idea of another counterattack, von Dellmensingen had not.[85]

He refused to accept the loss of the *Vorfeld* and at 6:00 p.m. launched another counterattack with artillery support. He ordered the *3rd RD* to commit its two available regiments (*34th FüR* and *49th RIR*). Dellmensingen may have interpreted the Canadian operation as a failed all-out assault. If true, the circumstances justified launching another counterattack with the southern *Eingreifdivision* to restore the *Vorfeld*. The *34th FüR* would retake the F-R Line and Upton Wood, with the *49th RIR* the sector south of the wood. With skirmishers leading small irregular columns ready to deploy, the enemy attack formation was conceptually similar to Canadian ones. The *34th* advanced to the D-Q Line before getting spotted. Then the Canadians fired off their SOS flares. With 168 pieces, the 1st Division's FA brigades pummelled the Germans, and they made only limited progress. The 3rd Brigade stopped the *49th RIR* well before it reached its objective. On the *34th FüR*'s front, they drove in the 12th Canadian Brigade's outposts and gained small positions in Orix Trench on the 5th Battalion's front. To do even this, it had to commit two companies of its reserve battalion. These were in turn thrown out. Overall, it was a meagre result for the use of an *Eingreifdivision*, which would have strong repercussions the next day. The *34th FüR* had to spread its *fusiliers* across the front in scattered groups with gaps in the line, made worse by the withdrawal of the battered *16th ID*. As a result, the *3rd RD* was not in a good position for the attack next morning.

The *34th FüR* history complained that the troops had to wear gas masks all night long because of the Canadian's gas shelling.[86] This was a constant refrain in German regimental histories throughout the battle, but none of the Canadian records indicate any gas employed, except for counter-battery fire. Given how close were the German positions to the Canadians, only 18-pounders could fire that close, and they had no gas shells. Neither side used gas on areas that they would attack in several hours.[87] The German complaints were a reaction to smoke shells which often accompanied gas attacks to disguise them.[88]

While these counterattacks wore down the Canadian's offensive edge, the losses, disorganisation, and demoralisation inflicted on the enemy was a net benefit. The Germans lost far more than they gained in them. Histories of units in the D-Q Line paint a distressing

85 Begau, *IR 28 in Weltkrieg*, pp.236-238; Pafferath, *Geschichte I.R. 68*, pp.732-734.

86 Pafferath, *Geschichte I.R. 68*, pp.732-734; Kraehe, *Füs. Reg. 34*, pp.432-434.

87 LAC: RG9 III-B-1 v875, A-53-3 v1 Ammunition and Gun States, August- September 1918; Tim Cook, *No Place to Run: The Canadian Corps and Gas Warfare in the First World War* (Vancouver: UBC Press, 1999), p.171; Albert Palazzo, *Seeking Victory on the Western Front: The British Army and Chemical Warfare in World War I* (Lincoln, Neb.: University of Nebraska Press, 2000), p.8.

88 *SS 175 Notes on the Use of Smoke (Revised Edition)* (General Staff, February 1918); Augustin M Prentiss, *Chemicals in War: A Treatise on Chemical Warfare* (New York: McGraw-Hill Book Company, 1937), p.290.

picture of the front-line forces reduced to a dispirited rabble by the morning of 2 September.[89] Effectively, von Dellmensingen burned out his forward divisions in ill-considered attacks that exposed them to intense artillery and machine gun fire with scant prospect of success. The defenders defeated every attack, so the Germans gained no ground and the counterattacking units were ground to dust. Later reports of the D-Q attackers meeting demoralised defenders corresponds to those units sorely tried in their futile counterattacks.

4th Canadian Division

The 12th Brigade's position was well short of the jump-off line. Through the day there was a constant struggle as both sides tried to improve their positions. German counterattacks hit the brigade, and generally 'the enemy fought fairly stoutly in his outpost positions.'[90] Low-key efforts by the brigade to reach the jump-off line were only partially successful. At 5:15 p.m. the division ordered MacBrien to 'make good' that line at all costs.[91] The 12th Brigade's battalions had a serious quandary in having to reach the jump-off line without burning out the battalion. Expecting a fierce fight for the D-Q line, the battalions wanted to keep their troops fresh, so they assigned limited forces with limited results.

In the hand-off with the 3rd Battalion, the 72nd ended up holding Orix Trench and a few of the outposts beyond it. This left it 1,700 metres from its start line on a 500 metre front. Clark narrowly interpreted a brigade directive to attack with 2nd Brigade by only committing a single platoon. The platoon commander fell early in the action, and the situation remained obscure for the rest of the day. During the noon German counterattack, Clark took advantage of enemy disarray by sending another platoon to reach the jump-off line. The SOS barrages and constant fighting had demoralised the Germans and over 100 surrendered. Nevertheless, the battalion painted a bleak picture of its readiness for the morning attack. In the morning, the infantry would have to fight their way forward 400 metres to reach the jump-off line where they would pick up the artillery barrage. The *3rd RD*'s counterattack washed up against the 72nd, and Clark committed another two platoons to hold the fragile outpost line. Rather than waiting for the oncoming Germans, these two platoons attacked and in the words of the regimental historian appeared to 'somewhat dampen the ardour of the Germans.'[92]

Ottawa's 38th held its line with just one company. The earlier German counterattack did not affect the battalion, but the second did. The forward company commander died bringing up reinforcements, but they arrived in time to resist the attack. Prompt response of the artillery was the key factor. The barrage crashed down, and recoiling from the punishment, the Germans fell back. The battalion's losses were 36 all ranks.[93] Private C J P Nunney at the company HQ visited

89 See for instance, Seebohm, *Geschicte Nr. 167*, p.140.
90 LAC: 12th Brigade War Diary, Scarpe Operation, Capture of Drocourt Queant Line, 2 September 1918.
91 LAC: RG9 III-C-3 v4231, 23/4: 12th Brigade Operations Message Diary, 1 September 1918.
92 McEvoy, *72nd Battalion History*, pp.120-127; LAC: 12th Brigade War Diary, 72nd Battalion Scarpe Operation 29th Aug.- 3rd Sept. 1918; LAC: 72nd Bn WD, 31 August-1 September 1918; LAC: 12th Brigade War Diary, Scarpe Operation, Capture of Drocourt Queant Line, 2 September 1918.
93 LAC: 12th Brigade War Diary, 38th Battalion Report on Scarpe Operations 30th Aug-3rd Sep, 9 September 1918; Kenneth W. Reynolds, *Capital Soldiers: The History of the Cameron Highlanders of Ottawa* (Ottawa, ON: Cameron Highlanders of Ottawa, 2011), p.119; LAC: MG30 E153 v1: 38th

each of the outposts at considerable peril on his own initiative to encourage the defenders. This was the first set of actions over two days that led to his receiving a VC. Clearly an extraordinarily brave man, he was with Thain MacDowell when he won his VC at Vimy. Promotion to sergeant followed, but he was later convicted and sentenced to prison for striking an officer. While in transit, Nunney suffered burns to his hands and face trying to rescue a shot-down German pilot. For his courageous attempt, the authorities suspended his sentence to return to the battalion.[94]

In response to the divisional prodding, the 85th attacked with artillery support at 8:40 p.m. For once, a Canadian attack synchronised with the British. With three platoons committed, the attack gained only 120 metres before it broke down. The unit would dedicate several platoons and machine guns in the morning to deal with the German strongpoints causing havoc.[95]

The 4th Canadian Division informed Hayter, GOC 10th Canadian Brigade, of a new mission late on 31 August. It was to take over the 10th British Brigade's sector next evening. Later on 1 September, MacBrien learned from the British that they were not at the jump-off position but would get there later that evening. With so much uncertainty, Hayter at 8:00 p.m. reiterated to his battalion commanders to not wait for the British but to get into position immediately. It was clear from Canadian accounts that the British were fought out. At 10:00 p.m., the right (47th) and left (50th) battalions crossed the Sensée on duckboards. The British attack failed, so the Canadians had to reach the jump-off line on their own. More bad news was that the 12th Canadian Brigade was also not on its jump-off line. This hastily arranged relief and the problems with preparation were a symptom of the compressed time frames for open warfare and the challenges of dealing with multiple formations.

Communications were also breaking down before the battle began as there was no line from the brigade to the division headquarters located far to the rear.[96] Two brigades in line stretched the divisional signal company to the breaking point. Twin tyrannies of space and time conspired against a robust network. The division's headquarters was 11 kilometres in the rear and traffic, shelling, and German night bombing continually cut the signal lines. The signal company did not have enough linemen for the distance and the frequent breaks. As a result, communications suffered. Even use of radios was problematic because of the distances involved. The signal company had to establish a relay station to keep in touch, which slowed the information flow and tied-up personnel.[97] With eight FA brigades to manage, the signals system could not manage that load. The 3rd CFA suggested 'the task was too big for the CDA Signals to cope with it

Battalion History, 41; LAC: 12th Brigade War Diary, Scarpe Operation, Capture of Drocourt Queant Line, 2 September 1918.

94 'Claude Nunney VC DCM MM' <http://www.claudenunney.co.uk/index.php> (5 March 2019); 'Claude Joseph Patrick Nunney' <http://www.cmp-cpm.forces.gc.ca/dhh-dhp/gal/vcg-gcv/bio/nunney-cjp-eng.asp> (5 March 2019).

95 Hayes, *The Eighty-Fifth in France and Flanders*, pp.137-139; LAC: 85th Bn. W.D., 1 September 1918 and Recommendation for Major John MacIntosh Millar; LAC: 12th Brigade War Diary, 85th Battalion Report Scarpe Operation 30th Aug.-3rd Sept. 1918.

96 LAC: 10th Brigade WD, 10th Brigade Narrative of Operations Battle of Arras, 14 September 1918.

97 LAC: RG9 III-D-3 v5005: 4th Division Signal Company War Diary, Communication, 4th Canadian Div. Signals Coy., From 1st to 5th September 1918.

Brigadier General Ross Hayter in the centre and the staff of the 10th Canadian Brigade in May 1918. A British Army office although born in Canada, Currie promoted him to command the 10th when he learned Hayter was to receive a British brigade. (Canada. Dept. of National Defence/Library and Archives Canada/ PA-002827)

quickly.'[98] Many of the British FA brigades did not have CW radio sets so further complicating matters. This was a case where the Canadians had a major advantage.[99]

On the brigade's right, the 47th Battalion deployed east of St Servins Farm. Its CO was Lieutenant Colonel Herbert Keegan (30) who spent most of the war in another battalion. He joined the 50th Battalion early 1915 and served with it until April 1918, when he took over the 47th. Watson described him as good and cool in action and a disciplinarian. Possibly senior officers believed the battalion needed a hard taskmaster in command, hence his transfer.[100] The 47th quickly regained its strength after Amiens, so its fighting strength was at 29 officers and 770 men by 28 August.

98 LAC: RG9 III-C-1 v3911, 39/8: 3rd CFA, R.O.11, 11 September 1918.
99 LAC: RG9 III-C-1 v3911, 39/8: 4 CFA A.2864, 11 September 1918 and Short Report on Communications During Second Battle of Arras, 4th CDA, September 2-7 1918; LAC: RG9 III-C-1 v3912, 41/11: 4th CDA Report, 15 September 1918.
100 LAC: 4th Div Confidential Reports.

The battalion relieved the 2nd Dukes on the 10th Brigade's right flank by 2:00 a.m. It was not an easy relief.[101] It had a challenging time crossing the Sensée at Remy as the valley was under heavy bombardment by shells and gas. The unit suffered losses in the process. With forces from both sides mixed up, the support company captured nine Germans and four machine guns in the woods around St Servins Farm. The battalion then trickled forward to get as close as possible to the jump-off line. While doing so two men fell into enemy hands. In the morning, the 47th would attack with the barrage about 300 metres away so they would have to move fast to catch up to it.[102]

On the brigade's left, the 50th Battalion from Alberta experienced the same uncertainties. Heavy German shelling of the roads made the march difficult. One round hit a lorry full of ammunition as well as an ammunition dump on the road. 'The explosion shook the earth about us and several chaps were sprayed with flying shrapnel. The traffic was held up for more than six hours,' was Sergeant W W Wheeler's vivid description of the trip to the front.[103] It ended up 200 metres from its jump-off line. The 50th's CO was the experienced Lieutenant Colonel Lionel Frank Page (34) – in command since March 1917. He volunteered for the 5th Battalion in 1914 and served with it until assuming the command of the 50th. Watson rated him as a very capable commander, disciplinarian, and tactician. The unit had relatively heavy losses at Amiens at 14 officers and 231 men. Also, many men were sick from bad food and water in the battle's aftermath. Even Watson, the division's commander, got dysentery and was quite ill for several days. He complained about being 'awfully weak' as a result on 28 and 29 August.[104]

4th British Division

Matheson's division would spend 1 September adjusting to a single brigade front. The 12th Canadian Brigade took over a small portion of its right front, and the 10th Canadian Brigade would relieve the 10th British Brigade that night. The British division had two issues. First, the 11th British Brigade on its left had been in line for three days and needed a rest. Second, the division was not on the jump-off line on its right. The first step was the 12th British Brigade relieving the 11th, which took to daylight. The 10th British Brigade launched an early morning attack at 4:15 a.m. On its right, the 2nd Dukes advanced 350 metres and took Pear Trench. One company of Seaforths took but could not hold the sunken road on the left. The attackers claimed 53 prisoners and 3 machine guns from the much-tried *4th EzD*.[105] For more, see Map 9.9 4th British Division Operations: 31 August in the colour map booklet.

101 LAC: 10th Brigade WD, 47th Battalion Report on Operations from 1st September to 4th September, 1918, Inclusive; LAC: RG9 III-D-3 v4940: 47th Battalion War Diary, 10-28 August 1918.

102 LAC: 10th Brigade WD, 47th Battalion Report on Operations from 1st September to 4th September, 1918, Inclusive; LAC: 47th Bn WD, 1 September 1918; LAC: 10th Brigade WD, 10th Brigade Narrative of Operations Battle of Arras, 14 September 1918.

103 Victor W. Wheeler, *The 50th Battalion in No Man's Land: 50th Canadian Infantry Battalion (Alberta Regiment), Canadian Expeditionary Force, 1915-1919* (Ottawa: CEF Books, 2000), p.248.

104 LAC: Watson Diary, 28-29 August 1918; Wheeler, *50th Battalion*, pp.244-246; LAC: 50th Bn WD, Report on Operations, 2nd-4th September 1918 and 1 September 1918.

105 TNA: 10th Br Bde WD, Report on Operations Carried out by the 10th Infantry Brigade East of Monchy-les-Preux During August and September 1918.

The brigade was up to the jump-off line along its centre but not on the flanks. It needed another operation. The 10th British attacked along with the 85th Battalion at 8:40 p.m., but staff botched the arrangements. With forces so closely mixed, the artillery plan required the infantry to fall back. The Dukes did not receive that message.[106] The artillery barrage fell on and behind the troops, and the attack sputtered. One bright spot was 2nd Lieutenant James Huffam would win the VC for taking out a machine gun post in the morning and another in the evening attack with conspicuous gallantry.[107] As already described, the 85th Battalion could not advance south of the Arras-Cambrai road. Using this as an excuse, the British charged that the Canadians 'failed to get forward.' The Seaforths also could not take their objective. The result was the 10th Canadian Brigade would assume a most unfavourable situation.[108] With their relief, the 10th British went into reserve although its 2nd Seaforth's were attached to the 11th Brigade.

In its discussion of lessons learned, the 4th British Division blamed the delay in clearing St Servins Farm on poor coordination with the Canadians. Ironically, the 10th British Brigade also groused about synchronisation and thought the division should manage it, 'to ensure them operating for the good of all.'[109] The divisions, brigades, and battalions were unable to work together effectively. Reports from both sides reference failures of other units to support an operation, to keep up, or to coordinate. Clearly there was a breakdown of cooperation to the offensive's detriment. This was a consequence of the rapid tempo demanded of units and the limited coordination provided by the Corps. There is inevitably a tendency to blame the flanking forces for missteps, but forces coming from different armies, which the Canadians were increasingly becoming, magnified the tension. Canadian attitudes showed little appreciation of the limitations the British were operating under and there was often a disdain for their efforts. While sometimes deserved, this reaction was mostly unfair and ungenerous. The British also had justifiable reasons for complaints about the Canadian actions.

Results and Analysis

With three divisions and multiple brigades actively involved, the casualty totals jumped to 1,323 all ranks for the day. Prisoner totals increased to 213 all ranks, but with only two officers captured.[110] This total again underestimates the captives taken by the Corps. Even discounting for the usual exaggerations of prisoner totals claimed by battalions and brigades, this total is considerably lower. This again was likely the result of the reporting periods overlapping.

106 LAC: 10th Brigade WD, 10th Brigade Narrative of Operations Battle of Arras, 14 September 1918.
107 'Scottish Victoria Cross Awards' <http://www.scotlandswar.ed.ac.uk/sites/default/files/pdf_Scottish_VCs_0.pdf> (6 September 2019).
108 TNA: 10th Br Bde WD, Report on Operations Carried out by the 10th Infantry Brigade East of Monchy-les-Preux During August and September 1918.
109 LAC: 10th Brigade WD, Report on Operations Carried out by the 10th Infantry Brigade East of Monchy-les-Preux During August and September 1918.
110 LAC: POW Arras.

Table 9.2 Estimated Casualties For 1 September 1918

	Killed	Wounded	POW	Total
1st CID	137	574	5	716
2nd CID	10	7		17
3rd CID	8	5	1	14
4th CID	37	104	2	143
4th BID*	64	85		149
Tank Corps				0
Other†	5	279		284
Total	**261**	**1,054**	**8**	**1,323**

* 4th British Division totals do not include prisoners lost.
† Included in the Other category are Tank Corps wounded.

At the start of these two days, the crucial question for the Germans was whether they could maintain their *Vorfeld* and wear down the attackers. For the Canadian Corps would it reach its jump-off line without undue losses, and the extent of the 4th Canadian Division's involvement. The results were mixed. South of the Arras-Cambrai road, the Germans suffered a calamitous defeat. The 1st and 4th Canadian Divisions were at the jump-off line across most of the sector. Losses, while not minor, were manageable. They had ample reserves available while von Dellmensingen had used up his *Eingreifdivision*. His insistence on counterattacks had disorganised, demoralised, and gravely debilitated his forces. On the Canadian side, a combination of clever tactics, overwhelming firepower, and carefully regulated attacks by Macdonell delivered success at an acceptable cost. The only criticism was the poor coordination with the British divisions on each flank. Better synchronisation would have resulted in greater success, especially with the 4th British Division.

North of the Arras-Cambrai road, the Germans had partially succeeded. The 4th British Division had reached most of its jump-off line, but it had done so by overtaxing its 10th Brigade. As a result, the Corps had to commit an additional brigade of the 4th Canadian Division. This overturned existing plans and weakened the D-Q attack force. Matheson's division had success, but poor coordination with the Canadians meant the Germans rolled back some of their advances. The enemy was sensitive to threats along the Arras-Cambrai road and so reacted more strongly to the actions of the 10th British Brigade than the 11th. The *II Bavarian Korps* had achieved part of its objective, but it had done so at a heavy cost to the *4th EzD*. North of the road, the *4th EzD* and *2nd GRD* were in bad shape, but behind them was the crack, fresh *1st GRD*.

The stage was now set for the big push – the D-Q Line operation. The Corps had completed Task 3 across most of the front. The attackers and defenders were in place. The artillery was in position and ammunition available in vast quantities. A week of intense and unrelenting combat had worn down the Corps, however, and it now faced its greatest challenge – the D-Q Line.

The delays meant the Germans had more time to prepare. Horne wrote just prior to the attack: 'I fancy he is aware of that & has sent up as many troops as he can lay hands on to try and hold us.'[111] So, what was the plan to overcome this? That is the next chapter.

111 Robbins, *The First World War Letters of General Lord Horne* p.260.

Section Four

Breaking the D-Q Line

10

'Break the hinge'
Planning the D-Q Line Attack

We are trying to break the hinge of the German position, and if we are successful great and important results might reasonably follow.

Arthur Currie, 29 August 1918[1]

The Corps' objectives on 2 September were the capture of the D-Q Line and the Bourlon Wood heights. While the Corps broke the line, it reached none of its other objectives. Operations miscarry through the interactions of failures in planning, preparation, and execution, and enemy actions. At the D-Q Line, it was a combination of a flawed plan and an unexpected hostile reaction. Further, the operations on 2 September are the most misunderstood of the campaign. Two myths stand out. Taking the lead from the Canadian Official History, virtually every academic and popular account repeats the fallacy that a barrage suspended to assist Brutinel's CIF explains the 4th Canadian Division's failure to advance further.[2] The second relates to the potential of the CIF as an exploitation force, which some historians have called an all-arms battle group and Canada's first armoured unit.[3] Related to this was the view that Brutinel had hoodwinked Currie into employing it.[4]

To move past these myths, it is necessary to consider the process and thinking behind its plan. To do so, the chapter will follow an abbreviated form of the Canadian Forces Operational Planning Process altered to fit the Canadian Corps' circumstances.[5] What was the Corps'

1 LAC: Currie Diary, 29 August 1918.
2 Nicholson, *CEF*, p.438. Some examples include Jackson, 'British Empire on the Western Front' p.344; Cook, *Shock Troops*, p.48; Brennan, 'Major-General David Watson': pp.131-135; Dancocks, *Spearhead to Victory*, p.116; Schreiber, *Shock Army*, p.82.
3 Tremblay, 'Brutinel': p.64; Cameron Pulsifer, 'Canada's First Armoured Unit', *Canadian Military History* 10, no. 1 (2001), p.44; Michael R. McNorgan, 'My God Look at Them Houses Moving" Combined Arms at Iwuy, 10-11 October 1918 ' in Donald E. Graves and Robert H. Caldwell, (ed.), *More Fighting for Canada: Five Battles, 1760-1944* (Toronto: R. Brass Studio, 2004), p.204.
4 Brennan, 'Major-General David Watson': p.131; Cook, *Shock Troops*, p.484.
5 *The Canadian Forces Operational Planning Process, B-GJ-005-500/FP-000* (CFEC Joint Doctrine Branch 2008).

process was not visible in the records, so this approach provides a framework for examining how the plan broadly developed. This chapter will examine the process, the plan, and the myths that arose from a poor reading of the evidence.

Conceptual Challenge

Currie and his staff faced a major challenge. Since the offensive started, the Corps had advanced 12.5 kilometres, and this took seven days. Its mission on 2 September was to advance 15 kilometres in a single day. To do this, the Corps first had to break the formidable D-Q Line 3,000 metres away. It then had a 6,000 metre push to the Canal du Nord. It would have to storm across and break the Marquion Line on the far side. Finally, 6,000 metres away was Bourlon Wood. Loss of this would unhinge the centre of the German Western Front defences, so they were prepared to defend to the last, while the Corps' forces were inadequate for the task.

Currie had at his disposal 3 divisions, 7 tank companies (54 tanks), 20 FA brigades (480 pieces), 11 HA brigades (192 pieces), 13 RAF squadrons, and the CIF. The 1st Canadian Division, although tired after three days of fighting, was in good shape. The 4th Canadian having had just entered the line was fresh, but the exhausted 4th British comprised only two effective brigades. Tentatively, he also had the 1st British Division deployed around Wancourt and Guémappe on 1 September.[6] It was, however, in army reserve until late on 1 September.[7]

A series of considerations and constraints shaped the D-Q Line plan. The first consideration was that the Germans intended to defend the D-Q Line to the end. Currie firmly believed the enemy would fight hard for it, and all officer prisoner interrogations and captured documents supported that view.[8] Next, the D-Q Line was a redoubtable fortified zone. Early reports suggested it was in good repair overall and that the wire was in excellent condition.[9] There were, also, serious concerns that tunnels linked the trench lines that the Germans would use to retake positions.[10] This fortified zone comprised the D-Q Line ran generally north-south across the Corps' direction of advance, along with three other defensive zones – the remaining parts of the Vis-en-Artois Switch, the Éterpigny Line, and the Buissy Switch. Undiscussed in planning, the Germans had fortified the deep cellars of the towns of Cagnicourt and Villers-lès-Cagnicourt and the Factory along the Arras-Cambrai road. On the 4th British Division's front, Prospect Farm was another important fortified strongpoint.

Planners assumed based on the above points that the enemy would deploy any arriving reinforcements in the D-Q Line. Those not deployed there would act as counterattack forces. This was especially so as Canadian intelligence had identified the *4th EzD* and *2nd GRD* defending the D-Q Line. With both rated lowly and having already suffered heavy losses, any

6 TNA: Cdn. Corps GS WD, Warning Order G.798/19-13, 30 August 1918; TNA: 1st British Division WD, 1 September 1918.
7 TNA: First Army GS WD 178-3, First Army G.161, 1 September 1918.
8 LAC: Currie Diary, 30 August 1918.
9 See for instance, LAC: RG9 III-C-1 v3932, 20/1: Canadian Corps POW Cage, CC166, 1 September 1918.
10 For example, see LAC: 4th Canadian Div WD, 4 Canadian Division OO No.107, 1 September 1918; LAC: 1st Divison W.D., Drocourt-Queant Operations Instructions No. 1, 31 August 1918; TNA: Cdn. Corps GS WD, Canadian Corps OO No. 234, 31 August 1918; LAC: Hindenburg Line Notes from Chief Engineer, January 1918.

The dense wire obstacles before the D-Q Line. Note they are low-lying so as not to interfere with traversing machine gun fire. (Canada. Dept. of National Defence/Library and Archives Canada/ PA-003280)

reinforcements would likely bolster them. The conclusion, therefore, was the operation's most difficult phase would be the fight for the D-Q Line. As Odlum, GOC 11th Brigade, phrased it, the task set the 4th Canadian Division assumed 'the enemy would break as soon as the QUEANT-DROCOURT line was passed.'[11] The planners locked these assumptions into the artillery plan. It would take two-and-a-half hours to reach the first objective – the D-Q line – but about the same time to advance to the second one, which was three times farther.[12] They expected this rate because of the lack of fixed defences beyond the D-Q Line. Thus, if the Corps broke through, the advance thereafter would be rapid.

It was vital to quickly capture bridges over the canal before the enemy destroyed them. This canal sector was only partially flooded, and it would be difficult to do an assault crossing there. Later, when the Corps had to assault across the canal, it moved south to a dry section.[13] At the most optimistic advance rates, the infantry would only reach the canal by noon. It was,

11 LAC: Currie Diary, 30 August 1918.
12 TNA: Cdn. Corps GS WD, Canadian Corps Barrage Map 'A', August 1918.
13 Nicholson, *CEF*, p.443.

Dropped bridge near Sauchy-Cauchy on the Canal Du Nord from 1919. It was imperative for the Corps' plan to seize the bridges before the Germans destroyed them. (Canada. Dept. of National Defence/ Library and Archives Canada/PA-004514)

therefore, imperative that a mobile force establish a bridgehead within an hour of the breaking of the D-Q Line before the Germans destroyed the bridges over the canal.

Four critical constraints of forces, artillery range, tanks, and flanking forces shaped the planning. At the jump-off line, the front was 8,500 metres, expanding to 16,200 at the second objective. The 4th British Division effectively consisted of two brigades, so the force comprised 24 Canadian and 7 British battalions.[14] Of these, 11 Canadian and 4 British battalions had attacked in the past four days. GHQ's 1918 offensive manual recommended attacking with a density of 3 to 5 men per metre.[15] The figure for the D-Q Line was 1.30 men per metre for the 1st Canadian Division, 2.24 for the 4th Canadian, and 1.05 for the 4th British Division.[16] This was significantly below the recommendation, and this against a strongly fortified position. Currie had no choice, however. He had to attack with what the high command assigned him as Haig rejected his request for a shorter front. The barrage's realistic depth was 2,500 metres, which was the first objective. With German anti-tank measures improving steadily, GHQ

14 One battalion from the 10th British Brigade served with the 11th British Brigade.

15 LAC: RG24 v22007: SS 135 The Training and Employment of Divisions, 1918, January 1918, p.26.

16 This is based on 8 battalions attacking the D-Q Line for the two Canadian divisions and 3 for the British division. Battalion strengths are averaged at 700 men for the Canadian divisions and 600 for the British. This is generous.

A Mark V in action. These tanks packed a powerful punch packaged in a glass jaw. They were far fewer of them than the Germans believed. (Canada. Dept. of National Defence/Library and Archives Canada/PA-003152)

mandated tanks were to follow the infantry and not to advance beyond the barrage.[17] This limited them to the first objective.

Tank losses were rising alarmingly with the improved German anti-tank measures. As early as 10 August, GHQ noted that two days of fighting reduced one battalion of 42 tanks to 2 machines with the loss of 60 percent of its personnel.[18] A lesson from Amiens was the fewer tanks committed and weaker the artillery support, the greater the casualty rate. The First Army issued instructions on 1 September that attackers should only use tanks for breaking the enemy's main line of resistance.[19] It instructed senior officers to review plans with the tank commanders because of their experience. The problem was that majors and captains commanding tank companies had to try to convince stubborn brigadier-generals of what was feasible.

The Canadian Corps had limited contact with tanks.[20] It showed. Only the 2nd Division had used them on the Somme and at Vimy. Every battalion had at least one day of tank training before Amiens, but this was not enough to understand their proper employment. The commander of

17 LAC: MG30 E300 v23: Odlum Fonds, Tank Corps Notes from the Battle 21st/23rd August 1918, 23 August 1918.
18 TNA: GHQ GS WD, GS Note A.34, 10 August 1918.
19 LAC: MG30 E300 v23: Odlum Fonds, First Army OA 109, 1 September 1918.
20 Hammond, 'Tank Cooperation' p.350; Bill Rawling, 'A Resource Not to Be Squandered: The Canadian Corps on the 1918 Battlefield,' in Peter Dennis, (ed.), *1918 Defining Victory* (Army History Unit, 1999), pp.2-3.

the 14th Tank Battalion stated he mistakenly thought the 1st Division's experiences at Amiens would have opened their eyes to the limits and possibilities of tanks.[21] He found they had learned nothing.

Finally, overlooking the Canadian's right flank was high ground 500 to 1,000 metres south of the Corps' boundary from which German fire could sweep deep into the 1st Division's advance. Therefore, it was imperative that the XVII Corps attack to eliminate this menace.

German Situation

Overall, the German situation was poor. Dellmensingen had six divisions facing three attacking formations. Four of his divisions (*3rd RD*, *4th EzD*, *2nd GRD*, and *16th ID*) were exhausted, weak, and demoralised. Only the *1st GRD* was at full strength and battle ready. The other division, the *111th ID*, had only two regiments on the Canadian front, and its *73rd FüR* comprised two battalions. The D-Q Line, however, would act as a significant force multiplier as long as the defenders' morale held. As a comparison, the *Second Armee* prior to Amiens had two divisions with six regiments fully capable of fighting whereas the *II Bavarian Korps* had four similarly rated regiments for a front a quarter as wide embedded in strong defences.[22]

Generalmajor Paul Tiede commanded the full-strength *1st GRD*. An elite formation, the *1st GRD* was instrumental in stopping both the 4th Canadian and British Divisions on 2 September and inflicting heavy casualties. (Ernst von Eisenhart Rothe, *Deutsche Infanterie: Das Ehrenmal Der Vordersten Front,* (Zeulenroda: Sporn Verlag, 1939).)

21 TNA: WO 95-105-5: History of the Fourteenth Battalion, Tank Corps
22 Alexander Fasse, 'Im Zeichen Des „Tankdrachen". Die Kriegführung an Der Westfront 1916-1918 im Spannungsverhältnis Zwischen Einsatz Eines Neuartigen Kriegsmittels Der Alliierten Und Deutschen Bemühungen Um Seine Bekämpfung' (PhD, Humboldt-Universität zu Berlin, 2007), p.279.

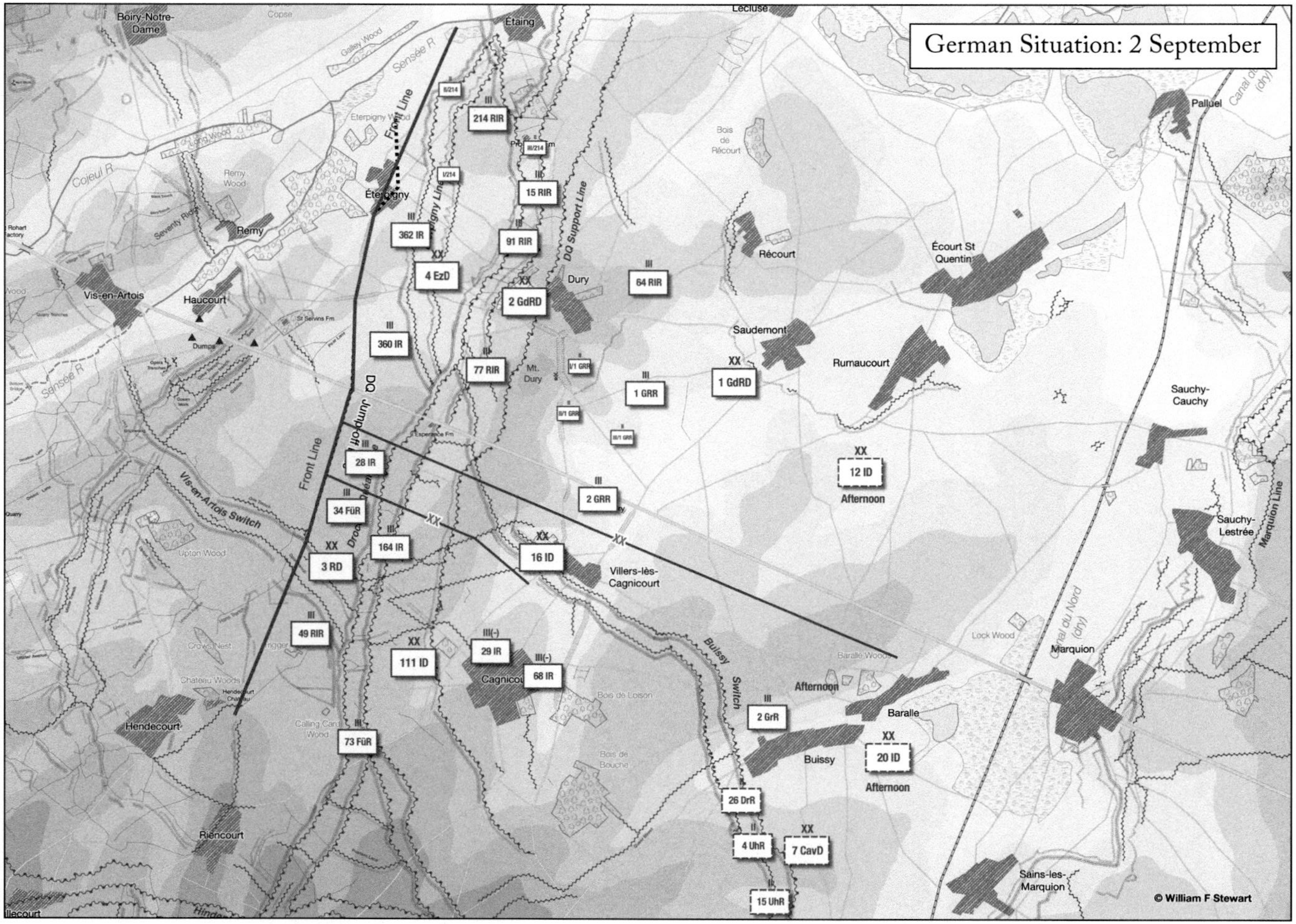

Map 32. II Bavarian Korps' deployment on 2 September. Dellmensingen's carefully laid out three-fold organisation was in dangerous disarray south of the Arras-Cambrai road. (Author's map)

The *II Bavarian Korps*' situation on its left was precarious. Its repeated counterattacks had consumed the southern *Eingreifdivision* – *3rd RD* – and wrecked the *16th ID*. The *49th RIR and 34th FüR* of the *3rd RD* and the *28th IR* held the *Vorfeld*. The *34th FüR* reported it held a two-kilometre front with just two battalions. It had no contact with the *49th RIR* on its left, and there was a 1,000 metre gap between it and the *28th IR* on its right.[23] Two regiments of the *111th ID* defended the D-Q Line along with the rest of the *28th IR*.[24] For reserves, only the scattered survivors of the *29th IR* and *68th IR* were available in the deep cellars of Cagnicourt.[25] In the rear on the southern boundary was the *7th Schützen Division*, a regimental strength formation. Early in the battle, v Dellmensingen moved the *2nd GrR* to the Baralle-Buissy area as the only battle-worthy reserve on the southern sector.[26]

North of the Arras-Cambrai road, the situation was better. The *4th EzD* still defended the *Vorfeld* and the Éterpigny Line north to Étaing. Defending the D-Q Line, the *2nd GRD's* three regiments had the strength of a battalion or less each. The one saving grace was the crack *Eingreifdivision*, *1st GRD*, was uncommitted and fresh. Dellmensingen had it deploy to the immediate east of the D-Q Support Line. Further to the rear were the *12th ID* and *20th ID* that would intervene in the later part of the day.

Decisions

The Corps was familiar with breaching operations, so the D-Q Line attack was straightforward. Critically, what was it to do when the barrage ended? At that point, it was 4,400 metres from the second objective. There were three possible actions: continue without pause; wait to fire another barrage; or pass through reserves and attack with attached FA brigades. The Germans did not pause but fought on. The German offensive manual was adamant: 'Leading infantry should avoid all halts which are not absolutely necessary.'[27] This was not in the Canadian doctrine, and the Corps had not practised this approach, so this was not a viable option.

The second alternative was to pause and bring up the field artillery for another barrage. This had the advantage of providing the infantry with powerful support to advance another 2,500 metres and would likely be successful. It had, however, three serious drawbacks. First, it would delay the advance by four to six hours.[28] It would entail moving 1,400 wagons, limbers, and pieces, with some having to cross two rivers, with only a handful of overloaded crossing points. A likely delay of six hours would mean the infantry would not reach the canal until 6:00 p.m. at the earliest, without time to reach the final objectives in daylight. Second, there were considerable risks associated in moving the pieces, their accuracy, and determining the starting line. Finally, if the assumption that the fiercest battle would be for the D-Q Line were correct, the Corps' infantry would be idle for six hours. Given the underlying assumptions of how the enemy would defend, rejecting this approach was an obvious decision.

23 Kraehe, *Füs. Reg. 34*, pp.434-435.
24 Szczepanski, *Geschicte FüR No. 73*, pp.155-156; Begau, *IR 28 in Weltkrieg*, pp.237-238.
25 Pafferath, *Geschichte I.R. 68*, pp.734-738.
26 Gottberg, *Grenadier-Regiment Nr. 2*, pp.456-457.
27 CWM: Experience of Recent Fighting; LAC: RG24 v22001, 34: The Attack in Position Warfare, 1 January 1918.
28 LAC: 5th CFA WD, 2 September 1918.

The final course of action, and the one selected, was to leapfrog the assault troops with reserves and continue. The gunners would support via batteries attached to brigades and guns to battalions. They would not fire another barrage but would directly shell point targets. This approach had the advantage of only a 30-minute delay before the advance resumed and no risks of a hastily arranged barrage. This option was the best choice as long as the assumptions of how the Germans were to defend the D-Q Line held true.

Planning Process

The opening discussion of the D-Q Line operation was a conference at the Corps headquarters with on 28 August. Attending were Horne, Haig, Webber, Currie, and the commander of the Cavalry Corps, Lieutenant General Sir Charles Kavanagh.[29] Currie intended to attack with three divisions in two days' time when the artillery finished the wire-cutting. He assumed the Corps would reach the jump-off line that day. The only contentious point was he planned to use the 3rd Cavalry Division as an exploitation force. Kavanagh, however, wanted to employ his full corps of two divisions. Neither Horne nor Currie wanted to use this balky force, despite Haig's desire to see it engaged. The reason was the cavalry would have to use the Arras-Cambrai road because of the cut-up terrain, but it was the Corps' main supply route.[30] Marching an entire cavalry corps consisting of two cavalry divisions, two CMMG brigades, a motorised infantry brigade and supply columns would gridlock the route for most of a day. Just one cavalry division took up 18.5 kilometres of road space and would require almost 4 hours to pass a point – assuming no disruptions.[31] Demonstrating his value as an army commander, Horne challenged the use of the cavalry. He suggested using a single division initially, with the rest of the cavalry echeloned back. Haig, unconvinced, instructed Kavanagh to recommend a solution.[32]

The Corps could now start the detailed planning involving the divisions, arms and services.[33] Likely on 28 August, in preparation for this meeting, the Corps' staff created the first draft of the attack plan – typed with pencilled changes. The plan sketched out the scheme's broad outline that was recognisably the final instructions. It had four objectives. The first, the Red Line, was about 3,000 metres from the expected jump-off line. This lay mainly on the reverse slope of the ridge running from Étaing to the Corps' southern boundary. After a 30-minute pause, a further advance of 6,000 metres would bring the Corps to high ground commanding the Canal du Nord – the Green Line. The third objective was high ground on the east side of it – the Blue Line. It would entail crossing the canal, penetrating the Marquion Line and advancing 3,000 to 3,500 metres. The final objective – Brown Line – involved a further push of 3,200 metres to Bourlon Wood overlooking Cambrai.[34]

29 Also attending were the GOC, 3rd Tank Brigade and GOC, 1st Brigade RAF. TNA: First Army GS WD, Notes of Conference at Canadian Corps Headquarter, 28 August 1918.

30 See for instance, LAC: GOCRA WD, Report of the Action of Close Support Brigades of 5th Canadian Divisional Artillery During Operations Commencing Aug. 26 1918.

31 War Office General Staff, *Field Service Pocket Book, 1914* (London: His Majesty's Stationary Office, 1914), pp.37-42.

32 TNA: First Army GS WD, Notes of Conference at Canadian Corps Headquarter, 28 August 1918.

33 LAC: GOCRA WD, 28 August 1918.

34 LAC: RG9 III-C-1 v3911, 39/8: Draft Outline of Plan of Attack, Undated [28? August 1918].

Canadian engineers building a bridge over the Canal du Nord later in September. (Canada. Dept. of National Defence/Library and Archives Canada/PA-003456)

With this scheme in place, the other branches could start planning. The engineers had a myriad of tasks, including how to bridge the canal, investigating dugouts, and providing water for masses of troops and animals.[35] The sappers had to throw multiple bridges across the canal suitable for infantry, horse-drawn transport, and heavy lorries.[36] Members of the former tunnelling companies would probe dugouts for booby traps and tunnels. Daily, the engineers had to deliver 1.5 million litres of water for 20,000 animals and almost a million for the Corps' 95,793 men.[37] The logistics staffs had to supply massive quantities of matériel. For instance, the 450 rounds per 18-pounder required 1,500 standard GS wagon loads for the 360 pieces.[38] These had to move on a road system close to collapse.

35 LAC: RG9 III-D-3 v4990: 1st Brigade Canadian Engineeers War Diary, 31 August, 1 September 1918.
36 LAC: GOCRE WD, Engineer Instructions No. 5, 1 September 1918.
37 LAC: Rations Issued at Refilling Points, 25 August and 1 September 1918; TNA: First Army AQ WD, Supply Situation, September 1918.
38 LAC: Canadian Corps AAQMG WD, 29 August 1918; LAC: Ammo Loads by Vehicle.

While this detailed planning by the various branches continued, Currie had further daily conferences with Horne, Kavanagh, and their staffs. Continued problems with wire-cutting and gaining the jump-off line forced further postponements eventually to 2 September.[39] The one major remaining issue was the exploitation force, as Kavanagh's solution did not find favour.[40] Instead, Currie proposed, likely at the 30 August conference, to use Brutinel's CIF. It comprised cavalry, cyclists, both CMMG brigades, artillery, mortars, armoured cars, a logistics train, and a wireless section. It had great defensive firepower, with 80 machine guns, 4 truck-mounted medium trench mortars, and six 18-pounder guns and was, in theory, highly mobile. In mid-May, Currie had the CLH, 1st CMMG, and the cyclists conduct a joint training scheme as an exploitation force.[41] There was not enough follow up to develop a common doctrine and understanding of the formation's limitations and possibilities. At Amiens, however, Brutinel's unit performed creditably, so there was a precedent for use.[42]

The CIF served a vital explicit and implicit purpose.[43] Once the Corps broke the defences of the D-Q line, the CIF would charge down the Arras-Cambrai road and bounce the canal – the explicit reason. Brutinel expected it would face only scattered defences, and the unit's machine guns could defend the bridgehead until relieved.[44] The implicit reason was to deflect Haig and his desperation to see his cumbersome Cavalry Corps employed. With the CIF, Currie could claim he had an exploitation force that freed the cavalry to carry out even deeper penetration missions.

Matheson's notice on 31 August threw Currie's careful planning into disarray. He had four unfavourable options. He could demand Matheson continue as planned, but Currie would need a compelling reason and there were no such grounds. Replacing Matheson's division was not realistic as there were no ready, fresh divisions.[45] Also, it would mean a further delay, which was unacceptable. The Canadian Corps had to strike on 2 September. He could reduce the attack by one brigade front. The Corps had to be in contact with the Third Army, so the only alternative was on the left flank. A narrower breakthrough risked the enemy strangling the advance with flanking fire, and the left flank already worried Horne.[46] The only realistic choice was to commit the 4th Canadian Division's 10th Canadian Brigade at the cost of blunting the thrust to the Green and Blue lines.

Meanwhile, the War Cabinet believing the Allies could not win the war that year wanted to conserve forces.[47] At the prime minister's direction, the Chief of the Imperial General Staff

39 TNA: First Army GS WD, First Army, G110, 29 August 1918.
40 TNA: First Army GS WD, Notes of Conference at Canadian Corps Headquarter, 29 August 1918; TNA: First Army GS WD, Notes of Conference at Canadian Corps Headquarter, 30 August 1918.
41 LAC: RG9 III-D-3 v4955: Canadian Light Horse War Diary, 15 May 1918.
42 Nicholson, *CEF*, pp.397-398, 405, 413.
43 See for instance, Brennan, 'Major-General David Watson': p.131.
44 LAC: RG9 III-C-1 v3943, 55/3: Canadian Independent Force Plan, Undated [31 August 1918].
45 TNA: First Army GS WD, Notes of Conference at Canadian Corps Headquarter, 30 August 1918; TNA: First Army GS WD, 1 September 1918.
46 TNA: First Army GS WD, Notes of Conference at Canadian Corps Headquarter, 29 August 1918.
47 Keith Jeffery, *Field Marshal Sir Henry Wilson: A Political Soldier* (Oxford, England: Oxford University Press, 2006), p.225; Brock Millman, *Pessimism and British War Policy, 1916-1918* (London: F. Cass, 2001), pp.262-266.

privately warned Haig on 31 August against any operation that would incur serious casualties.[48] Contrary to the cabinet, Haig thought it was possible to win in 1918. He, however, needed Horne's assurance of success, so he sent his chief of staff, Lieutenant General Sir Henry Lawrence. Lawrence told the First Army commander that, 'he was only to attack if he and his troops were satisfied that they could carry the enemy's position tomorrow.'[49] Initially 'none too optimistic about the attack,' Horne changed his opinion after visiting Currie and the division commanders and reported to Haig he was sure of success.[50] Currie asked for a reduction in the Corps' frontage, but Haig refused. The Corps had to attack on its entire front, and the British divisions on the Corps' right were too weak to take over any ground. He promised to decrease the Corps' front after the attack.[51] That Currie did not press harder was a mistake.

It was critical that the XVII Corps on the right captured the high ground south of the army boundary. The poor relationship with flanking units continued, as the British proved uncooperative. On 30 August, Horne requested Byng's support.[52] The Third Army would only do so if it had tank support, but GHQ was unwilling to provide any.[53] Byng informed Horne that without them the XVII Corps would not cooperate, but it would look for an opportunity to slip around the flank.[54] Currie, understandably concerned, met Fergusson on 31 August, who bluntly told him he would not move until the Canadians had captured the D-Q Line.[55] Fergusson agreed to position a 57th Division brigade on the right flank behind the attackers. If the Canadians took the line, it would follow the advance and swing south to capture the high ground but would not start until 0+90 minutes.[56]

While all the echelons were planning, Task 4, the cutting of the barbed wire before the D-Q Line, continued. The 15th Battalion's regimental history characterised the wire's impact as 'That vast sea of rusted malignancy loomed fiercely in all minds.'[57] The wire-cutting took longer than expected despite the heavy guns spending all day cutting wire.[58] Multiple factors contributed to the delays. Most of the field artillery was too distant until close to the assault date.[59] The gunners had to rely on RAF observation for accurate shooting, but poor weather grounded many flights. With pieces close to their maximum range, their predicted fire was less accurate. There were changes to the program with 4 of 12 lanes abandoned and new ones added. Vital 6-inch howitzers supported the jump-off line attacks which diverted them from blasting lanes.

48 Lloyd George denied doing so in his unreliable memoirs. Woodward, *Lloyd George and the Generals*, p.331; TNA: WO 158-25: Wilson to Haig, 85 HW, 31 August 1918.
49 NLS: Haig Diary, 31 August 1918.
50 LAC: Breaking the Quéant-Drocourt Line, p.124; TNA: First Army GS WD 178-3, 31 August 1918; LAC: Currie Diary, 1 September; LAC: Watson Diary, 1 September 1918; NLS: Haig Diary, 1 September 1918.
51 McGill: MG4027 C1, 13: Urquhart Fonds, General Lawrence Comments, 1934.
52 TNA: First Army GS WD, First Army, G134, 30 August 1918.
53 TNA: GHQ GS WD, GS Note, 31 August 1918.
54 TNA: First Army GS WD, MSG GSO 1, 31 August 1918.
55 LAC: Currie to Borden, 26 November 1918; LAC: Currie Diary, 31 August 1918.
56 TNA: 57th Division GS WD, Amendment to XVII Corps Order No.155, 1 September 1918; TNA: 57th Division GS WD, Instructions for the Employment of 63rd (Naval) Division, 1 September 1918; LAC: RG9 III-D-2 v4799, 111: CWNS XVII Corps 1st to 30th September.
57 Beattie, *48th Highlanders*, p.345.
58 LAC: RG9 III-D-3 v4966: 3rd CFA War Diary, 1 September 1918.
59 LAC: 1st CDA W.D., 30 August 1918.

In the end, the artillery created sufficient breaks but, especially north of the Arras-Cambrai road, the infantry often had to cut their own lanes.[60]

Corps' Plans

The plan's basic concept was to break through the D-Q Line astride the Arras-Cambrai road. Its flanking divisions would station their reserves on the inside flanks and use them to roll up the enemy line. According to the clipped language of the plan they would advance 'with view to pushing through gap and then swinging outwards.'[61] Most of the expected 54 tanks in seven companies would concentrate at the point of rupture. They would assist the rolling up action by pushing along the D-Q Line. The attack to the second and subsequent objectives would not receive tank support except along the Buissy Switch. The two flanking divisions (1st Canadian and 4th British Divisions) would each attack on a two-brigade front with the centre division (4th Canadian Division) employing one brigade. Zero Hour was 5:00 a.m. The initial plan did not provide details on how the Corps was to capture the next objectives. There were two significant modifications to the final version issued on 31 August.[62] First was the 4th Canadian Division taking over a brigade front. Second was a revision to the Red Line to shift to the west of Cagnicourt, likely at the request of Macdonell.[63] For more, see Map 10.2 Canadian Corps' Plan for 2 September in the colour map booklet.

Morrison had 20 FA and 11 HA brigades. While a powerful artillery force, it was not overpowering given the defences, the attack frontage, and low operational rates. The Corps would employ 672 pieces, but only 559 were in action. With a front of 8,500 metres, the overall density of the barrage based on the number of operational 18-pounders was a meagre 27.5 metres per gun.[64] Guns breaking down from the continuous fighting and German counter-battery fire gravely affected the operational rate. The 26th Canadian Ordnance Workshop reported as early as 21 August that the 'Rapid rate of fire is causing these guns to wear out very quickly.'[65] The 82nd Canadian Workshop (Light) in September repaired the equivalent of three FA brigades of 18-pounders, two of 4.5-inch howitzers, and two batteries of 60-pounders.[66]

Morrison assigned eight FA brigades (192 pieces) to the 4th Canadian Division, seven to the 1st Division (168) pieces, and five (120 pieces) to the 4th British Division. This meant each division differed in the density of its barrage with the 4th Canadian and 4th British having the greatest because of their missions. Each division also received an HA brigade to bombard defensive positions, villages, and expected strongpoints. The CBSO would command seven HA

60 LAC: RG9 III-C-1 v3911, 39/8: Wire Cutting on Queant-Drocourt Line 30th August to 1 Septr Inclusive. See for instance, LAC: 10th Brigade WD, Report Operation of 47th Canadian Battalion From 1 September to 4th September, 1918 Inclusive, 6 September 1918.

61 LAC: Draft Outline of Plan, Undated.

62 TNA: Cdn. Corps GS WD, Canadian Corps OO No. 234, 31 August 1918.

63 LAC: RG9 III-C-1 v3855, 75/3: Canadian Corps G.908, 1 September 1918.

64 LAC: Artillery Statistics by Date.

65 LAC: RG9 III-D-3 v5046: 26th Canadian Ordnance Workshop War Diary, 21 August 1918.

66 LAC: RG9 III-D-3 v5046: 82nd Canadian Workshop (Light) War Diary, September 1918 Summary.

brigades with one assigned directly under the CCHA.[67] Two army HA brigades with long-range pieces would shell distant rail centres and important German transportation nodes.[68]

The heavy artillery support was markedly weaker than on 26 August, with fewer batteries at a lower operational rate. By establishment, there were 48 fewer pieces but 73 fewer fired. The combination of eight days of intense operations and the difficulties in getting the heavier pieces forward meant a lower firepower concentration. The CCHA ordered the heavy and super heavy pieces to remain in position as they clogged the roads.[69] As the post-battle artillery analysis noted, heavy howitzers' movement placed a serious strain on road management and tied-up trucks better used to supply forward pieces.[70]

The counter-battery office had a serious challenge with multiple factors reducing its effectiveness. McNaughton had 30 percent fewer heavy artillery pieces of all categories and

Brigadier General Andrew McNaughton was responsible for the Corps' counter-battery efforts. The German artillery pull-back, repositioning of enemy batteries, poor weather, and reduced means for identification meant the Corps' counter-battery was not as effective as on the first day of Amiens. (Canada. Dept. of National Defence/ Library and Archives Canada/ PA-034150)

67 LAC: RG9 III-C-3 v4245, 7/3: GOCRA Artillery Instructions No. 3, 1 September 1918.
68 LAC: RG9 III-C-1 v3943, 55/3: First Army Artillery Instructions No.39, 1 September 1918.
69 LAC: CCHA WD, Amendment to No.1 to CCHA Order No. 136, 1 September 1918.
70 LAC: Artillery Notes on Operations - August 26th to Sept. 4th 1918.

60 percent fewer of the vital 8-inch and 6-inch howitzers than on 26 August.[71] These were the pieces needed to reach the German artillery moved to the rear. Moreover, the counter-battery office had trouble identifying the enemy positions. The Germans constantly moved their pieces complicating identification.[72] In open warfare conditions, often the only means of locating enemy batteries were with spotter aircraft.[73] With poor weather grounding many flights and a contested air space, it was difficult to locate the enemy guns. In addition, the Germans deployed more barrels. On 26 August, the attackers faced initially 12 field artillery batteries in the German divisional artillery.[74] In the afternoon, it was a further 15 batteries. On 2 September, the hostile artillery comprised 51 field artillery batteries. A further 18 joined the defence during the day. While these batteries had suffered equipment casualties, they still outnumbered those of the first day by a significant margin.

There were four significant groupings of German artillery. Two were well north of Éterpigny, another around Saudemont and Récourt west of the canal, and the fourth in the valley from Cagnicourt north to the Arras-Cambrai road.[75] The counter-battery plan called for intense neutralising fire on known hostile batteries until the field artillery barrage reached within 600 metres. Morrison revised the plan with the addition of the CIF by adding a 500 metre no-fire zone on each side of the Arras-Cambrai road.[76] The enemy battery concentrations were well away from this no-fire zone. None of the Counter-Battery Office orders mentioned any provision for a barrage to support the infantry.

XVII Corps' Plan

On the Corps' right flank, the 57th Division would position its 172nd Brigade behind the 1st Brigade. It would follow it starting at 0+30 minutes and at 0+90 wheel south. It was to do its utmost to capture the high ground south of the Corps' boundary, but the decision to move was conditional on the Canadians breaking through. Clearly, the British had doubts as to the Canadians' ability to break the D-Q Line. Although not mentioned in the orders, the 57th expected tank support. Trailing the 172nd Brigade, the 63rd (Royal Naval) Division would pass around the left of the brigade and advance south-east towards Inchy-en-Artois. The XVII Corps plan, hedged with conditional orders and unrealistic expectations of tanks, promised to disappoint the 1st Division. Given Fergusson's refusal to attack without tanks, it was the best the Corps could expect, but it would still leave the Canadians' flank unprotected.[77]

71 LAC: Artillery Statistics by Date.
72 CWM: GS Report 30 Aug-6 Sep 1918.
73 LAC: Organisation CBSO 1919.
74 Six field gun and three field howitzer batteries of the *214th ID* and two field gun batteries and one field howitzer battery of the one regiment of the *39th ID* facing the Corps.
75 CWM: GS Report 30 Aug-6 Sep 1918.
76 LAC: RG9 III-C-1 v3912, 41/1: CBO Order No. 80 and 80 (Continued), 30 August- 1 September 1918.
77 LAC: RG9 III-D-2 v4799, 111: CWNS XVII OO No. 155, 31 August 1918; TNA: 57th Division GS WD, Amendment to XVII Corps Order No.155, 1 September 1918, Addendum to XVII Corps Order No.155, 1 September 1918; TNA: 57th Division GS WD, Instructions for the employment of 63rd (Naval) Division, 1 September 1918; TNA: 57th Division GS WD, 57th Division Narrative of

1st Canadian Division's Plan

The Buissy Switch, the XVII Corps' limited assistance, and that all three of its brigades recently fought complicated the 1st Canadian Division's planning. Macdonell's solution was to attack with two brigades, each on a relatively narrow sector where the artillery had cut breaches in the wire. On the division's right, the 3rd Brigade would take the Red Line and the remaining portion of Vis-en-Artois Switch held by the Germans. It would then advance to capture Cagnicourt, Bois du Loison, Bois du Bouche, and the Buissy Switch from south of Buissy to the Corps' boundary. This entailed an advance of 6,500 metres at its farthest and with its right flank wide open until the British caught up. On the left, the 2nd Brigade had an even more daunting task. It was to capture the Red Line, the Factory complex on the Arras-Cambrai road, Villers-lès-Cagnicourt, and the Buissy Switch to Buissy. These were 6,200 metres away, almost all of which meant fighting through fortifications. The 1st Brigade would take the villages of Buissy and Baralle and garrison the Green Line objective. The scheme did not discuss the 1st Brigade crossing the Canal du Nord.

A key component of the plan was the use of tanks. The division would use two companies of the 14th Tank Battalion with 18 machines. The divisional instructions emphasised keeping tanks alive so 'Tanks will, therefore, not precede the Infantry unless the Infantry is confronted by trench systems.'[78] There was no provision for tanks to support the 57th Division. Both Loomis and Macdonell betrayed their ignorance of proper tank tactics in the 2nd Brigade's scheme. The issue was Loomis decided arbitrarily to reject the doctrinally sound approach agreed to between the tank commanders and the divisional and brigade staff. In his view, the tank company was under his command. According to doctrine, responsibility for tank planning resided at the divisional level and not the brigade. Loomis wanted the company to deploy five tanks forward and have three in reserve, so they would replace any losses. Loomis did not explain how the reserve tanks would learn they were needed and what to do. His plan betrayed his ignorance of tanks and doctrine. He tried to browbeat the tank company commander, Major Raikes, who rightly refused to accept such a poor plan. Loomis was so angry that in his diary he twice called him impossible.[79] Raikes also said, given the late hour, it was impractical to communicate the changes. Loomis ignored the point. Finding out about the clash, the 14th Tank Battalion commander, Lieutenant Colonel G A Sceales visited Macdonell at the divisional headquarters to say they could not change the plan in time. Macdonell ordered the tank commander to do as Loomis wanted. The division GOC in a later article claimed he 'soon straightened it out.'[80] Feeling Loomis's demands were 'unsound and hardly possible', Sceales ordered the reserve section to closely follow the forward machines and replace them if stopped.[81] The rule for tanks was the fewer committed, the more enemy action disabled. So, by effectively reducing

Operations August 20th to September 7th 1918; Douglas Jerrold, *The Royal Naval Division* (London: Hutchinson & Co., 1923), p.308.

78 LAC: 1st Div GS WD, Drocourt-Queant Operations Instructions No. 1, 31 August 1918.

79 BWRA: Loomis Diary, 1 September 1918.

80 A.H. Macdonell, 'The Old Red Patch at the Breaking of the Drocourt-Queant Line, the Crossing of the Canal Du Nord and the Advance on Cambrai, 30 Aug.--2nd Oct. 1918, Part 2', *Canadian Defence Quarterly* IV, no. 1 (1928), p.7.

81 TNA: 14th Tk. Bn. WD, History of the Fourteen Battalion, Tank Corps, [January 1919].

the forward tanks by almost 50 percent, Loomis guaranteed their losses would be higher than necessary. This was an example of what Balck talked about with stubborn seniors refusing to heed the greater knowledge of junior officers in technical matters.[82] Sceales would state the infantry little understood tank operations and that much study and practice was necessary to develop that understanding.[83]

The division's artillery support would comprise seven FA brigades with 114x18-pounders and 42x4.5-inch howitzers firing a rolling barrage. Two 18-pounder batteries would not take part in the barrage, with one each serving as mobile batteries for the two assault brigades. The barrage's actual density was 28.5 metres per 18-pounder which, given the vaunted strength of the D-Q Line, was thin. There was no pre-planned field artillery barrage after the Red Line.[84] There was, also, no indirect machine gun barrage. Instead, the 1st Machine Gun Battalion attached three batteries to each brigade for direct fire. With no barrage after the Red Line, it was of 'the utmost importance for the Machine Guns, from then on, to provide the principal neutralising and covering fire.'[85]

Macdonell's plan was more a skeleton than a fully developed scheme. It reflected his confidence in his brigade commanders and the lack of time to develop comprehensive instructions. The plan did not correspond to Currie's operational concept of rolling up the defences. Macdonell's division positioned its reserve brigade on the outer flank. The 2nd Brigade would roll up the Buissy Switch, but it was also to strike north to take objectives up to the divisional boundary. This was not the only curious aspect of the plan. The 1st Brigade's orders did not correspond to the Corps' objective lines. Further, the 1st Division's scheme made no mention of crossing the canal. What these plans illustrate was the evolving nature of the instructions, as the brigade commanders fleshed out the bare skeleton of the Corps' and divisional orders. This was a major departure from the comprehensive attack instructions from 1917 where the higher echelons decided all key details. From the division and brigade plans, there was little remaining of Currie's scheme.

Canadian Independent Force's Plans

The force's task was to advance down the Arras-Cambrai road at top speed to seize crossings over the Canal du Nord at Marquion. Once relieved, the force was to press towards Cambrai and the north-east. At a minimum, it was to occupy the Green Line. The plan stationed the head of the column on the Wancourt-Guémappe road just off the Arras-Cambrai route. It was to cross the Red Line at 8:00 a.m.[86] To assist the advance, Brutinel arranged a no-fire zone of 500 metres

82 Balck, *Development of Tactics--World War*, p.256; Blaber, 'A Diminishing Resource', pp.349-350; LAC: RG9 III-D-2 v4798, 103: CWNS 3rd Tank Brigade, Report on Operations with the Canadian Corps - 2nd September 1918, 18 September 1918; TNA: WO 95-103-4: 14th Tank Battalion War Diary, Report on the Operations of September 2nd, in co-operation with the 1st Canadian Division.

83 TNA: 14th Tank Bn History.

84 LAC: 1st CDA W.D., 1st Division Artillery Instructions No. 36 (3), 1 September 1918; LAC: 1st Div GS WD, 1st CDA Report of Operations 28 August to 4th September 1918.

85 LAC: RG9 III-C-4 v4031, 3/3: 1st MG Battalion DQ Operations: Instructions No. 2, 1 September 1918.

86 LAC: RG9 III-D-3 v4981: Corps Machine Gun Officer War Diary, BH Instructions No. 2, 1 September 1918; LAC: CIF Plan.

on each side of the Arras-Cambrai road to Marquion. The planners made a significant error in not taking any measures to suppress the Factory complex just south of the Arras-Cambrai road beyond the Red Line. The Germans were certain to convert it into a fortress and could easily stop the road-bound force.

Brutinel divided the CIF into three groups: Leading, No. 1, and No. 2. The Leading Group, commanded by the CO of the British 10th Royal Hussars, Lieutenant Colonel FHDC Whitmore, consisted of that cavalry regiment, half of the CLH, six heavy and two light armoured cars, an 18-pounder gun section, and 10 motorcyclists for communications.[87] No. 1 Group comprised 1st CMMG Brigade, eight of the nine platoons of the CCCB, another 18-pounder section, and four truck-mounted Newton mortars, plus motorcyclists for communications. Lieutenant Colonel W K Walker, CO of the 1st CMMG Brigade, led the No. 1 Group. Walker (30) was another interesting figure in the Canadian Corps. Born in England, 'Tiny' Walker was a tall Anglican missionary at the war's start. He commanded the Canadian Cavalry Brigade's machine gun squadron when Currie spotted him in April 1918. He was looking for a strong disciplinarian to take over the 1st CMMG Brigade after dissatisfaction with the incumbents.[88] During the March offensive, he and the 1st CMMG Brigade performed with great credit in fighting on the Fifth Army front. No. 2 Group never got into action on 2 September.

4th Canadian Division's Plan

The centrepiece of Currie's initial plan was the 4th Canadian Division's punching through the D-Q Line. Supported by a powerful group of 32 tanks, Watson's division would make the decisive breakthrough.[89] Watson and his GSO 1, Lieutenant Colonel E Panet, met Currie on 29 August for a briefing. As Watson's biographer, explained, 'Having embraced risky attacks in the past, Watson was nonetheless taken aback when he and Panet were briefed.'[90] Watson confided in his diary: 'It is a very ambitious programme & I doubt if it can be carried through to the extent they have laid down.'[91] Either he did not express his concerns to Currie, or he did not press them. Nor did he raise any concerns when Horne visited him on 1 September.[92]

Matheson's announcement meant a massive recasting of plans. On 1 September, Watson's division, with its front now extended to 2,500 metres, had to issue new attack orders. The 10th and 12th Brigades would take the Red Line using their existing front-line battalions. The 11th trailing behind the 12th would leapfrog it at 0+3 hours and advance east to take the Green and Blue Lines. One battalion each of the 10th and 12th Brigades would fill-in alongside it and push to the canal. This committed all the division's battalions and left no fresh reserves in the case of a setback.

87 The other half of the CLH was providing traffic control and despatch riders to the Corps. Stephanie Elizabeth Potter, '"Smile and Carry On:" Canadian Cavalry on the Western Front, 1914-1918' (PhD, University of Western Ontario, 2013), p.313.

88 Cameron Pulsifer, 'Death at Licourt: An Historical and Visual Record of Five Fatalities in the 1st Canadian Motor Machine Gun Brigade, 25 March 1918', *Canadian Military History* 11, no. 3 (2002), p.52.

89 LAC: 4th Canadian Div WD, Scarpe Instruction No.2, 31 August 1918.

90 Brennan, 'Major-General David Watson': p.131.

91 LAC: Watson Diary, 29 August 1918.

92 LAC: Watson Diary, 1 September 1918.

The tank concentration was one every 90 metres that exceeded GHQ's recommended density of 100 to 200 metres.[93] Artillery support consisted of eight FA brigades and one HA brigade. At 17.4 metres per gun with 144x18-pounder guns, the field artillery barrage was dense. When it ended at the Red Line, the 4th and 5th CDA would remain under divisional command and supply one brigade each to the 10th and 11th Brigades.[94] For machine gun support, the plan assigned one company less a battery to each brigade with the three detached batteries providing an indirect machine gun barrage.[95]

The spearhead of the overall offensive, the 12th Brigade, would assault on a 1,500-metre front with right to left 72nd, 38th, and 85th Battalions and 22 tanks from the 9th Tank Battalion.[96] 'Owing to the extreme importance of the task as shown above it was decided to use three Bns. in the first phase of the attack,' according to MacBrien's report.[97] The 12th Brigade was responsible for a major portion of the Blue Line, which meant its battalions had multiple assignments. It would advance over seven kilometres and have its frontage more than doubled when it reached the canal. The scheme had four phases. Three assault battalions would take the Red Line. At 8:00 a.m., the 78th Battalion would leapfrog and would advance to a spur of high ground 2,600 metres south-east of the Red Line. The 38th and 72nd Battalions would then pass through it, take the Green Line, and seize bridgeheads. Finally, the 85th Battalion would advance to the Blue Line.[98]

The plan was complex and depended on reusing all but one battalion to reach the objectives. It was only workable if the main fight was for the D-Q Line and the rest a pursuit. Second, the CIF would have to clear out most of the defenders along the Arras-Cambrai road. MacBrien, however, had little choice in having to rely on already committed units given the distant objectives he received.

Hayter and his staff had barely 24 hours to recast their plan, rearm the troops, move them into place, and prepare for a major offensive, all while fighting for the jump-off line. The 47th and 50th Battalions would break the Éterpigny and the D-Q Line on the brigade's 1,000 metre front with the support of 10 tanks. Then, the 46th Battalion would leapfrog through and take the D-Q Support Line, the village of Dury, and the Red Line. Nine tanks from the 11th Tank Battalion supported this phase. At 0+3 Hours, the 44th Battalion would advance on the Green and Blue Lines. In the rush, both the 4th Canadian and 4th British Divisions issued orders to capture Palluel on the Canal du Nord.[99] Beyond the problem of the conflicting boundaries, the brigade had only a single battalion advancing beyond the Red Line, instead of the entire brigade with obvious consequences in the battle.

93 LAC: RG24 v22020: SS 204 Infantry and Tank Cooperation and Training, March 1918.
94 LAC: 4th Canadian Div WD, OO No.107, 1 September 1918; LAC: 4th Canadian Div WD, Scarpe Instruction No. 3, 1 September 1918.
95 LAC: RG9 III-D-3 v4986: 4th Machine Gun Battalion War Diary, OO No. 55, 31 August 1918; LAC: 4th MG Bn WD, 4th Battalion Report on Operations 1, to 5th. September 1918.
96 LAC: 12th Brigade War Diary, Scarpe Instructions No.1, 31 August 1918.
97 LAC: 12th Brigade War Diary, Scarpe Operation, Capture of Drocourt Queant Line, 2 September 1918.
98 LAC: 12th Brigade War Diary, Scarpe OO No.157, 1 September 1918; LAC: 12th Brigade War Diary, Addenda No 1 to Scarpe OO No. 157, 1 September 1918.
99 LAC: 10th Brigade WD, OO 152, 31 August 1918; LAC: 10th Brigade WD, OO No 107, 1 September 1918; LAC: 10th Brigade WD, OO No 153, 1 September 1918.

Brigadier General Victor Odlum was an aggressive and energetic officer with determined views on how to fight battles. (Canada. Dept. of National Defence/Library and Archives Canada/PA-002117)

Brigadier General Victor Odlum, GOC 11th Brigade, and his staff had an intense two days of planning. They issued five sets of instructions and an amendment between 31 August and 1 September. Adding to the difficulty, the brigade-major was ill with dysentery and an inexperienced officer replaced him.[100] There were errors as a result. For instance, the instructions and accompanying map differed in the dispositions of the 54th and 102nd Battalions.[101] The brigade would move forward at 0+1 hour and assemble on a north/south line running through the Mt Dury ridge. This was another poor decision, as it meant the battalions would mass for their attack exposed to any Germans on the reverse slope of the ridge. At 0+3 hours, it would advance on a front of three battalions from right to left 54th, 75th, and 87th Battalions. In reserve was the 102nd Battalion. These three would take the Green Line, 6,000 metres away. Once captured, the 54th on the right and the 102nd on the left would storm across the canal and take the Blue Line. This was another advance of 3,500 metres.

The 54th's deployment was another puzzling decision. It would initially advance on a narrow 200 metre front for two kilometres. At that point, its front would expand to 600 metres. Apparently, the planners tried to shoe-horn in the battalion without disrupting the existing

100 LAC: RG9 III-D-3 v4903: 11th Brigade War Diary, 1 September 1918.

101 LAC: 11th Brigade WD, Scarpe Instructions 1-4 31 August 1918; LAC: 11th Brigade WD, "11 Scarpe" Instructions No. 5, 1 September 1918; LAC: 11th Brigade WD, OO No 150, 1 September 1918.

plans for the other two battalions. The 54th's operational order, however, had it in reserve until the Green Line fell.[102]

Two factors shaped the 11th Brigade's battle. First, its battalions were to be ready to intervene when the Red Line fell. They were, however, to wait for Odlum's order to advance. He reinforced this proviso in an early morning meeting on 2 September.[103] He left an opening that in 'special circumstances' they could advance without his approval.[104] The second issue was the 75th Battalion's Harbottle was on thin ice with Watson and Odlum. Just prior to Amiens, Watson chewed him out over the way he ran the battalion and his CO responsibilities.[105] Watson's confidential report critiqued his inability to delegate, his officer evaluations, and penchant for raising minor objections.[106] This was unusual, as Watson's 1919 confidential reports were almost always entirely positive. While the battalion had done well at Amiens, the Harbottle was likely still eager to improve his position with his superiors.

4th British Division's Plans

The British would take the Red Line with a two-battalion attack by the fresh 12th British Brigade but would avoid Étaing.[107] A heavy artillery barrage, smoke, and a 48-machine gun barrage would smother the village to prevent any interference. The 11th British Brigade reinforced by the 1st Seaforths would leapfrog at 0+3 hours and push on with three battalions. It was to take the high ground overlooking the Canal du Nord as the second objective – the Green Line. It would then continue on to take the Blue Line, including Lécluse and Palluel on the canal. The 12th British Brigade would advance on Étaing with any surviving tanks later in the day. Eight tanks would support the 12th, but they were not to pass beyond the D-Q Support Line. They had to assemble 1,000 metres south of Éterpigny in the 4th Canadian Division's sector. This awkward arrangement was necessary because of the marshy terrain in the area. They would have to hurry to catch up to the advancing infantry.[108]

Five FA brigades (120 pieces) supported the initial attack phase, but ironically none were its own gunners. Their position meant they were part of the right group assigned to support the Canadians. After the barrage, the 4th Division Artillery (DA) would control six FA brigades. The gun density was a powerful 16.7 metres per gun, which was much greater than the rest of the Corps' front – likely because of the fortifications and weak state of its infantry. Unlike the two Canadian divisions, the British did not assign any field artillery to the assault infantry. Possibly, it was their lack of training in open warfare artillery tactics.[109]

102 LAC: 54th Battalion WD, Map A Secret 175/4.
103 LAC: RG9 III-D-3 v4905: 11th Brigade War Diary, 54th Battalion Narrative of Operations Carried Out on the 2nd and 3rd of September 1918, 11 September 1918.
104 LAC: 11th Bde WD, 54th Battalion Narrative of Operations Carried Out on the 2nd and 3rd of September 1918, 11 September 1918.
105 LAC: Watson Diary, 5 August 1918.
106 LAC: 4th Div Confidential Reports.
107 TNA: WO 95-1497-1: 1st Rifle Brigade War Diary, Operation Order No 76, 30 August 1918.
108 TNA: 4th British Div GS WD, Instructions for Offensive Instruction No. 1, 31 August 1918; TNA: 4th British Div GS WD, Instructions for the Offence No. 1 [revised], 1 September 1918.
109 TNA: 4th British Divisional Artillery War Diary, 4th Divisional Artillery Order No. 127, 31 August 1918; TNA: 4th British Divisional Artillery War Diary, 4th Divisional Artillery Order No. 128, 1

The 12th British Brigade had a front of 750 metres with an advance of 2,700 metres to the Red Line. Its challenge was to punch through the two sets of trenches of the Éterpigny Line, two more of the D-Q Line, and one more for the D-Q Support Line. The planners counted on the barrage density, the eight tanks, and the feeble defenders for a successful operation.[110] The 11th British Brigade would leapfrog it at 0+3 hours with its 1st right, 1st Hampshire centre, and the 1st Somerset Light Infantry (SLI) left. It had a 1,500-metre front, with a maximum advance to Palluel of 7,400 metres.[111] The Germans would have their backs to the wall if the D-Q Support Line fell, as their line of communications were to the north across a handful of bridges. There was a genuine possibility of trapping large numbers of Germans and their guns. Thus, the artillery plan included provisions for supplying gunners to man trapped German pieces.[112]

The Corps' reserve was the 1st British Division, but it was under First Army control until 6:00 p.m. on 1 September. It was to advance along the Arras-Cambrai road to the Green Line without waiting for orders. Then, depending on the situation, the Corps would direct it to cross the canal and advance to the Brown Line.[113] This plan gave the British division the flexibility to move forward without delays, but it did not account for any misfires in the offensive. The result was the 1st British Division, through no fault of its own, ended up tangling up with the rear of the 4th Canadian.

Analysis

Currie's plan was bold, rigid, risky, demanding, and the product of grave over-confidence. The triumphs of the Corps at Amiens and Arras so far had reinforced the Canadian conceit of their superiority. The D-Q Line situation superficially resembled that of the first day of Amiens. There, once the Corps smashed through the defensive crust, the battle was a series of meeting engagements where Canadian training and firepower vanquished the scattered, battered, and demoralised defenders. The D-Q Line was much stronger than the defences at Amiens and the defenders prepared.

It was rash, as the force margin did not favour the attackers. The density of artillery support was less than half of what the Corps employed at Passchendaele for defences that were by reputation as strong as any on the Western Front. The concentration of infantry was also inadequate given the width and the depth of the expected advance. With 15 of the 31 battalions committed to the battle having already fought in the preceding four days, the infantry was not at full strength or effectiveness. Only in tanks was the Corps adequately provided. Currie had asked to reduce his frontage, but Haig rejected this request.

September 1918; TNA: 4th British Divisional Artillery War Diary, Narrative of Operations of 4th Divisional Artillery From 26th August to 4th September, 1918.

110 TNA: 11th Br Bde WD, Operation Order No. 70, 1 September 1918.

111 TNA: 11th Br Bde WD, Operation Order No. 70, 1 September 1918.

112 TNA: 4th British Divisional Artillery War Diary, 4th Divisional Artillery Order No. 128, 1 September 1918.

113 TNA: 1st British Division WD, Canadian Corps OO No. 234, 31 August 1918; TNA: 1st British Division WD, 1 September 1918.

The plan was rigid and made little allowance for unexpected results. Currie, his staff, and his senior commanders expected the Germans to fight hard but were certain in the Canadian's superiority. This certainty veered into over-confidence that resulted in an overly ambitious scheme. The rate of the advance after breaking the D-Q Line based on the heavy artillery plan had to assume a virtual absence of resistance. The artillery plan indicated the infantry would take two hours to advance from the Red to the Green Line, yet on 3 September they took three to four hours to cover the same ground against no direct resistance.[114]

For all the plan's flaws, it is difficult to envision any plan that could have achieved Haig's goals. He assigned the Corps a task that was too great for it. If the Corps had paused to fire another barrage, it was almost a certainty that the attack would have succeeded at a fraction of the cost of 2 September. The problem was that this program would not have resulted in the Canadians crossing the canal before darkness. Pausing for a second barrage was to admit that the Corps could not carry out Haig's mission.

Ultimately, Haig was responsible for two major errors and Currie for one. First, Haig did not provide sufficient forces. He should have paid more attention to reinforcing the assault than trying to press the ineffective Cavalry Corps on the Canadians. The density of assault infantry and artillery support was far below standard doctrine. Second, Haig's mission required the Corps to smash a powerful defensive zone, cross a canal, and advance 15 kilometres – a distance greater than on 8 August. Only a German collapse would make this possible. The *II Bavarian Korps* was staggering, but it was far from foundering. There were no indications that Currie evinced any doubts as to the possibility of large-scale success, especially considering Haig directed Horne to solicit such from his subordinates. That Horne went from being doubtful to being confident suggests no one in the Corps raised concerns with him. Currie's error was to carry out an operation with a significant degree of risk to meet its goals. The plan was rash and required the Germans to fight the battle the way the Canadians expected. This was usually a dangerous policy.

This chapter proves the CIF was filling an absolutely necessary role if the Corps was to achieve its objectives. Whether it was suitable for the purpose was a different matter to be discussed in the next chapter. The account has also established that at no point did the Corps or divisional planners envision a rolling barrage beyond the Red Line. The no-fire zone for the CIF was too distant from the 4th Canadian Division's battlefield to affect the battle. Thus, Brutinel's force was carrying out a necessary task and did not interfere with the artillery support for Watson's division.

The Corps had set its plans and its forces moved into position. 'It was a cold quiet morning and my teeth were dancing,' wrote Private Foster, an aid man in the 38th Battalion waiting for Zero Hour.[115] At 5:00 a.m., with a hellacious roar, 559 artillery pieces opened fire on the Germans. This was the signal for the 6,600 infantry of the 11 assault battalions to rise from their shell holes or hop the bags and advance. Behind them, thousands more moved forward. The

114 The 44th Battalion took three hours and the 2nd Brigade four hours. LAC: 10th Brigade WD, 10th CIB Narrative of Operations Battle of Arras, 14 September 1918; LAC: 2nd Brigade War Diary, 2 September 1918 and 2nd Brigade Narrative of Operations East of Arras August 25 to September 3, 1918.

115 LAC: MG30 E393 v1: Foster Fonds, Private Foster Memoirs, 25.

battle was now in their hands, along with the tank crews and support forces. How they fared is the subject of the next two chapters.

11

„Herr Leutnant, der Tommy ist hier" 1st Division and CIF, 2 September

The battle today has been a great success. I think it is one of the biggest things of the war.

Henry Horne, 2 September 1918[1]

Whilst the primary thrust of the Canadian attack was on the 4th Canadian Division's front, the 1st Division and CIF had a critical role. The 1st Division had to capture the D-Q Line and Buissy Switch to protect Watson's flank. Brutinel's force had the vital mission of capturing bridges over the Canal du Nord at Marquion. A rigid plan with multiple dependencies meant any reversal would unhinge its execution and possibly derail the offensive. Both formations had a daunting task and one that would stretch their capabilities to the limit. The 1st Division responded, while the CIF floundered. This chapter looks at the outcomes of the two formations' endeavours and how the enemy reacted.

Flanking Forces

The 57th Division would assist the Corps by using one brigade to pass through the Canadian breakthrough. It would then wheel south to advance down both branches of the D-Q Line to reach its junction with the Hindenburg Line. British and Canadian reports diverged significantly. Canadian accounts gave a quite negative view of the 172nd Brigade's performance, and its delay in taking the vital high ground. From the start, the plan broke down. For instance, the 1st Royal Munster Fusiliers (RMF) waited for tanks that were not assigned. The 15th Battalion was scathing on the Munsters 'This Regiment which seemed to be badly lost right from the jumping off, caused us an immense amount of trouble. They did everything from getting mixed up with our troops in the Drocourt-Quéant Line to bombing our Battalion Headquarters in the Crow's Nest.'[2] A Canadian staff officer working on the Canadian Official History thought the 57th Division 'attacked without a very clear idea of their job.'

1 Robbins, *The First World War Letters of General Lord Horne* p.260.
2 LAC: CWNS Millen to Rennie.

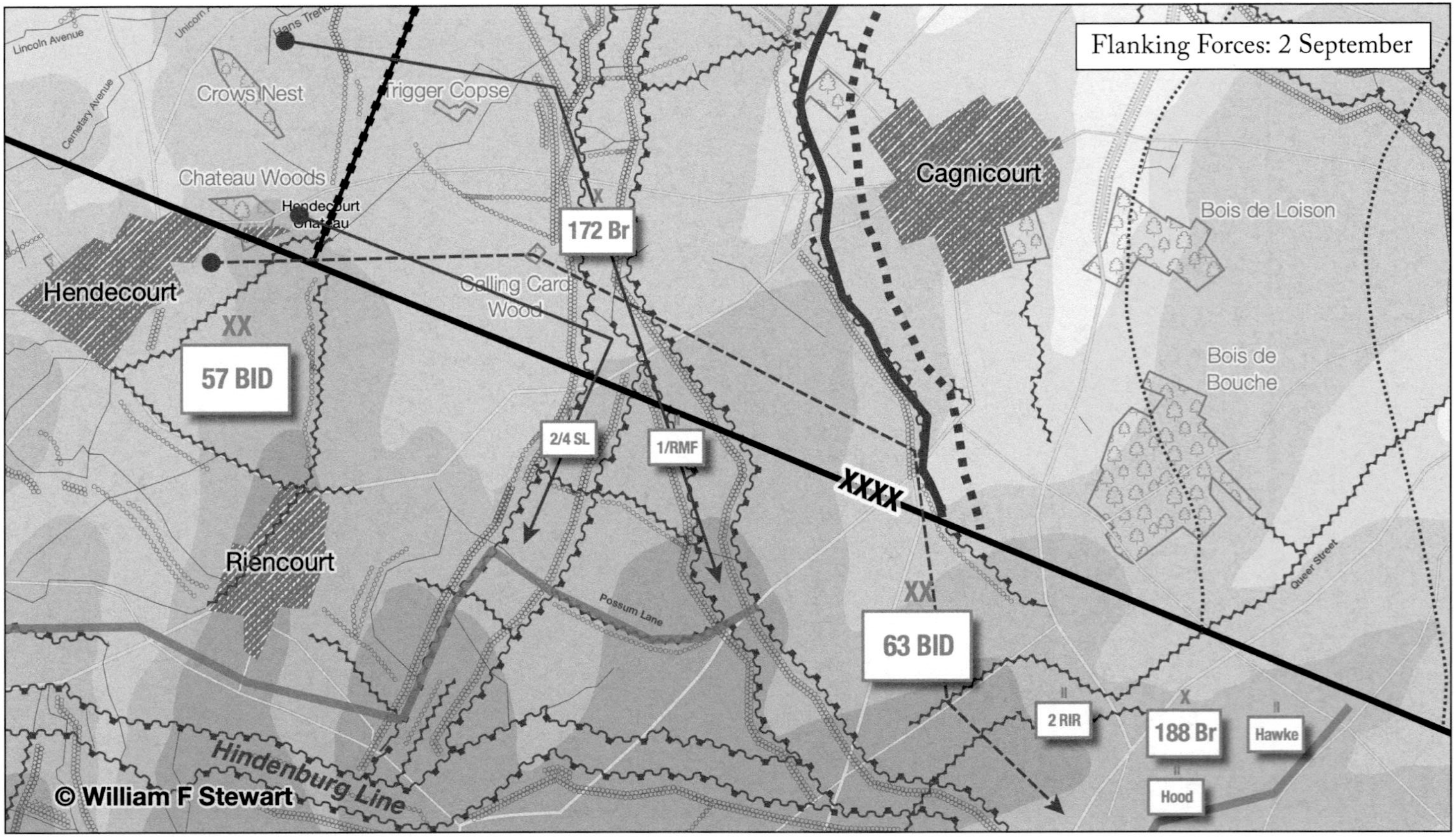

Map 33. The 172nd Brigade wheeled south and eventually took the high ground in the afternoon. The 63rd (Naval) Division followed and met up with the 1st Division along the railway embankment late in the afternoon. (Author's map)

The 2/4th South Lancashire Regiment on the right and 1st RMF on the left pushed south at 7:15 a.m. under a barrage but without tanks. Initially, they made good time as they advanced down the two sets of D-Q Line trenches. Once the barrage ended at 8:00 a.m., resistance stiffened, and the attack slowed. The 1st RMF reported taking all its objectives by 8:40 a.m. This was unlikely given the repeated claims by the Canadians of being subjected to heavy fire from the high ground the Munsters claimed to occupy.[3] More likely they reached 500 to 700 metres short of the third objective in the afternoon. Lieutenant Colonel H H Mathews, a senior 1st Division staff officer who toured the front, maintained the situation only cleared up when the 63rd (Royal Naval) Division attacked.[4] The 63rd followed the 172nd but did not cross the D-Q Line until 11:45 a.m.[5] It reached the ridge immediately south of the Red Line by 1:40 p.m., and then pushed on to the railway embankment which they reached at 5:45 p.m.[6]

In summary, the 1st Division was reliant on the XVII Corps neutralising the threat from the high ground. The British eventually did so, but only later in the afternoon. Given its lack of combat power, the XVII's only alternative was to swing through the Canadian sector. This, however, would inevitably take too long, even if everything went according to schedule. The result was a sharp check and drag on the Corps' advance until the afternoon. Macdonell and Tuxford believed the issues with the right flank were the reason the division did not reach the canal.[7] The flank was the British problem, but past experience showed it would end up being a Canadian problem – which it did. The larger issue was the insufficient forces to carry out the offensive, so there was little the two could do.

3rd Brigade

On the division's far right, the 3rd Brigade attacked with the 16th Battalion on the right and 13th on the left. The 16th entered Amiens with a veteran officer corps. All its platoon leaders were with the battalion from at least January 1918, and 30 out of 47 officers were rankers in the battalion before commissioning. It did superbly at Amiens and arrived at Arras with a strength of 32 officers and 803 other ranks. This total included 125 men transferred from the 5th and 13th Battalions.[8] The 16th's commander was the rotund but combative Lieutenant Colonel Cy Peck (47). Reputedly, 'He feared nothing that walked or talked.'[9] He took command of the battalion in November 1916, so by September 1918 Peck was an experienced and effective

3 LAC: CWNS XVII Corps.
4 LAC: Matthews Report.
5 Urquhart, *16th Battalion*, p.240.
6 LAC: 3rd Bn Report 28 August-1 September; Jerrold, *The Royal Naval Division*, pp.311-312; LAC: CWNS XVII Corps; TNA: 57th Division GS WD, 57th Division Narrative of Operations August 20th to September 7th 1918; LAC: XVII General Staff War Diary, Appendix 304 Map C.
7 LAC: 15th Battalion War Diary, Report on Operations of 2 September 1918 on Queant-Drocourt Line; LAC: 1st Divison W.D., Arras Operations Night 28/29 August to Night 4/5 September 1918.
8 Urquhart, *16th Battalion*, p.240; LAC: RG9 III-D-3 v4925: 16th Battalion War Diary, Narrative of Second Battle of Arras, 2nd September, 1918, Undated [September 1918]; LAC: RG9 III-C-3 v4082, 8/10: 16th Battalion Strength, 4-30 August 1918.
9 Greg Dickson Mark Forsythe, *From the West Coast to the Western Front: British Columbians and the Great War* (Madeira Park, BC: Harbour Publishing, 2014), pp.47-49, 96-97; 'War Hero' <https://matthewkbarrett.com/2015/10/19/the-war-hero/> (17 April 2019).

Cy Peck the rotund, but combative commander of the 16th Canadian Scottish Battalion. He is shown wearing his VC. (Canada. Dept. of National Defence/Library and Archives Canada/ PA-006713)

commander.[10] For more, see Map 11.2 The 1st Division Responds: 2 September 1918 in the colour map booklet.

The 16th Battalion, thanks to 'the valour and discipline of the troops' and the extraordinary gallantry of two men, overcame major obstacles.[11] It illustrated how battles could hinge on the actions of two outstanding personalities – each received a VC. That this level of conspicuous courage was necessary, however, suggested a planning failure. The Canadians had won earlier victories at Arras 1918 that did not require this level of bravery. With its right on the Hendecourt-Cagnicourt road, the battalion formed on a two-company front. Its regimental history reported the battlefield was: 'A perfect shambles. The place fearfully cut-up. The dead, the rifles and the equipment of both sides scattered around.'[12] According to Canadian reports, the operation caught the Germans preparing for a 6:00 a.m. counterattack.[13] Once again the enemy exposed

10 Cook, *The Madman and the Butcher*, pp.278-279.
11 LAC: 16th Battalion War Diary, Narrative of Second Battle of Arras, 2nd September, 1918, Undated [September 1918].
12 Urquhart, *16th Battalion*, p.288.
13 There are no German records available to prove or deny these claims.

their infantry to the full fury of Canadian artillery fire, and this left them demoralised. Peck observed, 'I have never seen the enemy so cowardly; prisoners surrendered in shoals.'[14]

Initially, the only significant resistance was from Trigger Copse on the left, but skilful manoeuvring outflanked it and the defenders capitulated. The Highlanders then reached the D-Q Line where the first of the 16th Battalion's VC actions occurred. Stalled in front of uncut wire, enemy machine gun fire drove the troops into shell holes. They were unsuccessful in attracting the attention of nearby tanks. Signaller Lance-Corporal W H Metcalf jumped up and used his signal flag to get a tank to notice. Despite 17 machine guns firing on him, he walked along the trench pointing out targets to destroy. The tank knocked them out and inflicted heavy losses. A brief wind dispersed the smoke, so that the *73rd FüR* regimental staff watched in horror as the tank attack wiped out its *I Battalion*'s headquarters.[15] German fire wounded Metcalf, but he survived the battle to receive his well-earned Victoria Cross. With the front cracked, the Highlanders poured into the D-Q Line and seized it.

Peck and his troops then had the daunting prospect of having to cross an 800 metre valley and charge up a slope to the D-Q Support Line. The delay in front of the first set of trenches meant it had lost the barrage. The 16th had to contend with massed machine gun fire from emboldened Germans in the support line and from a long-exposed right flank. After a brief pause, the battalion renewed the advance. It gained only 200 metres before the heavy fire in front and right forced it into shell holes. Peck recognised the only way to get the attack going was to involve three nearby tanks. Not a slender man, Peck stood up and tried to flag them down. They

Signaller Lance Corporal W H Metcalf wearing his well-earned VC. Despite the fire of multiple machine guns, he successfully attracted the attention of a tank and directed it to knock-out German positions with his signal flag. (Canada. Dept. of National Defence/Library and Archives Canada/PA-006727)

14 LAC: 16th Battalion War Diary, Narrative of Second Battle of Arras, 2nd September, 1918, Undated [September 1918].
15 Szczepanski, *Geschicte FüR No. 73*, pp.155-158.

ignored him even when he stood in front, all while being fired on. They then trundled off to their rallying point. Understandably, Peck thought the tanks gave poor service in comparison with Amiens. What he did not realise was they were not to move beyond the D-Q Line. Peck hustled back to the D-Q Line to arrange artillery support and gather up troops there. The assigned single gun or 'sniper' piece never appeared, so the artillery was of no assistance. He arranged for the attached machine gun battery to take on the German positions on his right. The fight to neutralise that threat was hard and the battery could only crew five of its eight guns after. He re-energised the troops in the line walking up and down jocularly telling them, 'She's a bear boys, by God, she's a bear.'[16]

After an hour, Peck observed the 14th Battalion on the left entering Cagnicourt and that enemy fire had slackened. The *73rd FüR* facing the 16th Battalion withdrew as the village's fall uncovered their right rear. As all good leaders do, Peck recognised the opportunity, and he struck. The 16th quickly overran the support line. After reorganising, the 16th moved up and eventually occupied the line along Queer Street facing south-east. Macdonell said Peck had 'performed prodigies of valour and leadership that materially helped the right flank.'[17] For this courageous command, Peck received a VC.[18] Given the volume of fire it received, the battalion's losses were astonishingly low at 203 for its full tour, with about 500 prisoners and 3 field guns taken. Peck believed the Germans 'outnumbered us vastly and had they made a determined stand could have hindered our advanced to a considerable degree.'[19] The failed counterattacks of the previous days had mangled the defenders and their morale.

On the brigade's left, the 13th Battalion's strength after Amiens had dropped to 34 officers and 867 men.[20] It was another experienced battalion with a strong leadership cadre. Its commander, Lieutenant Colonel G E McCuaig (33) was a stockbroker in his family's firm. He joined the battalion at the start of the war and took it over in September 1916. Clearly a capable and active officer with considerable experience, McCuaig relieved Rennie as commander of the 4th Brigade in September for the rest of the fighting.[21]

Its men had had no hot food for four days before the battle, owing to German shelling and gas bombardment. Despite this handicap, the battalion surged forward at Zero Hour on a two-company front and behind an efficient barrage. It sliced through the defending *34th FüR*, *49th RIR*, and *164th IR* meeting little resistance. Many defenders chose prudence over pluck and hid in their dugouts. It would take 1,000 prisoners, almost all in the morning action, and a complete artillery battalion (12x77mm guns). The D-Q Line fell rapidly. At this point,

16 Macdonell, 'Old Red Patch 2', p.10.
17 Macdonell, 'Old Red Patch 2', p.10.
18 LAC: CWNS, VC Winners.
19 LAC: MG30 E134: Peck Fonds, Cy Peck Diary, 2 September 1918; Mark Zuehlke, *Brave Battalion: The Remarkable Saga of the 16th Battalion (Canadian Scottish) in the First World War* (Mississauga, Ont.: J. Wiley & Sons Canada, 2008), pp.216-223; LAC: 16th Battalion War Diary, Narrative of Second Battle of Arras, 2nd September, 1918, Undated [September 1918]; Urquhart, *16th Battalion*, pp.287-300; LAC: 3rd Brigade WD, Narrative of Events- 26th August - 3rd September 1918.
20 R. C Fetherstonhaugh, *The 13th Battalion Royal Highlanders of Canada, 1914-1919*: 13th Battalion, Royal Highlanders of Canada, 1925), p.260; LAC: RG9 III-D-3 v4922: 13th Battalion War Diary, 30 August 1918.
21 The battalion war diary reports him competing in the battalion's athletic events in the 100 yard dash and another category. LAC: 13th Battalion War Diary, 5 May 1918.

a party of the 1st RMF blundered into the 13th Battalion's sector a kilometre and a half from their zone. McCuaig had to redirect them to their proper course. Meanwhile the 13th, after a brief stop to reorganise the ranks, overran its final objective, the D-Q Support Line by 7:10 a.m. At 8:00 a.m., the 14th leapfrogged to continue the offensive. The 13th followed and heavy fire from Villers-lès-Cagnicourt and Buissy Switch hit it hard while in support. Ordered to take Buissy Switch at 3:00 p.m., the 13th could not fight its way through the German standing barrage east of the woods. It remained there until 3:30 a.m. when the 1st Brigade relieved it. The Montrealers suffered 232 casualties for its entire tour, with about 170 in the battle.[22] It was a textbook attack and with a demoralised foe, the speed and violence of the assault gave them no time to recover. The 13th likely lost more troops in following up the 14th Battalion when there was no cover of a barrage.[23]

Not mentioned in the 3rd Brigade's reports was the fortuitous intervention of the 3rd Battalion. It was to trail the 3rd Brigade by 1,500 metres to ensure it did not get engaged. It was to assault through the 15th Battalion and take the high ground overlooking the canal. The unit was late leaving owing to its troops' exhaustion and had no touch with forces on its flanks or Tuxford's Brigade. Thus, it did not learn of the 16th's rebuff until 8:20 a.m. when wounded men informed it. It kept pushing forward and got tangled up in the front-line fight. Like the 16th, German machine gun fire from the south badly harassed it, and it lost officers, men, and coherence. By 9:30 a.m. it was at the Hendecourt-Cagnicourt road. When the reserve and support companies arrived, they raised its strength to just 14 officers and 250 men. The rest were casualties or stragglers. Mason, the CO, decided to continue. The battalion, with the 15th on its left flank and slightly ahead, aimed at the spur south of the Bois du Bouche. Without its attached machine gun battery or sniper gun, it had to rely on the raw courage of its troops, their training, and their immediate leadership. It reached Queer Street along the Corps' boundary at 12:15 p.m. and had to reorganise its platoons into two Lewis Gun sections because of casualties. It then reached the railway embankment by 2:00 p.m. on its second attempt. With its right flank open, the battalion's Lewis Gunners were busy taking on German batteries and bodies of troops and 'had a hot time.' It suffered the loss of 238 men and officers in its tour, but only 113 that day. Given the severity of the fighting, this was low. It played a valuable role in covering the 15th Battalion's flank. Without its unexpected aid, it was unlikely the 15th would have made the gains it did.[24]

The 15th Battalion followed the 16th. Its fighting the previous day had fatigued and depleted it. For instance, its companies had only three officers instead of the normal four or five. Girvan after returning from an early morning briefing at the brigade received a call from the brigade-major who extended the battalion's assignment to capturing the Buissy Switch. All this left little time to disseminate orders and brief the troops, so it reached its assembly position only thirty

22 This is based on a ratio derived from the number killed before 2 September from the CWGC database.
23 LAC: 13th Battalion War Diary, 13th Battalion 2 September Report, 3 September 1918; LAC: 13th Battalion War Diary, 1-2 September 1918; LAC: 13th Battalion War Diary, Statement of Guns and Howitzers Captured During Week Ending 7 September 1918; Fetherstonhaugh, *13th Battalion*, pp.266-269.
24 LAC: 3rd Bn Report 28 August-1 September; Goodspeed, *Battle Royal*, pp.249-251; LAC: CWNS Millen to Rennie; LAC: 1st Brigade Report 28 August-1 September.

minutes before Zero Hour. The hurried preparations resulted in Girvan expecting the tanks would follow when the 15th leapfrogged at the Red Line. The tanks had no such instructions.[25]

At Zero, the 15th followed the 16th Battalion by 500 metres. The German gunners fired a scattered and ineffective barrage. Girvan skilfully kept the 15th unengaged while the 16th fought its way forward. He could not do much about the galling fire from the south. Once through the 16th, the 15th advanced on the Bois du Bouche squatting on 'a high hill, dominating and ugly.'[26] To reach the wood, the 15th forged on with section and platoon rushes, while fired on from the front, right, and right rear. They had a difficult fight in the woods but punched through. On debouching, enemy fire from multiple directions assailed them, but they persevered with platoons led by lance corporals. Without artillery, tank, or machine gun support, the battalion reached the railway embankment that dominated the nearby terrain by 1:30 p.m. with the assistance of the 3rd Battalion.[27] With both flanks open, there was no possibility of a further push to the Buissy Switch, and it remained there. Girvan reported the enemy surrendered readily and the 'booty was enormous,' including six artillery pieces. It lost 13 officers and 240 men but claimed the capture of more enemy than its strength. Relentless fighting by the troops, strong leadership from junior NCOs, and determination drove the battalion for a gain of 3,200 metres. The Germans were staggering.

The 14th Battalion trailed the 13th on the brigade's left and leapfrogged it at the Red Line. Its objective was the Buissy Switch 3,500 metres away, and it would attack on a two-company front. Waiting to start the next phase, it had to pause and met an 'impressive silence. Men remarked on this and eyed the distant objectives uneasily. Silence, after storming one of the most formidable positions on the Western Front, seemed unwholesome, and the men wondered what evil the absence of noise might cloak.'[28] Worrall, the battalion CO, decided the best policy was to strike quickly before the Germans recovered from the bombardment. The 14th swept aside a last-stand of enemy cooks, pioneers, and artillerymen on its way to Cagnicourt.[29] The most effective resistance was fire from Buissy Switch and Villers-lès-Cagnicourt, as the 2nd Brigade was not up. Lieutenant McKean, the scout officer and already holding a VC, led his men around the village and herded Germans streaming from it back into Cagnicourt. It resulted in trapping a thousand enemy and a battalion headquarters in the cellars all to fall captive. The battalion also captured six 150mm howitzers east of the village.

The battalion advanced again across a small valley and up to and through the Bois du Loison by 9:00 a.m. Up to this point, the battalion had few casualties. Once it emerged from the woods, it contended with heavy fire from machine guns and directly firing artillery from its front, left, and rear left. The slow pace of the 2nd Brigade meant a difficult situation for the 14th. At one point, a German field gun battery clattered up, unlimbered, and opened fire. The crews gallantly served their pieces until the battalion's Lewis Gunners cut them down. They

25 LAC: 15th Battalion War Diary, OO No. 44, 2 September 1918.

26 Beattie, *48th Highlanders*, p.357.

27 LAC: 15th Battalion War Diary, Report on Operations of 2 September 1918 on Queant-Drocourt Line; LAC: 15th Battalion War Diary, OO No. 44 and 45, 2 September 1918; LAC: 3rd Brigade WD, Narrative of Events - 26th August - 3rd September 1918 3rd Bde; Beattie, *48th Highlanders*, pp.356-365; LAC: 3rd Bn Report 28 August-1 September; LAC: 15th Battalion War Diary, FM73, 3 September 1918 and FM35, 5 September 1918.

28 Fetherstonhaugh, *13th Battalion*, p.238.

29 Pafferath, *Geschichte I.R. 68*, pp.734-745.

also thwarted attempts to retrieve the cannon. Captain Brewer then led two companies forward due east up the slight slope to the Buissy Switch, while the other two covered the flank. Using sectional rushes, the two companies took the first trench line but could not get further. Worrall noted the 'Huns' seemed 'to be wandering around with no set purpose, and a very hazy idea as to the situation.'[30] An English-speaking German officer asked Worrall incredulously why the Canadians stopped as the Germans were on the run. The answer was, with both flanks exposed and under heavy fire, the 14th did not have the strength to keep pushing. Later in the afternoon, Brewer would fall back 500 metres as the Germans threatened to encircle his lodgement. Relief did not arrive until the evening when the 10th Battalion attacked down the Buissy Switch.

The battalion lost an estimated 13 officers and 260 men over the two days, the majority after it advanced beyond the Bois du Loison. The constant fighting was wearing away the battalion's combat edge. Since the start of the Amiens offensive, it had lost 8 company commanders, its signal officer, scout officer, the entire intelligence section, 37 other officers, 4 company sergeant-majors, and almost all the senior NCOs. It could not easily replace this loss of expertise and experience. Despite this, its performance was exemplary. Like most in the brigade, Worrall believed the failure of the flanking forces to keep up lost a major opportunity.[31]

German Southern Sector

Dellmensingen ordered the *2nd GrR* to the Baralle-Buissy area in the morning. With the loss of the D-Q Line, it received orders at 9:00 a.m. to retake the heights west of Villers-lès-Cagnicourt. Before it could attack, however, the situation had so deteriorated that its instructions changed to occupy the Buissy Switch. The German high command could not keep up with the pace of events, so outstripping its orders. The regiment occupied the defences while survivors of other units poured through. It had no contact with organised forces on either flank. Interspersed with the regiment was a 'porridge' of troops from six broken regiments of the *3rd RD*, *16th ID*, and the *111th ID*.[32] The 10th Battalion's assault, to be described later, crumpled its right flank and inflicted heavy casualties. The attack reduced one company to only 20 men, and this from the strongest regiment in the battle. As the only remaining formed and combat-ready force on the southern front, it provided the rearguard when the Germans retreated over the canal.[33]

The available German regimental histories confirm Canadian reports that the *49th RIR* was quickly and comprehensively overrun. According to the *73rd FüR* history, the barrage was stronger than previous days and the smoke obscured everything. The 13th Battalion broke through on the right of the *I/73rd FüR*. Then, the Canadians rolled it up using tanks to kill and suppress strongpoints while assault troops wiped out the defenders. The *73rd* account suggested that it stopped frontal thrusts but had no answer for outflanking actions. Peck's and later the 172nd Brigade attacks drove the *III/73rd FüR* south down the D-Q Line. It only re-joined the regiment two days later. Seeing the catastrophe developing, the regimental headquarters fell

30 LAC: 14th Battalion War Diary, Report on Operation of September 2nd, 1918, 6 September 1918.

31 LAC: Matthews Report; LAC: 14th Battalion War Diary, Report on Operation of September 2nd, 1918, 6 September 1918; LAC: 3rd Brigade WD, Royal Montreal Regiment Report on Operations of September 2nd 1918, 6 September 1918; Fetherstonhaugh, *13th Battalion*, pp.237-242.

32 Szczepanski, *Geschicte FüR No. 73*, pp.155-156.

33 Gottberg, *Grenadier-Regiment Nr. 2*, pp.456-458.

back to the Buissy Switch. It deployed its last reserve, the regimental *Sturm* company, on the ridge east of Cagnicourt. This company together with cannon firing over open sights held the 14th's initial strike but not the second. Only small fragments of the regiment under a lieutenant made it back to the Switch. Pulled out of the line and with everyone available called to refill the ranks, the regiment comprised only 12 officers and 290 men after the battle.[34]

While the D-Q Line was falling, the *29th* and *68th IR* huddled in the cellars and dugouts of Cagnicourt. At 7:00 a.m., the commander of the *29th IR* learned that the D-Q Line was under threat and ordered his regiment to garrison the support line. The bombardment was so severe, however, that it trapped them in their cellars. Stray troops, including artillerymen, cooks, and pioneers, attempted to hold back the surging 14th Battalion, but could not. Seeing the situation as hopeless, the headquarters of the *29th IR* fell back to the Buissy Switch – dodging shells as they ran. At 10:00 a.m., the Canadians engulfed the town and captured hundreds of Germans. In one case, a lookout laconically announced to his company commander that ‚Herr Leutnant, der Tommy ist Hier' (Lieutenant, Tommy is here).[35] This was effectively the end of the *68th IR*, with all its battalion staffs wiped out. Hard combat reduced it to 14 officers and 160 men the next day. A few more survivors joined it the following day and raised its strength to just 256 other ranks, this was still barely more than a company's manpower. The division's commander ordered an inquiry into the regiment's performance. The regimental commander responded with an excoriating condemnation of the senior leadership, their policies, and their effect on the regiment's efficiency.[36]

2nd Brigade

The 7th Battalion led the 2nd Brigade's attack. At Amiens, it suffered relatively few losses and was at full strength when it arrived at Arras.[37] The 7th's commander was another improbable CO, Lieutenant Colonel W F Gilson (41). Born William Forbes Gilchrist, the British regular army dismissed him as captain in 1912 for absence without leave. After this disgrace, he changed his name and settled in Vancouver. He enlisted in the 7th Battalion in 1914 as a colour sergeant and rose rapidly through the ranks to take over the battalion in early October 1916. This made him one of the most experienced COs in the Corps. He also earned the Distinguished Service Order and two bars – an impressive total. His performance resulted in the British authorities alter his British Army record to him having resigned his commission in 1912.[38]

The battalion would attack on a two-company front, with the objectives of the D-Q Support Line and a small portion of the Buissy Switch in the 2nd Brigade's sector. Owing to the 5th Battalion's ongoing battle, they advanced to contact from Opal and Orix Trenches to reach the jump-off line. With such short notice there was no opportunity to change the barrage, so

34 Szczepanski, *Geschicte FüR No. 73*, pp.155-158.
35 Pafferath, *Geschichte I.R. 68*, p.738.
36 Pafferath, *Geschichte I.R. 68*, pp.734-745.
37 LAC: RG9 III-D-3 v4917: 7th Battalion War Diary, 2 September 1918.
38 Harvey, 'An Army of Brigadiers' pp.76-77; "West India Regiment - Commissioning Corporal William F. Gilchrist," *London Gazette*, 7 December 1900; "West African Regiment - Local Rank of Captain," *London Gazette*, 3 July 1903; "Kings Own Yorkshire Light Infantry - Removed from Service," *London Gazette*, 4 October 1912; "Kings Own Yorkshire Light Infantry - Resigns His Commission," *London Gazette*, 29 April 1919.

Private WL Rayfield of the 7th Battalion, shown here as a sergeant, repeatedly rushed German strongpoints taking multiple prisoners. (Canada. Dept. of National Defence/Library and Archives Canada/ PA-006711)

the 7th would have to fight for its start line. The supporting tanks caught up to the battalion and led the way into the D-Q Line. Their presence greatly reduced opposition, and the line's two trenches fell easily with many captives. Machine gun posts defended the last objective, the support line, and the 7th deftly isolated and overwhelmed them. The left company used fire and movement tactics to capture its portion of the Buissy Switch with many prisoners by 7:30 a.m. It then had to employ its concentrated firepower to defeat close-range machine guns and cannon in the woods west of Villers-lès-Cagnicourt.[39]

Using artillery, smoke, tanks, and infantry with fire and movement tactics resulted in heavy losses to the Germans and few for the battalion. The outstanding courage of its troops, best exemplified by the actions of Private W L Rayfield who won a VC, aided the attack. Moving ahead of his company, he rushed a German trench, bayonetted two enemies, and captured 10 others. Continuing his exploits, he neutralised an enemy sniper who had caused many casualties, then rushed the sniper's trench with such intrepidity he took a further 30 captives. Finally, he left cover under heavy machine gun fire to carry in a badly wounded comrade.[40] The battalion received credit for capturing 202 prisoners but claimed the total was 600 to 700, with 6 field guns, and 80 to 100 machine guns. Its own casualties were 127 all ranks for the day with 174 during the full tour. The failed counterattacks on 1 September had clearly demoralised

39 LAC: 7th Battalion War Diary, OO No. 162, 2 September 1918; LAC: 7th Battalion War Diary, 7th Battalion Narrative of Operations from 28th August to 4th September, 1918.

40 LAC: CWNS, VC Winners.

the Germans. Relevant German regimental histories indicate the 7th struck a gap in the line that allowed it to pour into the German rear and outflank the defences.[41] The tanks provided significant assistance in disheartening the defenders. According to Gilson, 'They cut down our opposition very materially.'[42] The defence had to rely on the extreme courage of men who could evade the tanks' and infantry fire to throw a bundle of grenades that might damage the tank. There were not many of these men left in the German regiments. The 11th Tank Battalion reported: 'There is no question that German Infantry will not fight Tanks.'[43] German man-portable anti-tank weapons knocked only 4 out of 753 French tanks destroyed or badly damaged from July to November 1918.[44]

Leapfrogging the 7th Battalion was the 10th. It arrived at Arras in high fettle after its success at Amiens. One soldier explained: 'We had quite a thrill for the simple reason that we had gone so far. You know, when you'd been to Ypres, and you'd been around the Somme, when you got 200 yards or 100 yards, you thought you were making a wonderful advance. But here, we'd gone *miles*. It was unbelievable.'[45] The commander of the 10th Battalion was the youngest permanent CO in the Canadian Corps at 26 and the most heavily decorated officer in the unit. Lieutenant Colonel Eric MacDonald, an accountant, had limited Militia service and took over the battalion in June 1918. While relatively inexperienced, his decorations and rapid rise mark a gallant and savvy commander, with a 'forceful personality' according to the regimental historian.[46]

The battalion received the brigade's orders overnight. Instead of starting to move to the assembly area immediately, MacDonald let the men rest as long as possible. This was prudent as it would have a protracted, hard 15 hours of fighting. The immediate result was it had to hustle to get into position in time, with companies moving up separately, navigating by compass. It was a measure of their training and competence they executed it properly. The unit advanced at Zero and, after a short wait at Upton Wood, reached the Red Line in ample time. Two and half companies attacked, and artillery, four tanks, and machine guns reinforced it. The unit stalled at 8:45 a.m., and MacDonald moved up to investigate. He found a tough situation. The Germans were pounding the battalion from the front, left, and left rear. Enemy guns firing over open sights had knocked out all four tanks as they crossed over a ridge crest. MacDonald decided the 10th would advance methodically, using fire and movement tactics to grind forward. The attached 18-pounder battery was instrumental in knocking out strongpoints. Supporting machine guns were useful as their limbers kept up to provide ammunition. The unit struggled forward, but it was a time-consuming process. It had no other choice considering the defences and defenders. The enemy resisted stoutly from the fortified Villers-lès-Cagnicourt and Factory on the Arras-Cambrai road with masses of machine guns. In one strongpoint, thanks to the 'wonderful courage and initiative of Pte FENWICK and L/Cpl HOLMES' the 10th captured 61 prisoners and 13 machine guns plus liberating a captured armoured car crew. The Factory did

41 Kraehe, *Füs. Reg. 34*, pp.435-436.
42 LAC: 7th Battalion War Diary, 7th Battalion Narrative of Operations from 28th August to 4th September, 1918.
43 LAC: 3rd Tank Brigade Report.
44 Michel Goya, *Flesh and Steel During the Great War: The Transformation of the French Army and the Invention of Modern Warfare* (Barnsley: Pen & Sword, 2014), p.225.
45 Quoted in Dancocks, *Gallant Canadians*, p.178.
46 'Lt. Col. EW MacDonald' <https://matthewkbarrett.com/2017/11/02/lt-col-e-w-macdonald/> (22 April 2019); Dancocks, *Gallant Canadians*, pp.163, 177, 219.

The 10th Battalion's senior leadership in January 1919. At Arras 1918, the battalion fought an epic 15 hour battle to take the Buissy Switch, Villers-lès-Cagnicourt, and the Factory on the Arras-Cambrai road. (Canada. Dept. of National Defence/Library and Archives Canada/PA-004081)

not fall until 4:00 p.m. Fire from the CIF, especially its 6-inch Newton trench mortars, assisted the battalion. It took only 12 prisoners there along with 8 machine guns suggesting most of the crews fought to the death. It took all morning and the afternoon to take Villers-lès-Cagnicourt with two companies from both the east and the west. The battalion had now reached a line running north and south, just east of Villers-lès-Cagnicourt. It had been in intense fighting for eight hours, and it was still less than halfway along its planned advance. For the next phase, MacDonald had arranged through Loomis a supporting barrage by the 2nd CFA at 6:00 p.m.

The 2nd CFA had moved up to within 1,800 metres of the front by 1:45 p.m. and had already registered. The artillery brigade commander, Lieutenant Colonel S B Anderson, had reported to the 2nd Brigade headquarters in the morning. Thus, Loomis and Anderson could quickly arrange the barrage's details. Two 18-pounder batteries would shell down the Buissy Switch while a third did so along the Arras-Cambrai road on a 400-metre front. It was a sparse 66.7

metres per gun against the road and not much better along the trenches.[47] Anderson had to visit each battery to give them their fire orders because of the tight time frames. Thacker, the 1st CDA commander, would report: 'An exceptionally large number of enemy dead were found on following up the barrage.'[48] Most of them had head wounds.

MacDonald dispensed with the slow methodical advance and ordered a faster pace. He used two companies led by his second-in-command to move along and above the trenches along the Switch. Its progress was steady and linked up with the 3rd Battalion along Queer Street by 11:00 p.m. This meant the battalion had a 15-hour battle that Loomis expected would take two hours. Losses so depleted it that everyone at the battalion headquarters, other than the CO, one other officer, and a batman, moved forward.[49] Unlike elsewhere, according to the battalion report, the 'enemy appeared to have exceptionally good troops in this Area. They fought bitterly until the end in almost every instance and in many cases were killed rather than be captured.'[50] These were primarily from the *2nd GrR*.

The battalion estimated it killed 500 enemy and took 700 prisoners, 22 guns, and 150 machine guns for the loss of 233 all ranks. It was another superb performance. It defeated a force stronger than itself and embedded in strong defences. The authorities recognised its action with a shower of awards. These comprised 1 Victoria Cross, 3 DSOs, 6 Military Crosses, 11 Distinguished Conduct Medals, and 37 Military Medals for a total of 58 awards. In contrast, the battalion received 22 awards for service on the Somme 1916 for multiple engagements. Part of the reason it was successful was the limited role the German artillery played in the battle. Only 15 percent of the battalion's losses were due to shells.[51]

Sergeant Arthur Knight earned the battalion's VC, but at the cost of his life. An acting sergeant, he led a bombing section forward after an unsuccessful attack on a trench near Villers-lès-Cagnicourt. When German fire stopped them as well, he charged ahead despite the heavy fire and bayonetted several members of a machine gun and trench mortar crew. The rest fled, and Knight brought up a Lewis Gun to fire on those fleeing. Not done, he spotted a group of 30 retiring into a long tunnel. He dashed forward alone again and killed an officer and two NCOs and accepted the surrender of 20 Germans – a few escaped. A third time, he routed an enemy strongpoint holding up the advance in the face of heavy fire. He later suffered a mortal wound and died the next day. It would be difficult for any force to withstand an enemy that showed such courage and self-sacrifice.[52]

The 10th Battalion's operation required hard, epic fighting, because of Loomis's poor planning. By being so parsimonious with his forces, Loomis was guaranteeing the only way the 10th could succeed was with cool, careful, and measured tactics that resulted in a slow pace.

47 LAC: 2 CFA WD, OO No. 20, 2 September 1918; LAC: 2 CFA WD, Report on Operations from August 27th to Sept. 6th, 1918; LAC: 2 CFA WD, 2 September 1918.

48 LAC: RG9 III-D-3 v4958: 1st Canadian Division Artillery War Diary, Report of Operations 28 August to 4th September 1918.

49 'Andrews, Alfred Herbert John Diary: 1918' <http://www.canadianletters.ca/content/document-8448> (18 April 2017).

50 Dancocks, *Gallant Canadians*, pp.181-186; LAC: RG9 III-C-3 v4052, 22/6: Narrative of Operations Carried out by the 10th Canadian Battalion from 28-8-1918 to 4-9-18, 6 September 1918; LAC: RG9 III-D-3 v4921: 10th Battalion War Diary, 2 September 1918; 'Andrews Diary'.

51 Dancocks, *Gallant Canadians*, pp.95, 186.

52 LAC: CWNS, VC Winners.

Sergeant Arthur Knight earned his Victoria Cross by charging and routing three machine gun posts at the cost of a mortal wound. (Canada. Dept. of National Defence/Library and Archives Canada/ PA-006724)

The artillery supporting the 2nd Brigade – the 2nd CFA – played an important role in its success. It provided close and effective fire support through the day, including firing a barrage at its end. Even though hastily arranged and sparse in comparison with other barrages, it made a major difference in demoralising and killing Germans.

The 8th Battalion was in support and one company got involved in the battle for Villers-lès-Cagnicourt, taking 46 prisoners. An incident in this struggle highlights the spreading demoralisation in some German units. A strongpoint's officer refused to capitulate when several of his troops tried to do so. One of his men shot him, and the group surrendered. The 8th then covered the left flank of the 10th as it attacked down the Buissy Switch. It was not glamorous but necessary work.[53]

1st Brigade

The 1st Brigade was to trail Tuxford's reserves by 1,500 metres. That distance turned out to be too small. The 3rd Brigade's battle sucked in one battalion entirely and parts of two others. As a result, Griesbach lost control over most of his brigade during the morning. He had to pull companies of the 1st and 4th Battalions out of combat to get two intact battalions available if called upon. A central concern of command was reserve positioning. Too close, they end up in the forward battle and the commander loses control; but too far back they cannot intervene in time. Griesbach recommended increasing the trailing distance to 3,000 metres. The 4th Battalion took over the weakened 3rd Brigade's front that night.[54] The 2nd Battalion ended up in a mass of nine other battalions in the area south of Villers-lès-Cagnicourt and east of the

53 BWRA: Loomis Diary, 1 September 1918; LAC: 8th Bn WD, Narrative of Events- Phase II [September 1918]; LAC: 8th Bn WD, 2-3 September 1918.

54 LAC: 4th Bn Report, 28 August-1 September; LAC: 4th Bn. WD, 2 September 1918.

Red Line.[55] Its report captured the situation well with 'The clouds of obscurity were very heavy indeed' and the division was 'mixed up into one great jumble.'[56]

Air Operations

Just as the RAF concentrated 13 squadrons on the Canadian front, the German Air Service reinforced the sector. See Appendix III Formations, Units, Commanders, and Staff for the RAF's Order of Battle. The outcome was a contested air space where neither side could seriously interfere with the other's primary tasks. RAF reports indicated that the Corps wing ran photographic, contact, and spotting missions 'with little molestation.'[57] Even when the Germans shot down balloons, the balloon companies had new ones up in short order.[58] The result was RAF spotter aircraft could identify 111 battery firing positions during the day. Planes also bombed Cambrai and the northern canal crossing points to stop reinforcements, and four squadrons conducted ground support missions. They dropped 573 bombs and strafed so were a nuisance, but the effects were not material.[59]

Beyond the inherent dangers of enemy fighters and ground fire from both sides, low-flying aircraft had to contend with the constant peril of an artillery shell knocking them down. The heavy employment of smoke in attacks meant spotting aircraft had to fly dangerously low and thus expose themselves to increasingly sophisticated ground fire and shells. Flying strafing or spotting missions was a hazardous profession. The Corps' supporting No. 5 Squadron RAF lost three aircraft to enemy ground fire and another to Canadian shells alone on 8 August.[60] In addition, it was common to have aircraft return so damaged as to be unrepairable.[61] Finally, the extensive use of camouflage meant machine gun posts were unspotted until they opened up. While outnumbered, the German Air Service could take over air control when they concentrated their aircraft. They would attack smaller RAF groupings and inflict disproportionate losses.[62]

The German approach was to focus on ground missions. Groups of 20 to 40 aircraft would streak across the front to strafe and bomb Corps units and positions, then scramble back before the RAF could respond. Canadian infantry were understandably bitter at this experience, and the 2nd, 3rd, and 11th Brigade reports made pointed comments about the RAF.[63] While it was impossible to prevent these raids, the actual effects were similarly limited as the RAF's strafing.

55 Elements of the 8th Battalion, and the 10th Battalion, 1st, and 3rd Brigades.
56 LAC: 2nd Bn Report 28 August-1 September; Murray, *2nd Battalion History*, pp.286-288.
57 LAC: RG9 III-C-3 v4197, 1/2: First Army No.G.S.769, 9 September 1918.
58 LAC: RG9 III-D-3 v4919: 10th Battalion War Diary, 1 September 1918; LAC: First Army No.G.S.769, 9 September 1918; LAC: 3rd Brigade WD, Narrative of Events - 26th August - 3rd September 1918.
59 LAC: RG9 III-D-2 v4801, 130: CWNS RAF Reports-Arras.
60 LAC: RG24 v1839, GAQ 10-20: No. 5 Squadron Work under Command of Major C. H Gardner from July 1918 to November 11th 1918, 12 January 1919.
61 LAC: RG9 III-D-2 v4798, 105: 5th Squadron RAF Narrative of Operations 8-8-18 to 11-11-18, 12 January 1919.
62 S. F Wise, *Canadian Airmen and the First World War* (Toronto: University of Toronto Press, 1980), 1, p.555.
63 LAC: 11th Bde WD, Narrative of Operations Carried out between September 2nd and Sept. 5th, 1918, 8 August 1918.

The cost of airpower. Troops from a Canadian Highland battalion inspect the bodies of dead aviators with their aircraft burning a short distance away. (Canada. Dept. of National Defence/Library and Archives Canada/PA-003182)

The 1st RAF Brigade assigned two squadrons to the task, and so the enemy attackers badly outnumbered them.[64]

Canadian Independent Force

At 8:20 a.m., Brutinel ordered Whitmore, the Leading Group's commander, near St Rohart's Factory to advance. This meant it was already behind schedule, as it was supposed to cross the Red Line at 8:00 a.m. The accounts of the battle embodied in the war diaries and reports radically diverge how far they got. Whitmore claimed the lead cavalry squadron reached the Red Line, while the CLH, part of the Leading Group, stated the group reached the crossroads

64 LAC: CWNS RAF.

at l'Esperance Farm about 1,400 metres before the Red Line.[65] Only patrols penetrated beyond. Given the cavalry's sensitivity about stopping in the enemy's view, the bulk of the group remained at the crossroads. Whitmore then sent detachments to scout the way ahead. German guns knocked out two pairs of armoured cars from the 17th Tank Battalion sent down the road – their purpose baffled the defenders.[66] The cavalry's minimal casualties of three wounded indicates small parties probed forward with little aggressiveness. Also, the information they obtained was misleading, as they failed to note cut down trees across the road. They either were incompetent, and did not notice the trunks, or badly misjudged how far they advanced. Alternatively, and most likely, they never pushed far but turned back when the patrols suffered minor losses. Regardless, the cavalry performed poorly. Brutinel was scathing: 'In my opinion the resistance was not at that time properly tested. The Cavalry was extremely reluctant to test it and did not do it. Patrols were withdrawn early, and their reports were of negative value.'[67]

After the war, Whitmore responded with a critique of the plan in the British *Cavalry Journal*. He argued Brutinel had limited the area of manoeuvre to the no-fire zone and a fight for the bridgehead would have meant dismounting, but there was no secure place to do so for the horses.[68] Essentially, he contended that the cavalry required no movement restrictions and that it needed a safe spot for its animals if it were to fight. Not surprisingly, his article omits his regiment's weak performance in the battle. David Kenyon in his book rehabilitating British cavalry accepted Whitmore's criticisms.[69] He did not, however, discuss the 10th Royal's Hussars poor effort or Whitmore's unrealistic demands. For more, see Map 11.3 The CIF Flounders: 2 September in the colour map booklet.

Shortly after 9:00 a.m., Walker's No. 1 Group caught up to the rear of the Leading Group, and Brutinel ordered it to take over the advance at 10:15 a.m. Before deciding what to do, Walker sent out patrols to assess the situation as he evidently did not trust the cavalry report. When the scouts returned, he instructed E Battery under Captain F F Worthington and two platoons of cyclists to push beyond the 78th Battalion's positions in the D-Q Support Line.[70] This was the first of a series of decisions to send small detachments one at a time instead of using his concentrated force. Cut tree trunks stymied attempts to move down the road, and cyclists had to clear them. Walker sent out further machine gun batteries and cyclist parties, but Germans in the fortified Factory stopped all advances. To neutralise them, Walker summoned two of the truck-mounted Newton trench mortars. They quickly engaged them and landed

65 TNA: WO 95-1142-6: 10th Royal Hussars War Diary, Appendix 1, Report on Operations East of Arras in Which the 10th (POW) Royal Hussars Took Part on Sept. 2nd, 1918; LAC: CMGO WD, Summary of Operations of Canadian Independent Force, 2-9-18 to 4-9-18; LAC: RG9 III-D-3 v4055: Canadian Light Horse War Diary, Operations Report, September 1918.

66 TNA: WO 95-116-3: 17th Tank Battalion War Diary, Report on Operations 2nd & 3rd September 1918; Hauptstaatsarchiv Stuttgart: M109 Bü49 2009: Note from 51st (K.W.) Reserve Infantry Brigade to the 121st Reserve Infantry Regiment,19 September 1918.

67 LAC: CMGO WD, CIF Notes on Recent Fighting, September 1918.

68 Lieutenant-Colonel F.H.D.C. Whitmore, 'Drocourt-Queant Line, September 2, 1918', *Cavalry Journal* XXV, no. January to October (1925).

69 David Kenyon, *Horsemen in No Man's Land: British Cavalry and Trench Warfare, 1914-1918* (Barnsley: Pen & Sword Military, 2011), e-Book, loc.5617.

70 Worthington, called the father of the Canadian Armoured Corps, remained in the Permanent Force after the war and was instrumental in developing Canada's tank forces in the Second World War.

Lieutenant Colonel W K 'Tiny' Walker sitting in the centre with his officers of the 1st CMMG Brigade in January 1919. Based on his performance at Arras 1918 and Brutinel's sharp criticism, it was somewhat surprising he kept his command. (Canada. Dept. of National Defence/Library and Archives Canada/PA-004050)

their 25-kilogramme mortar rounds on the buildings and defensive positions. With twice the explosive filling of a 6-inch howitzer shell, the Newton's rounds were devastating. They played a role in the 10th Battalion's capture of the complex later in the afternoon. The trucks remained in action until 4:15 p.m. when a German battery found its range and knocked them out.[71] Walker eventually deployed three machine gun batteries and six cyclist platoons, but they could not capture the Factory. At 4:00 p.m., Brutinel sent the cavalry to the rear and later pulled back the CIF as it was apparent that any opportunity was gone.[72]

In Walker's battle narrative, he claimed his group intrepidly penetrated 2,000 metres beyond the infantry. He asserted it definitely captured the crossroads east of the Factory, and he strongly

71 LAC: RG9 III-C-1 v3932, 18/1: Independent Force Recommendations for Honours, 25 September 1918.

72 LAC: RG9 III-D-3 v4987: 1st Canadian Motorised Machine Gun Brigade War Diary, 2 September 1918; LAC: RG9 III-C-1 v3944, 56/4: Narrative of Operations Group No. 1 Canadian Independent Force, September 2nd 1918.

implied the Factory, as well.[73] Brutinel's official report had the CIF reach those crossroads and that the infantry occupied the empty Factory at 4:00 p.m.[74] He suggested this was due to the actions of the CIF. He took a much different stance in a stinging rebuke to Walker. In it, he doubted whether there was even an attempt to take the position. Both the 2nd Brigade and 10th Battalion were insistent that the infantry captured the Factory.[75] They do not mention the CIF at all. On the 4th Division side, both the 72nd and 78th Battalions, which operated near the Arras-Cambrai road, dismissed Brutinel's force. The 72nd's report stated: 'In order to be of any value an Independent Force must have dash and be prepared to risk casualties.'[76] Based on this, the most likely scenario was the group engaged the German defenders at the Factory and area. They did not capture it or reach the crossroads. The Newton mortars helped soften up the complex. They also helped draw fire from the positions attacked by the 10th Battalion, but it was the infantry who captured it.

After the battle, Brutinel argued the force structure was fit for its purpose.[77] He believed the Germans were reeling and the CIF would have succeeded if the 10th Royal Hussars were not so loss averse. While his complaints about the cavalry had much merit, there was no opportunity for a road-bound unit to breakout in the face of heavy opposition. An earlier gap in the line was closed by this point according to the Germans.[78] Plus, the fierce resistance to the infantry advance at the Red Line well before 8:00 a.m. disproves Brutinel's assertion. Later in the document, he contradicted his statement of the force's fitness by requesting permanently attached cavalry and an additional 1,200 cyclists. He also wanted considerably more training. He was correct that five types of mobile troops assembled at the last minute would find it difficult to fight together effectively.

Why the failure? First, the CIF was not fit for its task, despite Brutinel's claims. Its road-bound, extemporised composition, and insufficient numbers of infantry meant almost any level of opposition could stop it. Only the cavalry when dismounted and the cyclists could advance under enemy fire. Cyclists amounted to little more than a reinforced company in strength, so the force lacked the infantry it needed to fight forward. The machine guns were too immobile and too conspicuous a target on the move to be effective when advancing.

The two group leaders' weak leadership limited their group's potential. Whitmore's cavalry performed badly and accomplished nothing. Walker made poor use of his auxiliary units by calling up his mortars well after his force ceased advancing and never used the attached artillery. The assigned artillery battery fought its own battle – it carried out no fire missions for the CIF.[79] He dissipated his effort into small packets and scattered them in ineffective detachments across the front. Brutinel excoriated Walker for this.[80] Essentially, Walker failed in every respect in

73 LAC: No.1 CIF Narrative.
74 LAC: CMGO WD, Summary of Operations of Canadian Independent Force, 2-9-18 to 4-9-18.
75 LAC: 10th Battalion Narrative.; LAC: 2nd Brigade War Diary, Narrative of Operations East of Arras August 25 to September 3, 1918.
76 LAC: 12th Brigade War Diary, 72nd Battalion Scarpe Operation 29th Aug.-3rd Sept. 1918; LAC: 12th Brigade War Diary, 78th Battalion Report Scarpe Operation 30th Aug- 3rd September 1918.
77 LAC: CMGO WD, CIF Notes on Recent Fighting, September 1918.
78 Tiede, *Die 1. Garde-Reserve-Division*, p.20.
79 LAC: RG9 III-C-1 v3944, 56/4: 30th Battery Report on Operations September 2nd to September 4th 1918.
80 LAC: CMGO WD, MG-G 18-1/337, 10 September 1918.

Lorries of the 1st CMMG Brigade waiting for the order to advance on 2nd September. Note the white markers on the hoods for aircraft identification and the narrow tires that severely limited the tactical mobility of the force. (Canada. Dept. of National Defence/Library and Archives Canada/PA-003398)

leading his formation. It was surprising he kept his position. The lack of drive is evident in the casualty totals for the force. Where infantry battalions in the same sector were suffering casualty rates of 30 to 50 percent, the 1st CMMG Brigade and CCC Battalion each lost about 10 percent of its strength. The cavalry suffered even less – 3 wounded. Total losses for the CIF were 13 officers and 85 men.[81] While casualty totals are not an infallible measure of effort, they suggest a lack of enterprise given both the few losses and minimal gains of these units.

The underlying premise of the 2 September plan, that the major challenge was seizing the D-Q Line and not the advance afterwards, turned out to be faulty. Instead, the Germans defended in-depth extending thousands of metres beyond the D-Q Line. Thus, the CIF would have to fight through what the 12th Brigade reported as 'the most severe Machine Gun opposition which this Brigade has ever encountered.'[82] Finally, the planners erred in not suppressing the Factory, the only structures between the Red Line and the canal on the road. The Germans

81 LAC: CCCB Arras Report.
82 LAC: 12th Brigade War Diary, Scarpe Operation, Capture of Drocourt Queant Line, 2 September 1918.

turned it into a fortress that took hours to capture by the infantry. It is difficult to envision any set of reasonable circumstances where the CIF could have fulfilled its mission.

Analysis

Macdonell's division decisively defeated eight German regiments and parts of two more and reduced most to the strength of a reinforced company. The Germans fought fiercely at times and cravenly at others. They still put up enough resistance to justify the awarding of four Victoria Crosses to the division. It claimed 2,312 prisoners with 98 percent of them unwounded, indicating most did not fight hard. The division's casualties were 1,118, which, given the fierce combat after the D-Q Line fell, was surprisingly low. Any battle where the attacker's losses are less than half of the defender's fixed in strong defences was outstanding. The division, however, achieved only a partial victory. Only on the extreme right did it even approach its second objective. The rest of the gains while well in advance of the Red Line was still 1,100 to 2,200 metres short of the Green Line. Still, Currie wrote his diary: 'Their performance since coming into the line, August 29th, has been quite remarkable.'[83] Haig visited Macdonell after the battle and told him, 'You broke the line and got through; the whole thing was simply magnificent and it was wonderful.'[84]

Serious German command errors, the poor state of the D-Q Line, the power of the barrage, the intermittent assistance of tanks, and superior tactics aided the division. Planning failures, breakdowns in attached machine gun, artillery, and tank support, and issues with command and control in the reserve brigade, however, handicapped it. Dellmensingen's poor command decisions materially aided Macdonell's attack. It is clear from the German regimental accounts that von Dellmensingen's determination to hold the *Vorfeld* burned out and disorganised the forward forces. On 30 August, he wrote in his diary that the *Korps* should never have allowed the enemy to approach so close to the D-Q Line. The *167th IR* regimental history in reserve spoke of leaderless forward troops without ammunition hiding in shelters to the point the regiment considered itself to be the front-line unit.[85] While these operations wore down the 4th British Division, they did not affect the 1st Canadian sufficiently. Despite German claims, the *34th FüR* and *49th RIR* put up a negligible resistance after the punishment they received the previous day. Had they remained in reserve; they would have been far better prepared to resist.

The D-Q Line was not as formidable as feared. Lieutenant Colonel H H Matthews, the 1st Division's GSO 2, toured the battlefield and stated the trenches while deep were not in good repair. 'To my mind, the line was not nearly as formidable an obstacle as had been anticipated' he wrote.[86] The 3rd Battalion reported the wire protecting the line was 'old and not much effort put into it.'[87] Line construction started in the summer of 1917, but the Germans did not complete it. The *II Bavarian Korps* did not have the time or manpower to refurbish it once the Canadian offensive began on 26 August. Thus, the combination of demoralised, exhausted, and disorganised defenders in dilapidated defences resulted in a rapid overrun.

83 LAC: Currie Diary, 2 September 1918.
84 LAC: Macdonell Biography, 175.
85 Seebohm, *Geschicte Nr. 167*, p.140.
86 LAC: Matthews Report.
87 LAC: 3rd Bn Report 28 August-1 September.

The artillery had three key roles on 1st Division's front: barrage, counter-battery, and point fire by attached guns. It performed superbly in the first two and far less successfully with the third, which demonstrated how much it still had to learn about open warfare. On this front, the artillery barrage was thin but effective in crushing enemy morale, as attested by the masses of prisoners taken. The 6th CFA's barrage supporting the 10th Battalion's attack testified to the efficacy of this form of shelling in killing, suppressing fire, and isolating defenders.

German gunnery noticeably slackened during the morning. The advancing infantry and counter-battery efforts forced them to pull their pieces back.[88] The greatest contribution the enemy gunners made was in their desperate use of cannon firing over open sights as the Canadian infantry closed on them. At times their fire was effective, but it was costly as the number of guns captured indicates. Canadian gunners across the front had the satisfaction of using 15 captured field guns and 3 howitzers on their former owners.[89]

The 14th Tank Battalion's contribution to the battle was 17 tanks. Three of them broke down or ditched before reaching the enemy line. Of the 14 remaining vehicles, Germans knocked out half, with 5 of these burned out, and only 7 rallied. They provided good service in assisting the infantry in taking the D-Q Line. The 14th Tank Battalion's history claimed: 'The Tanks undoubtedly broke down the main resistance of the DROCOURT line, the garrison surrendering en bloc, and gave good material and moral support to the Infantry.'[90] They were of limited assistance after the D-Q Line as breakdowns, casualties, and exhaustion took their toll. Instead of being used in mass, they advanced in small packets or single tanks, with German guns knocking them out. When employed after their initial assignment, the infantry found them difficult to direct, as Peck's experience attests.

The plan was rigid and had no allowances for delays or failures. Once one part of the operation stumbled, it negatively affected its neighbours which in turn influenced others. For instance, while the 10th Battalion was ultimately successful, flanking fire from the Buissy Switch slowed the advance of the 3rd Brigade. Griesbach and Tuxford were both adamant that with protected flanks, the division would have reached the canal. German regimental accounts confirm their appreciation. The consistent Canadian unit reports of operating with both their flanks open attested to the sparsity of forces south of the Arras-Cambrai road. The 1st Division committed insufficient troops in this first phase to take the D-Q Line and Buissy Switch rapidly. This was essential if it were to reach the canal. Loomis's decision to assign a single battalion to the later phases of the action was an example of insufficient forces. Macdonell, with the benefit of hindsight, should have used all or a significant part of the 1st Brigade in this initial phase. This would have protected the inner flanks of the 2nd and 3rd Brigades and freed up forces to cover the right flank. It should have been apparent that the British could not cover that zone in time and that 1st Division needed to take additional measures. This was the conundrum that Macdonell faced as the only way to guarantee a rapid capture of both systems was to commit all three of his brigades. In doing so, however, he would not have the fresh forces needed to cross the canal. Only the superb training and leadership of the 1st Division's battalions got the

88 LAC: 1st CDA W.D., 2 September 1918; LAC: 2 CFA WD, 2 September 1918; LAC: GOCRA WD, 2 September 1918.
89 LAC: Artillery Notes on Operations - August 26th to Sept. 4th 1918.
90 TNA: 14th Tk. Bn. WD, History of the 14th Tank Battalion; LAC: CWNS 3rd Tank Brigade, Report on Operations with the Canadian Corps - 2nd September 1918, 18 September 1918.

division as far as it did once it passed beyond the barrage. Fundamentally, Macdonell did not have the force to quickly carry the two lines, and to storm across the canal with fresh forces.

Another issue of the rigid plan was a timing-based advance by reserves. The problem was how to keep them from slamming into the forward forces' fight, while remaining close enough to intervene when needed. When the schemes broke down, there was a strong tendency for them to get sucked into battle or at least interfere with the rear areas. Brigade commanders routinely lost control of their battalions and ended up 'mixed up in one great jumble' as according to the 2nd Battalion's commander.[91] The issue was programmatic movement of follow-on force was necessary because of imperfect communications. If they waited for orders, they would miss opportunities. If they advanced on a schedule and there was a delay, they prematurely engaged as what happened with the 1st Brigade.

While there were sterling examples of support weapons contributing, the usual story was of poor coordination, missed opportunities, and minimal assistance. Too often they failed to find their battalion, could not keep up, ran out of ammunition, or mysteriously turned away. A key issue with the machine gun arm was its crews' inability to haul all the rounds needed for an engagement. Using limbers like the battery that supported the 10th Battalion solved that problem, but there were risks. These were vulnerable targets if they followed too closely. Machine gun fire caught limbers of B Battery of the 1st Machine Gun Battalion passing through Cagnicourt.[92] The infantry rarely understood the tankers' orders or their limitations. Overall, this was a symptom of the trade-off between dedicated support weapon systems tied to a specific unit or pools of weapons attached as necessary. The latter gave greater flexibility and efficiency but at the cost of less effectiveness. A close read of post-battle reports indicates a significant gap in understanding between the different arms.

Generally, the use of mobile or sniper guns attached to the infantry was not a success. In multiple instances, the cannon did not show up or ended up in the wrong location. The gunners complained that it was difficult for single pieces to make an impact. It was hard to distinguish positions, tanks interfered, and the infantry could not provide meaningful targets. They also pointed out the difficulty of control of a gun by a single officer. He could either be with it or with the battalion headquarters but not both. The recommendation was for single guns to proceed on their own and pick out their own targets.[93]

South of the road, the battle had gone substantially in the Canadian's favour with two critical exceptions. The CIF had not delivered on its promise and the 1st Division did not reach the canal. Brutinel's force had accomplished little. Macdonell's division shredded the enemy line and swept the defenders from the board. Fortunately for the *II Bavarian Korps*, reinforcements were in place in the afternoon to cover a retreat if necessary. They had lost a strong defensive position and there were no organised fortifications until the canal. The German situation was perilous. The 1st Division had not suffered crippling losses, but four days of constant fighting had exhausted it. This following brief exchange between two 2nd and 3rd Brigade officers captured its accomplishments. Captain Alfred Andrews of the 10th Battalion reported: 'We

91 Murray, *2nd Battalion History*, p.288.
92 LAC: 1st Bn CMGC Report.
93 LAC: Artillery Notes on Operations - August 26th to Sept. 4th 1918; LAC: 2nd CDA Narrative; LAC: RG9 III-D-3 v4969: 6th CFA War Diary, Close Support of Infantry Commencing 26 August, September 1918.

spread out and connected with the 3rd Brigade. While there was a row started in the switch and I said to the 3rd Brigade officer, that is our boys taking the switch. He laughed and said that it couldn't be done.'[94] But they did do it. Across the 1st Division's front, the indomitable spirit, training, and skill of its infantry pulled off the improbable. What happened next was highly contingent on how the battle progressed north of the Arras-Cambrai road. Would the two 4th Divisions enjoy greater success than the 1st and decisively break the German line or was there a different dynamic at play.

94 'Andrews Diary'.

12

'The most severe machine gun opposition' 4th Canadian and 4th British Divisions, 2 September 1918

The task set ...was based on the assumption that the enemy would break as soon as the QUEANT-DROCOURT line was passed.

11th Canadian Brigade, 8 September 1918[1]

Both the 4th Canadian and 4th British Division had great initial success capturing the D-Q Line. The two formations captured the line with surprising ease but then faced unprecedented masses of machine guns that stopped them. Dellmensingen did not deploy his reserves as the Corps' plan depended on. Instead of passing through green fields, Canadian and British infantry met a multitude of machine guns, trench mortars, and artillery. Despite courage and determination, the troops could not make headway. The result was heavy casualties and limited gains. As the 78th Battalion report declared, 'Resistance was met where it was apparently least anticipated and was less where it had been anticipated.'[2]

12th Canadian Brigade

On the 4th Canadian Division's right, the 12th Brigade was the offensive's spearhead. Its success was paramount if the Corps were to attain its objectives. Critically, it needed to capture the D-Q Line and clear the path for the 11th Canadian Brigade to cross the Canal du Nord. Failure would derail the Corps' plans. It took the enemy outpost and main line of resistance but not the rear zone. The combination of no barrage, no tanks, and German resistance with 'Exceedingly strong M.Gun opposition from the North, South and East' stopped its advance.[3] For more, see Map 12.1 The D-Q Line Broken: 2 September in the colour map booklet.

1 LAC: 11th Bde WD, Narrative of Operations Carried out between September 2nd and Sept. 5th, 1918, 8 September 1918.
2 LAC: 12th Brigade War Diary, 78th Battalion Report Scarpe Operation 30th Aug-3rd September 1918.
3 LAC: 12th Brigade War Diary, Scarpe Operation, Capture of Drocourt Queant Line, 2 September 1918.

The *II Bavarian Korps* exerted tremendous effort on 1 September to secure and maintain the D-Q Line's *Vorfeld*. As a result, it held the entire front in-depth with portions west of the jump-off line. In the D-Q Line, the resistance was inconsistent with some groups fighting to the end and others surrendering freely. Usually, the defenders folded when the assault troops reached close quarters.

The early reports to the brigade spoke of rapid success, many prisoners, and little ammunition expended. This showed the already exhausted *4th EzD* and *2nd GRD* collapsed. Adding to the good news was that the German shelling started after 6:30 p.m. to fade away. The real battle developed in the fight for the rear zone, extending from Mt Dury to a depth of 3,000 metres. MacBrien's, GOC 12th Brigade, report characterised it as 'the most severe Machine Gun opposition which this Brigade has ever encountered.'[4] The Germans positioned them in-depth in a mesh of posts that swept the bare reverse slope of Mt Dury. Firing obliquely and indirectly, the defenders generated a kill zone that no infantry tactics could master. Contrary to claims that the Germans occupied 'a warren of bunkers' and defences constructed in-depth to the canal, the Germans extemporised the strongpoints as a detailed German trench map showed.[5] Canadian tactics depended on facing one or two machine gun strongpoints on a platoon front. Assault troops could suppress these posts with their weapons. Smoke would screen one position while the platoon outflanked and then rushed the other. With multiple positions outside the range of infantry weapons and smoke devices, the enemy brought too much firepower to overcome. The result was the 4th Canadian Division suffered the highest death toll of all four Canadian divisions during Arras 1918, although it was in line for the shortest time.[6]

MacBrien had poor communications with his forward forces and the reports lagged the developments at the front. It was not until 2:25 p.m. that he reported the brigade could not advance without further artillery and tank support. This was six hours after his brigade had definitively halted. He advised Watson fresh troops were necessary as his disorganised battalions were too weak to attack. All four battalions had fought and suffered that day and needed time to reorganise before another attempt.[7]

On the brigade's right, the 72nd attacked on a two-company front south of the Arras-Cambrai road in the *28th IR*'s sector. As soon as the barrage crashed down, the Germans in the outpost zone hurriedly pulled back as per doctrine. There was considerable wild machine gun fire; indicating the damage done to the *28th IR*. The Highlanders found their way through the wire with the enemy surrendering readily. Under a barrage that was 'perfect and very accurate,' the first line fell easily.[8] The formidable D-Q Line proved to be feeble as the Germans had not completed many of the concrete MEBUs. What little fight left in the German infantry evaporated with eight behemoths looming out of the smoke and dust after catching up to the unit. The battalion claimed it reached the Red Line about 6:30 a.m. and pushed out lightly

4 LAC: 12th Brigade War Diary, Scarpe Operation, Capture of Drocourt Queant Line, 2 September 1918.
5 Geoffrey Jackson, 'The British Empire on the Western Front: A Transnational Study of the 62nd West Riding Division and the Canadian 4th Division' (PhD, University of Calgary, 2013), p.351; Abtlg.-9, 'Biache St Vaast, Croisselles, Sheet 1440' Hauptstaatsarchiv Stuttgart, (23.8.18).
6 See Chapter 14 Analysis for more details on loss rates. Based on 'Find War Dead' <http://www.cwgc.org/find-war-dead.aspx?cpage=1> (4 March 2018).
7 LAC: RG9 III-B-1 v2284, O-12-30 v2: 11th Brigade Field Messages.
8 LAC: 72nd Bn WD, 2 September 1918.

manned posts along it. By 8:00 a.m., enemy reinforcements arrived, however, and there was a major increase in machine gun fire – as the regimental history framed it, 'no longer was the fire wild.' The outpost line suffered heavy losses from this. The defenders had turned a sunken road on the reverse slope of Mt Dury into a hastily fortified position that commanded the slopes. Sergeant K Q Campbell, a platoon commander, worked his way with two men, outflanked it, and cleared part of the trench. This was part of a process where multiple units had a role in taking the road. The battalion claimed the capture of 6 officers and 442 other ranks. Thus, it took more prisoners than its 268 casualties for the period 1-3 September.[9] It repeated the point that the hastily attached support units added little value owing to the lack of training together.[10]

In the brigade's centre, the 38th Battalion was to attack on a 500 metre front with two companies to take the D-Q Line and another two would advance to the Red Line. Private Arthur Foster wrote that at Zero 'hundreds of eighteen pounders seemed to scream over our heads, and burst in a splashing form, a hundred yards ahead of us.'[11] German infantry were in

The infamous windmill on the reverse slope of Mt Dury, which was won, lost and won again repeatedly in fierce fighting on 2 September. (Canada. Dept. of National Defence/Library and Archives Canada/ PA-004397)

9 McEvoy, *72nd Battalion History*, pp.130-132.
10 LAC: 12th Brigade War Diary, 72nd Battalion Scarpe Operation 29th Aug.-3rd Sept. 1918.
11 LAC: Private Foster Memoirs.

no shape to put up much resistance, and the combination of rifle grenades, Lewis Guns, and tanks suppressed what little there was. Most Germans bolted or surrendered from the first three lines. After the capture of the D-Q Line, C/38th and D/38th leapfrogged and found considerably more enemy machine gun and artillery fire in the valley leading to the support line. They still took it. In crossing over the slight rise of the shoulder of Mt Dury they met the full fury of German fire from multiple directions. This included guns firing over open sights from Saudemont and machine guns from a windmill on the reverse slope.

These two companies ahead of the other battalions were the focus of hostile attention. The Germans held the sunken road in strength 275 metres east of Mt Dury. The two companies had to either take the road or fall back over the ridge. Private Foster reported few casualties until they reached this position, when a 'terrible barrage of machine gun fire' knocked men 'over like nine pins.' Using fire and movement, the two companies wiped out the garrison. The Germans responded with devastating trench mortar fire that forced the two companies in support to send reinforcements. Arriving 11th Brigade troops bolstered the thinning defenders but at the disadvantage of a congested zone. Men from every battalion of the 12th Brigade, and many from the 10th and 11th Brigades, crammed the road. At 3:00 p.m. MacBrien, seeing the futility of any further advances, ordered the 38th to fall back and reorganise.

In a repeated theme in the after-action narrative, Edwards, the battalion commander, claimed the machine guns made no contribution. The battalion claimed 325 prisoners, 4 trench mortars, and 40 machine guns while they lost 9 officer and 269 other ranks or a 39 percent loss rate. The authorities acknowledged the battalion's performance with the award of 30 decorations, including a Victoria Cross to Private Claude Nunney.[12] On 2 September, Nunney was well ahead of this company by as much as 50 to 75 metres taking on the enemy single-handedly. Wounded early in the morning, he declined evacuation and fought on. He captured four machine guns and killed at least 25 Germans during the day. Injured again in the afternoon, he still refused to go to the rear but eventually did so under compulsion. He reached the hospital but died from his wounds on 23 September. It was evident by his actions he desired redemption and to clear his record after his striking an officer.[13]

On the brigade left, the 85th Battalion's task was difficult. It had to take five trenches to reach the Red Line and had to use all four companies. Complicating matters was that it was up to 1,000 metres from the jump-off line and the Germans defended in strength. It was too late to adjust the barrage, so the battalion had to overrun this zone without gunnery support. Expecting two tanks to assist, Millar, the battalion commander, assigned two platoons to clear it out. The tanks were late, so the platoons completed the job substantially on their own but at a high cost. Millar estimated half his unit's losses came here. Two of the strongpoints resulted in the capture of 78 prisoners and 18 machine guns. The *4th EzD* clearly was holding the *Vorfeld* in greater strength than doctrine allowed. The barrage was excellent, and the tanks' 'work in the attack on the DROCOURT-QUEANT System was extremely effective and greatly appreciated by the troops.' Two companies took the D-Q Line by 6:15 a.m. Then a reinforced company battled to the D-Q Support Line, with the German machine gunners providing most of the

12 LAC: 12th Brigade War Diary, 38th Battalion Report on Scarpe Operations 30th Aug-3rd Sep, 9 September 1918.
13 LAC: CWNS, VC Winners.

Private Claude Nunney VC was likely seeking redemption in his daring actions over 1 and 2 September. (Canada. Dept. of National Defence/Library and Archives Canada/PA-006859)

resistance. According to the 85th's history, they 'exhibited a courage of a high order.'[14] A single company leapfrogged and crossed over Mt Dury. There, the *1st GRD* met them with streams of fire from every weapon type. The assault staggered and stopped. The German positions were beyond the barrage's reach, and the tanks were not to go beyond the support line. Using its infantry weapons, the battalion fought its way forward. Rifle grenadiers infiltrated ahead and generated a smoke screen that covered sections to close with the sunken road. Using grenades and Lewis Gun fire, they drove out the defenders. The fighting was fierce as the enemy positions were only 100 metres from the Red Line. This type of combat was slow and costly, but they cleared the road by 9:30 a.m. At 11:00 a.m., the 11th Brigade relieved the depleted 85th to reduce congestion in the front positions.[15]

The Nova Scotia Highlanders had a much longer and tougher fight than expected after the fall of the support line. Lieutenant Clarence Gass of the battalion thought: 'It was certainly the

14 Hayes, *The Eighty-Fifth in France and Flanders*, p.140.

15 Hayes, *The Eighty-Fifth in France and Flanders*, pp.139-140; LAC: 12th Brigade War Diary, 85th Battalion Report Scarpe Operation 30th Aug.-3rd Sept. 1918; LAC: 85th Bn. W.D., 85th Battalion OO No. 171, 1 September 1918; LAC: 12th Bde Message Diary; LAC: 12th Brigade War Diary, Scarpe Operation, Capture of Drocourt Queant Line, 2 September 1918.

hardest scrap I've ever been through.'[16] The 85th punched through the *4th EzD* but could not do so against the far better *1st GRD*. It suffered 262 casualties but took 253 prisoners.[17] The CWGC database lists 82 fatalities, which is a 3 to 1 wounded to dead ratio, whereas the ratio for the battle was 4 to 1. This indicates the Highlanders endured more shelling from trench mortars and artillery than usual.

The 78th Battalion, initially in reserve, had a complex task of advancing beyond the Red Line at 8:00 a.m. to a spur north of the Arras-Cambrai road 2,500 metres from the Red Line. An artefact of the hurried nature of the changes to the plan was the Battalion's operational order had an unusual number of location reference errors.[18] These suggest an order hastily typed out and without time to review it properly. When the two assault companies crested the ridge, devastating German fire slammed them like the other battalions. The situation was 'confused on account of the mixing of Units' with the 78th Battalion, CIF, 72nd Battalion, and elements of the 11th Brigade all thrown into the mix.[19] The 78th remained in line until ordered back by the brigade at 7:30 p.m. Kirkcaldy complained the CIF arrived late and did little but hang around before falling back. His battalion suffered losses of 9 officers and 244 men showing the strength of the German resistance and that it made strenuous efforts to advance. Contrast its 33 percent loss rate with the 10 percent rate of the CIF's units attacking over the same sector.

10th Canadian Brigade

The 10th Brigade was to launch a crucial attack in complex and uncertain circumstances. It confronted intermittent communications, active fighting for its start line, and a hastily developed plan with aggressive objectives. The circumstances were so unclear that they had no touch with the 12th Brigade on their right on their jump-off line. It would use the 47th and 50th Battalions to take the four trenches of the Éterpigny and D-Q Lines. The 46th would leapfrog them to capture the D-Q Support Line and Dury. At 8:00 a.m., the 44th would pass through and strike to seize Palluel on the Canal du Nord.

Hayter's brigade's operation followed a similar trajectory as the other Corps' units. It rapidly overran the D-Q Line, suffered few casualties, and took many prisoners, but it had still to advance to the Red Line. Once the troops crossed the ridge crest line, the *1st GRD* stopped the advance. Unlike the other brigades, the 10th faced strongly pressed German counterattacks. The nature of the combat of early success and then a struggle appeared in the brigade's casualty figures. The 47th and 50th Battalions with strong tank and artillery support suffered 162 and 249 casualties. In comparison, the 44th and 46th Battalions lost 278 and 318 all ranks reflecting the cost of attacking without tanks and guns.[20]

As with the 12th Brigade, the initial reports were uniformly positive, with the Germans offering a weak artillery response and limited resistance. At 7:30 a.m., the brigade learned the

16 'Gass, Clarence Reginald Letter: 1918 September 9th'.
17 LAC: 12th Brigade War Diary, 85th Battalion Report Scarpe Operation 30th Aug.-3rd Sept. 1918.
18 LAC: RG9 III-D-3 v4944: 78th Battalion War Diary, 78th Battalion Scarpe OO No. 160, 1 September 1918.
19 LAC: 12th Brigade War Diary, 78th Battalion Report Scarpe Operation 30th Aug- 3rd September 1918.
20 LAC: 10th Brigade WD, 10th CIB Narrative of Operations Battle of Arras, 14 September 1918.

46th Battalion was pushing on to Dury as planned. The first disconcerting information was the 44th Battalion was incommunicado. Counterbalancing this was the 46th's report that it captured Dury at 8:30 a.m., albeit 30 minutes late. With signal delays of two to three hours, Hayter was unaware of how far the plan had unravelled. His description was 'the situation now began to get somewhat obscure.'[21] Shelling cut the wires to the division at 10:30 a.m., and the signal company did not restore them until the evening. Only early in the afternoon did some reliable information arrive that the D-Q Line was full of troops. They were suffering heavy losses, and machine gun fire held up the advance. A few minutes later, the errant 44th got in touch. It claimed to hold the road running east of Dury, but it was actually 500 metres west and north of its reported position in the British sector. It did not report its correct location until 5:00 p.m.[22] The last proof of the attack's collapse was a 2:45 p.m. report from the 46th Battalion that it was in a brutal dogfight for Dury facing multiple counterattacks.

On the brigade's right, the 47th Battalion attacked with two companies on a front of 500 metres. The barrage was excellent as it was accurate and dense. It, however, had only partially cut the sector's wire, so the troops made their own lanes with their rifle cutters. Despite the prompt enemy counter-barrage, the battalion advanced so rapidly that it suffered few losses from it. The unit quickly captured the first two trenches assisted by eight tanks crushing holdout positions and masking others with the smoke they generated. The remaining two trenches also fell with little difficulty. As was usually the case, the enemy machine gunners battled on while the infantry surrendered when the attackers closed with them. The battalion claimed 580 prisoners, and it suffered light losses of 7 officers and 155 men considering the D-Q Line's reputation. This loss rate was a function of fighting only as far as the first four line and not having to contend with the crack *1st GRD.*[23]

On the brigade's left, the 50th Battalion had to form up 200 metres from its expected start line and German machine gun nests untouched by the barrage would oppose them.[24] Between shelling and gas, the battalion lost 17 other ranks and a company commander before the battle began. Offsetting this, it reported the barrage was the 'most effective ever experienced by our troops.'[25] The leading waves jumped the forward machine gun posts and wiped them out before they could react. They caught up to the barrage at the first trench and then surged into the trench and overwhelmed the defenders, capturing hundreds of them. The 50th would claim 1,000 enemy captured in the battle with one company alone taking 450. The machine gunners fought well to the end, but according to the war diary 'all those found in the dugouts showed a willingness to surrender.' This reinforces Boff's argument on German morale that with deep dugouts 'Germans who wanted to surrender could relatively safely skulk and await being overrun.'[26]

21 LAC: 10th Brigade WD, 10th CIB Narrative of Operations Battle of Arras, 14 September 1918.
22 LAC: 10th Brigade WD, 10th CIB Narrative of Operations Battle of Arras, 14 September 1918.
23 LAC: RG9 III-D-3 v4923: 47th Battalion War Diary, 47th Battalion Report on Operations from 1st September to 4th September, 1918, Inclusive; LAC: 47th Battalion WD, 1-3 September 1918; LAC: 10th Brigade WD, 10th CIB Narrative of Operations Battle of Arras, 14 September 1918.
24 LAC: 50th Bn WD, 50th Battalion OO NO. 129, 1 September 1918.
25 LAC: RG9 III-C-3 v4215, 2/2: 50th Battalion Handwritten War Diary, 2nd September 1918.
26 Watson, *Enduring the Great War*, p.228; Boff, 'The Morale Maze: The German Army in Late 1918', p.875.

The 50th took all four of its trench lines on time and at little cost. The war diary justifiably called the operation 'the most brilliant attack ever made by the Battalion.' They did not always have their way, however. Sergeant Wheeler narrates an astonishing account of his company caught in the crossfire of three machine gun nests that stopped any further advance. The company commander sent a pair of runners back to get the attached artillery battery to knock them out, but both runners were hit. A second pair volunteered and shared the same fate. A third pair stepped forward, and one of them made it through the curtain of fire. An 18-pounder battery promptly engaged the nests and smashed them. It speaks to the high morale and dedication of the troops that two sets of runners would still volunteer knowing their likely fate.[27] The 50th suffered casualties of 4 officers and 210 men and claimed along with the masses of prisoners, 90 machine guns, and two trench mortars.[28] It reported prisoners from 16 battalions from 10 different regiments, suggesting the confused state of the German defences. The 50th's war diary narrative thought the tanks were of little assistance given the excellence of the gunnery support.

Major 'Jock' Rankin commanding the 46th Battalion was 'slightly scruffy and easy-going', but cared deeply about his men. (Canada. Dept. of National Defence/ Library and Archives Canada/ PA-007747)

27 Wheeler, *50th Battalion*, pp.251-252.
28 LAC: 10th Brigade WD, Report on Operations, 2nd-4th September 1918.

The 46th Battalion passed through at the D-Q Line. Ominously nicknamed the 'Suicide Battalion,' it had done well at Amiens and suffered only 120 casualties. It reached Arras at full strength of 45 officers and 1,072 men. Its long-standing commander was evacuated with the flu, and Major James 'Jock' Rankin (36) took over.[29] After long service with the battalion, he was completing the SOC Aldershot course when recalled on 29 August to take command. An experienced and courageous officer, he was 'slightly scruffy and easygoing' but cared deeply about his men.[30] This would be his first battle in command.

The 46th attacked on the full brigade front of 1,000 metres with two companies and four tanks. It had three obstacles to contend with: a 20-metre deep quarry blocking a third of its front, the D-Q Support Line, and the fortified village of Dury. Its mission was challenging. It was to advance on a kilometre front to a depth of 1,300 metres. This task illuminates the planners' expectations that the first two battalions would break the primary resistance. In addition, there was no choice but to use a single battalion given the 10th Brigade's other assignments.

The right-hand company breached the D-Q Line, but fierce opposition from the area of the windmill and the sunken road south of Dury stopped any further progress. Captain Brown of the supporting company flagged down and directed a tank to the strongpoints. The enemy promptly knocked it out. Brown then sent two sections through Dury to outflank the road while the rest of this company attacked. Surprised by the two sections emerging in their flank, the Germans immediately surrendered with 120 prisoners and 9 machine guns captured. That these sections could pass through the town without combat suggests that most of the defenders were cowering in their dugouts. Capturing this strongpoint along with the 85th's rifle grenade bombardment of the windmill, broke German resistance. The left company had an easier time reaching the Red Line by 7:30 a.m. and taking 300 prisoners. George Kenter of the battalion wrote the troops 'were surprised at the slight resistance offered.'[31] The final wave took the quarry and 100 captives. The company commander reported back that the enemy seemed badly disorganised. Unfortunately owing to the strictures of the pre-planned barrage, no advance was possible for another 30 minutes until the protective fire ended. This was enough time for the Germans to recover and manoeuvre fresh troops into position.

By 11:30 a.m., having moved up the reserves, the *1st GRD* counterattacked with two battalions of the *64th RIR* under a heavy barrage. This fire and assault wiped out several Canadian outposts and others went to cover. An hour later the counterattack drove back the left company 500 metres to the D-Q Support Line and inflicted heavy losses. Rankin rushed to the front bringing reserves, and the company threw itself on the Germans with great ferocity and pushed them back using flanking Lewis Gun fire and a bayonet charge. An outpost emerged from cover and caught the enemy in the flank and rear. The *64th RIR* had entered parts of Dury, but a lost 44th platoon cleared them out. The Canadians retook their positions by 2:10 p.m., along with two machine guns and 29 prisoners. While the enemy claimed to have held Dury until that night, it was more likely the Canadians drove them out of the town. They, however, remained close

29 James L. McWilliams, Steel, J. L., *The Suicide Battalion* (Edmonton: Hurtig, 1978), p.160; LAC: RG9 III-D-3 v4939: 46th Battalion War Diary, 10 and 31 August 1918.
30 McWilliams, *The Suicide Battalion*, p.183.
31 McWilliams, *The Suicide Battalion*, p.162.

to the village and harassed Odlum's brigade for most of the day.[32] The battalion captured 400 prisoners, 1 field gun, and just 15 machine guns. The number of guns taken was surprisingly low given the captive haul. This indicates that many were rear area troops who had fewer guns. The battalion's losses were 10 officers and 310 men.[33]

The 44th Battalion was a hard-luck unit suffering severely at the Somme and at Hill 70.[34] At Amiens its losses had exceeded its replacements by 100 men.[35] Its second-in-command, Major D B Martyn (30), led it on 2 September. A courageous leader, he received an MC and bar while a junior officer. By Arras, he was an experienced commander, but this would be his first battle in charge.

The brigade's insertion changed the role of the 44th from being a reserve to advancing to the Green Line and Palluel. The battalion was to attack on a two-company front and was to follow the 46th, leapfrog it when the latter reached the Red Line, and press on to the north-east. Ordered to advance at 7:15 a.m., the two leading companies had to squeeze in to avoid Dury laying athwart the line of advance. Two platoons went through Dury and, after losing their officers, remained to fight with the 46th for the rest of the day. German fire hit the advance hard, and the companies drifted left. They ended up 500 metres in the British sector. They had to battle their way forward through the various trenches to the D-Q Support Line by 10:00 a.m. The right company commander mistook the position of a small wood for another, leading to the erroneous location report. Strong enemy machine gun and artillery fire stopped every effort to push on. Even an attempt with the 12th British Brigade resulted in no gains and more losses. It still took 250 prisoners and one 100mm gun, but its casualties were significant at 7 officers and 271 other ranks.[36]

11th Canadian Brigade

The accounts of the 12th and 11th Brigades relate different battles that just happened to coincide on the same ground and at the same time. MacBrien's brigade's narrative as had it capture the sunken road but could not advance beyond. Odlum's brigade mistakenly believed it leapfrogged the 12th Brigade at the D-Q Support Line, and it captured the road. With leadership losses high and the fighting desperate, each battalion captured a portion of this road. As the Germans were at close quarters, attackers interpreted their fire as coming from the road. In the smoke, dust, and confusion, it was difficult to see where the enemy were firing from. Thus, units thought

32 LAC: 11th Bde WD, 11th Brigade Narrative of Operations Carried out between September 2nd and Sept. 5th, 1918, 8 August 1918.

33 LAC: RG9 III-D-3 v4940: 46th Battalion War Diary, 46th Battalion Report on Operations September 2nd - 4th 1918 inclusive, 9 September 1918; LAC: 46th Battalion War Diary, 1-2 September 1918; LAC: 46th Battalion War Diary, 46 Battalion Instructions No.1, 1 September 1918; McWilliams, *The Suicide Battalion*, pp.162-168.

34 For more on its unhappy Somme experience, see William F. Stewart, 'When the Learning Curve Falls: The Ordeal of the 44th Battalion, 25 October 1916', *British Journal for Military History* 2, no. 3 (2016).

35 LAC: RG9 III-D-3 v4939: 44th Battalion War Diary, 44th Battalion Report on Operations from 8:00 AM 10-8-18 to 3:30 AM 12-8-18; Russenholt, *6000 Canadian Men*, pp.169, 173.

36 LAC: 44th Battalion War Diary, Report on Operations, Midnight 1/2 to Midnight 3/4 Sept.1918; Russenholt, *6000 Canadian Men*, pp.175-177.

they took a position still held by the enemy. For more, see Map 12.2 The 4th Canadian and British Divisions Struggle: 2 September in the colour map booklet.

Odlum's brigade was to pass through the 12th Brigade at the Red Line at 8:00 a.m. and drive to and cross the Canal du Nord. It was, therefore, dependent on the 12th completing its mission on time. By 6:15 a.m., reports on the 12th's progress changed to a more positive tone. Odlum shortly after asked permission for his brigade and headquarters to move forward. He intended to stay close to the front so he could decide when to commit the brigade. The division replied the brigade could advance, but his headquarters was to remain. This was a fateful decision that took the battle out of Watson's control. With successes reported at 8:10 a.m., Watson ordered Odlum to send his brigade to the Red Line. This meant Watson already knew that the schedule was falling behind, as the plan had the brigade crossing the Red Line at 8:00 a.m. With permission to move, Odlum joined MacBrien at his headquarters on the Arras-Cambrai road. There the situation was unclear, and already out of control.[37]

By 11:00 a.m., Odlum, after a personal reconnaissance, discovered his 87th and 75th Battalions and a company of the 54th held the sunken road. Mixed in were elements of the 12th Brigade, and at no point was the Red Line occupied. Each CO gave him the doleful news that their units could not advance without more support and that their losses were excessive. Odlum reported to the division at 12:40 p.m. and requested the heavy artillery pound Récourt, Saudemont, and Rumaucourt from where German gunners were firing. The enemy front lines were too close to bombard with the field artillery. Poor communications also bedevilled him. It was impossible to maintain wire connections, and a shell destroyed the brigade's wireless set. German fire cut down many of the runners crossing over the bare slope of Mt Dury, so senior commanders knew little of the situation at the sharp end. With MacBrien's concurrence, he told Watson that no advance was possible without more gunnery and tank support. Watson concurred with his brigadiers' assessment and called off any additional attacks that day.[38]

On the brigade's right, the 54th Battalion was almost at full strength by 2 September.[39] The 54th's commander was another example of an officer with limited prewar military experience commanding a battalion. A civil engineer specialising in building dams, Lieutenant Colonel A B Carey (37) had a brief service in the Spanish-American and Boer Wars.[40] He served with a pioneer unit and the 102nd Battalion, before Odlum selected him to take over the 54th after court-martialling the incumbent commander.[41] Watson would rate him in 1919 as 'an outstanding bn [battalion] commander, good organiser, leader and hard fighter, has confidence of his men.' He recommended him for accelerated promotion, indicating a superb officer.[42]

37 LAC: 11th Bde WD, 11th Brigade Narrative of Operations Carried out between September 2nd and Sept. 5th, 1918, 8 August 1918; LAC: MG30 E300 v22: Odlum Fonds, Timetable for the 11th Brigade "Scarpe" Operations September 2nd and 3rd, 1918; LAC: 11th Brigade FM.

38 LAC: 11th Bde WD, 11th Brigade Narrative of Operations Carried out between September 2nd and Sept. 5th, 1918, 8 August 1918; LAC: Timetable Scarpe Operation; LAC: 11th Brigade FM.

39 LAC: 54th Battalion WD, 54th Battalion Operations August 1918.

40 He attended the University of Wisconsin and joined a volunteer regiment from there to fight.

41 The incumbent, Lt-Col VV Harvey, was court-martialled for an unauthorised leave of absence. 'The Court Martial' <http://54thbattalioncef.ca/?page_id=236> (21 April 2019).

42 'The Customs Collector' <https://matthewkbarrett.com/2016/03/31/the-customs-collector/> (21 April 2019); 'LCol Carey' <http://54thbattalioncef.ca/?page_id=429> (21 April 2019).

Lieutenant Colonel Colin Harbottle, CO 75th Battalion, made the fateful decision to commit his battalion and dragged along two others in a costly advance over Mt Dury. His action took the battle out of Watson's control. (Canada. Dept. of National Defence/Library and Archives Canada/PA-007308)

The 54th moved forward on Odlum's order from division and reached the second trench of the D-Q Line where it stopped. At 9:36 a.m., Carey directed his lead company to attack with the 75th, as that battalion's commander, Lieutenant Colonel Harbottle, would assault, regardless. It was critical to support his operation; otherwise, it risked being defeated in detail, thus Carey had little option but to bolster Harbottle. Two companies attacked and took a portion of the sunken road. They did so at bayonet point, reaching it using short rushes to minimise casualties. A/54th's report stated: 'The fighting in this area was most dogged, and enemy machine gunners serving their guns exceptionally well.'[43] With reports of heavy losses, crowding, and no chance to advance, Carey stopped the support company from crossing the ridge and adding to the casualty totals. Odlum instructed him to keep his two uncommitted companies in hand. Odlum told him to stand fast at 2:10 p.m. Carey's battalion took 100 prisoners and 17 machine guns but lost 14 officers and 153 men.[44] The ratio of machine guns to prisoners shows the concentration of these weapons on the 4th Canadian Division's sector.

The 75th Battalion was in the brigade's centre. It had done well at Amiens and had relatively few casualties. Its commander, Lieutenant Colonel Colin Harbottle (43), had a chequered past and his decisions on 2 September likely reflected a desire to overcome that history. From a prominent family, he moved in the highest social circles in Toronto, but in 1906 he was convicted of embezzlement and spent time in prison. He took over the 75th Battalion in April 1917. By Arras, he was a veteran officer but on thin ice with both Odlum and

43 LAC: 54th Battalion WD, Report of A Coy, [September 1918].
44 LAC: 54th Battalion WD, 2 September 1918; LAC: 54th Battalion WD, Narrative of Operations Carried by the Battalion on the 2nd and 3rd September 1918 in the Second Battle of Arras; Bailey], *Cinquante-Quatre*, p.26.

Watson over his management as previously discussed. He was in further trouble because he did not inform the brigade commander that he delayed an attack at Amiens. He included an abject apology in his report for failing to do so.[45]

The 75th was to take the Green Line after leapfrogging the 38th Battalion on the reverse slope of Mt Dury. The battalion started its move forward after 6:00 a.m. and stopped at the D-Q Line to wait for Odlum's order to advance. Harbottle received reports from his scout officer and patrols that the 12th Brigade had not advanced beyond the support line, and there was no sign of the 38th Battalion. Moreover, a few 12th Brigade stragglers dribbled back over the ridge. These details were critical in influencing his subsequent decision, but the information was wrong. At 7:45 a.m., he reported his situation but got no response from Odlum still well to the rear. Harbottle met with his fellow battalion commanders and demanded they advance. This despite Odlum's reinforced intentions of leaving the decision to commit to himself. Harbottle's reasoning was that as time was of the essence for the operation, they needed to reinvigorate the attack. Contributing to his decision was his belief that MacBrien's 38th and 78th Battalions had swerved around Mt Dury, leaving a gap in the line. What 12th Brigade troops he could see were obviously demoralised and disorganised. Harbottle believed that rather than waiting and taking casualties, it was better to take a positive action by invoking the loophole in Odlum's orders. An unstated factor might have been his desire to restore his reputation. From the subtext of the other battalions' reports, it was clear that he strongly argued to advance and that he intended to do so regardless of their support. Seeing his resolution, the commanders of the 54th and 85th Battalions had to aid his attack. Where one battalion would likely fail, three acting in unison were more likely to succeed. With this decision, Harbottle effectively took the battle out of his superiors' hands. It reduced the brigade commander to controlling three companies of the 102nd Battalion and two of the 54th – limiting what he could do. As the 11th Brigade was the sole reserve of the division, this deprived Watson of the resources to influence the operation. Thus, out of the division's 48 infantry companies, Watson could control five across two battalions.

At 8:00 a.m., two companies with one in support advanced. When they crossed the ridge crest, sheets of German fire from the front, flanks, windmill, and sunken road flayed them. Employing short rushes on a bare, open slope, the battalion advanced using Lewis Gun teams to infiltrate forward to deliver covering fire. One company reached the sunken road, already partially taken, and another then expanded its hold. Harbottle stationed himself and his headquarters on the crest line to monitor the engagement. He reported a prolonged battle for the windmill, as it was captured, lost, and recaptured repeatedly through the morning. By 9:45 a.m., the unit had pushed out 200 metres beyond the sunken road but could go no further. This was despite the help of Newton and Stokes mortars and strafing RAF aircraft. Shortly after noon Odlum visited Harbottle and ordered him to thin out his front but to keep striving to advance. The brigade commander would arrange for tank and artillery assistance. Neither were available, however. After the visit, Harbottle went forward to assess the situation, but on his way back, machine gun fire pinned him and his runner down. The gun caught him as he tried a short rush hitting him in both legs. After his wounding, the battalion reorganised and thinned out its front. Given its long casualty list, especially in officers, Odlum ordered the

45 LAC: RG9 III-D-3 v4943: 75th Battalion War Diary, Operation of 75th Canadian Infantry Battalion of August 8th/9th 1918.

Captain Bellenden Hutcheson of the 75th Battalion earned his Victoria Cross for outstanding courage in treating wounded under heavy and unrelenting fire on the bare slopes of Mt Dury <http://www.cmp-cpm.forces.gc.ca/dhh-dhp/gal/vcg-gcv/bio/hutcheson-bs-eng.asp> (17 August 2020).)

54th Battalion to relieve it. The 75th lost 24 officers and 301 men. It took 132 prisoners and 18 machine guns. Over 60 percent of the captives were wounded when the percentage for the campaign was roughly 10 percent. This shows these prisoners were primarily men hit in an early action and recovered by the 75th.[46]

Harbottle's decision effectively took Odlum out of the battle. Nevertheless, he still praised the battalion CO's leadership but criticised the choice to advance. Odlum was correct. The 11th Brigade accomplished nothing in the attack but add to the casualty total. With seven battalions congregated in the area around the sunken road, command and control was difficult, if not impossible. It would have been far better to wait to commit the 11th Brigade. What cannot be questioned was the courage of the officers and men of the battalion. The actions of its medical officer, Captain Bellenden Hutcheson, who earned a VC for his outstanding courage in treating wounded men under fire, exemplified this. He repeatedly attended badly wounded troops under heavy and unrelenting fire and remained until all were dressed and evacuated.[47]

46 LAC: 11th Bde WD, 75th Battalion Narrative of Operations, September 2nd to 5th, 1918, 8 September 1918; LAC: 75th Battalion War Diary, 2 September 1918; Timothy J. Stewart, *Toronto's Fighting 75th in the Great War 1915-1919* (Waterloo, ON: WLU Press, 2017), pp.287-298; LAC: 11th Bde WD, Casualty Phase August 31/September 1st to September 14/15th 1918.

47 LAC: CWNS, VC Winners; Stewart, *Toronto's Fighting 75th in the Great War 1915-1919*, p.302.

The 87th Battalion on the brigade's left had two significant engagements at Amiens but only suffered 152 casualties and was at full strength.[48] Lieutenant Colonel Kenneth Perry (34) was an experienced battalion commander, just not with the 87th. In May 1918, the authorities moved him to lead the 87th on the death of the incumbent. He was well-regarded by his seniors as witnessed by his promotion to battalion command, attendance at the SOC, and entrance into the first postwar Camberley staff college course.[49]

The battalion reached the area west of Mt Dury by 7:30 a.m. While pausing, the dominant sensory experience was the 'constant roar of shells.' Having met with Harbottle, Perry had the unit attack with the 75th and swung to the left to go around the 85th Battalion. In this way, it could dislodge the Germans and open the way for the brigade. Two companies pressed over the ridge crest and the usual torrent of fire met them from the front and flanks. After two hours of slow progress using short rushes, the two companies had advanced 200 metres beyond the sunken road. Their supporting firepower failed when a German shell knocked out the 6-inch Newton mortar and the Stokes ran out of ammunition. Thus, they had to rely on their infantry

Private J F Young VC repeatedly risked his life to care for and evacuate wounded men on the bare, exposed slope of Mt Dury. (Canada. Dept. of National Defence/Library and Archives Canada/ PA-006714)

48 LAC: RG9 III-C-3 v4221, 2/3: 87th Battalion Strength, September 1918; Archer Fortescue Duguid, *History of the Canadian Grenadier Guards, 1760-1964* (Montreal: Gazette Print. Co., 1965), p.194.

49 'Lt. Col. Perry' <https://matthewkbarrett.com/2017/07/30/lt-col-perry/> (23 April 2019).

weapons that lacked the range and firepower to suppress the defenders deployed in-depth. Perry advised Odlum early in the afternoon that there was no opportunity to advance without significant artillery and tank support. It could not make any more progress because of German resistance, its casualties, and disorganisation. It had lost any momentum. The engagement hit the unit hard. It reorganised the two assault companies into one because of losses of 10 officers and 331 men. This was from a battalion that went into action with a strength of 760 personnel. For its conduct, its personnel earned 1 VC, 3 MCs, and 22 MMs.[50]

Private John Francis Young, a stretcher-bearer, won the Victoria Cross for his courage and dedication to duty. He dressed and cared for wounded men on the bare, fire swept slope of Mt Dury for over an hour. He repeatedly crossed the open ridge to replenish his supply of dressings and to assist more men. When enemy fire slackened, he organised stretcher-bearers to evacuate the injured. The citation for his award credited him with saving the lives of many troops. Surprisingly given the lethal environment, he survived the battle.[51]

The 102nd Battalion in brigade reserve had few losses at Amiens.[52] Its commander, however, fell ill and the second-in-command, Major E J W Ryan (34), took over. Ryan was a major from a disbanded unit who had a brief tour with the 102nd Battalion. He must have impressed as the battalion kept him, unlike most other senior officers on these tours. He remained with the unit from March 1917 through the war and would win a DSO for his leadership.[53] The battalion followed the 87th by 1,000 metres. When the 87th advanced over the ridge, the lead company pressed onto just short of the crest. It sent a four-man scouting party to reconnoitre. After a long wait with no reports, the company crossed the crest and found the scouts all casualties. The company got sucked into the battle. Ryan pulled back the other three companies to the D-Q Line to ensure they remained uncommitted. He preserved at least a slight reserve. He also disengaged his lead company later in the morning. Overnight, Odlum ordered it to relieve the 72nd Battalion on the brigade's right. For the commitment of a single company, its losses of 8 officers and 178 men was a steep price.[54]

Unsupportive Support Weapons

The tank support for the 4th Canadian and 4th British Divisions consisted of the 9th and 11th Tank Battalions. Unlike the 1st Division, the various tank commanders met their infantry counterparts before the battle. From the 9th Tank Battalion, eight machines each supported the 72nd and 38th Battalions and six the 85th Battalion, with two more assisting the 10th

50 LAC: RG9 III-D-3 v4944: 87th Battalion War Diary, 2 September 1918; William J. Patterson, *Soldiers of the Queen: The Canadian Grenadier Guards of Montreal, 1859-2009* (Montréal: Canadian Grenadier Guards Corp., 2009), pp.145-147; LAC: 11th Bde WD, 87th Battalion, Narrative of Operations on September 2nd, 3rd, and 4th., 1918, 6 September 1918; Duguid, *Canadian Grenadier Guards*, pp.201-203.

51 LAC: CWNS, VC Winners.

52 LAC: RG9 III-D-3 v4944: 102nd Battalion War Diary, 2 September 1918; Gould, *From B.C.*, pp.101-103.

53 Stewart, *Embattled General*, pp.191-192; Gould, *From B.C.*, p.103.

54 LAC: 102nd Battalion War Diary, 2 September 1918; Gould, *From B.C.*, pp.103-106; LAC: 11th Bde WD, 102nd Battalion Narrative of Operations From Morning September 2nd. to Night September 5th, 1918, 7 September 1918.

Brigade. The tanks cleared out pillboxes, menaced Germans into surrender or crushed them, silenced field guns, and cut gaps in the wire. All but two – mechanical failures – reached the D-Q Line. The Germans knocked out five tanks with field artillery after that point. Thus, the overall loss rate, including the mechanical breakdowns, was 30 percent versus the 70 percent loss on 26 August. That the enemy killed no tanks with barrage protection clearly showed how much less vulnerable they were when used in mass and with proper artillery support. The 9th Tank Battalion reported 25 casualties with only four men killed in the operation, so a loss rate of 15 percent versus the infantry's 30 to 50 percent casualty rates.[55]

The 11th Tank Battalion assigned one company of nine machines each to the 4th British Division and to the 10th Canadian Brigade. It observed the only resistance was from enemy field piece anti-tank guns as: 'There is no question that German Infantry will fight Tanks.'[56] Of the 18 machines, 6 broke down in moving up, the Germans knocked out 6, and only 6 returned to the rally point. Here a lower concentration of tanks on the front resulted in a higher loss rate.

On completing the barrage, the artillery plan assigned one FA brigade to each infantry brigade, with one battery in close support under battalion control. From the various infantry and gunnery accounts, once the guns reached their new positions, there was little direction provided by the infantry. As a result, batteries found their own targets using their observers or employing direct fire.[57] They were easy to find as 'Targets were beyond the hope of the most optimistic gunner.'[58] Batteries in close support fired 470 to 1,000 rounds each with a devastating impact on enemy groups. They seemed to especially relish engaging enemy guns. While doing so, they were subject to considerable counter-battery fire and suffered accordingly. The German artillery effort at Arras was much stronger than at Amiens. For instance, the 3rd CFA suffered almost twice as many casualties on 2 September as in August 1918.[59]

The machine gun battalion's report admitted the gunners having to haul the bulky Vickers guns were vulnerable to enemy machine gun fire when on the move.[60] Horse-drawn limbers bringing up ammunition brought down fire and resulted in heavy animal losses. The five man crews, however, were too few to carry guns and ammunition any distance.[61] Even when the machine guns could get into position, they needed to shoot thousands of rounds to silence a

55 TNA: 9th Tank WD, Notes on Operations of the 9th Tank Battalion 2/9/18; TNA: 9th Tank WD, History of the 9th Tank Battalion From November 1916 to 31st Day of December 1918,; LAC: CWNS 3rd Tank Brigade, Report on Operations with the Canadian Corps - 2nd September 1918, 18 September 1918.

56 LAC: CWNS 3rd Tank Brigade, Report on Operations with the Canadian Corps - 2nd September 1918, 18 September 1918.

57 The 11th Battery reported its forward observer could not find the battalion it was supposed to support until noon. LAC: 3rd CFA War Diary, 3rd Brigade Canadian Field Arty. During Operations East of Arras [September 1918].

58 LAC: 4th CDA Report, 15 September 1918.

59 The brigade suffered casualties of 82 all ranks on 2 September 1918 versus 44 in August. LAC: 3rd CFA War Diary, 2 September 1918 and Third Battle of the Somme, 3rd CFA. undated [August 1918].

60 LAC: RG9 III-D-3 v4896: 4th Machine Gun Battalion War Diary, Lessons Learned from Operations 2nd to 5th. Sept. 1918.

61 LAC: 4th MG Bn WD, Report on Operations, No.2 Coy. 4th Battalion CMGC, [September 1918].

position such as the Factory or the windmill.[62] The machine gun battalion suffered substantial losses with 175 casualties. It also had eight guns destroyed.[63]

4th British Division

Depleted and fatigued, the 4th British Division's day mirrored the 4th Canadian Division's experience. It had early success with few casualties, with the follow-on forces unable to advance and suffering heavy losses. Reflecting the chaos of the battle, the divisional and brigade accounts were contradictory, confusing, and masked a major planning failure. The 12th British Brigade veered off-course and left a powerful strongpoint on its left flank that impeded both it and the 11th British Brigade's subsequent operations. This position, called Prospect Farm, appeared in every account as playing an outsized role in stopping the division's progress. Between the trenches of the D-Q Line 1,100 metres south of Étaing on high ground, it dominated the area south of it. The planners had overlooked its importance and had taken no special measures to neutralise it.

On the right, the 12th British Brigade's 2nd Essex overran the right flank of the *362nd IR* and the *I/214th RIR*. This assault annihilated the latter, with its battalion commander killed and the headquarters captured.[64] The Essex hugged the barrage which suppressed the demoralised defenders. The battalion reported only 70 casualties, showing the enemy's lack of fight and limited German shelling. Its greatest issue was the 44th Battalion's intrusion into its sector, leading to considerable crowding of trenches and problems with control.[65] On the left, the 1st KORL did not attack across its entire front but concentrated on the southern portion. This left the *II/214th RIR* unengaged, and it linked up with the reserve *III/214th* in the D-Q Line at Prospect Farm. As the British advanced, fire from there caused the troops to drift to the right. As a result, the KORL reached the D-Q Support Line on half of its front. This left the follow-on forces to contend with the threat from the strongpoint. The KORL's losses were minimal at just 56 all ranks.[66]

Initial reports spoke of striking early success with the D-Q Support Line reached by 6:45 a.m., with 95 percent of the 1,122 prisoners captured during the day seized in the morning. The situation, thus, looked excellent to Matheson. Although unknown to him, the *214th RIR*'s history described masses of field grey troops pouring through their position on their way to the north-east. In this stream were the *4th EzD*'s regimental headquarters trying to escape the British onslaught. The Corps' protective barrage prevented any further exploitation of the success, however. As a result, the Germans extracted five batteries deployed close to the Red Line. More seriously, it gave them time to recover their pluck and organise the defence. Thus, when the 11th British Brigade resumed the attack at 8:00 a.m., it faced a rejuvenated resistance.

62 LAC: 11th Bde WD, 11th Brigade Narrative of Operations Carried out between September 2nd and Sept. 5th, 1918, 8 August 1918.
63 LAC: 4th MG Bn WD, 4th MG Battalion Report on Operations 1st, to 5th. September 1918.
64 Bastanier, *Geschichte RIR 214*, p.416.
65 TNA: WO 95-1505-1: 2nd Essex War Diary, 2 September 1918.
66 TNA: WO 95-1506-1: 1st Kings Own Royal Lancashire War Diary, 2nd September 1918.

After, Matheson recommended that SOS barrages be on call instead of a protective barrage to exploit any enemy weakness.[67]

At 8:00 a.m., the 11th British Brigade was to capture the Green and Blue Lines. Instead, an off-course advance, hard fighting to reach the Red Line, and minimal gains accompanied by severe losses characterised the day. The German shelling was weak and inaccurate, but the opposite was true of the machine guns. Advancing on time, the brigade experienced difficulties in controlling its units. The 1st RB on the right found the barrage too slow, and it got caught up in the 2nd Essex's fight. Its two right-hand companies veered right and ended up battling in the 4th Canadian Division sector. At the same time, the two left-hand companies reached as far as the Dury-Lécluse crossroads 850 metres west of Bois de Récourt, where a later advance found their bodies. The unit could not secure any permanent gain beyond the support line and suffered staggering losses. The second hardest hit battalion in the campaign, the 1st RB lost 15 officers and 409 men with 81 killed.[68]

In the brigade centre, the 1st Hampshire got side-tracked by the fire from Prospect Farm and instead of advancing east, one company pushed north along the D-Q Support Line to outflank it. German pressure forced them to fall back, however. Enemy machine gun fire stopped any further advances. Its losses for the tour were moderate at 6 officers and 156 other ranks.[69] On the left, the 1st SLI entered the battle in poor shape. It had only 300 men available, and these were 'so exhausted that it was difficult to keep them awake.' The battalion skewed to the right to get away from Prospect Farm and ended up to the right of the 1st Hampshire – it should have been on the left. The unit claimed it reached the D-Q Support Line, but its reported position was 500 metres east of it. Either its map-reading skills were deficient, or its report was wrong – neither of which reflects well. Again, German machine gun fire prevented any lasting advance beyond the support line. Its losses during its tour were heavy at 15 officers and 313 men.[70] An operation of a company each of 1st KORL and 2nd Seaforths took Prospect Farm later in the morning. By that point there was no momentum left, and the division went no further. The division had taken only half of the support line and faced a hard struggle to push further if the Germans wished to contest the advance.[71]

Germans North of the Arras-Cambrai Road

The previous three days of hard fighting had exhausted and worn down the *28th IR* facing the 12th Canadian Brigade. Short of food because ammunition had first priority for resupply,

67 TNA: 4th British Div GS WD, Narrative of Operations of 4th Division from 26 August to 4th September 1918; TNA: 4th British Div GS WD, 2 September War Diary; Bastanier, *Geschichte RIR 214*, p.420.
68 TNA: 11th Br Bde WD, 2 September 1918; TNA: 11th Br Bde WD, 11th Brigade Account of Operations at Arras August 28th - September 2nd 1918; TNA: 11th Br Bde WD, 1 Rifle Brigade Report, [September 1918; 'CWGC'.
69 TNA: 11th Br Bde WD, 1st Battalion the Hampshire Regiment Report on Operations 28/8/18 - 4/9/18.
70 TNA: 1st Somerset Light Infantry War Diary, 1 September 1918; TNA: 1st Somerset Light Infantry War Diary, Account of Operations from 31-8-18 to 4-9-18, September 1918.
71 TNA: 4th British Div GS WD, Narrative of Operations of 4th Division from 26 August to 4th September 1918; TNA: 4th British Div GS WD, 2 September War 1918.

heavy shelling, and shell-hole defences primed the regiment for defeat. The previous days' counterattack had left the regiment's zone a confused jumble of troops. When the barrage opened up, orientation was impossible in the fog and smoke. The attack whittled the regiment down, and the *coup de grâce* was the arrival of four tanks. They suppressed German fire and enabled assault troops to close with defenders, which usually resulted in surrender. Only a handful of men escaped to the *II/28th IR* holding the D-Q Line. The battalion with no reserves could not stop the 12th Brigade. The regimental history claimed it was a day of honour as it was 'the last great battle of the regiment.' Its casualties were staggering – it lost all except one of its officers and over 90 percent of its personnel.[72]

The *4th EzD* after four days of exhausting fighting was at the end of its tether. The 4th Canadian and 4th British Divisions rapidly overran the defenders, with only the machine gunners putting up a fight. Deployed behind the *4th EzD* in the D-Q Line, the *91st RIR* insisted it stopped the first attack, but failures elsewhere forced its collapse. The regimental history's personal accounts, however, belie this rosy picture. For instance, the adjutant of one of its battalions claimed its morale was the 'worst imaginable.' The regiment did not put up much of a fight.[73]

The sector's *Eingreifdivision* – the *1st GRD* – delivered a much more effective defence. With its *2nd* and *1st GRR* deployed from south to north on the reverse slope of Mt Dury, it was in a good position to derail the Canadian attack. Early in the morning, the *III/1st GRR* received instructions to prepare to counterattack, but the division soon amended them to include the entire regiment. These orders also directed the *64th RIR* in reserve to retake Dury with two battalions. Before the *1st GRR* could execute the order, the 10th and 12th Canadian Brigades' troops surged over Mt Dury. The *1st* and *2nd GRR* shifted to a defensive posture which explains the Canadian accounts of German fire increasing in quantity and effectiveness over the morning. The *2nd GRR* had to stretch thinly to maintain contact with the *2nd GrR* on its left in the Buissy Switch. A later history admitted there was briefly a gap along the Arras-Cambrai road, but the *1st GRD* quickly closed it off well before the CIF was on the scene. The division had to commit all its force, leaving only a single company in reserve. In the fighting for the sunken road, the 4th Canadian Division destroyed the *I/1st GRR* and threatened the regiment with encirclement. Only with hard fighting was it saved from annihilation.[74]

On the guards' right, the *64th RIR* played a crucial role in blunting the advance of the 10th Canadian and the 11th British Brigades with a fierce counterattack. It hit the 46th Battalion holding Dury with two battalions (*I* and *III/64th RIR*) around noon. It rolled back the Saskatchewan troops briefly, but the Canadians drove them out. The *214th RIR* acknowledged the *64th*'s counterattack materially assisted its efforts to hold back the 4th British Division. While ultimately unsuccessful, the action drained away the attackers' momentum in this sector.[75]

The *1st GRD* performed brilliantly in stopping the advance north of the Arras-Cambrai road. It took advantage of the terrain and situation to create a kill zone that inflicted crushing losses and disorganisation on the attackers. The high command acknowledged the formation's

72 Begau, *IR 28 in Weltkrieg*, pp.237-244.
73 Kümmel, *Res.Inf.Regt. Nr. 91*, pp.428-431.
74 Tiede, *Die 1.Garde-Reserve-Division*, p.20; Brederlow, *1st Garde-Reserve-Regiments*, pp.313-314.
75 Julius Voight, *Das Garde-Reserve-Infanterie-Regiment Nr. 64 im Weltkriege* (Berlin: Gerhard Stalling, 1923), pp.140-141.

Major Tido Brederlow, commander of the *1st GRR*, received the *Pour le Mérite* for the superb performance of his regiment in stopping the 4th Canadian Division. (Tido von Brederlow, *Geschichte Des 1st Garde-Reserve-Regiments* (Berlin: Gerhard Stalling, 1926), p.336.)

achievement by granting the *Pour le Mérite* to the commanders of both the *1st* and *2nd GRR*.[76] It was a rare event for a single division to receive two such awards. The division paid a price for its success with 1,600 casualties. Its *1st GRR* lost 646 officers and men, most of whom the Canadians captured.[77] It was in the unusual situation in this battle in likely having inflicted as many casualties as it suffered. In most cases, the Germans' losses exceeded those of the Corps' formations.

Results and Analysis

Owing to the timing of casualty reporting, the results for 2 and 3 September are covered here. Second September was the hardest and most costly day of the battle, with the Corps' losses exceeding the next worst day (27 August) by almost 80 percent. The Corps suffered 4,312 casualties in the fighting with the 4th Canadian Division losing the most at 1,929 all ranks. The casualties rattled Watson, with Haig reporting Watson was 'disturbed at the report of the losses he had.'[78] Failure was costly, with the 1st Division's casualty toll for the day just 58 percent

76 Tiede, *Die 1.Garde-Reserve-Division*, p.20.
77 Brederlow, *1st Garde-Reserve-Regiments*, p.317; Tiede, *Die 1.Garde-Reserve-Division*, p.20.
78 NLS: Haig Diary, 2 September 1918.

and the 4th British 29 percent of Watson's division's total. The Corps recorded 3,346 prisoners captured on 2 September and another 1,666 on 3 September. The Corps reported another 1,988 casualties on 3 September, bringing its total for the two days up to 6,300. Many of these were likely suffered the previous day.

Table 12.1 Estimated Casualties 2 September 1918

	Killed	Wounded	POW	Total
1st CID	264	853	1	1,118
2nd CID	9	25		34
3rd CID	7	25		32
4th CID	641	1287	1	1,929
4th BID*	162	400		562
Tank Corps†				0
Other	29	608		637
Total	**1,112**	**3,198**	**2**	**4,312**

* 4th British Division totals do not include prisoners lost.
† Included in the Other category are Tank Corps wounded.

Although not a victory on the scale demanded by Haig, it was, nevertheless, a victory. The Corps captured almost all the enemy fortifications. Of the six German divisions at the start of the day, the attackers destroyed five and battered the sixth. The *II Bavarian Korps* had stopped the Canadian Corps' attack but at a grievous cost. Three German regimental histories describe the action as their last major battle in the war.[79] Certainly, the high command believed it a great victory. Henry Horne, writing his wife, called it 'one of the biggest things of the war.'[80] Currie wrote in his diary on 3 September, 'It is a question whether our victory of yesterday or of August 8th is the greatest, but I am inclined to think yesterday's was.'[81]

The standard explanation for the 4th Canadian Division's failure to advance beyond the Red Line was the artillery barrage's suspension. At no point in the planning process was a field artillery barrage beyond the Red Line contemplated. What the Corps suspended was the heavy artillery in the no-fire zone. At its closest, it was 1,700 metres from the Red Line and beyond the range of effective machine gun fire. Contrary to McNaughton's memories after 44 years' passage, enemy shelling from this sector was not a factor.[82] Only 6 percent of the batteries

79 Bastanier, *Geschichte RIR 214*, p.415; Begau, *IR 28 in Weltkrieg*, p.239; Pafferath, *Geschichte I.R. 68*, p.742.
80 Robbins, *The First World War Letters of General Lord Horne* p.260.
81 LAC: Currie Diary, 3 September 1918.
82 LAC: MG30 E133 v325: McNaughton Fonds, CBC McNaughton Interview.

the RAF spotted were in this sector, and those would shell the 1st Division's front.[83] The 4th Canadian Division's narrative was explicit that the most telling artillery fire came from areas well away from the zone.[84] None of the battalion, brigade, or division narratives discuss fire from there but emphasised it came from in front, the flanks, the windmill, the Factory, and Dury.

If the standard narrative is incorrect, why was the 4th Division stopped after taking the D-Q Line? The key factor was that von Dellmensingen did not pour all his reserves into the D-Q Line, as Currie's plan predicated. Instead, he kept the *Eingreifdivision* in the northern sector unengaged to make a counterattack. The Corps' assault comprehensively defeated the *4th EzD* and *2nd GRD* and disabled their headquarters so that little reliable information reached the German decision makers. Two regimental histories reference sending patrols forward to find out what was happening at the front. No one from them returned.[85] Fortunately for the Germans, the *1st GRD* was in a perfect position. When the assault battalions crossed over the ridge crest, a crack German division in great strength, reinforced with elite machine gun detachments and deployed in-depth, met them. The ground the Canadians had to advance on was bare and exposed. Without an artillery barrage and smoke to shield the assault troops, they were ideal targets for artillery, trench mortar, and machine gun fire.

The Canadian battalions had the support of individual batteries or sections of guns that could effectively deal with point targets, but they could not suppress a deep defensive zone. The Canadian machine gun batteries, if they showed up, could do little to neutralise the deep machine gun defensive zone the Germans had established. It was up to the infantry relying on their own weapons to advance in the face of masses of machine guns. Canadian platoon tactics were effective at dealing with one or two machine gun strongpoints. They were powerless when confronting six to eight posts deployed far beyond the range of their own weapons.

Contributing factors to the repulse was the Red Line's placement, the premature commitment of the 11th Brigade, and Watson's decision to place his headquarters so far to the rear. The Red Line on the reverse slope of Mt Dury was tactically unsound. Multiple brigade and battalion reports complained that the line's location was an error. Its positioning was on the supposition that the attack would have overcome all German resistance by that point. That was a dangerous assumption. Odlum lost control of his brigade depriving him and Watson of any substantial reserve to change the battle's course. He took the appropriate steps in his orders and briefing to emphasise the importance of waiting for him to commit the force. Watson's insistence on tying Odlum to his headquarters thwarted his ability to decide, and Harbottle forced the choice on him. By placing his headquarters so far to the rear and with the tenuous communication infrastructure, Watson took himself out of the battle. He and his staff received few messages over the over-stretched signals' line, so they had a poor understanding of the situation. Watson complained in his diary that 'Our Signal Communications were very bad.'[86] The battle effectively devolved to the battalion commanders who had few, if any, support weapons to assist their advance. By the time Watson understood what was happening, there was insufficient time for

83 LAC: RG9 III-C-1 v3923, 12/1: Counter Battery Office C.B.544/9, 3 September 1918.
84 LAC: 4th Canadian Div WD, 4th Canadian Division Report on Operations Scarpe, Sept. 2nd - 4th, 1918.
85 Kümmel, *Res.Inf.Regt. Nr. 91*, p.431; Brederlow, *1st Garde-Reserve-Regiments*, p.314.
86 LAC: Watson Diary, 2 September 1918.

him to arrange another barrage before the end of the day. Watson's challenge was that the correct choice in hindsight of pausing to arrange another barrage meant reaching the day's objective was impossible. In retrospect, the task set for Watson was beyond his division's capabilities and the responsibility for its failure in large part lay with Currie and his staff.

The 4th British Division had early success. Like the 4th Canadian Division, errors in planning, inadequate battlefield control, and hard fighting by the Germans stymied its advance. The protective barrage imposed by the Corps prevented the division from exploiting its success. Failing to neutralise Prospect Farm threw the entire operation off-kilter as battalions sheered right to escape its fire. The British did not engage the crucial high ground around the Farm until later in the morning. Instead of a coherent and coordinated push, its attack was a series of disjointed actions that interfered with their neighbours just as their neighbours hampered them. Units did not know where they were and provided erroneous reports of their position. Like the 4th Canadian Division, the lack of a barrage magnified by the lack of attached guns doomed the advance. Once the 'fire-roller' missed or passed them, the *II* and *III Battalions* of the *214th RIR* responded well and fought hard to slow and then stop the British advance. The pressure of the *64th RIR*'s counterattack centred on Dury gave the 'troops a noticeable relief.'[87] The day's action buttressed the British Official History's statement of the British infantry's reliance on the guns to advance successfully. Once the barrage ended, like the 4th Canadian, the division made no significant gains.

In the opening stages, there was little the Corps or Currie could do but to let the operation run its course. It had committed all its forces other than the heavy artillery assigned to counter-battery missions and the 1st British Division. Moreover, the latter already had instructions to follow the 4th Canadian Division automatically. The result was the only intervention made by Currie was an order to keep advancing issued at 3:00 p.m. Its basis was quantities of prisoners from numerous German units indicating great confusion in the enemy's lines. The instruction urged: 'Vigorous action this afternoon should lead to complete collapse of his organisation.'[88] This order demonstrated how quickly the intelligence branch could identify the enemy's order-of-battle and how little the Corps knew of its own units' condition. By 3:00 p.m., the 4th British and Canadian Divisions were incapable of an organised operation to take advantage of the confused German state. The 1st Division, while in better shape, had already committed most of its troops leaving only two battalions available.

The Corps had cracked the hinge but had not yet broken out. Two crucial questions would dictate the offensive's future course. First, could the Corps overcome the hurdles of confusion, casualties, and exhaustion and launch another powerful blow? Second, what would the Germans do? As a result of the day's action, Dellmensingen and his superiors had a stark choice. They could fall back behind the canal. This had wider ramifications as it would also mean the remainder of the *Seventeenth* and *Second Armees* to the south would have to withdraw as well. It meant giving up the last gains of the March offensive. The alternative was to retake the D-Q Line. They had no option but either to go forward or to fall back as their current line with their backs to the canal was untenable. The next chapter finishes the campaign with the answers to these two issues.

87 Bastanier, *Geschichte RIR 214*, p.421.
88 TNA: WO 95-1053-3: Canadian Corps G.938, 2 September 1918.

13

'Impresses importance of pushing on'
The Offensive Stalls, 3-5 September

I never thought we would get out alive when they caught us on the forward slope ...

Captain A H J Andrews, 3 September 1918[1]

At 10 minutes to Zero Hour on 3 September, Lieutenant Colonel Davies of the 44th Battalion noticed something gravely disquieting. The neighbouring British battalion was falling back when it was supposed to attack alongside his unit. On learning from them that the Corps had postponed the attack four and a half hours earlier, he sent his runners to prevent the massacre resulting from his companies advancing unsupported. They reached the companies just as they started, but surprisingly there was no German response. The day before, the Corps had driven the *II Bavarian Korps* from the D-Q Line. But it was just the first of the offensive's four objectives for that day. Currie's Corps would have to resume the assault, but much depended on the enemy's reaction. The next stage revolved around the Canadian Corps' ability to promptly deliver another strong blow despite its exhausted state and the German's decision whether to remain or retire. The Corps would have to overcome the inertia of a great victory, over 4,300 casualties, bone-weary staff, commanders, and troops, and serious disarray to make another effort. After their thrashing the previous day, the Germans too were staggering. Enormous numbers of prisoners and limited resistance at times showed a rot developing in the *II Bavarian Korps*. Would they stand or run?

Planning

Currie believed the Germans were vulnerable to a quick coordinated and artillery supported strike. His rationale was the Corps had just sliced through the D-Q Line and taken many prisoners from multiple formations – signs of a demoralised enemy. This chaotic mélange of units suggested the Germans were reacting desperately to the critical fracture in their line. Finally, the enemy had lost all their fixed fortifications other than on the right front of the 1st

1 'Andrews Diary' 3 September 1918.

Division. They held only weak shell-hole defences. Currie was also under considerable pressure from Horne to exploit the success based on Horne's orders. In a post-war article, Horne's MGGS critiqued the Corps for not taking aggressive steps to ensure its divisions launched a pursuit. He wanted a 'ruthless exploitation of success in battle.'[2] Horne, Anderson, and Currie were correct that the Germans were staggering, but so was the Corps. The 1st Canadian and 4th British Divisions were entering their fifth and sixth days of continuous action and all levels were dog-tired. Watson's division had suffered serious casualties. With its units badly scrambled in the fighting and with two brigades overlaid on each other, they needed time to reorganise. Finally, as Anderson acknowledged, the Corps believed that it had done enough.

Currie issued his orders at 6:00 p.m. on 2 September to resume the offensive across the Corps' front in the morning with the objective of gaining the Green Line and Étaing.[3] Currie did little to enforce his directive for coordinated action across the Corps. While Currie wanted a synchronised operation, Anderson in his post-war article strongly suggested the divisional commanders could not agree on a harmonised barrage.[4] Each formation made its own provisions, with the 4th British Division delegating artillery arrangements down to its brigades to organise.[5] Currie's order had no instructions to be on alert for a German retreat, thus showing the Corps did not expect one. This was a serious oversight, although it was unlikely the dog-tired commanders and troops would have aggressively kept in contact. Next, the order was less aggressive and more realistic than the D-Q Line plan, with only the Green Line as an objective. It reflected the weariness of the troops, the lack of time for artillery preparation, and the absence of tanks. Currie kept the 1st British Division in reserve. Having it replace the 4th British would delay the operation, and time was of the essence. Another factor was the advantage of having a fresh division to reinforce success and bull its way across the canal. While the 4th Canadian Division anticipated tank support, the Corps ordered that all the tanks were to withdraw and assemble under the command of the 3rd Tank Brigade.[6] Given the heavy losses, crew exhaustion, and distance from the rally points to the front, there was no chance they could take part.

Finally, the 1st Division made no provision to attack and its actions were consistent with a defensive posture.[7] Macdonell's lack of action was perplexing. Although the division was ahead of the 4th Canadian Division by the end of 2 September, it was still well short of the Green Line. Furthermore, by not attacking would expose the other two divisions to the concentrated firepower of the defenders and flanking fire. Likely, Macdonell figured his formation had done enough and was in no state to attack again.

2 LAC: Breaking the Quéant-Drocourt Line, p.126.
3 TNA: WO 95-1053-3: Canadian Corps General Staff War Diary, G.944, 2 September 1918.
4 LAC: Breaking the Quéant-Drocourt Line, p.126.
5 TNA: 4th British Div GS WD, Narrative of Operations of 4th Division from 26 August to 4th September 1918.
6 For instance, the 14th Tank Battalion commander ordered his surviving tanks to pull back to Wancourt on the night of 2 September 1918. TNA: 14th Tank Battalion War Diary, Report on the Operations of September 2nd, in co-operation with the 1st Canadian Division; LAC: 10th Brigade WD, 10th Brigade Narrative of Operations Battle of Arras, 14 September 1918; TNA: Cdn. Corps GS WD, Canadian Corps G.949, 2 September 1918.
7 LAC: 1st Brigade Report 28 August-1 September.

The multiple issues with this order suggest a breakdown in the Corps' ability to respond to the demanded tempo. Its staff, commanders, and troops were on the eighth straight day of continuous operations, and the command system was breaking down. Commanders and staff worked around the clock as witnessed by the orders issued at all hours of the night. The result was an exhausted command structure unable to sustain a high cadence.

4th Canadian Division

Watson's division, critical to the action, did not receive Currie's order until 7:15 p.m. 2 September – giving it little preparation time. Watson selected 5:00 a.m. as Zero Hour, likely to give as much daylight as possible. The 11th and 10th Brigades would advance on a front of three battalions (102nd, 54th, 87th) and two battalions (46th and 44th) respectively. Given the problems with signals, Watson sent Panet, his GSO 1, to each brigade commander to explain the scheme. What he learned was that they opposed it because of their weakened units, defender's strength, and lack of preparation time. This was obviously a surprise to Watson and his staff, indicating their inadequate situational understanding. Panet convinced Watson that their objections had merit. The divisional commander persuaded Currie that his formation needed time to recover.[8]

At 12:20 a.m., Currie, after getting Horne's permission, postponed the attack for a day.[9] One of the Corps commanders' strengths was his willingness to listen to his subordinates. He still wanted Matheson to take Étaing, if it was feasible. Also, the order enjoined, 'Close touch will be kept with the enemy and he must be followed up at once if he commences to withdraw.' The Corps issued this order too late as, by the time it reached most front-line units, it was almost dawn.

How this postponement reached the troops illustrated the ramshackle and unpredictable state of communications across all combatants. The 4th Canadian Division received the cancellation with little delay. Its 11th Brigade's battalions got the news with time to spare – not so with the 10th Canadian and 11th British Brigades. At 10:00 p.m., Hayter was on the line with Panet when a shell severed the line in mid-conversation. The divisional signal company could not restore it until the morning. As a result, the brigade did not receive Currie's order until 4:30 a.m., only 30 minutes before Zero Hour. Hayter got an inkling of the cancellation through the artillery channels but could not get confirmation. He cancelled the attack on his own authority an hour before the official notice arrived.[10] With the lines so poor to the battalions, Hayter's notice only reached the 46th Battalion shortly after Zero Hour. Davies. on learning from the British of the postponement, had to rush to stop his companies advancing. One company

8 LAC: 10th Brigade WD, 10th Brigade Narrative of Operations Battle of Arras, 14 September 1918; LAC: 44th Battalion War Diary, Report on Operations, Midnight 1/2 to Midnight 3/4 Sept. 1918.

9 TNA: Cdn. Corps GS WD, Canadian Corps G.958, 2 September 1918; Edmonds, *Military Operations, 1918* 4, p.416.

10 LAC: 10th Brigade WD, 10th Brigade Narrative of Operations Battle of Arras, 14 September 1918; LAC: 44th Battalion War Diary, Report on Operations, Midnight 1/2 to Midnight 3/4 Sept. 1918; LAC: 46th Battalion War Diary, 46th Bn Report on Operations September 2nd-4th 1918 Inclusive; LAC: Timetable Scarpe Operation; TNA: 11th Br Bde WD, 1st Rifle Brigade Account of Operations at Arras August 28th - September 2nd 1918; TNA: 4th British Div GS WD, Narrative of Operations of 4th Division from 26 August to 4th September 1918.

Lieutenant Colonel R D Davies commanding the 44th Battalion belatedly found out about the postponement of the attack on 3 September. This was an example of the difficulty of distributing orders in a timely fashion. (Canada. Dept. of National Defence/Library and Archives Canada/ PA-007009)

received the halt instruction 10 minutes after Zero Hour. The lack of a barrage and movement by other units must have puzzled them.

The answer to the first major chapter question was that the Corps could not launch another powerful blow. Macdonell's division made no preparations to attack, and Watson pushed back hard against making the effort. The result was a postponed operation that would leave the Corps having to wait another day. Horne did not like the delay. He issued his own directive at 8:00 a.m. stating he 'impresses importance of pushing on to secure high ground overlooking crossing over SENSEE and CANAL DU NORD before enemy has time to reorganise.'[11] Both Horne and Anderson believed that the commanders should have compelled their subordinates to attack as it would have brought great dividends. Had Currie been a professional officer leading a professional army, Horne's and Anderson's complaints may have had merit. The Corp's leaders could drive the troops hard but not that hard. Even if Currie had ordered the operation to proceed despite Watson's objections, it would not have mattered. By 5:00 a.m., the Germans had already retreated over the canal.

11 TNA: Cdn. Corps GS WD, First Army G.197, 3 September 1918.

Dellmensingen's Decision

With no answer to a 'fire-roller' barrage leading an infantry and tank assault, the *II Bavarian Korps*' situation was precarious, verging on disastrous. Of the six divisions at the start of 2 September, only the *1st GRD* had a semblance of battle-readiness. The Canadian Corps had reduced the other five to broken fragments, barely able to muster a battalion's strength with low morale. Further, except on the Baralle sector, the *II Bavarian Korps* had lost all the fortifications held in the morning. Dellmensingen had to expect another combined arms operation the next morning. The Canadians had done so on the last seven of eight days. If the *II Bavarian Korps* could not hold with strong fortifications and more troops, it was unlikely it would do so with battered forces and weak defences. The elements of two divisions reinforcing von Dellmensingen could not replace the massive losses already suffered. To remain in position risked the loss of all the artillery deployed west of the canal. The *Korps* was in no condition to retake the D-Q Line, so the only viable option was to withdraw.

Given the defeat's extent, *OHL* had little choice but to agree to a request from the army group and *Seventeenth Armee* to fall back. It ordered a large-scale retreat behind the Canal du Nord south to Peronne to take place overnight.[12] Dellmensingen's major concern was that the Canadians would try to rush the German positions.[13] It was imperative to withdraw overnight before the Canadians responded. Dellmensingen really did not have much to worry about. The Canadian Corps was so focused on its own problems that only one battalion sent out a patrol that found nothing untoward.[14] Currie and his staff did not take the actions that suggested they anticipated the Germans would retreat. As a result, the Germans disengaged successfully and pulled back across the canal with no interference. German pioneers blew up all the bridges except for one narrow wooden bridge in the 1st Division sector. This rendered any crossing unlikely.[15]

The *63rd IR* of the newly arrived *12th ID* crossed over the canal and held a bridgehead at Marquion while the forward forces retired.[16] On the British front, the *214th RIR* of the *4th EzD* pulled out at 12:30 a.m., without the British noticing their retirement.[17] The *2nd GrR* on the 1st Division sector provided the rearguard for the remnants of the *3rd RD* to cross over the canal unmolested. It left covering detachments that maintained the appearance that they were still defending the lines.[18] In the centre, the *1st GRR* pulled back at 1:00 a.m. with no interference.[19]

How the Corps discovered the withdrawal highlights a peculiar aspect of command in the war. Instead of the expected information flow from the front back, the middle echelon of brigades and divisions were the last to know. The Corps had access to reports from the Corps Survey Section and aircraft that were more immediate than through its subordinates. Dawn

12 Bundesarchive, Freiburg: Herman Von Kuhl Kriegserinnerungen, p.188.
13 Bundesarchiv, Freiburg: Feldzug 1918, 3 September 1918.
14 LAC: 11th Bde WD, 87th Battalion, Narrative of Operations on September 2nd, 3rd, and 4th., 1918, 6 September 1918.
15 LAC: 1st Div GS WD, 3 September 1918.
16 Franz Kaiser, *Das Konigl. Preuss. Infanterie Regiment Nr. 63 (4. Oberschlesisches)* (Berlin: Verlag Bernard & Graefe, 1940), p.226.
17 Bastanier, *Geschichte RIR 214*, p.421.
18 Gottberg, *Grenadier-Regiment Nr. 2*, p.458.
19 Brederlow, *1st Garde-Reserve-Regiments*, p.317.

contact aircraft patrols described a lack of activity suggesting the enemy had departed.[20] Based on RAF observation flights, the Third Army also communicated to GHQ in the morning that the Germans had retreated.[21] Battalions noticed the absence of fire, movement, and action on the other side and investigated. In trench warfare conditions, more responsibility switched to the Corps because it was better informed than the divisions. In open warfare, control shifted back to the divisions, but having to rely on delayed, inaccurate, and incomplete information from their subordinates handicapped them. Other than the 1917 German withdrawal after Vimy Ridge to the Oppy-Méricourt Line, the Corps had little experience in dealing with a retreating enemy.[22]

Strategic and Flanking Forces Situation 3-5 September

With the breaking of the D-Q Line and a German retreat, Haig on 3 September had a crucial decision. Should he continue to force the offensive or was it time to take a breather? While he did order his armies to press enemy rearguards, he also decided to not undertake large-scale deliberate operations in the near-term. Army commanders were to rest their troops, improve their communications, and conserve their resources.[23] On the Third Army's front, its centre and right wing were to maintain pressure on the enemy and 'take advantage of any opportunity for advancing.'[24] They found the enemy had retired, and they pushed towards the canal. The Fourth Army spent the day in rest and preparations for an assault crossing of the Somme along its front, while the French made only minor gains. On 4 September, the 63rd (Royal Naval) Division attempted to storm the canal with a single battalion. Not surprisingly, the Germans repulsed it. The 63rd blamed the failure on the Canadians on its left and the Guards Division on its right for being too far back. It was unlikely, however, that a single battalion action would have succeeded under any circumstances. This effort was far less than what First Army stated was the intent in its instructions to the Canadian Corps.[25] Other than minor actions, the Allies did not undertake any large-scale operations after this period until the resumption of the major offensive later in September.[26]

1st Division

Overnight 2-3 September, the 1st Division covered its front with only three battalions. Thus, the German retreat caught it at a disadvantage in comparison with the 4th Canadian and British Divisions. On the right, the 1st Brigade had relieved the exhausted 3rd Brigade that night. The 4th Battalion took over the entire sector with the 2nd Battalion in support. Heavy enemy fire

20 TNA: Cdn. Corps GS WD, 3 September 1918.
21 TNA: WO 158-227: Third Army GB 114, 3 September 1918.
22 Mike Bechthold, 'In the Shadow of Vimy Ridge the Canadian Corps in April and May 1917,' in Geoffrey Hayes, Andrew Iarocci, and Mike Bechthold, (ed.), *Vimy Ridge: A Canadian Reassessment* (Waterloo, Ont.: Wilfrid Laurier University Press, 2007).
23 TNA: WO 158-227: GHQ OAD 915, 3 September 1918.
24 Quoted in Edmonds, *Military Operations, 1918* 4, pp.417-418.
25 TNA: Cdn. Corps GS WD, First Army G.217, 3 September 1918.
26 Edmonds, *Military Operations, 1918* 4, pp.437-442; LAC: RG9 III-D-3 v5072: XVII Corps War Diary Excerpts; Jerrold, *The Royal Naval Division*, pp.313-314.

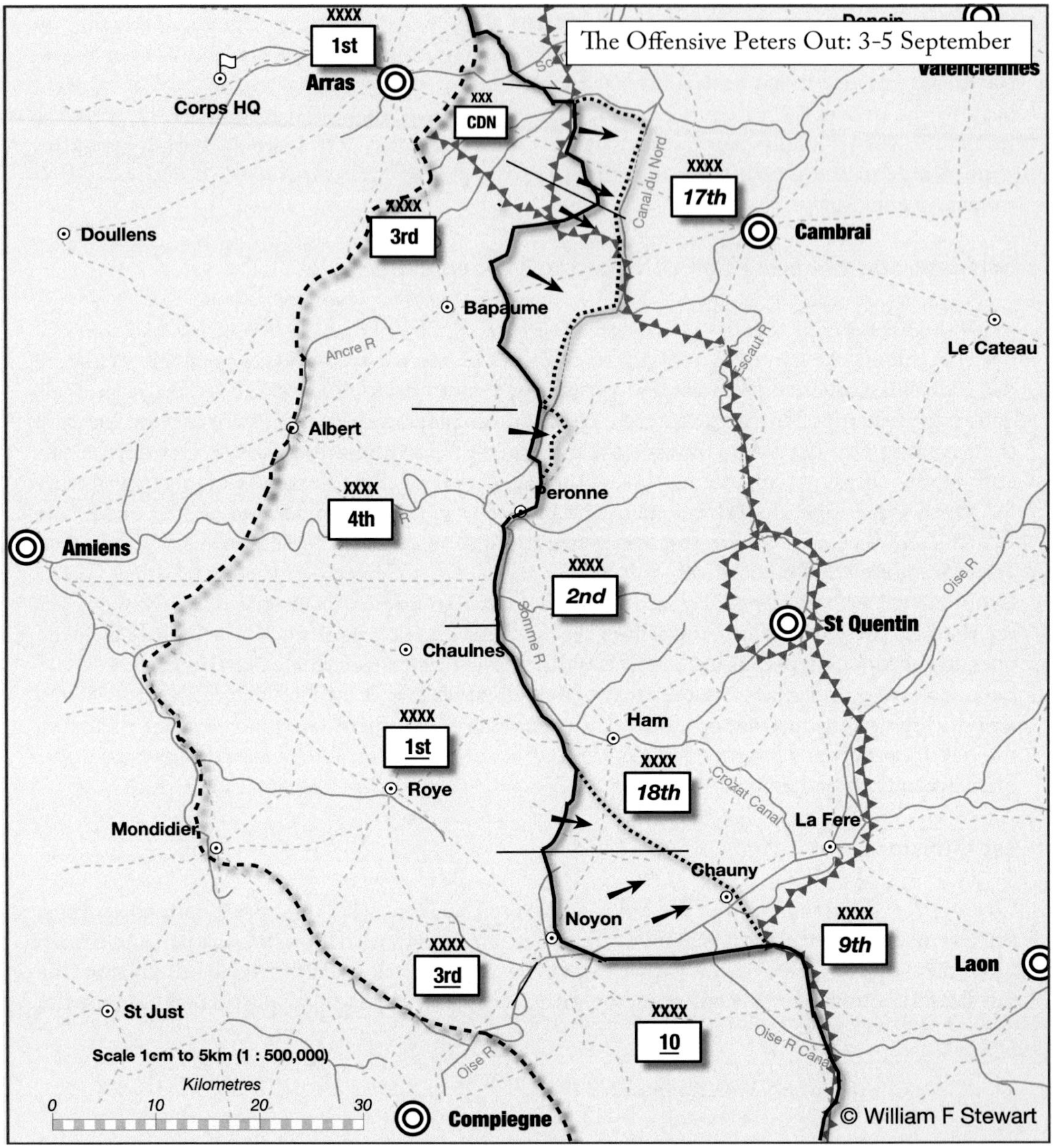

Map 34. The success of the Canadian Corps unhinged the German line and forced Ludendorff to order his forces to fall back across the Canal du Nord. To the south, the French made major gains east of Noyon. (Author's map)

hit the 4th Battalion overnight as the Germans were using up their ammunition and covering their retreat. The unit did not notice the drop in enemy activity. At 9:00 a.m., the battalion received orders to send out patrols, but machine gun fire from covering detachments from the *2nd GrR* stopped them. It then received orders first to take the remaining positions of Buissy Switch and another order to clear the ground to the canal.[27] The battalion did not move until the afternoon, and the Germans had set into their defences on the other side of the canal. They opened a heavy fire when the 4th crossed over the high ground east of the switch. It drifted to the left, and Griesbach ordered the 2nd Battalion to fill it. The 4th reached the canal by 6:50 p.m. The brigade commander noted much confusion on the German side of the canal as 'parties of enemy Machine Gunners, trudging stolidly forward to the Canal Bank, apparently oblivious to the retirement going on about them.'[28] Despite this turmoil, the 4th could not cross the canal when ordered to do so. Its losses were 1 officer and 53 men on 3-4 September in occupying terrain already abandoned, which was a steep price to pay.[29]

Originally in support, the 2nd Battalion moved to maintain touch with the British on the right. Like the 4th, hostile fire hit the 2nd hard as it crossed down the slope from Buissy Switch. The unit could only approach the canal by using section rushes. The enemy easily repulsed an attempt to rush a narrow wooden bridge covered by Lewis Gun fire. They could not develop the firepower necessary to suppress the enemy. Again, the lack of dedicated heavy machine guns limited Canadian infantry. The 2nd took 12 prisoners and one gun but lost 7 officers and 103 men wounded. This was an even steeper price than the 4th paid for taking over an abandoned enemy position.[30]

On the division's left, the 2nd Brigade's 10th Battalion protected the right, and the 8th guarded the long-left flank along the Arras-Cambrai road. The forward battalions sent out patrols in the morning of 3 September to find the enemy gone. Interestingly, the brigade war diary claimed this was in accordance with the previous evening's operation order, but the order did not say that.[31] The diarist tried to bury the fact the Germans caught the brigade napping. At 9:30 a.m., Loomis instructed both forward battalions to press on, but they took their time. The 10th did not reach the canal until about 5:00 p.m. – a rate of advance of half a kilometre an hour. This indicated how exhausted were the troops and their leaders. The battalion met heavy German fire when it crossed over the railway embankment running parallel to the canal. According to Captain Andrews: 'I never thought we would get out alive when they caught us on the forward slope of the hill above the canal.'[32] Despite the precautions, the battalion still lost 4 officers and 72 men on 3 September.[33]

The 8th Battalion was tired. It had expected a quiet morning, given there were two uncommitted battalions in the brigade. Instead, Loomis ordered it to advance along the Arras-Cambrai road

27 LAC: 1st Brigade War Diary, 1st Brigade G.1-8, 3 September 1918; LAC: 1st Brigade War Diary, 1st Brigade G.2-8, 3 September 1918.
28 LAC: 1st Brigade Report 28 August-1 September.
29 LAC: 4th Bn. WD, 3 September 1918; LAC: 4th Bn Report, 28 August-1 September.
30 LAC: 2nd Battalion WD, 3 September 1918; LAC: 2nd Bn Report 28 August-1 September.
31 LAC: 2nd Brigade War Diary, 3 September 1918 and OO 315, 2 September 1918.
32 'Andrews Diary' 3 September 1918.
33 LAC: RG9 III-C-3 v4052, 22/6: Narrative of Operations Carried out by the 10th Canadian Battalion from 28-81918 to 4-9-18, 6 September 1918; LAC: 2nd Brigade War Diary, 3 September 1918 and 2nd Brigade Narrative of Operations East of Arras August 25 to September 3, 1918.

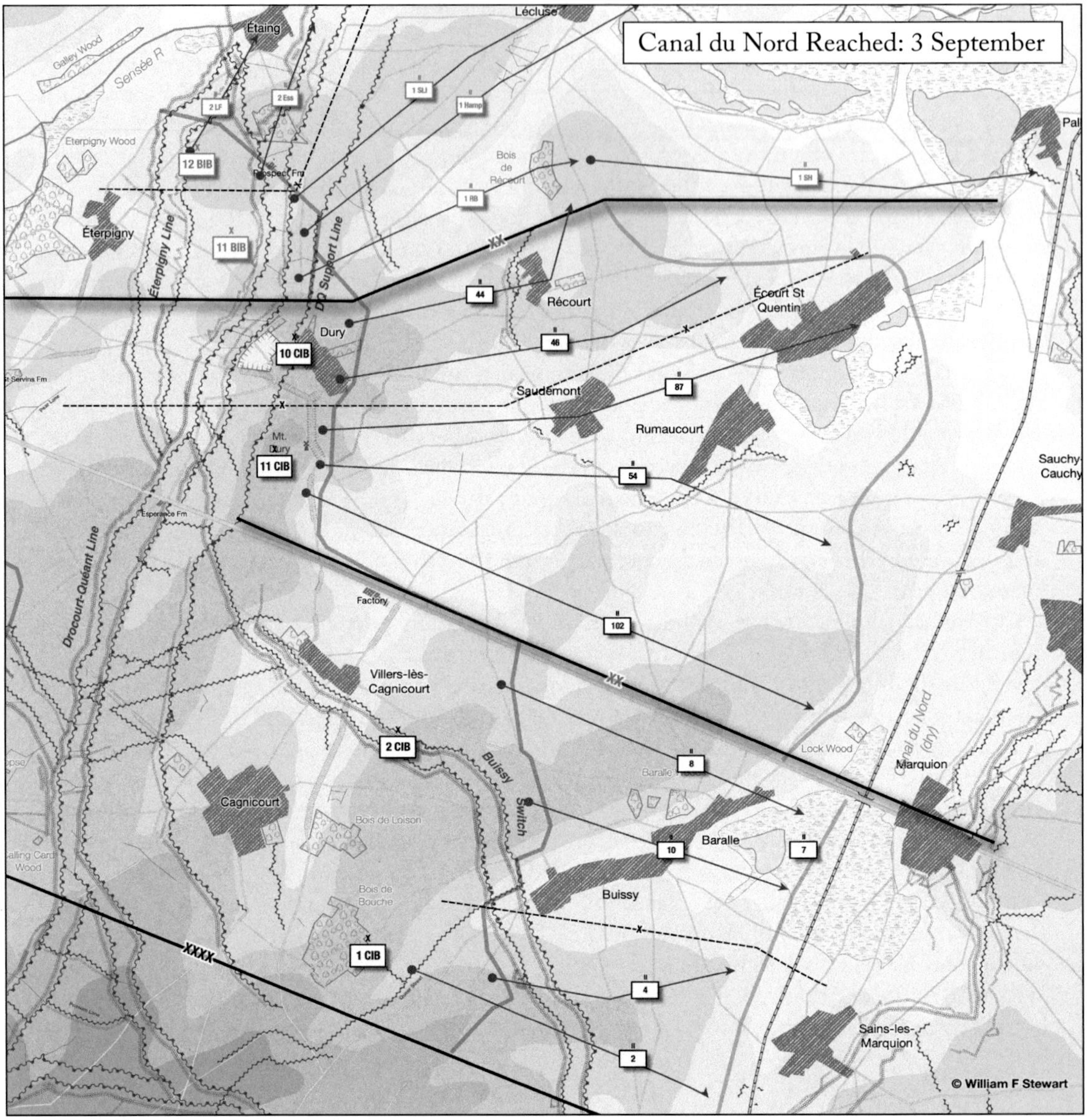

Map 35. The Canadian Corps' advance on the Canal du Nord after the Germans retired. (Author's map)

to the canal. Judging from the subtext of the diary entry, this additional assignment annoyed the 8th. Two companies sent out patrols while the battalion signallers scrambled to find enough wire to maintain communications. One advantage of a successful operation was the capture of enemy stores. In this case, three kilometres of captured German signalling wire fulfilled the purpose, and the headquarters could move and remain in touch with the brigade. When the battalion crossed the crest of the spur north of Baralle, heavy German fire sprayed it all the way to the canal. In the advance, the battalion lost 1 officer and 48 men.[34]

Initially Loomis was unsure of what the Germans were doing, so he took the precaution of directing the 7th Battalion to move up to support the 8th and 10th Battalions. It took over the front with two companies but found the position forward of the railway embankment terrible. The troops were exposed to heavy enemy fire and much of the ground was wet, marshy terrain where it was hard to find shelter. The 7th was only in the line for a short time before the 2nd Division's 31st Battalion relieved it overnight.[35] Its casualties were relatively light at 19 all ranks, as a result.

4th Canadian Division

Watson's division was in a better posture to respond to the German retreat. Early in the morning, the Corps passed on an RAF report about a lack of activity on the enemy front. Surprisingly, Watson did not order an immediate advance but waited until later in the afternoon before doing so.[36] Generally, the units at the front noticed the lack of movement in the German lines and lack of response to the movement and preparations for the dawn attack. They sent out patrols that found the enemy trenches abandoned. Once reported up the chain of command, the brigades ordered their units to push to the Green Line. Like the 1st Division, German fire repeatedly hit the 4th Canadian Division's battalions when spotters observed their movement from the high ground east of the canal. The enemy had particularly good views from the ridge spur where the village of Oisy-le-Verger sat. It was near a German artillery concentration, so fire was quickly and effectively brought to bear on the Canadian advance.

On the division's right, the 11th Brigade learned of the attack's cancellation well in time, so stood down by dawn. On the right, the 102nd Battalion relieved the 78th overnight and was still setting in when ordered to advance along the Arras-Cambrai road. They had to pick their way through scattered bodies of horses, mules, and knocked out armoured cars. They reached a line short of the canal by nightfall. In the centre, the 54th advanced cautiously on the front of a single company and pushed to within 1,000 metres of the canal by nightfall. In its move east, it met the Corps' first liberated French citizens from the nearby town of Rumaucourt. On the right, the 87th sent out its scouts again, who reported the ground clear all the way to Saudemont. The unit advanced on a one-company front to minimise losses and pushed on through Saudemont

34 LAC: 8th Bn WD, Narrative of Events-Phase II [September 1918]; LAC: 2nd Brigade War Diary, 3 September 1918 and 2nd Brigade Narrative of Operations East of Arras August 25 to September 3, 1918.

35 LAC: 7th Battalion War Diary, 3 September 1918 and Narrative of Operations from 28th August to 4th September, 1918.

36 LAC: 4th Canadian Div WD, 4th Canadian Division Report on Operations Scarpe, Sept. 2nd - 4th, 1918.

and took Écourt-St-Quentin on the Green Line by the early afternoon. Heavy fire stymied its efforts to reach the canal. German artillery pounded all three battalions but, as they had not gained ground as close to the canal as the 1st Division, their losses were fewer.[37]

Shortly before 8:00 a.m., Panet called the 10th Brigade to send out patrols as the 4th British Division had reported the Germans had left. The forward battalions also noticed the lack of activity and sent out scouts. Hayter's brigade-major went to meet the four-battalion commanders to plan. The 46th and 44th would press to the Green Line with the 47th and 50th to support, but at a distance. The 46th Battalion advanced in an open artillery formation to reduce casualties from shelling. It reached the Green Line by 12:40 p.m. after a move of five and half kilometres. The 44th on the left found Récourt empty, and it was a short push to reach the Green Line by noon. Curiously, the unit reported it anchored its line in the Bois de Récourt, which was in the British sector. Issues of boundaries continued to bedevil the actions of the two divisions. Both battalions sent out patrols and discovered the canal strongly defended. The 46th and 44th Battalions lost 106 and 45 all ranks respectively for occupying ground already abandoned by the enemy. Shockingly, the 47th and 50th Battalions that trailed the advance lost 80 and 45 men to enemy artillery fire. The German gunners were active and would open up on individuals.[38]

4th British Division

At 2:00 a.m., Matheson's division finally received Currie's postponement.[39] As with the 10th Canadian Brigade, this cancellation only reached the forward units 15 minutes before they were to attack – some were already on the move. In the 1st SLI, the men were completely exhausted but formed up, regardless. Thus, they must have welcomed the cancellation.[40] In accordance with the Corps commander's wishes, Matheson decided that the 12th Brigade would proceed with its attack on Étaing. The 12th attacked with the 2nd Lancashire Fusiliers on the left and the 2nd Essex on the right. It met negligible resistance, and the brigade claimed 80 prisoners.[41]

On the 11th Brigade's front, the brigade-major, Captain Lester, noticed the enemy lines appeared to be very still and led out a patrol to find the Germans gone. His initiative allowed the 11th Brigade to get a jump on pursuit. The brigade hastily ordered its units to advance. They

37 LAC: 54th Battalion WD, Narrative of Operations Carried by the Battalion on the 2nd and 3rd September 1918 in the Second Battle of Arras; LAC: 87th Battalion War Diary, 3 September 1918; LAC: 11th Bde WD, 87th Battalion, Narrative of Operations on September 2nd, 3rd, and 4th., 1918, 6 September 1918; LAC: 102nd Battalion War Diary, 3 September 918; LAC: 11th Bde WD, 102nd Battalion Narrative of Operations From Morning September 2nd. to night September 5th, 1918, 7 September 1918; LAC: Timetable Scarpe Operation.

38 LAC: 46th Battalion War Diary, 3 September 1918 and 46th Battalion Report on Operations September 2nd-4th 1918 Inclusive; LAC: 44th Battalion War Diary, Report on Operations, Midnight 1/2 to Midnight 3/4 Sept. 1918; LAC: 10th Brigade WD, 10 Brigade Report on Operations, Midnight 1/2 to Midnight 3/4 Sept.1918.

39 TNA: 4th British Div GS WD, Narrative of Operations of 4th Division from 26 August to 4th September 1918.

40 TNA: 1st Somerset Light Infantry War Diary, 3 September 1918.

41 TNA: WO 95-1504-1/5: 12th British Brigade War Diary, 3 September 1918; TNA: WO 95-1057-1/4: 2nd Lancashire Fusiliers War Diary, 3 September 1918.

reached the Green Line by noon and took most of the Blue Line in the afternoon.[42] Their move did not attract the same attention from the Germans as did the Canadians. This was likely due to the enemy lacking full observation over the area and that they were still settling in.

Offensive Sputters Out: 4-5 September

Late on 3 September, Horne directed the Corps to advance the next day. He emphasised it was 'Important to secure crossings over the CANAL DU NORD.' If the Germans held the canal with only rearguards, the Canadians were to force them back and pursue towards Cambrai. The Third Army would continue to advance, with its XVII Corps slated to take Cambrai, so the Canadians had to support the attack.[43] As discussed, however, the Fergusson's effort comprised a single battalion thrust. To deal with this demand, Horne and Currie shuffled boundaries and divisions. The 1st British Division replaced the worn-out 4th British, which moved into First Army reserve. Burstall's division started replacing Macdonell's exhausted formation. Lipsett's division started moving into position to do the same for the 4th Canadian Division on the night of September 4/5.[44] The Corps issued orders that the divisions were to try to gain bridgeheads.[45] The 1st Brigade planned overnight an operation for an assault crossing supported by artillery and smoke. Macdonell convinced Currie to cancel because of German firepower dominating the slope down to the canal, as this would lead to heavy losses in storming across.[46]

Macdonell was not the only one raising concerns, as Watson again faced strong resistance from his brigade commanders. This demonstrated the disconnect between the front-line commanders and the Corps' senior leadership. Panet called to relay orders that the 10th Brigade was to assault across the canal. Hayter objected. He set up a three-way call with Odlum of the 11th Brigade and Panet to voice their opposition. This was the second consecutive day that Watson's brigadiers pushed back. Panet passed on the objections, and Watson relayed these concerns to Currie. In response, he postponed the operation until after the XVII Corps had secured crossings. Likely, he was dubious of Fergusson's corps' commitment to storm the canal. The assumption that the Germans were in headlong retreat was faulty, so any attempts to seize bridgeheads were certain to fail in this sector. Reports to the Corps showed the canal filled with four feet of water and that the enemy had destroyed or broken all the bridges. A sniper would later wound Odlum while he scouted his front to assess the situation.[47] There was no realistic opportunity for continuing the offensive. Even so, there were still small pockets of Germans holding out on along the canal. Eradicating them was the final task. In the process, the 102nd Battalion lost 2 officers and 50 men forcing out the enemy holding Lock Wood 500 metres north of the Arras-Cambrai road on the canal.

42 TNA: 11th Br Bde WD, Summary of Operations of the 11th Infantry Brigade between 28th August and 3rd September, 1918, 6 September 1918; TNA: 11th Br Bde WD, 3 September 1918.
43 TNA: Cdn. Corps GS WD, First Army G.217, 3 September 1918.
44 TNA: Cdn. Corps GS WD, 3-4 September 1918.
45 The timing of this order may be in error as a later order with a later sequence number was issued before this one. TNA: Cdn. Corps GS WD, 3-4 September 1918 and G.18, 4 September 1918.
46 LAC: 1st Div GS WD, 4 September 1918; LAC: 1st Brigade Report 28 August-1 September.
47 LAC: 11th Bde WD, 5 September 1918.

The offensive was over. Currie's Corps would remain in position guarding the canal front while giving up the 1st British Division sector to the XXII Corps at midnight on 4/5 September. On 19 September in preparation for the next major offensive, the Corps slid south to a sector more suited to an assault crossing. On 27 September, the Canadian Corps undertook a daring operation to seize crossings over the Canal du Nord on a narrow front. Despite Horne's concerns over the plan's audacity, the Corps carried it off, finally seizing Bourlon Wood.

Section Five

Analysis

14

Analysis

You broke the line and got through; the whole thing was simply magnificent.

Douglas Haig to Macdonell, 2 September 1918[1]

Arras 1918 was eight days of continuous, brutal, and costly fighting until the Germans had no choice but to pull back across the canal. In the battle, the Corps launched 83 contested battalion attacks, with 67 carried out by Canadian units and 16 by British ones. This was 10 more than the Canadians launched in the 89 days they served on the Somme in 1916, thus testifying to the increased intensity of combat in the Hundred Days campaign. This chapter analyses the battle through its outcomes, casualties, and commanders. It starts with a comparison with Amiens to establish the degree to which Arras differed from the campaign's opening battle of the campaign. The engagement provides a unique lens on the conduct of battles in the early stages of the Hundred Days. It enables an evaluation of the relative contribution of different weapon systems and their effects on casualties. This forms the basis for the assessment of the primary reasons for the Corps' success in the conclusion.

Amiens-Arras 1918 Comparison

The great success of Amiens made it the gold-standard for the Hundred Days campaign, while Arras has the deserved reputation for hard-slogging.[2] Comparing the two reveals the differences were not so stark. Casualties were half again as great at Arras than at Amiens, but Arras had more days of active fighting. Based on active fighting days, the losses per day were slightly lower at Arras. On the same basis, Amiens had roughly one-third more prisoners per day than Arras. This reflected the operational surprise, massive tank support, weak defences, and a large-scale attack featuring two elite assault corps, plus British and French formations. These were factors absent at Arras 1918 and this after the 11,882 Canadian casualties of Amiens. The Corps took more guns at Amiens, because the Germans pulled much of their field artillery out of harms'

1 LAC: Macdonell Biography, 175.

2 For instance, Tim Cook's chapter titles for the Arras campaign include 'Hard Pounding', 'Hammer and tongs fighting' and 'It was murder to move and suicide to stay put.' Cook, *Shock Troops*, p.vii.

Tanks at Amiens advancing through a field. Tanks played a much larger role at Amiens than at Arras 1918 because of the numbers available. (Canada. Dept. of National Defence/Library and Archives Canada/PA-002879)

way and the Arras advance rate was slower. The result was fewer pieces taken but with less effective gunnery support for the German infantry. In contrast, the Corps seized a quarter more machine guns at Arras. These numbers represent the extent to which the Germans reinforced the sector. The key difference between the two battles' outcomes was that the first day at Amiens was so successful. In ground gained; the two battles were similar. This is especially so given that almost 60 percent of the gains at Amiens occurred on the opening day. Overall, the two battles' outcomes were broadly comparable.

Table 14.1 Amiens 1918 and Arras 1918 Comparison

	Amiens 8-14 August 1918*	Arras 26 August - 3 September 1918†
Days	7	9
Active Days‡	4	7
Casualties	11,822	17,587
Casualties/Active Day	2,956	2,512
Prisoners	9,074	10,514
Prisoners/Active Day	2,269	1,502
Guns taken	201	123
Machine guns taken	755	927
Penetration depth (Km)	22.5	21.5
Territory liberated (Km^2)	174	189

Sources

* Tim Cook, *Shock Troops: Canadians Fighting the Great War, 1917-1918* (Toronto: Viking Canada, 2008), pp.450-451; G.W.L. Nicholson, *Canadian Expeditionary Force, 1914-1919* (Ottawa: R. Duhamel, Queen's Printer, 1964), p.419.

† LAC, RG24 v1884, GAQ 11-5, General Statistics, April 1920; LAC, RG9 III-D-2 v4810, Arras (Drocourt-Queant Line).

‡ Active Days = Days on which major offensive actions took place.

Outcomes

The study assessed each of the 83 battalion assaults on its characteristics and outcome. This study defines a battalion attack as one with an operations order in which half or more of the unit advanced and the enemy contested directly. Repeated actions conducted by the same battalion to fulfil its original order do not count. An attack on the same objective but with a new operation order counts. Each battalion engagement was then appraised considering over 40 factors including strength, frontage, types of support, and results in casualties, outcomes, and prisoners taken. There were four outcomes. 'Fully successful' meant a unit took substantially all of its objective. 'Partially successful' was where some of the objective fell. 'Initially successful' represented a success permanently lost to a German counterattack. 'Failure' meant the unit took no part of its objective. The study also considered the opposition, including the unit's faced, their contemporary effectiveness rating, and state, whether fresh, tired, or exhausted.

In comparison with the Somme 1916, the Canadians at Arras 1918 were far more effective. On the Somme, roughly two-thirds of battalion attacks had some success, either partial or fully successful, while at Arras 1918 this was four-fifths with a much higher proportion of full success. This illustrates the increasing effectiveness of Canadian infantry and support arms, even accounting for variations in the opposition's strength and the decreasing power of German counterattacks. While on the Somme 12 percent of attacks were initially successful, only one British and no Canadian ones were so at Arras.

Table 14.2 Success Comparison Arras 1918 and Somme 1916

	All Corps Attacks		British Attacks		Canadian Attacks		1916 Somme
	#	%	#	%	#	%	%
Full Success	47	57%	4	25%	43	64%	42%
Partial Success	19	23%	8	50%	11	16%	25%
Initial Success	1	1%	1	6%			12%
Failure	16	19%	3	19%	13	19%	21%
Total	**83**		**16**		**67**		

Arras 1918 featured a significantly higher operational tempo than in 1916/1917. This was evident by the number of battalion-level attacks conducted by the Corps at Arras 1918. On the Somme, the Canadians carried out 57 contested attacks over 89 days or fewer than one per day. At Arras 1918, the Corps averaged 10 such attacks per day with 8 of these by Canadian units – a 13-fold increase. It also resulted in a higher daily Canadian casualty total of 957 compared with 267 per day for the Somme.

Tanks raised the success rate – fully or partially – of Canadian attacks to 95 percent from the average of 81 percent. To simplify the discussion, success rates from here are the combination of fully and partially successful actions. Attacks that employed both smoke and a barrage with a density less than 30 metres per gun had an even greater effect. They increased success to 100 percent and at a lower cost in casualties than tanks. If the gun density decreased to 30 or more metres per 18-pounder the success rate dropped to 61 percent and casualty rate increased. Somewhat surprisingly, all three different support weapons resulted in a higher casualty rate than the average attack. Tanks were almost 50 percent more. The reason for this was the Corps would only commit tanks, a barrage, and smoke when it expected severe opposition and strong defences. The three weapons were successful in improving the odds of success, but because the Corps used them in the most difficult situations, battalion losses would inevitably be greater. Failure in all instances was more costly.

Table 14.3 Support Weapons' Outcomes for Canadian Battalion Attacks

	With Tanks			Without Tanks		
	#	%	Losses/Attack	#	%	Losses/Attack
Full or Partial Success	19	95%	206	35	74%	105
Failure	1	5%	295	12	26%	225
Total	**20**		**210**	**47**		**136**

	With Barrage			Without Barrage		
	#	%	Losses/Attack	#	%	Losses/Attack
Full or Partial Success	37	88%	166	17	68%	80
Failure	5	12%	250	8	32%	219
Total	**42**		**177**	**25**		**124**

	With Smoke			Without Smoke		
	#	%	Losses/Attack	#	%	Losses/Attack
Full or Partial Success	26	100%	165	28	68%	116
Failure				13	32%	230
Total	**26**		**165**	**41**		**152**

The Tank Corps committed 83 tanks to support the Canadian Corps on 26-27 August and 2 September, of which 32 rallied – meaning they returned to their assembly point.[3] Of these, enemy shells damaged three and carbon monoxide poisoned one crew. The rally rate was 39 percent, although the workshops would recover and return to service some of the others. Effectively for every 10 tanks employed only four would be usable in the next two days. Typically, crews needed 48 hours to recover from the enervating conditions of the vehicles. Thus, tanks packed a powerful punch packaged in a glass jaw.

3 LAC: CWNS 3rd Tank Brigade, Report on Operations with the Canadian Corps - 2nd September 1918, 18 September 1918; TNA: 9th Tank WD, August 1918; TNA: 14th Tank Bn History; TNA: 14th Tk. Bn. WD, August 1918.

A common fate of tanks at Arras 1918. Destroyed tank on its side in a trap near Monchy-le-Preux. The picture was taken in April/May 1919. (Canada. Dept. of National Defence/Library and Archives Canada/PA-004506)

Table 14.4 Tank Commitment and Loss Rate, Arras 1918

	Tanks Committed	Tanks Rallied	Rally Rate
26 August	13	4	31%
27 August	13	4	31%
2 September	57	24	42%
Total	**83**	**32**	**39%**

Successful attacks by Canadian battalions resulted in significantly lower losses. One consequence of failure was losses on average were almost double of those that fully succeeded.

Table 14.5 Average Casualties per Canadian Battalion Attack Outcome

	Number of Attacks	Average Casualties per Attack
Full Success	43	128
Partial Success	11	182
Failure	13	230
Total	**67**	**157**

The Corps destroyed nine German divisions, defeated a further two, and engaged elements of six more during Arras 1918. Destroyed meant the division was so shattered that it was no longer fit to remain in the line. One of the destroyed divisions was elite, four were average, and four were poor. Defeated referred to divisions that the Corps drove from their positions and inflicted heavy casualties on but that were still capable of further resistance. Engaged signified that the Corps encountered elements of these divisions.

Table 14.6 German Divisions Defeated

	Division	Classification		Division	Classification
Destroyed			**Defeated**		
	*26th RD**	Elite		*1st GRD*	Elite
	3rd RD	Average		*48th RD*	Average
	16th ID	Average	**Engaged**		
	35th ID	Average		*20th ID*	Elite
	*111th ID**	Average		12th ID	Elite
	214th ID	Poor		*7th SD*	Average
	*39th ID**	Poor		*58th ID*	Average
	4th EzD	Poor		*22nd ID*	Average
	2nd GRD	Poor			

*Two-thirds of division destroyed by the Canadian Corps, with the other third on the Third Army front.

Some of the 10,514 prisoners captured during Arras 1918 marching to the rear. Two of them near the front appear to be quite young, highlighting the perilous state of German manpower. (Canada. Dept. of National Defence/Library and Archives Canada/PA-003148)

The Corps captured 10,514 Germans during Arras 1918, including 1,023 wounded.[4] It took almost 70 percent of its total captives after 31 August. The ratio of 1 dead to 10 wounded to unwounded suggests many surrendered without fighting to the end. The Canadians also claimed the capture of 123 artillery pieces, 99 trench mortars, and 927 machine guns.[5] On the Somme 1916, the Canadian forces captured 2,094 prisoners. Thus, for every contested battalion attack the Corps took 3.4 times more prisoners at Arras 1918 than on the Somme.

4 LAC: RG9 III-C-1 v3855, 75/1: POW Statement, 16 September 1918; LAC: RG9 III-D-2 v4810: Arras (Drocourt-Queant Line).

5 LAC: Arras (Drocourt-Queant Line).

Table 14.7 Prisoners Captured 2 August-15 September 1918*

Period	Officers	Other Ranks	All Ranks
24-31 August	84	3,566	3,650
31 August - 15 September	139	5,702	5,841
Sub-Total	**223**	**9,268**	**9,491**
All Ranks Wounded			1,023
Total			**10,514**

Sources:
*LAC, RG9 III-C-1 v3855, 75/1, POW Statement, 16 September 1918.

Casualties

The casualty totals for the Canadian Corps at Arras 1918 conflict and at times mislead. Typically, historians report just Canadian casualties, but claim prisoners, trophies, and ground taken for the Corps, including British formations.[6] These forces composed over a third of the Corps in active operations at Arras 1918.[7] This section reports casualties for the entire Corps but will also examine the Canadian losses compared to the Corps' experience on the Somme in 1916.[8] The exact daily casualty figures for the Corps are difficult to determine now. They will be, of necessity, an approximation of the actual numbers. Wounded totals come from the report of the Corps' medical system.[9] This excludes those wounded who remained at duty. The daily total of those wounded includes men who received mortal wounds and who died later but not men who ended up in another corps' system. Fatal statistics are based on the CWGC database filtered for Canadian units, the 51st (Highland) and 4th British Divisions while they served with the Corps, and British field artillery units in the Corps.[10] The period runs from 26 August to 10 September for those who died in France. These dates capture the majority of those who survived their initial wounding but were ultimately to succumb. The cut-off date ensures only a minimum of casualties from subsequent engagements were included. It excludes those who died of their wounds in France after the cut-off date or those who subsequently died in England. These totals are not, however, believed to be significant. The totals of Canadians captured are from the listings in Wigney's *Guests of the Kaiser.*[11]

6 Nicholson, *CEF*, p.440; Cook, *Shock Troops*, p.497.
7 Each division's service at the front with the Corps during the period 26 August to 3 September gives a total of 25 divisions-days of which British divisions served for 9.
8 The totals for deaths were adjusted by adding the missing figure minus known prisoners into the death totals. LAC: RG24 v1884, GAQ 11-5: General Statistics, April 1920.
9 LAC: Mds Report.
10 'CWGC'.
11 Wigney, *Guests of the Kaiser*.

Attending to the wounded at a Casualty Clearing Station near Arras. (Canada. Dept. of National Defence/Library and Archives Canada/PA-040218)

Table 14.8 Casualty Comparisons

	Arras 1918 Canadian Casualties	Arras 1918 British Casualties	Arras 1918 Total	1916 Somme Canadian Casualties
Dead	2,929	625	3,554	8,096
Wounded	11,387	2,600	13,987	15,636
Captured*	33	13	46	296
Total	**14,349**	**3,238**	**17,587**	**24,028**

* Does not include Tank Corps totals

One striking aspect of the battle was the marked increase in the ratio of wounded to dead of 3.94 to 1 – higher was better. The average for the war was just under 2.9 wounded for every soldier who died.[12] At the Somme 1916, this total was approximately two wounded to every one killed owing to harsher conditions, a longer campaign, and fewer successes.[13] Another factor

12 Nicholson, *CEF*, p.548.
13 Stewart, *Neglected Campaign*, p.299.

was the greater effectiveness of German artillery on the Somme.[14] At Arras 1918, the improved ratio reflects the decline in enemy gunnery, as machine gun and rifle bullets were less likely to kill than shells.

Table 14.9 Ratios of Canadian Wounded to Dead

Arras 1918 Ratio Wounded - Dead	1916 Somme Ratio Wounded - Dead	1914-1918 Ratio Wounded - Dead*
3.94	1.93	2.90

Sources:
* G.W.L. Nicholson, *Canadian Expeditionary Force, 1914-1919* (Ottawa: R. Duhamel, Queen's Printer, 1964), p.548.

Another facet of the improved performance was that the Corps suffered both actually and as a percentage significantly fewer casualties for greater success than in 1916. On the Somme, each battalion attack resulted on average in almost 300 casualties, with an officer loss rate of 74 percent and 54 percent for other ranks. At Arras 1918, this average was just 157 with an officer loss rate of 37 percent and 25 percent for other ranks. With better results, therefore, the Corps halved its casualty rate for each attack outcome.

Table 14.10 Arras 1918 and Somme 1916 Loss Comparison per Battalion Attack

	Arras 1918 Losses/Attack						1916 Somme Losses/ Attack*	
	Corps		British Units		Canadian Units†		Canadian Units	
	#	%	#	%	#	%	#	%
Officers	7	36%	7	31%	7	37%	16	74%
Other Ranks	149	26%	152	30%	150	25%	295	54%

Sources:
* William F. Stewart, *The Canadians on the Somme, 1916: Canada's Neglected Campaign* Wolverhampton Military Studies (Solihull, West Midlands, England: Helion, 2017), pp.297-299.
† Includes two attacks by the CIF

The losses were not, however, evenly distributed. On average, the 4th Division's battalions had an 80 percent higher loss rate than the other three Canadian divisions. There can be no question of the courage and fortitude of its troops, only the plan that put them in a situation of having to

14 Stewart, *Neglected Campaign*, pp.94-95, 285.

fight a dense mesh of machine guns almost unaided. This is further evidence that the Germans could inflict a costly defeat on the Canadians if the Corps did not use the right attack method.

Table 14.11 Average All Ranks Loss per Battalion by Canadian Division

	Arras 1918 AR Losses	Arras 1918 % Loss	Arras 1918 Number of Attacks
1st Division	149	24%	15
2nd Division	145	24%	20
3rd Division	128	21%	19
4th Division	259	38%	11
CIF	57	8%	2
Totals	**157**	**25%**	**67**

A great difference between the Somme 1916 and Arras 1918 was the significantly lower percentage of fatalities with no known grave. Whereas on the Somme, where 55 percent of fatal casualties were missing, this percentage was just under 14 percent at Arras.[15] This sharp decline in missing was due to greater success, a shorter campaign, fewer German shells, and better weather.

The Canadian Corps' infantry still paid the primary cost in deaths in the fighting, although slightly less than on the Somme. The major changes were an increase in the percentage of artillery and machine gunner fatalities as a whole. For the infantry and machine guns, the loss rate in comparison to their nominal strength declined significantly. In the infantry's case it dropped to almost a third of the rate at the Somme 1916.[16] Despite the reduced effectiveness of the German artillery, the more open warfare exposed gunners to more counter-battery and direct fire. This resulted in more deaths. Unlike on the Somme in 1916 where the machine gunners primarily fired indirect barrages or were in defensive positions, the machine guns were more active at Arras 1918. They were more exposed in the open warfare conditions and paid accordingly. Their loss rate was 3.6 times that of the Somme.

15 Stewart, *Neglected Campaign*, p.299.
16 This was calculated by multiplying the war establishment by the number of units of that type for the total of infantry and machine gunners.

Table 14.12 Canadian Fatalities by Arm 1916 and 1918[17]

	Arras 1918			Somme 1916		
	Deaths	**Percent**	**Percent of War Establishment**	**Deaths**	**Percent**	**Percent of War Establishment**
Infantry	2,987	87.5%	5.8%	7,543	93.2%	16.3%
Artillery	158	4.6%		208	2.6%	
Engineers	79	2.3%		173	2.1%	
Machine Guns	137	4.0%	2.0%	88	1.1%	3.2%
Misc.	51	1.5%		84	1.0%	
Total	**3,412**			**8,096**		

Commander Assessment

An important factor shaping the outcome of the campaign was the commanders' performance, from Haig down to the brigade GOCs. After four years of struggle, the Corps had generated a strong cadre of experienced and capable leaders. Their experience, however, was in the deliberate operations of 1916/1917. Not all could meet the new demands of open warfare, although most did.

At the most senior level of the BEF, Haig had improved as an operational commander. He would now shift the offensive to another sector rather than futilely prolonging an attack. He, also, trusted his army commanders to a greater degree and would listen when they advised stopping. Haig, however, still had weaknesses. For all his merits as a strategic and national force commander, he had a limited understanding of the factors of time, space, and enemy actions. This handicapped his operational command. He repeatedly underestimated the German Army's resiliency. He was right that Allies could defeat the Germans in 1918, but they did not collapse as Haig expected but instead were worn down. This was particularly the case with the operations at Arras 1918, where his expectations of the Canadians were unrealistic. Haig issued a general directive on 23 August admitting there would be a long, difficult battle to break through the enemy's line, but once through the pursuit must be vigorous.[18] The depth of the German defences and the capacity of even small bands of machine gunners to impede progress ensured this possibility never existed in the Canadian sector.

Related to his poor appreciation of the true conditions at the front was his continued attempts to foist the Cavalry Corps on the Canadians. It was apparent by both Byng's and Horne's actions that neither wanted the encumbrance. Both struggled to supply their forward forces, and the cavalry divisions would make it worse. Squadrons of cavalry positioned close to the front could

17 'CWGC'; Stewart, *Neglected Campaign*, p.300.
18 TNA: WO 158-227: OAD 912, GHQ to Armies, 23 August 1918.

have had tactical utility, but there was no opportunity for large bodies. Haig's generals, even a cavalry general like Byng, realised this but not the C-in-C.

His greatest error was when realigning the boundary between Horne's and Byng's army, he did not assign more forces to the Canadians. The Corps had too extended a front to meet Haig's demands in a timely fashion. His claim to Foch that the Corps had ample strength indicated he believed the Canadians were strong enough. By the GHQ's doctrine, the Corps had insufficient manpower and guns – more on this in the conclusion. He badly underestimated the task he set. Only belatedly did he realise that Currie had too wide a sector and inserted the XXII Corps. Even with its front significantly reduced, the Canadians lacked the forces to take on the D-Q Line and cross the canal. They needed more artillery and at least one extra division. Haig did not have the extra divisions and artillery that the Corps needed. Thus, he should have either scaled back the Canadians' objectives or reduced the scope of the other armies' offensives to free up forces.

Horne had mixed results in three important roles. He funnelled forces to Currie. His army defended a broad front with a bare minimum of troops, and this limited what he could do. Still, the Canadians' had insufficient forces. Horne acted as an advocate with Byng to gain greater cooperation, but he had little success. His failure contributed to the poor coordination between the Canadians and the flanking corps. Finally, he protected the Corps from having Haig impose on it the Cavalry Corps.

Currie's command had six distinct facets, including: planning, operations, coaching, training, organising, and a national force commander. The last facet was unique to the Portuguese, Canadian, and Australian Corps within the larger BEF. During Arras 1918, Currie and his staff generated two formal plans for deliberate assaults on 26 August and 2 September and an odd Future Policy of Operations document. The remainder of the Corps' orders were brief instructions, leaving the key decisions to the divisions. Both formal plans were simpler and briefer than the massive 1917 tomes. Given the issues of limited time to prepare and inadequate resources, the plan for 26 August worked well, as attested by the results. The Future Policy of attacking on the front of one brigade per division made little sense given the front's width. With both divisions each committing two brigades on the first day, the policy was immediately irrelevant. The plan for 2 September was flawed from its inception. It tried to solve an insolvable problem of insufficient forces to both break the D-Q Line and cross the Canal du Nord. One of Currie's great strengths in 1917 was his ability to prepare deliberate attacks. At Arras 1918, the results were mixed with an excellent plan for 26 August, the peculiar Policy document, and a defective D-Q Line plan. In his defence, having to attack with insufficient forces for the goals set by Haig compromised the D-Q Line scheme.

As a commander, Currie oversaw the execution of the Corps' plans, its day-to-day operations, and divisional coordination. In the latter, his performance was less than ideal. The Corps provided little direction resulting in disjointed attacks. The divisions tended to fight their own battles to their mutual detriment. Currie took too much of a hands-off policy and did not provide the vital oversight needed. For instance, he should have stepped in to ensure the 2nd and 3rd Division attacks on 27 August and the 4th British and 1st Canadian Division operations on 30 August meshed. This lack of cooperation also existed with the VI and XVII Corps. His decision to continue the offensive on 28 August with the battered 2nd Division was a serious mistake. In addition, the five postponements in the date for the D-Q Line attack indicated

Currie significantly underestimated the time needed to cut the barbed wire and reach the jump-off lines.

Currie as a coach had the responsibility of grooming the Corps' senior command cadre. He paid close attention to his major-generals and brigadier-generals with oversight on the selection of unit commanders down to the battalion level. Currie was active in this role. He monitored them closely for signs of a break down and would rotate them when before breaking.[19] For instance, he transferred one brigade GOC (Brigadier General F W Hill, 9th Brigade) prior to the Hundred Days and two more immediately after Arras 1918 (Rennie, 4th Brigade and Dyer, 7th Brigade) for this reason. He had a stable set of five major-generals – the four division commanders and the GOCRA.

Haig, Currie, and his division commanders in December 1918 in Bonn. Currie was on the left with Haig on the right. The four division commanders starting behind Currie are Macdonell, 1st Division, Watson, 4th Division, Loomis, 3rd Division, and Burstall, 2nd Division. Loomis replaced Lipsett as GOC 3rd Division in September. (Canada. Dept. of National Defence/Library and Archives Canada/ PA-004254)

19 Stewart, *Embattled General*, pp.277-278. The BEF transfer policy pre-dated this in mid-1917, but no Canadian officers were transferred until 1918. Trevor Harvey, "Turnover Amongst Brigade Commanders, 1917. The Real Reasons?, Stand To!', *Stand To!* , no. 109 (2017).

Only Burstall of Currie's five major generals turned in a disappointing performance during Arras 1918. Of the five, Currie was instrumental in selecting Macdonell of the 1st Division. Currie's role in brigade command selection was greater. Of the twelve infantry brigade GOCs, four were relatively recent appointments (Tremblay 5th Brigade, Bell 6th Brigade, Draper 8th Brigade, and Ormond 9th Brigade) in 1918, and only Tremblay performed poorly at Arras 1918. He would improve. Overall, Currie had a good record as a coach.

As a trainer, he prepared the Corps for the upcoming actions through rigorous training. He and his staff set the doctrine, the methods of instruction, and closely supervised the process. Currie was superlative in this function as the Corps took full advantage of its training time. He was active in enforcing the doctrine across the Corps. With the advantage of a semi-permanent force, he could ensure all the Corps' elements followed the same script. The combat achievements of the Corps were a testament to his ability.

As an organiser, Currie proposed changes to the Corps' establishment for GHQ approval. While British corps commanders could always suggest improvements, they had little say in what happened. Currie proposed, and mostly GHQ accepted them. One of Currie's greatest skills was in mapping the imperatives of the Western Front onto a changed structure for the Corps. These Corps' organisational alterations greatly aided its ability to keep fighting at a high level during the days of hard-slogging.

Finally, as a national force commander, Currie dealt with Haig on a different basis than a standard British corps GOC. He could raise a protest with Canadian political authorities against orders he strongly disagreed with. He could not play this card often or on minor matters, but it was effective when he did. The experience of the Corps' break-up and re-uniting demonstrated this. Why then did he not protest more strongly for more forces? He did prior to the D-Q Line attack and Haig rebuffed him. He likely did not escalate the matter for two reasons. First, because he did not believe it to be a fundamental matter. Second, he was still influenced by the great successes of the Corps in 1918.

Six divisional commanders, Canadian and British, served in the Corps during Arras 1918. Two performed brilliantly (Macdonell and Lipsett), two did well, (Matheson and Oldfield), one had issues but was not as bad as commonly asserted (Watson), and one did poorly (Burstall).[20] Macdonell's division fought superbly in grinding forward to reach the jump-off line for 2 September without getting worn out. His division's capture of the D-Q Line and most of the Buissy Switch with unfavourable force ratio was impressive. He was flexible in his planning in shifting from relying on the 1st Brigade to using all three of his brigades. Macdonell, however, did not challenge Currie over his inadequate force allocation for the D-Q Line operation. Given GHQ rejected Currie's request for more forces, the 1st Division commander was unlikely to succeed if he had protested. He also did not have a good understanding of tank tactics. Lipsett and his division also brilliantly conducted its operations. His one stumble was a misreading of the situation on 27 August when he sent a single brigade with a shallow barrage to break the F-R Line. His opening day attack and the attack on 28 August were first rate in exploiting Canadian advantages and German disadvantages to reach the objectives at a low cost. The 28 August attack was especially well-thought out and executed.

20 On Watson for instance, see Dancocks, *Spearhead to Victory*, p.115.

Both Matheson (4th British Division) and Oldfield (51st (Highland) Division) did satisfactorily, considering their straightened circumstances. They were operating with less well-trained troops and weaker divisions. Both had to carry out their missions without incurring heavy losses. Oldfield's final attack scheme that forced the Germans to abandon their positions on Hausa and Delbar Woods made excellent use of the limited force he had available. Still, it took too long for the 51st (Highland) to arrive at the correct formula, and the delays influenced the Corps' advance. Matheson's division had initial success. It took too many casualties, however, in attempting to reach the jump-off line on the front of the 10th British Brigade. This brigade's heavy losses reduced the 4th British Division to effectively two brigades for the D-Q Line operation. This compelled Currie to modify the D-Q Line operation that weakened it. Matheson's division's planning broke down on 2 September in not taking steps to neutralise Prospect Farm.

The decisions of the Corps' headquarters were the major factor in the 4th Canadian Division's issues on 2 September. The primary responsibility for failing to advance beyond the Red Line lay with Currie's scheme. Watson was dubious about its feasibility, but if he raised objections with Currie, there is no record of it. Watson erred in locating his headquarters so far to the rear. It meant his signal company had great difficulty in keeping the lines of communication open. As a result, he had a poor understanding of the situation with a limited means of control. His refusal to allow Odlum to move with his brigade was a symptom of this, as the 11th Brigade commander was the only one with whom he had reliable communications. The result was Odlum was out of his brigade's command loop at a critical point. It was clear that Watson had only a limited comprehension of the front conditions. To his credit, he would listen, and he persuaded Currie to call off attacks on 3 and 4 September.

Burstall's errors were many, although his division did well on the first day of the offensive. He mis-positioned his 5th Brigade, resulting in a long delay for the attack on 27 August. This late assault hampered the 3rd Division's operation. The 2nd Division repeated the delayed start the next day as well. While the opening stage of the second day's attack was successful, the subsequent attempt to bull rush the F-R Line without a barrage was a costly mistake. Burstall erred again in not objecting to the 28 August attack, given the exhausted and battered state of his division. His decision to use the 5th Brigade again on the third day demonstrated poor judgement, compounded by an unimaginative and poorly conceived attack plan. His surprising 'jubilant mood' in the afternoon of 28 August suggests a commander out of touch. Burstall, a gunner, was an officer who worked best in a deliberate operation where he and his staff could work out all the details in advance. He did not have the same facility in more fluid conditions.

Of the 12 Canadian infantry brigade commanders, eight did well or quite well at Arras 1918, with four having a more problematic or variable conduct. On the positive side, Bell and Draper performed particularly strongly on the opening day with innovative schemes that took their objectives with minimal casualties. Griesbach of the 1st Brigade executed a brilliant action to take the F-R Line on 30 August but almost squandered it through poor defensive arrangements. The hard fighting of his troops and battalion commanders saved him and the brigade. Loomis's brigade did well on 31 August and 1 September but his planning and use of tanks on 2 September were deeply flawed. Tremblay's decision to use the 22nd Battalion on 28 August and lack of opposition to the ill-considered attacks on the F-R Line were serious errors. Finally, despite his clear orders, Odlum lost control of his brigade owing to the decision of a battalion commander. This choice knocked the brigade out of action for the day with heavy losses.

In conclusion, Arras 1918 and Amiens were closer in results, outcomes, and casualties than is usually surmised. This is especially so considering the immense success of the opening day of the Amiens offensive. Arras 1918 was markedly more successful than Canadian operations on the Somme 1916, with more ground gained, a higher rate of battalion attack success, and more prisoners taken with fewer casualties. Increasing this was the Corps' deft use of tanks, barrages, and smoke, with the last an under-rated contributor to victories. The operational tempo was markedly greater than in previous years. Accompanying these improved results was the Corps' average loss rate per battalion attack was half of the Somme 1916 figure. This highlights the immense increase in the Corps' fighting prowess allied with a decline in German proficiency. The commanders, in the main, performed superbly, while Haig, Currie, Burstall, and Tremblay delivering more mixed to substandard results.

Conclusion

'The Hardest Battle'

Smashing of the Quéant-Drocourt Line was the turning point in the campaign.

Byng to Currie, 1918[1]

The Canadian Corps did not meet Haig's aggressive demands to capture Bourlon Wood. What it accomplished, however, was surprising, significant, and superb considering its many obstacles. Having to attack on too broad a front with inadequate forces, the Corps smashed through 15-kilometres of the best defences on the Western Front. For Currie, Arras 1918 was 'the hardest battle in its [Corps'] history.'[2] In his diary, he thought it a greater victory than Amiens.[3] It comprehensively destroyed nine German divisions, defeated another two, and reached the Canal du Nord. This forced a German multi-army retreat across the canal. The Corps encountered an alert enemy that channelled substantial reserves to repel it, but nothing they could do could stop it for long. The Canadian infantry employed sophisticated infiltration tactics integrated with powerful artillery support to overwhelm multiple strong defensive zones and defeat potent counterattacks. With multiple handicaps in manpower, organisation, and training, British divisions in the Corps also did well when properly supported. Their higher failure rate resulted from these disadvantages. Only when the Corps' generals deviated from employing an effective barrage with smoke supporting the infantry were its attacks repulsed. That the Germans could defeat these assaults demonstrated the importance of methods over manpower, morale, or matériel as the explanation for the Corps' success. The latter three had a role, but they were not the dominant factors.

This conclusion ties together the effects of the 12 threads that shaped the campaign. It also answers the question raised in the Introduction why the Corps was more successful at Arras 1918 than the British were in 1917. Extending this analysis, it looks at the larger reasons for the improved results in the Hundred Days or at least this period in the campaign when the Germans still had some limited chance to stop the advance. It concludes with whether Arras 1918 mattered.

1 Quoted in Cook, *Shock Troops*, p.499.
2 Kemp, *Report of the Ministry*, p.144.
3 LAC: Currie Diary, 3 September 1918.

Core Threads – Facilitators

At the campaign's core were 12 factors, with five facilitating success, six hindering, and one that did both. They were critical to how the campaign transpired. At every stage, these factors conditioned its conduct and outcome. The first beneficial factor was the use of smoke. It had a crucial and unsung role in the improved results at Arras 1918. The Corps used it in 26 out of 83 actions and all were full successes. The best measure of its impact was the 2nd Division's decision to not employ it in its assaults on 27 and 28 August. Burstall's division's full and partial success rate dropped from 100 percent when it used smoke on 26 August to 41 percent when it did not. While smoke was not the sole reason for the failures, its absence contributed. Contemporary German accounts consistently reported the demoralising impact of smoke. They described assault troops emerging from it to strike isolated defenders, allowing the attackers to manoeuvre, infiltrate, and overwhelm them. For German units with depressed morale, smoke was crucial in undermining their determination. Even elite formations suffered in these conditions. An additional influence was the fear that smoke masked the use of gas. Both sides used smoke to disguise poison gas shells, so when the Canadians utilised smoke the Germans had to mask up. This was a further burden on tired and worn down defenders.

The next facilitator was the centrepiece of the Corps' attacks – the barrage. They supported two-thirds of Canadian assaults, and they raised the success rate from 81 to 88 percent. If the barrage had a concentration of less than 30 metres per gun, then it rose to 100 percent. This aligns with after-action reports such as the 6th CFA's: 'It seems to be the general opinion also that so long as the artillery barrage is going the infantry find very little difficulty in progressing and that the hold-ups usually commence after the barrage has finished.'[4]

Paradoxically then, barrage supported attacks were more costly than non-barrage ones. An increase to 166 casualties per attack compared with the average of 139 for all battalion operations accompanied the improved results. The reason for this was the Corps fired them when facing stronger defences and defenders. In operations without artillery support, the success rate dropped to 67 percent – demonstrating their importance. It was not, however, enough to fire any barrage, because it had to be of sufficient density to be effective. Attacks supported by barrages with concentrations under 30 metres per gun resulted in a 97 percent partial or full success rate. That dropped to two-thirds partial or full success when the gun concentration exceeded 30 metres per gun. If there was no barrage, the failures increased to 33 percent. As the battle progressed, it was more and more difficult to reach a sufficient density of guns and attack the entire front. The increased front width, loss of guns to enemy fire and wear, and the difficulty of moving up the heavier pieces all contributed to decreasing firepower density.

4 LAC: 6th CFA War Diary, Close Support of Infantry Commencing 26 August, September 1918.

Table C.1 Effect of Barrages on Outcomes All Attacks

	Barrage Concentration less than 30 m/gun	Barrage Concentration greater than 30 m/gun	No Barrage
Full Success	31	2	14
Partial Success	3	10	6
Initial Success	1		
Failure		6	10
TOTAL	**35**	**18**	**30**

Barrages had profound physical and psychological effects. They inflicted losses, especially on defenders in the open. They screened the advance with shell bursts, and when supplemented by smoke, they were even more effective at screening. Barrages isolated the forward defences, allowing the aggressors to manoeuvre to outflank them. In daylight, the moving shell bursts indicated the line of advance to the assault troops. Psychologically, they raised the attackers' morale and depressed the defenders'. For troops with shaky morale, it was sufficient reason to hide in their dugouts to surrender later.[5]

If barrages were so effective, why then were they not always employed? Factors of range, time to organise, ammunition supply, ground devastation, and poor judgement limited their use. The effective reach of the 18-pounder, the workhorse of the field artillery barrage, was 2,500 metres. Guns equipped with the new air-recuperator could extend that up to 3,500 metres, but only a portion of the Corps' field guns were of that model. Further, the more they fired, the less accurate they were at extreme ranges, so it was better to err on the side of caution and use shorter ranges.[6] Thus, the useful range was 2,500 metres, which meant penetrating only the Germans' *Vorfeld* and, depending on the situation, part of the *HWL*. Therefore, with planned advances of greater depth than this, the planners had two choices. They could wait the hours to move up the artillery for another barrage or continue the attack without one. Barrages took hours to arrange, and this assumes the batteries were already in position and supplied. It was difficult and only rarely attempted for a FA brigade to fire a barrage, move, and fire another in a day. This differed from firing on point targets.

Barrages used a lot of shells. One 18-pounder battery of six pieces firing a standard barrage at a concentration of 25 metres per gun to its full depth would expend 900 rounds.[7] The battery would consume a further 360 rounds firing a protective barrage for 60 minutes at a rate of fire of 1 round per minute. Thus, the battery would need 1,260 rounds or 12 GS Wagon loads of

5 Tim Cook, 'The Politics of Surrender: Canadian Soldiers and the Killing of Prisoners in the Great War', *The Journal of Military History* 70(2006), p.646.

6 LAC: 26th Canadian Ordnance Workshop War Diary, 20 August 1918; LAC: 1st CDA War Diary, 1st CDA G.1-476, 20 August 1918.

7 Six pieces firing 2 rounds per minute, reaching a depth of 2,500 metres, in 100 metre lifts every 3 minutes at a concentration of 25 metres per 18-pounder.

ammunition for a 150-metre section of front. The shells cut-up the ground and made it difficult to move through the destruction zone. The artillery had learned to minimise the devastation by sparingly firing HE shells that left big craters. Even with this care, barrages damaged the terrain and that slowed resupply and movement. Considering the time to organise, the logistical strain, and the destruction, commanders almost always decided not to fire another barrage when the first reached its end. They relied on the infantry's firepower, manoeuvre capabilities, and attached artillery firing to overcome defences. While justified at Amiens given the weak defences and defenders, it was usually a mistake at Arras 1918 with its great depth of fortifications.

Another major aid was the small unit tactics employed by the Canadians. German accounts highlighted the importance of infiltration, fire and movement, and how smoke enabled these approaches to work so effectively. The Canadian after-action reports, with a few exceptions, give the impression of the steady advance of well-dressed waves. The reality was that of a loose collection of platoons broken down into sections, fluidly moving around strong points and striking them from the flank and rear. A consistent theme in the German regimental histories was of brave forces holding out heroically against all direct attacks but falling victim to flanking assaults. The consistency of these statements in contemporary and postwar accounts strongly suggests this was a genuine phenomenon.

A series of enemy mistakes aided the Corps' operations. These errors arose from inadequate intelligence and desperation. German intelligence poorly served von Dellmensingen and contributed to his defective decisions. The capture of only 33 Canadians hampered it, as prisoners, according to Markus Pöhlman, provided the 'bulk of the day-to-day intelligence' for the Germans.[8] The Canadian efforts at communications silence also misled German signals intelligence. They made three key gaffes in missing the move north of the Canadian Corps, the likely location of Haig's next blow, and the number of divisions deployed against the *II Bavarian Korps*. The Germans did not identify the Canadians on the Arras front until the third day, thus delaying the recognition that the front south of the Scarpe was at risk. They also did not expect that the offensive would extend from Neuville-Vitasse north to the Scarpe, so they mis-positioned their reserve. This left the *II Bavarian Korps* front with inadequate counterattack resources on 26 August. The misevaluation of where the BEF would strike was curious. The blow south of the Scarpe would outflank the Hindenburg Line, while one north of it would not immediately threaten anything vital. Finally, by exaggerating how many divisions faced the *II Bavarian Korps*, German intelligence misled von Dellmensingen into making a bigger effort to retain the *Vorfeld* than was prudent. Believing the attackers had committed all their divisions, the German commander ordered an all-out effort to recapture the forward zone. Dellmensingen might have been more cautious about expending his reserves if he knew the Canadian Corps was gaining ground with just two and later three divisions.

Dellmensingen's policy of attempting to retake the *Vorfeld* was a grave mistake. He burned out his best units in futile efforts to restore the zone. In doing so, he exposed his forces to Canadian firepower, so the attackers suffered excessive casualties, fatigue, and disorganisation. The German's defensive doctrine's centrepiece was the counterattack. A properly conceived blow by an *Eingreifdivision* against an over-extended, exhausted, and weakened attacker could

8 Markus Pöhlman, 'German Intelligence at War, 1914-1918', *The Journal of Intelligence History*, no. 5 (2005), pp.47, 50.

be devastating. At Arras 1918, however, these actions were unsuccessful. Both Canadian and German sources discuss multiple counterattacks, but the Germans only made 12 in sufficient strength to appear in both sides' chronicles. Of those well-attested counterattacks, half were initially successful, a quarter were fully successful, and a quarter were failures. Thus, three-quarters of the attacks had no lasting success or were outright defeats and rendered these units incapable of putting up much resistance. Four attacks stand out in particular in highlighting their declining power. These were made on 26 August, 30 August, and two on 1 September. All featured a multi-regimental assault against vulnerable troops, but the Canadians defeated them with catastrophic effects. These counterattacks should have been successful, but they failed with large losses, leaving them vulnerable when the Corps attacked the next day. The common reasons for these failures include the defender's improved artillery support and signals, increased infantry firepower, and better training with German launch delays and less capable troops. The one major exception was the attack of the *64th RIR* on 2 September, as it played a key role in stabilising the German position north of Mt. Dury, even though it permanently retook no ground.

Assisting the Corps was that German artillery did not contribute as effectively as it had done in the 1916/17 battles. Beyond the larger issue of munition shortages, two decisions adversely affected the German artillery's performance. Roughly one-fifth to one-quarter of the German field artillery deployed in the *HWL* zone to defend against Allied tank attacks. Jonathon Boff

German 77 mm field gun that did not get away near Buissy. One of 123 pieces captured by the Corps. (Canada. Dept. of National Defence/Library and Archives Canada/PA-003106)

in his work on the Third Army asserted the exposure of this many field pieces to direct attack was a mistake.[9] Given the repeated statements in contemporary German documents of the critical importance of providing the infantry with anti-tank resources, it was an appropriate use. Although they lost many guns, the Germans could replace them but not their infantry. Many of the 123 guns captured by the Canadians served in this role. Even if overrun, these pieces still put up a fight and inflicted losses. More importantly, the availability of many anti-tank weapons forced the BEF to adjust its tank tactics. The German anti-tank measures reduced the effectiveness of the tank arm. As a result, it had to fight under the cover of a barrage and with an infantry screen. Thus, the decision was appropriate.

Less justifiable was the decision to shift the field artillery to the rear. Although it resulted in fewer guns lost, it eliminated much of the gunnery support defending the *Vorfeld*. This undermined the German defensive arrangements and was most evident on 26 August when the Canadians took the entire zone rapidly with few casualties. The entire purpose of the *Vorfeld* was an economy of force delaying action to wear down the attackers at a minimal cost. With the guns deployed too far to the rear, the artillery could not grind down the attackers caught in the open. A post-battle analysis by the *II Bavarian Korps* admitted this approach was an error.[10]

The Canadian Corps had crucially important advantages in structure, status, manpower, resources, training, and reputation that contributed significantly to its success. Structurally, retaining the four-battalion brigade, and the Corps' unique tramways units, engineer brigades, Corps Survey Section, extra truck companies, additional field artillery brigades, and a larger signal service all strengthened it and made it more combat capable than a British corps. The semi-permanent and semi-independent status ensured the Corps could form and enforce its own variations on the BEF's doctrine. Confidence and experience of fighting alongside welded together a powerful force. This status also contributed to the Canadians receiving GHQ's permission to change its organisation. Sufficient manpower to maintain and increase the establishments was the necessary precondition for the approvals – a luxury not available to British formations. The ready supply of trained replacements to the end of Arras 1918 enabled the Corps to keep fighting after Amiens without either a long rest or diminished effectiveness. Moreover, unlike the British, the Canadians did not have to radically reduce personnel standards. The Corps had more matériel. It had more wireless sets, permanently assigned trucks, machine guns, and field artillery, and even typewriters that increased its effectiveness. Fusing all these advantages together and enabling the 1st, 3rd, and 4th Divisions to exploit fully the new tactical opportunities was the intensive open warfare training from May to July. This instruction was instrumental in the Corps' ability to drive a rapid tempo and employ bold infiltration tactics with smoke-led barrages. The issues with the 2nd Division's inadequate pace and not using smoke in its barrages demonstrated the open warfare training's importance. This period was also critical in resting the Corps, so it was far fresher than almost every other formation at the start of the Hundred Days campaign. Finally, the Corps' and its commander's reputation was an immense benefit. This manifested itself in three key respects. Haig's confidence in Currie was instrumental in granting the Canadian requests for a modified organisation. As a result of their reputation for victories in 1917, the Canadians received greater leeway to ask for more time,

9 Boff, 'British Third Army' pp.176-177.
10 Jonathan Boff, 'Combined Arms During the Hundred Days Campaign, August--November 1918', *War in History* 17, no. 4 (2010), p.177.

guns, shells, and resources than the typical British formation. Given the Canadian's success, Horne granted considerable operational autonomy to Currie.

Core Themes – Hindrances

Not all the factors helped, with six being detrimental to the Corps' operations. The most crucial of these was insufficient forces. Contrary to Haig's confidence in his message to Foch, the Corps did not have sufficient tanks, troops, and guns for its assignment based on GHQ's own doctrine.[11] This was particularly true given the aggressive nature of the mission and the nature of the defences. The C-in-C wanted it to advance further than in the Amiens offensive without the advantages of surprise and an exhausted enemy lacking robust defences. These factors argued for providing resources at the high end of the doctrine's scale of force requirements. Instead, it received less, much less.

Rather than the German image of masses of tanks supporting the Canadians, only a little over a quarter of the Corps' assaults had any tank support. Of these, only 10 battalion operations had a concentration of vehicles that met the recommended GHQ figure of 100 to 200 metres per tank.[12] Eight of these were on 2 September and two on 27 August. Thus, the vast majority of the Corps' engagements had either no tanks or insufficient numbers. The 3rd Tank Brigade had to stop all actions for five days to even reach 43 percent of its nominal strength on 2 September. The problem was that the entire Tank Corps was short of vehicles and crews, and GHQ's penchant to scatter the limited number across all the attacking forces exacerbated this. Rather than concentrating on key sectors, GHQ scattered them and lessened their impact.

The Corps had too much front for its infantry. According to the GHQ offensive manual, the recommended density was three to five men per metre.[13] Given the defences' sophistication, the Corps should have had five men per metre. Only the 4th Canadian Division on 2 September met the low-end figure. The other attacks were well below three men per metre, while in contrast the Canadian Corps attacked on 8 August with a concentration of 3.12 men per metre against far weaker defences. At times during Arras 1918, the Canadian divisions conducted assaults on frontages suited for a defensive posture. The GHQ platoon manual called for a battalion attack frontage of 200 to 600 metres.[14] At Arras 1918, the average attack frontage was 815 metres – far in excess of the recommended figure. Even Haig eventually recognised how strained the Corps was when he inserted the XXII Corps to take over a major portion of the front.

11 TNA: Haig to Foch, 27 August 1918.
12 LAC: RG24 v22020: SS 214 Tanks and Their Employment in Co-Operation with Other Arms, August 1918.
13 LAC: SS 135 Training.
14 LAC: SS 143 Platoon, 24.

Table C.2 Force Density Arras 1917 and 1918 and Amiens

	Corps/ Divisions	Front	Divisions	Manpower	Density
Arras 1917	VII Corps	3,600	2	14,400	3.98
	VI Corps	3,770	3	21,600	5.73
	XVII Corps	2,400	1	7,200	3.00
Amiens 1918	Canadian Corps	10,760	4	33,600	3.12
	Australian Corps	7,040	3	25,200	3.58
	III Corps	8,800	3	16,200	1.84
Albert 21 August 1918	IV Corps	10,560	3	19,200	1.82
Arras 26 August 1918	Canadian Corps	9,800	3	22,200	2.27
Arras 2 September 1918	1st CID	3,500	1	8,400	2.40
	4th CID	2,500	1	8,400	3.36
	4th BID	2,200	1	4,200	1.91

Given the success of the Corps in breaking the D-Q Line, did the lack of troops matter? Yes, as it had to adopt risky plans. They often worked like the outflanking operations of the 8th and 6th Brigades on 26 August and the wheeling action of the 1st Brigade on 30 August. But the 2 September attacks of the 2nd and 3rd Brigades showed the consequences of having to attack with too low of a manpower density. They took almost all their initial objectives but with much delay. Buttressing this argument was the case of the fortuitous intervention of the 3rd Battalion. It allowed the 15th Battalion to make a greater gain than it would have had the 3rd not been present. Currie's use of Brutinel's brigade on 29 August indicates how stretched was the Corps. While the Corps broke the D-Q Line, it did so after seven days of hard fighting. Had it a narrower front or more forces, it could have made more rapid progress at less cost.

Finally, Haig did not provide the artillery concentration given to other British armies, though they were attacking weaker defences. On 30 August, the First Army had a force equal to 62 percent of the field artillery per metre of the Third and Fourth Armies and 68 percent of the heavy artillery. While only a portion of the First Army attacked, the discrepancy was still significant. GHQ's head of artillery on 30 August recommended it reinforce the First Army with four more field artillery and two heavy artillery brigades.[15]

Table C.3 Metres per Piece 30 August 1918*

	First Army†	Second Army	Third Army†	Fourth Army†	Fifth Army
FA	42	48	26	26	58
HA	93	109	63	61	180

Sources:
TNA, WO 95-21-4, GHQ General Staff War Diary, LtCol GS to MGO, 30 August 1918.

* Measured in metres per piece where a lower value is better
† Engaged in offensive operations

Four key command errors significantly hampered the Corps' operations. These mistakes all stemmed ultimately from Haig's demands to accomplish the impossible with insufficient forces. The first mistake was the flawed second phase attacks made by the 2nd and 3rd Divisions on 27 August. Both Burstall and Lipsett underestimated the strength of the German defences of the F-R Line. As a result, they tried to rush the trenches with inadequate forces. The result was a complete repulse. Currie's decision to continue the offensive with the battered 2nd Division on 28 August was an obvious mistake, even without the benefit of hindsight. Burstall compounded the blunder by executing a poorly conceived plan to assault with the same units that had failed the previous day, supplemented only by a weak barrage. The attackers had no chance to succeed. Finally, the 2 September attack plan was fundamentally flawed.

A consistent issue throughout the campaign was traffic congestion caused by insufficient road space and aggravated by poor road discipline and control. With only a single all-weather highway, the Corps depended on battle-damaged routes. Unlike Amiens, the ubiquitous trenches and barbed wire meant all but the infantry were road-bound. The results were delays, prolonged exposure to German shelling and bombing, and supply shortages. By the mid-point of the campaign, when the Corps moved two divisions in and two out on these overcrowded routes, the offensive risked strangulation. The artillery was not being adequately resupplied. There were ample quantities of shells at the Corps' dumps in the rear, but they could not be pushed through the road system. Thus, there was a real risk that, as on the Somme in 1916, logistics would slow the operational tempo. This would give the Germans more time to recover, to replace worn-out units, and to push up reserves. The saving grace was an unsung part of the Corps' advantage – the tramways system. It greatly relieved the strain on the road system and allowed the Corps to renew its daily attacks. It also aided the evacuation of the wounded, thus lowering the fatality rate.

15 TNA: GHQ GS WD, LtCol GS to MGO, 30 August 1918.

Signals depended on men like these on the move to carry the wire forward and maintain the lines under heavy shell fire. The man in front is carrying a reel of wire and the men behind appear to be carrying message flags. (Canada. Dept. of National Defence/Library and Archives Canada/PA-003131)

Notwithstanding the improvements in communications, they were still fragile and unreliable. The information flow back to the Corps was relatively quick, but there were continuing issues in getting orders forward. Commanders could not count on being able to receive reports from or send instructions to their subordinates. Moreover, there was little staff appreciation of the need to change their methods in a lean messaging environment. As a result, signals teetered on a knife edge through the Hundred Days. The signal service handled 20 percent more messages on the first day of Arras 1918 over that of 8 August and this despite having fewer divisions under its command.[16] By 30 August, the volume rose by 50 percent more. At Arras 1918, as at Amiens, the subordinate position of the signal service was clear as it could not influence the leadership to ease their load. The open warfare training had not properly weaned headquarters off their dependence on wired communications. For instance, the Corps' signal company drew

16 LAC: CWNS Canadian Signal Service.

2,300 kilometres of telegraph wire from stores from 24 to 31 August. Further, the signallers entered the Arras 1918 campaign already overtaxed from their exertions at Amiens. Unlike other branches that had rest periods while out of the line, the signal companies still had to provide communications. The service could barely keep up with demand when static, so having to advance resulted in an even greater burden. Still, the open warfare training, experience, and added signallers enabled the Corps to overcome the communications limitations and win great success.

Their support weapons did not serve the Canadian Corps' infantry in offensive operations as well as the Germans. The result was that Canadian infantry had less firepower than enemy stormtroopers. Without an artillery barrage, Canadian troops had to rely on their infantry weapons that lacked the punch and range to suppress deeply set machine gun zones. The heavy machine guns, trench mortars, and attached direct firing artillery all had significant restrictions when supporting infantry. The problem was once the barrage ended machine guns generally could not deliver 'the principal neutralising and covering fire' in open or semi-open warfare.[17] Three factors limited them. First, the organisation of machine guns into independent battalions interfered with infantry coordination. Too often, attached machine gun batteries failed to link up. If they did, there was a lack of teamwork because they did not train together. Secondly, machine guns had limited mobility. Not only were the weapons heavy, but the crews had to carry the large quantities of ammunition. Only occasionally were limbers or mules brought close to the front to keep the guns supplied. As a result, even if a battery linked with an infantry battalion and kept in touch, it would only fire briefly before running out of rounds. Finally, the machine gun arm had no dedicated signal resources, so it was difficult to command in open warfare conditions. For all their power in defensive situations, the structure of the machine gun arm was flawed and poorly provided for mobility, resupply, and communications in offensive situations.

The Canadian trench mortar arm made only a minor contribution to the Arras 1918 operation. Despite employing a weapon that weighed considerably less than the German version, the trench mortars could not keep up with the advance. If they did, they quickly ran out of ammunition. Only rarely were they able to employ their considerable firepower in open warfare.

Attached artillery were useful in their direct fire role but issues of control, coordination, and effectiveness constrained them. Artillery officers found them difficult to command as they had to be both at the infantry headquarters and with the guns. Like the machine guns, attached cannons did not always sync up. When they did, the infantry did not know how to get the most out of them. Finally, while valuable in firing on point targets, they could not suppress a deep machine gun zone as on 2 September. The GOCRA's notes on the operation summed up the problem with that a FA brigade firing a barrage 'materially assisted an advance' while firing on targets did not help.[18]

A striking feature of the campaign was the poor coordination within the Corps and with British formations. Repeated instances where the Corps did not synchronise attacks marred operations with the 4th British Division and the VI and XVII Corps. These problems also existed between the 2nd and 3rd Divisions. The Corps provided little to no oversight on the

17 LAC: 1st Bn CMGC Report.
18 LAC: Artillery Notes on Operations - August 26th to Sept. 4th 1918.

German trench mortar in its direct fire mode. Likely it was used as one of the many anti-tank pieces the Germans deployed to stop the tank menace. (Canada. Dept. of National Defence/Library and Archives Canada/PA-003066)

uncoordinated actions of the 4th British and its neighbouring Canadian formations. As a result, they fought their own battles to their mutual detriment. Being on the boundary between armies magnified the tensions with the flanking British corps. The dealings with the XVII Corps were particularly poor, with limited harmony and some unwillingness to work together on both sides. This was a case where Horne could have contributed more to ensuring closer cooperation.

Finally, the increased tempo of operations had consequences both negative and positive. The Corps had limited experience in a sustained operational cadence. As a result, the Canadians had to rely on junior officers conducting actions without the benefit of detailed instructions. The almost 12,000 casualties the Corps suffered at Amiens tested this dependence. In some cases, there was only time to issue verbal orders and never an opportunity to rehearse an attack. It entailed an unprecedented strain on staff and commanders who had to work around the clock. Fatigue was a constant factor. More than a normal number of errors resulted because of the compressed time frames and exhausted staff. Leaders had to make key decisions before knowing the day's results. These time pressures contributed to the Corps' poor coordination.

What was positive about this tempo was that it left the Germans having to scramble to stitch together defences after the Corps' assaults. They could not reset before the next attack struck.

For instance, von Dellmensingen left the *26th RD* in the line for an extra day as there was insufficient time to replace it. The regular hammer blows every morning but one, lacerated the defenders. Like a sumo wrestler who had lost the first struggle and could not find firm footing before the next, the enemy did not have a set defence when struck again. The problem with German guns pounding their own men at St Servins Farm was an example of this. Delaying assaults to make better preparations would have benefited the Germans more than the attackers.

Why the Greater Success of Arras 1918 versus Arras 1917?

On 9 April 1917, three British corps, with six divisions attacking plus more in reserve, assaulted the same sector as did the Canadian Corps with three divisions and no reserves on 26 August 1918.[19] While the British corps had to advance through an additional set of trenches to reach where Canadians launched their attack, the sectors roughly corresponded. The 1917 operation featured considerably more infantry battalions, artillery, and tanks than in 1918. Admittedly, the tanks in 1918 were more capable. Both attacks faced an equivalent number of German battalions. While these were numerically weaker with lower morale in 1918, they had more machine guns than in 1917. As well, the prolonged bombardment of German positions in 1917 depleted the defenders' numbers and spirit before the assault. In material terms, the raw combat power exerted in the 1917 offensive was much greater than in 1918. The results were, however, the reverse. The Canadian Corps gained more ground at a lower cost in casualties and with more prisoners taken per committed division per day.

19 To make the comparison equitable, reserve divisions, such as the 4th British, committed on the first day are not included.

Table C.4 Arras 1917 and 1918 Comparison*

	Arras 1917	Arras 1918	Ratio 1917:1918
Corps (Divisions)	XVII (9), VI (3, 12, 15), VII (14, 56)	Canadian Corps (2nd Cdn, 3rd Cdn, 51st)	
Divisions	6	3	2:1
Reserves	2 (37, 4)	None	
Battalions (front-line divisions only)	72	33	2.18:1
FA Brigades	28	16†	1.65:1
Heavy Artillery	439‡	270 (only 241 were operational)	1.23:1
Preliminary Bombardment (Days)	5	0	
Tanks (Opening day)	40	13	2.5:1
German Divisions	3	3	-
Casualties (Divisions in line on opening day)	19,648§	7,057‖	2.78:1
Days	38	9	4.22:1
Ground Gained	8,500 metres (39 Days)	10,500 metres (3 Days) 17,600 metres (8 Days)	1:2

Sources:

* Cyril Bentham Falls, *Military Operations: France and Belgium, 1917* [London: Macmillan, 1940), 1, pp.201-230.

† Canadian field and heavy artillery from LAC, RG9 III-D-2 v4800, 126, Artillery Statistics by Date.

‡ Heavy artillery totals were derived by splitting each corps' total number of pieces equally between its front-line divisions to arrive at a fair total of the heavy artillery support available.

§ This total includes only losses for the first tour of the 3rd and 14th Divisions. The 4th British Division losses are not included in the Arras 1917 totals as it was not in the front-line at the opening of the offensive. Cyril Bentham Falls, *Military Operations: France and Belgium, 1917* [London: Macmillan, 1940), 1, p.559.

‖ Note the 51st (Highland) Division's losses begin before and extend after its service in the Canadian Corps, but they were not significant. TNA, WO 95-2849-1/4, 51st Division AAQMG War Diary, August Casualties.; LAC, RG9 III-D-2 v4794, 54, 2nd Division Report Battle of Arras.; LAC, RG9 III-D-3 v4858, 3rd Division AAQMG War Diary, Statement of Casualties from Aug. 25th to Aug. 29th ,1918.

The first-order reasons for these improved results were a faster operational tempo, better weather, more effective forces, and a weaker enemy. Each of these factors, other than weather, resulted from multiple transformations in the BEF's methods, including the Canadians, and the effects of costly fighting of 1917 and 1918 on the Germans. Attacks almost every day characterised Arras 1918, while the British corps at Arras 1917 had to take long pauses to replenish ammunition and replace troops. These intervals gave time for the Germans to recover. In 1918, an improved infrastructure, the Canadian reliance on tramways, doctrine, and training accelerated battle planning and execution, coupled with better weather resulted in the rapid operational pace. A major contribution to the tempo was the structural change of increasing the engineers in a division to brigade strength. This dramatically reduced the infantry's workload and meant completing the vital engineering work faster and more efficiently. The junior and senior leadership cadres in the Canadian Corps were more experienced and better trained than in 1917 and so able to handle a swifter tempo.

Road condition during Arras 1917 such as this contributed to long pauses between attacks to move up supplies and reinforcements. (Canada. Dept. of National Defence/Library and Archives Canada/ PA-001238)

The open warfare training prior to Amiens, the increase in Lewis Guns, and the dynamic tactics and doctrine meant a more effective force than in 1917. Currie's changes to the Corps' structure made it more capable. Using predicted fire increased the artillery's potency and enabled operational and tactical surprise. Employing smoke had the effect of reducing casualties and boosting results.

While the weather interfered with air operations at Arras 1918, the ground conditions were far better than in 1917. There was not the deep mud, cold, and debilitating circumstances that wore out men, clogged the roads, and killed horses. There was no need to build up supplies that limited the operational tempo in 1917.

The Germans of 1918 were weaker than in 1917, with fewer personnel with a lower morale. The troops they had, however, had ample supplies of machine guns. Errors in command resulted in poorly positioned reserves. In the latter battle, intelligence failures meant the Germans missed the return of the Corps and where the next blow would fall. As a result, they mis-located reserves that could not promptly intervene in the battle's opening.

Matériel, Manpower, Morale or Method

The introduction submitted that a detailed examination of Arras 1918 would provide insight into the debate on the reasons for the Allied victory in 1918 and the German defeat. Various historians have proposed some combination of four main factors of matériel, manpower, morale, and method with one predominating. Those who favour matériel reference an overwhelming superiority in weapons, munitions, supplies, transport, and all the paraphernalia of war. Manpower advocates believe the hollowing out of German combat units as a result of the hecatombs of dead and wounded from the spring offensives. Those who champion morale argue for a collapse in the German willingness to fight. Method proponents contend the primary factor was an improvement in the Allies' fighting techniques.

If matériel was decisive, then its availability must have meaningfully changed between 1917 and 1918. Thus, there had to be an increase in Allied resources and/or a major decline in German ones in 1918 that altered the relative matériel balance. After the opening months of 1916, the Allies had a great advantage in almost every category but could not translate that massive edge into decisive victories. If matériel were the critical factor, this superiority had to be even greater in 1918. German accounts thought so and, in particular, with tanks. This section examines how the matériel factors at Arras 1918 compared to Arras 1917 and the Canadian assault at Passchendaele. This comparison analyses the key factors of artillery, machine guns, mortars, tanks, ammunition supply, and aircraft to determine if matériel was the prime reason for the greater success.

At Arras 1918, the Corps had 65 percent fewer artillery pieces than the three British corps at Arras 1917 but had 13 percent more than at Passchendaele. The battles in 1917 featured more heavy artillery with a significantly greater throw weight than at Arras 1918. Even Passchendaele, with fewer pieces overall, had a higher throw weight than at Arras 1918. Based on weapons per metre, gun support density was markedly higher in the two 1917 operations, with Arras 1917 65 percent higher and Passchendaele more than three times greater. Despite the lack of detailed figures for German guns, it was unlikely that they had less in 1918 than in 1917 on this sector. What had changed was the enemy policy of pulling back their field artillery so it could not intervene in the battles for the *Vorfeld*. That, however, was not a matter of matériel but of tactics.

The Allied counter-battery fire concerned the Germans, but they could still rapidly replace lost pieces.[20] Therefore, the Canadians did not have a greater matériel superiority over the Germans than in 1917 in terms of quantity of artillery.

Table C.5 Artillery Comparison Arras 1917, Passchendaele 1917, Arras 1918

	Battle	Field Artillery	Heavy Artillery	TOTAL	Differential
# Pieces	Arras 1917-Scarpe*	672	439	**1,111**	65%
	Passchendaele 1917†	360	227	**587**	-13%
	Arras 1918‡	480	192	**672**	
Throw Weight (Kg)§	Arras 1917-Scarpe	6,911	31,679	**38,590**	161%
	Passchendaele 1917	3,702	14,850	**18,552**	26%
	Arras 1918	4,891	9,882	**14,773**	
Concentration (lower is better)	Arras 1917-Scarpe	17	26	**10**	165%
	Passchendaele 1917	8	12	**5**	355%
	Arras 1918	24	60	**17**	

Sources:
* Cyril Bentham Falls, *Military Operations: France and Belgium, 1917* [London: Macmillan, 1940), 1, pp.204, 215, 226.
† Tim Cook, *Shock Troops: Canadians Fighting the Great War, 1917-1918* [Toronto: Viking Canada, 2008), p.321.
‡ LAC, RG9 III-D-3 v4821, Canadian Corps AAQMG War Diary, Appendix D, September 1918.
§ LAC, RG9 III-D-2 v4810, CWNS Comparison of German and Canadian Artillery.

Another point of comparison was the German *Michael* offensive. The Germans massed 96 pieces per kilometre against the British total of 39 – a differential of 2.5 to 1.[21] This does not include an additional 51 trench mortars per kilometre. In contrast, using a German front-wide average of 32 pieces per kilometre, the Canadian Corps' Arras 1918 figure was 58 guns and howitzers per kilometre. This amounted to a difference of 1.8 to 1.[22] Given the defences at Arras 1918 were markedly superior to those of the British, the Canadian edge was considerably less than in *Michael*. This buttresses the notion that the artillery advantage was not the dominant factor in the success in the Hundred Days.

With machine guns, the primary difference between 1917 and 1918 was that the Canadians closed the machine gun firepower gap. Using the estimate that a light machine gun was the

20 Boff, 'British Third Army' p.77.
21 Watson, *Ring of Steel*, p.294; Edmonds, *Military Operations, 1918* 1, pp.41, 114-115.
22 Boff, 'British Third Army' p.95.

Some of the close to one thousand machine guns captured by the Corps. While the Canadians had more machine guns, so did the Germans in 1918. (Canada. Dept. of National Defence/Library and Archives Canada/PA-003291)

equivalent of 20 riflemen and a heavy machine gun the equal of 40 rifles, a Canadian battalion was close to a German one in machine gun firepower in 1918.[23] Thus, while the Canadians deployed more machine guns than in 1917, so did the enemy. Moreover, this does not account for the number of machine gun sharpshooter detachments assigned to the front. The doubling of the number of Lewis Guns was an important addition to the Canadian infantry. It enabled platoons better to suppress enemy strongpoints and provided greater defensive resiliency against counterattacks. Nevertheless, the increase still left the enemy with a matériel advantage in machine guns and in the tactical employment of heavy machine guns in offensive operations. This meant the Germans still had an important edge in defensive actions.

23 Cron, *Imperial German Army*, p.113; Bidwell and Graham, *Fire-Power*, p.28.

Table C.6 Machine Gun Comparison

		Arras 1917-Scarpe Sector	Canadian Corps Passchendaele 1917	Arras 1918
Germans	LMG/Company	2	4	6
	HMG/Battalion	12	12	12
Canadians	LMG/ Company	4	4	8
	HMG/Battalion	4	5	6
German Firepower	LMG/Battalion	160	320	480
	HMG/Battalion	480	480	480
	Total Firepower Equivalent	**640**	**800**	**960**
Canadian Firepower	LMG/Battalion	320	320	640
	HMG/Battalion	160	200	240
	Total Firepower Equivalent	**480**	**520**	**880**
Differential		33.3%	53.8%	9.1%

LMG = Light Machine Gun
HMG = Heavy Machine Gun

With tanks, the Allies had a clear dominance. The new Mark V tanks were more mobile, mechanically more reliable, and faster. They had important limitations in that they were still slow, broke down, and poisoned their crews. Tanks, depending on the situation, could be an irresistible and profoundly demoralising force that destroyed with impunity. Or, if attacking in the clear, enemy guns and trench mortars would massacre them. The tanks were powerful but fragile and lacked endurance.

Despite these limitations, the tanks still had a talismanic quality to both the Allies and the Germans. German accounts are replete with masses of tanks when only a few were present or none. The XVII Corps repeatedly refused to attack the Hindenburg Line without tank support. The Germans had a poor understanding of tanks' potential and weaknesses, and only after repeated defeats were demonstrations run with captured British tanks to show the troops how to defeat them.[24] These had no effect on the Arras 1918 campaign but demonstrate the mesmerising impact of them as the troops did not realise their vulnerabilities. It also speaks to tank fright and its effects on morale. This effect had repercussions at the higher command levels. Post-battle, the *Seventeenth Armee* asserted that the enemy infantry 'were cowardly without tank

24 Fasse, 'Des „Tankdrachen"' p.280.

protection' and could not succeed without them.[25] It was patently not true. First, less than a quarter of the battalion attacks had any tank support at all. The average concentration of these was 300 metres per tank – well above the GHQ recommendation of no more than 200. Of the 72 battalion attacks without tanks, or where the concentration was below the GHQ minimum, 77 percent were fully or partially successful.

At Arras 1917, the initial attack employed 40 tanks while the Canadians used 13 on the first day of Arras 1918. The Canadians used none at Passchendaele, due to terrible field conditions. In 1918, they were a powerful addition to the arsenal, but the Corps had them available in only a minority of attacks. Further, contrary to the Germans' wildly exaggerated accounts of tank numbers, relatively few served with the Corps. They do not explain the major difference in results between 1917 and 1918.

As discussed in the section on support weapons, the Germans had more trench mortars and employed them more effectively, even though the Corps had better weapons. German mortars were heavy and awkward, but there were many more of them, and the Germans used them far more aggressively. Further, unlike the Canadian models, they could use direct fire. Therefore, in trench mortars there was no matériel superiority.

Where there was both a significant matériel advantage, and it was meaningful, was ammunition supply. Shell shortages limited German artillery.[26] The *Second Armee* on the Amiens front fired only 40-50,000 rounds a day in hard fighting.[27] Similar constraints likely affected the *Seventeenth Armee*. The evidence for this lies in the artillery regimental histories and that immediately after Arras 1918, the *Seventeenth Armee* warned about shortages.[28] The Canadian Corps in contrast expended an average of 95,000 rounds per day from 26 August to 3 September.[29] The Corps fired double the number of shells per day in comparison with a formation at least four times larger. While the Germans had fewer shells meaning fewer attacker casualties, this did not affect the Canadian artillery's tasks. The Canadian artillery still had to suppress the German defenders, and they did not have more ammunition than in 1917. At Passchendaele, the Corps fired 1,453,000 shells and at Arras 1918 1,267,000 shells. Thus, there was not a significant difference. Considering the depth and width of the front, however, the concentration of shells at Passchendaele was 25 times that of Arras 1918. Overall, the ammunition shortages restricted German counter measures and was a factor in their defeat, but it was not the primary reason.

By August 1918, the Allied air services heavily outnumbered the German one. At Arras, the Allies' edge was likely less than at Amiens. The RAF still had a clear superiority and generally successfully carried out their missions when the weather allowed. The Germans, however, could intervene effectively when they massed.[30] They could not do this consistently, but they were still inflicting disproportionate losses on the RAF.

25 Fasse, 'Des „Tankdrachen"' p.285.
26 *Der Weltkrieg* 14.1, p.574.
27 Boff, 'British Third Army' p.76.
28 Bundesarchiv, Freiburg: AOK 17 Radio Message to XVIII AK, 5 September 1918.
29 LAC: Canadian Corps AAQMG WD, Appendix D, September 1918.
30 Wise, *Canadian Airmen* 1, p.555.

Some of the 95,000 rounds fired per day by the Corps. This was a case where the Canadians had a decided matériel advantage over the Germans. (Canada. Dept. of National Defence/Library and Archives Canada/PA-003804)

Table C.7 Aircraft Numbers*

	Arras 1917-Scarpe Sector	Canadian Corps Passchendaele 1917	Amiens 1918
German Aircraft	195	600	365
Allied	365	840	1,904
Differential	1.9	1.4	5.2

Source:
* John Howard Morrow, *The Great War in the Air: Military Aviation from 1909 to 1921* [Washington: Smithsonian Institution Press, 1993), pp.215, 216, 303.

There was a clear advantage in numbers, but how that translated into battlefield results was not significant. Even at the height of 'Bloody April' in 1917 where the Germans were chopping British aircraft out of the sky in dispiriting numbers, the Royal Flying Corps still carried out its missions. The greater quantity of available aircraft allowed more spotting missions, but the bombing and strafing did not have a material effect. German regimental accounts rarely mention RAF attacks, and the multiple complaints in Canadian ones of German strafing their positions offsets this. In addition, the German night bombing, while having a limited physical effect, had an outsized psychological one.

In summary, while there were changes in matériel, they were not of a scale nor scope that explained the dramatically different results. The relative balance between the combatants had not changed significantly. Where there were differences, such as with aircraft and tanks, the limited firepower of aircraft and numbers of tanks restricted their effect. Ammunition shortages interfered with the German artillery response, but it did not account for the magnitude of the Allied victories.

Analysts who advocate for manpower shortages point to the severe losses the Germans suffered during the spring offensives. The enemy had two interrelated manpower problems. First, they did not have enough men. Most of their regiments were woefully under-strength. There were units, such as the *91st RIR*, that amounted to little more than a reinforced company. Most, however, were at one-third to one-half of their reduced establishment. But this was not the complete story. There were regiments like the *214th RIR*, *68th IR*, and *2nd GrR* that were at or almost at full strength after receiving troops from broken-up formations. Thus, unit strengths were highly variable, although the majority were weaker than in 1917. The second issue was the lack of time to train replacements and men received from other units. The regimental histories repeatedly complained that the short rest periods meant there was not enough training to weld the disparate elements into a cohesive and confident force. Even reinforced regiments comprised strangers who had not had time to build trust in their leaders. As a result, they lacked the resiliency that marked German infantry in previous years.

Nevertheless, despite the manpower woes, there were two counterbalancing factors. The lavish allocation of machine guns, as attested by the almost one thousand captured by the Corps, provided a formidable firepower increase. They could still inflict heavy casualties and stop an attack if the attackers did not employ all their advantages. Second, these weakened units mostly defended robust fortifications that required clever tactics, ample firepower, and intrepid troops to overcome. Even in their reduced state, they could put up a strong resistance if not tackled properly.

Did the reduced German morale explain the victories? The simplistic view has their morale was uniformly poor, but the 17,587 casualties and 16 failed battalion attacks demonstrate someone in the German Army was still fighting. A more considered view was that their morale was so variable and differentiated that no blanket statement was accurate, other than it was lower overall than in 1917. A German expert on the impact of tanks contradicted Ludendorff's claims about terror-struck troops fleeing at Amiens. In his view, there were examples of 'panic-stricken behaviour and vanishing will to fight, as well as cases of extraordinary valour and clear unbroken perseverance.'[31] This was true at Arras 1918 as well. One attacking battalion would face fierce resistance, and the one next to it would take prisoners in shoals. The Corps captured 10,514 prisoners. Some Germans did surrender but others could still put up a considerable fight.

31 Fasse, 'Des „Tankdrachen"' p.270.

One German who did not run away. A German machine gunner who fought to the end, with his light Machine Gun MG08/15 lying near him. (Canada. Dept. of National Defence/Library and Archives Canada/PA-003202)

Using the terminology coined by Clausewitz, soldiers' states of mind consisted of their spirit and mood.[32] Spirit was the underlying default morale modified by their mood where defeats, heavy casualties, and lack of food could depress the temper of even highly motivated troops. Rest, warm food, and some replacements could work wonders in recovering their mood. Based on Canadian reports, German units comprised three broad categories of spirit: elite, average, and poor. Elite units facing the Corps comprised machine gunners, artillery gunners, the Guards, and Württemberg regiments. Average ones were the line divisions such as the *35th ID* and *16th ID*. Poor were formations such as the *39th ID* and *91st RIR*.

Elite units were the least affected by adverse circumstances and tended to fight on despite the situation. Canadian reports were consistent in their praise of the dedication, skill, and die-hard nature of the German machine gunners and artillery. The performance of the *1st GRD* and the

32 Clausewitz, Howard, and Paret, *On War*, p.189.

26th RD and their ability to battle on despite Canadian manpower and matériel superiority highlighted their high morale. They were not invulnerable, however, to exhaustion, casualties, and surprise. Evidence of this was the rapid destruction of the *121st RIR* on 30 August. Of the 21 actions where the Canadians or British engaged elite units, the only successes were when facing an exhausted defender.[33] In every other instance, the Germans were successful in stopping the attack.

Average units fought well when they had the advantage, but their mood was more susceptible to collapse when exhausted or subjected to a barrage. A specimen of this was the *16th ID*, which launched a series of powerful counterattacks on 30 August that initially drove back the 1st Brigade. After these attacks, however, its *68th IR* dissolved into masses of prisoners when struck by the barrage supported attack on 1 September. Average and weak category units were counterintuitively more prone to surrender in larger numbers when there were deep dugouts available. These allowed defenders to shelter from the Canadian barrage and then submit with reduced risk. There was always a danger in surrendering but doing so after the heat of battle meant a greater chance of survival.[34] The Canadian Corps attacks had a 94 percent success rate where they encountered average morale units. Poor units started with a weak spirit. Unfavourable circumstances, such as a tank and barrage attack, greatly influenced them. Formations like the *2nd GRD* needed very advantageous conditions to resist, and any adversity caused a rapid disintegration.

Reflecting the overall state of the German Army, the *II Bavarian Korps* had too few elite units and too many poor ones at the front to provide a sustained and coherent resistance. With the switch to open warfare tactics, the Canadian attacks would exploit soft spots to strike the flanks and so totally overrun, overcome, and capture the defenders. Nevertheless, while the weaker morale contributed to the German defeat, it was not the only factor, or even the primary one. There were sufficient fragments of elite forces, like the Guards and machine gunners, to resist if not attacked effectively. Again, the Corps' defeats and casualties inflicted indicated many Germans continued to fight and fight well.

In order for the argument for method as the key factor to be credible, it must first be demonstrated that there was a major change in methods between 1917 and 1918. In every important dimension the methods employed by the Canadian Corps during the Hundred Days differed markedly from those in 1917, as Tables 3.1 and C.4 show. The tempo of operations accelerated from multiple days between major attacks to one every day. There was no time for the elaborate preparations that marked the set-piece attacks of 1917. The speed of the advance doubled or tripled, and its depth increased by up to 10 times. Troop and fire support densities dropped to half to a third. The artillery could rely on predicted fire to obviate the necessity of registration. Smoke was broadly and effectively used. Infiltration tactics were far more aggressive and reliant on outflanking the enemy than before. The Corps integrated weapons and support systems into an open or at least semi-open warfare model. Operational and tactical surprise was a common feature. Thus, by every important measure the Corps' methods had changed significantly between 1917 and 1918.

33 Five of these engagements were by the 2nd Division on 27 August. The division smashed the *39th ID* but the *26th RD* repelled the attack. Both sets of attacks were included in the database as a special case.

34 For more on this, see Cook, 'Politics of Surrender'.

CS Forester in his novel The General referred to British attacks in 1916 as 'the debate of a group of savages as to how to extract a screw from a piece of wood.'[35] Knowing only nails, they kept applying more and more force. The Germans' defensive methods in 1916/17 morphed in effect to a screw and thus would frustrate attacks expecting a nail. By 1918, the BEF and the Canadian Corps had learned how to deal with screws, but they at times did not apply those techniques and failed. Thus, the key factor for victory was if the Corps employed the appropriate technique, they would win. The enemy's reduced manpower and morale and the Allied matériel superiority boosted their efforts. But, if the Corps did not use the right approach, the advantages of morale, manpower, and matériel were not enough to defeat the Germans. The 16 battalion attack failures attest to this. If those elements were as critical as thought, then the method should not have mattered.

Assaults by the 5th Brigade and 116th Battalion on 27 August, the 4th and 5th Brigades again the next day, and the 4th Canadian Division on 2 September illustrate the criticality of method. The Canadians made all four assaults without either the support of smoke, an effective barrage, or with little to no tank support. The results were calamitous, with only three partially successful attacks and nine failures with a loss rate 60 percent greater than the Corps' average. For instance, the *26th RD* trounced Burstall's two attacks by the 5th Brigade. Yet, the 3rd Battalion successfully attacked the F-R Line head on with a narrower front than had the 5th Brigade. Admittedly, the prolonged defence had worn down the Germans, but they were still holding strong defences that had easily defeated the 5th Brigade. The difference was the 3rd Battalion had the benefit of a proper barrage covered by smoke, demonstrating again that method was the critical success element.

Did it Matter?

Did the Canadian Corps' capture of the D-Q Line have any large-scale consequences? Or, was it just a part of a series of blows that defeated the German army and so was not worthy of special comment? The commander of the Third Army, Sir Julian Byng, thought it was critical, as he told Currie that 'smashing of the Quéant-Drocourt Line was the turning point in the campaign.'[36] Had the Corps stumbled and not taken the D-Q Line the ramifications could have been enormous. A failure at the D-Q Line would likely have enabled British Prime Minister Lloyd George to finally unseat Haig. He had tried to displace Haig from the start of his premiership. Now, he would have the final evidence to convince the War Cabinet, especially, after the private warning to Haig to avoid heavy losses. Given Haig's possible fate, his replacement would have stopped the offensive and waited for 1919. Even if Lloyd George had not replaced Haig, the Canadian failure would have delayed the follow-on offensives. The BEF did not have the reserves to replace the Canadian Corps, so would have had to rely on it to finish the job. But it needed time to recover – at least two weeks to do so. This would have pushed back the Hindenburg Line attacks and given time for the Germans to revive, despite their problems both military and domestic. With the weather getting worse, any postponements would risk the main attack encountering adverse conditions. As it was, the British advance was on a thin logistical edge.

35 CS Forester, *The General* (Middlesex, UK: Penguin Books, 1936), p.173.
36 Quoted in Cook, *Shock Troops*, p.499.

Pushing it back well into November and December might have forced ending the onslaught because of logistics. Moreover, the second wave of the influenza epidemic struck in October and November. If it had hit while the fighting was still intense, it would have had a significant effect. All these factors would result in waiting to the spring to launch the 1919 offensives. Germany would still have lost but a further six months or more would have an incalculable impact on the postwar situation. Even with the conflict ending in November, there was a fervent, febrile, and destabilising temper with revolution, chaos, strikes, anger, and destruction of the old order. A further six months of fighting would have magnified these. The Allies would win but what would they have won? The Corps' victory was thus critical.

Four years before Arras 1918, the volunteers of Canada's First Contingent started arriving at camp at Valcartier in Quebec.[37] They were enthusiastic but virtually untrained, and their officers were even less prepared. Canada had no experience in sending and maintaining a large expeditionary force an ocean away. An unbiased observer would not have given this motley contingent much of a chance of emerging as a *nonpareil* force. Yet by the Hundred Days, the Canadian Corps had transformed into an elite formation and the equal of the best on the Western Front. Regarded within the BEF and by the Germans as in the first rank, the Corps was the spearhead on key offensives at Amiens and Arras 1918. What Arras 1918 illustrated was the immense progress the Canadian Corps had made from a disjointed, untrained, and poorly administered militia force to one capable of taking on and defeating the best the Germans could field. There were stumbles and failures, but the Corps performed superbly and demonstrated what Canadians can do, not only on the battlefield but at home and around the world, when unified by a common cause. A lesson that applied then and today and in the future.

37 The first volunteers started arriving on 18 August and the numbers at Valcartier rose to 20,089 on 27 August 1914. Duguid, *Canadian Forces in the Great War* 1, p.20; Duguid, *Canadian Forces in the Great War* 1, p.45.

Appendices

Appendix I

Historiographical Debate

Significant errors in the *Report of the Ministry* and the Canadian Official History mar the Arras 1918 historiography. Owing to their official status, they established a flawed narrative that subsequent studies have repeated. The *Report of the Ministry* was Currie's bid to set the standard narrative for the operations in 1918 – which it did.[1] Angry at how Max Aitken, later Lord Beaverbrook, had treated his command in previous works, Currie wanted to set the canonical version. To that end, Currie established the CWNS and populated it with experienced staff officers headed by Raymond Brutinel. At the time the CWNS was working on the *Report of the Ministry* after the Armistice, Currie was under intense stress and concerned about his reputation and how the British would bury the Corps' accomplishments in their histories.[2] Thus, the report would both highlight the Corps' achievements and provide a justification and defence for the Corps' 48,000 casualties suffered during the Hundred Days. CWNS wrote it with an eye to protect Currie's reputation. The resulting work was an anodyne product, with a tone giving it the imprimatur of an official history.[3] It remained the only substantive official Canadian account of the Hundred Days until the 1964 *Canadian Expeditionary Force.*

The *Report* went through two drafts, and in the process the writers modified the text to fit Currie's wishes, and so introduced errors. This despite Currie's and Brutinel's insistence that the text be 'complete and accurate.'[4] These errors were in some cases repeated in the Canadian Official History that added its own distortion in its account of 2 September. The *Report*'s first major error was misdating when Haig issued the more aggressive attack order. Both the *Report* and the Canadian Official History incorrectly state Haig issued this order on 22 August.[5] On 22 August, Horne issued instructions for the Canadian Corps to assault Orange Hill, and on 24 August, Haig expanded the operation to crossing the Canal du Nord – a far more ambitious objective. This was not just a simple error as an early draft had the right sequence, so Currie or Brutinel changed it. Possibly it was to simplify the sequence of events, but more likely it was to demonstrate that Currie and the Corps did not have to rush the operation.

1 Cook, *Clio's Warriors*, pp.34-35.
2 Cook, *The Madman and the Butcher*, pp.234-236, 260-261, 268-272.
3 Kemp, *Report of the Ministry*.
4 Cook, *Clio's Warriors*, p.34.
5 Kemp, *Report of the Ministry*, p.143; NLS: Haig Diary, 24 August 1918; LAC: Currie Diary, 24 August 1918; LAC: RG9 III-D-2 v4809: CWNS Battle of Arras Draft; Nicholson, *CEF*, p.426.

The *Report* erroneously claimed the 2nd Division attacked along with the 3rd Division at 4:55 a.m. on 27 August. It actually attacked five hours after the 3rd. Such a long delay would not look good, so the history covered it up. Similarly, the account for 28 August had the 3rd Division attacking at 9:00 a.m. and the 2nd at 12:30 p.m. The 3rd's first attack was at 5:00 a.m. The *Report* particularly garbled the D-Q Line operation dates stating the Corps issued the initial plans for the attack on 28 August with an intent on attacking on 1 September.[6] This meant Currie only postponed it once and for only one day. The first discussion of attacking the D-Q Line was late on 26 August with an expected date of 28 August in a First Army order.[7] There were five date shifts, so Currie wanted the account to ignore these delays as they could raise questions about competency.

The Canadian Official History took the timing of the orders for the initial attack from the *Report of the Ministry* and added another error that is now part of the standard narrative. Based on an interview with Andrew McNaughton in 1963, the Official Historian, GWL Nicholson, created a myth about the reason for the 4th Division's failure. Based on McNaughton's statement, the Nicholson claimed the artillery suspended the 4th Division's supporting barrage to allow Brutinel's CIF to advance down the Arras-Cambrai road. McNaughton also claimed RAF reports of CIF's armoured cars near Marquion prevented his heavy artillery from engaging enemy batteries located there. Even a cursory examination of the 4th Division's files shows the reason for the failure was fire from areas far removed from this zone. Why then did Nicholson accept McNaughton's statement? There were two factors at play – time and status. Nicholson had limited time to write the Official History and space was running out when he reached 1918. The description of Arras 1918 is the same length as a far less important action at Hill 70 in 1917. The result was errors in the maps and the narrative absent from the earlier chapters.[8] McNaughton was a revered figure with a lifetime of accomplishments, and he was the Corps' most senior officer alive in the early 1960s. The result was there was no one else to contradict McNaughton.

McNaughton's error stemmed from a faulty memory combined with professional clashes with Brutinel. He admitted that he had not consulted files, maps, or books for the interview.[9] The general was going from memory of events that occurred 44 years earlier, so errors were not surprising. Also, he had two serious professional disagreements with Brutinel in 1918 that he repeated in 1963. McNaughton was still angry that Brutinel claimed it was his advice to Currie that caused the Corps commander to argue for stopping the Amiens. Brutinel's claim that heavy German losses at Valciennes in November 1918 were the result of indirect machine fire rather than artillery fire upset him.

6 Kemp, *Report of the Ministry*, p.150.
7 TNA: First Army GS WD, First Army G.36, 26 August 1918.
8 For instance, the colour map for the battle shows the 19th Battalion attacking on 1 September when it was well to the rear. Nicholson, *CEF*, p.432.
9 CWM: "Flanders Fields" Transcribed Tapes by General A.G.L. McNaughton.

Appendix II

Comparison German and Canadian Divisions

This appendix compares the nominal establishment of a German division with a Canadian one.[1] While both would be under-strength in combat operations, the German formations were usually considerably weaker and especially in infantry.

A.1 German and Canadian Division Establishment Comparison

	German Division				Canadian Division			
Unit	**#**	**Unit Strength**	**Total**	**Category Total**	**#**	**Unit Establishment**	**Total**	**Category Total**
Division HQ	1	108	108	**108**	1	173	173	**173**
Infantry				**8,407**				**13,617**
Brigade HQ	1	13	13		3	33	99	
Regimental HQ	3	59	177				-	
Infantry Battalion	9	776	6,984		12	1,114	13,368	
Machine Gun Company	9	137	1,233				-	
Trench Mortar Battery			-		3	50	150	
Cavalry Squadron	1	170	170	**170**			-	
Artillery				**1,363**				**2,502**

1 LAC: RG9 III-D-2 v4801, 128: CWNS Intelligence German Divisions 100 Days.

Headquarters	1	25	25		1	24	24	
Field Artillery Regiment HQ	1	18	18				-	
Artillery Battalions/Brigades	3	440	1,320		2	828	1,656	
Trench Mortar					3		183	
Division Ammunition Column			1	639	639			
Pioneers/ Engineers				**838**				**3,136**
Headquarters	1	5	5		1	28	28	
Field Companies/ Battalions	2	268	536		3	1,014	3,042	
Searchlight	1	47	47					
Trench Mortar Company	1	250	250					
Bridging Transport Unit					1	66	66	
Division Troops				**747**				**3,322**
Telephone/Signal Coy	1	200	200		1	297	297	
Mechanical Transport Coy	1	100	100		1	436	436	
Bearer Company	1	250	250					
Field Hospital/ Ambulance	2	61	122		3	245	735	
Veterinary	1	75	75		1	22	22	
Employment Coy			-		1	275	275	
MG Battalion					1	1,557	1,557	
TOTAL				**11,463**				**22,750**

Appendix III

Formations, Units, Commanders, and Staff

This appendix lists the Canadian and British formations and units along with their commanders and staff where available and German divisions, their formations and units, and commanders. Included in the British formations are divisions, the 3rd Tank Brigade, and I Brigade RAF.

Canadian Units

This section lists Canadian formations, units, commanders, and staff.[1] The majority of the names come from a 28 September 1918 document. The list was updated to reflect, where known, the situation during Arras 1918. Units in italics, while part of the Corps or the CEF, did not serve with it during Arras 1918 or arrived after the offensive had ended.

Table A.2 Canadian Units, Commanders and Staff

Abbreviations

Ranks

LT	Lieutenant
CPT	Captain
MAJ	Major
LTC	Lieutenant Colonel
COL	Colonel
BG	Brigadier General
MG	Major General
LTG	Lieutenant General

1 CWM: 19801226-275 58 A1, 160.4: Currie Fonds, Command and Staff List, 28 September 1918; LAC: RG9 III-C-4 v4268, 2/5: Staff Appointments and Commanding Officers 3rd Division, 2 June 1918; Nicholson, *CEF*, pp.544-545.

Units and Positions

2i/c	2nd in command
a/	Acting
AAQMG	Assistant Adjutant-General and Quartermaster-General
ADC	Aide-de-Camp
ADJ	Adjutant
ADMS	Assistant Director of Medical Services
BM	Brigade Major
Bty	Battery
CBSO	Counter-Battery Staff Officer
CCC	Canadian Corps Cyclist
CCHA	Canadian Corps Heavy Artillery
CE	Canadian Engineers
CFA	Canadian Field Artillery
CGA	Canadian Garrison Artillery
CHB	Canadian Heavy Battery
CLH	Canadian Light Horse
CMG	Canadian Machine Gun Corps
CMGO	Corps Machine Gun Officer
CMMG	Canadian Motor Machine Gun
CRA	Commander, Royal Artillery
CRE	Commander, Royal Engineers
CSB	Canadian Siege Battery
CSO	Corps Signals Officer
D	Deputy
DAAQMG	Deputy Assistant Adjutant-General and Quartermaster-General
DAC	Division Ammunition Column
DDMS	Deputy Director Medical Services
DTMO	Deputy Trench Mortar Officer
FE	Field Engineer
H	Howitzer
OO	Orderly Officer
PBTU	Pontoon and Bridge Transport Unit
Recce	Reconnaissance
S&T	Supplies and Transport
SC	Staff Captain
SIO	Senior Intelligence Officer
SL	Staff Lieutenant
SO	Staff Officer
TMB	Trench Mortar Battery
TOPO	Topographic Officer

Designation	Unit	Position	Rank	Initials	Surname	Notes
Canadian Corps						
Canadian Corps		GOC	LTG	AW	Currie	
		ADC	MAJ	H	Willis O'Connor	
		ADC	LT	HR	Watt	
		ADC	CPT	WJ	Shaugnhessy	
		BGGS	BG	NW	Webber	
		GSO 1	LTC	MC	Festing	
		GSO 2	MAJ	TM	McAvity	
		GSO 2	LTC	RP	Clark	
		GSO 3	MAJ	FM	Bressey	
		SC	CPT	SA	Vernon	
		Topo	LT	WR	Flewin	
		SIO	CPT	CW	Erlebach	
		SIO	LT	CC	Brooks	
		DA&QMG	BG	GJ	Farmar	
		AQMG	LTC	WB	Anderson	
		DAQMG	MAJ	BW	Browne	
		DAAG	MAJ	W	Bovey	
		CSO	LTC	E	Forde	
		DDMS	COL	AE	Snell	
		Chemical Advisor	MAJ	WE	Harris	
Artillery						
	GOCRA	GOCRA	MG	EWB	Morrison	
		a/SO RA	MAJ	HDG	Crerar	
		SO Recce	CPT	G	Tyndal-Lea	
		SC RA	CPT	HD	Fripp	
		CBSO	LTC	AGL	McNaughton	
		SO CBO	CPT	LP	Napier	
	5th CDA	GOC	BG	WHO	Dodds	
	13th CFA	CO	LTC	EG	Hanson	
	52nd Bty					
	53rd Bty					
	55th Bty					

Designation	Unit	Position	Rank	Initials	Surname	Notes
	51st H Bty					
	14th CFA	CO	LTC	AT	Oglivie	
	60th Bty					
	61st Bty					
	66th Bty					
	58th H Bty					
	5th DAC	CO	LTC			
	8th CFA	CO	LTC	JC	Stewart	
	E Anti-Aircraft Bty	OC				
	CCHA	GOC	BG	RH	Massie	
		BM	MAJ	NW	Aitken	
		SC	CPT	M	Spencer-Smith	
		SL Recce	LT	AEW	Nesbitt	
		Intel	LT	FGH	Davidson	
	1st CGA	*CO*	LTC	WB	Prowse	
	1st CSB	*OC*	MAJ	WH	Dobbie	
	3rd CSB	*OC*	MAJ	W	Leggat	
	7th CSB	*OC*	MAJ	CJ	Macmillan	
	9th CSB	*OC*	MAJ	WG	Scully	
	2nd CGA	CO	LTC	FC	Magee	
	1st CHB	OC	MAJ	CF	Inches	
	2nd CHB	OC	MAJ	RJ	Leach	
	2nd CSB	OC	MAJ	HRN	Cobbett	
	4th CSB	OC	MAJ	LW	Barker	
	5th CSB	OC	MAJ	NP	MacLeod	
	6th CSB	OC	MAJ	TE	Ryder	
	3rd CGA	*CO*	*LTC*	*WG*	*Beeman*	
	8th CSB	*OC*	MAJ	RA	Ring	
	10th CSB	*OC*	MAJ	LC	Ord	
	11th CSB	*OC*	MAJ	SA	Heward	
	12th CSB	*OC*	MAJ	FM	Robertson	
Machine Guns						
	CMGO	GOC	BG	R	Brutinel	
		SO	MAJ	WB	Forster	

Designation	Unit	Position	Rank	Initials	Surname	Notes
		SC	CPT	JK	Lawson	
		SL Recce	LT	PH	Humme	
	1st CMMG	CO	LTC	WK	Walker	
	2nd CMMG	CO	LTC	HF	Meurling	
Engineers						
	Chief Engineer	GOC	BG	WB	Lindsay	
		SO	MAJ	FO	Hodgins	
		SC A	CPT	AT	McLean	
		SC S&T	CPT	ECG	Chambers	
		FE Tramways	MAJ	RP	Rogers	
		FE Roads	MAJ	RS	Smith	
		FE Defences	CPT	EP	Fetherstonhaugh	
	Corps Signal Coy	OC				
	Corps Survey Section	OC				
	1st-5th Army Troops Coy	OC				
	AA Searchlight Coy	OC				
	3rd Tunnelling Coy	OC				
	1st Tramways Coy	*OC*				
	2nd Tramways Coy	OC				
Cavalry						
	CLH	CO	LTC	IB	Leonard	
Cyclists						
	CCC Battalion	OC	MAJ	E	Humphrey	
1st Division						
DIVISION HQ						
	1st Division	GOC	MG	AC	Macdonell	
		GSO 1	LTC	JLR	Parsons	
		GSO 2 O	LTC	HH	Matthews	
		GSO 2 T	MAJ	WB	Wedd	
		GSO 3 O	CPT	JH	Chipman	
		GSO 3 I	MAJ	JCL	Young	
		AA&QMG	LTC	JS	Brown	

Designation	Unit	Position	Rank	Initials	Surname	Notes
		DAAG A	MAJ	BW	Browne	
		DAAG B	MAJ	FR	Phelan	
		DAQMG	MAJ	P	Hennessy	
ARTILLERY						
	1st CDA	CRA	BG	HC	Thacker	
		BM	MAJ	AH	Bick	
		SC A	CPT	ROG	Bennett	
		SC Q	LT	IM	Macdonell	
		SC for Recon	CPT	HH	Blake	
	1st CFA	CO	LTC	JG	Piercey	
		ADJ				
	1st Bty	OC				
	2nd H Bty	OC				
	3rd Bty	OC				
	4th Bty	OC				
	2nd CFA	CO	LTC	SB	Anderson	
		ADJ				
	5th Bty	OC				
	6th Bty	OC				
	7th Bty	OC				
	48th H Bty	OC				
	1st DAC	CO				
	1st DTMO	OC				
INFANTRY						
	1st Brigade	GOC	BG	WA	Griesbach	
		BM	MAJ	HWA	Foster	
		SC	MAJ	LT	Outerbridge	
		SC	CPT	JC	Matheson	
		OO	LT	LW	Taylor	
	1st TMB	OC				
	1st Battalion	CO	LTC	AW	Sparling	
		2nd i/c	MAJ	TR	Coleman	
		ADJ	CPT	AV	Yates	
	2nd Battalion	CO	LTC	L	McLaughlin	WIA
		CO	MAJ	R	Vanderwater	From 3/9

Designation	Unit	Position	Rank	Initials	Surname	Notes
		2nd i/c	MAJ	FP	Strachan	
		ADJ	CPT	WW	Murray	
	3rd Battalion	a/CO	MAJ	DHC	Mason	WIA
						From 2/9
		a/CO	MAJ	WH	Kippen	WIA
		a/CO	CPT	JK	Crawford	From 2/9
	4th Battalion	a/CO	MAJ	GG	Blackstock	
		ADJ	a/MAJ	SH	Griffin	
	2nd Brigade	GOC	BG	FOW	Loomis	
		BM	CPT	WD	Herridge	
		SC	MAJ	MK	Greene	
		SC	CPT	TS	Chutter	
		OO	CPT	HD	Ives	
	2nd TMB	OC				
	5th Battalion	CO	LTC	LPO	Tudor	
		2nd i/c	MAJ	E	Day	
		ADJ	LT	WT	Bobbington	
	7th Battalion	CO	LTC	WF	Gilson	
		2nd i/c	MAJ	RM	Harcourt	
		ADJ	CPT	JE	Mathews	
	8th Battalion	CO	MAJ	AL	Saunders	
		2nd i/c	CPT	DK	Turner	
		ADJ	CPT	CB	Smith	
	10th Battalion	CO	LTC	EW	MacDonald	
		2nd i/c	MAJ	HC	Ferguson	
		ADJ	CPT	HE	Pearson	
	3rd Brigade	GOC	BG	GS	Tuxford	
		BM	MAJ	AD	Wilson	
		SC	CPT	TB	Barrie	
		SC	CPT	NL	Lesueur	
		OO	LT	JA	Tuxford	
	3rd TMB	OC				
	13th Battalion	CO	LTC	GE	McCuaig	
		2nd i/c	MAJ	IMR	Sinclair	
		ADJ	LT	FC	Smith	

Designation	Unit	Position	Rank	Initials	Surname	Notes
	14th Battalion	CO	LTC	D	Worrall	
		2nd i/c	MAJ	CB	Price	
		ADJ	CPT	D	MacRitchie	
	15th Battalion	a/CO	MAJ	JP	Girvan	
		2nd i/c	CPT	GS	Winnifrith	
		ADJ	LT	HH	Donald	
	16th Battalion	CO	LTC	CW	Peck	
		2nd i/c	MAJ	RO	Bell-Irving	
		ADJ	CPT	JR	Paton	
ENGINEERS						
	1st CE Brigade	CRE	COL	A	Macphail	
		BM	LTC	JP	MacKenzie	
		SC A&Q	CPT	FJ	O'Leary	
		SC S&T	CPT	GR	Chatwynd	
	1st CE Battalion	CO	LTC	CB	Russell	
		2nd i/c	MAJ	L>T	Tweed	
		ADJ	CAPT	RH	Neilson	
	2nd CE Battalion	CO	LTC	JM	Rolsten	
		2nd i/c	MAJ	EF	Lynn	
		ADJ	LT	AM	Reid	
	3rd CE Battalion	CO	MAJ	E	Pepler	
		2nd i/c	MAJ	CB	North	
		ADJ	LT	GA	Bennet	
	1st PBTU	OC				
	1st Div Signal Coy	OC	MAJ	P	Earnshaw	
		2nd i/c	CPT			
SUPPORT SERVICES						
	1st Division Train	CO	LTC	CA	Corrigan	
		ADJ	CPT			
	1st Division Medical	ADMS	COL	RP	Wright	
	1st Field Ambulance	CO	LTC	GJ	Boyce	
	2nd Field Ambulance	CO	MAJ	HM	Barrett	
	3rd Field Ambulance	CO	LTC	AS	Donaldson	

Designation	Unit	Position	Rank	Initials	Surname	Notes
	1st CMG Battalion	CO	LTC	SW	Watson	
		2nd i/c	MAJ	R	Murdie	
		ADJ	CPT	LG	Francis	

2nd Division

Designation	Unit	Position	Rank	Initials	Surname	Notes
DIVISION HQ						
	2nd Division	GOC	MG	HE	Burstall	
		GSO 1	LTC	WR	Bertram	
		GSO 2 O	LTC	RO	Alexander	On Course
		GSO 2 T	LTC	W	Rae	
		GSO 3 O	MAJ	HF	Hall	
		GSO 3 I	MAJ	GI	Gwynn	4th Brigade BM
		AA&QMG	LTC	PJ	Montague	
		DAAG A	LTC	DWB	Spry	
		DAAG B	CPT	PE	Colman	
		DAQMG	MAJ	DEA	Rispin	
ARTILLERY						
	2nd CDA	CRA	BG	HA	Panet	
		BM	MAJ	JC	Ball	
		SC A	CPT	JL	Duncan	
		SC Q	CPT	W	Harty	
		SC for Recce	LT	AJ	Cowan	
	5th CFA	CO	LTC	CF	Constantine	
		ADJ				
	17th Bty	OC				
	18th Bty	OC				
	2nd Bty	OC				
	2nd H Bty	OC				
	6th CFA	CO	LTC	JF	McParland	
		ADJ				
	15th Bty	OC				
	16th Bty	OC				
	2nd Bty	OC				
	2nd H Bty	OC				
	2nd DAC	CO				

Designation	Unit	Position	Rank	Initials	Surname	Notes
	2nd DTMO	OC				
INFANTRY						
	4th Brigade	GOC	BG	R	Rennie	
		a/BM	MAJ	GI	Gwynn	
		SC	CPT	HW	Morgan	
		SC	CPT	HW	Scruton	
		OO	CPT	MS	Gooderham	
	4th TMB	OC				
	18th Battalion	CO	MAJ	JS	McIntosh	WIA
		a/CO	MAJ	JS	Bell	
		2nd i/c	MAJ	JS	Bell	
		ADJ	LT	C	Cook	
	19th Battalion	CO	LTC	LH	Millen	
		2nd i/c	MAJ	HC	Hatch	
		ADJ	CPT	RH	Bliss	
	20th Battalion	CO	MAJ	BO	Hooper	
		2nd i/c	MAJ	CJ	Inglis	
		ADJ	CPT	CEH	Medhurst	
	21st Battalion	CO	LTC	HE	Pense	
		2nd i/c	MAJ	CS	Bowerbank	
		ADJ	CPT	FD	Raymond	
	5th Brigade	GOC	BG	TL	Tremblay	
		BM	MAJ	JC	Kemp	
		SC	CPT	J	Black	
		SC	CPT	JF	McKay	
		OO	CPT	AS	Boa	
	5th TMB	OC				
	22nd Battalion	CO	Maj	AE	Dubuc	WIA 28 Aug
		a/CO	MAJ	GP	Vanier	WIA
		2nd i/c	CPT	H	Chasse	
		ADJ	LT	DA	DesLauriers	
	24th Battalion	CO	LTC	WH	Clark-Kennedy	WIA
		2nd i/c	MAJ	PL	Hall	
		ADJ	LT	EH	Hart	

Designation	Unit	Position	Rank	Initials	Surname	Notes
	25th Battalion	CO	LTC	FP	Day	
		2nd i/c	MAJ	CJ	Mersereau	
		ADJ	CPT	GW	Anderson	
	26th Battalion	CO	LTC	AEG	McKenzie	KIA
		a/CO	MAJ	CG	Porter	
		2nd i/c	MAJ	CG	Porter	
		ADJ	CPT	HG	Wood	
	6th Brigade	GOC	BG	AH	Bell	
		BM	MAJ	Hon FE	Grosvenor	
		SC	MAJ	AE	Duncanson	
		SC	MAJ	DF	Keith	
		OO	CPT	HN	Petty	
	6th TMB	OC				
	27th Battalion	CO	LTC	HJ	Riley	
		2nd i/c	MAJ	KL	Patton	
		ADJ	CPT	C	Curran	
	28th Battalion	CO	LTC	A	Ross	
		2nd i/c	MAJ	CF	Bond	
		ADJ	CPT	L G	Chance	
	29th Battalion	CO	MAJ	LS	Wilmot	
		2nd i/c				
		ADJ	CPT	EH	Daniel	
	31st Battalion	CO	LTC	ES	Doughty	
		2nd i/c	MAJ	N	Spencer	
		ADJ	CPT	GS	Robertson	
ENGINEERS						
	2nd CE Brigade	CRE	LTC	SH	Osler	
		BM	CPT	JAG	White	
		SC A&Q	CPT	RG	Saunders	
		SC S&T	CPT	WE	Bull	
	4th CE Battalion	CO	LTC	HDStA	Smith	
		2nd i/c	MAJ	AB	Ritchie	
		ADJ	CPT	VW	Price	
	5th CE Battalion	CO	LTC	CW	Allen	

Designation	Unit	Position	Rank	Initials	Surname	Notes
		2nd i/c	MAJ	JA	Morphy	
		ADJ	LT	RB	Gibson	
	6th CE Battalion	CO	LTC	AL	Mieville	
		2nd i/c	MAJ	EW	Harrison	
		ADJ	CPT	RD	Hague	
	2nd PBTU	OC				
	2nd Div Signal Coy	OC	MAJ	AA	Anderson	
		2nd i/c				
SUPPORT SERVICES						
	2nd Division Train	CO	LTC	C McA	Scott	
		ADJ				
	2nd Division Medical	ADMS	COL	RM	Simpson	
	4th Field Ambulance	CO	LTC	RH	Macdonald	
	5th Field Ambulance	CO	LTC	DK	Kappelle	
	6th Field Ambulance	CO	LTC	TJF	Murphy	
	2nd CMG Battalion	CO	LTC	JG	Weir	
		2nd i/c	MAJ	JE	McCorkell	
		ADJ	CPT	GN	Douglas	
3rd Division						
DIVISION HQ						
	3rd Division	GOC	MG	LJ	Lipsett	
		GSO 1	LTC	CM	Hore-Ruthven	
		GSO 2 O	MAJ	AF	Duguid	
		GSO 2 T	MAJ	APO	Meredith	
		GSO 3 O	MAJ	DFB	Gray	
		GSO 3 I	CPT	SL	Cunningham	
		AA&QMG	LTC	WWP	Gibsone	
		DAAG A	MAJ	GG	Blackstock	
		DAAG B	MAJ	RJ	Brock	
		DAQMG	MAJ	WA	Harrison	
ARTILLERY						
	3rd CDA	CRA	BG	JS	Stewart	
		BM	MAJ	JMcK	MacDonnell	

Designation	Unit	Position	Rank	Initials	Surname	Notes
		SC A	CPT	LStG	Kelly	
		SC Q	CPT	JE	Eastlake	
		SC for Recon	LT	JC	Carroll	
	9th CFA	CO	LTC	FT	Coghlan	
		ADJ	LT	TC	Wood	
	31st Bty	OC	MAJ	AC	Ryerson	
	33rd Bty	OC	MAJ	EV	Thompson	
	36th Bty	OC	MAJ	DA	McKinnon	
	45th Bty	OC	MAJ	LVM	Cosgrave	
	10th CFA	CO	LTC	GH	Ralston	
		ADJ	LT	TC	Wood	
	35th Bty	OC	MAJ	AT	Davidson	
	38th Bty	OC	MAJ	AWW	Ker	
	39th Bty	OC	MAJ	RT	Young	
	45th Bty	OC	MAJ	WD	Wilson	
	3rd DAC	CO	LTC	WG	Hurdman	
	3rd DAC	ADJ	CPT	JH	Strothers	
	3rd DTMO	OC	CPT	HO	Bennett	
INFANTRY						
	7th Brigade	GOC	BG	HM	Dyer	
		BM	MAJ	AG	Styles	
		SC	CPT	E	Osborne	
		SC	CPT	WJ	Wilby	
		OO	LT	D	McGillvray	
	7th TMB	OC	CPT	J	KeLTie	
	RCR Battalion	a/CO	MAJ	CRE	Willets	
		2nd i/c	CPT	RE	Balders	
		ADJ	CPT	FD	McCrae	
	PPCLI Battalion	CO	LTC	CJT	Stewart	
		2nd i/c	CPT	M	Tenbrocke	
		ADJ	LT	AR	Chapman	
	42nd Battalion	a/CO	MAJ	RLH	Ewing	
		2nd i/c	MAJ	CB	Topp	

Designation	Unit	Position	Rank	Initials	Surname	Notes
		ADJ				
	49th Battalion	CO	LTC	CY	Weaver	
		2nd i/c	MAJ	AP	Chattell	
		ADJ	CPT	GH	Nolan	
	8th Brigade	GOC	BG	DC	Draper	
		BM	MAJ	SC	Norsworthy	
		SC	MAJ	JK	Keefler	
		SC	CPT	JD	Craig	
		OO	LT	GW	Craig	
	8th TMB	OC	CPT	JW	Lewis	
	1st CMR Battalion	CO	LTC	B	Laws	
		2nd i/c	CPT	WE	Maxfield	
		ADJ	CPT	JA	Wotherspoon	
	2nd CMR Battalion	CO	LTC	GC	Johnston	
		2nd i/c	MAJ	LW	Miller	
		ADJ	CPT	CFHK	Douglas	
	4th CMR Battalion	CO	LTC	WR	Patterson	
		2nd i/c	MAJ	WV	Sifton	
		ADJ	CPT	G	Clark	
	5th CMR Battalion	CO	LTC	W	Rhoades	
		a/2nd i/c	CPT	JSE	Todd	
		ADJ	LT	HFC	Cocks	
	9th Brigade	GOC	BG	DM	Ormond	
		BM	CPT	L	Younger	
		SC	MAJ	GE	Leighton	
		SC	MAJ	RM	Redmond	
		OO	LT	FG	Rump	
	9th TMB	OC	CPT	AWG	Good	
	43rd Battalion	CO	LTC	WK	Chandler	
		2nd i/c				
		ADJ	CPT	R	Shankland	
	52nd Battalion	CO	LTC	DM	Sutherland	
		2nd i/c	MAJ	WT	Lawless	
		ADJ	CPT	GS	Rutherford	
	58th Battalion	a/CO	MAJ	RE	Smythe	

Designation	Unit	Position	Rank	Initials	Surname	Notes
		2nd i/c	MAJ	MD	Carmichael	
		ADJ	CPT	AT	Field	
	116th Battalion	a/CO	MAJ	J	Sutherland	KIA
		2nd i/c	Serving as acting CO			
		ADJ	CPT	AF	Hind	
ENGINEERS						
	3rd CE Brigade	CRE	LTC	HFH	Hertzberg	
		BM	CPT	CWU	Chivers	
		SC A&Q	CPT	JA	Creasor	
		SC S&T	LT	AN	Scott	
	7th CE Battalion	CO	LTC	JLH	Bogart	
		2nd i/c	MAJ	K	Stuart	
		ADJ	CPT	TP	MacKenzie	
	8th CE Battalion	CO	LTC	EJC	Schmidlin	
		2nd i/c	MAJ	WE	Manhard	
		ADJ	LT	FM	Dawson	
	9th CE Battalion	CO	MAJ	LNR	Robertson	
		2nd i/c	MAJ	HW	Tate	
		ADJ	LT	CMcN	Steeves	
	3rd PBTU	OC	LT	CStB	Sladen	
	3rd Div Signal Coy	OC	MAJ	A	Leavitt	
SUPPORT SERVICES						
	3rd Division Train	CO	LTC	WHd'A	Findlay	
		ADJ	CPT	WA	DeGrave	
	3rd Medical Services	ADMS	COL	AE	Snell	
	8th Field Ambulance	CO	LTC	ER	Selby	
	9th Field Ambulance	CO	LTC	CW	Vipond	
	10th Field Ambulance	CO	LTC	TMcC	Leask	
	3rd CMG Battalion	CO	LTC	WN	Moorhouse	
		2nd i/c	MAJ	GW	MacLeod	
		ADJ	CPT	JP	LeGallais	

Designation	Unit	Position	Rank	Initials	Surname	Notes
4th Division						
DIVISION HQ						
	4th Division	GOC	MG	D	Watson	
		GSO 1	LTC	ÉdeB	Panet	
		a/GSO 2 O	MAJ	CB	Lindsay	
		GSO 2 T	LTC	AA	Magee	
		GSO 3 O	MAJ	SD	Armour	
		GSO 3 I	MAJ	WE	Hahn	
		AA&QMG	LTC	KR	Marshall	
		DAAG A	MAJ	GS	Currie	
		DAAG B	CPT	JM	Pauline	
		DAQMG	MAJ	AE	Taylor	
ARTILLERY						
	4th CDA	CRA	BG	WBM	King	
		BM	MAJ	L C	Goodeve	
		SC A	CPT	EB	Savage	
		SC Q	CPT	J	O'Reilly	
		SC for Recon	LT	HL	McPherson	
	3rd CFA	CO	LTC	JA	McDonald	
		ADJ				
	10th Bty	OC				
	11th Bty	OC				
	12th Bty	OC				
	9th H Bty	OC				
	4th CFA	CO	LTC	MN	Ross	
		ADJ				
	13th Bty	OC				
	19th Bty	OC				
	27th Bty	OC				
	21st H Bty	OC				
	4th DAC	CO	LTC	ETB	Gillmore	
	4th DTMO	OC				
INFANTRY						
	10th Brigade	GOC	BG	RJF	Hayter	

Designation	Unit	Position	Rank	Initials	Surname	Notes
		BM	MAJ	ND	Perry	
		SC	MAJ	DJ	O'Donahoe	
		SC	MAJ	WO	White	
		OO	LT	HY	Hicking	
	10th TMB	OC				
	44th Battalion	CO	LTC	RD	Davies	
		2nd i/c	MAJ	DB	Martyn	a/CO 2/9
		ADJ	LT	JB	Gould	
	46th Battalion	CO	MAJ	JS	Rankin	
		2nd i/c	CPT	RW	Gyles	
		ADJ	LT	S	Lett	
	47th Battalion	CO	LTC	HL	Keegan	
		2nd i/c	MAJ	EGP	Baker	
		ADJ	LT	GCH	Lindsell	
	50th Battalion	CO	LTC	LF	Page	
		2nd i/c	MAJ	JLR	Parry	
		ADJ	CPT	TH	Prescott	
	11th Brigade	GOC	BG	VW	Odlum	
		a/BM	MAJ	AA	Aitken	
		SC	CPT	RH	Richardson	
		SC	CPT	TB	Barrie	
		OO				
	11th TMB	OC				
	54th Battalion	CO	LTC	AB	Carey	
		2nd i/c	MAJ	B	McDiarmid	
		ADJ	CPT	WG	Foster	
	75th Battalion	CO	LTC	CC	Harbottle	WIA
		2nd i/c	CPT	AB	Duncan	
		ADJ	CPT	RH	Wilson	
	87th Battalion	CO	LTC	KM	Perry	
		2nd i/c	MAJ	R	Bickerdyke	
		ADJ	CPT	GS	Stairs	
	102nd Battalion	a/CO	MAJ	EJW	Ryan	
		2nd i/c				

Designation	Unit	Position	Rank	Initials	Surname	Notes
		ADJ	CPT	SH	Okell	
	12th Brigade	GOC	BG	JH	MacBrien	
		BM	MAJ	TP	Jones	
		SC	CPT	VN	Smallpiece	
		SC	CPT	WC	Merston	
		OO	LT	WAH	MacBrien	
	12th TMB	OC				
	38th Battalion	CO	LTC	CM	Edwards	
		2nd i/c	MAJ	TH	Warren	
		ADJ	LT	W	Vernon	
	72nd Battalion	CO	LTC	JA	Clark	
		2nd i/c	MAJ	GH	Kirkpatrick	
		ADJ	CPT	WG	McIntosh	
	78th Battalion	CO	LTC	J	Kirkcaldy	
		2nd i/c	MAJ	JN	Semmens	
		ADJ	LT	AK	Harvie	
	85th Battalion	a/CO	MAJ	JMcI	Millar	
		2nd i/c				
		ADJ	CPT	AT	Croft	
ENGINEERS						
	4th CE Brigade	CRE	LTC	HT	Hughes	
		BM	CPT	MA	Pope	
		SC A&Q	CPT	RD	Sutherland	
		SC S&T	CPT	F	Alport	
	10th CE Battalion	CO	MAJ	HP	Wilgar	
		2nd i/c	MAJ	AW	Davis	
		ADJ	LT	SH	Hawkins	
	11th CE Battalion	CO	MAJ	HL	Trotter	
		2nd i/c	MAJ	AJ	McPherson	
		ADJ	LT	RD	Kinmond	
	12th CE Battalion	CO	LTC	JTC	Thompson	
		2nd i/c	MAJ	GH	Shaw	
		ADJ	LT	TD	Henderson	
	4th PBTU	OC				
	4th Div Signal Coy	OC	MAJ	FG	Mallock	

Designation	Unit	Position	Rank	Initials	Surname	Notes
		2nd i/c				
SUPPORT SERVICES						
	4th Division Train	CO	LTC	WD	Greer	
		ADJ				
	4th Medical	ADMS	COL	CA	Peters	
	11th Field Ambulance	CO	LTC	S	Paulin	
	12th Field Ambulance	CO	LTC	PG	Bell	
	13th Field Ambulance	CO	LTC	WHK	Anderson	
	4th CMG Battalion	CO	LTC	MA	Scott	
		2nd i/c	MAJ	EW	Sansom	
		ADJ	CPT	H	Ward	

British Units

This appendix lists the two British divisions and their formations, units, commanders, and staff that served actively in the Canadian Corps during Arras 1918.

Table A.3 British Units, Commanders, and Staff

Abbreviations

Ranks

LT	Lieutenant
CPT	Captain
MAJ	Major
LTC	Lieutenant Colonel
COL	Colonel
BG	Brigadier General
MG	Major General

Units and Positions

a/	Acting
AA&QMG	Assistant Adjutant-General and Quartermaster-General

BM	Brigade Major
CO	Commanding Officer
CRA	Commander Royal Artillery
CRE	Commander, Royal Engineers
DAQMG	Deputy Adjutant-General and Quartermaster-General
DAAQMG	Deputy Assistant Adjutant-General and Quartermaster-General
DAC	Division Ammunition Column
GOC	General Officer Commanding
GSO	General Staff Officer
RFA	Royal Field Artillery Brigade
TMB	Trench Mortar Battery

Designation	Unit	Position	Rank	Initials	Surname
4th British Division					
DIVISION HQ					
	4th British Division	GOC	MG	TG	Matheson
		GSO 1	LTC	L	Carr
		GSO 2 O	MAJ	H	Hallett
		AA&QMG	LTC	H	Street
ARTILLERY					
	4th Division Artillery	CRA	BG	CA	Sykes
	29th RFA	CO	LTC	JL	Poston
	32nd RFA	a/CO	LTC	CES	Bower
INFANTRY					
	10th Brigade	GOC	BG	J	Greene
		BM	CPT	LM	Taylor
	10th TMB	OC			
	1st Royal Warwickshire	CO	MAJ	J	Kennington
	2nd Duke of Wellington's	CO	LTC	F	Pawlett
	2nd Seaforth Highlanders	CO	LTC	NC	Orr (WIA)
		a/Co	MAJ	AA	Macfarlane-Grieve
	11th Brigade	GOC	BG	TH	Wade
		BM	MAJ	HW	Lester
	11th TMB	OC			
	1st Somerset Light Infantry	CO	LTC	VHB	Majendie
	1st Hampshire	CO	LTC	JFC	Mordaunt

Designation	Unit	Position	Rank	Initials	Surname
	1st Rifle Brigade	CO	LTC	RT	Fellowes (WIA)
		a/CO	CPT	JA	Davidson
	12th Brigade	GOC	BG	EA	Fagan
		BM	CPT	D	MacCallum
	12th TMB	OC			
	1st KOR Lancashire	CO	LTC	CR	Carter
	2nd Lancashire Fusiliers	CO	LTC	HA	Kirby
	2nd Essex	CO	LTC	AE	Maitland
ENGINEERS					
	4th CRE	CRE	LTC	CR	Johnson
	400th Field Company	CO			
	401st Field Company	CO			
	402nd Field Company	CO			
	21st West Yorkshire Pioneers	CO	LTC	EHStL	Clarke
	4th Div Signal Coy	OC			
SUPPORT SERVICES					
	4th Battalion Machine Gun Corps	CO	MAJ	WR	Styles

51st (Highland) Division

Designation	Unit	Position	Rank	Initials	Surname
DIVISION HQ					
	51st (Highland) Division	a/GOC	BG	L	Oldfield
		GSO 1	LTC	RS	McClintock
		GSO 2 O	MAJ	JL	Willcocks
		AA&QMG	LTC	PF	FitzGerald
		DAAG	MAJ	SV	Kennedy
		DAQMG	MAJ	G	Fox
ARTILLERY					
	51st Division Artillery	a/CRA	BG	LM	Dyson
	255th RFA	CO	LTC	T	Davidson
	256th RFA	a/CO	LTC	RR	Will
INFANTRY					
	152nd Brigade	GOC	BG	WHE	Seagrave
		BM	CPT	R	Adam
	152nd TMB	OC			

Designation	Unit	Position	Rank	Initials	Surname
	1/5th Seaforth Highlanders	CO	LTC	W	Morrison
	1/6th Seaforth Highlanders	CO	LTC	JE	Laurie
	1/6th Gordon Highlanders	CO	LTC	JG	Gibb
	153rd Brigade	GOC	BG	W	Green
		BM	MAJ	WP	Wrathall
	153rd TMB	OC			
	1/6th Black Watch	CO	LTC	FR	Tarleton
	1/7th Black Watch	CO	LTC	J	Millar
	1/7th Gordon Highlanders	CO	LTC	J	Menzies
	154th Brigade	GOC	BG	GK	Buchanan
		a/BM	CPT	AR	Chapman
	154th TMB	OC			
	1/4th Gordon Highlanders	CO	LTC	AJ	Welsh
	1/4th Seaforth Highlanders	CO	LTC	JAJO	Hopkinson
	1/7th Argyll & Sutherland Highlanders	CO	LTC	L	Gartside
ENGINEERS					
	51st CRE	CRE	LTC	NW	Napier-Cavering
	400th Field Company	CO			
	401st Field Company	CO			
	402nd Field Company	CO			
	1/8th Royal Scots Pioneers	a/CO	MAJ	TB	Mitchell
	51st Div Signal Coy	OC			
SUPPORT SERVICES					
	51st Battalion Machine Gun Corps	CO	LTC	AS	Vernon

3rd Tank Brigade

Designation	Unit	Position	Rank	Initials	Surname
Brigade Headquarters					
	3rd Tank Brigade	GOC	BG	J	Hardress-Lloyd
	9th Tank Battalion	CO	LTC	HK	Woods
	11th Tank Battalion	CO	LTC	R	Pigot
	14th Tank Battalion	CO	LTC	GAMc	Sceales

Royal Air Force I Brigade

This listing provides the squadron's designation, the aircraft type flown, and when it joined the brigade if after 26 August.[2]

Type	Squadrons
Fighter	No. 40 SE5A, 54 Camel, 64 SE5A, 208 Camel, 209 Camel
Fighter Reconnaissance	No. 22 Bristol F2B
Day Bomber	No. 18 DH4
Night Bomber	No. 148 FE2b
Tank Cooperation	No. 8 FK 8*, 73 Camel*
Corps	No. 5 Bristol F2B, 6 RE8†, 52 RE8

* Added 27 August
† Added 28 August

German Units

The German Order of Battle is incomplete as assigned artillery, machine gun, *sturmtrupp*, and pioneer units are missing for the most part. Units marked with an asterisk * did not serve on the Canadian Corps front and those with † served on the front but did not engage.

Table A.4 German Units and Commanders

Abbreviations

Ranks

GM	Generalmajor
GLT	Generalleutenant

2 H. A. Jones, *The War in the Air: Being the Story of the Part Played in the Great War by the Royal Air Force* (Oxford: Clarendon Press, 1937), VI, p.484; 'A History of RAF Organisation' <http://www.rafweb.org/index.html> (25 April 2018); LAC: CWNS RAF.

Units

EB	Ersatz Brigade
EzD	Ersatz Division
FAR	Field Artillery Regiment
FtABn	Foot Artillery Battalion
FtAR	Foot Artillery Regiment
FüR	Füsilier Regiment
GRB	Guards Reserve Brigade
GRD	Guards Reserve Division
GRFAR	Guards Reserve Artillery Regiment
GrR	Grenadier Regiment
GRR	Guards Reserve Regiment
IB	Infantry Brigade
ID	Infantry Division
IR	Infantry Regiment
RD	Reserve Division
RFAR	Reserve Field Artillery Regiment
RFtAR	Reserve Foot Artillery Regiment
RIR	Reserve Infantry Regiment
SD	Schützen (Dismounted Cavalry) Division

Division	Commander	Infantry	Artillery	Machine Gun
39th ID	GLT Julius Ritter und Edler von Davans	61st IB, 126th IR*, 132nd IR, 172nd IR	39th Artillery Command - 80th FAR, 406th FtABn	19th Marksman Detachment
214th ID	GM Maercker	214th IB - 50th, 358th, 363rd IR	214th Artillery Command - 44th FAR, I/15th FtAR + assigned II/246th FAR, I/76th FAR, 31st Infantry Gun Bn, Bavarian 20th FtABn	
48th RD	GLT Konrad von Hippel	96th RB - 221st, 222nd, 223rd RIR	48th Artillery Command - 48th RFAR, I/23rd FtAR	
35th ID	GM Albert von Kemnitz	87th IB - 61st, 141st, 176th IR	35th Artillery Command - 71st FAR, I/18th RFtAR	46th Marksman Detachment
26th RD	GLT e. D. Albert Hermann von Fritsch	51st RB - 119th, 121st, 180th* RIR	122nd Artillery Command - 26th RFAR, 69th FtABn	

4th EzD	GLT Friedrich Bronsart von Schellendorf	13rd EB - 214th RIR, 360th, 362nd IR	139th Artillery Command - 90th FAR, 119th FtABn	
58th ID	GLT Woldemar Graf Vitzthum von Eckstädt	116th IB - 103rd RIR, 106th, 107th IR	57th Artillery Command - 115th RFAR, 97th FtABn	
16th ID	GLT Paulus von Stolzman	30th IB - 28th, 29th, 68th IR	16th Artillery Command - 23rd FAR, 32nd FtABn	
2nd GRD	GM Wigand von Cramer	38th RIB - 15th, 77th, 91st RIR	116th Artillery Command - 20th RFAR, II/23rd FtAR	65th Marksman Detachment
1st GRD	GM Paul Tiede	1st GRB - 1st, 2nd GRR, 64th RIR	8th Guards Artillery Command - 1st GRFAR, II/1st FtAR	
3rd RD	GLT Rudolf Rusche	5th RB - 2nd GrR, 34th FüR, 49th RIR	73rd Artillery Command - 3rd RFAR, IV/11th RFtAR	
111th ID	GM Johannes von Busse	221st IB - 73rd FüR, 76th*, 164th IR	111th Artillery Command - 94th FAR, II/25th FtAR	
7th SD (Dismounted)	GLT Hans von Heuduck	28th Rifle Command - 11th 14th Uhlans, 4th Uhlans 30th Rifle Command - 15th, 25th Dragoons, 9th Hussars 41st Rifle Command - 5th Cuirassiers, 26th Dragoons, 4th Uhlans	5th FAR - (x2nd batteries)	
22nd ID†	GLT Otto Neubaur	43rd IB - 82nd, 83rd, 167th IR	22nd Artillery Command - 11th FAR, 50th FtABn	
20th ID†	GLT Wilhelm Zwenger	40th IB - 77th, 79th, 92nd IR	20th Artillery Command - 46th FAR, 155th FtABn	32nd Marksman Detachment
12th ID†	GLT Arnold Lequis	24th IB - 23rd, 62nd, 63rd IR	12th Artillery Command - 21st FAR, 68th FtABn	

Appendix IV

Detailed Canadian Corps Orders of Battle, 26 August 1918

The order of battle extending from north to south lists all the units committed and engaged during the day.

2nd Division

Infantry Committed

4th Brigade - 18th, 19th, 20th, 21st Battalions
6th Brigade - 27th, 28th, 29th Battalions

Engineers

2nd Engineer Brigade - 4th, 5th, 6th Engineer Battalions

Field Artillery - Opening Barrage[1]

Assigned to division: 2nd CDA (5th CFA, 6th CFA), 15th DA (70th RFA, 71st RFA), 39th DA (174th RFA, 186th RFA), 282nd AFA
Barrage = 126x18-pdr, 42x4.5-inch howitzers
Mobile = 36x18-pounder, 12x4.5-inch howitzers

Field Artillery - After Barrage

Assigned to division: 2rd CDA (5th CFA, 6th CFA), 39th DA (174th RFA, 186th RFA), 282nd AFA Pieces = 90x18-pdr, 30x4.5-inch howitzers

1 Artillery order of battle from LAC: Chronological Table.

Heavy Artillery

Morning: 91st HA, 78th HA= 28x6-inch howitzers, 6x8-inch howitzers, 4x9.2-inch howitzers (38 pieces)
Afternoon: 48th HA = 12x60-pounder, 12x6-inch howitzers (24 pieces)

Machine Guns

2nd Machine Gun Battalion, 2xBatteries Life Guards Machine Gun Battalion, 4xBatteries 1st CMMG Brigade = 144 machine guns

Tanks

B/9th Tank Battalion - 8xMk V Tanks

Cavalry

2 troops CLH

3rd Division

Infantry Committed

7th Brigade - RCR, PPCLI, 42nd, 49th Battalions
8th Brigade- 1st, 2nd, 4th, 5th CMR Battalions

Engineers

3rd Engineer Brigade - 7th, 8th, 9th Engineer Battalions

Field Artillery - Opening Barrage

Assigned to division: 3rd CDA (9th CFA, 10th CFA), 52nd AFA, 126th AFA
Mobile artillery: 5th CDA (13th CFA, 14th CFA)
Barrage only: 16th DA (31st FA, 32nd FA), 256th AFA
Barrage = 126x18-pdr, 42x4.5-inch howitzers
Mobile = 36x18-pounder, 12x4.5-inch howitzers

Field Artillery - After Barrage

Assigned to division: 3rd CDA (9th CFA, 10th CFA), 5th CDA (13th CFA, 14th CFA), 52nd AFA, 126th AFA
Barrage = 108x18-pdr, 36x4.5-inch howitzers

Heavy Artillery

Morning: 19th HA, 50th HA= 40x6-inch howitzers, 8x8-inch howitzers (48 pieces)
Afternoon: 42nd HA = 12x60-pounder, 12x6-inch howitzers (24 pieces)

Machine Guns

3rd Machine Gun Battalion, 2xBatteries Life Guards Machine Gun Battalion = 112 machine guns

Tanks

Composite Company 11th Tank Battalion = 5xMk V tanks

Cavalry

2xTroops CLH

51st (Highland) Division

Infantry Committed

152nd Brigade - 1/6th Gordon Highlanders
153rd Brigade - 1/6th Black Watch, 1/7th Black Watch, 1/7th Gordon Highlanders

Engineers and Pioneers

400th, 401st, 404th Field Companies, 1/8th Royal Scots

Field Artillery

51st DA (255th RFA, 256th RFA), 177th AFA, 180th AFA = 72x18-pounder, 24x4.5-inch howitzer

Heavy Artillery

2nd CGA - 6x60 pounder, 6x6-inch howitzers, 6x8-inch howitzers, 4x9.2-inch howitzers = 22 pieces

Machine Guns

51st Machine Gun Battalion, 2 Companies/Life Guards Machine Gun Company=96 machine guns

GOCRA

CBSO

Morning - 2nd CGA, 53rd HA, 81st HA, 42nd HA, 48th HA Pieces= 54x60-pounder, 60x6-inch howitzers, 18x6-inch howitzers, 8x6-inch howitzers (140 pieces)
Afternoon - 2nd CGA, 53rd HA, 81st HA Pieces= 30x60-pounder, 36x6-inch howitzers, 18x8-inch howitzers, 8x9.2-inch howitzers (92 pieces)

CCHA

Afternoon - 19th HA, 78th HA, 50th HA, 91st HA Pieces= 24x60-pounder, 42x6-inch howitzers, 12x8-inch howitzers, 6x9.2-inch howitzers (84 pieces)

Field Artillery Reserve after exploitation

39th DA (174th RFA, 186th RFA), 52nd AFA, 126th AFA, 282nd AFA
Pieces = 90x18-pdr, 30x4.5-inch howitzer

CIF

2xBatteries 1st CMMG Brigade = 16 machine guns
2xPlatoons Canadian Corps Cyclist Battalion

First Army Heavy Artillery

26th Army HA, 31st Army HA = 1x14-inch gun, 1x12-inch gun, 1x12-inch howitzer, 3x6-inch guns and 10x8-inch guns=16 pieces

Appendix V

Detailed Canadian Corps Orders of Battle, 2 September 1918

The order of battle lists all units committed during the day.

1st Division

Infantry Committed

1st Brigade - 1st, 3rd, 4th Battalions
2nd Brigade - 7th, 8th, 10th Battalions
3rd Brigade - 13th, 14th, 15th, 16th Battalions

Engineers

1st Engineer Brigade - 1st, 2nd, 3rd Engineer Battalions

Field Artillery[1]

Assigned to division: 1st CDA (1st CFA, 2nd CFA), 2nd CDA (5th CFA, 6th CFA less 1x18-Pdr. Battery), 39th (174th RFA, 186th RFA), 282nd AFA = 120x18-pdr, 42x4.5-inch howitzers

Heavy Artillery[2]

91st HA, 3x6-inch howitzers Batteries, 1x8-inch howitzer Battery = 36x6-inch howitzers, 6x8-inch howitzers (42 total)

Machine Guns

1st Machine Gun Battalion = 96 machine guns

1 Field artillery order of battle from LAC: Chronological Table.
2 Heavy artillery order of battle from LAC: CCHA WD, Amendment to No. 1 to CCHA OO No. 136, 1 September 1918.

Tanks[3]

2xComposite Companies 14th Tank Battalion = 18xMk V tanks

Cavalry

2xTroops CLH

4th Division

Infantry Committed

10th Brigade - 44th, 46th 47th, 50th Battalions
11th Brigade - 54th, 75th, 87th, 102nd Battalions
12th Brigade - 38th, 54th, 72nd, 85th Battalions

Engineers

4th Engineer Brigade - 10th, 11th, 12th Engineer Battalions

Field Artillery - Opening Barrage

Assigned to division: 4th CDA (3rd CFA, 4th CFA), 5th CDA (13th CFA, 14th CFA), 4th DA (29th, 32nd RFA), 52nd AFA, 126th AFA = 144x18-pdr, 48x4.5-inch howitzers

Heavy Artillery

78th HA, 3x6-inch howitzers batteries, 1x8-inch howitzer battery= 36x6-inch howitzers, 6x8-inch howitzers (42 total)

Machine Guns

4th Machine Gun Battalion = 96 machine guns

Tanks

9th Tank Battalion, Composite Company 11th Tank Battalion = 31xMk V tanks

Cavalry

2xTroops CLH

3 LAC: 3rd Tank Brigade Report.

4th British Division

Infantry Committed

11th Brigade - 2nd SLI, 1st Rifle Brigade, 1st Hampshire
12th Brigade - 1st KORL, 2nd Essex Battalions

Engineers and Pioneers

9th, 406th, 536th Field Companies and 21st West Yorkshire Pioneer Battalion

Field Artillery

3rd CDA (9th CFA, 10th CFA), 5th CDA (13th CFA, 14th CFA), 8th CFA = 90x18-pounder, 30x4.5-inch howitzer

Heavy Artillery

50th HA - 18x6-inch howitzers, 6x6-inch howitzers (24 total)

Machine Guns

4th Machine Gun Battalion = 64 machine guns

Tanks

Composite Company, 11th Tank Battalion = 9xMk V tanks

GOCRA

CBSO

19th HA, 29th HA, 42nd HA (-), 48th HA, 53rd HA, 77th HA, 81st HA (-) Pieces= 60x60-pounder, 104x6-inch howitzers, 6x8-inch howitzers = 170 total

CCHA

40th HA (-) Pieces= 6x6-inch howitzers

CIF

See the detailed Appendix VI CIF Order of Battle, 2 September for a more detailed order of battle

1st CMMG Brigade= 40 machine guns
2nd CMMG Brigade = 40 machine guns
Canadian Corps Cyclist Battalion
10th Royal Hussars
17th Tank Battalion = 6 Armoured Cars
30th Battery 6th CFA = 6x18 pounder
2xSections 5th CDA Trench Mortar Battery = 4x6-inch Newton Trench Mortar
6xTroops CLH

First Army Heavy Artillery

26th Army HA, 31st Army HA = 1x14-inch Gun, 1x12-inch Gun, 1x12-inch howitzer, 3x6-inch guns and 10x8-inch guns=16 total

Appendix VI

Canadian Independent Force Order of Battle, 2 September 1918[1]

Commander: BG R Brutinel
Officers: 3 Staff, 1 Signalling, I Intelligence, 1 Supply Column
Units: 10 Motorcyclists, 3 Orderlies, 1 Platoon Canadian Corps Cyclist Battalion, 1 Corps Wireless Signal Station

Leading Group

Commander LTC FHDC Whitmore, 10th Royal Hussars
10th Royal Hussars (12 troops)
Canadian Light Horse (6 troops)
1 section/30 CFA (2x18-pdr)
Detachment 17th Tank Battalion (6 Heavy Armoured Cars)
Section/2 CMMG Brigade (2 Light Armoured Cars)
10 Motorcyclists (1st and 2nd CMMG Brigade)

2nd Group

Commander: LTC WK Walker (1st CMMG Brigade)
2 Sections/2 CMMG Brigade (4 Light Armoured Cars)
Canadian Corps Cyclist Battalion (less one platoon)
1st CMMG Brigade (5xMotor Machine Gun Batteries=40 MG)
1 section/30 CFA (2x18-pdr)
2 Sections/5 CDA TM Battery (4x6-inch Newton TM)
20 Motorcyclists (1st and 2nd CMMG Brigade)

3rd Group

Commander a/LTC HF Meurling (2nd CMMG Brigade)
2nd CMMG Brigade (5xMotor Machine Gun Batteries=40 MG)

1 LAC: CMGO WD, BH Instructions No.1, 1 September 1918.

1 section/30 CFA (2x18-pdr)
20 Motorcyclists (1st and 2nd CMMG Brigade)

Supply Column

Commander: Major G Arnold
1 Water lorry
1 Supply lorry
1 Ammunition lorry
1 Fuel and Oil lorry
Trains of 1st and 2nd CMMG Brigades
5 Motorcyclists for liaison

Bibliography

Primary Sources

Black Watch Regiment Archives, Montreal
F.O.W. Loomis Diary

Bundesarchiv, Freiburg (Germany)

PH 81	*26th Reserve Division* Files
RH61	

Canadian War Museum, Ottawa

19801226-277	Currie Fonds
19870027-001	Morrison Fonds

Directorate of History and Heritage, Department of National Defence, Ottawa

DHH 2001/10	Duguid Fonds

Hauptstaatsarchiv, Stuttgart (Germany)
M93
M109

Library and Archives Canada, Ottawa

RG9 III A	OMFC ministerial records
RG9 III B	Administrative records
RG9 III C	Canadian Corps files
RG9 III D	Canadian Corps War Diaries and Canadian War Records Office files
RG24	Official History preparation, and officer comments
RG150	Service files
RG41	CBC *In Flanders Fields* radio program interviews
MG26 H	Borden Fonds
MG30 E5	Bovey Fonds
MG30 E6	Burstall Fonds
MG30 E15	Griesbach Fonds

MG30 E20	A.C. Macdonell Fonds
MG30 E32	West Fonds
MG30 E40	Erlebach Fonds
MG30 E46	Turner Fonds
MG30 E69	Watson Fonds
MG30 E75	Urquhart Fonds
MG30 E81	Morrison Fonds
MG30 E60	Matthews Fonds
MG30 E100	Currie Fonds
MG30 E117	Parsons Fonds
MG30 E133	McNaughton Fonds
MG30 E134	Peck Fonds
MG30 E300	Odlum Fonds
MG30 E345	Wilson Fonds
MG30 E351	Craig Fonds
MG30 E378	Morris Fonds
MG30 E393	Foster Fonds
MG30 E432	Sinclair Fonds
MG30 E537	Sansom Fonds

McGill University Archives, McGill University, Montreal

MG 4027 Urquhart Fonds

National Library of Scotland, (UK)

No. 96, Haig's Autograph Great War Diary, Haig Papers

The National Archives (UK), London

CAB 37	Despatches
CAB 45	Comments British Official History
WO 95	Orders
WO 158	War Diaries

University of British Columbia Archives

D547.M3 L63 1919a. Logan Fonds

Electronic Resources

'6. Rheinisches Infanterie-Regiment Nr. 68.' http://genwiki.genealogy.net/IR_68 (6 October 2018).

'35. Infanterie-Division 1914-1918.' http://www.militaerpass.net/35id.htm (12 December 2017).

'39. Infanterie-Division 1914-1918.' http://www.militaerpass.net/39id.htm (12 December 2017).

'48. Reserve-Division 1914–1918.' http://www.militaerpass.net/48rd.htm (12 December 2017).

'1915 Battlefield Commissions for Two Future RMR Co's.' http://www.royalmontrealregiment.com/1915-battlefield-commissions-for-two-future-rmr-cos/ (31 January 2019).

'Akte Nr. 256. Übersichtskarte Des Chefs Des Generalstabes Des Feldheeres – Abteilung Fremde Heere Zur Verteilung Der Französischen, Englischen Und Belgischen Streitkräfte an Der Westfront Vom 25.08.1918.' http://tsamo.germandocsinrussia.org/de/pages/39222/map (6 March 2018).

'Andrews, Alfred Herbert John Diary: 1918.' http://www.canadianletters.ca/content/document-8448 (18 April 2017).

'Basic Fighting Unit of the AEF the Square Division.' http://www.worldwar1.com/dbc/squarediv.htm (10 February 2018).

'The Bug.' https://matthewkbarrett.com/2015/04/17/the-bug/#more-1480 (29 January 2019).

The Canadian Forces Operational Planning Process, B-GJ-005-500/FP-000, (CFEC Joint Doctrine Branch 2008).

'Charles Smith Rutherford.' Directorate of History and Heritage, http://www.cmp-cpm.forces.gc.ca/dhh-dhp/gal/vcg-gcv/bio/rutherford-cs-eng.asp (4 June 2018).

'Claude Joseph Patrick Nunney.' http://www.cmp-cpm.forces.gc.ca/dhh-dhp/gal/vcg-gcv/bio/nunney-cjp-eng.asp (5 March 2019).

'Claude Nunney VC DCM MM.' http://www.claudenunney.co.uk/index.php (5 March 2019).

'The Clear Grit.' https://matthewkbarrett.com/2014/12/15/the-clear-grit/ (5 August 2019).

Commonwealth War Graves Commission. 'Find War Dead.' http://www.cwgc.org/find-war-dead.aspx?cpage=1 (4 March 2018).

'The Court Martial.' http://54thbattalioncef.ca/?page_id=236 (21 April 2019).

'The Customs Collector.' https://matthewkbarrett.com/2016/03/31/the-customs-collector/ (21 April 2019).

'Dictionary of Canadian Biography Online - Sir David Watson.' http://www.biographi.ca/009004-119.01-e.php?id_nbr=8411 (19 March 2013).

'Flag Bearer.' https://matthewkbarrett.com/2015/07/01/the-flagbearer/ (30 January 2019).

'Foster, Kenneth Walter Memoir.' The Canadian Letters and Images Project, http://www.canadianletters.ca/content/document-4021 (18 April 2017).

'A History of RAF Organisation.' http://www.rafweb.org/index.html (25 April 2018).

'The Iron Man.' https://matthewkbarrett.com/2015/11/14/the-ironman/ (6 February 2019).

'Kings Own Yorkshire Light Infantry - Removed from Service.' *London Gazette*, 4 October 1912, 7295.

'Kings Own Yorkshire Light Infantry - Resigns His Commission.' *London Gazette*, 29 April 1919, 5481.

'LCol Carey.' http://54thbattalioncef.ca/?page_id=429 (21 April 2019).

'Lieutenant Colonel Royal Ewing, D.S.O., M.C.' https://matthewkbarrett.com/2017/11/06/lt-col-ewing/ (1 August 2018).

'Louis James Lipsett.' http://www.biographi.ca/en/bio/lipsett_louis_james_14E.html (7 July 2016).

'Lt-Col Lionel Herbert Millen, DSO (1876–1956).' https://www.argylls.ca/history/millen.html (29 July 2018).

'Lt. Col. EW MacDonald.' https://matthewkbarrett.com/2017/11/02/lt-col-e-w-macdonald/ (22 April 2019).

'Lt. Col. Perry.' https://matthewkbarrett.com/2017/07/30/lt-col-perry/ (23 April 2019).

'Lt.-Col. Charles Richard Edward Willets, D.S.O.' http://regimentalrogue.com/rcr_great_war_officers/rcr_offr_willets_cre.html (1 August 2018).
'M.G. Barrage Map No. 25, 24 August 1918.' McMaster University, 1918.
'Major C. Y. Weaver, D.S.O. 49th (Edmonton Regiment) Battalion.' https://matthewkbarrett.com/2018/05/03/lt-col-weaver/ (1 August 2018).
'Mason, Douglas Herbert Campbell.' https://qormuseum.org/soldiers-of-the-queens-own/mason-d-h-c/ (7 February 2019).
'Memorable Manitobans - Hugh Marshall Dyer.' http://www.mhs.mb.ca/docs/people/dyer_hm.shtml (7 March 2016).
'Memorable Manitobans: William Kellman Chandler (?-1948).' www.mhs.mb.ca/docs/people/chandler_wk2.shtml (26 July 2018).
'MGen Sir EWB Morrison KCMG, CB, DSO.' http://www.rcamuseum.com/English/Great%20Gunners/morrison.htm (26 April 2013).
'Morrison, Sir Edward Whipple Bancroft.' http://www.biographi.ca/009004-119.01-e.php?BioId=41976 (26 April 2013).
Pariseau, Jean. 'Stewart, Charles James Townshend.' http://www.biographi.ca/en/bio/stewart_charles_james_townshend_14E.html (1 August 2018).
Project, Canadian Letters and Images. 'Gass, Clarence Reginald Letter: 1918 September 9th.' http://www.canadianletters.ca/content/document-3142?position=29&list=HmFlanQ-eZfN91UMM7eNscggOzGQwPovdkOhB0MLVUc (12 April 2018).
Project, Canadian Letters and Images. 'Maharg, Ivan Clark Diary: 1918 August.' http://www.canadianletters.ca/content/document-9511 (18 April 2017).
Project, Canadian Letters and Images. 'Wilson, Andrew Diary: 1918 September 1st.' http://www.canadianletters.ca/content/document-2201?position=312&list=epFid7A8SEhIegQkhQL_b_xvfyKN_K2Nr20IiYMYOOY (12 April 2018).
'The Professional.' https://matthewkbarrett.com/2014/09/15/the-professional/ (4 August 2019).
'Red Baiter.' http://matthewkbarrett.com/2015/10/07/the-red-baiter/ (4 December 2015).
'Reid, Donald Calderwood Letter: 1918 August 24th.' The Canadian Letters and Images Project, http://www.canadianletters.ca/content/document-6437?position=92&list=of77sNO263Y0LsfRfsi9NzXeugSiZuhy7PN7ewfmIVs (12 April 2018).
'Robert Rennie.' http://qormuseum.org/soldiers-of-the-queens-own/soldier-bios-q-r-s-t-u/soldiers-bios-r/rennie-robert/ (26 February 2013).
'Savage, Charles Henry Memoir: 1936.' The Canadian Letters and Images Project, http://www.canadianletters.ca/content/document-8359 (24 September 2017).
'Scottish Victoria Cross Awards.' http://www.scotlandswar.ed.ac.uk/sites/default/files/pdf_Scottish_VCs_0.pdf (6 September 2019).
'Senior Officers' Course Confidential Report on Major J.A. McIntosh, 3 March 1918.' https://18thbattalioncef.wordpress.com/soldiers-listed-in-diary/mcintosh-john-alexander-major/ (27 September 2018).
Sheldon, Jack. 'German Rating of BEF Divisions.' http://1914-1918.invisionzone.com/forums/index.php?/topic/34342-british-v-dominion/&page=2#comment-277580/jack (9 February 2017).
'Tribute To: Colonel Burnett Laws.' http://www.rcmpveteransvancouver.com/tribute-to-colonel-burnett-laws/ (31 July 2018).

Viser, Jonathan. 'Otto Von Below.' http://prussianmachine.com/aok/below_o.htm (26 March 2017).

Viser, Jonathan. 'Otto Von Stettin.' http://prussianmachine.com/akb/stetten.htm (27 May 2018).

'War Hero.' https://matthewkbarrett.com/2015/10/19/the-war-hero/ (17 April 2019).

'William Reginald Patterson DSO.' http://www.doingourbit.ca/profile/william-patterson-dso (30 July 2018).

Williamson, John L. 'Dictionary of Canadian Biography Online - McKenzie, Archibald Ernest Graham.' http://www.biographi.ca/en/bio/mckenzie_archibald_ernest_graham_14E.html (26 September 2018).

Official Histories and Documents

Department of Militia and Defence. *The Quarterly Militia List of the Dominion of Canada (Corrected to June 30, 1914)*. Ottawa: Department of Militia and Defence, 1914.

Der Weltkrieg 1914 Bis 1918. Vol. 14.1, Berlin: Ernst Siegfried Mittler and Sohn, 1944.

Der Weltkrieg 1914 Bis 1918, Beilagen. Vol. 14.2, Berlin: Ernst Siegfried Mittler and Sohn, 1944.

Duguid, A. Fortescue. *The Canadian Forces in the Great War 1914-1919*. Chronology, Appendices and Maps ed. Vol. 1, Ottawa: Minister of National Defence, 1938.

Edmonds, J.E. *Military Operations: France and Belgium, 1918*. Vol. 4, London: Macmillan and Co., Limited, 1947.

Edmonds, J.E. *Military Operations: France and Belgium, 1918*. Vol. 1, London: Macmillan and Co., Limited, 1935.

Edmonds, J.E. *Military Operations: France and Belgium, 1918*. Vol. 2, London: Macmillan and Co., Limited, 1937.

Falls, Cyril Bentham. *Military Operations: France and Belgium, 1917*. Vol. 1, London: Macmillan, 1940.

Falls, Cyril Bentham. *Military Operations: France and Belgium, 1917*. Vol. II, Nashville: Battery Press, 1948. 1991.

General Staff, War Office, Field Service Pocket Book, 1914, (London: His Majesty's Stationary Office, 1914).

Henniker, A. M. *Transportation on the Western Front 1914-1918*. London: HMSO, 1937.

Historical Sub-section General Staff, A.E.F. *Survey of German Tactics 1918*. Verdun Press, 1918. Kindle.

Jones, H. A. *The War in the Air: Being the Story of the Part Played in the Great War by the Royal Air Force*. Vol. VI, Oxford: Clarendon Press, 1937.

Kemp, A.E. *Report of the Ministry, Overseas Military Forces of Canada, 1918*. London: Printed by authority of the Ministry, Overseas Military Forces of Canada, 1919.

Nicholson, G.W.L. *Canadian Expeditionary Force, 1914-1919*. Ottawa: R. Duhamel, Queen's Printer, 1964.

Snell, Arthur Evans. *The C.A.M.C. With the Canadian Corps During the Last Hundred Days of the Great War*. Ottawa: Canadian Army Medical Corps, 1924.

The Quarterly Army List for the Quarter Ending 31 March 1914. London: HMSO, 1914.

Wise, S. F. *Canadian Airmen and the First World War*. Vol. 1, Toronto: University of Toronto Press, 1980.

Secondary Sources

Adjutant, The. *The 116th Battalion in France.* Toronto: E.P.S. Allen, 1921.

Anderson, Hastings. 'The Breaking of the Quéant-Drocourt Line by the Canadian Corps, First Army.' LAC.

Anon. *Canada in the Great World War: An Authentic Account of the Military History of Canada from the Earliest Days to the Close of the War of the Nations.* Toronto: United Publishers of Canada, Limited, 1918.

Anon. *The Story of the Sixty-Sixth C.F.A.* Edinburgh: Turnbull & Spears, 1919.

Asprey, Robert B. *The German High Command at War: Hindenburg and Ludendorff Conduct World War I.* 1st ed. New York: W. Morrow, 1991.

Bailey, JBB John Beswick. *Cinquante-Quatre; Being a Short History of the 54th Canadian Infantry Battalion.* 1919.

Balck, W. *Development of Tactics--World War.* Fort Leavenworth, Kansas,: General Service Schools Press, 1922.

Barrett, Michael B. 'Below, Otto Von (1857-1944).' In *The Encyclopedia of World War I*, edited by Spencer C. Tucker. Santa Barbara, CA: ABC-CLIO, 2005.

Bastanier, Hanns. *Geschichte Des Großherzoglich Mecklenburgischen Reserve-Infanterie-Regiments Nr. 214.* Dessau: Selbstverlag, 1933.

Beattie, Kim. *48th Highlanders of Canada, 1891-1928.* Canada: The Highlanders, 1932.

Bechthold, Mike. 'In the Shadow of Vimy Ridge the Canadian Corps in April and May 1917.' In Geoffrey Hayes, Andrew Iarocci and Mike Bechthold (ed.), *Vimy Ridge: A Canadian Reassessment.* 239-56. Waterloo, Ont.: Wilfrid Laurier University Press, 2007.

Begau, Paul Münstermann and Robert. *Infanterie-Regiments von Goeben (2. Rhein.) Nr. 28 im Weltkrieg 1914-1918.* Monchen Gladbach: Buch- und Kunstdruckerei Küppers and Knoben, 1932.

Bennett, S. G. *The 4th Canadian Mounted Rifles, 1914-1919.* Toronto: Murray Printing, 1926.

Bewsher, F.W. *The History of the 51st (Highland) Division 1914-1918* Edinburgh: William Blackwood and Sons, 1921.

Bidwell, Shelford, and Dominick Graham. *Fire-Power: British Army Weapons and Theories of War, 1904-1945.* London: Allen and Unwin, 1982.

Bilton, David. *Germans at Arras (Images of War).* Barnsley: Pen & Sword, 2009. e-Book.

Blaber, Roger. 'Tanks in the 'Hundred Days' 1918 - A Diminishing Resource.' *British Journal for Military History* 2, no. 1 (2015).

Blaxland, Gregory. *Amiens: 1918.* London: W.H. Allen, 1981.

Boff, Jonathan. 'Combined Arms During the Hundred Days Campaign, August--November 1918.' *War in History* 17, no. 4 (2010): 459-478.

Boff, Jonathan. *Haig's Enemy: Crown Prince Rupprecht and Germany's War on the Western Front.* Oxford: Oxford University Press, 2018. e-Book.

Boff, Jonathan. 'The Morale Maze: The German Army in Late 1918.' *The Journal of Strategic Studies* 37, no. 6-7 (2014): 855-878.

Boff, Jonathan. *Winning and Losing on the Western Front: The British Third Army and the Defeat of Germany in 1918.* Cambridge: Cambridge University Press, 2012.

Borden, Robert Laird. *Letters to Limbo.* Toronto: University of Toronto Press, 1971.

Borden, Robert Laird, and Henry Borden. *Robert Laird Borden: His Memoirs*. 2 vols Toronto,: The Macmillan Company of Canada, Limited, 1938.

Brederlow, Tido von. *Geschichte Des 1st Garde-Reserve-Regiments*. Berlin: Gerhard Stalling, 1926.

Brennan, Patrick. 'Byng's and Currie's Commanders: A Still Untold Story of the Canadian Corps.' *Canadian Military History* 11, no. 2 (2002): 5-16.

Brennan, Patrick. 'From Amateur to Professional: The Experience of Brigadier General William Antrobus Griesbach.' In Briton C. Busch (ed.), *Canada and the Great War: Western Front Association Papers*. Montreal & Kingston: McGill-Queen's University Press, 2003.

Brennan, Patrick. 'Major-General David Watson: A Critical Appraisal of Canadian Generalship in the Great War.' In Andrew B. Godefroy (ed.), *Great War Commands: Historical Perspectives on Canadian Army Leadership 1914-1918*. Kingston: Canadian Defence Academy Press, 2010.

Buckley, Francis. *Q.6.A and Other Places: Recollections of 1916, 1917 and 1918*. London: Spottiswoode, 1920.

Burns, E. L. M. *General Mud: Memoirs of Two World Wars*. Toronto: Clarke, Irwin, 1970.

Calder, Donald George Scott. *The History of the 28th (Northwest) Battalion, C. E. F. (October 1914-June 1919) from the Memoirs of Brigadier General Alexander Ross*. Regina, Sask.: Regina Rifle Regiment, 1961.

Campbell, David. *It Can't Last Forever: The 19th Battalion and the Canadian Corps in the First World War*. Waterloo, ON: WLU Press, 2017.

Cane, Bruce. *It Made You Think of Home: The Haunting Journal of Deward Barnes, Canadian Expeditionary Force: 1916-1919*. Toronto: The Dundurn Group, 2004.

Chaballe, Joseph. 'Courcelette, the Glorious Battle Fought by the 22nd French-Canadian Battalion.' *La Canadienne*, no. October & November (1920: 15-35.

Christie, N. M. *The Canadians at Amiens, August 8th to 16th, 1918: A Social History and Battlefield Tour*. Ottawa: CEF Books, 1999.

Churchill, Allen L. *The Story of the Great War Victory with the Allies*. Vol. VIII, NY: PF Collier and Son, 1920.

Clausewitz, Carl von, Michael Howard, and Peter Paret. *On War*. Princeton, N.J.: Princeton University Press, 1976.

Clements, Robert N., and B. D. Tennyson. *Merry Hell: The Story of the 25th Battalion (Nova Scotia Regiment), Canadian Expeditionary Force 1914-1919*. Toronto: University of Toronto Press, 2013.

Cook, Tim. *Clio's Warriors: Canadian Historians and the Writing of the World Wars*. Vancouver: UBC Press, 2006.

Cook, Tim. '"Literary Memorials": The Great War Regimental Histories, 1919-1939.' *Journal of the Canadian Historical Association / Revue de la Société historique du Canada* 13, no. 1 (2002): 167-190.

Cook, Tim. *The Madman and the Butcher*. Toronto: Allen Lane, 2010.

Cook, Tim. *No Place to Run: The Canadian Corps and Gas Warfare in the First World War*. Vancouver: UBC Press, 1999.

Cook, Tim. 'The Politics of Surrender: Canadian Soldiers and the Killing of Prisoners in the Great War.' *The Journal of Military History* 70 (July 2006): 637-666.

Cook, Tim. *Shock Troops: Canadians Fighting the Great War, 1917-1918*. Toronto: Viking Canada, 2008.

Corrigall, David James. *The History of the Twentieth Canadian Battalion (Central Ontario Regiment) Canadian Expeditionary Force: In the Great War, 1914-1918*. Toronto: Stone & Cox Limited, 1935.

Cron, Hermann. *Imperial German Army 1914-18: Organisation, Structure, Orders-of-Battle*. 2006 ed. Solihull, UK: Helion and Company, 1937.

Daly, James. *Portsmouth's World War One Heroes: Stories of the Fallen Men and Women*. Stroud, UK: The History Press, 2013.

Dancocks, Daniel G. *Gallant Canadians: The Story of the Tenth Canadian Infantry Battalion, 1914-1919*. Calgary: Calgary Highlanders Regimental Funds Foundation, 1990.

Dancocks, Daniel G. *Legacy of Valour: The Canadians at Passchendaele*. Edmonton: Hurtig, 1986.

Dancocks, Daniel G. *Sir Arthur Currie: A Biography*. Toronto: Methuen, 1985.

Dancocks, Daniel G. *Spearhead to Victory: Canada and the Great War*. Edmonton: Hurtig, 1987.

Davies, WJK. *Light Railways of the First World War: A History of Tactical Rail Communications on the British Fronts, 1914-18*. Newton Abbot (Devon): David & Charles, 1967.

Delaney, Douglas E. 'Mentoring the Canadian Corps: Imperial Officers and the Canadian Expeditionary Force, 1914-1918.' *Journal of Military History* 77, no. 3 (July 2013): 931-954.

Dennis, Patrick. 'A Canadian Conscript Goes to War—August 1918: Old Myths Re-Examined.' *Canadian Military History* 18, no. 1 (2009).

Dennis, Patrick M. *Reluctant Warriors: Canadian Conscripts and the Great War*. Vancouver: UBC Press, 2017.

Dickson, Paul. 'Leadership and Innovation: Andrew McNaughton and the Counter-Battery Staff Office.' In Andrew B. Godefroy (ed.), *Great War Commands: Historical Perspectives on Canadian Army Leadership 1914-1918*. Kingston: Canadian Defence Academy Press, 2010.

Duguid, Archer Fortescue. *History of the Canadian Grenadier Guards, 1760-1964*. Montreal: Gazette Print. Co., 1965.

Durflinger, Serge Marc, Douglas E. Delaney, and Nikolas Gardner. *Capturing Hill 70: Canada's Forgotten Battle of the First World War*. Vancouver: UBC Press, 2016.

Farr, Don. *The Silent General: Horne of the First Army, A Biography of Haig's Trusted Great War Comrade-in-Arms*. Solihull: Helion, 2007.

Ferland, Raphaël Dallaire. 'Patriotism and Allegiances of the 22nd (French Canadian) Battalion, 1914-1918.' *Canadian Military Journal* 13, no. 1 (2012): 51-60.

Ferris, John. 'The British Army and Signals Intelligence in the Field During the First World War.' *Intelligence and National Security* 3, no. 4 (1988): 23-48.

Fetherstonhaugh, R. C. *The 13th Battalion Royal Highlanders of Canada, 1914-1919*. 13th Battalion, Royal Highlanders of Canada, 1925.

Fetherstonhaugh, R. C. *The 24th Battalion, C.E.F., Victoria Rifles of Canada, 1914-1919*. Montreal: Gazette Print. Co., 1930.

Fetherstonhaugh, R. C. *The Royal Montreal Regiment: 14th Battalion, C.E.F. 1914-1925*. Montreal: The Gazette Printing Co. Limited, 1927.

Fetherstonhaugh, R.C., Stevens, G.R.B. *The Royal Canadian Regiment*. London, Ont.: London Print. & Lithographing Co., 1936.

Foran, Max. 'W.A. "Billy" Griesbach and World War One.' *Alberta History* 32, no. 3 (1984): 1-8.

Forester, CS. *The General*. 1975 ed. Middlesex, UK: Penguin Books, 1936.

Fowler, T. Robert. 'The Canadian Nursing Service and the British War Office: The Debate over Awarding the Military Cross, 1918.' *Canadian Military History* 14, no. 4 (2012): 31-42.

Fox, Colin. *Monchy Le Preux - Arras (Battleground Europe)*. Barnsley: Pen & Sword, 2000.

Gary Sheffield, John Bourne, ed. *Douglas Haig: War Diaries and Letters, 1914-1918*. London: Weidenfeld & Nicolson, 2005.

General Staff Intelligence Section. *Two Hundred and Fifty-One Divisions of the German Army Which Participated in the War (1914-1918)*. Government Publishing Office, 1920.

Gerster, Matthäus. *Das Württembergische Reserve-Infanterie-Regiment Nr. 119 im Weltkrieg 1914-1918*. Stuttgart: Chr. Belsersche Verlagsbuchhandlung, 1920.

Godefroy, Andrew B. 'Portrait of a Battalion Commander: Lieutenant-Colonel George Stuart Tuxford at the Second Battle of Ypres, April 1915.' *Canadian Military Journal*, no. Summer (2004): 55-61.

Goodspeed, D. J. *Battle Royal: A History of the Royal Regiment of Canada, 1862-1979*. 2nd ed. Toronto: Royal Regiment of Canada Association, 1979.

Gordon, Andrew. 'Ratcatchers and Regulators at the Battle of Jutland.' In G. Sheffield (ed.), *The Challenges of High Command*. 26-33. London: Palgrave Macmillan, 2003.

Gottberg, Döring von *Das Grenadier-Regiment König Friedrich Wilhelm IV (1. Pommersches) Nr. 2 im Weltkrieg*. Berlin: Verlag Tradition Wilhelm Kolk, 1928.

Gould, L. McLeod. *From B.C. To Baisieux: Being the Narrative History of the 102nd Canadian Infantry Battalion*. Victoria, B.C.: T.R. Cusack, 1919.

Gould, R.W., and S.K. Smith. *The Story of the Fighting 26th*. St. John News Co., 1918.

Goya, Michel. *Flesh and Steel During the Great War: The Transformation of the French Army and the Invention of Modern Warfare*. Translated by Andrew translator Uffindell. English ed. Barnsley: Pen & Sword, 2014.

Grafton, C.S. *The Canadian "Emma Gees": A History of the Canadian Machine Gun Corps*. London, ON: Canadian Machine Gun Corps Association, 1938.

Granatstein, J. L. *The Greatest Victory: Canada's One Hundred Days, 1918*. Oxford: Oxford University Press, 2014.

Greenhalgh, Elizabeth. *Foch in Command: The Forging of a First World War General*. Paperback ed. Cambridge: Cambridge University Press, 2013.

Greenhalgh, Elizabeth. 'General Ferdinand Foch and United Allied Command in 1918.' *Journal of Military History* 79, no. 4 (2015): 997-1023.

Greenhalgh, Elizabeth. *Victory through Coalition: Britain and France During the First World War*. Cambridge: Cambridge University Press, 2005.

Griffith, Paddy. *Battle Tactics of the Western Front: The British Army's Art of Attack, 1916-18*. New Haven: Yale University Press, 1994.

Harris, J. P., and Niall Barr. *Amiens to the Armistice: The BEF in the Hundred Days' Campaign, 8 August-11, November 1918*. 1st English ed. London ; Washington: Brassey's, 1998.

Harvey, A.D. 'Trench Mortars in the First World War.' *The RUSI Journal* 174, no. 4 (2012): 86-92.

Harvey, Trevor. 'Turnover Amongst Brigade Commanders, 1917. The Real Reasons?, Stand To!'. *Stand To!* , no. 109 (June/July 2017): 97-105.
Hayes, Geoffrey, Michael Bechthold, Andrew Iarocci, and Laurier Centre for Military Strategic and Disarmament Studies. *Vimy Ridge: A Canadian Reassessment.* Waterloo, Ont.: Wilfrid Laurier University Press, 2007.
Hayes, Joseph. *The Eighty-Fifth in France and Flanders.* Halifax N.S.: Royal Print & Litho, 1920.
Hertzberg, H.F.H. 'The Re-Organization of the Engineering Troops of a Canadian Division - Great War 1914-1918.' *Canadian Defence Quarterly* 1, no. 4 (1923).
Hirschel, Dr. Otto. *Standhaft Und Treu! Geschichte Des Reserve-Infanterie-Regiments 221.* Berlin: Verlag Gehard Stalling, 1925.
Hodder-Williams, Ralph Wilfred. *Princess Patricia's Canadian Light Infantry.* Vol. 2, Toronto: Hodder and Stoughton, 1923.
Hodges, Paul Dominick. "They Don't Like It up 'Em!': Bayonet Fetishization in the British Army During the First World War.' *Journal of War and Culture Studies* 1, no. 2 (2008): 123-138.
Holtz, George vom. *Das Württembergische Reserve-Infanterie-Regiment Nr. 121 im Weltkrieg 1914-1918*. Stuttgart: Chr. Belsersche Verlagsbuchhandlung, 1922.
Horn, Bernd. *Establishing a Legacy: The History of the Royal Canadian Regiment, 1881-1953.* Toronto: Dundurn Press, 2008.
Horne, Bernd, ed. *Fortune Favours the Brave: Tales of Courage and Tenacity in Canadian Military History.* Toronto: Dundurn Press, 2009.
Hutchison, Paul P. *Canada's Black Watch: The First Hundred Years, 1862-1962.* Bloomfield, Ont.: Museum Restoration Service, 1987.
Hyatt, A. M. J. *General Sir Arthur Currie: A Military Biography.* Toronto: University of Toronto Press, 1987.

Innes-Robbins, Simon. 'Henry Horne as Corps Commander on the Somme.' In Spencer Jones (ed.), *At All Costs: The British Army on the Western Front 1916*. 252-269. Warwick: Helion & Company, 2018.
Instructor, An. *The Complete Lewis Gunner.* Aldershot: Gale & Polden, 1918.
Irian, Glenn. *In the Trenches, 1914-1918*. Kenora: Artbookbindery, 2008.

Jeffery, Keith. *Field Marshal Sir Henry Wilson: A Political Soldier.* Oxford, England: Oxford University Press, 2006.
Jerrold, Douglas. *The Royal Naval Division*. London: Hutchinson & Co., 1923.
Johnston, G. Chalmers. *The 2nd Canadian Mounted Rifles (British Columbia Horse) in France and Flanders*. 1st ed. Vernon, B.C.: Vernon News Printing & Publishing Co., 1931.
Jones, Simon. 'Yellow Cross: The Advent of Mustard Gas In 1917.' https://simonjoneshistorian.com/2014/02/04/yellow-cross-the-advent-of-mustard-gas-in-1917/ (22 June 2017).

Kaiser, Franz. *Das Konigl. Preuss. Infanterie Regiment Nr. 63 (4. Oberschlesisches).* Berlin: Verlag Bernard & Graefe, 1940.
Karl Dieterich, Oscar Winter. *Das Niedersächsische Feld-Artillerie-Regiment Nr. 46 im Krieg 1914-1918*. Braunschweig: George Westermann, 1934.

Kearsey, A. *The Battle of Amiens, 1918, and Operations 8th August–3rd September, 1918*. Naval and Military Press, 2009.

Keegan, John. *The Face of Battle*. London: J. Cape, 1976.

Kempling, James S. 'Birth of a Regiment: Princess Patricia's Canadian Light Infantry 1914-1919.' MA, University of Victoria, 2011.

Kenyon, David. *Horsemen in No Man's Land: British Cavalry and Trench Warfare, 1914-1918*. Barnsley: Pen & Sword Military, 2011. e-Book.

Kitchen, Martin. *The German Offensives of 1918*. Charleston, SC: Tempus, 2001.

Klaus, Max. *Das Württembergische Reserve-Feldartillerie-Regiment Nr. 26 im Weltkrieg 1914-1918*. Stuttgart: Chr. Belse AG, 1929.

Kraehe, Generalleutnant a.D. *Das Füsilier-Regiment Königin Victoria Von Schweden (Pommersches) Nr. 34 im Weltkriege*. Stettin: Verlag von F. Heffenland, GmbH, 1931.

Kümmel, Adolf. *Res.Inf.Regt. Nr. 91 im Weltkriege 1914-1918*. Berlin: Verlag Gehard Stalling, 1926.

Livesay, John Frederick Bligh. *Canada's Hundred Days. With the Canadian Corps from Amiens to Mons, Aug. 8-Nov. 11, 1918*. Toronto: Thomas Allen, 1919.

Lloyd, Nick. *Hundred Days: The Campaign That Ended World War I*. New York: Basic Books, 2014.

Lothar Gitterman, Ernst Zillmer, Martin Grunau. *Das Feldartillerie-Regiment Nr. 71 Groß-Komtur im Weltkriege*. Zeulenroda: Sporn Verlag, 1936.

Ludendorff, Erich von. *Ludendorff's Own Story, August 1914 - November 1918*. New York: Harper and Brothers Publishers, 1919. e-Book.

Lupfer, Timothy T. *The Dynamics of Doctrine: The Changes in German Tactical Doctrine During the First World War*. Vol. 4, Fort Leavenworth, Kan.: Combat Studies Institute, U.S. Army Command and General Staff College, 1981.

Macdonell, A.C. 'The Old Red Patch at the Breaking of the Drocourt-Queant Line, the Crossing of the Canal Du Nord and the Advance on Cambrai, 30 Aug.--2nd Oct. 1918.' *Canadian Defence Quarterly* IV, no. 4 (1927).

Macdonell, A.H. 'The Old Red Patch at the Breaking of the Drocourt-Queant Line, the Crossing of the Canal Du Nord and the Advance on Cambrai, 30 Aug.--2nd Oct. 1918, Part 2.' *Canadian Defence Quarterly* IV, no. 1 (1928).

MacGowan, S. Douglas, Harry M. Heckbert, and Byron E. O'Leary. *New Brunswick's Fighting 26th: A History of the 26th New Brunswick Battalion, C.E.F., 1914-1919*. Saint John, N.B.: Neptune Publishing Company, 1994.

Mark Forsythe, Greg Dickson. *From the West Coast to the Western Front: British Columbians and the Great War*. Madeira Park, BC: Harbour Publishing, 2014.

McAllister, Anthony. *The Greatest Gallantry: The Story of the Newfoundland Regiment at Monchy Le Preux*. St. John's, Nfld.: DRC Pub., 2011.

McCluskey, Alistair, and Peter Dennis. *Amiens 1918: The Black Day of the German Army*. Oxford: Osprey, 2008.

McCulloch, Ian M. 'Batty Mac - Portrait of a Brigade Commander of the Great War, 1915-1917.' *Canadian Military History* 7, no. 4 (1998): 11-28.

McCulloch, Ian M. 'Crisis in Leadership: The Seventh Brigade and the Nivelles "Mutiny", 1918.' *The Army Doctrine and Training Bulletin* 3, no. 2 (Summer 2000).

McCulloch, Ian M. 'The "Fighting Seventh": The Evolution and Devolution of Tactical Command and Control in a Canadian Infantry Brigade of the Great War.' MA, Royal Military College of Canada, 1997.

McEvoy, Bernard. *History of the 72nd Canadian Infantry Battalion, Seaforth Highlanders of Canada*. Vancouver: Cowan & Brookhouse, 1920.

McNorgan, Michael R. 'My God Look at Them Houses Moving' Combined Arms at Iwuy, 10-11 October 1918 '. In Donald E. Graves and Robert H. Caldwell (ed.), *More Fighting for Canada: Five Battles, 1760-1944*. Toronto: R. Brass Studio, 2004.

McWilliams, James L., and R. J. Steel. *Amiens: Dawn of Victory*. Toronto: Dundurn Press, 2001.

McWilliams, James L., Steel, J. L. *The Suicide Battalion*. Edmonton: Hurtig, 1978.

Messenger, Charles. *The Day We Won the War: Turning Point at Amiens, 8 August 1918*. London: Weidenfeld & Nicolson, 2008.

Millman, Brock. *Pessimism and British War Policy, 1916-1918*. London: F. Cass, 2001.

Montgomery, A.A. *The Story of the Fourth Army in the Battle of the Hundred Days, August 8th to November 11th, 1918*. London: Hodder & Stoughton, 1920.

Morrow, John Howard. *The Great War in the Air: Military Aviation from 1909 to 1921*. Smithsonian History of Aviation History. Washington: Smithsonian Institution Press, 1993.

Morton, Desmond. *A Peculiar Kind of Politics*. Toronto: University of Toronto Press, 1982.

Murray, W. W. *The History of the 2nd Canadian Battalion (East. Ontario Regiment), Canadian Expeditionary Force, in the Great War, 1914-1919*. Ottawa: Published for the Historical Committee, 2nd Canadian Battalion, C.E.F., 1947.

Nichol, Stephen J. *Ordinary Heroes: Eastern Ontario's 21st Battalion C.E.F. In the Great War*. Almonte, ON: Stephen J. Nichol, 2008.

Nicholls, Jonathan. *Cheerful Sacrifice: The Battle of Arras 1917*. Barnsley, South Yorkshire: Pen & Sword, 2008. e-Book.

Nicholson, G.W.L. *The Gunners of Canada: The History of the Royal Regiment of Canadian Artillery*. Toronto: McClelland and Stewart, 1967.

Norris, Marjorie, ed. *Medicine and Duty: The World War I Memoir of Captain Harold W. McGill, Medical Officer, 31st Battalion, C.E.F.* Calgary: University of Calgary Press, 2007.

O'Keefe, David R. '"A Brutal, Soul Destroying Business:" Brigadier-General F.O.W. Loomis and the Question of 'Impersonal Generalship'.' In Andrew B. Godefroy (ed.), *Great War Commands: Historical Perspectives on Canadian Army Leadership 1914-1918*. 87-110. Kingston: Canadian Defence Academy Press, 2010.

Osborn, Patrick R., and Marc Romanych. *The Hindenburg Line*. Bloomsbury Publishing Plc, 2016. e-Book.

Otto Mathies, Karl Guth, Urn Bunnemann. *Geschichte Des 3. Oberelsässisch. Feldartillerie-Regiments Nr. 80*. Berlin: Druck und Verlag von Gerhard Stalling, 1928.

Pafferath, Fritz. *Die Geschichte Des 6. Rheinischen Infanterie-Regiments Nr. 68 im Weltkriege 1914-1918*. Berlin: Druck und Verlag Franz Weber, 1930.

Palazzo, Albert. *Seeking Victory on the Western Front: The British Army and Chemical Warfare in World War I*. Lincoln, Neb.: University of Nebraska Press, 2000.

Patterson, William J. *Soldiers of the Queen: The Canadian Grenadier Guards of Montreal, 1859-2009*. Montréal: Canadian Grenadier Guards Corp., 2009.

Pépin, Carl. 'The Need to Advance: The Battle of Chérisy and the Massacre of Québécois Troops (August 1918).' *Canadian Military Journal* 15, no. 3 (2006): 37-43.

Pöhlman, Markus. 'German Intelligence at War, 1914-1918.' *The Journal of Intelligence History*, no. 5 (2005): 33-62.

Poland, Franz Theodor. *Das Kgl. Sächs. Reserve-Infanterie-Regiment Nr. 103*. Dresden: Wilhelm und Bertha von Baensch Stiftung, 1922.

Prentiss, Augustin M. *Chemicals in War A Treatise on Chemical Warfare*. New York: McGraw-Hill Book Company, 1937.

Preusser, Wilhelm. *Das 9. Westpreussische Infanterie-Regiment Nr. 176 im Weltkrieg*. Berlin: Tradition Wilhelm Kolk, 1931.

Pugsley, Christopher. 'Haig and the Implementation of Tactical Doctrine on the Western Front ' In *Sandhurst Occasional Papers*. Royal Military Academy, Sandhurst, 2011.

Pulsifer, Cameron. 'Canada's First Armoured Unit.' *Canadian Military History* 10, no. 1 (2001): 44-57.

Pulsifer, Cameron. 'Death at Licourt: An Historical and Visual Record of Five Fatalities in the 1st Canadian Motor Machine Gun Brigade, 25 March 1918.' *Canadian Military History* 11, no. 3 (2002).

Radley, Kenneth. *We Lead, Others Follow: First Canadian Division 1914-1918*. St. Catharines, Ont.: Vanwell Pub., 2006.

Rawling, Bill. 'A Resource Not to Be Squandered: The Canadian Corps on the 1918 Battlefield.' In Peter Dennis (ed.), *1918 Defining Victory*. Army History Unit, 1999.

Rawson, Andrew. *The Arras Campaign*. Barnsley: Pen and Sword Military, 2017.

Reynolds, Kenneth W. *Capital Soldiers: The History of the Cameron Highlanders of Ottawa*. Ottawa, ON: Cameron Highlanders of Ottawa, 2011.

Robbins, Simon. *British Generalship on the Western Front 1914-18: Defeat into Victory*. London: Frank Cass, 2005.

Robbins, Simon, ed. *The First World War Letters of General Lord Horne*. London: History Press for the Army Records Society, 2009.

Rothe, Ernst von Eisenhart. *Deutsche Infanterie: Das Ehrenmal Der Vordersten Front*. Zeulenroda: Sporn Verlag, 1939.

Roy, Reginald Herbert. *For Most Conspicuous Bravery: A Biography of Major-General George R. Pearkes, V.C., through Two World Wars*. Vancouver: University of British Columbia Press, 1977.

Russenholt, Edgar Stanford. *Six Thousand Canadian Men: Being the History of the 44th Battalion Canadian Infantry 1914-1919*. Winnipeg: De Montfort Press, 1932.

Schreiber, Shane B. *Shock Army of the British Empire: The Canadian Corps in the Last 100 Days of the Great War*. Westport, Conn.: Praeger, 1997.

Schulemann, Edmund. *Das Kulmer Infanterie-Regiment Nr. 141 im Weltkriege*. Berlin: Gerhard Stalling, 1926.

Seebohm, Walter. *Geschichte Des Oberelsässischen Infanterie-Regiments Nr. 167.* Jena: Walter Viedermann, 1932.

Shackleton, Kevin R. *Second to None: The Fighting 58th Battalion of the Canadian Expeditionary Force.* Toronto: Dundurn Group, 2002.

Sheffield, G. D. *Command and Morale: The British Army on the Western Front 1914-1918.* Barnsley: Praetorian Press, 2014. e-Book.

Sheffield, Gary. *The Chief: Douglas Haig and the British Army.* Aurum Press, 2011. e-Book.

Sheffield, Gary. *Forgotten Victory: The First World War: Myths and Realities.* London: Review, 2002.

Showalter, Dennis E. *Instrument of War: The German Army 1914-18.* Osprey Publishing, 2016. e-book.

Simkins, Peter. *From the Somme to Victory: The British Army's Experience on the Western Front 1916-1918.* Barnsley: Pen & Sword, 2014. e-Book.

Smithson, Jim. *A Taste of Success: The First Battle of the Scarpe 9-14 April 1917: The Opening Phase of the Battle of Arras, 9-14 April 1917.* Solihull, West Midlands, England: Helion & Company, 2017.

Speaight, Robert. *Vanier: Soldier, Diplomat and Governor General: A Biography.* London: Collins, 1970.

Stanley, George F. G. *In the Face of Danger: The History of the Lake Superior Regiment.* Port Arthur, Ont.: Lake Superior Scottish Regiment, 1960.

Steele, W Arthur. 'Wireless Telegraphy in the Canadian Corps in France Part II Open Warfare.' *Canadian Defence Quarterly* VIII, no. 3 (April 1931).

Steele, W Arthur. 'Wireless Telegraphy in the Canadian Corps in France Part II Open Warfare.' *Canadian Defence Quarterly* VII, no. 4 (1930).

Stenger, Alfred. *Geschichte Des Kgl. Preuß. Trierschen Feldartillerie-Regiments Nr. 44, 1899-1919.* Freiburg: Poppen & Ortmann, 1934.

Steuer, Joseph. *Das 1. Unter-Elsassische Infanterie-Regiment Nr. 132 im Weltkriege.* Berlin: Tradition Wilhelm Kolk, 1931.

Stevens, G. R. *A City Goes to War; [History of the Loyal Edmonton Regiment (3 PPCLI).* Brampton: Charters Publishing Co., 1964.

Stevenson, D. *With Our Backs to the Wall: Victory and Defeat in 1918.* Paperback ed. London: Allen Lane, 2012.

Stewart, John Smith. *Memoirs of a Soldier: Brigadier-General John Smith Stewart.* Lethbridge, AB: S.I., 1979?

Stewart, Timothy J. *Toronto's Fighting 75th in the Great War 1915-1919.* Waterloo, ON: WLU Press, 2017.

Stewart, William F. '"Byng Boys": A Profile of Senior Commanders of Canadian Combat Units on the Somme 1916.' *War in History* 23, no. 1 (2016): 55-78.

Stewart, William F. *The Canadians on the Somme, 1916: Canada's Neglected Campaign.* Wolverhampton Military Studies. Solihull, West Midlands, England: Helion, 2017.

Stewart, William F. *The Embattled General: Sir Richard Turner and the First World War.* Montreal & Kingston: McGill-Queen's University Press, 2015.

Stewart, William F. '"The Most Vivifying Influence:" Operation Delta in Preparing the Canadian Corps for the Hundred Days.' *Canadian Military History* 27, no. 2 (Summer/Autumn 2018).

Stewart, William F. 'When the Learning Curve Falls: The Ordeal of the 44th Battalion, 25 October 1916.' *British Journal for Military History* 2, no. 3 (2016): 24-46.

Strohn, Matthias. 'German Tactical Doctrine and the Defensive Battle on the Western Front.' In Matthias Strohn (ed.), *World War I Companion*. Oxford: Osprey Publishing, 2013.

Stümke, Generalmajor. *Die 26. (Württembergische) Reserve-Division im Weltkrieg 1914-1918*. Vol. II, Stuttgart: Bergers Literaisches Büro und Verlagsanstalt, 1935.

Sydow, Herbert von *Das Infanterie-Regiment Hamburg (2. Hanseatisches) Nr. 76 im Weltkriege 1914/1918*. Berlin: Gerhard Stalling, 1922.

Szczepanski, Max von *Erinnerungsblätter Aus Der Geschichte Des Füsilier-Regiments Generalfeldmarschall Prinz Albrecht Von Preußen (Hann.) Nr. 73 Während Des Weltkrieges 1914-1918*. Berlin: Druck und Verlag von Gerhard Stalling, 1923.

Tascona, Bruce. *From the Forks to Flanders Field: The Story of the 27th City of Winnipeg Battalion, 1914-1918*. Bruce Tascona, 1995.

Tascona, Bruce. *Little Black Devils: A History of the Royal Winnipeg Rifles*. Winnipeg: Published by Frye Pub. for Royal Winnipeg Rifles, 1983.

Thompson, RR. *The Fifty-Second (Lowland) Division 1914-1918*. Glasgow: Maclehose, Jackson & Co. , 1923.

Tiede, Paul. *Die 1.Garde-Reserve-Division im Weltkriege 1914-1919*. Berlin: M. Galle, 1922.

Todman, Daniel. 'The Grand Lamasery Revisited.' In Gary Sheffield and Daniel Todman (ed.), *Command and Control on the Western Front: The British Army's Experience, 1914-1918*. Staplehurst: Spellmount, 2004.

Topp, C. Beresford. *The 42nd Battalion, C. E. F., Royal Highlanders of Canada, in the Great War*. Montreal: Gazette Printing Co., Limited, 1931.

Tremblay, Yves. 'Brutinel: A Unique Kind of Leadership.' In Bernd Horne and Stephen Harris (ed.), *Warrior Chiefs*. 57-70. Toronto: Dundurn Press, 2001.

Urquhart, H. M. *The History of the 16th Battalion (the Canadian Scottish)*. Toronto: MacMillan, 1932.

Urquhart, Hugh MacIntyre. *Arthur Currie, the Biography of a Great Canadian*. Toronto: J.M. Dent & Sons (Canada), 1950.

Vines, Anthony John. 'The Heroic Manager: An Assessment of Sir Douglas Haig's Role as a Military Manager on the Western Front.' PhD, King's College London, 2015.

Vischer, Alfred. *Das Württ. Infanterie-Regiment Nr. 180 im Weltkrieg 1914 - 1918*. Stuttgart: Belser, 1921.

Vogt, Dr. Otto Vogt and Karl. *3. Niederschlesisches Infanterie-Regiment Nr. 50 1914-1920* Berlin: Bernard & Graefe, 1931.

Voight, Julius. *Das Garde-Reserve-Infanterie-Regiment Nr. 64 im Weltkriege*. Berlin: Gerhard Stalling, 1923.

Watson, Alexander. *Enduring the Great War: Combat, Morale and Collapse in the German and British Armies, 1914-1918*. Cambridge: Cambridge University Press, 2008.

Watson, Alexander. *Ring of Steel: Germany and Austria-Hungary at War, 1914-1918*. London: Allen Lane, 2014.

Wegener, Hans. *Die Geschicte Des 3. Ober-Elsässischen Infanterie-Regiments Nr, 172*. Zeulenroda: Bernard Sporn, 1934.

Wheeler, Victor W. *The 50th Battalion in No Man's Land: 50th Canadian Infantry Battalion (Alberta Regiment), Canadian Expeditionary Force, 1915-1919*. Ottawa: CEF Books, 2000.

Whitmore, Lieutenant-Colonel F.H.D.C. 'Drocourt-Queant Line, September 2, 1918.' *Cavalry Journal* XXV, no. January to October (1925): 171-6.

Wigney, Edward H. *Guests of the Kaiser: Prisoners of War of the Canadian Expeditionary Force 1915-1918*. Ottawa: CEF Books, 2008.

Williams, Jeffery. *First in the Field: Gault of the Patricias*. St. Catharines, Ont.: Vanwell Publishing, 1995.

Woodward, David R. *Lloyd George and the Generals*. Newark, London: University of Delaware Press; Associated University Presses, 1983.

Zabecki, David T. *The German 1918 Offensives: A Case Study in the Operational Level of War*. London: Routledge, 2006.

Zabecki, David T. 'Operational Art and the German 1918 Offensives.' PhD, Cranfield University, 2004.

Zuehlke, Mark. *Brave Battalion: The Remarkable Saga of the 16th Battalion (Canadian Scottish) in the First World War*. Mississauga, Ont.: J. Wiley & Sons Canada, 2008.

Theses

Boff, Jonathan. 'British Third Army, the Application of Modern War, and the Defeat of the German Army, August-November 1918.' PhD, King's College London, 2010.

Brown, Ian Malcolm. 'Lieutenant-General Sir Arthur Currie and the Canadian Corps 1917-1918: The Evolution of a Style of Command and Attack.' Masters, University of Calgary, 1991.

Campbell, David Charles Gregory. 'The Divisional Experience in the C.E.F.: A Social and Operational History of the 2nd Canadian Division, 1915-1918.' PhD, University of Calgary, 2003.

Dagenais, Maxime. 'Une Permission!...C'est Bon Pour Une Recrue, Discipline and Illegal Absences in the 22nd (French-Canadian) Battalion 1915-1919.' Masters, University of Ottawa, 2006.

Fasse, Alexander. 'Im Zeichen Des „Tankdrachen". Die Kriegführung an Der Westfront 1916-1918 im Spannungsverhältnis Zwischen Einsatz Eines Neuartigen Kriegsmittels Der Alliierten Und Deutschen Bemühungen Um Seine Bekämpfung.' PhD, Humboldt-Universität zu Berlin, 2007.

French, Craig. 'The 51st (Highland) Division During the First World War.' PhD, University of Glasgow, 2006.

Hall, Brian N. 'The British Expeditionary Force and Communications on the Western Front, 1914-1918.' PhD, University of Salford, 2009.

Hammond, Christopher Byrnley. 'The Theory and Practice of Tank Cooperation with Other Arms on the Western Front in the First World War.' PhD, University of Birmingham, 2005.

Harris, Paul Martin. 'The Men Who Planned the War: A Study of the Staff of the British Army on the Western Front 1914-1918.' PhD, King's College London, 2013.

Harvey, Trevor Gordon. "An Army of Brigadiers' British Brigade Commanders at the Battle of Arras 1917.' PhD, University of Birmingham, 2016.

Hughes, Jackson. 'The Monstrous Anger of the Guns: The Development of British Artillery Tactics 1914 - 1918.' PhD, University of Adelaide, 1992.

Jackson, Geoffrey. 'The British Empire on the Western Front: A Transnational Study of the 62nd West Riding Division and the Canadian 4th Division.' PhD, University of Calgary, 2013.

Jenkins, Dan. 'Winning Trench Warfare: Battlefield Intelligence in the Canadian Corps, 1914-1919.' PhD, Carleton University, 1999.

Mepham, Leslie P. 'Making Their Mark: Canadian Snipers and the Great War. 1914-1918.' Masters, University of Windsor, 1997.

Miedema, Aaron Taylor. 'Bayonets and Blobsticks: The Canadian Experience of Close Combat 1915-1918 ' Masters, Royal Military College of Canada, 2010.

Potter, Stephanie Elizabeth. '"Smile and Carry On:" Canadian Cavalry on the Western Front, 1914-1918.' PhD, University of Western Ontario, 2013.

Radley, Kenneth. 'First Canadian Division, C.E.F., 1914-1918: Ducimus (We Lead).' PhD, Carleton University, 2000.

Robbins, Simon. 'British Generalship on the Western Front, 1914-1918.' PhD, King's College London, 2001.

Ryan, Michael Patrick. 'Supplying the Material Battle: Combined Logistics in the Canadian Corps, 1915-1918.' Masters, Carleton University, 2005.

Stewart, William F. 'Attack Doctrine in the Canadian Corps, 1916-1918.' Masters, University of New Brunswick, 1982.

Index

INDEX OF BATTLES AND CAMPAIGNS

Amiens 1918, Battle of 21–22, 27, 32, 36–38, 40–41, 49–50, 58, 66, 68–69, 76–78, 80, 86, 89, 91–94, 97, 99–103, 105, 110, 112–113, 115, 121, 129, 133, 138–139, 142–145, 148–151, 153–154, 156–158, 160–161, 165–167, 176, 178–179, 181–184, 191, 200–201, 224, 231, 233, 246, 248, 251, 261, 264, 266–268, 274–275, 277, 281–282, 291–292, 297, 307–308, 313, 316, 319–320, 322, 344–345, 347–348, 350–352, 374–376, 391–392, 395, 397–403, 407, 411–413, 417, 420

Arras 1917, First Battle of 22–23, 34, 60, 83, 89, 160, 230, 399, 404–408, 411

Arras 1918, Second Battle of 21–27, 30, 32, 38, 41, 43–44, 46, 49–50, 52–53, 60, 62, 64, 70, 73–74, 78, 80, 83, 85–86, 93, 98, 100, 103, 113, 115, 138, 169, 191, 198, 222, 230, 233, 248, 261, 268, 275, 314, 337, 374, 376–377, 379–393, 395–399, 401–402, 404–408, 410–411, 413, 417, 419–420

Hill 70, Battle of 22, 38, 42, 246, 345, 420

Hundred Days, Campaign of 22–23, 27, 40, 66, 70, 86, 92–93, 95, 100, 139, 144, 152, 198, 246, 374, 388, 392, 397, 401, 408, 415, 417, 419

Marne, Second Battle of 58, 76, 101, 230

Mt Sorrel, Battle of 36, 41

Passchendaele, Third Battle of 21, 32, 35, 38, 41–42, 50, 56, 58, 80, 87, 90, 92–94, 128, 142, 191, 251, 308, 407–408, 410–412

Somme, 1916 Campaign of 77, 264, 324, 376–377, 381, 383–386, 391

St Eloi Craters, Battle of 38

Vimy Ridge. Battle of 21, 38, 41–42, 280, 291, 365

Ypres 1915, Second Battle of 35, 38, 40, 42, 256, 268

INDEX OF MILITARY CONCEPTS

Air operations 24, 103, 115, 128, 268, 301, 326, 407, 411

Barrage 23, 26, 50, 75, 80–81, 83–84, 92–93, 98–99, 101, 108, 117, 126–131, 133, 140, 142–143, 147–150, 153–154, 156, 159, 162, 165, 176, 179–188, 190, 192, 194–195, 201, 204–214, 218–220, 223, 244–246, 248–254, 258, 266, 269, 273–275, 277–279, 282–283, 287, 290–291, 294–295, 299, 301, 303, 305, 307–309, 313, 315–320, 323–325, 332–334, 336–337, 339–340, 342, 344, 352–355, 357–359, 361, 363–364, 377–378, 389–390, 392–395, 397, 400, 402, 415–416, 420

Casualties 25–26, 36, 58, 75–76, 81, 85, 89–90, 101, 103, 121, 134, 138, 142–143, 148–149, 153–154, 157–158, 160–164, 179, 181–183, 185, 187, 191–194, 200, 203, 208, 211–212, 214–217, 220–223, 231, 233–234, 236–239, 246, 248, 252–254, 256, 264–269, 274–275, 284, 298, 301, 317–319, 321, 328, 330, 332–333, 336, 338–339, 341, 343–345, 347–348, 350–353, 355–357, 359–361, 369–370, 374, 376–377, 380, 382–385, 390–391, 393, 395, 397, 403–405, 407, 411, 413–415, 419

Counter-battery 51–53, 75–76, 93, 100–101, 128–129, 137, 147, 165, 174, 213, 239, 245, 253, 259, 278, 299–301, 333, 352, 359, 385, 408

Counterattack 61, 75, 78–80, 84, 101, 138, 147, 156, 158–159, 161–162, 165, 174, 190–191, 203, 214–217, 226, 228, 230, 241, 249–252, 254, 256–257, 263, 266, 271, 274, 276–279, 288, 314, 344, 355, 358–359, 376, 395

Doctrine 24, 53, 60, 73–74, 78–80, 85, 94–95, 97–98, 110, 144, 156, 158–159, 294, 297, 302, 309, 337, 339, 387, 389, 395, 397–398, 406–407

Eingreifdivision 100, 135, 203, 230, 243, 249, 252, 261, 271, 273, 278, 284, 294, 355, 358, 395

Firepower 32, 46, 49, 55, 74–75, 79, 92, 101, 103, 156, 160, 162, 195, 220, 236, 252, 284, 297, 300, 308, 321, 337, 350–351, 361, 367, 371, 393, 395–396, 402, 408–410, 413
Fog 47, 50, 75, 101, 154, 248, 275, 355
Fortification 21–22, 71, 151, 154, 210, 241, 288, 290, 322, 328, 338, 344

Infiltrate 77, 95, 151, 165, 193, 220, 248, 277, 348, 392–393, 397, 415

Logistics 23–24, 35, 46, 57, 83, 87, 89, 192, 259, 296–297, 395, 400, 416–417

Morale 22–23, 28, 45, 50, 60, 69, 71, 74, 76–78, 85, 90, 137, 148, 152, 160, 164–165, 214, 248, 268, 274, 292, 316, 333, 342–343, 355, 364, 392–394, 404, 407, 410, 413–416

Prisoners of war 56, 103, 105, 135, 140, 143, 148, 151–153, 161–164, 167, 175, 179–180, 182, 185–186, 189, 193–194, 214–218, 220–221, 236, 239, 246–247, 251, 253–254, 256, 265, 274–278, 282, 315–316, 321–325, 332–333, 337–339, 341–345, 347, 349, 353, 357, 359–360, 367, 370, 374, 376, 381–382, 391, 395, 404, 413, 415

Senior Officers Course (SOC) 156, 158, 190, 251, 264, 344, 350
Signals 25, 38, 46, 57, 115, 150, 155, 216, 245, 261, 280, 309, 315, 319, 342, 358, 362, 390, 397, 401–402
Smoke 23, 47, 50–51, 74–77, 81, 92–93, 95, 128, 142, 150–151, 164, 176, 190, 205, 213, 223, 244–245, 248–249, 252, 274, 278, 307, 315, 319, 321, 326, 337, 340, 342, 345, 355, 358, 371, 377–378, 391–395, 397, 407, 415–416

Tactics 23–24, 32, 49–50, 53, 71, 75, 77, 79–80, 83–84, 86, 92, 94–95, 100–101, 140, 151, 164–165, 190, 192, 207–208, 220, 248–249, 274, 277, 284, 302, 307, 321–322, 324, 332, 337, 358, 389, 392, 395, 397, 407, 413, 415
Tanks 22–23, 26, 49–50, 74, 76, 90, 92–93, 95, 99–101, 105, 108, 110, 112, 121, 123, 131–134, 140, 143–145, 156–158, 162, 165, 170, 175–178, 186, 190–192, 194, 201, 206, 211, 217, 223, 244, 288, 290–292, 299, 301–305, 307–308, 311, 313, 315–316, 318–319, 321–322, 332–334, 336, 339–344, 352, 355, 361, 377–379, 390–391, 398, 404–405, 407, 410–411, 413
Tempo 23, 32, 38, 66, 83, 92, 94–95, 121, 148–149, 169, 174, 188, 195, 283, 362, 377, 391, 397, 400, 403, 406–407, 415
Training 23–24, 37–39, 42, 45, 58, 71, 77, 79, 86–87, 92, 94–98, 103, 110, 112, 134, 139, 149, 151, 160, 163, 165, 176, 182–183, 190, 208, 230–231, 238, 246, 251, 275, 291, 297, 307–308, 317, 322, 330, 333, 335, 338, 387, 389, 392, 396–397, 401–402, 406–407, 413

Wireless 54, 56, 115, 150, 297, 346, 397

INDEX OF MILITARY UNITS AND FORMATIONS

Armies, British
- First Army 24, 32–33, 58, 66, 83, 91–92, 95, 98–99, 105, 110, 113, 115, 117–118, 123–124, 169–170, 198, 200, 223, 226, 237, 239, 291, 298, 308, 365, 371, 399–400, 420
- Second Army 54, 100, 400
- Third Army 24, 33, 60, 70, 75, 83–84, 89, 98–100, 103, 105–106, 108, 110, 112–113, 115, 117–118, 123–126, 131, 137–139, 175–176, 196, 203, 228, 241, 261, 269, 273, 297–298, 365, 371, 397, 400, 416
- Fourth Army 60, 100, 103, 123, 196, 241, 261, 365, 400
- Fifth Army 113, 304, 400

Armies, German
- *Second Armee* 78, 292, 411
- *Seventeenth Armee* 68, 70, 78, 87, 89, 123, 135, 137–138, 218, 243, 261, 271, 359, 364, 410–411
- *Sixth Armee* 60, 70, 78

Artillery, British
- 4th DA 307
- 50th HA 234

Artillery, Canadian
- 1st CDA 51, 67, 230, 324
- 2nd CDA 51, 147
- 2nd CFA 244, 250, 323, 325
- 3rd CFA 280, 352
- 5th CDA 113, 150, 305
- 5th CFA 179, 223
- 6th CFA 147, 179, 333, 393

8th CFA 113
10th CFA 213
General Officer Commanding Royal Artillery (GOCRA) 51, 53, 55, 128, 174, 388, 402
Artillery, Germans
26th RFAR 186
44th FAR 203
71st FAR 159, 217

Battalions/Regiments, British
1st Hampshire 234, 308, 354
1st Rifle Brigade (RB) 254, 354
1st Royal Warwickshire 234
1st Somerset Light Infantry (SLI) 234, 254, 266, 308, 354, 370
2nd Essex 353–354, 370
2nd Lancashire Fusiliers 370
9th Tank Battalion 132, 305, 351–352
10th Royal Hussars 304, 330
11th Tank Battalion 134, 156, 305, 322, 352
14th Tank Battalion 177, 292, 302, 333
17th Tank Battalion 328
39th Machine Gun Battalion 237
51st Machine Gun Battalion 129, 153
101st Life Guards Machine Gun Battalion 234, 237
Argyll and Sutherland Highlanders 238
Black Watch Regiment 134, 161–162, 268
Gordon Highlanders 162–163, 192–193, 238
King's Liverpool Regiment 269, 271
King's Own Royal Lancaster Regiment 228, 353–354
Royal Munster Fusiliers (RMF) 311
Seaforth Highlanders Regiment 193, 253, 266, 282–283, 307, 354
Battalions/Regiments, Canadian
1st Battalion 246, 249–251
2nd Battalion 43, 98, 244, 246, 250–252, 256, 325, 334, 365, 367
3rd Battalion 40, 85, 244, 247–249, 256, 263, 279, 317–318, 324, 332, 399, 416
4th Battalion 250–252, 325, 365, 367
5th Battalion 38, 274, 277–278, 282, 320
7th Battalion 44, 320, 322, 369
8th Battalion 38, 41, 249, 263–265, 277, 325, 367
10th Battalion 42, 319, 322, 324, 329–330, 333–334, 367
13th Battalion 96, 316–317, 319
14th Battalion 50, 77, 275–276, 316–318, 320
15th Battalion 273–275, 298, 311, 317–318, 399
16th Battalion 58, 313–316, 318
18th Battalion 25, 132, 145, 148–149, 184, 186, 206, 210–211
19th Battalion 25, 32, 132, 144–145, 148–149, 184–186, 210–211
20th Battalion 26, 132, 144, 149, 206, 210–211, 271, 294, 380
21st Battalion 132, 143–144, 210–211
22nd Battalion 25, 40, 179–180, 183–184, 186, 205–210, 222, 224, 271, 380, 390
24th Battalion 179, 182, 184, 205, 207–209
25th Battalion 178–179, 206–208, 222
26th Battalion 179, 181, 207
27th Battalion 131, 142–143, 147–149
28th Battalion 120–121, 131, 142–143, 147–148, 163, 206, 249, 251, 265, 271, 273–274, 277–278, 294, 337, 354–355
29th Battalion 83, 132, 163, 179, 207, 250–251, 263, 271, 276–278, 294, 320, 332
31st Battalion 41, 117–118, 206, 369
38th Battalion 267–268, 279, 305, 309, 338–339, 348, 351
42nd Battalion 156, 160–161, 191, 215–217, 234
43rd Battalion 22, 140, 188–189, 191–192, 213, 218–220
44th Battalion 159, 203, 268, 305, 341–342, 344–345, 353, 360, 362, 370
46th Battalion 230, 305, 341–342, 344–345, 355, 362, 370
47th Battalion 280–282, 305, 341–342, 370
49th Battalion 37, 156, 158, 187, 213–214, 217, 271, 278, 294, 316, 319, 332
50th Battalion 208, 281–282, 342
52nd Battalion 188, 215
54th Battalion 306–307, 346–349, 362, 369
58th Battalion 188, 190, 192, 214–217, 228, 243, 271, 380
72nd Battalion 45, 267, 277, 279, 305, 330, 337, 341, 351
75th Battalion 306–307, 346–350
78th Battalion 267–268, 305, 328, 330, 336, 341, 348, 369
85th Battalion 30, 267–268, 280, 283, 305, 339–341, 344, 348, 350–351
87th Battalion 306, 346, 350–351, 362, 369
102nd Battalion 96, 306, 346, 348, 351, 369, 371
116th Battalion 188, 190, 192, 215, 416
1st Canadian Mounted Rifles (CMR) 150, 153–155
2nd CMR 58, 150, 153, 161, 187, 191–192, 219–220
4th CMR 150, 153, 213–215
5th CMR 41
Princess Patricia's Canadian Light Infantry

(PPCLI) 156–159, 162, 213, 216–217
Royal Canadian Regiment (RCR) 156–157, 159, 161, 215, 217
2nd Engineer Battalion 66
1st Machine Gun Battalion 244, 259, 303, 334
2nd Machine Gun Battalion 129, 179
4th Machine Gun Battalion 268
Canadian Corps Cyclist Battalion (CCCB) 145, 172, 234, 236, 328–329
Canadian Light Horse 259, 304, 327

Brigades, British
3rd Tank Brigade 361, 398
10th British Brigade 233, 265–266, 280, 282–284, 390
11th British Brigade 237, 266, 282, 307–308, 353–354
12th British Brigade 282, 307–308, 345, 353
34th Brigade 237
152nd Brigade 162, 193, 221
153rd Brigade 162–163, 192, 221
154th Brigade 221, 238
156th Brigade 175, 179
157th Brigade 175
171st Brigade 261, 269
172nd Brigade 204, 261, 301, 311, 313, 319
Brigades, Canadian
1st Brigade 37, 226, 231, 241, 244, 246, 248–250, 252, 255–257, 263, 273–274, 301–303, 317, 325, 333–334, 365, 371, 389–390, 399, 415
2nd Brigade 30, 37–38, 41, 263, 268, 274, 276, 279, 302–303, 318, 320, 323, 325, 330, 367
3rd Brigade 38, 207, 231, 250, 271, 273–275, 278, 302, 313, 317, 325, 333–335, 365
4th Brigade 25, 39–40, 128, 132, 142–145, 148–149, 172, 175–176, 180, 184, 201, 203, 205–206, 209–210, 316, 388
5th Brigade 40, 43, 126, 145, 170, 172, 175, 177–180, 186, 188, 194, 204–206, 211, 249, 389–390, 416
6th Brigade 41, 115, 117–120, 130–131, 142–143, 145, 147–149, 172, 179, 205–206, 222, 389
7th Brigade 36, 41, 132, 134, 154–156, 158–160, 163, 172, 187, 213, 216–218, 236, 388
8th Brigade 41–42, 115, 126, 132, 134, 150, 154–155, 159, 187, 213–214, 218–220, 389
9th Brigade 42, 98, 172, 187–188, 192, 194, 213–214, 216–218, 388–389
10th Brigade 44, 233–234, 253–254, 282, 284, 341, 344, 370–371
11th Brigade 44, 234, 237, 254, 283, 289, 306–307, 326, 339–341, 348–349, 358, 362, 369–371, 390
12th Brigade 44, 266–267, 279, 305, 331, 336–337, 339, 341, 345–346, 348, 355, 370
1st CMMG 145, 297, 304, 331
2nd CMMG 234–235

Corps, British
Australian Corps 100, 103, 113, 137, 387, 399
Canadian Corps 21–27, 30–31, 35, 37–38, 42–43, 45–47, 49, 53, 55–56, 58–60, 78, 80, 83, 85–86, 90–92, 94, 97, 99, 101, 103, 108, 110, 112–113, 121–123, 127, 131, 135, 137, 139–140, 142, 151, 167, 169, 172, 192, 212, 226, 228, 234, 236–237, 244, 256, 258, 271, 284, 287, 291, 297, 299, 304, 322, 357, 360, 364–365, 372, 378, 382, 385, 392, 395, 397–398, 402, 404–406, 408, 410–412, 415–417, 419
Cavalry Corps 33, 83, 123, 170, 226, 237, 295, 297, 309, 386–387
VI Corps 90, 95, 105, 110, 115, 117, 120–121, 399
XVII Corps 89, 98, 100, 106, 108, 110, 113, 115, 131, 140, 142, 170, 172, 175, 196, 204, 228, 232–233, 239, 241, 261, 273, 292, 298, 301–302, 313, 371, 387, 399, 402–403, 410
XXII Corps 198, 237–239, 372, 387, 398
Korps, Germans
II Bavarian Korps 68, 70–71, 73–74, 79–80, 100, 135, 138, 159, 174, 203, 212, 230, 243, 251, 261, 263, 271, 284, 292, 294, 309, 332, 334, 337, 357, 360, 364, 395, 397, 415
XVIII AK 271

Divisions, British
1st British Division 288, 308, 359, 361, 371–372
3rd Cavalry Division 295
4th British Division 198, 200, 233–234, 236–237, 239, 241, 252–253, 256, 264–265, 269, 282–284, 288, 290, 299, 307, 332, 336, 352–353, 355, 359, 361, 370, 390, 402
51st (Highland) Division 27, 30, 47, 53, 58, 60, 84–85, 113, 126, 129, 134–135, 153, 158, 162–164, 169, 192–194, 213–214, 221–222, 226, 237–239, 243, 253, 382, 390, 405
52nd Division 71, 117, 120–121, 126, 131, 140, 147, 204
56th Division 108, 115
57th Division 137, 175, 204–205, 222, 224, 228, 241, 244, 249, 261, 298, 301–302, 311
63rd Royal Naval Division 301, 313, 365
Guards Division 233, 365

Divisions, Canadian
1st Division 30, 35–36, 38, 44, 94, 121, 172, 198, 200–201, 205, 222–224, 226, 228, 230, 232–234, 236, 239, 241, 244, 252, 255, 263, 265, 269, 273–274, 277–278, 292, 299, 301, 303, 311, 313–314, 332–335, 351, 356, 358–359, 361, 364–365, 369–370, 380, 385, 389
2nd Division 32, 38, 43, 50, 79, 90, 92, 95, 113, 115, 117, 120–121, 125, 128, 132, 135, 137, 140, 142, 145, 147, 149–150, 156, 161, 163, 170, 172, 175–176, 179, 182, 184, 187–189, 191–196, 198, 200–201, 203–205, 212–213, 219, 221–224, 230–231, 244–245, 291, 369, 385, 387, 390, 393, 397, 400, 420
3rd Division 41, 79, 95, 110, 113, 128, 132–133, 137, 145, 148–150, 154, 159, 163, 170, 172, 184, 187, 192, 194, 196, 198, 200, 203, 210, 212–213, 218, 221, 223–224, 233–234, 237–238, 385, 387, 390, 420
4th Division 101, 233–234, 266, 299, 307, 330, 358, 384–385, 420
Divisions, German
1st GRD 174, 243, 261, 273, 284, 292, 294, 340–342, 344, 355, 358, 364, 380, 414
2nd GRD 174, 203–204, 230, 243, 261, 271, 284, 288, 292, 294, 337, 358, 380, 415
3rd RD 243, 261, 271, 278–279, 292, 294, 319, 364, 380
4th EzD 203, 221, 228, 230, 241, 243, 249, 255–256, 261, 266, 271, 273, 282, 284, 288, 292, 294, 337, 339, 341, 353, 355, 358, 364, 380
7th Schützen Division (SD) 228, 230, 241, 243, 380
12th ID 78, 294, 364, 380
16th ID 77, 174, 203, 230, 243, 249, 251–252, 255–256, 261, 263, 271, 273, 276, 278, 292, 294, 319, 380, 414–415
20th ID 271, 294, 380
22nd ID 271, 380
26th RD 138–139, 165, 174, 180, 185–186, 194–195, 203, 223, 228, 230, 241, 243, 249, 251, 255–256, 380, 404, 415–416
35th ID 138, 156–160, 165, 174, 186, 189–190, 194–195, 203, 213, 217, 221, 223, 228, 236, 243, 380, 414
39th ID 135, 137–138, 142, 179–180, 193, 195, 203, 380, 414
48th RD 134–135, 137, 139, 162, 174, 193, 237–238, 271, 380
58th ID 228, 243, 271, 380
111th ID 174, 203, 230, 243, 261, 271, 292, 294, 319, 380
214th ID 74, 137, 140, 158–159, 174, 194–195, 380

High Command, British
British Expeditionary Force (BEF) 23–24, 30, 32, 34, 45, 50, 58, 66, 83, 90–91, 94, 100–101, 112–113, 121, 123, 167, 196, 233, 386–387, 395, 397, 406, 416–417
Commander-in-Chief 21, 35, 84, 86, 90, 101, 105, 115, 123, 131, 169, 201, 387, 398
General Headquarters (GHQ) 24, 32, 45–47, 53, 55, 57, 66, 80, 83, 86–87, 90–91, 94–95, 99, 108, 110, 112–113, 121, 125–126, 128, 167, 198, 200, 234, 243, 271, 273, 290–291, 298, 305, 365, 387, 389, 397–398, 400, 411
Royal Air Force (RAF) 24, 159–160, 204, 288, 298, 326–327, 348, 358, 365, 369, 411, 413, 420
High Command, Canadian
Canadian Expeditionary Force 24, 97, 419
Overseas Military Forces of Canada (OMFC) 91
High Command, German
Oberste Heeresleitung (OHL) 45, 69–70, 73, 75, 77–78, 87, 89, 100, 105, 114–115, 135, 196, 230, 243, 271, 273, 364

Miscellaneous, British
No.5 Squadron RA 326
Miscellaneous, Canadian
Corps Survey Section 56, 128, 364, 397
Leading Group 304, 327–328
No. 1 Group 304, 328
Tramways 54, 66–67, 129, 174, 397, 400, 406

Regiments, German
1st GRR 355–356, 364
2nd GrR 271, 294, 319, 324, 355, 364, 367, 413
2nd GRR 355-356
26th Dragoon Regiment 241
28th IR 249, 251, 265, 271, 273–274, 277, 294, 337, 354–355
29th IR 250–251, 263, 271, 276–277, 294, 320
34th FüR 271, 278, 294, 316, 332
49th RIR 271, 278, 294, 316, 319, 332
50th IR 132, 138, 151–152, 174, 194
61st IR 159, 174, 189, 192, 203, 214–215, 217
63rd IR 364
64th RIR 344, 355, 359, 396
68th IR 77, 79, 249–251, 271, 273, 275–276, 278, 294, 320, 413, 415
73rd FüR 203, 292, 315–316, 319
76th IR 203
91st RIR 139, 204, 273, 355, 413–414

103rd IR 228, 241
103rd RIR 228
107th IR 228
119th RIR 138, 174, 184, 186, 203, 211, 219–220, 228, 230, 243, 254
121st RIR 59, 174, 203–204, 207, 211–212, 228, 243, 247–249, 256, 265, 415
132nd IR 135, 137, 143, 147, 165, 174, 185
141st IR 158–159, 162, 174, 190, 203, 214, 217–218
164th IR 316
167th IR 332
171st IR 203
172nd IR 174, 180
176th IR 137, 174–175, 186, 190–191, 203, 215, 217–218
180th RIR 138
214th RIR 230, 243, 254, 353, 355, 359, 364, 413
221st RIR 75
222nd RIR 139
358th IR 174
360th IR 230
362nd IR 203, 221, 230, 246, 353
363rd IR 132

INDEX OF OPERATIONS

Delta, Operation 92, 94–95, 97–98
Mars, Operation 88–89, 132, 138, 233
Michael, Operation 87–88, 273, 408
Thistle, Operation 98, 105, 108–110, 115, 124, 126, 129

INDEX OF PEOPLE

Anderson, Lieutenant Colonel S B 323
Anderson, Major General Hastings 33–34, 118, 120, 361, 363

Balck, Herman 50, 303
Barnes, Corporal Deward 32, 149, 211
Bell, Brigadier General A H 41, 117–118, 131, 147, 205, 389–390
Below, *General der Infantrie* Otto v 68, 70–71, 121, 189, 217, 290, 309, 398, 411
Bertram, Lieutenant Colonel William 38–39, 170, 187, 195, 200, 206–207
Blackstock Lieutenant Colonel G G 251
Borden, Robert 91
Brutinel, Brigadier General Raymond 25–26, 49, 129, 234, 236–237, 287, 297, 303–304, 309, 311, 327–330, 334, 399, 419–420
Burns, Captain E L M 154–155, 280
Burstall, Major General Sir Henry 38–39, 52, 113, 117–118, 120–121, 124–125, 130–131, 145, 147–148, 169–170, 172, 175, 179, 194, 196, 198, 201, 204–205, 210, 213, 222–223, 249, 371, 389–391, 393, 400, 416
Byng, General Sir Julian 99, 105–106, 113, 118, 121, 123, 131, 241, 298, 386–387, 392, 416

Carey, Lieutenant Colonel A B 346–347
Chandler, Lieutenant Colonel W K 191
Clark, Lieutenant Colonel J A 267, 279
Clarke-Kennedy VC, Lieutenant Colonel W H 179, 182, 184, 208
Constantine, Lieutenant Colonel C F 179
Currie, Lieutenant General Sir A W 21–27, 30–33, 36–38, 41, 44, 49, 57–58, 71, 86, 90–91, 94, 96–97, 99–100, 103, 110, 113, 115, 118, 120–121, 123–126, 128, 130–131, 157, 165–166, 169–170, 172, 174, 187, 195–196, 198, 200–201, 205, 212, 221–224, 228, 231, 233–234, 237–239, 257, 259, 266, 274, 287–288, 290, 295, 297–298, 303–304, 308–309, 332, 357–364, 370–372, 387–392, 397–400, 407, 416, 419–420

Davies, Lieutenant Colonel R D 360, 362
Day, Lieutenant Colonel F P 206
Dellmensingen, *General der Artillerie* Konrad Krafft v 68, 70–71, 135, 138, 180, 195, 203, 212, 217, 228, 241, 243, 245, 251–252, 256–257, 261, 271, 273, 278–279, 284, 292, 294, 319, 332, 336, 358–359, 364, 395, 404
Dill, Brigadier General John 46, 126, 128
Draper, Brigadier General D C 42, 132, 153–154, 218, 220, 389–390
Dubuc, Lieutenant Colonel A E 167, 183–184
Dyer, Brigadier General Hugh Marshall 'Daddy' 41, 155–156, 158, 160, 388

Edwards, Lieutenant Colonel Cameron 268, 339
Ewing, Major Royal 160

Fergusson, Lieutenant General Sir Charles 106, 108, 131, 170, 175, 228, 298, 301, 371
Foch, Marshal Ferdinand 35, 90–91, 100–101, 103, 105, 112–113, 167, 169, 387, 398
Foster, Lance Corporal Ken 98, 309, 338–339
Fritsch, *Generalleutenant* Freiherr v 255

Gilson, Lieutenant Colonel W F 320, 322
Girvan, Major J P 273–275, 317–318
Greene, Brigadier General J 266
Griesbach, Brigadier General W A 'Billy' 37, 47, 226, 244–245, 248–250, 252, 257, 325, 333,

367, 390

Haig, Field Marshal Douglas 21, 23, 31–35, 58, 83–86, 89–92, 98–101, 103, 105, 110, 112, 115, 117, 121, 123–125, 131, 137, 139–140, 167, 169–170, 172, 187, 196, 198, 200–201, 205, 222, 224, 226, 228, 233, 237, 261, 290, 295, 297–298, 308–309, 332, 356–357, 365, 374, 386–387, 389, 391–392, 395, 397–400, 416, 419
Harbottle, Lieutenant Colonel C 307, 347–350, 358
Hayter, Brigadier General Ross 44, 280, 305, 341–342, 362, 370–371
Hindenburg, *Field Marshal* Paul v 69, 73, 83, 98, 117, 121, 123, 131, 135, 137, 140, 170, 172, 175, 179, 196, 204, 226, 311, 395, 410, 416
Hooper, Lieutenant Colonel B 144, 149
Hore-Ruthven, Lieutenant Colonel C M 41, 213
Horne, General Sir Henry 32–34, 58, 91, 98–100, 106, 108, 113, 115, 117, 120–121, 123–124, 131, 170, 196, 198, 201, 221–222, 241, 285, 295, 297–298, 304, 309, 311, 357, 361–363, 371–372, 386–387, 398, 403, 419
Humphrey, Major A E 236
Hutchenson VC, Captain Bellenden 154, 156, 178, 207, 220, 319–320, 328, 334, 344, 349, 360, 367, 370

Johnston, Lieutenant Colonel G C 'Whizbang' 153

Kavanagh, Lieutenant General Sir Charles 295, 297
Keegan, Lieutenant Colonel H L 281
Kemnitz, *Generalmajor* v 217
Kemp, Sir Edward 91, 180
Kirkcaldy, Lieutenant Colonel James 268, 341
Knight VC, Sergeant Arthur 324
Kuhl, *Generalleutnant* Herman v 69–70, 218, 271

Lawrence, General Sir Henry 298
Laws, Lieutenant Colonel Burnett 154
Lester, Major H W 370
Lipsett, Major General Louis 21, 41, 110, 115, 132, 145, 154–155, 170, 172, 187, 194, 196, 201, 212–213, 216–217, 221–223, 233, 371, 389, 400
Lloyd, George 91, 416
Loomis, Brigadier General F O W 3 7, 263–265, 302–303, 323–324, 333, 367, 369, 390
Ludendorff, *General* Erich 35, 45, 69–71, 74, 78, 87, 89–90, 103, 105, 218, 241, 413

MacBrien, Brigadier General James Howden 44, 267, 279–280, 305, 337, 339, 345–346, 348
MacDonald, Lieutenant Colonel Eric 322–324
Macdonell, Major General Sir Archibald Cameron 36–37, 41, 94, 224, 226, 230–231, 241, 244–245, 248, 250, 252, 257, 263–264, 273, 284, 299, 302–303, 313, 316, 332–334, 361, 363, 371, 374, 389
Martyn, Major D B 345
Mason, Major Douglas 248, 317
Matheson, Major General T G 200, 233–234, 266, 282, 284, 297, 304, 353–354, 362, 370, 389–390
Matthews, Lieutenant Colonel H H 332
McCuaig, Lieutenant Colonel G E 316–317
McIntosh, Major J 186
McKenzie, Lieutenant Colonel A E G 181, 207
McLaughlin, Lieutenant Colonel Lorne 246, 250, 252
McNaughton, Lieutenant Colonel G L 53, 56, 128, 300, 357, 420
Metcalf VC, Lance Corporal W H 315
Millar, Major John 268, 339
Millen, Lieutenant Colonel Lionel 148, 184, 186
Morrison, Major General E W B 51, 57, 128, 299, 301

Nunney VC, Private Claude 279–280, 339

Odlum, Brigadier General Victor 44, 289, 306–307, 345–349, 351, 358, 371, 390
Oldfield, Brigadier General L 134, 221, 238, 389–390
Ormond, Brigadier General Dan 42, 187–188, 192, 389

Page, Lieutenant Colonel L F 282
Panet, Brigadier General H A 176–177
Panet, Lieutenant Colonel Édouard 43–44, 176, 304, 362, 370–371
Patterson, Lieutenant Colonel William 153
Peck VC, Lieutenant Colonel Cy 313, 315–316, 319, 333
Pense, Lieutenant Colonel H E 143
Perry, Lieutenant Colonel Kenneth 350–351
Pétain, Marshal 90, 101, 113

Raikes, Major 302
Rankin, Lieutenant Colonel J S 'Jock' 344
Rawlinson, General Sir Henry 100–101, 103
Rayfield VC, Private R L 42, 61, 80, 139–140, 186, 191, 219, 268, 274, 279, 309, 321, 338–339, 351, 416
Reid, Private Donald 139–140
Rennie, Brigadier General Robert 39, 145,

148–149, 186, 205–206, 210–211, 316, 388
Rhoades, Lieutenant Colonel W 151
Riley, Lieutenant Colonel Harold 142
Ross, Lieutenant Colonel Alex 44, 89, 120, 143
Rupprecht, *Field Marshal* Crown Prince 68–70, 105
Rutherford VC, Lieutenant Charles 151–153, 165
Ryan, Major E J W 351

Saunders, Major Alex 'Bug' 264–265
Sceales, Lieutenant Colonel G A 302–303
Smythe, Major Rolsa 190, 215–216
Sparling, Lieutenant Colonel A W 246, 251
Stewart, Brigadier General J S 187
Stewart, Lieutenant Colonel Charlie 157–158, 187, 217
Sutherland, Lieutenant Colonel D M 188–191, 238
Sutherland, Major John 190

Thacker, Brigadier General H C 244, 324
Tremblay, Brigadier General T L 40–41, 170, 172, 178–180, 183, 196, 205–209, 222, 389–391
Tudor, Lieutenant Colonel L P O 277
Tuxford, Brigadier General George 38, 273, 313, 317, 325, 333

Vanier, Major Georges 184, 208

Walker, Lieutenant Colonel W K 304, 328–330
Watson, Major General Sir David 42–44, 77, 257–258, 266, 268, 281–282, 304, 307, 309, 311, 337, 346, 348, 356–359, 361–363, 369, 371, 389–390
Weaver, Lieutenant Colonel C Y 158
Webber, Brigadier General Norman 'Ox' 32, 53, 117–118, 120, 126, 145, 165, 170, 172, 295
Wheeler, Sergeant W W 282, 343
Whitmore, Lieutenant Colonel F H D C 304, 327–328, 330
Willets, Lieutenant Colonel C R E 156–157
Worrall, Lieutenant Colonel Dick 50, 258, 275–276, 318–319

Young VC, Private J F 39–40, 351

INDEX OF PLACES

Agnez-lès-Duisan 231
Arras-Cambrai road 60–61, 66, 73, 117, 123–124, 127, 132, 135, 145, 147–148, 150, 156, 161, 171, 175, 179, 186, 188, 191, 203, 213, 228, 230, 234, 239, 241, 243, 251–254, 256, 259, 261–262, 264–266, 268, 271, 283–284, 288, 293–295, 297, 299, 301–305, 308, 322–323, 330, 333, 335, 337, 341, 346, 354–355, 367, 369, 371, 420
Artillery hill 187–188, 191, 214–215

Bapaume 103, 105–107, 203, 228
Baralle 302, 364, 369
Boiry trench 216
Boiry-Notre-Dame 84, 132, 156, 172, 187–190, 203, 213–217, 224, 234, 237, 253
Bois de Récourt 354, 370
Bois du Bouche 302, 317–318
Bois du Loison 302, 318–319
Bois du Sart 84, 156–157, 159, 187–188, 190, 215
Bois du Vert 187–188, 191
Bourlon wood 21, 226, 287–288, 295, 372, 392
Buissy 73, 288, 299, 302–303, 311, 317–321, 323, 325, 333, 355, 367, 389, 396
Buissy Switch 73, 288, 299, 302–303, 311, 317–321, 323, 325, 333, 355, 367, 389

Cagnicourt 176, 203, 271, 278, 288, 294, 299, 301–302, 316, 318, 320, 334
Cambrai 21, 27, 66, 83, 86, 94, 122–123, 142, 198, 201, 295, 302–303, 326, 371
Canal du Nord 21, 72–73, 86, 112, 123, 125, 146, 154, 242, 271, 288, 290, 295–296, 302–303, 305, 307, 311, 336, 341, 346, 363–364, 366, 368, 371–372, 387, 392, 419
Chapel hill 62–63, 65, 99, 109, 132, 150, 172, 179
Chateau wood 274
Chérisy 84, 147, 175, 182–184, 206
Cojeul river 63, 65, 71, 83, 98, 132, 138, 143, 145, 147, 149, 174–175, 177, 184, 191–192, 203, 213, 220, 234, 237
Crow's Nest 147, 172, 224, 231, 241, 273–274, 311

Delbar wood 63, 135, 193, 226, 238, 390
Dury village 132, 187, 271, 305–306, 337–342, 344–351, 355, 358–359, 396

Étaing 187, 213–214, 230, 243, 271, 294–295, 307, 353, 361–362, 370
Éterpigny 221, 230, 243, 253–254, 261, 288, 294, 301, 305, 307–308, 341
Éterpigny Line 261, 288, 294, 308

Factory 84, 161, 288, 302, 304, 322–323, 327–331, 353, 358
Feuchy-Wancourt Line 71, 83, 123, 126
Flanders 24, 42, 58, 85, 92, 99, 105, 138,

147–148, 200, 268, 280, 340, 420
Fontaine-lès-Croisilles 175, 179
Fresnes-Rouvroy Line 71, 73, 111, 132, 138, 156, 167, 169, 171, 173–177, 179–196, 198–201, 203–206, 209–214, 216, 218–220, 223–224, 226, 231–233, 238, 241, 244, 246, 248–250, 253, 256, 263, 265–266, 271, 273, 278, 389–390, 400, 416

Greenland hill 61–62, 84, 135, 162, 192–193, 226, 238, 253
Guémappe 84, 132, 144–145, 148–149, 186, 288

Hamel 94, 100
Hans trench 180, 275–276
Hatchet wood 190, 203
Haucourt 124, 201, 206, 234, 271
Hauptwiderstandlinie (HWL) 71, 74, 138, 174, 214, 394, 396
Hausa wood 63
Hendecourt Chateau 273–274
Hendecourt-Dury road 179, 250–251, 277
Hénin 98–99, 106, 109, 115, 118, 123–125, 142–143, 175
Héninel 83, 98, 142
Hindenburg Line 73, 83, 98, 117, 121, 123, 131, 137, 140, 170, 172, 175, 179, 196–197, 204, 226–227, 288, 311, 395, 410, 416

Jigsaw wood 138, 156–157, 159, 187–188, 213, 216–218

Lady Lane 214–215
Lock wood 371
Long wood 220

Marquion 169, 288, 295, 303-304, 311, 364, 420
Monchy-le-Preux 61–63, 71, 83–85, 89, 115, 123, 127–128, 132, 134–135, 138, 145–148, 150–152, 154, 156–157, 159, 175, 190, 192, 226, 379
Mt Dury 306, 337–340, 346–351, 355, 358, 396
Mt Pleasant 63, 97, 126, 128, 135, 158, 162

Neuville-Vitasse 60, 82–83, 98–99, 117–121, 131, 135, 174, 395
Nova Scotia trench 132, 143, 209, 340

Olive trench 185, 205–206, 211, 248
Opal trench 246–247, 276, 320
Orange hill 62–63, 83, 89, 98–100, 109–110, 112, 115, 132–134, 150, 153, 156, 160, 172, 174, 419
Orix trench 246, 264, 276–279, 320
Ox trench 32, 53, 117, 210–211, 244, 248

Palluel 305, 307–308, 341, 345
Pelves 84, 157–158, 172, 199, 203, 213
Plouvain 84, 238
Prospect farm 288, 353–354, 359, 390

Queer Street 316–317, 324

Rake trench 149
Récourt 301, 346, 354, 370
Remy 187, 192, 213, 219–220, 234, 282
Remy wood 187, 213, 219
Riencourt 73, 175, 224, 228, 232, 271
Roeux 63, 84, 163, 230

Saudemont 243, 301, 339, 346, 369
Scarpe river 22, 33, 46, 60–61, 63, 66, 82–84, 88–89, 98–99, 109, 132–135, 137–139, 148–150, 153, 158, 162–163, 165, 167, 169, 174, 184, 186, 193, 198, 210, 212, 221, 223, 226, 233–234, 236–239, 243, 258, 267, 279–280, 304–306, 330–331, 336–341, 346, 358, 362, 369–370, 395
Sensée river 60, 63, 65, 75, 147, 171, 175–176, 178–180, 182–187, 200, 205, 207, 210–211, 213, 219–220, 223–224, 226, 228, 234, 237, 253, 280, 282
Seventy ridge 213, 234
St Servins Farm 187, 201, 213, 221, 253–254, 256, 261, 264–266, 281–283, 404

Trigger Copse 274, 315
Trinquis Brook 60, 216–218, 228, 243

Ulster trench 182, 206–207, 247–248
Unicorn 206–207, 247, 251
Union 204, 206–207, 247
Upton wood 179, 182, 246, 249–251, 263, 273, 278, 322

Villers-lès-Cagnicourt 2 30, 249, 288, 317–319, 321–323, 325
Vimy Ridge 21, 38, 41–42, 90, 98, 239, 280, 291, 365
Vis-en-Artois 71, 75, 105–106, 115, 175, 184–186, 192, 211, 244, 246, 248, 250–251, 263, 274, 276, 288, 302
Vis-en-Artois Switch 244, 246, 248, 250–251, 263, 274, 276, 288, 302
Wancourt 65, 83, 106, 131, 142–143, 145, 147, 259, 288, 361
Wancourt Tower 142, 145, 147
Western Front 21, 30–32, 34–35, 37, 39, 44–45,

49, 56, 59, 62, 66–67, 69–70, 78, 84, 87, 90, 94, 100, 122–123, 131–132, 137, 139, 204, 237, 243, 271, 277–278, 287–288, 304, 308, 313, 318, 337, 389, 392, 417

INDEX OF WEAPONS

18-pounder gun 48, 51, 53, 101, 128, 142, 150, 176, 204, 213, 238, 245, 278, 296–297, 299, 303–304, 322–323, 343, 377, 394
4.5-inch howitzer 51, 53, 80, 128, 150, 176, 206, 244–245, 253, 299, 303
6-inch howitzer 52, 160, 174, 206, 234, 298, 301, 323, 329, 350
60-pounder gun 51–52, 160, 174, 299
8-inch howitzer 73, 234, 301
Lewis Gun 46–47, 49, 81, 143–144, 147, 151–152, 159–160, 211, 220, 236, 248, 252, 317–318, 324, 339–340, 344, 348, 367, 407, 409
Mortars 45–46, 48, 74, 87, 95, 132, 143, 151–152, 220, 234, 243, 297, 304, 323, 328, 330, 336, 339, 341, 343, 348, 381, 402, 407–408, 410–411
Vickers Heavy Machine Gun 46, 48–49, 235, 252, 352

The Hardest Battle

The Canadian Corps and the Arras 1918 Campaign

Map book

William F. Stewart

Helion & Company

Helion & Company Limited
Unit 8 Amherst Business Centre
Budbrooke Road
Warwick
CV34 5WE
England
Tel. 01926 499 619
Email: info@helion.co.uk
Website: www.helion.co.uk
Twitter: @helionbooks
Visit our blog at blog.helion.co.uk

Published by Helion & Company 2023
Designed and typeset by Mary Woolley (www.battlefield-design.co.uk)
Cover designed by Paul Hewitt, Battlefield Design (www.battlefield-design.co.uk)

ISBN 978-1-915113-66-5

British Library Cataloguing-in-Publication Data.
A catalogue record for this book is available from the British Library.

Contents

Legend IV

Map C1. Opening Day Plan: 26 August 1918 V
Map C2. 2nd Division Success VI
Map C3. 3rd Division Takes Monchy-le-Preux: Morning VII
Map C4. 7th Brigade Frustrates *35th ID* Counterattack: Afternoon VIII
Map C5. 51st (Highland) Division Captures Mt Pleasant IX
Map C6. 2nd Division Mixed Success: 27 August X
Map C7. 3rd Division Makes Only Limited Gains: 27 August XI
Map C8. 51st (Highland) Division Stopped Before Greenland Hill: 27 August XII
Map C9. 2nd Division Repelled: 28 August XIII
Map C10. 3rd Division Breaks the F-R Line: 28 August XVI
Map C11. 4th British Division and Brutinel's Brigade: 29 August XV
Map C12. Highlanders: 29 August XVI
Map C13. 1st Brigade Attacks: 30 August XVII
Map C14. 1st Brigade: German Counterattack XVIII
Map C15. 4th British Division: 30 August XIX
Map C16. 1st Division and Flanking Forces: 31 August XX
Map C17. 4th British Division Takes St Servins Farm: 31 August XXI
Map C18. 1st Division and Flanking Forces: 1 September Morning XXII
Map C19. 1st Division and Flanking Forces: 1 September Afternoon XXIII
Map C20. 4th British Division Operations: 1 September XXIV
Map C21. Canadian Corps' Plan for 2 September XXV
Map C22. The 1st Division Responds: 2 September XXVI
Map C23. The CIF Flounders: 2 September XXVII
Map C24. The D-Q Line Broken: 2 September XXVIII
Map C25. The 4th Canadian and British Divisions Struggle: 2 September XXIX

Legend

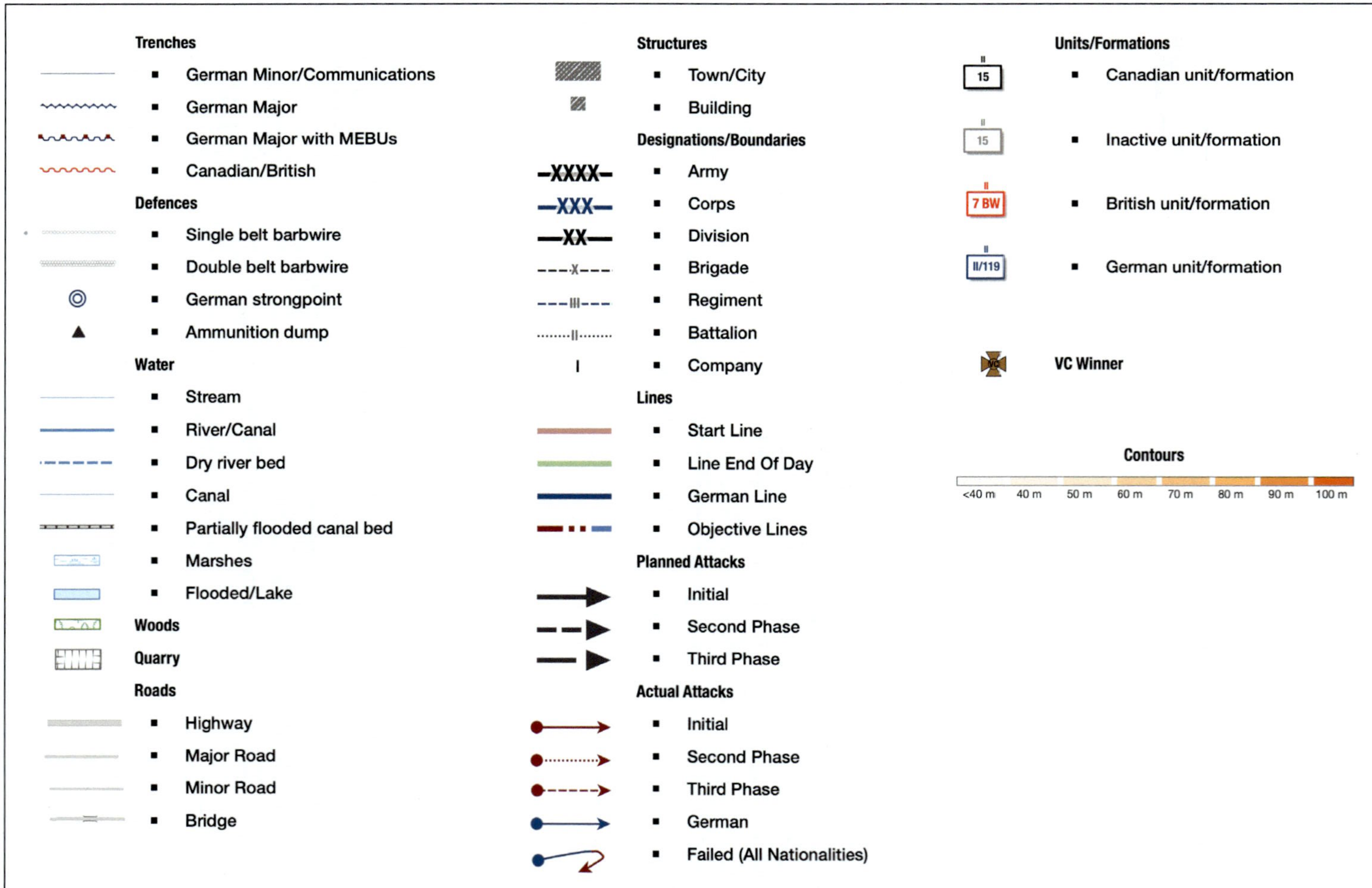
Trenches
German Minor/Communications
German Major
German Major with MEBUs
Canadian/British
Defences
Single belt barbwire
Double belt barbwire
German strongpoint
Ammunition dump
Water
Stream
River/Canal
Dry river bed
Canal
Partially flooded canal bed
Marshes
Flooded/Lake
Woods
Quarry
Roads
Highway
Major Road
Minor Road
Bridge
Structures
Town/City
Building
Designations/Boundaries
XXXX
Army
XXX
Corps
XX
Division
X
Brigade
III
Regiment
II
Battalion
I
Company
Lines
Start Line
Line End Of Day
German Line
Objective Lines
Planned Attacks
Initial
Second Phase
Third Phase
Actual Attacks
Initial
Second Phase
Third Phase
German
Failed (All Nationalities)
Units/Formations
15
Canadian unit/formation
15
Inactive unit/formation
7 BW
British unit/formation
II/119
German unit/formation
VC
VC Winner
Contours
<40 m
40 m
50 m
60 m
70 m
80 m
90 m
100 m

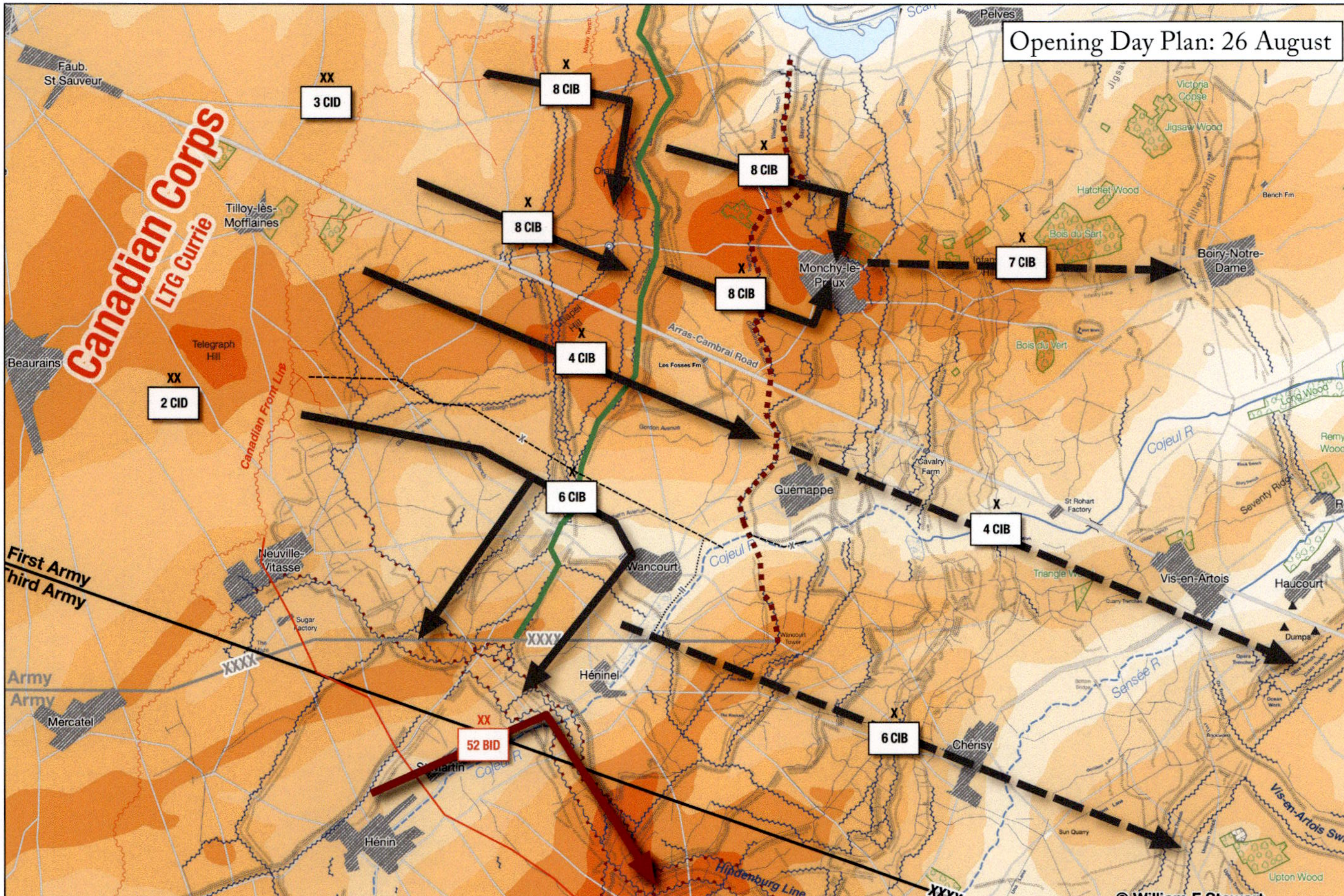

Map C1. The plan for the first day of the offensive. The detailed preparations only went as far as the Red Dotted Line. After this point, the infantry would have to fight forward using their own resources.

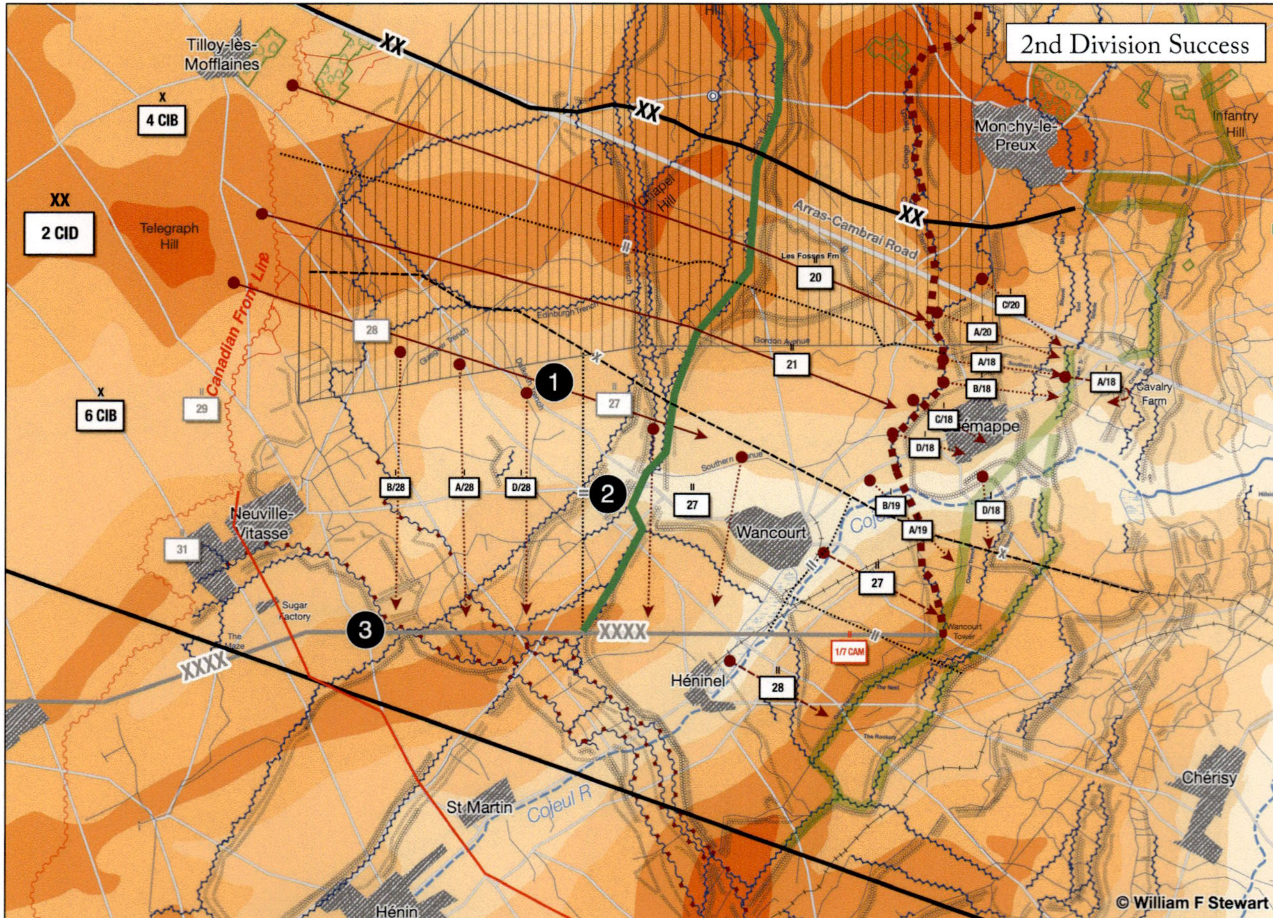

Map C2. 2nd Division operations on 26 August

1. Initial attack of the 6th Brigade
2. Strike south by the 27th and 28th Battalions
3. Former boundary of the First and Third Armies

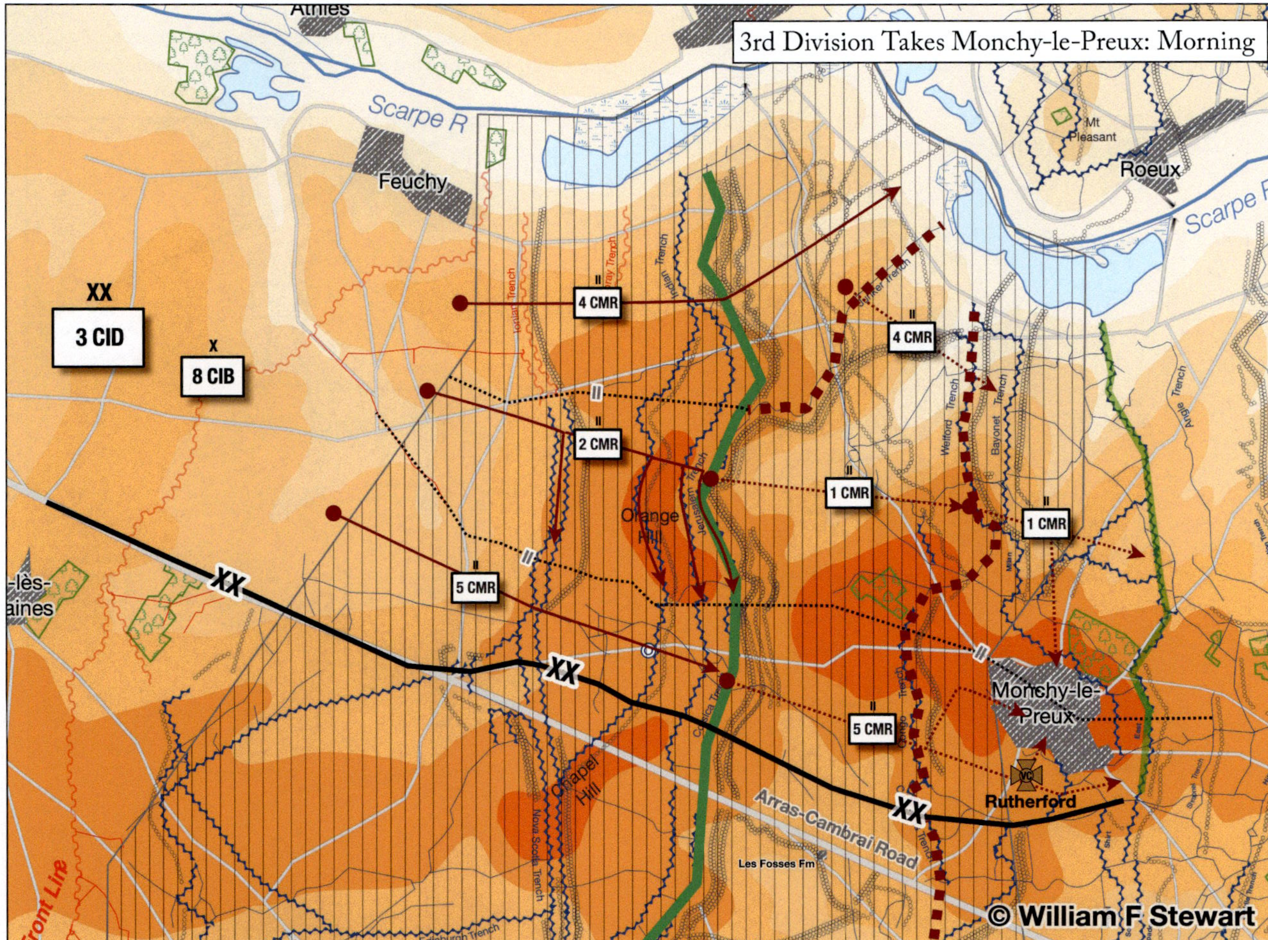

Map C3. Morning operations of the 3rd Division. The 8th Brigade's clever infiltration tactics outflanks the German defences at Orange Hill and Monchy-le-Preux. The grey lines represent the extent of the barrage. Note the Victoria Cross awarded to Lieutenant CS Rutherford of the 5th CMR.

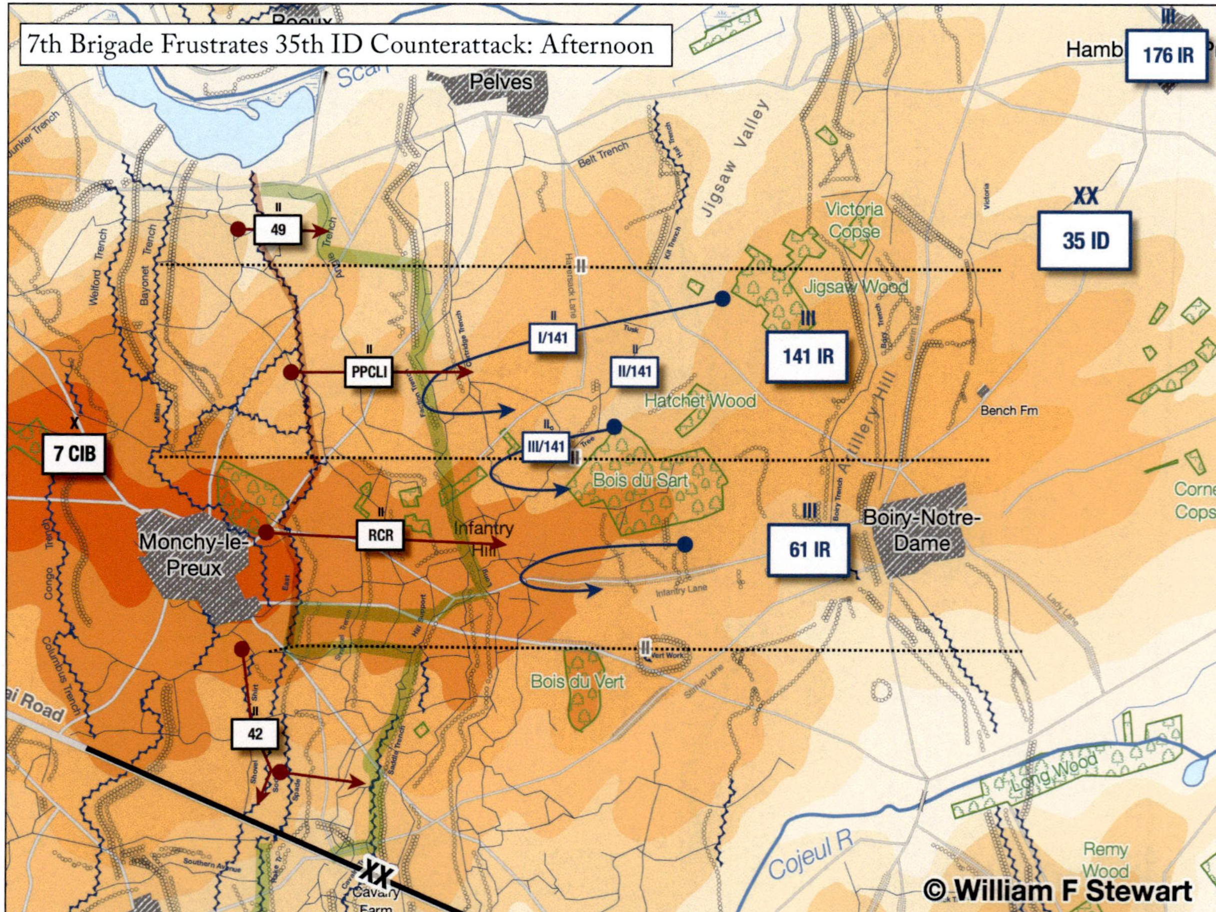

Map C4. Afternoon operations of the 3rd Division. The 7th Brigade meets the arriving *35th ID* and is unable to make major headway. It defeats a strong German counterattack on the same ground that resulted in the destruction of the Royal Newfoundland and Essex Regiments in the First Battle of Arras in April 1917.

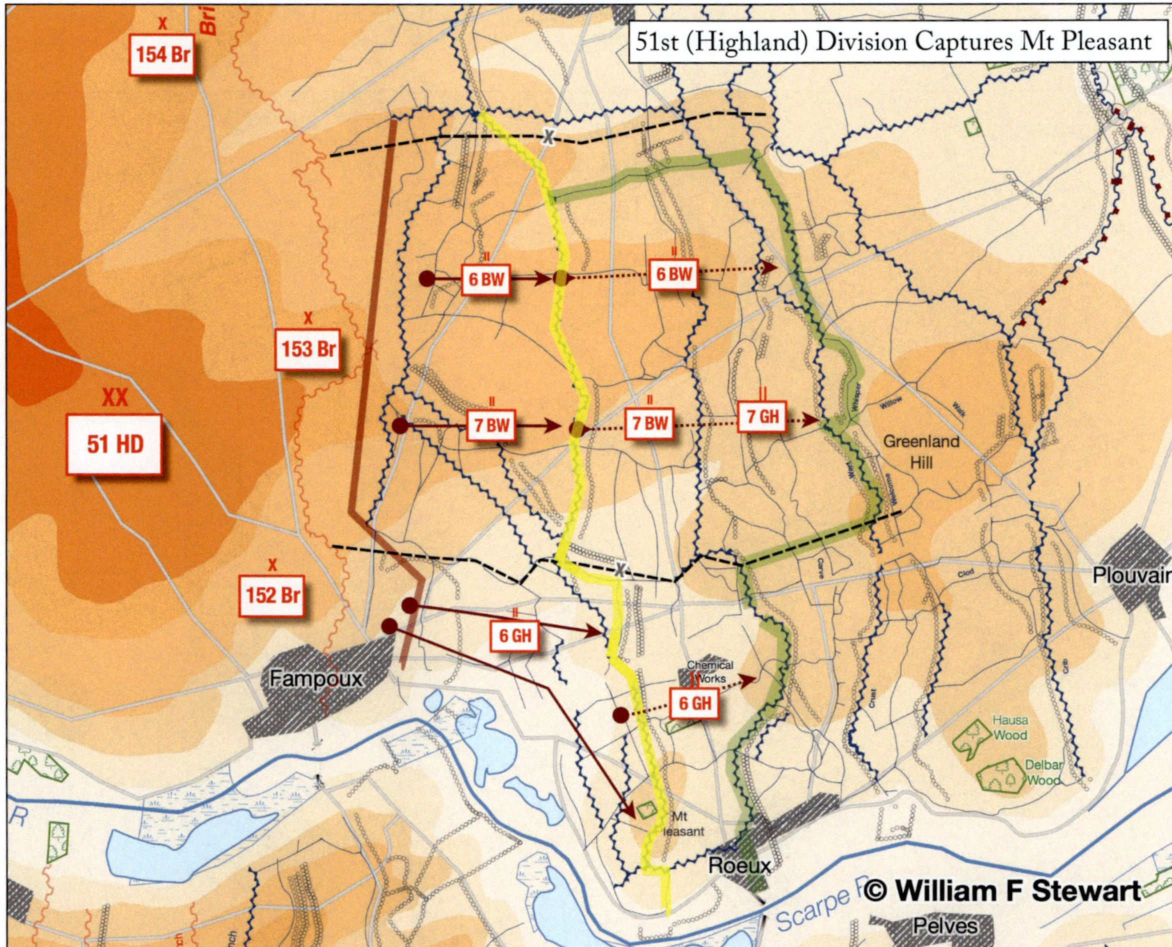

Map C5. The 51st (Highland) Division despite no great superiority over the *48th RD* captures Mt Pleasant and makes gains towards the capture of Greenland Hill.

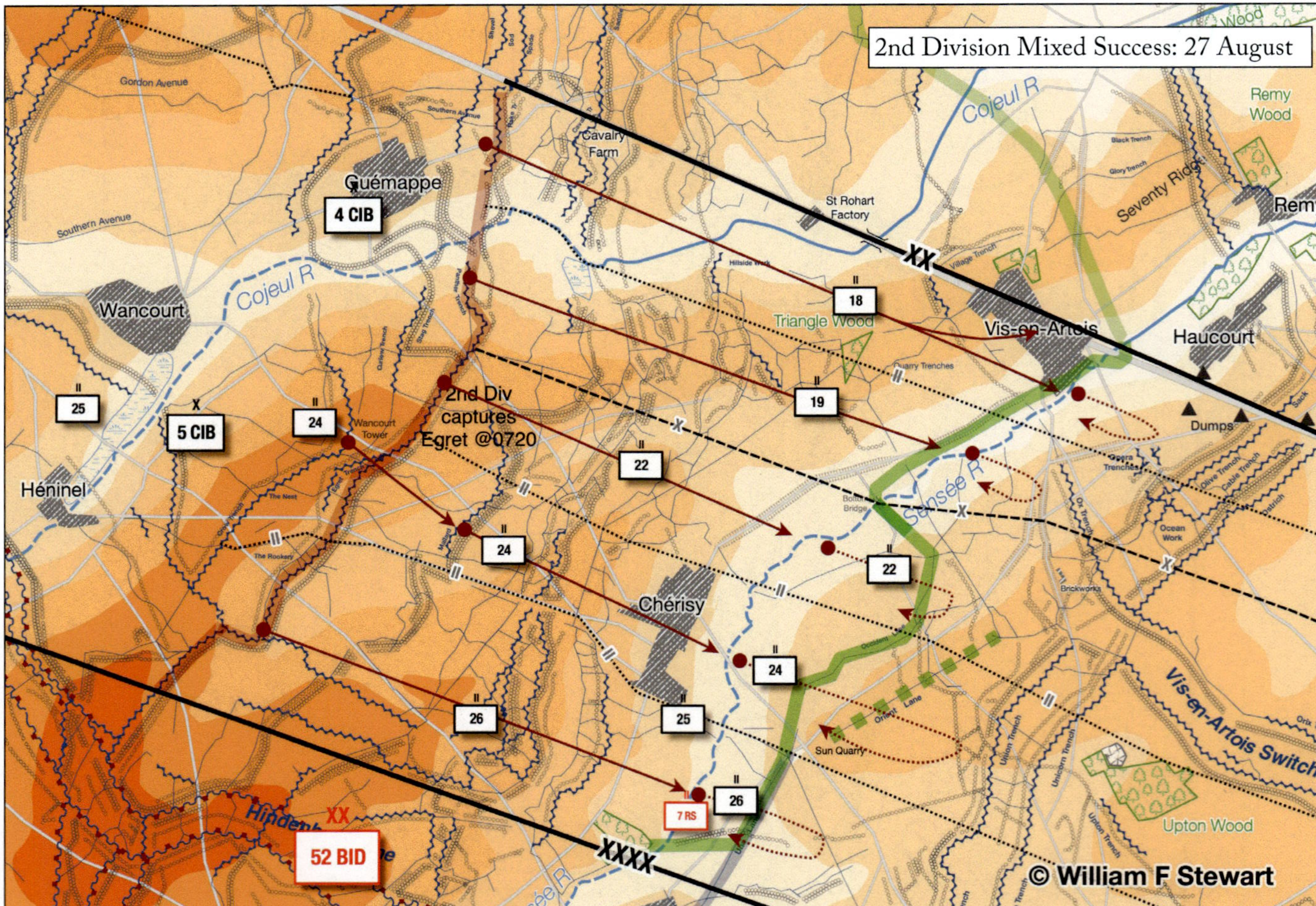

Map C6. 2nd Division's operations on 27 August were initially successful and then the attackers ran into the crack *26th Reserve Division* embedded in the F-R Line. The tough Württembergers shot the attack to pieces.

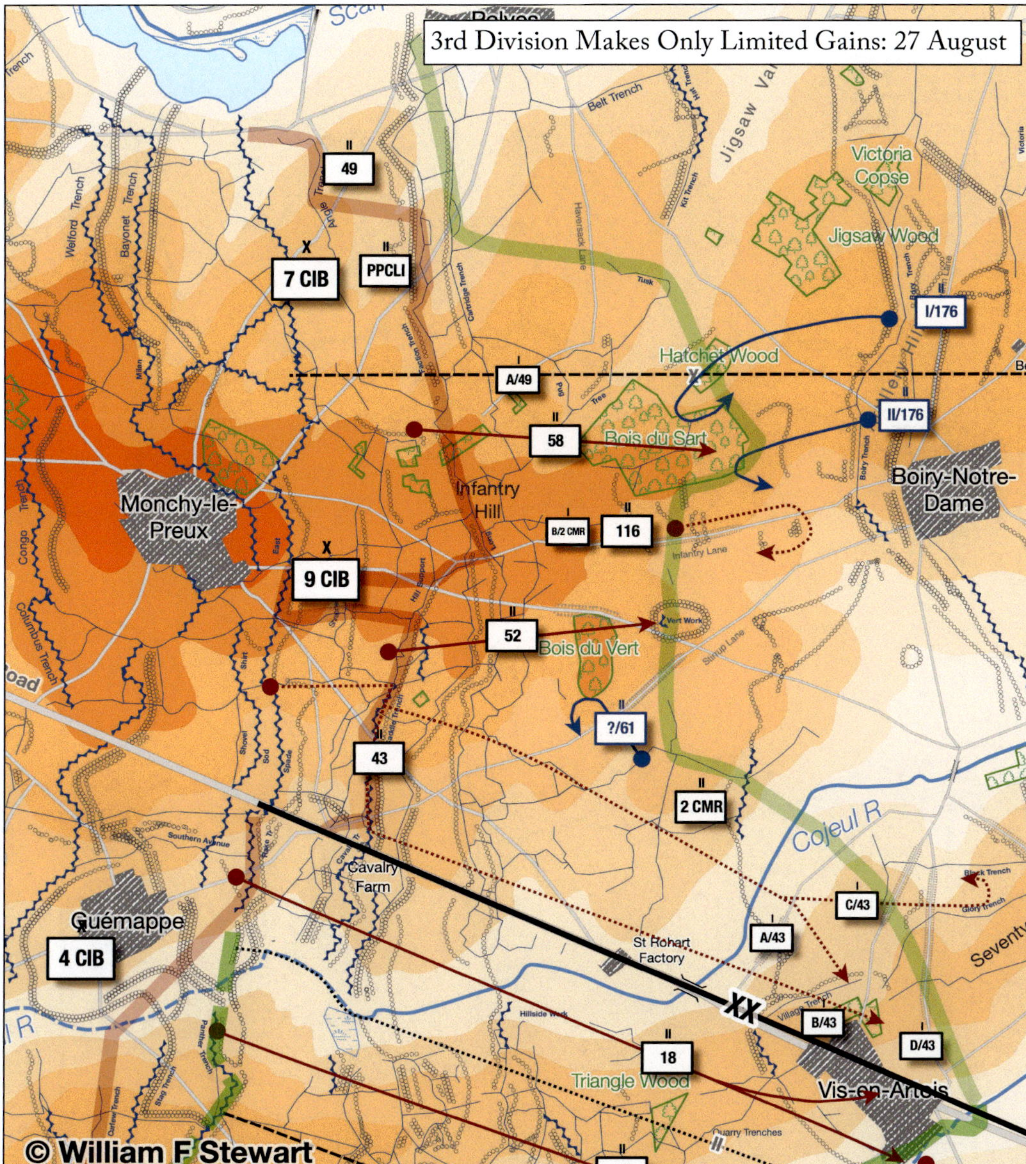

Map C7. The 3rd Division takes its first objectives but is stymied in front of the F-R Line.

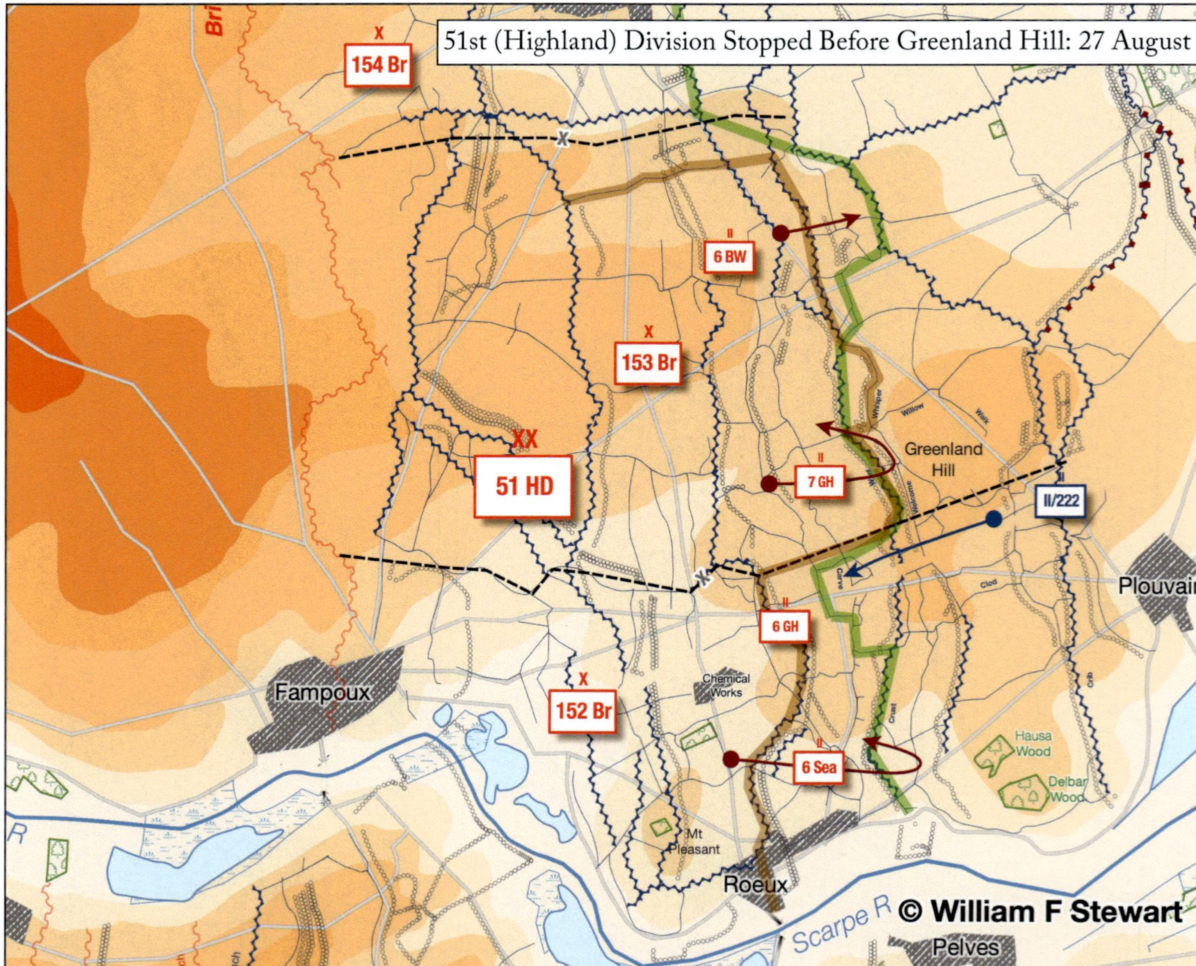

Map C8. The 51st (Highland) Division attempts but fails to take the high ground of Greenland Hill and Hausa and Delbar Woods.

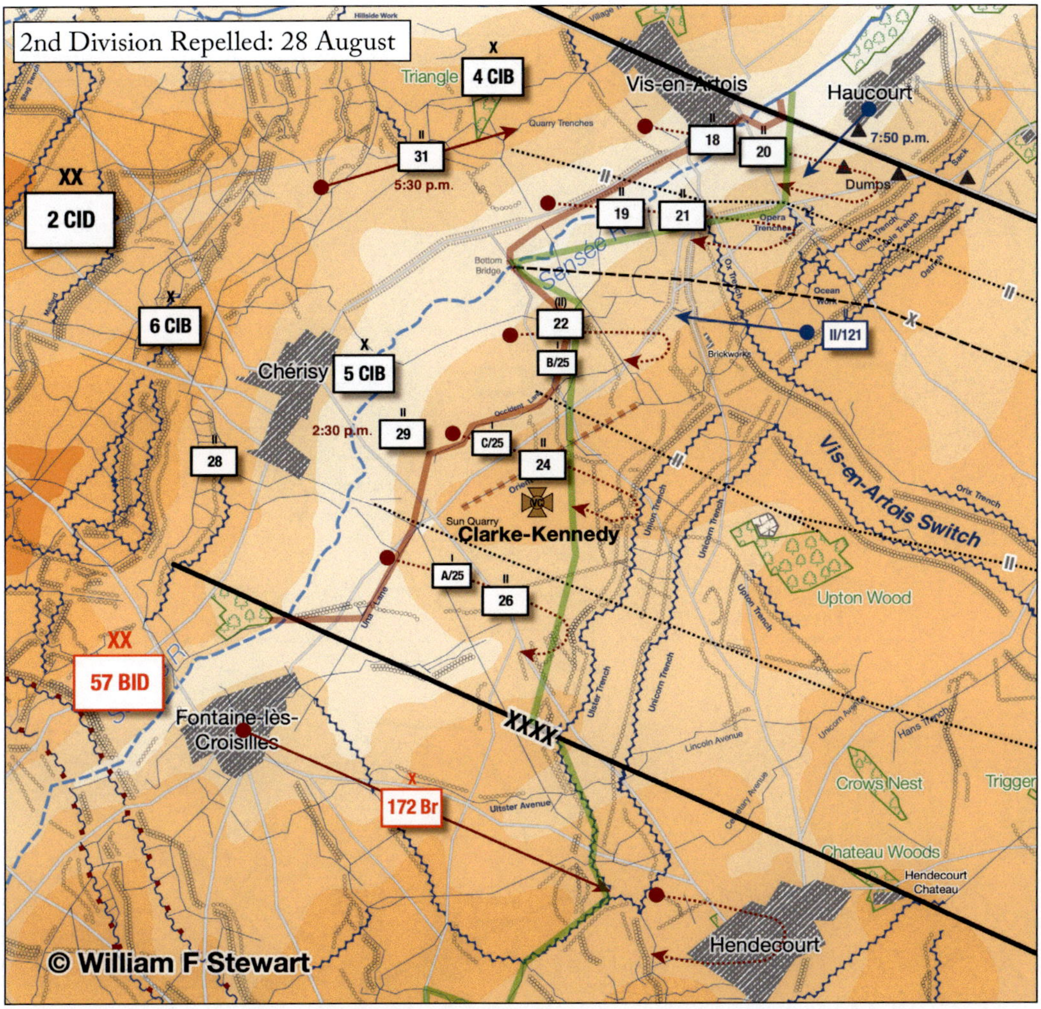

Map C9. 2nd Division's operations on 28 August were characterised by heavy casualties and no significant gains. The *26th RD* decisively stopped Burstall's division. To the south, the British 172nd Brigade briefly capture Hendecourt but had more success than the Canadian formation. Note the Victoria Cross won by Lieutenant-Colonel W Clarke-Kennedy of the 24th Battalion.

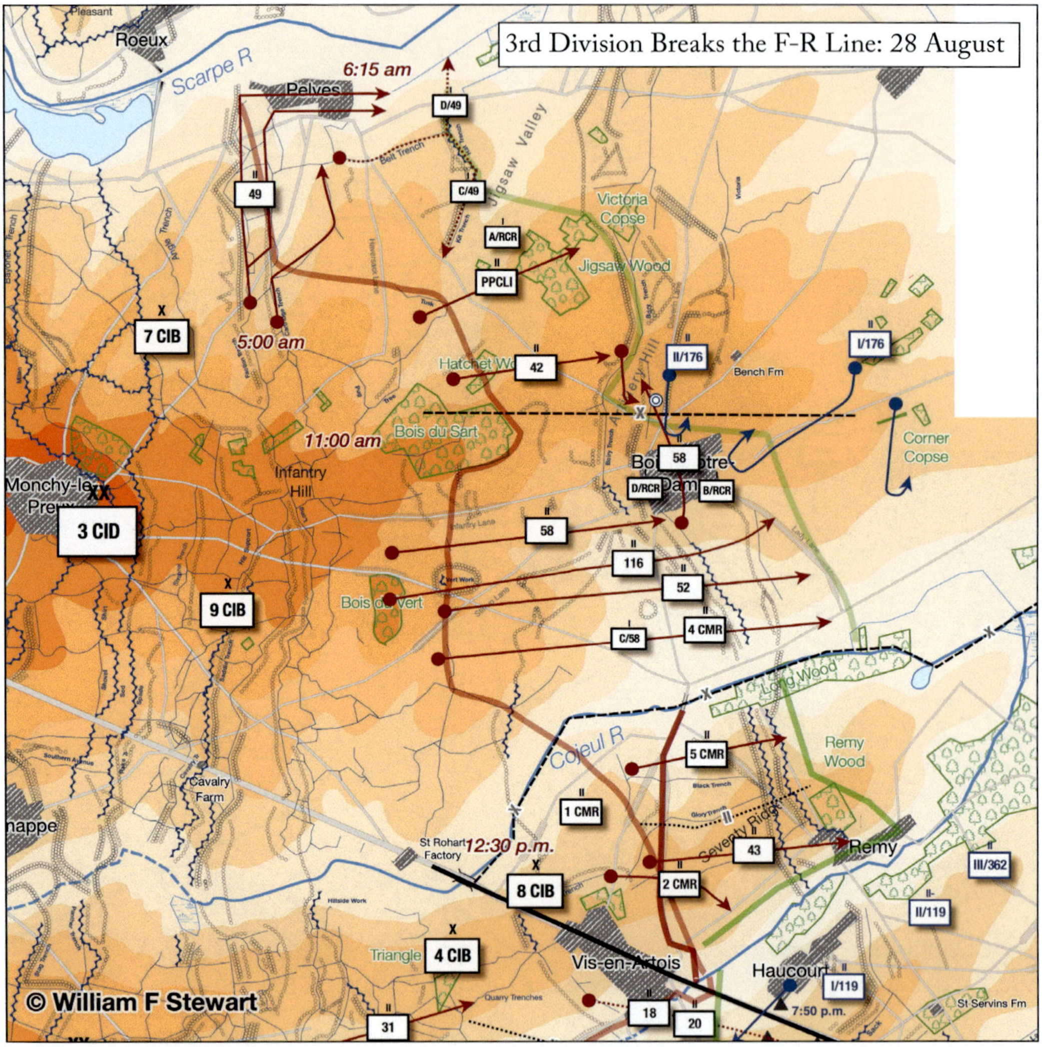

Map C10. The 3rd Division through a series of cleverly constructed consecutive strikes destroyed the *35th ID* and broke through the F-R Line north of the Sensée River.

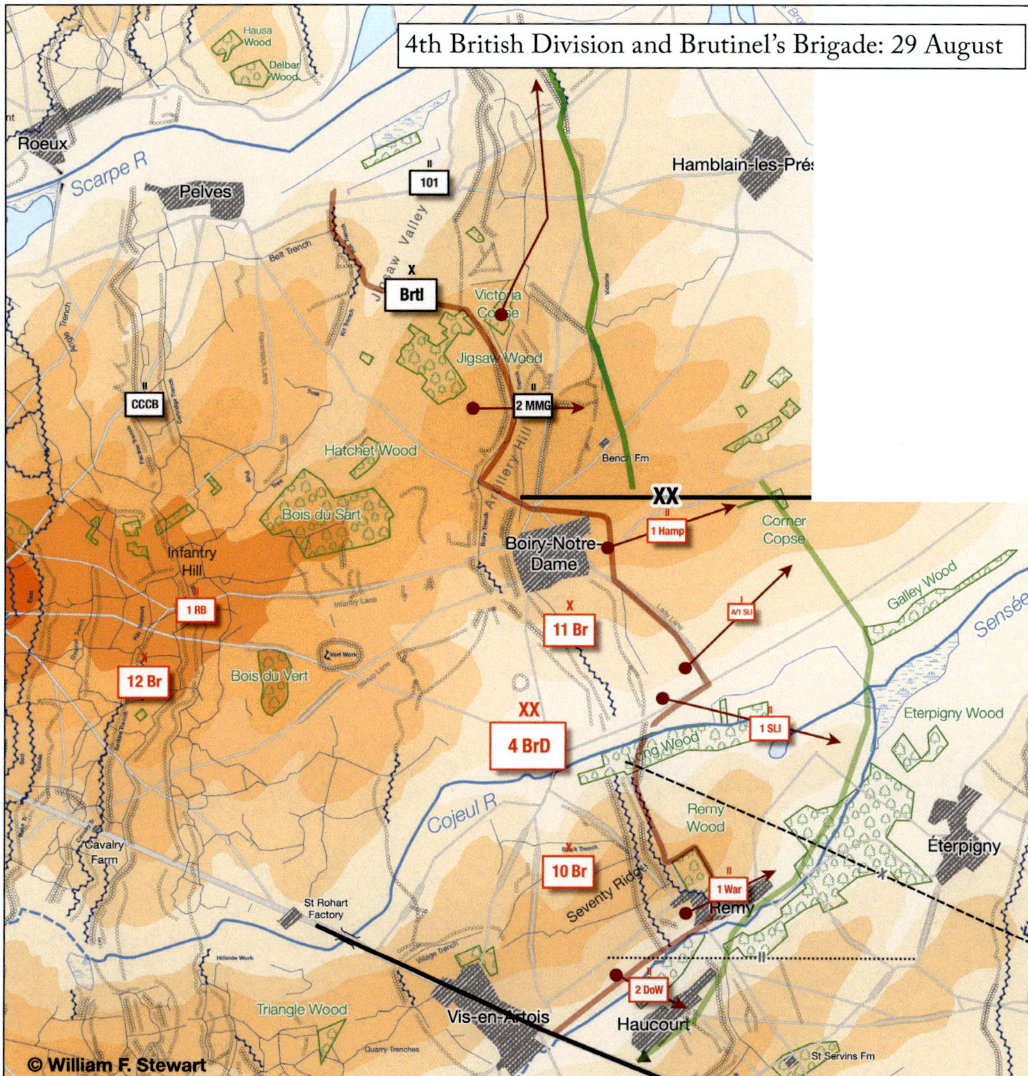

Map C11. The 4th British Division relieved the 3rd Division. Matheson's division took Haucourt and pushed to the Sensée River. Brutinel's Brigade took over the front north of Boiry-Notre-Dame and made a small advance.

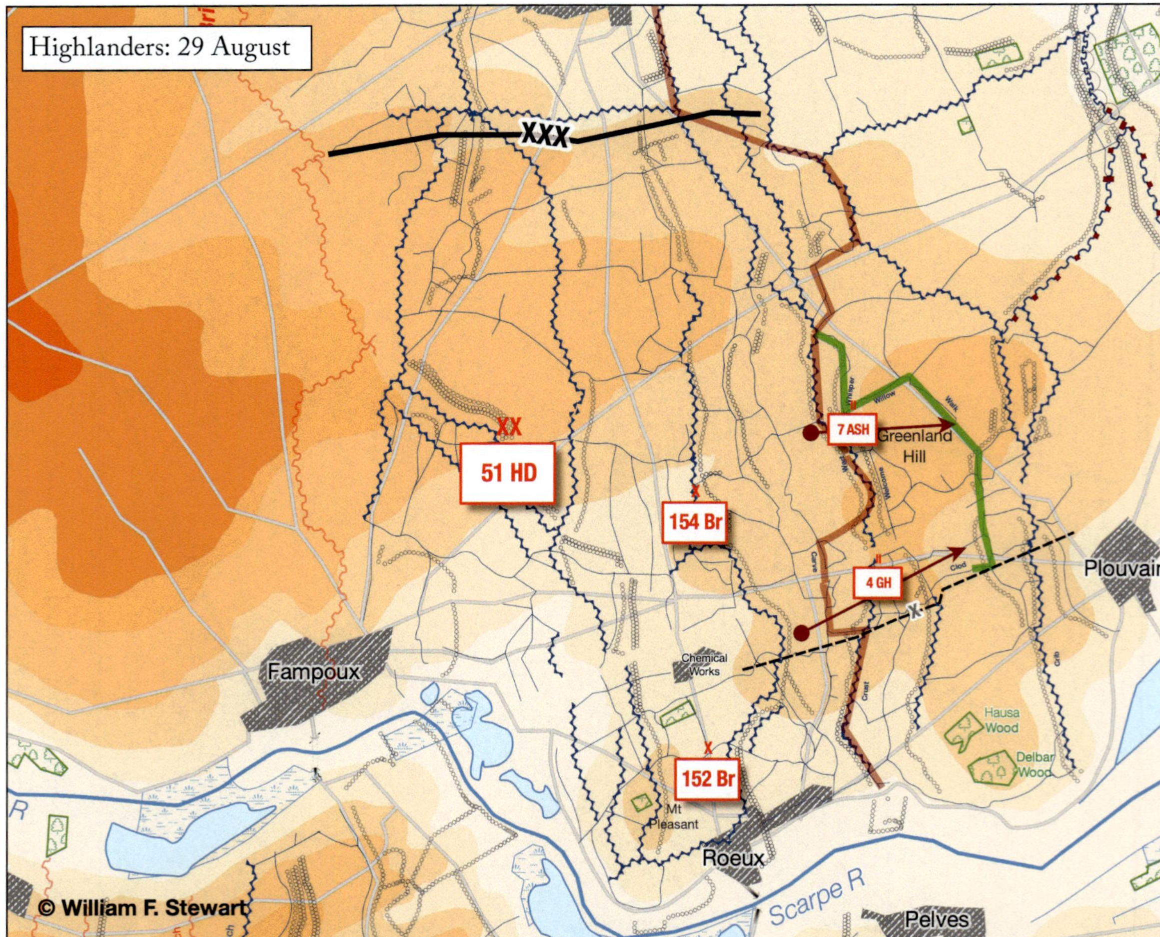

Map C12. 51st (Highland) Division's 154th Brigade captured Greenland Hill and forced the German defenders of Hausa and Delbar Woods to fall back. The Canadian Corps was no longer at risk from German observation from high ground north of the Scarpe River.

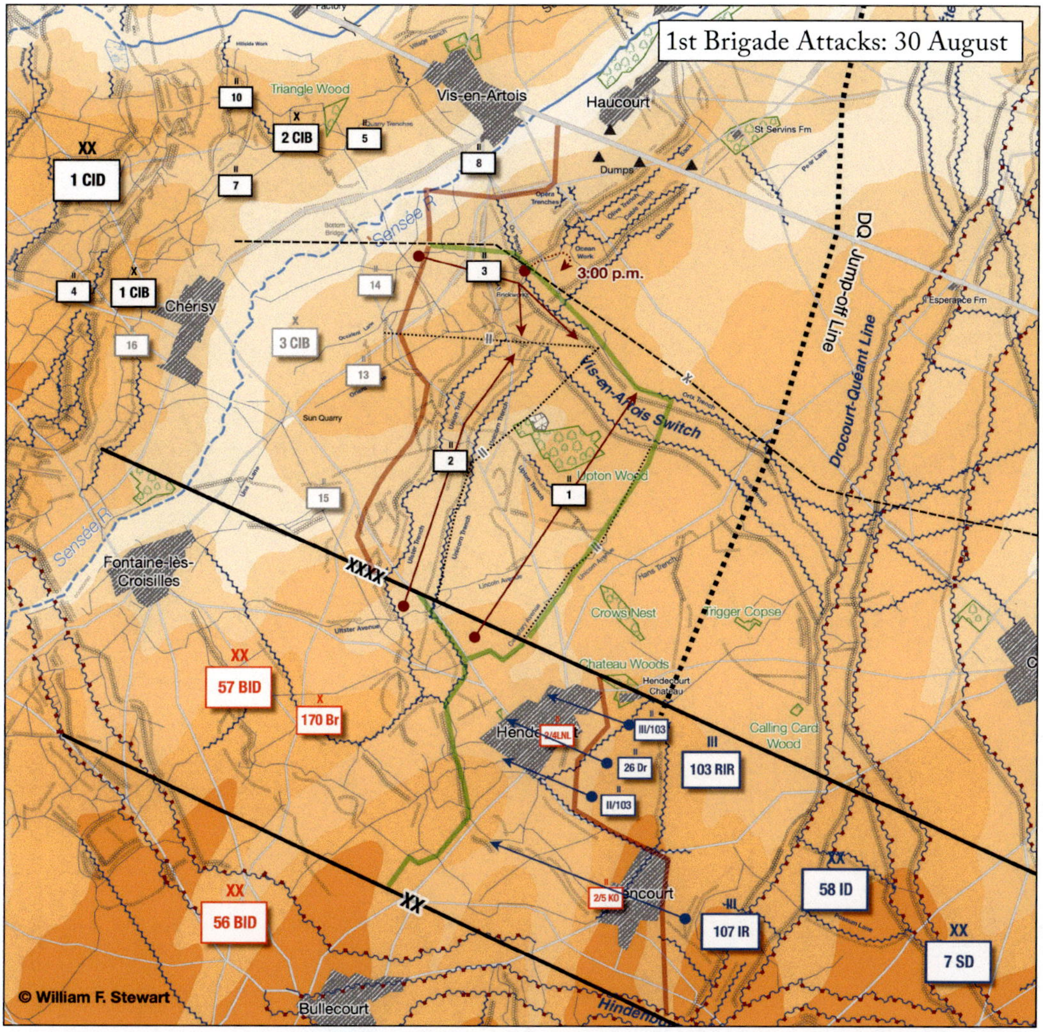

Map C13. During the night of 29/30 August the *58th ID* retook Hendecourt and Riencourt. Despite this setback, the 1st Brigade successfully launched its daring outflanking attack rolling up the F-R Line and effectively destroying *121st RIR* plus two battalions of the *4th EzD*.

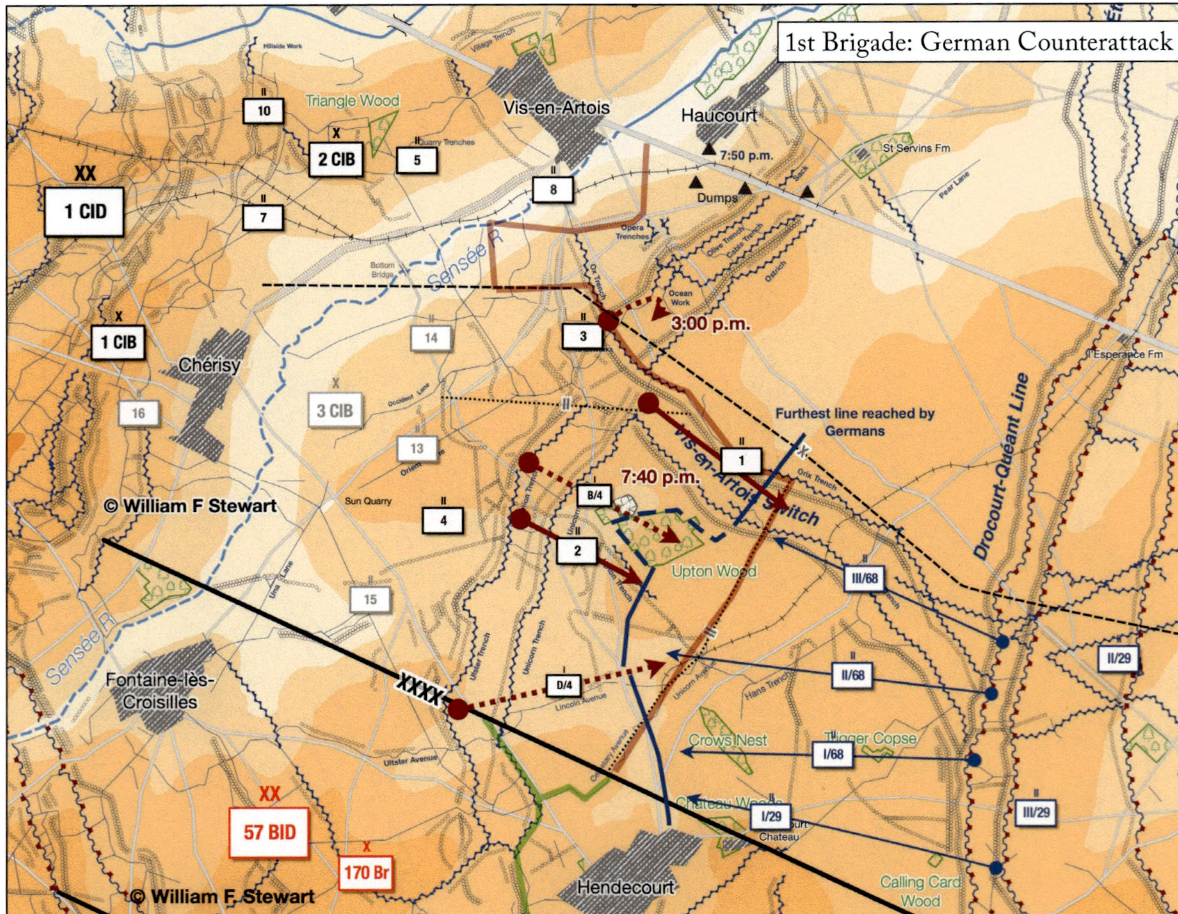

Map C14. In the afternoon, the *16th ID* launched a dangerous counterattack that rolled up the mispositioned 1st Brigade. Through strong leadership, hard fighting, and massive firepower, Griesbach's brigade first slowed, then stopped, and finally drove back the attackers inflicting heavy losses and disorganisation on them.

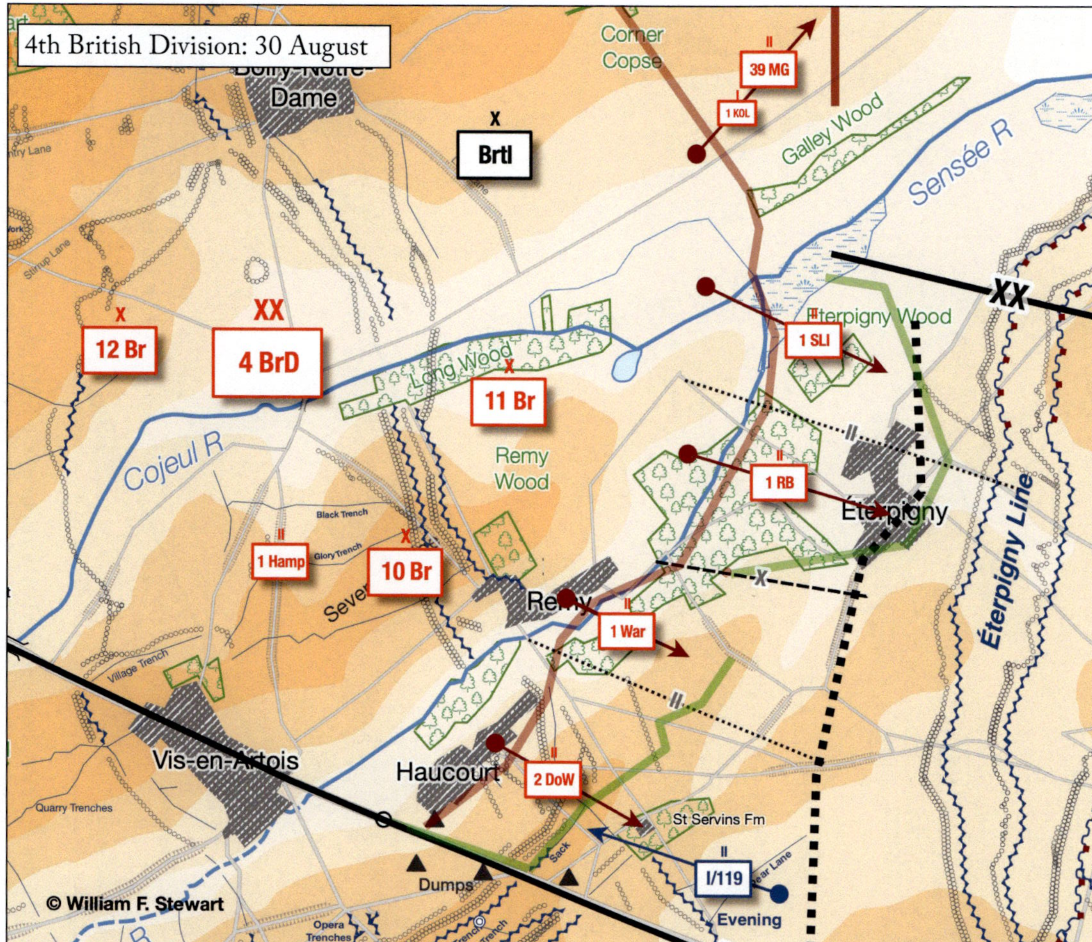

Map C15. The 11th British Brigade advanced to the jump-off line for the D-Q Line attack but the 10th stumbled. It took reached about halfway to its objective. It captured St Servins Farm but lost it to a German counterattack in the evening.

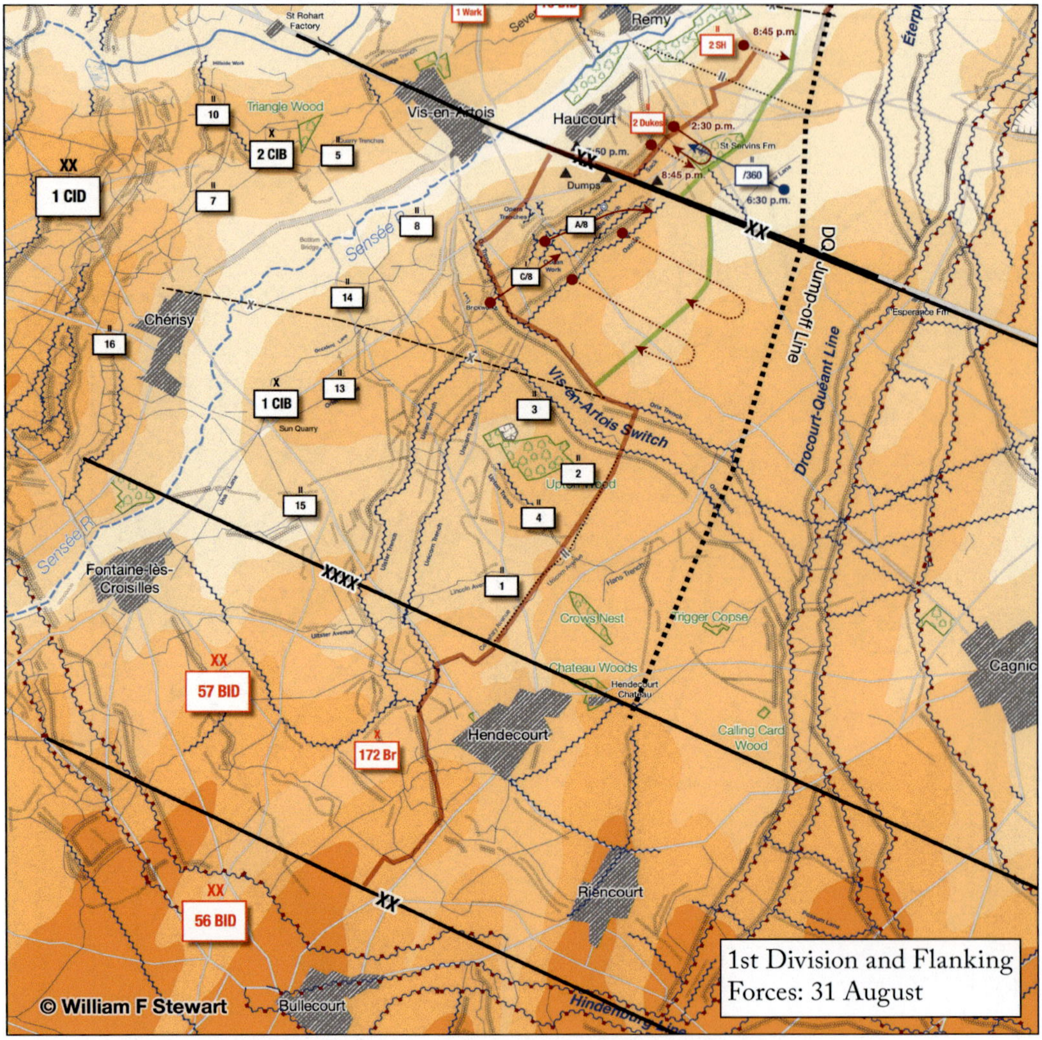

Map C16. The 8th Battalion captured the last portions of the F-R Line held by the Germans. The 57th Division's 172nd Brigade relieved the forward forces.

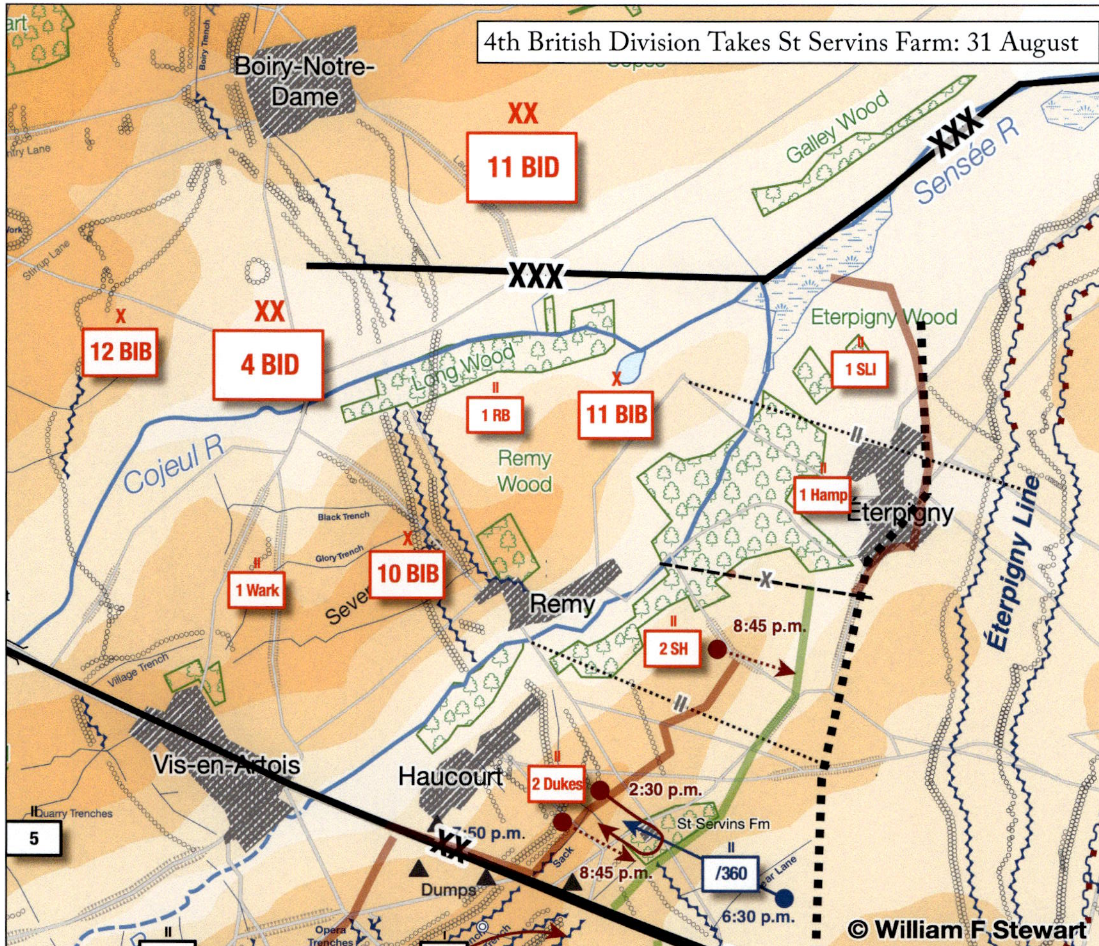

Map C17. The 10th British Brigade spent the day fighting to gain the jump-off line for the D-Q Line attack. After a day of see-saw fighting, St Servins Farm finally fell.

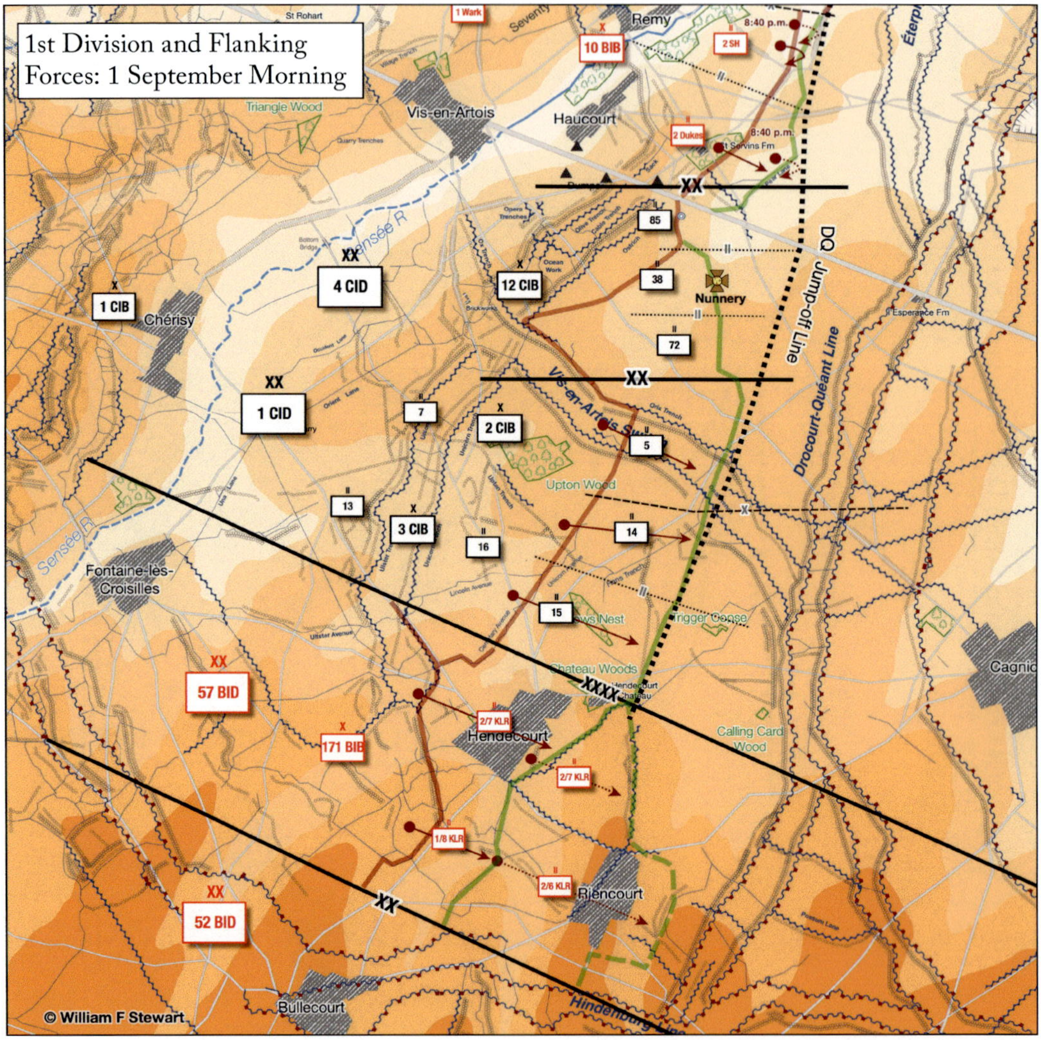

Map C18. The 4th Canadian Division entered the line and the 1st Division launched a three-battalion attack to reach the jump-off line for the D-Q Line. The morning's operations were successful with heavy losses inflicted on the Germans. On the flank, the 57th Division captured Hendecourt and Riencourt to keep up with the Canadians.

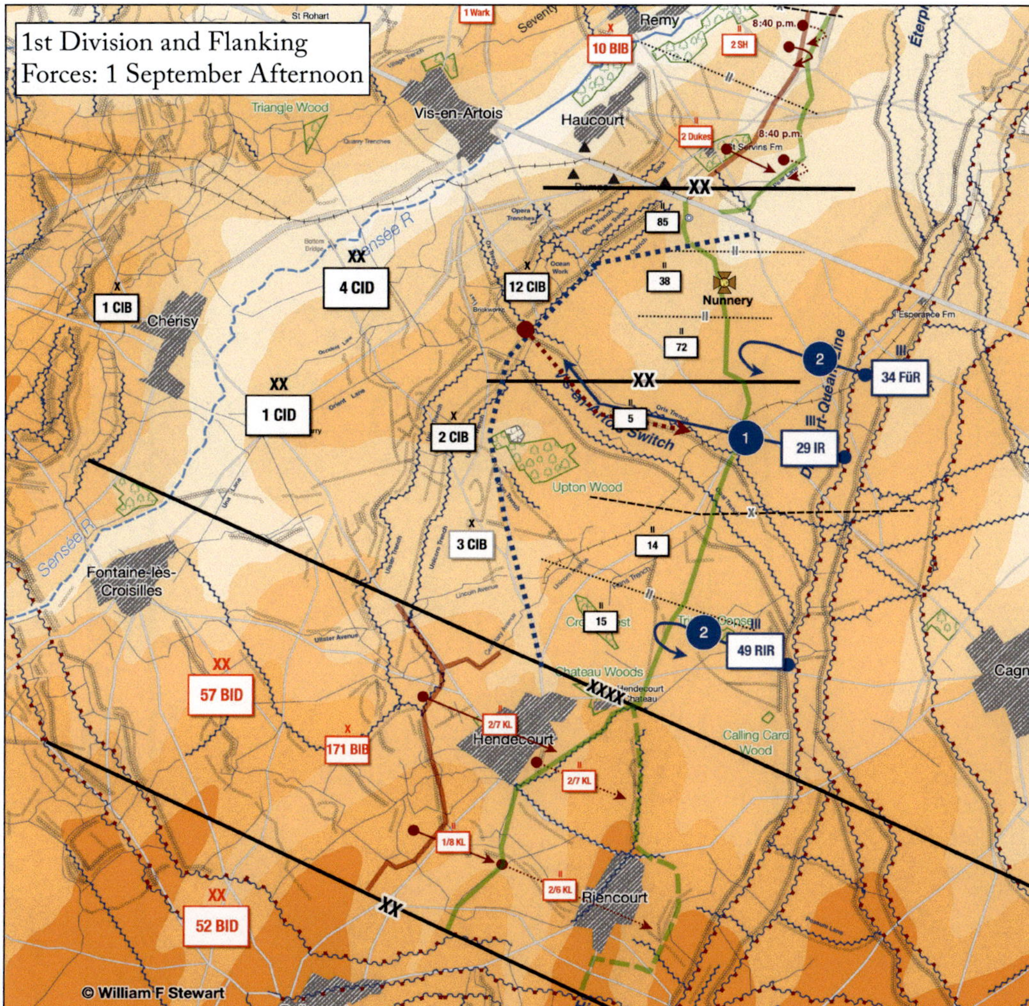

Map C19. The *II Bavarian Korps* launched two abortive counterattacks in response to the 1st Division's attack. Note the Victoria Cross awarded to Private C Nunnery of the 38th Battalion.

1. The *29th IR* and elements of the *28th IR* had initial success in rolling back the 5th Battalion. It counterattacked and regained all the lost ground.
2. The *3rd RD* attacked with two regiments and Canadian firepower smashed the two regiments inflicting heavy losses and disorganisation on the attackers.

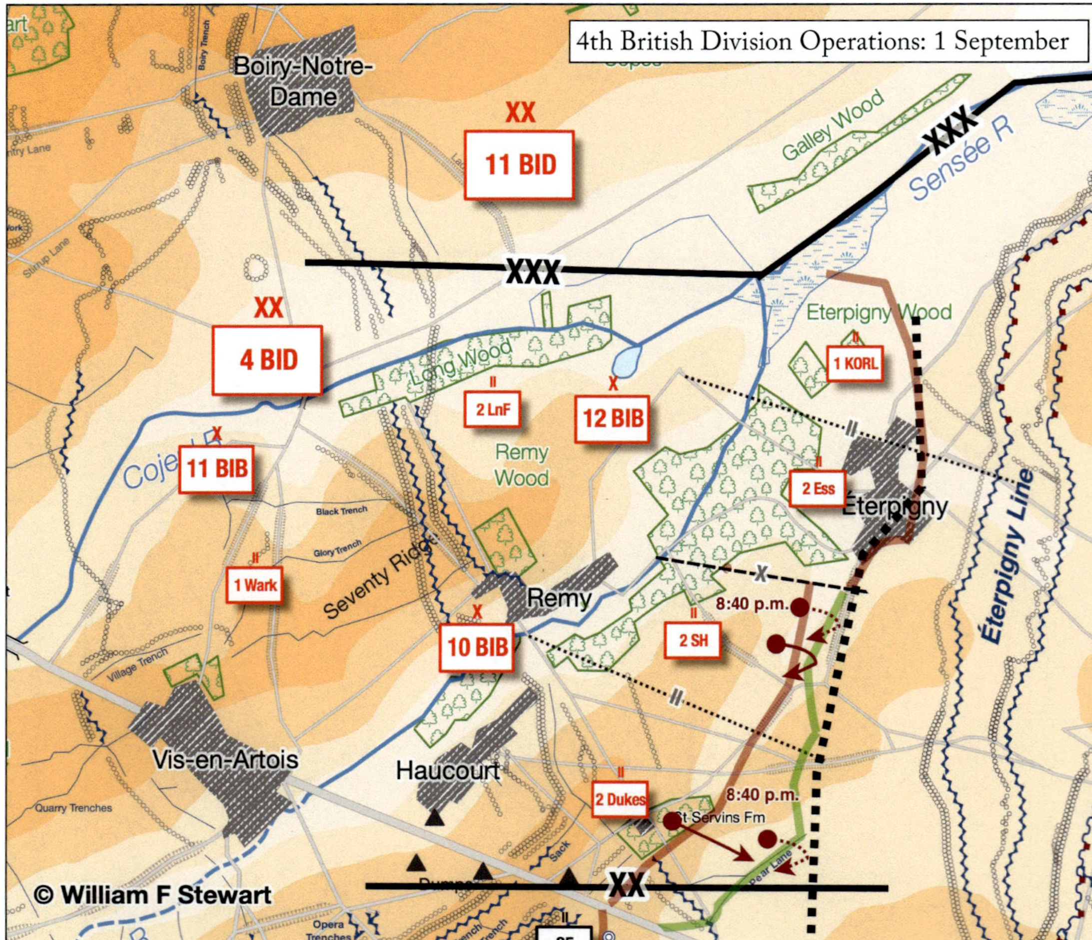

Map C20. The 10th British Brigade continued to try to reach the jump-off line before handing over its line to the 10th Canadian Brigade. Exhausted after four days of fighting, it struggled to reach its target.

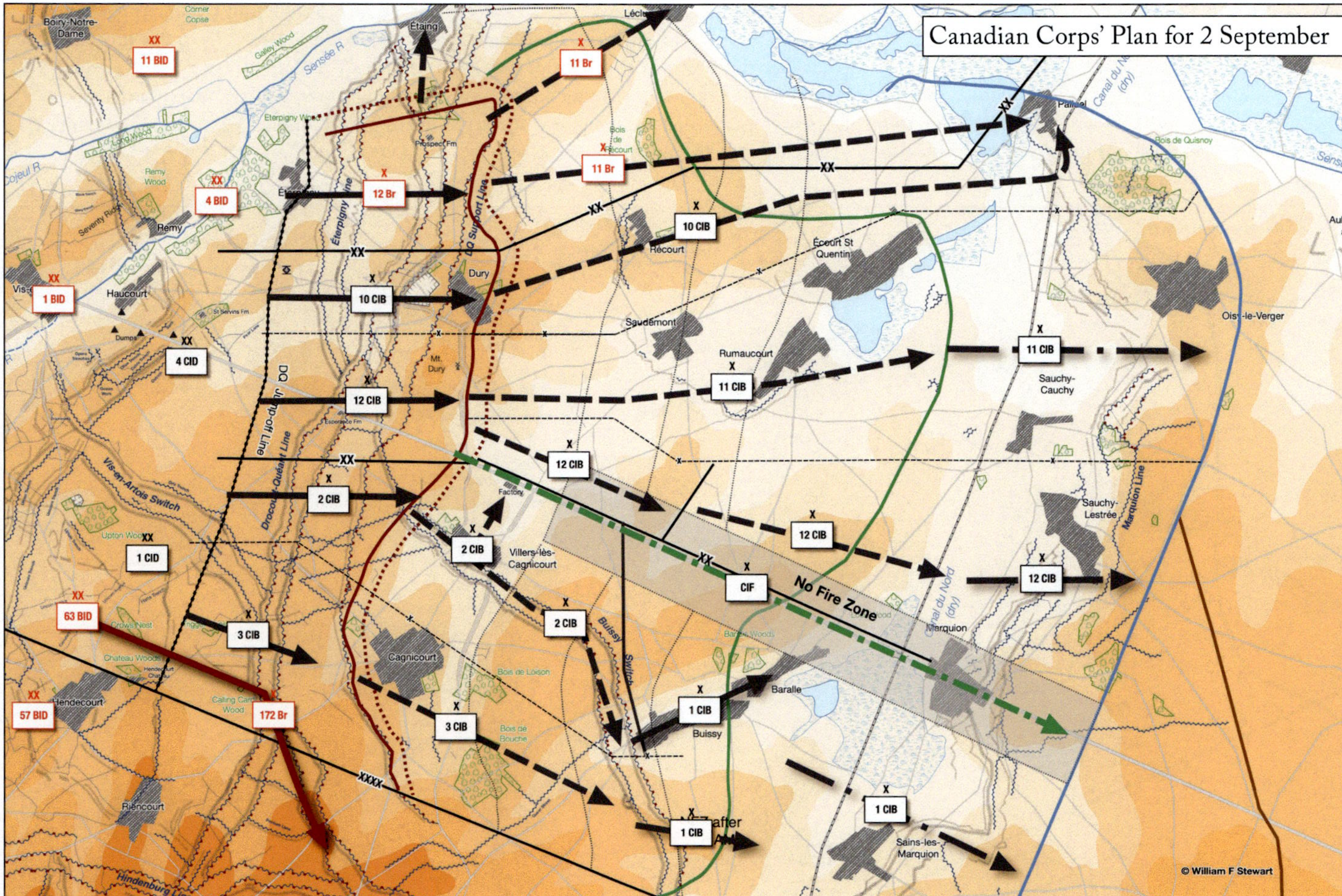

Map C21. The Canadian Corps' aggressive plan for breaking the hinge of the D-Q Line. Note the No Fire Zone along the Arras-Cambrai road and the route of the Canadian Independent Force.

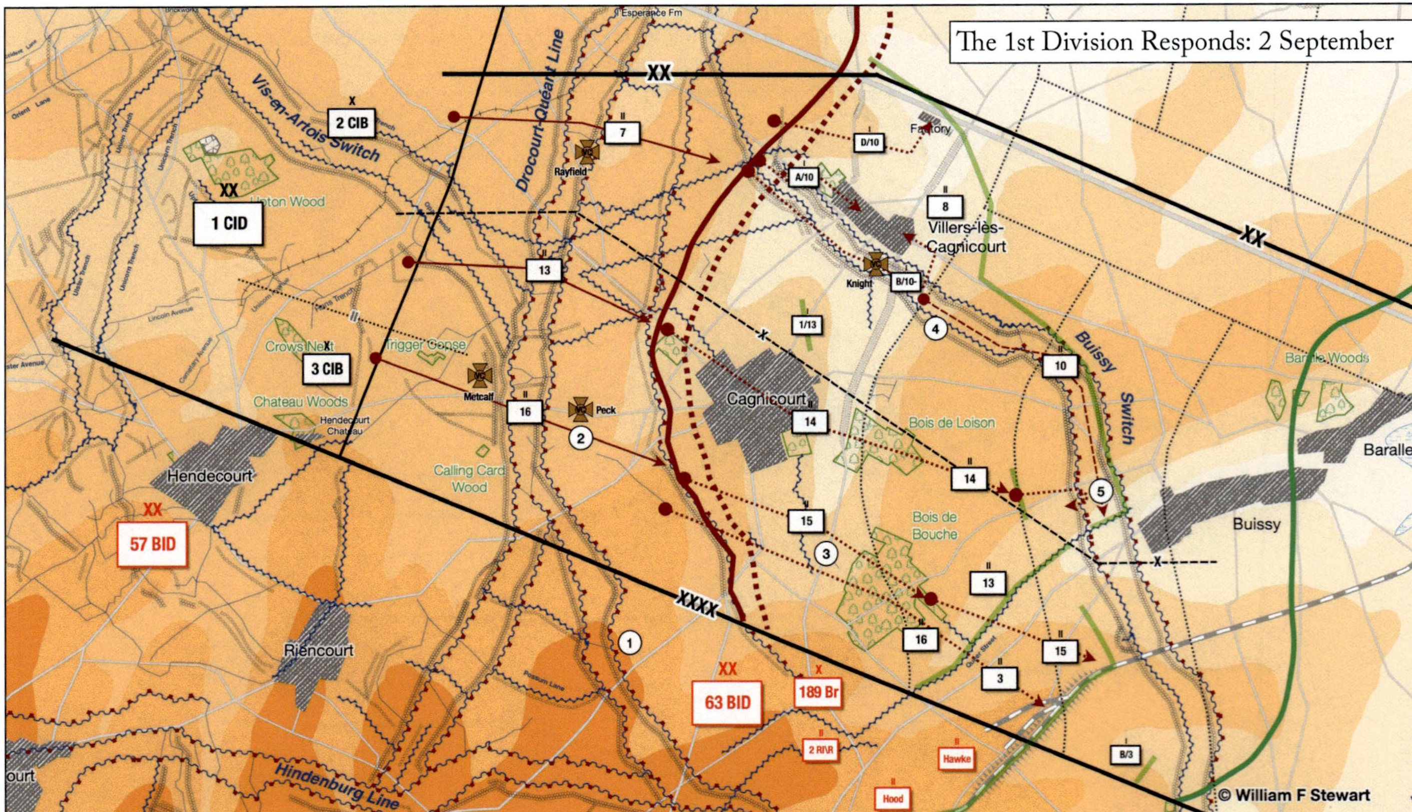

Map C22. The 1st Division advanced to the Buissy Switch. Note the four Victoria Crosses awarded to the 1st Division this day.

1. Machine gun fire from high ground south of the division boundary inflicted casualties and disorganisation
2. Lieutenant-Colonel Cy Peck re-energised his battalion and led it to take the D-Q Support Line
3. The CO of the 14th, 15th, and 16th Battalions met to plan how to reach their objectives
4. Fire from the Buissy Switch impeded the advance of the 14th Battalion
5. The 14th Battalion took part of the Switch in the 2nd Brigade's sector but had to fall back. The 10th Battalion fought its way down the Switch to reach Queer Street by 11:00 p.m.

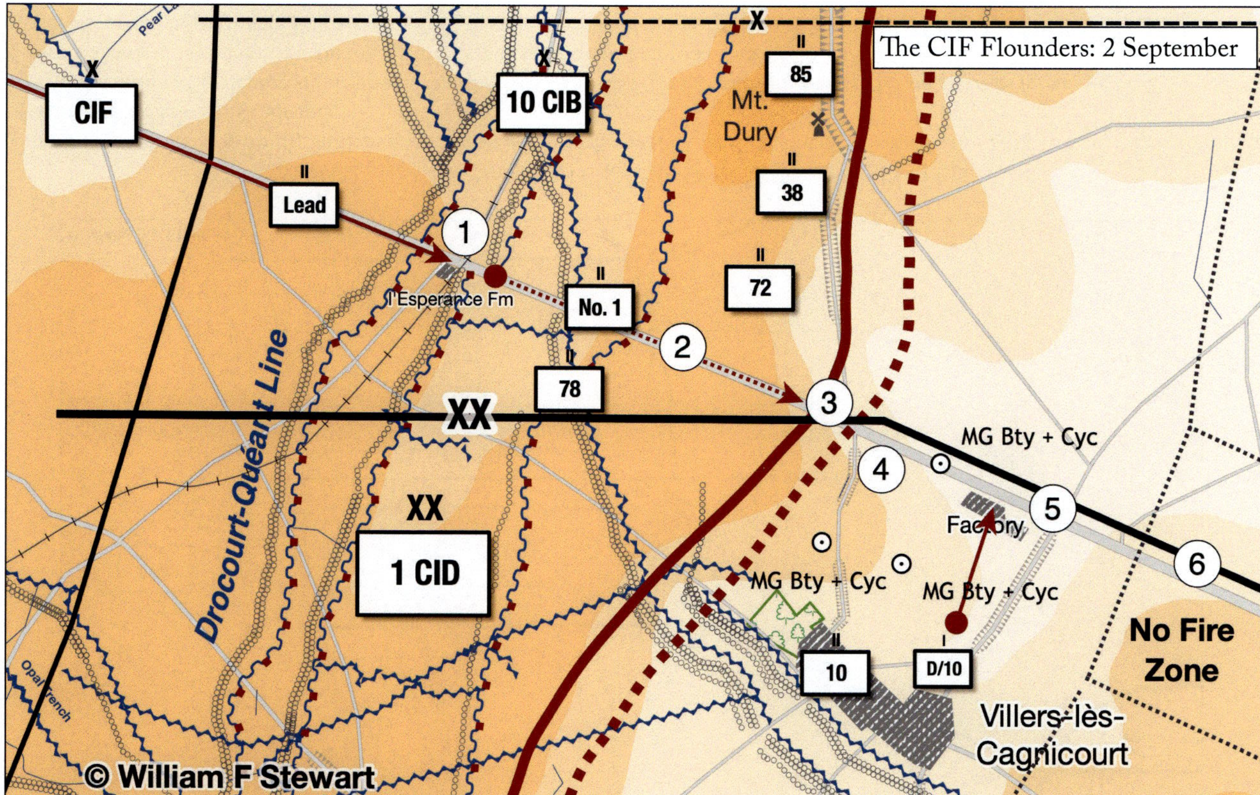

Map C23. Brutinel's CIF failed to advance.

1. Lead Group stops at l'Esperance Farm and sent out patrols that return after a few casualties and with misleading information
2. 10th Royal Hussars failed to notice trees cut down across the Arras-Cambrai road. This was also the position reached by the main body of No. 1 Group
3. Claimed position for Lead Group
4. No 1 Group commander sent out three parties of a machine gun battery and two cyclist platoons each. They made little headway
5. Brutinel's claim of how far the CIF penetrated
6. Position claimed by No. 1 Group commander

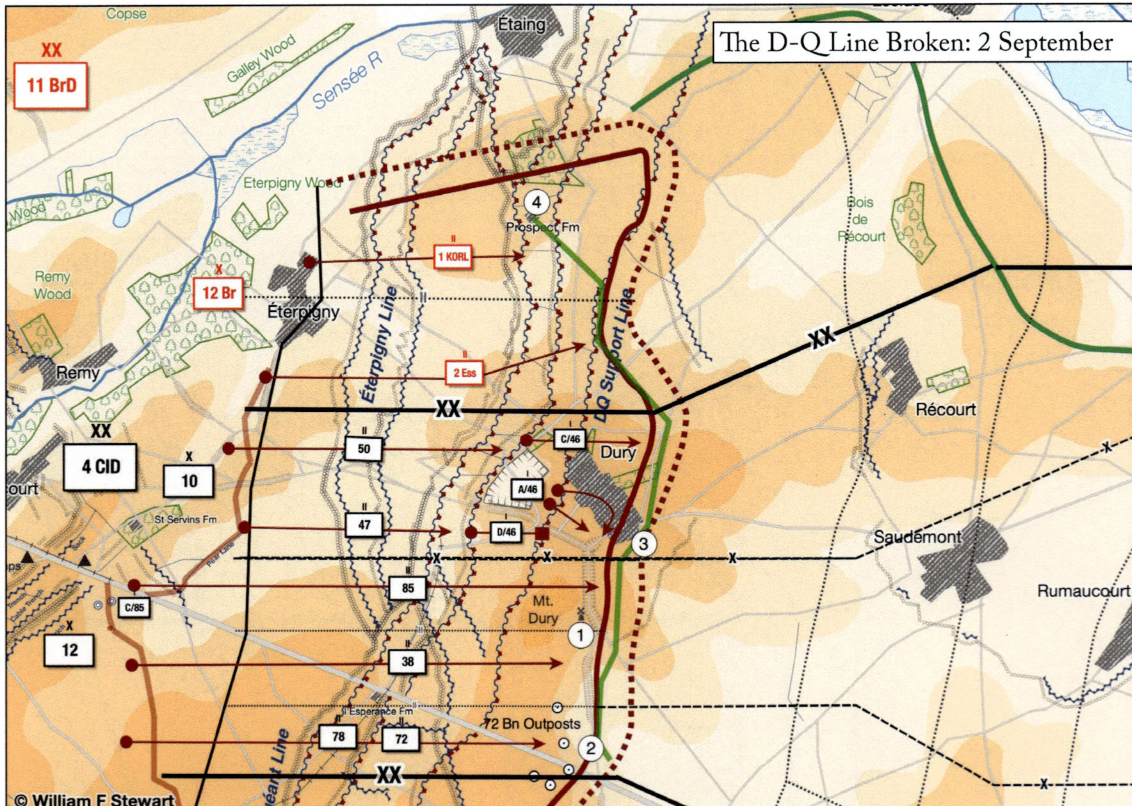

Map C24. The 4th British and Canadian Divisions break the D-Q Line.

1. German fire from the Windmill, Sunken road and villages in the distance inflicted heavy losses on the 12th and 10th Brigades and disrupted the 4th Canadian Division's advance
2. The 72nd Battalion only deployed outposts along the Red Line and other battalions believed it only got as far as the D-Q Support Line
3. The 46th Battalion has an epic battle to capture Dury and the Sunken road south of it
4. Prospect Farm defenders forced British battalions to sidle south to avoid its fire and this movement disrupted the 4th British Division's advance

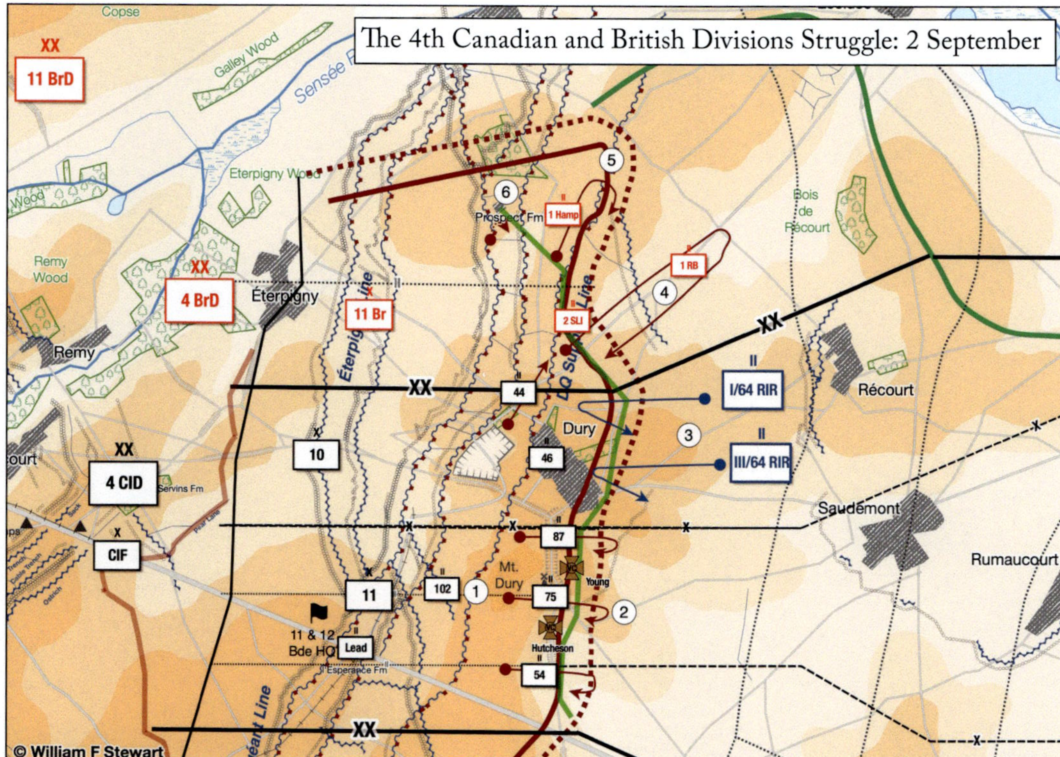

Map C25. The 4th Canadian and 4th British Division encountered fierce resistance and could not advance.

1. Lieutenant-Colonel Harbottle, CO 75th Battalion, decided to advance without waiting for the brigade order. The COs of the 54th and 87th agreed to support him
2. A torrent of German fire from the front, flanks, and distant villages shredded the 11th Brigade's advance
3. Around noon, the *64th RIR* counterattacked, drove back the 46th Battalion, and took part of Dury. The 46th recovered and retook the village
4. Elements of the 1st RB penetrated as far as the crossroads. The SLI erroneously reported its position as along the trench east of the D-Q Support Line. It was actually in the support line
5. Parties of the 1st Hampshire and 2nd SLI pushed up the D-Q Support Line but the Germans drove them back
6. Later in the morning, the 4th British Division took Prospect Farm